Handbook of Market Research

Christian Homburg • Martin Klarmann •
Arnd Vomberg
Editors

Handbook of Market Research

Volume 2

With 211 Figures and 130 Tables

Editors
Christian Homburg
Department of Business-to-Business
Marketing, Sales, and Pricing
University of Mannheim
Mannheim, Germany

Martin Klarmann
Department of Marketing & Sales Research
Group
Karlsruhe Institute of Technology (KIT)
Karlsruhe, Germany

Arnd Vomberg
Marketing & Sales Department
University of Mannheim
Mannheim, Germany

ISBN 978-3-319-57411-0   ISBN 978-3-319-57413-4 (eBook)
ISBN 978-3-319-57412-7 (print and electronic bundle)
https://doi.org/10.1007/978-3-319-57413-4

© Springer Nature Switzerland AG 2022
This work is subject to copyright. All rights are reserved by the Publisher, whether the whole or part of the material is concerned, specifically the rights of translation, reprinting, reuse of illustrations, recitation, broadcasting, reproduction on microfilms or in any other physical way, and transmission or information storage and retrieval, electronic adaptation, computer software, or by similar or dissimilar methodology now known or hereafter developed.
The use of general descriptive names, registered names, trademarks, service marks, etc. in this publication does not imply, even in the absence of a specific statement, that such names are exempt from the relevant protective laws and regulations and therefore free for general use.
The publisher, the authors, and the editors are safe to assume that the advice and information in this book are believed to be true and accurate at the date of publication. Neither the publisher nor the authors or the editors give a warranty, expressed or implied, with respect to the material contained herein or for any errors or omissions that may have been made. The publisher remains neutral with regard to jurisdictional claims in published maps and institutional affiliations.

This Springer imprint is published by the registered company Springer Nature Switzerland AG.
The registered company address is: Gewerbestrasse 11, 6330 Cham, Switzerland

Preface

Already in 2015, the *Wall Street Journal* claimed that companies sit on a treasure trove of market data. They have an ever-increasing amount of data at their disposal. However, it is not only about access to data. Companies need to develop strong empirical and analytical skills to turn their data into a competitive advantage. Traditional market research firms and hundreds of new startup companies specializing in "Data Science" and analytics support companies in building and maintaining customer relationships, developing strategies to increase customer satisfaction, improving sales strategies, personalizing the marketing mix, and automating marketing processes in real time. The *Handbook of Market Research* seeks to provide material for both, firms specialized in data analysis and firms hiring those firms. On the one hand, it seeks to provide in-depth coverage of established and new marketing research methods. On the other hand, by giving examples throughout, it aims to be as accessible as possible.

The *Handbook of Market Research* helps readers apply advanced market research methods in their projects and provides them with a valuable overview of various analytical techniques. It targets three groups: graduate students, scholars, and data science practitioners. Graduate students obtain an introduction to diverse market research topics. Scholars can use the handbook as a reference, supporting their research and teaching. Practitioners receive a state-of-the-art overview of scientific practices.

What is special about the *Handbook of Market Research*?

- Chapters in this handbook are not purely technical but also offer an intuitive account of the discussed methodologies.
- Many chapters provide data and software code to replicate the analyses. Readers can find such supplementary material on the handbook's online site (https://link.springer.com/referencework/10.1007/978-3-319-05542-8).
- Nearly all chapters in this handbook have gone through a friendly review process. The friendly reviewers helped to improve all chapters of this handbook further.
- We publish the handbook dynamically. Novel chapters will appear continuously on the handbook's online site. Moreover, authors have the opportunity to update existing chapters online to respond to emerging trends and new methods.

The handbook has three parts: Data, Methods, and Applications. The Data part supports readers in collecting and handling different types of data. The Method part outlines how readers can analyze structured and unstructured data. The Application part equips readers with knowledge on how they can use data analytics in specific contexts.

Our special thanks go to the authors of the chapters for their willingness to share their knowledge and experience with the readers. Furthermore, we would like to take this opportunity to thank the friendly reviewers who have helped further to increase the high quality of the individual contributions. We want to thank Dr. Prashanth Mahagaonkar, Veronika Mang, and Barbara Wolf from Springer Verlag for their excellent cooperation.

Mannheim, Germany	Christian Homburg
Karlsruhe, Germany	Martin Klarmann
Germany	Arnd Vomberg
November 2021	

List of Reviewers

Last Name	First Name	Title	Description	Institution
Artz	Martin	Prof. Dr.	Professor for Management Accounting and Control	University of Münster
Atalay	Selin	Prof. Dr.	Professor of Marketing	Frankfurt School of Finance and Management
Becker	Jan-Michael	Dr.	Associate Professor at the Marketing Department	BI Norwegian Business School
Bhattacharya	Abhimanyu	Ph.D.	Assistant Professor at the Marketing Department	University of Alabama, Tuscaloosa
Bruno	Hernán	Prof. Dr.	Professor of Marketing and Digital Environment	University of Cologne
Colicev	Anatoli	Ph.D.	Assistant Professor at the Marketing Department	Bocconi University
De Vries	Thom	Dr.	Assistant Professor at the Faculty of Economics and Business	University of Groningen
Dehmamy	Keyvan	Dr.	Post-Doctoral Researcher at the Marketing Department	Goethe University Frankfurt
Delre	Sebastiano	Dr.	Associate Professor at the Marketing, Sales and Communication Department	Montpellier Business School
Dew	Ryan	Ph.D.	Assistant Professor at the Marketing Department	Wharton School of the University of Pennsylvania
Dinner	Isaac	Ph.D.	Director of Econometric Modeling	Indeed
Draganska	Michaela	Ph.D.	Associate Professor at the Marketing Department	Drexel University
Entrop	Oliver	Prof. Dr.	Professor of Finance and Banking, Chair of Finance and Banking	University of Passau

(continued)

Last Name	First Name	Title	Description	Institution
Fuchs	Christoph	Prof. Dr.	Professor of Marketing and Chair of Marketing	University of Vienna
Fürst	Andreas	Prof. Dr.	Chair of Business Administration (Marketing)	Friedrich-Alexander-Universität Erlangen-Nürnberg
Gensler	Sonja	Prof. Dr.	Extraordinary Professor at the Chair for Value-Based Marketing	University of Münster
Gijsenberg	Maarten J.	Prof. Dr.	Full Professor at the Marketing Department	University of Groningen
Groening	Christopher	Ph.D.	Associate Professor at the Marketing Department	Kent State University
Haans	Hans	Dr.	Marketing Department, Director Econasium	Tilburg University
Hahn	Carsten	Prof. Dr.	Professor für Innovation und Entrepreneurship	Karlsruhe University of Applied Sciences
Hartmann	Jochen	Dr.	Post-doctoral Researcher at the Chair Marketing and Branding	University of Hamburg
Hattula	Stefan	Dr.	Market analyst	Robert Bosch GmbH
Henseler	Jörg	Prof. Dr.	Chair of Product-Market Relations	University of Twente
Hohenberg	Sebastian	Dr.	Assistant Professor at the Marketing Department	University of Texas at Austin
Junc	Vanessa	Dr.	Senior CRM Analyst	Douglas GmbH
Kamleitner	Bernadette	Prof. Dr.	Marketing Department	WU Vienna
Klarmann	Martin	Prof. Dr.	Professor of Marketing	Karlsruhe Institute of Technology
Klein	Kristina	Prof. Dr.	Professor of Marketing	University of Bremen
Landwehr	Jan	Prof. Dr.	Professor of Marketing and Chair for Product Management and Marketing Communications	Goethe University Frankfurt
Lanz	Andreas	Dr.	Assistant Professor at the Marketing Department	HEC Paris
Lemmens	Aurélie	Dr.	Associate Professor of Marketing	Rotterdam School of Management, Erasmus University
Ludwig	Stephan	Dr.	Associate Professor at the Department of Management and Marketing	University of Melbourne
Mayer	Stefan	Prof. Dr.	Assistant Professor of Marketing Analytics	University of Tübingen
Miller	Klaus	Dr.	Assistant Professor at the Marketing Department	HEC Paris

(continued)

List of Reviewers

Last Name	First Name	Title	Description	Institution
Mooi	Erik	Dr.	Associate Professor at the Department of Management and Marketing	University of Melbourne
Nitzan	Irit	Dr.	Assistant Professor of Marketing	Coller School of Management
Osinga	Ernst Christiaan	Ph.D.	Associate Professor of Marketing	Singapore Management University
Otter	Thomas	Prof. Dr.	Professor of Marketing	Goethe University Frankfurt
Papies	Dominik	Prof. Dr.	Professor of Marketing	University of Tübingen
Roelen-Blasberg	Tobias		Co-Founder	MARA
Sarstedt	Marko	Prof. Dr.	Chair of Marketing	Otto von Guericke University Magdeburg
Schlereth	Christian	Prof. Dr.	Chair of Digital Marketing	WHU – Otto Beisheim School of Management
Schulze	Christian	Prof. Dr.	Associate Professor of Marketing	Frankfurt School of Finance and Management
Sichtmann	Christina	Prof. Dr.	Research Associate for the Chair of International Marketing	University of Vienna
Stahl	Florian	Prof. Dr.	Professor of Marketing at the Department of Business Administration	University of Mannheim
Totzek	Dirk	Prof. Dr.	Chair of Marketing and Services	University of Passau
Van Heerde	Harald	Ph.D.	S.H.A.R.P. Research Professor of Marketing	University of South Wales
Vomberg	Arnd	Prof. Dr.	Professor of Marketing	University of Mannheim
Weeth	Alexander	Dr.	Engagement Manager	McKinsey & Company
Weijters	Bert	Ph.D.	Associate Professor in the Department of Work, Organization and Society	Ghent University
Wentzel	Daniel	Prof. Dr.	Chair of Marketing	RWTH Aachen University
Yildirim	Gokham	Dr.	Associate Professor of Marketing	Imperial College London

Contents

Volume 1

Part I Data 1

Experiments in Market Research 3
Torsten Bornemann and Stefan Hattula

Field Experiments 37
Veronica Valli, Florian Stahl, and Elea McDonnell Feit

Crafting Survey Research: A Systematic Process for Conducting Survey Research 67
Arnd Vomberg and Martin Klarmann

Challenges in Conducting International Market Research 121
Andreas Engelen, Monika Engelen, and C. Samuel Craig

Fusion Modeling 147
Elea McDonnell Feit and Eric T. Bradlow

Dealing with Endogeneity: A Nontechnical Guide for Marketing Researchers 181
P. Ebbes, D. Papies, and H. J. van Heerde

Part II Methods 219

Cluster Analysis in Marketing Research 221
Thomas Reutterer and Daniel Dan

Finite Mixture Models 251
Sonja Gensler

Analysis of Variance 265
Jan R. Landwehr

Regression Analysis 299
Bernd Skiera, Jochen Reiner, and Sönke Albers

Logistic Regression and Discriminant Analysis 329
Sebastian Tillmanns and Manfred Krafft

Multilevel Modeling 369
Till Haumann, Roland Kassemeier, and Jan Wieseke

Panel Data Analysis: A Non-technical Introduction for Marketing Researchers 411
Arnd Vomberg and Simone Wies

Applied Time-Series Analysis in Marketing 469
Wanxin Wang and Gokhan Yildirim

Modeling Marketing Dynamics Using Vector Autoregressive (VAR) Models 515
Shuba Srinivasan

Volume 2

Structural Equation Modeling 549
Hans Baumgartner and Bert Weijters

Partial Least Squares Structural Equation Modeling 587
Marko Sarstedt, Christian M. Ringle, and Joseph F. Hair

Automated Text Analysis 633
Ashlee Humphreys

Image Analytics in Marketing 665
Daria Dzyabura, Siham El Kihal, and Renana Peres

Social Network Analysis 693
Hans Risselada and Jeroen van den Ochtend

Bayesian Models 719
Thomas Otter

Choice-Based Conjoint Analysis 781
Felix Eggers, Henrik Sattler, Thorsten Teichert, and Franziska Völckner

Exploiting Data from Field Experiments 821
Martin Artz and Hannes Doering

Mediation Analysis in Experimental Research 857
Nicole Koschate-Fischer and Elisabeth Schwille

Part III   Applications **907**

Measuring Customer Satisfaction and Customer Loyalty 909
Sebastian Hohenberg and Wayne Taylor

Market Segmentation 939
Tobias Schlager and Markus Christen

Willingness to Pay 969
Wiebke Klingemann, Ju-Young Kim, and Kai Dominik Füller

Modeling Customer Lifetime Value, Retention, and Churn 1001
Herbert Castéran, Lars Meyer-Waarden, and Werner Reinartz

Assessing the Financial Impact of Brand Equity with Short Time-Series Data 1035
Natalie Mizik and Eugene Pavlov

Measuring Sales Promotion Effectiveness 1055
Karen Gedenk

Return on Media Models 1073
Dominique M. Hanssens

Index 1097

About the Editors

Prof. Christian Homburg holds the Chair of Business-to-Business Marketing, Sales and Pricing at the University of Mannheim. He is also Distinguished Professorial Fellow of the University of Manchester (UK) and Director of the Institute for Market-Oriented Management (IMU) at the University of Mannheim. He specializes in market-oriented management, customer relationship management, and sales management. Professor Homburg has published numerous books and articles at the national and international levels and has thus established a research portfolio that places him as one of the leading German management professors and most productive scholars in the marketing discipline. In 2019 and 2020, WirtschaftsWoche honored Professor Homburg for his Lifetime Achievement as the leading management professor in Germany, Austria, and Switzerland.

He is currently a member of the editorial boards of five scientific journals in the United States and Europe. Since April 2011, he works as the first German area editor for the *Journal of Marketing*. Professor Homburg received several awards for his scientific research from the American Marketing Association, the world's leading scientific association in the area of marketing, and is the first European university professor to be honored as an AMA Fellow for his lifetime achievement in marketing research. In 2021, Professor Homburg ranked fourth in the American Marketing Association's global ranking, which is based on the number of publications in the most important marketing journals.

Prior to his academic career, Professor Homburg was Director of marketing, controlling, and strategic planning in an industrial company that operates globally.

xv

In addition to his academic position, he is Chairman of the scientific advisory committee of Homburg & Partner, an international management consultancy.

Prof. Martin Klarmann is Professor of Marketing at the Karlsruhe Institute of Technology (KIT), Germany. Professor Klarmann's research is centered around three core themes: marketing using new technologies, marketing methods, and B2B sales management. His research has been published in several leading journals of the field, including the *Journal of Marketing*, the *Journal of Marketing Research*, the *Journal of the Academy of Marketing Science*, and the *International Journal of Research in Marketing*. Professor Klarmann has received several awards for his research, including an overall best paper award at the American Marketing Association's Winter Educators' Conference.

Prof. Arnd Vomberg is Professor of Digital Marketing and Marketing Transformation at the University of Mannheim, Germany. Professor Vomberg has also been an Associate Professor (with tenure) at the Marketing Department of the University of Groningen, The Netherlands. Professor Vomberg's research focuses on digital marketing and marketing transformation. He studies omnichannel strategies, online pricing, marketing automation, agile transformation, marketing technology, and marketing's impact on employees. His research has been published in several leading journals of the field, including *Journal of Marketing*, *Journal of Marketing Research*, *Strategic Management Journal*, *Journal of the Academy of Marketing Science*, and *International Journal of Research in Marketing*. Professor Vomberg has received several awards for his research, including the Ralph Alexander Best Dissertation Award from the Academy of Management.

Contributors

Sönke Albers Kuehne Logistics University, Hamburg, Germany

Martin Artz School of Business and Economics, University of Münster, Münster, Germany

Hans Baumgartner Smeal College of Business, The Pennsylvania State University, State College, PA, USA

Torsten Bornemann Department of Marketing, Goethe University Frankfurt, Frankfurt, Germany

Eric T. Bradlow The Wharton School, University of Pennsylvania, Philadelphia, PA, USA

Herbert Castéran Humanis Institute, EM Strasbourg Business School, Strasbourg, France

Markus Christen Faculty of Business and Economics (HEC) University of Lausanne, Lausanne, Switzerland

Daniel Dan Department of New Media, Modul University Vienna, Vienna, Austria

Hannes Doering School of Business and Economics, University of Münster, Münster, Germany

Daria Dzyabura New Economic School and Moscow School of Management SKOLKOVO, Moscow, Russia

P. Ebbes HEC Paris, Jouy-en-Josas, France

Felix Eggers University of Groningen, Groningen, The Netherlands

Siham El Kihal Frankfurt School of Finance and Management, Frankfurt, Germany

Andreas Engelen TU Dortmund University, Dortmund, Germany

Monika Engelen TH Köln, Cologne University of Applied Science, Köln, Germany

Elea McDonnell Feit LeBow College of Business, Drexel University, Philadelphia, PA, USA

Kai Dominik Füller Karlsruhe Institute of Technology, Institute for Information Systems and Marketing – Services Marketing, Karlsruhe, Germany

Karen Gedenk University of Hamburg, Hamburg, Germany

Sonja Gensler Marketing Center Münster – Institute for Value-based Marketing, University of Münster, Münster, Germany

Joseph F. Hair University of South Alabama, Mobile, AL, USA

Dominique M. Hanssens UCLA Anderson School of Management, Los Angeles, CA, USA

Stefan Hattula Department of Marketing, Goethe University Frankfurt, Frankfurt, Germany

Till Haumann South Westphalia University of Applied Sciences, Soest, Germany

Sebastian Hohenberg McCombs School of Business, The University of Texas, Austin, TX, USA

Ashlee Humphreys Integrated Marketing Communications, Medill School of Journalism, Media, and Integrated Marketing Communications, Northwestern University, Evanston, IL, USA

Roland Kassemeier Marketing Group, Warwick Business School, University of Warwick, Coventry, UK

Ju-Young Kim Goethe University Frankfurt, Department of Marketing, Frankfurt, Germany

Martin Klarmann Department of Marketing & Sales Research Group, Karlsruhe Institute of Technology (KIT), Karlsruhe, Germany

Wiebke Klingemann Karlsruhe Institute of Technology, Institute for Information Systems and Marketing – Services Marketing, Karlsruhe, Germany

Nicole Koschate-Fischer University of Erlangen-Nuremberg, Nuremberg, Germany

Manfred Krafft Institute of Marketing, Westfälische Wilhelms-Universität Münster, Muenster, Germany

Jan R. Landwehr Marketing Department, Goethe University Frankfurt, Frankfurt, Germany

Lars Meyer-Waarden School of Management, CRM CNRS University Toulouse 1 Capitole, IAE Toulouse, Toulouse, France

Natalie Mizik Foster School of Business, University of Washington, Seattle, WA, USA

Thomas Otter Goethe University Frankfurt am Main, Frankfurt am Main, Germany

D. Papies School of Business and Economics, University of Tübingen, Tübingen, Germany

Eugene Pavlov Foster School of Business, University of Washington, Seattle, WA, USA

Renana Peres School of Business Administration, Hebrew University of Jerusalem, Jerusalem, Israel

Werner Reinartz University of Cologne, Köln, Germany

Jochen Reiner Goethe University Frankfurt, Frankfurt, Germany

Thomas Reutterer Department of Marketing, WU Vienna University of Economics and Business, Vienna, Austria

Christian M. Ringle Hamburg University of Technology (TUHH), Hamburg, Germany

Faculty of Business and Law, University of Newcastle, Callaghan, NSW, Australia

Hans Risselada University of Groningen, Groningen, The Netherlands

C. Samuel Craig New York University, Stern School of Business, New York, NY, USA

Marko Sarstedt Otto-von-Guericke University, Magdeburg, Germany

Faculty of Business and Law, University of Newcastle, Callaghan, NSW, Australia

Henrik Sattler University of Hamburg, Hamburg, Germany

Tobias Schlager Faculty of Business and Economics (HEC) University of Lausanne, Lausanne, Switzerland

Elisabeth Schwille University of Erlangen-Nuremberg, Nuremberg, Germany

Bernd Skiera Goethe University Frankfurt, Frankfurt, Germany

Shuba Srinivasan Boston University Questrom School of Business, Boston, MA, USA

Florian Stahl University of Mannheim, Mannheim, Germany

Wayne Taylor Cox School of Business, Southern Methodist University, Dallas, TX, USA

Thorsten Teichert University of Hamburg, Hamburg, Germany

Sebastian Tillmanns Westfälische Wilhelms-Universität Münster, Muenster, Germany

Veronica Valli University of Mannheim, Mannheim, Germany

Franziska Völckner Department of Marketing and Brand Management, University of Cologne, Köln, Germany

Jeroen van den Ochtend University of Zürich, Zürich, Switzerland

H. J. van Heerde School of Communication, Journalism and Marketing, Massey University, Auckland, New Zealand

Arnd Vomberg Marketing Department, University of Groningen, Groningen, The Netherlands

Wanxin Wang Imperial College Business School, Imperial College London, London, UK

Bert Weijters Faculty of Psychology and Educational Sciences, Department of Work, Organization and Society, Ghent University, Ghent, Belgium

Simone Wies Goethe University Frankfurt, Frankfurt, Germany

Jan Wieseke Sales Management Department, University of Bochum, Bochum, Germany

Gokhan Yildirim Imperial College Business School, Imperial College London, London, UK

Structural Equation Modeling

Hans Baumgartner and Bert Weijters

Contents

Introduction	550
The Core Structural Equation Model and Its Submodels	551
Model Estimation	556
Testing the Global Fit of Models	558
Respecifying Models That Do Not Pass the Global Fit Test	562
Assessing the Local Fit of Models	564
Measurement Model	564
Latent Variable Model	567
The Problem of Endogeneity	567
Extensions of the Core Structural Equation Model	569
Measurement Model Extensions	569
Latent Variable Model Extensions	571
Models That Incorporate Population Heterogeneity	572
Empirical Illustration of Structural Equation Modeling	574
Conceptual Model	574
Measurement Model	575
Latent Variable Model	579
Multi-Sample Analysis	581
Concluding Comments	581
Cross-References	583
References	584

H. Baumgartner (✉)
Smeal College of Business, The Pennsylvania State University, State College, PA, USA
e-mail: HansBaumgartner@psu.edu

B. Weijters
Faculty of Psychology and Educational Sciences, Department of Work, Organization and Society, Ghent University, Ghent, Belgium
e-mail: bert.weijters@ugent.be

© Springer Nature Switzerland AG 2022
C. Homburg et al. (eds), *Handbook of Market Research*,
https://doi.org/10.1007/978-3-319-57413-4_14

Abstract

This chapter presents an overview of the process of structural equation modeling, involving the steps of model specification, model estimation, overall fit evaluation, model respecification, and local fit assessment (including interpreting the parameters of the model). Various extensions of the core structural equation model are described to enable more general representations of measurement and latent variable models as well as applications of the model to heterogeneous populations. An empirical example is provided to illustrate the process of structural equation modeling and to demonstrate some of the complexities that may arise in practical applications.

Keywords

Structural equation modeling · Confirmatory factor analysis · Measurement models · Path analysis · Multi-sample analysis

Introduction

Only a few decades ago structural equation modeling (SEM) was regarded as an advanced statistical methodology that was used primarily by academic researchers to conduct sophisticated measurement analyses or to test the validity of theoretical models based on empirical data (Bagozzi 1980). Nowadays, SEM is a standard data analysis method that is employed widely by both academic and industry researchers (e.g., Chapman and Feit 2019). The success and rapid adoption of SEM is likely due to the following three reasons. First, SEM allows researchers to take into account measurement error (both random and systematic) when estimating correlations or structural relationships between constructs. Since observed measures in practical applications are usually measured with error, the suspect assumption of perfect measurement in conventional correlation and regression analysis is circumvented (see chapter ▶ "Regression Analysis" by Skiera, Reiner, and Albers, this volume, for a discussion of regression analysis). For example, it is unlikely that constructs such as the quality or value of a product or the satisfaction experienced by a customer can be measured well with single items, and even when multiple measures of these constructs are averaged (which corrects for unreliability of measurement to some extent), this does not provide much insight into the quality of measurement of the constructs by their measures. Second, researchers are often interested in estimating and testing models in which the dependence of multiple constructs on different sets of antecedents is modeled simultaneously and the process through which one construct influences another is investigated. SEM enables researchers to study complex conceptual frameworks in an integrative fashion and avoids the piecemeal testing of chains of effects as in conventional regression analysis. For example, a researcher may want to investigate both the antecedents of customer satisfaction such as expectations, perceived quality, and perceived value, and the consequences of customer satisfaction such as loyalty and complaints, as well as the mediating role of satisfaction in this process. Third, researchers who want to study the invariance of model parameters across discrete populations (e.g., different demographic groups, industries, or countries) or test hypotheses about specific group differences can specify models for multiple populations in which both the homogeneity and heterogeneity of parameters can be investigated in a straightforward manner.

Although SEM is widely used, it is not always used well. A first goal of this chapter is to present an overview of the methodology, with special emphasis on issues that are sometimes misunderstood in applications of the technique (e.g., global fit testing). SEM is a rather vibrant research domain, and the core model has been extended in a variety of ways. A second goal of this chapter is to bring these developments to the attention of a wider audience and to encourage additional applications of SEM. Although we will not be able to cover advanced topics in using SEM in any detail, we will raise several important issues and point interested readers to the relevant literature. The final goal is to offer an empirical illustration of many of the issues discussed in this chapter, which will hopefully demonstrate the power of SEM for data analysis and convince researchers who have not used SEM to apply it in their own research. The data set used in the illustration and the code necessary to run the models in R, using the package lavaan (Rosseel 2012) and various supporting packages, are available for download on Github (https://github.com/HansBaum129/SEM).

The Core Structural Equation Model and Its Submodels

A full structural equation model consists of two parts: a model specifying the structural relationships between the substantive variables or constructs of interest (called the latent variable model because the constructs in one's model often cannot be observed and measured directly), and a model specifying the relationships between the constructs and their hypothesized observed (manifest) measures or indicators (called the measurement model). We will assume that the latent variable underlying a set of observed variables is equal to the construct of interest, and we will therefore use the terms construct and latent variable interchangeably. However, a researcher should carefully evaluate whether this assumption is justified when a structural equation model is specified for a particular substantive context. In the simplest case, the latent variable model is like a regression model (although the variables in the model are usually unobserved or latent), but in more complex models, the latent variable model could be comprised of a series of regression models, one for each construct to be explained in one's conceptual framework or theory. If a researcher is willing to assume that a construct is measured perfectly by a single indicator (where the single indicator could be an average of several observed measures), then an explicit measurement model is superfluous (i.e., the construct is identical to the observed measure). However, in many (most) cases, this is a tenuous assumption, and often (usually) researchers will want to specify a measurement model which enables a thorough investigation of the measurement quality of the indicators of the constructs of interest.

Two types of measurement models can be formulated (e.g., MacKenzie et al. 2011). In a reflective measurement model, the observed variables (effect indicators) are specified as a function of (and thus a reflection of) hypothesized latent variables, which presumably represent the substantive variables the researcher is interested in. For example, a customer's satisfaction with a product may be measured with semantic differential scales such as satisfied-dissatisfied or happy-sad and these observed measures are assumed to be (fallible) reflections of respondents' satisfaction. In a formative measurement model, the observed variables (cause indicators) are specified as determinants of hypothesized latent variables, which means that constructs are formed by their indicators. For example, a customer's satisfaction with a service may depend on the friendliness, knowledgeability, and responsiveness of the sales staff and these service attributes are all assumed to contribute to a respondent's overall satisfaction. In general, a formatively measured construct is not completely captured by its indicators (i.e., the construct is measured with error), but sometimes it is assumed that the formative construct is equal to a linear combination of its indicators; Bollen (2011) refers to the two types of indicators as cause and composite indicators, respectively.

Formative indicators are frequently misspecified as reflective indicators (Jarvis et al. 2003; MacKenzie et al. 2005), and such measurement model misspecifications can have various negative consequences (see Diamantopoulos et al. 2008 for a summary). Indicators should therefore be evaluated carefully before a reflective measurement model is specified (usually almost by default). Jarvis et al. (2003) and MacKenzie et al. (2005) recommend that researchers ask themselves the following four questions about each indicator: Is the indicator a manifestation of the underlying construct (rather than a defining characteristic of it)? Is a given indicator conceptually interchangeable with the other indicators of the same construct? Will the indicators of the construct necessarily covary? And does each indicator have the same antecedents and consequences as the other indicators of the same construct? If the answer to these questions is yes, the measurement model is reflective; if the answer is no, it is formative. Although formative indicators should not be misspecified as being reflective (Rhemtulla et al. 2020), it is difficult to recommend formative measurement models for general use because they give rise to many difficult problems (see the recent discussion in Baumgartner and Weijters 2019). Since formative measures can sometimes be reformulated to make them reflective, it might be preferable to ensure that the measures used are truly reflective, rather than specifying a formative measurement model. Alternatively, the presumed formative indicators can be specified as (possibly errorful) determinants of the overall (formative) construct, although the construct has to be directly measured by reflective indicators in this case. In the sequel, we will focus on reflective measurement models, but we will briefly return to the difference between reflective and formative measurement models when discussing how to assess the quality of construct measurement.

Formally, a structural equation model can be specified as follows:

$$\eta = B\eta + \Gamma\xi + \varsigma \tag{1}$$

$$y = \Lambda^y \eta + \varepsilon \tag{2}$$

$$x = \Lambda^x \xi + \delta \tag{3}$$

Equation (1) is the latent variable model in which the vector η (eta) contains the endogenous constructs (i.e., constructs that are functions of other constructs in the proposed model) and the vector ξ (ksi) contains the exogenous constructs (i.e., constructs that are not affected by other constructs in the model). The matrix **B** (Beta) contains the coefficients representing the effects of endogenous on other endogenous constructs (i.e., β_{ij} is the effect of η_j on η_i, and the diagonals of this matrix are zero since a variable cannot influence itself); the matrix Γ (Gamma) contains the coefficients representing the effects of exogenous on endogenous constructs (i.e., γ_{ij} is the effect of ξ_j on η_i). The vector ς (zeta) contains the errors in equations (structural disturbances) associated with each endogenous construct. If **B** is subdiagonal (i.e., all the coefficients above and on the diagonal are zero) and the error terms in ς are pairwise uncorrelated, the model is called recursive. In a recursive model, there are no reciprocal effects between the endogenous constructs and no feedback loops from one endogenous construct to itself, and the errors in equations are uncorrelated (i.e., there are no unobserved variables causing the endogenous variables to be correlated). Most structural models encountered in practice are recursive models, although they are often not realistic representations of reality.

Equations (2) and (3) are the measurement models (confirmatory factor models) for the endogenous (η) and exogenous (ξ) constructs, respectively; y is a vector containing the (mean-centered) measures of the endogenous constructs, and x is a vector containing the (mean-centered) measures of the exogenous constructs. The coefficients expressing the effects of the endogenous and exogenous constructs on their observed measures (called factor loadings) are contained in the matrices Λ^y and Λ^x (Lambda-y and Lambda-x), respectively. The vectors ε (epsilon) and δ (delta) contain the unique factors (measurement errors) corresponding to the observed measures. The variance-covariance matrices of ξ, ε, and δ are called Φ (Phi), Θ^ε (Theta-epsilon) and Θ^δ (Theta-delta), respectively. We will not discuss the model assumptions in detail, but it is important that ς, ε, and δ are uncorrelated with η and ξ.

If only a single measure is available for each construct (or multiple measures are averaged to form a single composite) and measurement error in observed variables is ignored, Eqs. (2) and (3) are not needed and the analysis is based on Eq. (1); this is the conventional econometric simultaneous equation model. If a researcher is only interested in conducting a measurement analysis, Eq. (3) is sufficient.

Many different measurement models can be specified, depending on whether an observed variable is allowed to load on multiple constructs, whether method factors are considered in addition to the substantive factors (as in multi-trait multi-method analyses), and whether measurement errors (unique factors) are specified to be correlated or uncorrelated (so-called correlated uniquenesses). Usually (at least in the first step), each observed measure is hypothesized to load on a single latent variable (the so-called target factor, which is thought to represent the substantive construct of interest), and while the variances of the unique factors are allowed to differ across observed measures, all unique factors are specified to be pairwise uncorrelated. This is called a congeneric factor model.

The model specification in Eqs. (1) to (3) is very general, but if the model parameters are to be unique, it is necessary to impose some restrictions on the model (i.e., a researcher has to make sure that the model is identified). Identification rules for structural equation models in general do not exist, but some guidelines can be offered. First, a necessary condition for a model to be identified is that the number of free model parameter not be greater than the number of distinct elements in the variance-covariance matrix of the observed variables. If this is the case, the degrees of freedom of the model will be nonnegative. Second, it is useful to break down model identification into two parts. In the first step, ignore the specific structural specification expressed by Eq. (1) and consider a (congeneric) measurement model for all the constructs and observed measures, in which the constructs are freely correlated. If there are no directed relationships between the constructs, all constructs can be treated as exogenous constructs and the measurement model can be specified using Eq. (3). Since all the variables on the right-hand side of Eq. (3) are latent, the scale in which each construct in ξ is measured has to specified; this can be done by setting either the loading of one observed measure per construct or the variance of each construct in ξ to one. If there are at least two indicators per construct, a (congeneric) measurement model with at least two correlated factors is identified. If a construct is measured by a single indicator, the variance of the unique factor corresponding to this indicator has to be set to zero (or another assumed value). If there are at least three indicators per construct, the constructs do not have to be correlated, and when a construct is measured by at least four indicators, even a single-factor model is overidentified (i.e., the model has a positive number of degrees of freedom, which implies that the fit of the model to data can be tested).

In the second step, once the measurement model has been shown to be identified, the identification status of the structural specification of interest should be checked. Recursive models (see the earlier discussion) are known to be identified, but demonstrating identification for more complex models (e.g., by using the rank rule) is more difficult. Frequently, researchers rely on empirical identification strategies, which basically means that they trust that the computer program used for estimation will issue a warning when a model is not identified.

Figure 1 is a graphical depiction of the SEM model that will be used later in the chapter to illustrate the process of structural equation modeling. The model represents the core constructs in the so-called Technology Acceptance Model (TAM) (Davis 1989) and consists of two endogenous latent variables (or etas), perceived usefulness (PU) and behavioral intention to use the new technology (BI), and one exogenous construct (or ksi), perceived ease of use (PEOU). By convention, latent variables of substantive interest are shown as ellipses (or circles). Directed arrows show causal effects, so the model assumes that PU is caused by PEOU (the strength of this relationship is expressed by γ_{11}) and BI is caused by PEOU and PU (the strength of these relationships is expressed by γ_{21} and β_{21}, respectively). PEOU is not expected to account for all the variation in PU, and PEOU and PU are not expected to account for all the variation in BI, so errors in equations (structural disturbances) are associated with each endogenous variable; the variances of these errors (zetas) are called psis and are shown as double-headed arrows. Since the structural errors are not connected with two-headed arrows (which can refer to either variances or covariances), it means that they are specified to be uncorrelated. This is a highly restrictive (and unrealistic) assumption, since it implies that there are no other unobserved variables that may cause PU and BI to be correlated. Unfortunately, a model with correlated structural errors is not identified in the present case since the latent variable model is saturated (see below), so the assumption cannot be relaxed. Because there are no feedback loops (as in PEOU → PU → BI → PEOU) or reciprocal relationships (e.g., PU ⇄ BI), and since the errors in equations are uncorrelated (i.e., there is no double-headed arrow between ζ_1 and ζ_2), the model is recursive.

PEOU and PU are each measured by four indicators (PEOU1-PEOU4 and PU1-PU4), and BI is measured by two indicators (BI1-BI2). By convention, observed measures are shown as rectangles or squares. The strength of the relationships between the latent variables and their indicators is given by the lambdas (λ_{ij}), which are the factor loadings. Associated with each observed variable is a unique factor (or error of measurement), either epsilon or delta, and the variances of the unique factors are called thetas (again indicated by double-headed arrows). All unique factors are pairwise uncorrelated.

The graphical model specification shown in Fig. 1 is equivalent to the algebraic model formulation shown in Table 1. There are two latent model equations corresponding to the two endogenous latent variables (PU and BI) and 10 measurement equations corresponding to the 10 observed variables.

Since the latent variable model is saturated, the model in Fig. 1 is equivalent to a confirmatory factor model in which PEOU, PU, and BI are freely correlated. Each

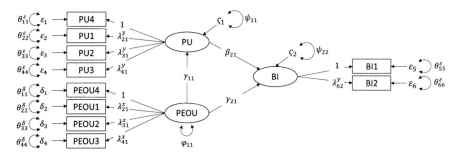

Fig. 1 Illustrative structural equation model

Table 1 Algebraic formulation of the model in Fig. 1

Latent variable model:
PU = γ_{11}PEOU + ς_1
BI = β_{21}PU + γ_{21}PEOU + ς_2
with VAR(PEOU) = φ_{11}, VAR(ζ_1) = ψ_{11}, VAR(ζ_2) = ψ_{22}, and COV(ζ_1, ζ_2) = 0.
Measurement model:
PEOU4 = PEOU + δ_1
PEOU1 = λ^x_{21}PEOU + δ_2
PEOU2 = λ^x_{31}PEOU + δ_3
PEOU3 = λ^x_{41}PEOU + δ_4
PU4 = PU + ε_1
PU1 = λ^y_{21}PU + ε_2
PU2 = λ^y_{31}PU + ε_3
PU3 = λ^y_{41}PU + ε_4
BI1 = BI + ε_5
BI2 = λ^y_{62}BI + ε_6

with VAR(δ_i) = θ^x_{ii}, VAR(ε_i) = θ^y_{ii}, and all δ_i, ε_i, and ζ_i mutually uncorrelated. All observed and latent variables are assumed to be mean-centered, so intercepts are not included in the model specification.

observed variable loads on a single factor and the unique factors are uncorrelated, so the confirmatory factor (or measurement) model is congeneric. For identification, one loading per factor (e.g., λ^x_{11}, λ^y_{11}, and λ^y_{52}) has to be constrained to one, or the factor variances have to be set to unity. In a confirmatory factor model, it is best to set the factor variances to one because this yields significance tests and readily interpretable factor loadings for all indicators, and the factor covariances are actually correlations; in a full structural equation model, the variances of PU and BI are functions of other model parameters, so it is better to set one loading per factor to one. Since all constructs are measured with at least two indicators and the measurement model is congeneric, the confirmatory factor model is identified as long as the correlation of BI with the other constructs is nonzero. The latent variable model is also identified because it is a recursive model (i.e., there are no feedback loops or reciprocal effects between PEOU, PU, and BI, and the covariance between the structural disturbances ζ_1 and ζ_2 is zero). The variance-covariance matrix of the 10 observed variables consists of 55 distinct elements (10 × 11/2 = 55, i.e., 10 variances and 45 covariances), and since the model in Fig. 1 (or Table 1) contains 23 free parameters (7 loadings, 10 unique factor variances, the variance of PEOU, three structural coefficients, and 2 structural disturbance variances), the model is overidentified with 32 degrees of freedom.

Model Estimation

The goal of estimation is to find values for all model parameters such that the variance-covariance matrix implied by the estimated parameters is as close as possible to the sample variance-covariance matrix. Structural equation models are usually estimated using the maximum likelihood (ML) method under the assumption that the observations are sampled independently from an underlying multivariate normal distribution. Before estimating the model, a researcher should ascertain that the assumption of multivariate normality is not too badly violated by graphically examining the data (e.g., checking the symmetry of the variable distributions via histograms, doing normal probability plots, etc.) and computing statistics such as skewness and kurtosis (both univariate and multivariate), and possibly conducting formal tests of normality. In order for normality to hold, the variables have to be continuous, which is rarely the case, so the hope is that the results based on ML will be robust to (moderate) violations of underlying assumptions. Although estimation procedures are available that do not require normality (e.g., so-called asymptotically distribution-free procedures), they have been shown not to perform well unless the sample size is very large. There are also estimation procedures that lessen the influence of unusual observations (outliers), but these are not used very often. Structural equation models can also be estimated using partial least squares (PLS) estimation, but we will not discuss PLS estimation in this chapter because it is based on a different statistical model; the reader is referred to the chapter ▶ "Partial Least Squares Structural Equation Modeling" by Sarstedt, Ringle, and Hair (this volume).

In theory (i.e., when the underlying assumptions are satisfied), ML estimation is attractive because the ML estimator is consistent, asymptotically unbiased, asymptotically efficient, and asymptotically normally distributed. In practice, the parameter estimates themselves tend to be reasonably robust (close to the true parameters, at least in simulations), but this robustness does not hold for the overall test of model fit and the estimates of the standard errors of the parameters, which are needed for the statistical tests conducted on individual parameters or sets of parameters. Possible solutions to this problem are discussed below in the context of model testing.

Since the desirable properties of the ML estimator only hold asymptotically, the question arises how large the sample size should be so that one can have confidence in the estimates and statistical tests. Few reliable guidelines are available. Existing sample size recommendations are based on rules of thumb such as the sample size should be at least 200, there should be at least 5–10 observations per estimated parameter, or at least 10 cases should be available per observed variable (see Muthén and Muthén 2002 and Wolf et al. 2013 for references). Since there is no magic cutoff above which the desirable properties of ML suddenly kick in, the usefulness of these rules of thumb may be questioned. Furthermore, research has shown that the required sample size depends on a host of factors, including the number of observed and latent variables, the distribution of the observed variables, the reliability of the measures, the strength of the relationships between the latent variables, the type of model (CFA models vs. models with a latent variable specification), and the amount of missing data (Muthén and Muthén 2002; Wolf et al. 2013). Finally, the required sample size depends on the magnitude of the bias in parameter and standard error estimates that the researcher is willing to tolerate, the desired accuracy of the coverage rate of confidence intervals (how often, say, a 95% confidence interval includes the true parameter value), and the power for detecting specific effects or sets of effects that the researcher wants to achieve.

Instead of relying on questionable rules of thumb, a researcher can use a Monte Carlo analysis to determine the required power. To provide a specific example, consider the model in Fig. 1. Assume that each indicator has a reliability of 0.64 (i.e., with standardized observed variables, all loadings are 0.80), and the standardized path coefficients between PEOU and PU, PEOU and BI, and PU and BI are all 0.5. Thus, the amounts of variance explained in PU and BI are 25% and 75%, respectively. To conduct the analysis, a large number of samples of a given size is generated from the assumed population, for each data set the model is estimated, and the performance of the estimator at a given sample size is assessed. Specifically, Muthén and Muthén (2002) and Wolf et al. (2013) propose the following two-step procedure for determining sample size. First, the bias of both the parameter and standard error estimates should not exceed a certain percentage (e.g., the ratio of the value estimated for a given sample minus the population value over the population value should be within, say, 5% of the true value on average). In addition, the 95% confidence interval should include the true value in, say, at least 90% of the replications. Second, the estimated power for the parameter(s) of interest should be, say, at least 80% (i.e., the estimated parameter should be significant in at least 80% of samples). For the illustration, we used Mplus to conduct an analysis for 10,000 replications (the results are available on Github). Even at a sample size of only 100, most parameters had little bias (with the exception of the effects of PEOU and PU on BI, as well as the indirect effect). The same was true for standard error bias. The minimum coverage accuracy was 0.929, and power was at least 95%. At a sample size of 200, bias, coverage, and power were at acceptable levels for all parameters.

Two problems may arise during the estimation of the model. First, the estimation procedure may fail to converge within a given number of iterations or within a given time limit. For example, in the sample size simulation, the nonconvergence rate was 0.33% at a sample size of 100. Second, even if the estimation does converge, the solution may not be admissible. For example, estimated correlations may be greater than one in absolute magnitude or variance estimates may be negative. The causes of both problems include poorly specified models, few observed indicators per factor, small sample sizes, and bad starting values. It is possible to constrain questionable parameters so that inadmissible estimates are impossible, but this may lead to nonconvergence. Another possibility is to fix inadmissible estimates to a certain value (e.g., +1 or −1 for correlations that exceed 1 in absolute value or 0 for negative variance estimates); this may be defensible when the confidence interval about the estimated parameter includes the boundary of the parameter space (+1 or −1 for correlations, 0 for negative variance estimates).

Testing the Global Fit of Models

When a model is overidentified (i.e., when the degrees of freedom are positive), the fit of the model to data can be tested with a chi-square goodness-of-fit test. The null hypothesis for the test is that the model fits perfectly, whereas the alternative hypothesis is that the fit is less than perfect (i.e., the model fits less well than the saturated model with zero degrees of freedom). The test statistic (which we will call T_{ML} in the case of maximum likelihood estimation based on the multivariate normal distribution) is compared to the critical value of a reference distribution (e.g., a chi-square distribution with df degrees of freedom), and if T_{ML} exceeds the critical value, the null hypothesis of perfect fit is rejected. The test assumes that (a) the assumptions on which the chosen estimation procedure is based are satisfied (e.g., in the case of maximum likelihood, it is assumed that the observations are independently and identically distributed and are sampled from a multivariate normal distribution) and (b) the sample size is large (because the test is only asymptotically valid). In practice, the chi-square test may not be useful because (a) it is not robust to violations of the underlying assumptions; (b) it requires a large sample size and the available sample may not be large enough to yield a trustworthy test; and, maybe most importantly, (c) the null hypothesis assumes that the specified model fits perfectly in the population, which is likely not a realistic assumption since most models are at best only approximately true. If the model is only an approximation, a large enough sample will invariably lead to the decision that the model does not fit perfectly. Sample size is thus a two-edged sword: on the one hand, a large sample is required for the chi-square test to be valid, but on the other hand, when the specified model is not literally true in the population, a large sample will lead to the rejection of the specified model. If the reasons for the departure from perfect fit could be reliably detected and sensibly corrected, this would not be a problem, but unfortunately, there are often small discrepancies in many different parts of the model that defy easy rectification.

Modified test statistics for assessing overall model fit have been suggested to deal with both a violation of normality and a small sample size. When multivariate normality is violated, the Satorra-Bentler rescaled (mean-adjusted) test statistic (T_{MLM}) is commonly used (Satorra and Bentler 2001). Unfortunately, research has shown that correct models are rejected too frequently by this test statistic when the number of variables is large and/or the sample size is small (i.e., the type I error rate is too high). Other modifications of T_{ML} to correct for non-normality (e.g., mean- and variance-adjusted test statistics) have been proposed as well.

To deal with small samples, Bartlett suggested multiplying the minimum of the ML discrepancy function not by (N-1) but by a different factor that depends on the number of observed variables and the number of factors. This modification was initially introduced for exploratory factor models, but it has been applied to confirmatory factor models and more general structural equation models as well. Furthermore, the correction has also been applied to T_{MLM}. Modified versions of the Bartlett correction have been proposed as well.

Yang, Jiang and Yuan (2018) studied the performance (in terms of type I error rates) of 11 modifications of the conventional T_{ML} statistic (including T_{MLM} and the Bartlett correction) for a correctly specified SEM model across different numbers of observed variables (15–80), different sample sizes (70–2500), and different population distributions (normal, elliptical, skewed, and rescaled skewed). The degrees of freedom for the models studied ranged from 76 to 3066, so model complexity was much higher than in many models encountered in practice. Yang et al. found that T_{MLM} showed the worst performance among all the modifications of T_{ML} and the Bartlett correction applied to T_{MLM} showed the best performance (although some other modifications performed similarly well). The performance of the test statistics that performed well depended on all three factors studied (number of observed variables, sample size, and distribution of the observed variables), although when the number of observed variables did not exceed 30, the performance of T_{MLM} with the Bartlett correction was good in general. When the number of observed variables was large and the sample size small, none of the test statistics yielded trustworthy results.

A different small-sample correction was recently proposed by McNeish (2020), who suggested that an F-distribution (rather than a chi-square distribution) be used as the reference distribution. Specifically, the chi-square statistic has to be divided by the degrees of freedom of the model (df) and the resulting ratio is then compared to an F-distribution with df and (sample size minus 1) degrees of freedom. This is based on the fact that as the denominator degrees of freedom of an F-distribution go toward infinity (i.e., as the sample size becomes very large), the F-distribution converges to a chi-square distribution divided by the numerator degrees of freedom. When the data are not normal, T_{MLM}, rather than T_{ML}, should be compared to an F-distribution.

An alternative to tests of overall model fit based on T (either T_{ML} or the various modifications discussed above) is to rely on various alternative fit indices. Generally, these do not enable inferential tests of model fit (although some, such as RMSEA, do) and instead quantify the degree of fit on a continuous scale. In order to judge fit based on these alternative fit indices, researchers need guidelines on how to interpret the scale on which fit is measured. Different researchers have proposed various cutoff values for different fit indices, based on either personal experience or simulation evidence. Initially, researchers hoped that general cutoff criteria could be developed that would be independent of model and data characteristics. For example, based on extensive simulations in which they varied sample size, distributional characteristics (normal distribution and different types of non-normality), estimation method, and type of misspecification (of either the factor loadings or the factor correlations), Hu and Bentler (1998, 1999) made recommendations about (a) which estimation procedure researchers should use (ML is preferable to generalized least squares or GLS and asymptotically distribution-free or ADF methods); (b) which fit indices researchers can rely on (among the preferred fit indices are the standardized root mean residual [SRMR], the root mean squared error of approximation [RMSEA], the confirmatory fit index [CFI], and the Tucker-Lewis index [TLI], although some caution is required for RMSEA and TLI when the sample size is 250 or smaller); and (c) what cutoffs researchers should employ to evaluate fit. In particular, they suggested that researchers use a two-index presentation strategy in which SRMR is combined with one of the other recommended fit indices, primarily because SRMR was particularly effective in detecting structural model misspecification (misspecification of the factor correlations), while the other fit indices were more effective in detecting measurement model (loading) misspecification. In their words, "our results suggest a cutoff value close to .95 for the ML-based TLI ... [and] CFI ...; a cutoff value close to .08 for SRMR; and a cutoff value close to .06 for RMSEA, before one can conclude that there is a relatively good fit between the hypothesized model and the observed data" (Hu and Bentler 1998, p. 449). Note that low values of RMSEA and SRMR and high values of CFI and TLI are indicative of good fit.

Unfortunately, subsequent research has shown that the distribution of the various fit indices depends on many different model and data characteristics, including the number of indicators per factor, the number of factors, the magnitude of the factor loadings, and the sample size (in addition to degree of misspecification, degree of normality, etc.). This implies that these model and data characteristics have to be taken into account when formulating guidelines for model fit. This has led to the development of so-called flexible cutoffs (Niemand and Mai 2018). In addition, researchers must take into account to what extent they are concerned about type I (rejecting a correct model) or type II (failing to reject an incorrect model) errors. A website (www.flexiblecutoffs.org) is available that readers can use to derive cutoffs for specific models of interest.

To summarize the discussion, it is unfortunate that, in spite of the voluminous research on the topic, generally applicable guidelines for overall fit assessment ("golden rules") remain elusive (Marsh et al. 2004). It also seems doubtful that flexible cutoffs will prove to be a fully satisfactory solution to the fit conundrum. Furthermore, since even a well-fitting model based on the most stringent standards (e.g., the standard chi-square goodness-of-fit test) is not necessarily the "true" model, an acceptable overall model fit should never be used as the sole (or primary) arbiter of whether a proposed theory is correct (especially since usually most of the overidentifying restrictions come from the measurement model, not the latent variable model). This is especially true when alternative fit indices are used to adjudge model fit because the cutoffs for the alternative fit indices are essentially arbitrary.

Our recommendation is twofold. First, lack of fit based on the chi-square goodness-of-fit test (or more robust alternatives) should instigate a search for major and correctable misspecifications. Second, if a respecified model still does not meet the stringent requirements of the chi-square test (after readily correctable misspecifications have been implemented), alternative fit indices (probably in combination with flexible cutoff values) may be used to justify the conclusion that the hypothesized (or respecified) model is good enough to evaluate the local fit of the model and interpret the parameters of interest. The guidelines offered by Hu and Bentler (1998) may be used as rough rules of thumb to judge model fit (i.e., if RMSEA <0.06, SRMR <0.08, CFI > 0.95, and TLI >0.95, the model fits reasonably well), but they should not be employed dogmatically and supplemented with flexible cutoff values. Finally, instead of evaluating a single model, it is usually preferable to compare several plausible competing models and to determine which model is most consistent with the data. Information criteria such as the Bayesian Information Criterion (BIC) can be helpful when comparing alternative models (Bollen et al. 2014), especially when non-nested models are to be compared.

Respecifying Models That Do Not Pass the Global Fit Test

Based on our own experience with estimating numerous structural equation models, it is rare that the originally hypothesized model will provide an acceptable fit to the data. If all the fit indices indicate that the fit is poor, the model should not be interpreted before appropriate modifications are introduced. Frequently, the situation is complicated by the fact that some fit indices indicate that the fit is acceptable, while others suggest that the fit is questionable. It is not unusual to read papers in which the authors' primary concern seems to be to defend their favored model by selectively focusing on the fit indices that imply acceptable fit. Obviously, a better approach is for researchers to be skeptical of their own models and to thoroughly investigate potential sources of misfit before moving on to a substantive interpretation of the results.

The two primary tools for model modification are residual analysis and inspection of the modification indices and expected parameter changes. Residuals are the differences between the observed covariances or correlations and the covariances or correlations implied by the estimated model. A positive residual indicates that an observed covariance or correlation is underfitted, whereas a negative residual signals overfitting. In our experience, modification indices are easier to use and provide more useful information, so we will focus on them. A modification index (MI), also called Lagrange multiplier or LM statistic in some programs, is the expected decrease in the chi-square statistic (e.g., T_{ML}) when a previously fixed parameter is freely estimated or an equality constraint is relaxed. If a MI exceeds the critical value of a chi-square distribution with one degree of freedom (e.g., 3.84 for a significance level of 0.05), relaxing the constraint in question will significantly improve the fit of the model. Associated with each MI is an expected parameter change (EPC) statistic, which is the predicted estimate when a parameter is freely estimated in the revised model. When the model is reasonably complex and the sample size relatively large, many MI's can be significant, and it may not be straightforward to decide how to modify the model. Parameters should be freed one at a time in a stepwise fashion, and model modifications should be strongly guided and tempered by conceptual considerations. Sometimes, potential revisions to the model suggested by highly significant MI's make no conceptual sense, and simulations have shown that data-driven specification searches frequently fail to identify known misspecifications (e.g., MacCallum 1986; MacCallum et al. 1992). It is also important to check the EPC's associated with significant MI's to ascertain whether a suggested model modification is practically relevant and substantively interpretable. For example, the MI for a nontarget loading or an error covariance may be highly significant, but if the EPC is negligible (e.g., a standardized nontarget loading of 0.05), it is probably not meaningful to add an additional parameter to the model. Finally, researchers should compare the substantively important parameter estimates in the original model (or the model in which the major misspecifications, if any, were corrected) with those in the final, modified model, ideally one that is judged acceptable on all (or most) fit criteria. If there are no substantively important differences, the simpler model might be preferable even when it fits the data less well than the more complex model, especially if some of the parameter estimates in the more complex model are difficult to interpret or explain.

The most common model modifications are the following. In the measurement model, observed variables often have nonzero loadings on factors other than the target factor on which each observed variable is supposed to load. It can happen that these nontarget loadings are actually stronger than the target loading, in which case the measurement model has to be revised or the offending indicator has to be dropped from the model (although this may cause other problems, such as a restriction of the domain of content of the construct). Another problem in the measurement model could be that some correlations between the unique factors (error terms) associated with different observed variables are nonzero, or that additional factors are needed to fully account for the correlations between the observed variables. For example, if some indicators are coded such that a higher score indicates a higher standing on the construct of interest (so-called regular items), whereas for other items a lower score indicates a higher standing on the underlying construct (so-called reversed items), the keying direction of the items may lead to correlated uniquenesses or require the inclusion of a method factor (or several method factors) to model this source of covariation (see Baumgartner and Weijters 2019).

In the latent variable model, the covariances between the exogenous variables are usually freely estimated, so there should be no misspecification in this part of the model. However, a saturated structural model in which all possible pairwise relationships between constructs are estimated is not parsimonious, and since researchers prefer simple models, usually some relationships between exogenous and endogenous constructs, or between endogenous constructs, are specified to be zero. For example, construct M may be hypothesized to fully mediate the relationship between constructs X and Y, in which case the direct path from X to Y should be zero. However, it is possible that the mediation is only partial in the data analyzed. This means that the MI for the direct path from X to Y will be significant (see also chapter ▶ "Mediation Analysis in Experimental Research" by Koschate-Fischer and Schwille, this volume). Such a misspecification is easily rectified. However, significant modification indices are not always informative. For example, in a panel data set in which construct X is measured at time t and construct Y is measured at (t + 1), the MI for the path from Y to X might be significant, but such a relationship is of course impossible. The goal is to find a latent variable specification that is as simple as possible and as complex as required (see Anderson and Gerbing 1988 for details).

Often, some of the covariances or paths between constructs will be nonsignificant. If a relationship was hypothesized a priori, it is best to retain the nonsignificant path in the final model. If a relationship is not of explicit interest, one may prune the model by dropping the nonsignificant path, but the overall goodness-of-fit test is no longer interpretable as an a priori test. Ideally, modified models should be tested on new data to avoid that misleading conclusions are derived from data sets that happen to contain idiosyncratic associations.

Assessing the Local Fit of Models

Even if a model explains the covariances between the observed variables very well (as shown by a nonsignificant chi-square goodness-of-fit test), this does not mean that the constructs are measured validly and reliably, that the relationships between the constructs are consistent with the researcher's hypotheses, or that a significant proportion of the variance in the endogenous variables is accounted for. Answers to these questions require a more detailed assessment of the local fit of the estimated model. We recommend a two-step process in which the quality of the measurement model is evaluated first and then the latent variable model is investigated in detail (Anderson and Gerbing 1988). Unless the constructs are measured appropriately, it will be difficult to interpret the relationships between the constructs with confidence. Although a measurement analysis can be conducted for the model in which a particular structure is imposed on the relationships between the constructs, it is advantageous to start with a measurement model in which both the endogenous and exogenous variables are allowed to be freely correlated. In such a model, the latent variable model is saturated so that a structural misspecification will not distort the measurement relations. Once the measurement model is deemed acceptable (using the measurement model modification strategies described earlier), the hypothesized structural specification can be implemented, and after the latent variable model has been adapted, if necessary, the parameters of substantive interest can be interpreted.

Measurement Model

We will assume that a congeneric factor model fits the data adequately. If the model contains nontarget loadings or correlated uniquenesses (correlated errors), some of the discussion below may not be applicable (e.g., the computation of composite reliability).

The first step is to check the parameter estimates for the loadings, factor correlations, and error variances (i.e., the variances of the unique factors). There should be no improper solutions (e.g., the factor correlations should not exceed one in absolute magnitude, the error variances should be nonnegative), and the factor loadings should be positive (assuming all items are keyed such that higher scores reflect a higher standing on the construct of interest), significant, and substantial.

The second step is to compute various statistics related to reliability and convergent validity. Conceptually, reliability refers to the degree of convergence of measures that are very similar (they have perfectly correlated true scores) but may be distorted by random error; convergent validity refers to the degree of convergence between measures that are less similar (e.g., they might be based on different methods for measuring a construct) and may contain nonrandom error. It is often difficult to draw a sharp distinction between the two, and we will mostly use the term reliability to refer to both reliability and convergent validity. Three measures of reliability are commonly reported. As the name suggests, individual-item reliability

(IIR) refers to the reliability of a single indicator as a measure of the target construct; conceptually, it is the squared correlation between an indicator and the underlying construct, and it is computed as the square of the completely standardized loading (i.e., the loading from a factor model in which both the constructs and the observed measures are standardized to a variance of one). A summary measure for the average individual-item reliability of all measures of a construct is called average variance extracted (AVE; Fornell and Larcker 1981). For example, if a construct is measured by four items, the AVE would be the average of the four IIRs. The final reliability measure is called composite reliability (CR), and it refers to the squared correlation between an unweighted sum (or average) of all measures of a construct and the construct. It can be computed as follows:

$$CR_{\Sigma x_i} = \frac{(\Sigma \lambda_{ij})^2 \varphi_{jj}}{(\Sigma \lambda_{ij})^2 \varphi_{jj} + \Sigma \theta_{ii}}, \qquad (4)$$

where the subscripts i and j refer to the ith measure of construct j. If, in the previous example, the four items measuring the construct of interest were averaged (or summed), CR would be the estimated reliability of that composite. Composite reliability can be computed for both observed variables in their original metric or standardized observed variables; the results will differ (corresponding to the difference between a coefficient alpha based on the original or standardized variables), and if the observed variables are measured on very different scales, standardization is preferable. Since multiple measures are generally more reliable than single measures, CR will usually be larger than IIR or AVE.

We hesitate to provide guidelines about desirable levels of reliability, because reliability depends greatly on various item characteristics that do not necessarily reflect differences in measurement quality. For example, a series of more or less identical items administered one after the other will likely exhibit high reliability because respondents will fail to see the difference between the items and there are strong demands for consistency; in contrast, items that cover the domain of an intended construct more broadly and comprehensively may demonstrate less consistency. Of course, reliability assumes that the items are exchangeable, but in practice, convergent validity is probably the more appropriate concept (because measures should not be obviously redundant). Available recommendations also differ widely, particularly with respect to IIR. For IIR and AVE, 0.5 is frequently proposed as a lower limit of acceptability (i.e., observed measures should contain, on average, at least 50% trait variance). This criterion may not sound very stringent, but it frequently is not satisfied in practice. For CR, the same guidelines as for coefficient alpha apply (the two tend to be very similar in magnitude); thus, values below 0.6 are probably unacceptable, and values of 0.8 or higher are often deemed desirable.

The third step is to assess the discriminant validity of the constructs in one's model. The idea is that constructs should not correlate too highly, otherwise they may not be distinct. An important goal of discriminant validity assessment is to avoid construct proliferation. The primary and most defensible test of discriminant validity is that the disattenuated correlation between each pair of constructs (i.e., the factor correlation corrected for the downward bias in observed correlations due to measure unreliability) should be significantly different from unity (i.e., constructs should not be perfectly correlated). The most straightforward way to conduct this test is to construct confidence intervals around the estimated factor correlations; if the confidence interval does not include one, discriminant validity is satisfied. The major problem with this criterion is that rather high correlations will differ from one when the test is sufficiently powerful and that constructs may not be distinct for practical purposes (i.e., statistical significance is not the same as practical significance). Ultimately, it is up to the researcher to decide whether a conceptual distinction between two highly correlated constructs is justified; the final arbiter of this decision should not be a statistical test. Many researchers also evaluate discriminant validity using a criterion originally proposed by Fornell and Larcker (1981). It is not a statistical test (although a statistical test could be conducted), but a numerical comparison of the squared (disattenuated) correlation between two constructs and the AVEs of the constructs involved in the correlation. If the squared correlation between two constructs is smaller than the AVE of both constructs, discriminant validity is said to be satisfied. Alternatively (and equivalently), the factor correlation can be compared with the square root of AVE. The idea is that a construct should share more variance with its own measures (as assessed by AVE) than with other (supposedly distinct) constructs. On the one hand, since the squared correlation between constructs is compared to AVE rather than unity, the Fornell and Larcker criterion is more stringent than the test of whether two constructs are perfectly correlated. On the other hand, since the Fornell and Larcker criterion usually involves only a numerical comparison, it is less stringent than a statistical test of whether two constructs are perfectly correlated (which takes into account the uncertainty involved in this decision).

If two constructs lack discriminant validity, the model has to be respecified. The two constructs may be combined (if a conceptual argument can be constructed supporting this integration), one construct may be dropped, or better measures for one of the constructs (or both constructs) may have to be developed.

So far we have only discussed discriminant validity at the construct level. At the item level, discriminant validity means that an item is solely (or at least primarily) related to its target construct, not to other, related constructs. In general, nontarget loadings are undesirable, and if they are too high, the indicator in question is probably not a good measure of the intended construct.

Once an appropriate measurement model is in place, the restrictions contained in the latent variable model can be implemented and the reliability statistics should be recomputed. The differences in the values of these statistics between the two specifications should be minor, but the measurement analysis should be reported for the final model.

It should be noted that the measurement analysis described for reflective measurement models is inappropriate for formative indicators models. Formative indicators need not be highly (positively) correlated, and error resides in the latent variable, not the indicators, so the conventional reliability indices are not applicable. Furthermore, the notion of reliability is questionable with formative indicators, and convergent validity is the more relevant concept. Convergent validity of individual formative indicators can be assessed by the strength of the relationship between each formative indicator and the construct it measures, and the convergent validity of the formative indicators as a set can be expressed by the variance accounted for in the formatively measured construct by its indicators. Discriminant validity at the construct level can be assessed by testing whether the correlations between the constructs differ from one (as with reflective measurement models), but the conventional Fornell and Larcker criterion is not applicable. More detail is provided in Baumgartner and Weijters (2019) and MacKenzie et al. (2011), as well as the references given there.

Latent Variable Model

In studies in which SEM is used to test conceptual frameworks, the latent variable model will be of primary substantive interest. The research was probably motivated by the desire to investigate particular relationships between constructs, so the researcher will look at the sign and magnitude of the relevant parameter estimates and their statistical significance (or, preferably, the confidence interval around the estimated parameters). To get a sense of the explanatory power of the proposed framework, it is also useful to look at the variance accounted for in each endogenous construct. The chi-square goodness-of-fit test is sometimes used for evaluating the explanatory power of a framework, but as stated earlier, this is inappropriate because (a) usually most of the overidentifying restrictions tested by the chi-square test are derived from the measurement model and the chi-square test does not directly test the overidentifying restrictions contained in the latent variable model, and (b) the "explanatory" variables may explain little variation in the endogenous constructs even when the model fits well based on the chi-square test.

Sometimes, hypotheses to be tested involve indirect effects. For example, if it is hypothesized that M mediates the effect of X on Y, the indirect effect of X→M and M→Y is of interest. All programs used for SEM enable the estimation and testing of indirect effects. However, the tests are usually based on normal-theory approximations (similar to the Sobel test), which are inferior to other alternatives such as bootstrapping or Bayesian procedures. These should be used in preference to the normal-theory tests. MacKinnon et al. (2002) compared 14 methods to test the statistical significance of an indirect effect and they concluded that the "best balance of Type I error and statistical power ... is the test of the joint significance of the two effects comprising the intervening variable [indirect] effect" (p. 83).

The Problem of Endogeneity

A model may have to be respecified not only when it fails to pass a global fit test, but also when local fit tests indicate that something is amiss. A key assumption for both the measurement and latent variable models is that the error term in each equation is uncorrelated with the explanatory variables in that equation. If this assumption is violated, a so-called endogeneity problem exists (see chapter ▶ "Dealing with Endogeneity: A Nontechnical Guide for Marketing Researchers" by Ebbes, Papies, and Van Heerde, this volume, for details). Common causes of endogeneity include measurement error in the explanatory variables; omitted variables that are correlated with the included explanatory variables and become part of the error term when not considered in the model; and reciprocal effects between the dependent variable and an explanatory variable. The usual way to deal with endogeneity is to use instrumental variables for the endogenous explanatory variables (Wooldridge 2016). An instrumental variable is a variable that is correlated with the endogenous explanatory variable (instrument relevance) but does not have a direct effect on the dependent variable and is uncorrelated with the error term in the equation of interest (instrument exogeneity). When a researcher anticipates that there might be an endogeneity problem, a so-called auxiliary variable (Bollen 2012) can be used as an instrument. For example, assume that a researcher is interested in the effect of schooling on earnings (Wooldridge 2016). When (unobserved) ability is not included in the regression, schooling is likely endogenous because ability is expected to be related to both schooling and earnings. A researcher might use proximity to a college/university or father's (mother's) education as an instrument, although one may question both choices because it is not clear that these variables are actually uncorrelated with the error term in the earnings-schooling regression. Bollen (2012, 2018) shows that observed variables included in a model can also serve as instrumental variables (so-called model-implied instrumental variables or MlIVs). We do not have the space to discuss MlIVs in detail but want to briefly present the basic idea. Consider the model in Fig. 1 and Table 1 and rewrite the measurement equations for the marker variables (i.e., the observed variables whose loading is set to 1) so that the latent variable appears on the left-hand side and the observed variable on the right-hand side (e.g., for PEOU this yields PEOU = PEOU4 − δ_1). Then substitute this expression for all occurrences of PEOU. Do the same for PU4 and BI1. For the two latent variable equations in the model this yields the following two equations:

$$PU4 = \gamma_{11}PEOU4 - \gamma_{11}\delta_1 + \varepsilon_1 + \varsigma_1 = \gamma_{11}PEOU4 + u_1 \qquad (5)$$

and

$$\begin{aligned}BI1 &= \beta_{21}PU4 + \gamma_{21}PEOU4 - \gamma_{21}\delta_1 - \beta_{21}\varepsilon_1 + \varepsilon_5 + \varsigma_2 \\ &= \beta_{21}PU4 + \gamma_{21}PEOU4 + u_2.\end{aligned} \qquad (6)$$

Note that if we regressed PU4 on PEOU4 and BI1 on PU4 and PEOU4, the coefficient estimates would be inconsistent because the explanatory variables in both equations are correlated with the (composite) error terms u_1 and u_2. However, we might be able to use other observed variables in the model as instruments for the endogenous explanatory variables PEOU4 and PU4. For example, an instrumental variable for PEOU4 in Eq. (5) would have to correlated with PEOU4 but uncorrelated with u1 (i.e., δ_1, ε_1, and ζ_1). It turns out that PEOU1, PEOU2, and PEOU3 are suitable instruments for PEOU4 in Eq. (5), and PEOU1, PEOU2, PEOU3, PU1, PU2, and PU3 are suitable instruments for PEOU4 and PU4 in Eq. (6), assuming that the specified model is correct. The MlIVsem package in R (Fisher et al. 2020) can be used to identify model-implied instrumental variables and to estimate the coefficients in both the measurement and latent variable model equations using two-stage least squares (2SLS). The advantage of using 2SLS estimation rather than a system-wide procedure such as ML is that the 2SLS estimator is less dependent on the normality assumption and that misspecifications in other parts of the model are less likely to affect the estimation of the parameters in a specific model equation (Bollen 2018). Furthermore, if an equation is overidentified (i.e., there are more instruments than endogenous explanatory variables), a χ^2 test is available to test the null hypothesis that the MlIVs are uncorrelated with the equation error (the so-called Sargan test). If the null hypothesis is rejected, the assumptions embedded in the specified model must be questioned (e.g., because the MlIVs implied by the model are apparently not valid instrumental variables) and the model may have to be respecified. Further details will be provided in the empirical section.

Extensions of the Core Structural Equation Model

We do not have the space to discuss in detail the many extensions of the core structural equation model that have appeared in the literature. However, we will briefly mention various models that significantly expand the scope of SEM and point the interested reader to the relevant literature.

Measurement Model Extensions

The extension from reflective to formative indicator models has already been mentioned and we will not discuss it further. The interested reader can consult sources such as Baumgartner and Weijters (2019), Bollen (2011), Diamantopoulos (2011), Diamantopoulos et al. (2008), Diamantopoulos and Winklhofer (2001), Edwards (2011), Howell et al. (2007), Jarvis et al. (2003), Kline (2013), MacCallum and Browne (1993), MacKenzie et al. (2005), MacKenzie et al. (2011), and Wilcox et al. (2008).

The (reflective) measurement model described so far assumes that the observed variables are continuous and measured on an interval scale. This assumption is violated in nearly all applications of SEM. Extensions to ordered-categorical (discrete-ordinal) observed variables (e.g., Likert-type scales) are available and deserve more widespread use. The conventional measurement model for continuous observed variables still applies, but the assumption is that continuous observed variables are not directly observed and only discretized versions of these variables are available. Although the statistical theory underlying these models has been around for a long time, and even though it is relatively easy these days to estimate these models in existing computer programs, they do introduce various complications, including the fact that the interpretation of the parameters of the model is less straightforward.

Fortunately, in many circumstances, methods developed for continuous data based on normal theory maximum likelihood estimation provide acceptable answers when robust corrections are applied to the test statistics and standard errors (this is necessary because categorical data are by definition non-normal). Specifically, based on an extensive simulation study, Rhemtulla et al. (2012) concluded that for scales with at least five answer categories, "reliance on continuous methodology in the presence of ordinal data will produce acceptable results" (p. 371).

One way in which researchers can improve the continuousness of their indicators is to form item parcels (i.e., sums or averages of sets of individual items within scales or subscales) and to use these item parcels as indicators. Measurement experts commonly agree that parceling should not be used in scale development and/or validation studies, or when the factor structure of a set of items is not well-understood, but when the number of items used to measure a construct is relatively large (e.g., greater than, say, 5), it may be impractical or even infeasible to specify a measurement model for the individual items. Furthermore, item parceling has several advantages, including better variable to sample size ratios, improved distributional properties and reliability of the parceled indicators, and more stable parameter estimates (Bandalos and Finney 2001). Usually, items are allocated to parcels in a (quasi-)random fashion, but there are situations in which strategic parceling is preferable (Weijters and Baumgartner, forthcoming). One complication that arises when using parceling is that, depending on how the parcels are formed (i.e., which specific items are allocated to a given parcel), the results may differ, and research has shown that the resulting parcel allocation variability can be non-negligible (Sterba 2011; Sterba and Pek 2012; Sterba and Rights 2017). It is therefore necessary to investigate parcel allocation variability, for example, by computing the average goodness-of-fit and the average parameter estimates across many different parcel allocations. The semTools package in R can be used for this purpose.

In the congeneric factor model, each indicator is allowed to load on a single construct and nontarget loadings are restricted to zero. This is a rather strong assumption that is frequently violated. Two extensions weaken this assumption. One is exploratory structural equation modeling (ESEM), where the usual confirmatory (congeneric) factor (measurement) model is replaced with an exploratory factor model (see Marsh et al. 2014). The other is Bayesian structural equation modeling (BSEM), where nontarget loadings are freely estimated but informative priors with a mean of zero and small variance are specified for the nontarget loadings to identify the model (see Muthén and Asparouhov 2012). Readers are referred to Baumgartner and Weijters (2019) and the original sources for more detail.

A final extension of the measurement model relates to situations in which substantive factors are not the only source of covariation between the indicators. Frequently, there are systematic, non-substantive influences on observed measures that are due to the method of measurement, which can cause dependencies between the items. Collectively, these are called method effects (MacKenzie and Podsakoff

2012; Podsakoff et al. 2003; Podsakoff et al. 2012), and the concern is that shared method variance may distort substantive relationships (i.e., common method bias). For example, some respondents may have a tendency to use certain response categories (e.g., the extremes, the positive or negative side, or the midpoint of the response scale), regardless of what they are being asked; shared characteristics of items, such as their keying direction (i.e., whether the item is a regular or reversed item), may lead to variance overlap; and common features of the measurement instrument or the context in which an instrument is administered may induce correlations between (some of) the items (see Podsakoff et al. 2003). To avoid common method bias, method factors or correlated uniquenesses can be included in the measurement model; method effects can be explicitly measured and accounted for in the measurement model or modeled implicitly via method factors or correlated uniquenesses; and method effects can be considered at the factor level or the level of individual items (see Baumgartner and Weijters 2019; Baumgartner and Weijters forthcoming; and Podsakoff et al. 2003 for details, as well as chapter ▶ "Crafting Survey Research: A Systematic Process for Conducting Survey Research" by Vomberg and Klarmann, this volume, for a discussion of survey research more generally).

Latent Variable Model Extensions

So far we have assumed that the relationships in the latent variable model are linear. This limits the applicability of SEM because theoretical frameworks sometimes specify nonlinear relationships between constructs. Here we will briefly discuss one type of nonlinear relationship in the latent variable model, namely, interactions between the exogenous latent variables (although quadratic effects could be considered as well). For concreteness, assume that instead of hypothesizing that PU partially mediates the effect of PEOU on BI, a researcher instead wants to test whether PEOU and PU have a multiplicative effect on BI, that is,

$$\text{BI} = \gamma_0 + \gamma_1 \text{PU} + \gamma_2 \text{PEOU} + \gamma_3 \text{PEOU} * \text{PU} + \varsigma_1 \qquad (7)$$

The problem that arises in this type of model is that products of normally distributed variables do not have a normal distribution, which implies that BI and the indicators of BI are also non-normal. Starting with the work of Kenny and Judd (1984), many different approaches for modeling latent interaction effects have been considered (see Cortina et al. 2021 for a recent review). The most promising approach appears to be one suggested by Klein and Moosbrugger (2000), which has been implemented in Mplus and is also available in the nlsem package in R (Umbach et al. 2017). Basically, Klein and Moosbrugger (2000) show that the density of the observed variables can be expressed as a continuous mixture of normal densities and that this density can be approximated by a finite mixture of normal densities. The parameters can then be estimated with the EM algorithm. In contrast to other methods, this approach does not require that products of observed variables be used as indicators of the latent interaction term, and it has performed well in simulation studies (maybe partly because it minimizes non-normality since products of observed variables are not used as indicators).

Models That Incorporate Population Heterogeneity

The single-sample structural equation model assumes that the observations are sampled from a single homogeneous population. One way the core model can be extended to multiple populations is to assume that there are G populations, and even though the same measurement and latent variable model applies to each of the G populations, the values of the model parameters may differ across populations. The model can be written as follows:

$$\eta^g = \alpha^g + B^g \eta^g + \Gamma^g \xi^g + \varsigma^g \tag{8}$$

$$y^g = \tau^{yg} + \Lambda^{yg} \eta^g + \varepsilon^g \tag{9}$$

$$x^g = \tau^{xg} + \Lambda^{xg} \xi^g + \delta^g \tag{10}$$

where the superscript g refers to the gth population (g = 1, ..., G). This is the multi-sample analogue of the model in Eqs. (1)–(3), except that the model includes a latent variable model intercept term α^g (alpha) and measurement intercept terms τ^{yg} and τ^{yg} (tau). In single-sample models, the latent and observed variables are assumed to be mean-centered, but in multi-sample models, it is possible to specify a mean structure, which expresses the means of the observed variables as a function of the latent means of ξ^g (denoted by κ^g) and which requires the inclusion of intercepts in the three equations. For identification, the measurement intercept of the indicator whose loading on the target construct is set to one is restricted to zero (although other identification constraints are possible).

There are two primary uses for this model. One is to assess the invariance of parameters across groups. This is particularly important for multi-sample measurement models, because comparing construct means and relationships between constructs across groups is only meaningful if the measurements are comparable across groups. The details are spelled out in Steenkamp and Baumgartner (1998) and Vandenberg and Lance (2000), as well as other sources, but stated briefly: (a) if relationships between constructs are to be compared across groups, at least two loadings per construct have to be invariant and (b) if latent means are to be compared across groups, at least two loadings and two intercepts per construct have to be invariant. Chi-square difference tests can be used to check whether the loadings and intercepts are invariant. For example, for invariance of the loadings, the model in which all loadings are freely estimated is compared with the model in which the loadings are constrained to be equal across groups. If the first model fits significantly better than the second model, the hypothesis of invariance of all loadings has to be rejected, and modification indices can be used to free the loadings that are not invariant. When the sample sizes are rather large, it may be more meaningful to base model comparisons on alternative fit indices; information criteria such as BIC can be especially useful for this purpose.

The second use of multi-sample models, already hinted at in the previous paragraph, is to test substantive hypotheses about differences in latent means and structural relationships between different groups. For example, a researcher may want to test whether US respondents are more individualistic (less collectivistic) than Chinese respondents, or whether attitudes are a stronger influence on behavioral intentions than social norms for US respondents, whereas the opposite is the case for Chinese respondents. Multi-sample analysis thus enables the testing of moderator effects as long as the moderator is discrete (see also chapter ▶ "Challenges in Conducting International Market Research" by Engelen, Engelen, and Craig, this volume, for further details about international marketing research).

In multi-sample structural equation models, the model parameters are treated as fixed effects. A second way in which population heterogeneity can be modeled is to assume that the groups for which data are available are randomly sampled from a larger number of populations and that the parameters in a particular population are specific realizations of a parameter distribution with a certain mean and variance (see chapter ▶ "Multilevel Modeling" by Haumann, Kassemeier, and Wieseke, this volume). Such hierarchical (or multilevel) random effect models, in which the individual observations are nested within higher-level groups, are usually used when the number of groups is relatively large, because they only require the estimation of the means and (co)variances of the parameters and are thus more parsimonious than fixed-effect models, in which separate parameters have to be estimated for all groups (see Muthén and Asparouhov 2011 for details).

Several special cases of hierarchical models deserve mention. When repeated observations for the same units are available over time, where the number of units is relatively large and the number of time periods is limited (e.g., respondents' materialism is measured on several occasions, or sales data are recorded across a large cross-section of brands for several years), a latent (growth) curve model can be specified. In this case, the repeated observations over time are nested within some higher-level unit (e.g., respondents, brands). Latent curve models simultaneously model both the aggregate change trajectory across all units and individual differences in this average trajectory across entities. The factors representing the individual curve parameters can also be related to other variables of interest so that it becomes possible to investigate hypotheses about systematic influences on individual change processes and to specify individual differences in change as antecedents of other constructs. For example, latent curve models provide answers to the following types of research questions: What is the average trajectory of materialism over time for a sample of respondents (where different functional forms can be specified for this average trajectory)? How much individual variation is there about this average trajectory? Do the trajectories of different variables covary (e.g., does increasing loneliness over time lead to an increase in materialism)? Which unit-level covariates (e.g., gender, social class) can explain different trajectories over time? See Bollen and Curran (2006) for further details.

Hierarchical models are also useful in a cross-sectional context when respondents provide ratings of multiple stimuli. An application that is particularly relevant for marketers is conjoint analysis (see chapter ▶ "Choice-Based Conjoint Analysis" by Eggers et al., this volume). In a typical conjoint study, respondents' rate (or choose from) multiple product profiles, where the product profiles (orthogonally) vary attributes such as price, brand name, or quality. In this case, the multiple ratings per respondent are nested within respondent, and a hierarchical model produces the distribution (means, variances, and covariances) of the part-worth utilities expressing the influence of the different levels of the design attributes on respondents' overall ratings (or choices). The individual-level part-worth utilities can also be related to various antecedents and consequences. See Weijters and Baumgartner (2019) for details.

Multi-sample analysis and hierarchical modeling represent situations in which the group membership of different observations is known a priori. This is called observed population heterogeneity. In models for unobserved population heterogeneity, the goal of the analysis is to uncover the number of populations from which the observations are sampled and to determine the likely membership of observations in each group. Such models may be valuable in areas such as segmentation analysis, although they are not used much in theory-guided research. See Muthén (2001) for details.

Empirical Illustration of Structural Equation Modeling

In this section, the concepts and procedures described above are illustrated with an empirical example. The example uses publicly available data from a study by Diop et al. (2019), who surveyed 762 Chinese respondents (i.e., drivers who held a valid driver license at the time the study was conducted) about various issues related to road guidance through Variable Message Sign (VMS) information. The R code for all analyses reported below (which also includes access to the data file directly from the PLOS ONE website) is available at https://github.com/HansBaum129/SEM.

Conceptual Model

A VMS system uses electronic traffic signs that can be dynamically updated to provide travelers with information about such things as road blockages, congestion, and alternative routes to get to a destination. In line with the Technology Acceptance Model or TAM (Davis 1989), a driver's behavioral intention (BI) to use electronic message signs can be explained by the perceived usefulness (PU) and perceived ease of use (PEOU) of VMS information, with PU additionally acting as a partial mediator of the effect of PEOU on BI. Figure 1 shows a graphical representation of this conceptual model. In the paper by Diop et al. (2019), the conceptual model contains additional variables specific to the VMS context (familiarity with the road network, information quality, and attitude toward route diversion), but we will focus

Measurement Model

The constructs PEOU, PU, and BI were measured with multiple items (four items each for PEOU and PU, and three items for BI) using five-point Likert scales ranging from "extremely disagree" to "extremely agree," with "neutral" as the mid-point anchor. The individual items are reported in Table 2. Several comments can be offered about them. The PEOU items are clearly reflective measures of the underlying construct. However, the first three PU items are probably formative indicators, because avoiding congestion, arriving at the destination on time, and making better routing and departure time choices (which is a double-barreled question) are probably contributing factors to PU. In contrast, the fourth PU item is clearly a reflective measure of the underlying construct. For both PEOU and PU, the fourth indicator is an overall assessment of perceived ease of use or perceived usefulness, respectively, whereas the other indicators refer to more specific aspects of each construct (esp. for PU). Finally, although the three measures of BI may be treated as reflective indicators, the third indicator does not measure behavioral intentions to use VMS information, but intentions to recommend the VMS system. These are different constructs. All these issues may create problems for model fit and may require an alternative measurement model specification, as discussed below.

Figure 2 displays the measurement model used for the confirmatory factor analysis (CFA), which is the model assumed by Diop et al. (2019). For identification,

Table 2 Items used to measure PEOU, PU, and BI

Construct	Item	Wording
Perceived ease of use	PEOU1	Using VMS information does not require a lot of mental effort.
	PEOU2	It is easy to learn how to use VMS information.
	PEOU3	VMS information is easy to understand.
	PEOU4	Overall, I find VMS information easy to use.
Perceived usefulness	PU1	Using VMS information helps me in avoiding congestion.
	PU2	Using VMS information helps me in arriving to my destination on time.
	PU3	Using VMS information helps me make better routing and departure time choices.
	PU4	Overall, I find VMS information useful.
Behavioral intention	BI1	I would consider using VMS information as long as it is available.
	BI2	I will very likely use VMS information if it is available.
	BI3	I would recommend others to use VMS information for their trips.

Source: Diop et al. (2019)

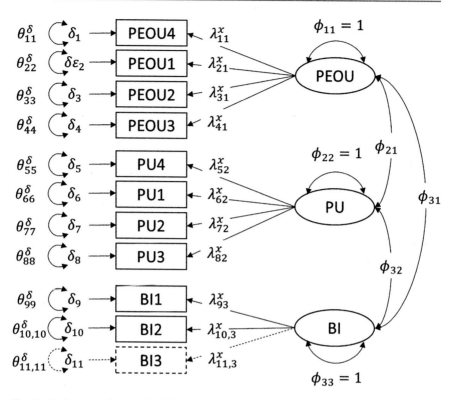

Fig. 2 Confirmatory factor analysis (measurement) model for the TAM constructs. Note: Item BI3 was eventually dropped from the model based on the measurement analysis

either one factor loading per factor needs to be fixed to one (e.g., $\lambda^x_{11} = 1$, $\lambda^x_{52} = 1$, $\lambda^x_{93} = 1$) or the factor variances have to be fixed to one ($\phi_{11} = 1$, $\phi_{22} = 1$, $\phi_{33} = 1$); as explained earlier, the latter is preferable in measurement models, as shown in Fig. 2. The null hypothesis that the model fits the data perfectly must be rejected since T_{ML} exceeds the critical value of the chi-square distribution; in particular, T_{ML} with 41 degrees of freedom is 265.25, $p < 0.0001$. The alternative fit indices are: RMSEA = 0.085 (90% CI = [0.075,0.095]); SRMR = 0.047; CFI = 0.960; and TLI = 0.947. Using conventional cutoff criteria (e.g., Hu and Bentler 1999), these indices suggest that the model shows acceptable fit (especially in terms of CFI and SRMR) or nearly acceptable fit (in terms of RMSEA and TLI) to the data. On the other hand, none of the indices meet the cutoffs suggested by www.flexiblecutoffs.org (assuming non-normality): RMSEA <0.023; SRMR <0.03; CFI > 0.982; and TLI > 0.977.

It is common in marketing research to treat five-point Likert-type item responses as continuous, interval-scaled, and normally distributed variables. Strictly speaking, this is incorrect and it may be useful to consider using an estimation and testing approach that accounts for the non-normality of the data. Using the Satorra-Bentler correction for non-normality (i.e., the MLM estimator in lavaan) gives slightly better fit results: $T_{\text{MLM}} = 187.448$ with 41 degrees of freedom, $p < 0.001$; Robust RMSEA = 0.081 (90% CI = [0.070,0.093]), SRMR = 0.047; Robust CFI = 0.963; and Robust TLI = 0.951. However, the fit is far from perfect. Since the sample size is fairly large, the small-sample correction due to Bartlett should not have a strong effect on the result, which was indeed the case; the Bartlett correction applied to the regular chi-square statistic yielded $T_{\text{ML}}^{\text{Bm}} = 262.64$ and the Bartlett correction applied to the Satorra-Bentler chi-square statistic yielded $T_{\text{MLM}}^{\text{Bm}} = 185.85$. The small-sample correction procedure based on the F-distribution suggested by McNeish (2020) also leads to the decision that the model does not fit the data well (i.e., the p-values based on the F-distribution using either T_{ML} or T_{MLM} are essentially zero).

To diagnose the sources of misfit, one can look at the (asymptotically) standardized residuals and/or modification indices. A total of 19 residuals are significantly different from 0 at a Bonferroni-adjusted p-value of 0.0009 (the nominal alpha of 0.05 divided by the number of off-diagonal elements of 55). The four largest residuals are for PU1-PU2, PEOU2-PU1, BI1-BI2, and PEOU2-PU2. There is one very large modification index for the error covariance between PU1 and PU2 (MI = 70.88, EPC = 0.064) and three additional large modification indices for the nontarget loading of BI3 on PEOU (MI = 40.87, EPC = 0.284) and the error covariances of BI1-BI2 and PU3-PU4 (MI's of 36.93 and 33.15 and EPCs of 0.085 and 0.040, respectively).

These results suggest the following. First, the positive residual for PU1 and PU2 and the corresponding large MI show that these measures share variance that is not fully captured by the model. This is likely due to the fact that the items refer to avoiding congestion and arriving at the destination on time (which are very similar), whereas the remaining PU items are more general measures of perceived usefulness. The large residuals for PU1 and PU2 on the one hand and PEOU2 on the other hand may indicate the same problem (i.e., the closer correspondence of PU1 and PU2 relative to the other PU items). A researcher wanting to correct this problem could add a residual covariance term between PU1 and PU2, drop one of the two items (probably the item with the lower loading), or combine the two items. Alternatively, since this source of misfit is unlikely to affect the substantive findings, the problem may be ignored, which avoids overfitting and aids parsimony. After all, the items are not flagged as invalid or unreliable indicators of the construct; they merely correlate more strongly with each other than with other items measuring the same construct.

Second, the significant positive residual between BI1 and BI2 and the MI for the residual covariance between BI1 and BI2 indicate that BI1 and BI2 correlate more strongly with each other than they do with BI3. As pointed out earlier, BI3 is not a valid measure of intention to use VMS technology because it refers to intending to recommend the use of this technology to others. It may therefore be advisable to drop this item from the model, or to specify two different intention constructs, intention to use and intention to recommend the technology. The problem with the latter approach is that only a single measure of intention to recommend is available. The significant MI for the nontarget loading of BI3 on

Table 3 Composite reliability, shared variance, average variance extracted and factor correlations

	CR	SV/AVE/CORR			
		PEOU	PU	BI
PEOU	0.89	**0.67**	*0.47*	*0.58*
PU	0.90	0.22	**0.70**	*0.59*
BI	0.90	0.33	0.35	**0.81**

Note: *CR* Composite reliability, *SV* Shared variance (below diagonal, underlined); *AVE* Average variance extracted (diagonal, in bold), *CORR* factor correlation (above diagonal), *PEOU* Perceived ease of use, *PU* Perceived usefulness, *BI* Behavioral intention

PEOU may also hint at the fact that BI3 does not measure the same construct as BI1 and BI2.

For illustrative purposes, and because a construct that confounds intention to use and intention to recommend lacks conceptual appeal, we respecified the original model by dropping BI3 as an indicator of behavioral intention to use the VMS technology. The revised model still shows significant misfit ($T_{ML} = 201.908$ with 32 degrees of freedom, $p < 0.001$), but this should not come as a surprise since the major misspecification in the previous model (the stronger correlation between PU1 and PU2 compared to the other indicators of PU) was not corrected. The alternative fit indices show that the fit of the model has improved somewhat (RMSEA = 0.083; 90% CI = [0.073,0.095]); SRMR = 0.038; CFI = 0.967; TLI = 0.954, but particularly the RMSEA is still rather high.

In the revised CFA model, all (completely standardized) factor loadings are large (greater than 0.74) and statistically significant ($p < 0.001$). Table 3 displays the average variance extracted (AVE) and composite reliability (CR) for each of the three constructs as well as the shared variance (SV) and factor correlations between each pair of constructs. The AVE's are at least 0.67, so the indicators are quite reliable on average; the CR's are around 0.9, which indicates high internal consistency of the indicators of each construct; and the SV is well below 1 and smaller than the AVE for each pair of factors, which supports discriminant validity.

There is another measurement model specification that may be appropriate for these data. As already mentioned, the last indicator of both PEOU and PU is a global measure of each construct while the first three indicators tap into more specific aspects of ease of use and usefulness. Since all indicators are strongly related to the underlying construct, one may consider forming parceled indicators for PEOU and PU that consist of averages of the first three items. This model (see the R code for details) fits the data quite well, even though the chi-square statistic is still significant: $T_{ML} = 25.63$ with 6 degrees of freedom, $p < 0.001$; RMSEA = 0.066 (90% CI = [0.041, 0.093]); SRMR = 0.012; CFI = 0.993; and TLI = 0.983.

It is likely that many researchers would ignore the lack of fit indicated by the significant chi-square statistic in the original model (as did Diop et al.), and in some cases, this will probably not materially affect the substantive conclusions. However, the example illustrates that a detailed investigation of the sources of misfit can yield important insights into the measurement quality of different indicators, which should prove valuable in future research. The previous analysis also shows that while some misspecifications can be corrected and justified based on conceptual considerations, others defy simple correction and ready explanation. Although a researcher should make every effort to find a model that approximates the observed covariances as well as possible, there are other considerations (e.g., the attempt to capture the full breadth of a construct) that place limits on the degree of fit that can be achieved in practice, because SEM imposes very stringent standards on model-data fit. We do not believe that researchers should restrict the domain of a construct to a single question (even if it is asked repeatedly in more or less the same way) simply to attain a good model fit.

Latent Variable Model

Since the measurement model in Fig. 2 (not including BI3 as an indicator of BI) seems reasonable, we can now consider a structural model specifying directed relationships (rather than correlations) between the constructs. As shown in Fig. 1 and Table 1, we used the fourth indicators of PEOU and PU as marker variables whose loadings were fixed to one since they are both overall measures of perceived ease of use and perceived usefulness. The structural model is saturated (i.e., there are as many path coefficients between the factors as there are factor correlations in the CFA model), so the fit of the structural equation model is identical to that of the revised CFA model. If this were not the case (i.e., if the latent variable model contained overidentifying restrictions), the fit of the structural equation model would have to be evaluated relative to the fit of the CFA model (e.g., by using a chi-square difference test). If the structural equation model were to fit the data significantly more poorly than the CFA model, the structural model would have to be revised (e.g., by relying on the modification indices for the structural paths that are fixed to zero).

Figure 3 reports standardized path coefficients (as well as estimates of indirect and total effects) with bootstrapped confidence intervals. Bootstrapped confidence intervals are preferred to assess the significance of the indirect (and total) effects, but in the present case, the confidence intervals based on MLM estimation are

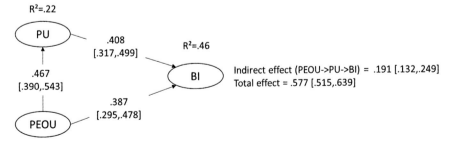

Fig. 3 Standardized estimates (with 95% confidence intervals) and R^2 values for the latent variable model

very similar to the bootstrapped confidence intervals for all parameters (the regular ML-based confidence intervals are somewhat too narrow). In line with the Technology Acceptance Model, BI is significantly and positively related to both PU and PEOU. In addition, PEOU has an indirect effect on BI, mediated by PU. The model explains 46% of the variance in BI and 22% of the variance in PU (the R^2 values are computed by subtracting the standardized structural residual variance of a factor from 1). One caveat should be kept in mind, however. All constructs were measured at the same time using the same questionnaire, so it is difficult to draw strong causal inferences from these results. Although it is intuitively plausible that perceived ease of use and perceived usefulness determine a driver's intention to use VMS technology, and the Technology Acceptance Model strongly supports these relationships, panel data in which PEOU and PU are measured prior to BI would provide stronger support for the predicted cause-effect relationships. The hypothesized causal effect from PEOU to PU is on particularly shaky grounds because one could certainly imagine that the two constructs simply covary or that PU affects PEOU. Moreover, the relations between the factors in the model may show upward bias due to common method variance (Baumgartner et al. 2021). Ideally, common method variance should be countered by using different methods for measuring different constructs (e.g., different types of questions, different response scales) or, if that is not possible, controlling for the presence of common method variance post hoc (e.g., by measuring potential sources of common method bias directly and including these measures as control variables; see Baumgartner and Weijters forthcoming). Finally, it should be noted that the only (substantive) sources of covariation between PEOU, PU, and BI are the direct and indirect effects of PEOU and PU on BI. It is quite unlikely that there are no other influences on the covariation between the three constructs, but since the model is saturated, it is impossible to include additional sources of covariation. Diop et al. (2019) consider other variables in their model (e.g., attitude toward route diversion is specified as an antecedent of, and thus confounding influence on the relationship between, perceived usefulness and behavior intention), but it is debatable whether the inclusion of these variables is an effective control of potential confounds.

To investigate potential endogeneity problems, we used the MIIVsem package in R to identify model-implied instrumental variables for all measurement and latent variable model equations and estimated the coefficients using 2SLS. The differences in the two types of estimates were generally small, except for the effect of PEOU on PU (the ML estimate was 0.39 whereas the 2SLS estimate was 0.45). Substantively, the results were the same. However, based on the Sargan test (even when adjusted for multiple comparisons), the null hypothesis that the model-implied instruments are uncorrelated with the equation error was rejected for every single measurement and latent variable model equation. This result is probably not too surprising since the chi-square test of model fit indicated that the model was inconsistent with the data and several large MIs suggested that some of the error correlations were highly significant. Thus, not all model-implied instruments are suitable instruments in the present case.

As an alternative to the mediation model in Fig. 1, we also estimated the interaction model in Eq. (5). The interaction was not significant, so the data provide no evidence that PEOU and PU have a multiplicative effect on BI (see the files on Github for details).

Multi-Sample Analysis

The structural model can be estimated simultaneously for multiple groups of respondents. To illustrate such an analysis, imagine that a researcher is interested in investigating the moderating effect of a driver's gender on the relations between PEOU, PU, and BI. To be able to meaningfully compare structural relationships across men and women, metric invariance has to be established first (Steenkamp and Baumgartner 1998). This requires the estimation and comparison of two two-group CFA models: a model in which the factor loadings are freely estimated in both gender groups, and a model in which corresponding factor loadings are constrained to be equal in the male versus female subsamples. The fit indices are: (a) $T_{ML} = 312.74$ with 64 degrees of freedom, RMSEA $= 0.101$, SRMR $= 0.040$, CFI $= 0.953$, and TLI $= 0.934$ for the unconstrained model, and (b) $T_{ML} = 330.66$ with 71 degrees of freedom, RMSEA $= 0.098$, SRMR $= 0.046$, CFI $= 0.951$, and TLI $= 0.938$ for the model of metric invariance. The fit of the baseline model (i.e., the unconstrained model) is marginal at best, so the results need to be interpreted with caution. The chi-square difference test comparing the unconstrained model to the metric invariance model is significant ($\Delta T_{ML} (7) = 17.927, p = 0.0123$), which implies that the model of full metric invariance fits the data significantly worse than the unconstrained model (the alternative fit indices RMSEA and TLI, which penalize less parsimonious models, actually show a slight improvement, while CFI and SRMR show a slight deterioration when metric invariance is imposed). The lack of invariance is primarily due to the loading of PEOU3 on PEOU, which has a large MI. Freeing this loading results in $T_{ML} = 316.02$ with 70 degrees of freedom, RMSEA $= 0.096$, SRMR $= 0.041$, CFI $= 0.953$, and TLI $= 0.940$. Table 4 reports the standardized structural parameter estimates for the male versus female subsamples. The results show that gender significantly moderates the effects of PEOU on PU, such that the effect is stronger for men (as compared to women). The effect of PU on BI is marginally stronger for men than women.

Concluding Comments

Structural equation modeling is used primarily in survey-based research and, particularly when applied to cross-sectional self-report data, it has encountered a fair amount of criticism because some researchers believe that it is difficult or even impossible to derive causal conclusions from structural equation models. In the early days, SEM was sometimes billed (or oversold) as causal modeling, and in complex models consisting of many exogenous and endogenous constructs, the final

Table 4 Standardized path coefficients for male versus female subsamples

Variable		Males			Females			Difference		
DV	IV	Est.	SE	p-value	Est.	SE	p-value	Est.	SE	p-value
PU	PEOU	0.568	0.036	<0.001	0.320	0.060	<0.001	0.248	0.070	0.001
BI	PU	0.471	0.045	<0.001	0.338	0.057	<0.001	0.134	0.073	0.065
BI	PEOU	0.323	0.047	<0.001	0.432	0.054	<0.001	−0.109	0.072	0.131

Note: *DV* Dependent variable, *IV* Independent variable, *PEOU* Perceived ease of use; *PU* Perceived usefulness, *BI* Behavioral intention, *Est.* Parameter estimate, *SE* Standard error

specification from which the substantive conclusions were derived often came across as ad hoc. The ambiguities associated with global goodness-of-fit tests, the problem of equivalent models (i.e., the fact that different models with very different substantive implications may fit the data equally well), the stringent assumptions imposed by multi-indicator measurement models (which have stimulated the development of very narrow measures of sometimes complex concepts), and a host of other problems have led to disillusionment about the value of SEM among (some) researchers. However, some of these issues are not unique to SEM (e.g., regression analysis faces similar problems of causality), and the ability to (a) represent the correspondence between observed measures and their presumed underlying constructs more explicitly and (b) model the relationships between constructs in a more integrative fashion are important advantages of SEM. Structural equation models can also be used in experimental contexts, in which the exogenous variables are manipulated, and particularly when the processes underlying hypothesized effects are investigated, SEM offers many benefits over regression analysis that have not been exploited by researchers. Finally, when moderators are discrete, multi-sample SEM is superior to regression-based methods, particularly when moderated mediation hypotheses are to be tested, and other approaches to modeling population heterogeneity may also be valuable.

Our discussion has focused on covariance-based SEM, but a prominent alternative (particularly in the marketing strategy and information systems literatures) is variance-based partial least squares (PLS) path modeling. Similar to Rönkko et al. (2016), we believe that PLS is mainly relevant when the emphasis is on predictive rather than explanatory modeling (see Reinartz et al. 2009). The reader is referred to Hair et al. (2017) for an introduction to PLS-SEM (see also chapter ▶ "Partial Least Squares Structural Equation Modeling" by Sarstedt, Ringle, and Hair, this volume).

Cross-References

- ▶ Bayesian Models
- ▶ Challenges in Conducting International Market Research
- ▶ Choice-Based Conjoint Analysis
- ▶ Crafting Survey Research: A Systematic Process for Conducting Survey Research
- ▶ Dealing with Endogeneity: A Nontechnical Guide for Marketing Researchers
- ▶ Finite Mixture Models
- ▶ Mediation Analysis in Experimental Research
- ▶ Multilevel Modeling
- ▶ Panel Data Analysis: A Non-technical Introduction for Marketing Researchers
- ▶ Partial Least Squares Structural Equation Modeling
- ▶ Regression Analysis

Acknowledgments Financial support from the Smeal Chair Endowment is gratefully acknowledged. The authors would like to thank two reviewers and the editors for helpful comments on a previous version of this chapter.

References

Anderson, J. C., & Gerbing, D. W. (1988). Structural equation modeling in practice: A review and recommended two-step approach. *Psychological Bulletin, 103*(3), 411–423.

Bagozzi, R. P. (1980). *Causal models in marketing*. New York: Wiley.

Bandalos, D. L., & Finney, S. J. (2001). Item parceling issues in structural equation modeling. In G. A. Marcoulides & R. E. Schumacker (Eds.), *New developments and techniques in structural equation modeling* (pp. 269–296). Mahwah: Erlbaum.

Baumgartner, H., & Weijters, B. (2019). Measurement in marketing. *Foundations and Trends® in Marketing, 12*(4), 278–400.

Baumgartner, H., & Weijters, B. (forthcoming). Dealing with common method variance in international marketing research. *Journal of International Marketing*. in press.

Baumgartner, H., Weijters, B., & Pieters, R. (2021). The biasing effect of common method variance: Some clarifications. *Journal of the Academy of Marketing Science, 49*(2), 221–235. https://doi.org/10.1007/s11747-020-00766-8.

Bollen, K. A. (2011). Evaluating effect, composite, and causal indicators in structural equation models. *MIS Quarterly, 35*(2), 359–372.

Bollen, K. A. (2012). Instrumental variables in sociology and the social sciences. *Annual Review of Sociology, 38*, 37–72.

Bollen, K. A. (2018). Model implied instrumental variables (MIIVs): An alternative orientation to structural equation modeling. *Multivariate Behavioral Research, 54*(1), 31–46.

Bollen, K. A., & Curran, P. J. (2006). *Latent curve models: A structural equation perspective*. Hoboken: Wiley.

Bollen, K. A., Harden, J. J., Ray, S., & Zavisca, J. (2014). BIC and alternative Bayesian information criteria in the selection of structural equation models. *Structural Equation Modeling, 21*(1), 1–19.

Chapman, C., & Feit, E. M. D. (2019). *R for marketing research and analytics* (2nd ed.). Springer: Cham.

Cortina, J. M., Markell-Goldstein, H. M., Green, J. P., & Chang, Y. (2021). How are we testing interactions in latent variable models? Surging forward or fighting shy? *Organizational Research Methods, 24*(1), 26–54.

Davis, F. D. (1989). Perceived usefulness, perceived ease of use, and user acceptance of information technology. *MIS Quarterly, 13*(3), 319–340.

Diamantopoulos, A. (2011). Incorporating formative measures into covariance-based structural equation models. *MIS Quarterly, 35*(June), 335–358.

Diamantopoulos, A., & Winklhofer, H. (2001). Index construction with formative indicators: An alternative to scale development. *Journal of Marketing Research, 38*(May), 269–277.

Diamantopoulos, A., Riefler, P., & Roth, K. P. (2008). Advancing formative measurement models. *Journal of Business Research, 61*(12), 1203–1218.

Diop, E. B., Zhao, S., & Duy, T. V. (2019). An extension of the technology acceptance model for understanding travelers' adoption of variable message signs. *PLoS One, 14*(4), e0216007.

Edwards, J. R. (2011). The fallacy of formative measurement. *Organizational Research Methods, 14*(2), 370–388.

Fisher, Z. F., Bollen, K. A., Gates, K., & Ronkko, M. (2020). *MIIVsem: Model implied instrumental variable (MIIV) estimation of structural equation models*. R package version 0.5.5.

Fornell, C., & Larcker, D. F. (1981). Evaluating structural equation models with unobservable variables and measurement error. *Journal of Marketing Research, 18*(1), 39–50.

Hair, J. F., Hult, G. T. M., Ringle, C. M., & Sarstedt, M. (2017). *A primer on partial least squares structural equation modeling (PLS-SEM)* (2nd ed.). Thousand Oaks: Sage.

Howell, R. D., Breivik, E., & Wilcox, J. B. (2007). Reconsidering formative measurement. *Psychological Methods, 12*(2), 205–218.

Hu, L., & Bentler, P. M. (1998). Fit indices in covariance structure modeling: Sensitivity to underparameterized model misspecification. *Psychological Methods, 3*(4), 424–453.

Hu, L., & Bentler, P. M. (1999). Cutoff criteria for fit indexes in covariance structure analysis: Conventional criteria versus new alternatives. *Structural Equation Modeling, 6*(1), 1–55.

Jarvis, C. B., MacKenzie, S. B., & Podsakoff, P. M. (2003). A critical review of construct indicators and measurement model misspecification in marketing and consumer research. *Journal of Consumer Research, 30*(2), 199–218.

Kenny, D. A., & Judd, C. M. (1984). Estimating the nonlinear and interactive effects of latent variables. *Psychological Bulletin, 96,* 201–210.

Klein, A., & Moosbrugger, H. (2000). Maximum likelihood estimation of latent interaction effects with the LMS method. *Psychometrika, 65*(December), 457–474.

Kline, R. B. (2013). Reverse arrow dynamics: Feedback loops and formative measurement. In G. R. Hancock & R. O. Mueller (Eds.), *Structural equation modeling: A second course* (2nd ed., pp. 39–76). Greenwich: Information Age Publishing.

MacCallum, R. C. (1986). Specification searches in covariance structure modeling. *Psychological Bulletin, 100*(1), 107–120.

MacCallum, R. C., & Browne, M. W. (1993). The use of causal indicators in covariance structure models: Some practical issues. *Psychological Bulletin, 114,* 533–541.

MacCallum, R. C., Roznowski, M., & Necowitz, L. B. (1992). Model modification in covariance structure analysis: The problem of capitalization on chance. *Psychological Bulletin, 111*(3), 490–504.

MacKenzie, S. B., & Podsakoff, P. M. (2012). Common method bias in marketing: Causes, mechanisms, and procedural remedies. *Journal of Retailing, 88*(4), 542–555.

MacKenzie, S. B., Podsakoff, P. M., & Jarvis, C. B. (2005). The problem of measurement model misspecification in behavioral and organizational research and some recommended solutions. *Journal of Applied Psychology, 90*(4), 710–730.

MacKenzie, S. B., Podsakoff, P. M., & Podsakoff, N. P. (2011). Construct measurement and validation procedures in MIS and behavioral research: Integrating new and existing techniques. *MIS Quarterly, 35*(June), 293–334.

MacKinnon, D. P., Lockwood, C. M., Hoffman, J. M., West, S. G., & Sheets, V. (2002). A comparison of methods to test mediation and other intervening variable effects. *Psychological Methods, 7*(1), 83–104.

Marsh, H. W., Hau, K.-T., & Wen, Z. (2004). In search of golden rules: Comment on hypothesis-testing approaches to setting cutoff values for fit indexes and dangers in overgeneralizing Hu and Bentler's (1999) findings. *Structural Equation Modeling, 11*(3), 320–341.

Marsh, H. W., Morin, A. J., Parker, P. D., & Kaur, G. (2014). Exploratory structural equation modeling: An integration of the best features of exploratory and confirmatory factor analysis. *Annual Review of Clinical Psychology, 10,* 85–110.

McNeish, D. (2020). Should we use F-tests for model fit instead of chi-square in over-identified structural equation models? *Organizational Research Methods, 23,* 487–510.

Muthén, B. (2001). Latent variable mixture modeling. In G. A. Marcoulides & R. E. Schumacker (Eds.), *New developments and techniques in structural equation modeling* (pp. 1–33). Mahwah: Erlbaum.

Muthén, B., & Asparouhov, T. (2011). Beyond multilevel regression modeling: Multilevel analysis in a general latent variable framework. In J. Hox & J. K. Roberts (Eds.), *Handbook of advanced multilevel analysis* (pp. 15–40). New York: Taylor and Francis.

Muthén, B., & Asparouhov, T. (2012). Bayesian structural equation modeling: A more flexible representation of substantive theory. *Psychological Methods, 17*(3), 313–335.

Muthén, L. K., & Muthén, B. (2002). How to use a Monte Carlo study to decide on sample size and determine power. *Structural Equation Modeling, 9*(4), 599–620.

Niemand, T., & Mai, R. (2018). Flexible cutoff values for fit indices in the evaluation of structural equation models. *Journal of the Academy of Marketing Science, 46,* 1148–1172.

Podsakoff, P. M., MacKenzie, S. B., Lee, J.-Y., & Podsakoff, N. P. (2003). Common method biases in behavioral research: A critical review of the literature and recommended remedies. *Journal of Applied Psychology, 88*(5), 879–903.

Podsakoff, P. M., MacKenzie, S. B., & Podsakoff, N. P. (2012). Sources of method bias in social science research and recommendations on how to control it. *Annual Review of Psychology, 63,* 539–569.

Reinartz, W., Haenlein, M., & Henseler, J. (2009). An empirical comparison of the efficacy of covariance-based and variance-based SEM. *International Journal of Research in Marketing, 26*(4), 332–344.

Rhemtulla, M., Brosseau-Liard, A. E., & Savalei, V. (2012). When can categorical variables be treated as continuous? A comparison of robust continuous and categorical SEM estimation methods under suboptimal conditions. *Psychological Methods, 17*(3), 354–373.

Rhemtulla, M., van Bork, R., & Borsboom, D. (2020). Worse than measurement error: Consequences of inappropriate latent variable measurement models. *Psychological Methods, 25*(1), 30–45.

Rönkko, M., McIntosh, C. N., Antonakis, J., & Edwards, J. R. (2016). Partial least squares path modeling: Time for some serious second thoughts. *Journal of Operations Management, 47–48* (November), 9–27.

Rosseel, Y. (2012). lavaan: An R package for structural equation modeling. *Journal of Statistical Software, 48*, 1–36.

Satorra, A., & Bentler, P. M. (2001). A scaled difference chi-square test statistic for moment structure analysis. *Psychometrika, 66*(4), 507–514.

Steenkamp, J.-B. E. M., & Baumgartner, H. (1998). Assessing measurement invariance in crossnational consumer research. *Journal of Consumer Research, 25*(June), 78–90.

Sterba, S. K. (2011). Implications of parcel-allocation variability for comparing fit of item-solutions and parcel-solutions. *Structural Equation Modeling, 18*(4), 554–577.

Sterba, S. K., & Pek, J. (2012). Individual influence on model selection. *Psychological Methods, 17*(4), 582–599.

Sterba, S. K., & Rights, J. D. (2017). Effects of parceling on model selection: Parcel-allocation variability in model ranking. *Psychological Methods, 22*(1), 47–68.

Umbach, N., Naumann, K., Brandt, H., & Kelava, A. (2017). Fitting nonlinear structural equation models in R with package nlsem. *Journal of Statistical Software, 77*(7), 1–20. https://doi.org/10.18637/iss.v077.i07.

Vandenberg, R. J., & Lance, C. E. (2000). A review and synthesis of the measurement invariance literature: Suggestions, practices, and recommendations for organizational research. *Organizational Research Methods, 3*(January), 4–69.

Weijters, B., & Baumgartner, H. (2019). Analyzing Policy Capturing Data Using Structural Equation Modeling for Within-Subject Experiments (SEMWISE). *Organizational Research Methods, 22*(3), 623–648.

Weijters, B., & Baumgartner, H. (forthcoming). On the use of balanced item parceling to counter acquiescence bias in structural equation models. *Organizational Research Methods*. in press.

Wilcox, J. B., Howell, R. D., & Breivik, E. (2008). Questions about formative measurement. *Journal of Business Research, 61*, 1219–1228.

Wolf, E. J., Harrington, K. M., Clark, S. L., & Miller, M. W. (2013). Sample size requirements for structural equation models: An evaluation of power, bias, and solution propriety. *Educational and Psychological Measurement, 73*(6), 913–934.

Wooldridge, J. M. (2016). *Introductory econometrics: A modern approach* (6th ed.). Boston: Cengage Learning.

Yang, M., Jiang, G., & Yuan, K.-H. (2018). The performance of ten modified rescaled statistics as the number of variables increases. *Structural Equation Modeling, 25*(3), 414–438.

Partial Least Squares Structural Equation Modeling

Marko Sarstedt, Christian M. Ringle, and Joseph F. Hair

Contents

Introduction	588
Principles of Structural Equation Modeling	590
Path Models with Latent Variables	590
Structural Theory	591
Measurement Theory	592
Path Model Estimation with PLS-SEM	594
Background	594
The PLS-SEM Algorithm	595
Additional Considerations when Using PLS-SEM	598
Evaluation of PLS-SEM Results	601
Procedure	601
Stage 1.1: Reflective Measurement Model Assessment	603
Stage 1.2: Formative Measurement Model Assessment	606
Stage 2: Structural Model Assessment	608
Research Application	612
Corporate Reputation Model	612
Data	613

M. Sarstedt (✉)
Otto-von-Guericke University, Magdeburg, Germany

Faculty of Business and Law, University of Newcastle, Callaghan, NSW, Australia
e-mail: marko.sarstedt@ovgu.de

C. M. Ringle
Hamburg University of Technology (TUHH), Hamburg, Germany

Faculty of Business and Law, University of Newcastle, Callaghan, NSW, Australia
e-mail: c.ringle@tuhh.de

J. F. Hair
University of South Alabama, Mobile, AL, USA
e-mail: jhair@southalabama.edu

© Springer Nature Switzerland AG 2022
C. Homburg et al. (eds), *Handbook of Market Research*,
https://doi.org/10.1007/978-3-319-57413-4_15

Model Estimation 615
Results Evaluation 616
Conclusions 621
Cross-References 623
References 623

Abstract

Partial least squares structural equation modeling (PLS-SEM) has become a popular method for estimating path models with latent variables and their relationships. A common goal of PLS-SEM analyses is to identify key success factors and sources of competitive advantage for important target constructs such as customer satisfaction, customer loyalty, behavioral intentions, and user behavior. Building on an introduction of the fundamentals of measurement and structural theory, this chapter explains how to specify and estimate path models using PLS-SEM. Complementing the introduction of the PLS-SEM method and the description of how to evaluate analysis results, the chapter also offers an overview of complementary analytical techniques. A PLS-SEM application of the widely recognized corporate reputation model illustrates the method.

Keywords

Partial least squares structural equation modeling · PLS-SEM · Path model analysis · Composite modeling · Results evaluation

Introduction

In the 1970s and 1980s, the Swedish econometrician Herman Wold (1975, 1982, 1985) "vigorously pursued the creation and construction of models and methods for the social sciences, where 'soft models and soft data' were the rule rather than the exception, and where approaches strongly oriented at prediction would be of great value" (Dijkstra 2010, p. 24). One method that emerged from Wold's efforts was partial least squares path modeling, which later evolved to partial least squares structural equation modeling (PLS-SEM; Hair et al. 2011). PLS-SEM estimates the parameters of a set of equations in a structural equation model by combining principal component analysis with regression-based path analysis (Mateos-Aparicio 2011). Wold (1982) proposed his "soft model basic design" underlying PLS-SEM as an alternative to Jöreskog's (1973) covariance-based SEM (chapter ▶ "Structural Equation Modeling"), also referred to as factor-based SEM. Covariance-based SEM has been labeled as hard modeling because of its comparably restrictive assumptions in terms of data distribution and sample size. Importantly, "it is not the concepts nor the models nor the estimation techniques which are 'soft', only the distributional assumptions" (Lohmöller 1989, p. 64).

A common goal of PLS-SEM analyses is to identify key success factors and sources of competitive advantage (Albers 2010; Hair et al. 2012a) for important target constructs such as customer satisfaction and customer loyalty (e.g., Fornell et al. 1996) or behavioral intentions and user behavior (Venkatesh et al. 2003). For creating and estimating complex path models with latent variables and their relationships, PLS-SEM has achieved widespread popularity in the social sciences. Indeed, as evidenced in numerous studies that have reviewed PLS-SEM publications in a variety of disciplines, applications have increased substantially in recent years (Table 1). PLS-SEM applications have also gained prominence in other fields of scientific inquiry, such as agriculture, engineering, environmental sciences, geography, and medicine (Sarstedt 2019).

In light of the increasing maturation of the field, researchers have also started exploring the knowledge infrastructure of methodological research on PLS-SEM by analyzing the relationships between authors, countries, and co-citation networks (Hwang et al. 2020; Khan et al. 2019). As a result of these developments, a growing number of textbooks (e.g., Garson 2016; Hair et al. 2018b, 2022; Henseler 2021; Mehmetoglu and Venturini 2021; Ramayah et al. 2016; Wong 2019) and edited books on the method (e.g., Avkiran and Ringle 2018; Esposito Vinzi et al. 2010; Latan and Noonan 2017) have been published, further popularizing PLS-SEM (Ringle 2019).

A key methodological reason for PLS-SEM's attractiveness is that the approach follows a causal-predictive paradigm, in which the aim is to test the predictive power of a model carefully developed on the grounds of theory and logic (Chin et al. 2020).

Table 1 Review articles on the use of PLS-SEM in different disciplines (Hair et al. 2022). (Reprinted by permission of the publisher (SAGE Publications))

Discipline	References
Accounting	Lee et al. (2011)
	Nitzl (2016)
Construction management	Zeng et al. (2021)
Entrepreneurship	Manley et al. (2020)
Family business	Sarstedt et al. (2014)
Higher education	Ghasemy et al. (2020)
Hospitality and tourism	Ali et al. (2018)
	do Valle and Assaker (2016)
	Usakli and Kucukergin (2018)
Human resource management	Ringle et al. (2020)
International business research	Richter et al. (2016)
Knowledge management	Cepeda-Carrión et al. (2019)
Management	Hair et al. (2012a)
Management information systems	Hair et al. (2017a)
	Ringle et al. (2012)
Marketing	Hair et al. (2012b)
Operations management	Bayonne et al. (2020)
	Peng and Lai (2012)
Psychology	Willaby et al. (2015)
Software engineering	Russo and Stol (2021)
Supply chain management	Kaufmann and Gaeckler (2015)

In addition, PLS-SEM enables researchers to estimate very complex models with many constructs and indicator variables, with considerably smaller sample size requirements compared to factor-based SEM methods. PLS-SEM also offers much flexibility in estimating multifaceted model relationships such as in conditional process models (Sarstedt et al. 2020a) or higher-order models (Sarstedt et al. 2019). A final reason is the accessibility of user-friendly software with a graphical interface such as ADANCO, PLS-Graph, SmartPLS, and XLSTAT, as well as the statistical computing software environment R that includes cSEM, matrixpls, SEMinR, and semPLS as complements to other programs.

The objective of this chapter is to explain the fundamentals of PLS-SEM. Building on Hair et al. (2022), this chapter first provides an introduction to the fundamentals of measurement and structural model specification as a basis for the use of the the PLS-SEM method. Next, we discuss the evaluation of results, provide an overview of complementary analytical techniques, and conclude by describing an application of the PLS-SEM method to a well-known corporate reputation model using SmartPLS 3 (Ringle et al. 2015), the most comprehensive and up-to-date software for conducting PLS-SEM analyses (Sarstedt and Cheah 2019).

Principles of Structural Equation Modeling

Path Models with Latent Variables

A path model is a diagram that displays the hypotheses and variable relationships to be estimated in a structural equation modeling analysis (Bollen 2002). Figure 1 shows an example of a path model with three latent variables (Y_1, Y_2, and Y_3) and their indicators.

Latent variables, also referred to as constructs, are elements in statistical models that represent conceptual variables that researchers define in their theoretical models.

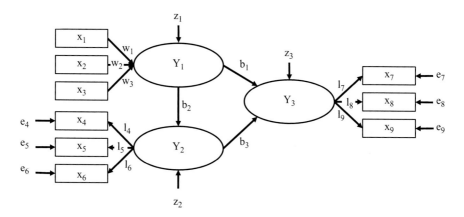

Fig. 1 Path model with latent variables

Examples of typical social sciences constructs include job satisfaction, organizational commitment, trust, and customer loyalty. Constructs are visualized as circles or ovals (Y_1 to Y_3) in path models, linked via single-headed arrows that represent causal-predictive relationships. The indicators, often also named manifest variables or items, are directly measured or observed variables that represent the raw data (e.g., respondents' answers to a questionnaire). They are represented as rectangles (x_1 to x_9) in path models and are linked to their corresponding constructs through arrows. Constructs in most instances are represented by a minimum of three or more indicators to ensure they are valid measures of the concept. Researchers sometimes include single-item constructs in their models. As construct and indicator are equivalent in this case, the relationship between construct and indicator is typically represented by a line rather than an arrow.

A path model consists of two elements. The structural model represents the causal-predictive relationships between the constructs, whereas the measurement models represent the relationships between each construct and its associated indicators. In PLS-SEM, the structural model is sometimes referred to as the inner model and the measurement models are sometimes referred to as outer models. To develop path models, researchers need to draw on both structural theory and measurement theory, which indicate the relationships between the elements of a path model.

Structural Theory

Structural theory specifies the latent variables to be considered in the analysis of a certain phenomenon and their relationships. The location and sequence of the constructs are based on theory and on the researcher's experience and accumulated knowledge (Falk and Miller 1992). When researchers develop path models, the sequence is typically from left to right. The latent variables on the left side of the path model are independent variables, and any latent variable on the right-hand side is the dependent variable (Fig. 1). However, latent variables can also serve as both independent and dependent variables in the model (Haenlein and Kaplan 2004).

When a latent variable only serves as an independent variable, it is called an exogenous latent variable (Y_1 in Fig. 1). When a latent variable only serves as a dependent variable (Y_3 in Fig. 1), or as both an independent and a dependent variable (Y_2 in Fig. 1), it is called an endogenous latent variable. Endogenous latent variables always have error terms associated with them. In Fig. 1, the endogenous latent variables Y_2 and Y_3 have one error term each (z_2 and z_3), which reflect the sources of variance not predicted by the respective antecedent construct(s) in the structural model. The exogenous latent variable Y_1 also has an error term (z_1) but in PLS-SEM, this error term is constrained to zero because of the way the method treats the (formative; i.e., arrows point from indicators to construct) measurement model of this particular construct (Diamantopoulos 2011). Therefore, this error term is typically omitted in the display of a PLS path model. In case an exogenous latent variable draws on a reflective measurement model theory (arrows point from construct to indicator), there is no error term attached to this particular construct.

The strength of the relationships between latent variables is represented by path coefficients (i.e., b_1, b_2, and b_3), and the coefficients are the result of regressions of each endogenous latent variable on their direct antecedent constructs. For example, b_1 and b_3 result from the regression of Y_3 on Y_1 and Y_2.

Measurement Theory

Measurement theory specifies how to measure latent variables. Researchers can generally choose between two different types of measurement models (Diamantopoulos and Winklhofer 2001; Sarstedt et al. 2016): reflective measurement models and formative measurement models.

Reflective measurement models have direct relationships from the construct to the indicators and treat the indicators as error-prone manifestations of the underlying construct (Bollen 1989). The following equation formally illustrates the relationship between a latent variable and its observed indicators:

$$x = l \cdot Y + e, \tag{1}$$

where x is the observed indicator variable, Y is the latent variable, the loading l is a regression coefficient quantifying the strength of the relationship between x and Y, and e represents the random measurement error. This equation is a bivariate regression with x being the dependent variable and Y being the independent variable. The latent variables Y_2 and Y_3 in the path model shown in Fig. 1 have reflective measurement models with three indicators each. When using reflective indicators (also called effect indicators), the items should be a representative sample of all items of the construct's conceptual domain (Nunnally and Bernstein 1994). If the items stem from the same domain, they capture the same concept and, hence, should be highly correlated (Edwards and Bagozzi 2000).

In contrast, in a formative measurement model, a linear combination of a set of indicators forms the construct (i.e., the relationship is from the indicators to the construct). Hence, "variation in the indicators precedes variation in the latent variable" (Borsboom et al. 2003, p. 208). Indicators of formatively measured constructs do not necessarily have to correlate strongly as is the case with reflective indicators. Note, however, that strong indicator correlations can also occur in formative measurement models and do not necessarily imply that the measurement model is reflective in nature (Nitzl and Chin 2017).

When referring to formative measurement models, researchers need to distinguish two types of indicators: causal indicators and composite indicators (Bollen 2011). Constructs measured with causal indicators have an error term, which implies that the construct has not been perfectly measured by its indicators (Bollen and Bauldry 2011). More precisely, causal indicators show conceptual unity in that they correspond to the researcher's definition of the concept (Bollen and Diamantopoulos 2017). But researchers will hardly ever be able to identify all indicators relevant for adequately capturing the construct's domain (e.g., Bollen and Lennox 1991). The error term captures all the other "causes" or explanations of the construct that the set of causal indicators do not capture (Diamantopoulos 2006). The existence of a construct's error term in causal indicator models suggests that the construct can, in principle, be equivalent to the conceptual variable of interest, provided that the model has perfect fit (e.g., Grace and Bollen 2008). If the indicators x_1, x_2, and x_3 represent causal indicators, Y_1's error term z_1 would capture these other "causes" (Fig. 1). A measurement model with causal indicators can formally be described as.

$$Y = \sum_{k=1}^{K} w_k \cdot x_k + z, \qquad (2)$$

where w_k indicates the contribution of x_k ($k = 1, \ldots, K$) to Y, and z is an error term associated with Y.

Composite indicators constitute the second type of indicators associated with formative measurement models. When measurement models are specified with composite indicators, researchers assume that the indicators define the construct in full (Sarstedt et al. 2016). Hence, the error term, which in causal indicator models represents "omitted causes," is set to zero in formative measurement models with composite indicators ($z_1 = 0$ in Fig. 1). A measurement model with composite indicators takes the following form, where Y is a linear combination of indicators x_k ($k = 1, \ldots, K$), each weighted by an indicator weight w_k (Bollen 2011; McDonald 1996):

$$Y = \sum_{k=1}^{K} w_k \cdot x_k. \qquad (3)$$

According to Henseler (2017, p. 180), measurement models with composite indicators "are a prescription of how the ingredients should be arranged to form a new entity," which he refers to as artifacts or emergent variables (Henseler 2021). That is, composite indicators define the construct's empirical meaning. Henseler (2017) identifies Aaker's (1991) conceptualization of brand equity as a typical conceptual variable with composite indicators (i.e., an artifact) in advertising research, comprising the elements brand awareness, brand associations, brand quality, brand loyalty, and other proprietary assets. The use of artifacts is especially prevalent in the analysis of secondary and archival data, which typically lack a comprehensive substantiation on the grounds of measurement theory (Hair et al. 2019a; Rigdon 2013). For example, a researcher may use secondary data to form an index of a company's communication activities, covering aspects such as online advertising, sponsoring, or product placement. Alternatively, composite indicator models can be thought of as a means to capture the essence of a conceptual variable using of a limited number of indicators (Sarstedt et al. 2016). For example, a researcher may be interested in measuring the salient aspects of a company's corporate social responsibility using a set of five (composite) indicators that capture important features relevant to the particular study.

More recent research contends that composite indicators can be used to measure any concept including attitudes, perceptions, and behavioral intentions (Nitzl and Chin 2017), as long as they operationally define the concept. But composite indicators are not a free ride for careless measurement. Instead, "as with any type of measurement conceptualization, researchers need to offer a clear construct definition and specify items that closely match this definition – that is, they must share conceptual unity" (Sarstedt et al. 2016, p. 4002). Thus, composite indicator models view construct measurement as approximation of conceptual variables, acknowledging the practical problems which arise with measuring unobservable conceptual variables that populate theoretical models (Rigdon et al. 2017, 2019).

Path Model Estimation with PLS-SEM

Background

Different from factor-based SEM (chapter ▶ "Structural Equation Modeling"), PLS-SEM explicitly calculates case values (construct scores) for the latent variables as part of the algorithm. For this purpose, the "unobservable variables are estimated as exact linear combinations of their empirical indicators" (Fornell and Bookstein 1982, p. 441) such that the resulting composites capture most of the variance of the exogenous constructs' indicators that is useful for predicting the endogenous constructs' indicators (e.g., McDonald 1996). PLS-SEM uses these composites to represent the constructs in a PLS path model, considering them as approximations of the conceptual variables under consideration (e.g., Hair and Sarstedt 2019; Rigdon 2012; Rigdon et al. 2017).

Since PLS-SEM-based model estimation always relies on composites, regardless of the measurement model specification, the method can process reflectively and formatively specified measurement models without identification issues (Hair et al. 2011). Identification of PLS path models only requires that each construct is linked to the nomological net of constructs (Henseler et al. 2016a). This characteristic also applies to model settings in which endogenous constructs are specified formatively as PLS-SEM relies on a multistage estimation process, which separates measurement from structural model estimation (Rigdon et al. 2014).

Three aspects are important for understanding the interplay between data, measurement, and model estimation in PLS-SEM. *First*, PLS-SEM handles all indicators of formative measurement models as composite indicators. Hence, a formatively specified construct in PLS-SEM does not have an error term as is the case with causal indicators in factor-based SEM (Diamantopoulos 2011).

Second, when the data stem from a common factor model population (i.e., the indicator covariances define the data's nature), PLS-SEM's parameter estimates deviate from the prespecified values. This characteristic, often incorrectly referred to as PLS-SEM bias, suggests the method overestimates the measurement model parameters and underestimates the structural model parameters (e.g., Chin et al.

2003). The degree of over- and underestimation decreases when both the number of indicators per construct and sample size increase (consistency at large; Hui and Wold 1982). The term PLS-SEM bias is a misnomer, however, as it implies that the data stem from a factor model population in which the indicator covariances define the nature of the data (e.g., Marcoulides et al. 2012; Rigdon 2016; Sarstedt et al. 2016). Numerous studies have shown that when the data stem from a composite model population where linear combinations of the indicators define the data's nature, PLS-SEM estimates are unbiased and consistent (Cho and Choi 2020; Hair et al. 2017b; Sarstedt et al. 2016). Apart from that, research has shown that the bias produced by PLS-SEM when estimating data from common factor model populations is low in absolute terms (e.g., Reinartz et al. 2009), particularly compared to the bias that common factor-based SEM produces when estimating data from composite model populations. Specifically, Sarstedt et al. (2016) find that the bias produced by factor-based SEM is, on average, 11 times higher than the bias produced by PLS-SEM when using each method on models inconsistent with what the methods assume (i.e., factor-based SEM on composite models and PLS-SEM on common factor models).

Third, PLS-SEM's use of composites not only has implications for the method's philosophy of measurement but also for its area of application. In PLS-SEM, once the weights are derived, the method always produces a single specific (i.e., determinate) score for each case per construct. This characteristic sets PLS-SEM apart from factor-based SEM, where construct scores are indeterminate, which can have considerable negative consequences for the validity of the results (Rigdon et al. 2019). Using these determinate scores as input, PLS-SEM applies a series of ordinary least squares regressions, which estimate the model parameters so they maximize the endogenous constructs' explained variance (i.e., their R^2 values). While this estimation process maximizes explanatory power, the computation of determinate construct scores makes PLS-SEM particularly well-suited for prediction where the aim is to apply model parameters estimated from a training sample to generate falsifiable predictions for other observations (hold out cases) not used in the model estimation (Hwang et al. 2020). Several studies have offered evidence of PLS-SEM's efficacy for prediction (Becker et al. 2013a; Evermann and Tate 2016; Cho et al. 2021). Hence, by using PLS-SEM, researchers simultaneously gain an understanding of the causal relationships derived from theory and logic (explanation) and also the model's predictive power, which is fundamental for establishing its practical relevance (Hair and Sarstedt 2021b; Shugan 2009).

The PLS-SEM Algorithm

Model estimation in PLS-SEM draws on a three-stage approach that belongs to the family of (alternating) least squares algorithms (Mateos-Aparicio 2011). Figure 2 illustrates the PLS-SEM algorithm as presented by Lohmöller (1989). Henseler et al. (2012) offer a graphical illustration of the SEM algorithm's stages.

Initialization

Stage 1: **Iterative estimation of weights and latent variable scores**
Starting at step #4, repeat steps #1 to #4 until convergence is obtained.

#1 Inner weights (here obtained by using the factor weighting scheme)

$$v_{ji} = \begin{cases} \text{cov}(Y_j; Y_i) & \text{if } Y_j \text{ and } Y_i \text{ are adjacent} \\ 0 & \text{otherwise} \end{cases}$$

#2 Inside approximation

$$\tilde{Y}_j := \sum_i b_{ji} Y_i$$

#3 Outer weights; solve for

$$\tilde{Y}_{jn} = \sum_{k_j} \tilde{w}_{k_j} x_{k_j n} + d_{jn} \quad \text{in a Mode A block}$$

$$x_{k_j n} = \tilde{w}_{k_j} \tilde{Y}_{jn} + e_{k_j n} \quad \text{in a Mode B block}$$

#4 Outside approximation

$$Y_{jn} := \sum_{k_j} \tilde{w}_{k_j} x_{k_j n}$$

Stage 2: **Estimation of outer weights, outer loadings, and path coefficients**

Stage 3: **Estimation of location parameters**

Fig. 2 The basic PLS-SEM algorithm. (Adapted from Lohmöller 1989, p. 29)

The algorithm starts with an initialization stage in which it establishes preliminary latent variable scores. To compute these scores, the algorithm typically uses unit weights (i.e., 1) for all indicators in the measurement models (Hair et al. 2022).

Stage 1 of the PLS-SEM algorithm iteratively determines the inner weights (i.e., the path coefficients) and latent variable scores by means of a four-step procedure. Step #1 uses the initial latent variable scores from the initialization of the algorithm to determine the inner weights b_{ji} between the adjacent latent variables Y_j (i.e., the dependent one) and Y_i (i.e., the independent one) in the structural model. Literature suggests three approaches to determine the inner weights (Chin 1998; Lohmöller 1989; Tenenhaus et al. 2005). In the centroid scheme, the inner weights are set to +1 if the covariance between Y_j and Y_i is positive and − 1 if this covariance is negative. In case two latent variables are unconnected, the weight is set to 0. In the factor weighting scheme, the inner weight corresponds to the covariance between Y_j and Y_i and is set to zero in case the latent variables are unconnected. Finally, the path weighting scheme takes into account the direction of the inner model relationships

(Lohmöller 1989). Chin (1998, p. 309) notes that the path weighting scheme "attempts to produce a component that can both ideally be predicted (as a predictand) and at the same time be a good predictor for subsequent dependent variables." As a result, the path weighting scheme leads to slightly higher R^2 values in the endogenous latent variables compared to the other schemes and should therefore be preferred. In most instances, however, the choice of the inner weighting scheme has very little bearing on the results (Lohmöller 1989; Noonan and Wold 1982).

Step #2, the inside approximation, computes proxies for all latent variables $\tilde{Y}_j$ by using the weighted sum of its adjacent latent variables scores Y_i. Then, for all the indicators in the measurement models, Step #3 computes new outer weights, which indicate the strength of the relationship between each latent variable $\tilde{Y}_j$ and its corresponding indicators. To do so, the PLS-SEM algorithm uses two different estimation modes. When using Mode A (i.e., correlation weights), the bivariate correlation between each indicator and the construct determine the outer weights. In contrast, Mode B (i.e., regression weights) computes indicator weights by regressing each construct on its associated indicators.

By default, estimation of reflectively specified constructs draws on Mode A, whereas PLS-SEM uses Mode B for formatively specified constructs. However, Cho et al. (2021) show that this reflex-like use of Mode A and Mode B is not optimal when using PLS-SEM for prediction purposes. Their simulation study shows that Mode A provides higher degrees of out-of-sample prediction in situations commonly encountered in empirical research (see also Becker et al. 2013a).

Figure 2 shows the formal representation of these two modes, where x_{k_jn} represents the raw data for indicator k ($k = 1,\ldots,K$) of latent variable j ($j = 1,\ldots, J$) and observations n ($n = 1,\ldots,N$); $\tilde{Y}_{jn}$ are the latent variable scores from the inside approximation in Step #2, $\tilde{w}_{k_j}$ are the outer weights from Step #3, d_{jn} is the error term from a bivariate regression, and e_{k_jn} is the error term from a multiple regression. The updated weights from Step #3 (i.e., $\tilde{w}_{k_j}$) and the indicators (i.e., x_{k_jn}) are linearly combined to update the latent variables scores (i.e., Y_{jn}) in Step #4 (outside approximation). Note that the PLS-SEM algorithm uses standardized data as input and always standardizes the generated latent variable scores in Step #2 and Step #4. After Step #4, a new iteration starts. The algorithm terminates when the weights obtained from Step #3 change marginally from one iteration to the next (typically $1 \cdot 10^{-7}$), or when the maximum number of iterations is achieved (typically 300).

Stages 2 and 3 use the final latent variable scores from Stage 1 as input for a series of ordinary least squares regressions. These regressions compute the final outer loadings, outer weights, and path coefficients as well as related elements such as indirect, and total effects, R^2 values of the endogenous latent variables, and the indicator and latent variable correlations (Lohmöller 1989).

Research has proposed several variations of the original PLS-SEM algorithm. Lohmöller's (1989) extended PLS-SEM algorithm, for example, allows assigning more than one latent variable to a block of indicators and imposing orthogonality restrictions among constructs in the structural model. Becker and Ismail (2016) developed a modified version of the original PLS-SEM algorithm that uses sampling (post-stratification) weights to correct for sampling error. Their weighted PLS-SEM approach considers a weights vector defined by the researcher in order to ensure correspondence between sample and population structure (Cheah et al. 2020). Furthermore, Bentler and Huang's (2014) PLSe algorithm as well as Dijkstra and Henseler's (2015a, b) consistent PLS (PLSc) approach both represent modified versions of Lohmöller's (1989) original PLS-SEM algorithm that produce unbiased and consistent estimates of common factor models. That is, PLSe and PLSc both follow a composite modeling logic, but introduce a correction factor to produce results that mimic those of factor-based SEM. That is, PLSe and PLSc assume the data stem from common factor model population. But in fact, PLS-SEM does not produce biased estimates per se; the only exception is when the method is used to estimate common factor models, similar to when factor-based SEM produces biased estimates when used to estimate composite models (Sarstedt et al. 2016). In light of this concern, Hair et al. (2017a, p. 443) note: "It is unclear why researchers would use these alternative approaches to PLS-SEM when they could easily apply the much more widely recognized and validated CB-SEM [i.e., factor-based SEM] method."

Additional Considerations when Using PLS-SEM

Research has witnessed a considerable debate about situations that favor or hinder the use of PLS-SEM (e.g., Goodhue et al. 2012; Hair et al. 2019b; Marcoulides et al. 2012; Marcoulides and Saunders 2006; Henseler et al. 2014). In the following sections, we complement our previous discussion of the method's treatment of latent variables and the consequences for measurement model specification and estimation by introducing further relevant aspects to consider when using PLS-SEM, which have been discussed in the literature (e.g., Hair et al. 2013, 2019a). Where necessary, we refer to differences between factor-based SEM and PLS-SEM even though such comparisons should not be made indiscriminately (e.g., Marcoulides and Chin 2013; Rigdon 2016; Rigdon et al. 2017; Hair et al. 2017b).

Distributional Assumptions

Many researchers indicate they prefer the non-parametric PLS-SEM approach because their data's distribution does not meet the rigorous requirements of the parametric factor-based SEM approach (e.g., Hair et al. 2012b; Nitzl 2016; do Valle and Assaker 2016). However, this line of reasoning does not consider that maximum likelihood estimation in factor-based SEM is fairly robust against violations of normality (e.g., Chou et al. 1991; Olsson et al. 2000) and comes with a variety of estimators that are robust against nonnormality (Lei and Wu 2012). Thus, justifying the use of PLS-SEM solely on the grounds of data distribution is not sufficient.

Statistical Power

When using PLS-SEM, researchers benefit from the method's greater statistical power compared to factor-based SEM, even when estimating data generated from a common factor model population. Because of its greater statistical power, the

PLS-SEM method is more likely to identify an effect as significant when it is indeed present in the population.

The characteristic of higher statistical power makes PLS-SEM particularly suitable for exploratory research settings where theory is less developed. As Wold (1980, p. 70) notes, "the arrow scheme is usually tentative since the model construction is an evolutionary process. The empirical content of the model is extracted from the data, and the model is improved by interactions through the estimation procedure between the model and the data and the reactions of the researcher."

Model Complexity and Sample Size

PLS-SEM works efficiently with small sample sizes when models are complex (e.g., Hair et al. 2017b; Sarstedt et al. 2016; Willaby et al. 2015). Prior reviews of SEM applications show that the average number of constructs per model is clearly higher in PLS-SEM (approximately eight constructs; e.g., Hair et al. 2017a; Kaufmann and Gaeckler 2015; Ringle et al. 2012) compared to factor-based SEM (approximately five constructs; e.g., Shah and Goldstein 2006; Baumgartner and Homburg 1996). Similarly, the number of indicators per construct is typically higher in PLS-SEM compared to factor-based SEM, which is not surprising considering the negative effect of more indicators on χ^2-based fit measures in factor-based SEM. Different from factor-based SEM, the PLS-SEM algorithm does not simultaneously compute all the model relationships, but instead uses separate ordinary least squares regressions to estimate the model's partial regression relationships – as implied by its name. As a result, the overall number of model parameters can be extremely high in relation to the sample size as long as each partial regression relationship draws on a sufficient number of observations. Reinartz et al. (2009), Henseler et al. (2014), and Sarstedt et al. (2016) show that PLS-SEM provides solutions when other methods do not converge, or develop inadmissible solutions, regardless of whether using common factor or composite model data. However, as Hair et al. (2013, p. 2) note, "some researchers abuse this advantage by relying on extremely small samples relative to the underlying population" and that "PLS-SEM has an erroneous reputation for offering special sampling capabilities that no other multivariate analysis tool has." PLS-SEM can be applied with smaller samples in many instances when other methods fail, but the legitimacy of such analyses depends on the size and the nature of the population (e.g., in terms of its heterogeneity). No statistical method – including PLS-SEM – can offset a badly designed sample. To determine the necessary sample size, researchers should run power analyses that take into account the model structure expected effect sizes and the significance level (e.g., Marcoulides and Chin 2013) and provide power tables for a range of path model constellations. In addition, Kock and Hadaya (2018) proposed the inverse square root method, which considers the probability that the ratio of a path coefficient and its standard error will be greater than the critical value of a test statistic for a specific significance level – see Hair et al. (2022) for illustrations of the method.

While much focus has been devoted to PLS-SEM's small sample size capabilities (e.g., Goodhue et al. 2012), discussions often overlook the method's suitability for analyzing large datasets, such as those generated by Internet research, social media, and social networks (e.g., Akter et al. 2017; Hair and Sarstedt 2021a). Analyses of social media data typically focus on prediction, rely on complex models with little theoretical substantiation (Stieglitz et al. 2014), and often lack a comprehensive substantiation on the grounds of measurement theory (Hair et al. 2019a; Rigdon 2013). PLS-SEM's non-parametric nature, its ability to handle complex models with many (e.g., say eight or considerably more) constructs and indicators along with its high statistical power, make it a valuable method for social media analytics and the analysis of other types of large-scale data.

Goodness-of-Fit and Prediction

PLS-SEM does not have an established goodness-of-fit measure. As a consequence, some researchers conclude that PLS-SEM's use for theory testing and confirmation is limited (e.g., Westland 2019). Recent research has, however, started reexamining goodness-of-fit measures proposed in the early days of PLS-SEM (Lohmöller 1989) or suggesting new ones, thereby broadening the method's applicability (e.g., Dijkstra and Henseler 2015a). One of the earliest proposed measures is the goodness-of-fit index (GoF), proposed by Tenenhaus et al. (2005, p. 173) as "an operational solution to this problem as it may be meant as an index for validating the PLS model globally." Henseler and Sarstedt (2013) challenged the usefulness of the GoF both conceptually and empirically, showing that the metric does not represent a goodness-of-fit criterion for PLS-SEM. Other measures include the standardized root mean square residual (SRMR), the root mean square residual covariance (RMS_{theta}), and the exact fit test (Dijkstra and Henseler 2015a; Lohmöller 1989; Henseler et al. 2014). But, while simulation studies sought to demonstrate their efficacy for PLS-SEM-based model fit testing (Schuberth et al. 2018), Hair et al. (2022) note that these measures have proven ineffective in detecting model misspecifications in settings commonly encountered in applied research.

In addition, literature casts doubt on whether measured fit – as understood in a factor-based SEM context – is a relevant concept for PLS-SEM (Hair et al. 2022; Lohmöller 1989; Rigdon 2012). Factor-based SEM follows an explanatory modeling perspective in that the algorithm estimates all the model parameters based on the objective of minimzing the divergence between the empirical covariance matrix and the model-implied covariance matrix. In contrast, the PLS-SEM algorithm follows a causal-prediction modeling perspective in that the method aims to maximize the amount of explained variance of the endogenous latent variables. Explanation and prediction are two distinct concepts of statistical modeling and estimation (e.g., Hair et al. 2019b). "In explanatory modeling the focus is on minimizing bias to obtain the most accurate representation of the underlying theory. In contrast, predictive modeling seeks to minimize the combination of bias and estimation variance, occasionally sacrificing theoretical accuracy for improved empirical precision" (Shmueli 2010, p. 293). Correspondingly, a grossly misspecified model can yield superior predictions whereas a correctly specified model can perform extremely poor in terms of prediction – see the Appendix in Shmueli (2010) for an illustration.

Researchers using PLS-SEM overcome this seeming dichotomy between explanatory and predictive modeling since they expect their model to have high predictive

Table 2 Reasons for using PLS-SEM

Reasons for using PLS-SEM
• The goal is to predict and explain a key target construct and/or to identify its relevant antecedent constructs. • T5he path model is relatively complex as evidenced in many constructs per model (six or more) and indicators per construct (more than four indicators), • The path model includes formatively measured constructs. • The sample size is limited (e.g., in business-to-business research) and also when it is large. • The research is based on secondary or archival data, which lack a comprehensive substantiation on the grounds of measurement theory. • The objective is to use latent variable scores in subsequent analyses..

accuracy, while also being grounded in well-developed causal explanations. Gregor (2006, p. 626) refers to this interplay as explanation and prediction theory, noting that this approach "implies both understanding of underlying causes and prediction, as well as description of theoretical constructs and the relationships among them." This perspective corresponds to Jöreskog and Wold's (1982, p. 270) understanding of PLS-SEM in which they labeled the method as a "causal-predictive" technique, meaning that when structural theory is strong, path relationships can be interpreted as causal. Hence, validation using goodness-of-fit measures is also relevant in a PLS-SEM context but less so compared to factor-based SEM. Instead, researchers should primarily focus on the assessment of their model's predictive performance (e.g., Rigdon 2012), for example, on the grounds of Shmueli et al.'s (2016) $PLS_{predict}$ procedure and Liengaard et al.'s (2021) cross-validated predictive ability test (CVPAT).

Table 2 summarizes the rules of thumb researchers should consider when determining whether PLS-SEM is the appropriate statistical tool for their research.

Evaluation of PLS-SEM Results

Procedure

Evaluating PLS-SEM results involves completing two stages, as illustrated in Fig. 3. Stage 1 addresses the examination of reflective measurement models (Stage 1.1), formative measurement models (Stage 1.2), or both. If the evaluation provides support for the measurement quality, the researcher continues with the structural model evaluation in Stage 2 (Hair et al. 2022). In brief, Stage 1 examines the measurement theory, while Stage 2 covers the structural theory that addresses the relationships among the latent variables, representing the proposed hypotheses.

Researchers have developed numerous guidelines for assessing PLS-SEM results (Chin 2010; Hair et al. 2019a, 2022; Roldán and Sánchez-Franco 2012), which may be summarized under the general term confirmatory composite analysis (CCA; Hair et al. 2018a, 2020). While the following illustrations draw on Hair et al. (2020), there

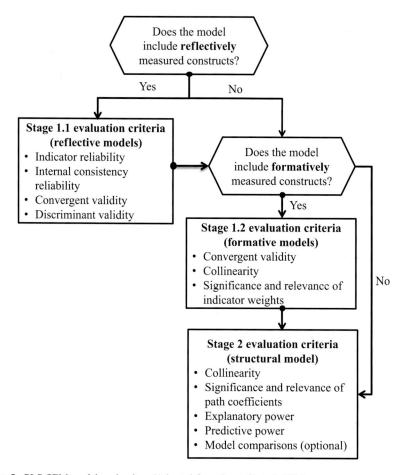

Fig. 3 PLS-SEM model evaluation. (Adapted from Sarstedt et al. 2014)

is disagreement as to which analysis steps define a confirmatory composite analysis (Henseler 2021; Henseler and Schuberth 2020; Schuberth et al. 2018). Hair et al.'s (2020) approach does not emphasize fit, but focuses on the assessment of the model's predictive power using Shmueli et al.'s (2016) $PLS_{predict}$ procedure. In contrast, Schuberth et al.'s (2018) approach requires fit but does not refer to out-of-sample prediction – see also Henseler (2021) and Henseler and Schuberth (2020). In this chapter, we follow the CCA steps recommended by Hair et al. (2020).

Starting with the measurement model assessment and continuing with the structural model assessment, the following guidelines offer rules of thumb for interpreting the adequacy of the results. Note that a rule of thumb is a broadly applicable and easily applied guideline for decision-making that should not be strictly interpreted for every situation. Therefore, the threshold for a rule of thumb may vary depending on the research context.

Stage 1.1: Reflective Measurement Model Assessment

In the case of reflectively specified constructs, a researcher begins Stage 1 by examining the indicator loadings. Loadings above 0.708 indicate the construct explains more than 50% of the indicator's variance, demonstrating that the indicator exhibits a satisfactory degree of item reliability.

The next step involves the assessment of the constructs' internal consistency reliability. When using PLS-SEM, internal consistency reliability is generally evaluated using Jöreskog's (1971) composite reliability ρ_c, which is defined as follows (for standardized data):

$$\rho_c = \frac{\left(\sum_{k=1}^{K} l_k\right)^2}{\left(\sum_{k=1}^{K} l_k\right)^2 + \sum_{k=1}^{K} var(e_k)}, \quad (4)$$

where l_k symbolizes the standardized outer loading of the indicator variable k of a specific construct measured with K indicators, e_k is the measurement error of indicator variable k, and $var(e_k)$ denotes the variance of the measurement error, which is defined as $1 - l_k^2$.

For the composite reliability criterion, higher values indicate higher levels of reliability. For instance, researchers can consider values between 0.60 and 0.70 as acceptable in exploratory research, whereas results between 0.70 and 0.95 represent satisfactory to good reliability levels (Hair et al. 2022). However, values that are too high (e.g., higher than 0.95) are problematic, as they suggest that the items are almost identical and redundant. The reason may be (almost) the same item questions in a survey or undesirable response patterns such as straight lining (Diamantopoulos et al. 2012).

Cronbach's alpha is another measure of internal consistency reliability that assumes the same thresholds but yields lower values than the composite reliability (ρ_c). This statistic is defined in its standardized form as follows, where K represents the construct's number of indicators and $\bar{r}$ the average non-redundant indicator correlation coefficient (i.e., the mean of the lower or upper triangular correlation matrix):

$$Cronbach's\ \alpha = \frac{K \cdot \bar{r}}{[1 + (K - 1) \cdot \bar{r}]}. \quad (5)$$

Generally, in PLS-SEM Cronbach's alpha is considered the lower bound, while ρ_c defines the upper bound of internal consistency reliability when estimating reflective measurement models with PLS-SEM. Hence, the actual reliability of a construct likely falls between Cronbach's alpha and the composite reliability ρ_c.

As an alternative and building on Dijkstra (2010), subsequent research has proposed the exact (or consistent) reliability coefficient ρ_A (Dijkstra 2014; Dijkstra and Henseler 2015b), which is defined as

$$\rho_A := (\widehat{w}'\widehat{w})^2 \cdot \frac{\widehat{w}'(S - diag(S))\widehat{w}}{\widehat{w}'(\widehat{w}\widehat{w}' - diag(\widehat{w}\widehat{w}'))\widehat{w}'} \tag{6}$$

where $\widehat{w}$ represents the indicator weights estimates, *diag* indicates the diagonal of the corresponding matrix, and S the sample covariance matrix. The ρ_A reliability metric usually lies between Cronbach's α and the composite reliability ρ_c, and is therefore considered a good compromise between these other two measures (Hair et al. 2019a).

The next step in assessing reflective measurement models addresses convergent validity, which is the extent to which a construct converges in its indicators by explaining the items' variance. Convergent validity is assessed by the average variance extracted (AVE) across all items associated with a particular reflectively measured construct and is also referred to as communality. The AVE is calculated as the mean of the squared loadings of each indicator associated with a construct (for standardized data):

$$\text{AVE} = \frac{\left(\sum_{k=1}^{K} l_k^2\right)}{K}, \tag{7}$$

where l_k and K are defined as explained above. An acceptable threshold for AVE is 0.50 or higher. This level or higher indicates that, on average, the construct explains (more than) 50% of the variance of its items.

Once the reliability and the convergent validity of reflectively measured constructs have been successfully established, the final step is to assess their discriminant validity. This analysis reveals to which extent a construct is empirically distinct from other constructs both in terms of how much it correlates with other constructs and how distinctly the indicators represent only this single construct. Discriminant validity assessment in PLS-SEM involves analyzing Henseler et al.'s (2015) heterotrait-monotrait ratio (HTMT) of correlations. The HTMT criterion is defined as the mean value of the indicator correlations across constructs relative to the (geometric) mean of the average correlations of indicators measuring the same construct. The HTMT of the constructs Y_i and Y_j with, respectively, K_i and K_j indicators is defined as follows:

$$\text{HTMT}_{ij} = \underbrace{\frac{1}{K_i K_j} \sum_{g=1}^{K_i} \sum_{h=1}^{K_j} r_{ig,jh}}_{\substack{\text{average} \\ \text{heterotrait--} \\ \text{heteromethod} \\ \text{correlation}}} \div \underbrace{\left(\frac{2}{K_i(K_i-1)} \cdot \sum_{g=1}^{K_i-1} \sum_{h=g+1}^{K_i} r_{ig,jh} \cdot \frac{2}{K_j(K_j-1)} \cdot \sum_{g=1}^{K_j-1} \sum_{h=g+1}^{K_j} r_{jg,jh} \right)^{\frac{1}{2}}}_{\substack{\text{geometric mean of the average monotrait-heteromethod} \\ \text{correlation of construct } Y_i \text{ and the average} \\ \text{monotrait-heteromethod correlation of construct } Y_j}},$$

(8)

where $r_{ig,jh}$ represents the correlations of the indicators (i.e., within and across the measurement models of latent variables Y_i and Y_j). Figure 4 shows the correlation matrix of the six indicators used in the reflective measurement models of constructs Y_2 and Y_3 from Fig. 1.

Therefore, high HTMT values indicate discriminant validity problems. Based on prior research and their simulation study results, Henseler et al. (2015) suggest a threshold value of 0.90 if the path model includes constructs that are conceptually very similar (e.g., affective satisfaction, cognitive satisfaction, and loyalty); that is, an HTMT value above 0.90 depicts a lack of discriminant validity. However, when the constructs in the path model are conceptually more distinct, researchers should consider 0.85 as threshold for HTMT (Henseler et al. 2015).

In addition, researchers can (and should) use bootstrap confidence intervals (see next section for a discussion of the bootstrapping concept) to test if the HTMT is significantly lower than 1.00 (Henseler et al. 2015) or another threshold value such as 0.90 or 0.85. The concrete thershold should be defined based on the study context (Franke and Sarstedt 2019). For example, assuming a threshold of 0.85 and assuming a significance level of 5%, researchers need to assess whether the upper boundary of the one-sided 95% bootstrap confidence interval (i.e., UB_{95}) is lower than 0.85. This upper boundary can also be inferred from a two-sided 90% bootstrap confidence interval. In order to obtain the bootstrap confidence intervals, in line with Aguirre-Urreta and Rönkkö (2018), researchers should generally use the percentile method. However, when the reliability coefficient's bootstrap distribution is skewed, the bias-corrected and accelerated (BCa) method should be preferred to obtain bootstrap confidence intervals. The recommended number of bootstrap samples researchers should use is 10,000 (Streukens and Leroi-Werelds 2016). We discuss the different bootstrap confidence interval types and parameter settings in greater detail in the next section.

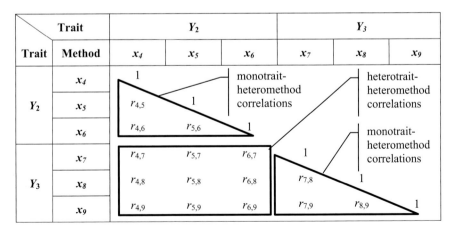

Fig. 4 Correlation matrix example

Stage 1.2: Formative Measurement Model Assessment

Formatively specified constructs are evaluated differently from reflectively measured constructs. Their evaluation involves the examination of (1) the convergent validity, (2) indicator collinearity, and (3) statistical significance and relevance of the indicator weights – see Fig. 3.

In formative measurement model evaluation, convergent validity refers to the degree to which the formatively specified construct correlates with an alternative measure of the same concept. Originally proposed by Chin (1998), the procedure is referred to as redundancy analysis. To execute this procedure for determining convergent validity, researchers must plan ahead in the research design stage by including an alternative measure of the formatively measured construct in their questionnaire. Cheah et al. (2018) show that a single item, which captures the essence of the construct under consideration, is generally sufficient as an alternative measure – despite limitations with regard to criterion validity (Diamantopoulos et al. 2012). When the model is based on secondary data, an available variable measuring a similar concept would be used (Houston 2004). Hair et al. (2022) suggest the correlation of the formatively measured construct with the reflectively measured item(s) should be 0.708 or higher, which implies that the construct explains (more than) 50% of the alternative measure's variance (Carlson and Herdman 2012).

Collinearity assessment involves computing each item's variance inflation factor (VIF) by running a multiple regression of each indicator in the measurement model of the formatively measured construct on all the other items of the same construct. The R^2 values of the k-th regression facilitates the computation of the VIF for the k-th indicator, using the following formula:

$$VIF_k = \frac{1}{1 - R_k^2} \qquad (9)$$

Higher R^2 values in the k-th regression imply that the variance of the k-th item can be explained by the other items in the same measurement model, which indicates collinearity issues. Likewise, the higher the VIF, the greater the level of collinearity. As a rule of thumb, VIF values above 3 are indicative of collinearity among the indicators. However, collinearity issues can also occur at lower VIF values of 3 (e.g., Mason and Perreault 1991). Hence, when the analysis produces unexpected sign changes in the indicator weights, researchers should reconsider the model set-up in an effort to reduce the collinearity.

The third step in assessing formatively measured constructs is examining the statistical significance and relevance (i.e., the size) of the indicator weights. In contrast to regression analysis, PLS-SEM does not make any distributional assumptions regarding the error terms that would facilitate the immediate testing of the weights' significance based on the normal distribution. Instead, the researcher must run bootstrapping, a procedure that draws a large number of subsamples (typically 10,000) from the original data. The model is then estimated for each of the subsamples, yielding a high number of estimates for each model parameter.

Using the subsamples from bootstrapping, the researcher can construct a distribution of the parameter under consideration and compute bootstrap standard errors, which allow for determining the statistical significance of the original indicator weights. More precisely, bootstrap standard errors allow for computing t-values (and corresponding p-values). When interpreting the results, reviewers and editors should be aware that bootstrapping is a random process, which yields different results every time it is initiated. While the results from one bootstrapping run to the next generally do not differ fundamentally when using a large number of bootstrap samples such as 10,000 (Streukens and Leroi-Werelds 2016), bootstrapping-based p-values slightly lower than a predefined cut-off level should give rise to concern. In such a case, researchers may have repeatedly applied bootstrapping until a certain parameter has become significant, a practice referred to as p-hacking.

As an alternative, researchers can use the bootstrapping results to construct different types of confidence intervals. Aguirre-Urreta and Rönkkö (2018) show that the percentile method performs very well in a PLS-SEM context in terms of coverage (i.e., the proportion of times the population value of the parameter is included in the 1-α% confidence interval in repeated samples) and balance (i.e., how α% of cases fall to the right or to the left of the interval). If a weight's confidence interval includes zero, this provides evidence that the weight is not statistically significant, making the indicator a candidate for removal from the measurement model. However, instead of mechanically deleting the indicator, researchers should first consider its loading, which represents the indicator's absolute contribution to the construct. While an indicator might not have a strong relative contribution (e.g., because of the large number of indicators in the formative measurement model), its absolute contribution can still be substantial and meaningful (Cenfetelli and Bassellier 2009). Based on these considerations, the following rules of thumb apply (Hair et al. 2022):

- If the weight is statistically significant, the indicator is retained.
- If the weight is nonsignificant, but the indicator's loading is 0.50 or higher, the indicator is still retained if theory and expert judgment support its inclusion.
- If the weight is nonsignificant and the loading is low (i.e., below 0.50), the indicator should be deleted from the measurement model.

Researchers must be cautious when deleting formative indicators based on statistical outcomes for at least the following two reasons. First, the indicator weight is a function of the number of indicators used to measure a construct: The higher the number of indicators, the lower their average weight. In other words, formative measurement models have an inherent limit to the number of indicators that can retain a statistically significant weight (e.g., Cenfetelli and Bassellier 2009). Second, as formative indicators define the construct's empirical meaning, indicator deletion should be considered with caution and should generally be the exception. Content validity considerations are imperative before deleting formative indicators (e.g., Diamantopoulos and Winklhofer 2001).

Having assessed the formative indicator weights' statistical significance, the final step is to examine each indicator's relevance for shaping the construct. In terms of relevance, indicator weights are standardized to values that are usually between −1 and +1, with weights closer to +1 (or −1) representing strong positive (or negative) relationships, and weights closer to 0 indicating weak relationships. Note that values below −1 and above +1 may technically occur, for instance, when collinearity is at critical levels.

Stage 2: Structural Model Assessment

Provided the measurement model assessment indicates satisfactory quality, the researcher moves to the assessment of the structural model in Stage 2 of the PLS-SEM evaluation process (Fig. 3). After checking for potential collinearity issues among the constructs, this stage considers the significance and relevance of the structural model relationships (i.e., the path coefficients) as well as the model's explanatory and predictive power. Some research situations call for the computation and comparison of alternative models, which can emerge from different theories or contexts. PLS-SEM facilitates the comparison of alternative models using criteria that are well known from the regression literature, as well as more recent out-of-sample prediction metrics. As model comparisons are not relevant for every PLS-SEM analysis, this assessment is optional.

Computation of the path coefficients linking the constructs is based on a series of regression analyses. Therefore, the researcher must first ascertain that collinearity issues do not bias or distort the regression results. This step is analogous to the formative measurement model assessment, with the difference that the scores of the exogenous latent variables serve as input for the *VIF* assessments. *VIF* values above 3 are indicative of collinearity among sets of predictor constructs. However, as indicated in the context of formative measurement model assessment, collinearity can also occur at lower *VIF* values.

Subsequently, the strength and significance of the path coefficients is evaluated regarding the relationships (structural paths) hypothesized between the constructs. Similar to the assessment of formative indicator weights, the significance assessment builds on bootstrapping standard errors as a basis for calculating *t*-values and *p*-values of path coefficients, or – as recommended in the literature – their percentile confidence intervals (Aguirre-Urreta and Rönkkö 2018). A path coefficient is significant at the 5% probability of error level if zero does not fall into the 95% percentile confidence interval. For example, a path coefficient of 0.15 with 0.1 and 0.2 as lower and upper bounds of the 95% percentile confidence interval would be considered significant since zero does not fall into this confidence interval. On the contrary, with a lower bound of −0.05 and an upper bound of 0.35, we would consider this coefficient as not significant.

In terms of relevance, path coefficients are usually between −1 and +1, with coefficients closer to +1 representing strong positive relationships, and those closer to −1 indicating strong negative relationships (note that values below −1 and above +1 may technically occur, for instance, when collinearity is at critical levels). A path coefficient of say 0.5 implies that if the independent construct increases by one standard deviation unit, the dependent construct will increase by 0.5 standard deviation units when keeping all other independent constructs constant. Determining whether the size of the coefficient is meaningful should be decided within the research context. When examining the structural model results, researchers should also interpret total effects. The total effect corresponds to the sum of the direct effect and all the indirect effects between two constructs in the path model. With regard to the path model shown in Fig. 1, Y_1 has a direct effect (b_1) and an indirect effect ($b_2 \cdot b_3$) via Y_2 on the endogenous construct Y_3. Hence, the total effect of Y_1 on Y_3 is $b_1 + b_2 \cdot b_3$. The examination of total effects between constructs, including all their indirect effects, provides a more comprehensive picture of the structural model relationships (Nitzl et al. 2016).

The next step involves reviewing the coefficient of determination (R^2). The R^2 measures the variance explained in each of the endogenous constructs and is therefore a measure of the model's explanatory power (Shmueli and Koppius 2011), also referred to as in-sample predictive power (Rigdon 2012). The R^2 ranges from 0 to 1, with higher levels indicating a higher degree of explanatory power. As a rough rule of thumb, the R^2 values of 0.75, 0.50, and 0.25 can be considered substantial, moderate, and weak (Henseler et al. 2009; Hair et al. 2011). Acceptable R^2 values are based on the context. In some disciplines an R^2 value as low as 0.10 is considered satisfactory, for example, when predicting stock returns (Raithel et al. 2012). In other contexts, scientists usually expect higher R^2 values above 0.65. An example is the customer satisfaction construct in American Customer Satisfaction Index model applications (Fornell et al. 1996; chapter ▶ "Measuring Customer Satisfaction and Customer Loyalty").

More importantly, the R^2 is a function of the number of predictor constructs – the greater the number of predictor constructs, the higher the R^2. Therefore, the R^2 should always be interpreted relative to the context of the study based on the R^2 values from related studies and models of similar complexity. R^2 values can also be too high when the model overfits the data. Model overfit is present when the partial regression model is too complex, which results in fitting the random noise inherent in the sample rather than reflecting the overall population. The same model would likely not fit as well on another sample drawn from the same population (Sharma et al. 2018). When measuring a concept that is inherently predictable, such as physical processes, R^2 values of 0.90 might be plausible. Similar R^2 value levels in a model that predicts human attitudes, perceptions and intentions likely indicate model overfit (Hair et al. 2019a).

In addition to evaluating the R^2 values of all endogenous constructs, the change in the R^2 value when a specified exogenous construct is omitted from the model can be used to evaluate whether the omitted construct has a substantive impact on the endogenous constructs. This measure is referred to as the f^2 effect size and can be calculated as

$$f^2 = \frac{R^2_{included} - R^2_{excluded}}{1 - R^2_{included}} \qquad (10)$$

where $R^2_{included}$ and $R^2_{excluded}$ are the R^2 values of the endogenous latent variable when a selected exogenous latent variable is included in or excluded from the model. Technically, the change in the R^2 values is calculated by estimating a specific partial regression in the structural model twice (i.e., with the same latent variable scores). First, the model is estimated with all exogenous latent variables included (yielding $R^2_{included}$) and, second, with a selected exogenous latent variable excluded (yielding $R^2_{excluded}$). As a guideline, f^2 values of 0.02, 0.15, and 0.35, respectively, represent small, medium, and large effects (Cohen 1988) of an exogenous latent variable. Effect size values of less than 0.02 indicate that there is no effect.

To assess a PLS path model's predictive power, also referred to as out-of-sample predictive power, researchers can draw on Shmueli et al.'s (2016) PLS$_{predict}$ procedure. PLS$_{predict}$ executes k-fold cross-validation by randomly partitioning the dataset into k subsets (folds). In the following, PLS$_{predict}$ then combines $k - 1$ subsets into a single analysis sample that is used to predict the indicator values of a specific target constructs in the remaining data subset (i.e., the holdout sample). This process is repeated k times such that each subset serves as holdout sample once. Shmueli et al. (2019) recommend setting $k = 10$, but researchers need to make sure the analysis sample for each subset (fold) meets minimum sample size guidelines. PLS$_{predict}$ can also be run repeatedly to alleviate the impact of potentially extreme samples resulting from the random partitioning of the data into k folds. As a rule of thumb, researchers should generally run PLS$_{predict}$ with ten repetitions.

To quantify the degree of prediction error, researchers can draw on several prediction statistics. The default statistic is the root mean squared error (RMSE), which weights large prediction errors more strongly than small errors. When the prediction error distribution is highly nonsymmetric, researchers may use the mean absolute error (MAE), which measures the average magnitude of the errors in a set of predictions without considering their direction (over or under). Both RMSE and MAE cannot be interpreted absolutely as their values depend on the measurement scale of the indicators under consideration. For example, an indicator measured on a scale from 0 to 100 can cover a much greater range of prediction errors than a 7-point Likert scale.

Hence, researchers need to compare the RMSE (or MAE) values with a linear regression model (LM) benchmark to generate predictions for the manifest variables by running a linear regression of each of the dependent construct's indicators on the indicators of the exogenous constructs in the PLS path model (Danks and Ray 2018). In comparing the RMSE (or MAE) values with the LM values, the following guidelines apply (Shmueli et al. 2019):

1. If *all* indicators in the PLS-SEM analysis have lower RMSE (or MAE) values compared to the naïve LM benchmark, the model has high predictive power.
2. If the *majority* (or the same number) of indicators in the PLS-SEM analysis yields smaller prediction errors compared to the LM, this indicates medium predictive power.
3. If the *minority* of the dependent construct's indicators produces lower PLS-SEM prediction errors compared to the naïve LM benchmark, this indicates that the model has low predictive power.

4. If the PLS-SEM analysis (compared to the LM) yields lower prediction errors in terms of the RMSE (or the MAE) for *none* of the indicators, this indicates that the model lacks predictive power.

Researchers can also assess the $Q^2_{predict}$ statistic, which indicates whether the PLS-SEM-based predictions outperform the most naïve benchmark, defined as the indicator mean from the holdout samples. A $Q^2_{predict}$ larger than zero indicates the PLS path model outperforms this most naïve benchmark. Importantly, when interpreting PLS$_{predict}$ results, researchers should focus on the model's key endogenous construct rather than examining the prediction errors for the indicators of all endogenous constructs. Shmueli et al. (2019) present a systematic application of the PLS$_{predict}$ procedure including the $Q^2_{predict}$ criterion and the LM benchmark.

In a final, optional step, researchers may be interested in comparing different model configurations resulting from different theories or research contexts. Sharma et al. (2018) and Danks et al. (2020) compared the efficacy of various metrics for model comparison tasks and found that Schwarz's (1978) Bayesian information criterion (BIC) and Geweke and Meese's (1981) criterion (GM) achieve a sound tradeoff between model fit and predictive power in the estimation of PLS path models. These (Information Theoretic) model selection criteria facilitate the comparison of models in terms of model fit and predictive power without having to use a holdout sample, which is particularly useful for PLS-SEM analyses that often draw on small sample sizes. In applying these metrics, researchers should estimate each model separately and select the model that minimizes the value in BIC or GM for a certain target construct. While BIC and GM exhibit practically the same performance in model selection tasks, BIC is easier to compute. Hence, focusing on this criterion is sufficient in most model comparison tasks. The BIC for a certain model *i* is defined as follows:

$$BIC_i = n[\log(\frac{SSE_i}{n}) + \frac{p_j \cdot \log(n)}{n}], \qquad (11)$$

where SSE$_i$ is the sum of squared errors for the *i*-th model in a set of alternative models, *n* is the sample size, and p_j is the number of predictors of the construct of interest plus 1.

One issue in the application of the BIC is that – in its simple form (i.e., raw values) – the criterion does not offer any insights regarding the relative weights of evidence in favor of models under consideration (Burnham and Anderson 2002). More precisely, while the differences in BIC values are useful in ranking and selecting models, such differences can often be small in practice, leading to model selection uncertainty. To resolve this issue, researchers can use the BIC values to compute Akaike weights, which indicate a model's relative likelihood, given the data and a set of competing models (Danks et al. 2020) – see Wagenmakers and Farrell (2004) for an application.

A further advancement in the field of prediction-oriented model comparisons in PLS-SEM is Liengaard et al.'s (2021) CVPAT, which proves valuable for developing and validating theories from a prediction standpoint (Hair et al. 2022). Future extensions of CVPAT will allow researchers to test the predictive power of their models on a standalone basis (Hair et al. 2020).

Research Application

Corporate Reputation Model

The empirical application builds on the corporate reputation model and data that Hair et al. (2022) use in their book *Primer on Partial Least Squares Structural Equation Modeling (PLS-SEM)*, and that Hair et al. (2018b) also employ in their *Advanced Issues in Partial Least Squares Structural Equation Modeling* book. The PLS path model creation and estimation was executed using the SmartPLS 3 software (Ringle et al. 2015). The model files, datasets and software used in this market research application can be downloaded at https://www.smartpls.com.

Figure 5 shows the corporate reputation model as displayed in SmartPLS 3. Originally presented by Eberl (2010), the goal of this model is to explain the effects of corporate reputation on customer satisfaction (*CUSA*) and, ultimately, customer loyalty (*CUSL*). Corporate reputation represents a company's overall evaluation by its stakeholder (Helm et al. 2010), which comprises two dimensions (Schwaiger

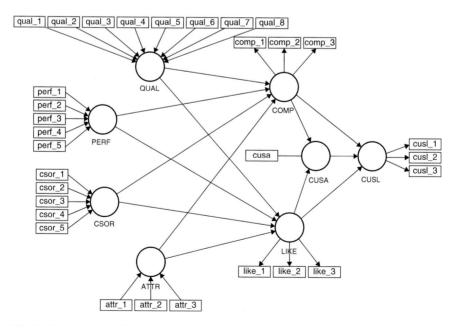

Fig. 5 Corporate reputation model in SmartPLS 3

2004). The first dimension captures cognitive evaluations of the company, and the construct is the company's competence (*COMP*). The second dimension captures affective judgments, which determine the company's likeability (*LIKE*). This two-dimensional reputation measurement has been validated in different countries and applied in various research studies (e.g., Eberl and Schwaiger 2005; Raithel and Schwaiger 2015; Schloderer et al. 2014). Research has shown that the approach performs favorably (in terms of convergent validity and predictive validity) compared with alternative reputation measures (e.g., Sarstedt et al. 2013). Schwaiger (2004) also identified four exogenous constructs that represent the key sources of the two corporate reputation dimensions: (1) the quality of a company's products and services, as well as the quality of its customer orientation (*QUAL*); (2) the company's economic and managerial performance (*PERF*); (3) the company's corporate social responsibility (*CSOR*); and (4) the company's attractiveness (*ATTR*).

In terms of construct measurement, *COMP*, *LIKE*, and *CUSL* have reflectively specified measurement models with three items. *CUSA* draws – for illustrative purposes – on a single-item measure. The four exogenous latent variables *QUAL*, *PERF*, *CSOR*, and *ATTR* have formative measurement models. Table 3 provides an overview of all items' wordings.

Data

The model estimation draws on data from four German mobile telecommunications providers. A total of 344 respondents rated the questions related to the items on a 7-point Likert scale, whereby a value of seven always represents the best possible judgment and a value of one the opposite. The most complex partial regression in the PLS path model has eight independent variables (i.e., the formative measurement model of *QUAL*). Hence, following Cohen's (1992) recommendations for multiple ordinary least squares regression analysis or running a power analysis, one would need only 54 observations to detect R^2 values of around 0.25, assuming a significance level of 5% and a statistical power of 80%. When considering the more conservative inverse square root method suggested by Kock and Hadaya (2018), the minimum sample size requirement is approximately 275, assuming a minimum path coefficient of 0.15 at a 5% probability of error level.

The dataset has only 11 missing values, which are coded with the value -99. The maximum number of missing data points per item is 4 of 334 (1.16%) in *cusl_2*. Since the relative number of missing values is very small, we continue the analysis by using the mean value replacement of missing data option. Box plots diagnostic by means of IBM SPSS Statistics (Sarstedt and Mooi 2019) reveals influential observations, but no outliers. Finally, the skewness and excess kurtosis values, as provided by the SmartPLS 3 data view, show that all the indicators are within the -2 and $+2$ acceptable range (George and Mallery 2019).

Table 3 Item wordings (Hair et al. 2022)

Attractiveness (ATTR) - formative	
attr_1	[the company] is successful in attracting high-quality employees.
attr_2	I could see myself working at [the company].
attr_3	I like the physical appearance of [the company] (company, buildings, shops, etc.).
Competence (COMP) - reflective	
comp_1	[the company] is a top competitor in its market.
comp_2	As far as I know, [the company] is recognized worldwide.
comp_3	I believe that [the company] performs at a premium level.
Corporate Social Responsibility (CSOR) - formative	
csor_1	[the company] behaves in a socially conscious way.
csor_2	[the company] is forthright in giving information to the public.
csor_3	[the company] has a fair attitude toward competitors.
csor_4	[the company] is concerned about the preservation of the environment.
csor_5	[the company] is not only concerned about profits.
Customer loyalty (CUSL) - reflective	
cusl_1	I would recommend [company] to friends and relatives.
cusl_2	If I had to choose again, I would choose [company] as my mobile phone services provider.
cusl_3	I will remain a customer of [company] in the future.
Customer satisfaction (CUSA) - single item	
Cusa	If you consider your experiences with [company], how satisfied are you with [company]?
Likeability (LIKE) – Reflective	
like_1	[the company] is a company that I can better identify with than other companies.
like_2	[the company] is a company that I would regret more not having if it no longer existed than I would other companies.
like_3	I regard [the company] as a likeable company.
Quality (QUAL) – Formative	
qual_1	The products/services offered by [the company] are of high quality.
qual_2	[the company] is an innovator, rather than an imitator with respect to [industry].
qual_3	[the company]'s products/services offer good value for money.
qual_4	The services [the company] offers are good.
qual_5	Customer concerns are held in high regard at [the company].
qual_6	[the company] is a reliable partner for customers.
qual_7	[the company] is a trustworthy company.
qual_8	I have a lot of respect for [the company].
Performance (PERF) - formative	
perf_1	[the company] is a very well-managed company.
perf_2	[the company] is an economically stable company.
perf_3	The business risk for [the company] is modest compared to its competitors.
perf_4	[the company] has growth potential.
perf_5	[the company] has a clear vision about the future of the company.

Model Estimation

The model estimation uses the basic PLS-SEM algorithm by Lohmöller (1989), the path weighting scheme, a maximum of 300 iterations, a stop criterion of 0.0000001 (or $1 \cdot 10^{-7}$), and equal indicator weights for the initialization (default settings in the SmartPLS 3 software). After running the algorithm, it is important to ascertain that the algorithm converged (i.e., the stop criterion has been reached) and did not reach the maximum number of iterations. However, with sufficiently high numbers of maximum iterations (e.g., 300 and higher), the PLS-SEM algorithm practically always converges in empirical studies, even in very complex market research applications.

Figure 6 shows the PLS-SEM results. The numbers on the path relationships represent the standardized regression coefficients while the numbers displayed in the circles of the endogenous latent variables are the R^2 values. An initial assessment shows that *CUSA* has the strongest effect (0.505) on *CUSL*, followed by *LIKE* (0.344) and *COMP* (0.006). These three constructs explain 56.2% (i.e., the R^2 value) of the variance of the endogenous construct *CUSL*. Similarly, we can interpret the relationships between the exogenous latent variables *ATTR*, *CSOR*, *PERF*, and *QUAL*, as well as the two corporate reputation dimensions *COMP* and *LIKE*. But before we address the interpretation of these results, we must assess the constructs' reflective and formative measurement models.

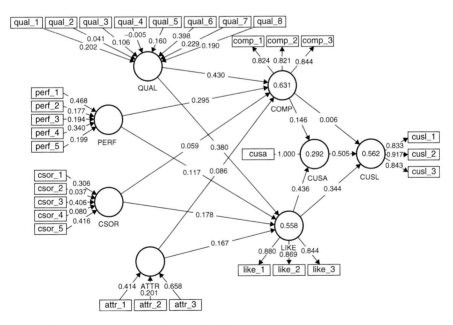

Fig. 6 Corporate reputation model and PLS-SEM results

Results Evaluation

Reflective Measurement Model Assessment

The evaluation of the PLS-SEM results begins with an assessment of the reflective measurement models (i.e., *COMP, CUSL,* and *LIKE*). Table 4 shows the results and evaluation criteria outcomes. We find that all three reflective measurement models meet the relevant assessment criteria. More specifically, all the outer loadings are above 0.708, indicating that all indicators exhibit a sufficient level of reliability. Furthermore, all AVE values are above 0.50, providing support for the measures' convergent validity. The composite reliability ρ_c has values of 0.869 and higher, which is clearly above the expected minimum level of 0.70. Moreover, the Cronbach's alpha values range between 0.776 and 0.831, which is acceptable. Finally, all composite reliability ρ_A values meet the 0.70 threshold. These results suggest that the construct measures of *COMP, CUSL,* and *LIKE* exhibit high levels of internal consistency reliability.

Finally, we assess the discriminant validity by using the HTMT criterion. All the results are clearly below the conservative threshold of 0.85 (Table 5). Next, we run the bootstrapping procedure with 10,000 samples with percentile bootstrap confidence intervals, and one-tailed testing at the 0.05 significance level (which corresponds to a two-sided 90% confidence interval). The results provide the HTMT confidence interval's upper bounds (i.e., UB_{95}) are below 0.85, suggesting that all the HTMT values are significantly different from this conservative threshold (Table 5). This even holds for *CUSA* and *CUSL* as well as *COMP* and *LIKE*, which are conceptually similar. We thus conclude that discriminant validity has been established.

The *CUSA* construct is not included in the reflective (and subsequent formative) measurement model assessment, because it is a single-item construct. For this construct, indicator data and latent variable scores are identical. Consequently,

Table 4 PLS-SEM assessment results of reflective measurement models

Latent variable	Indicators	Convergent validity			Internal consistency reliability		
		Loadings	Indicator reliability	AVE	Cronbach's alpha	Reliability ρ_A	Composite reliability ρ_c
		> 0.70	> 0.50	> 0.50	0.70–0.90	> 0.70	> 0.70
COMP	comp_1	0.824	0.679	0.688	0.776	0.786	0.869
	comp_2	0.821	0.674				
	comp_3	0.844	0.712				
CUSL	cusl_1	0.833	0.694	0.748	0.831	0.839	0.899
	cusl_2	0.917	0.841				
	cusl_3	0.843	0.711				
LIKE	like_1	0.880	0.774	0.747	0.831	0.836	0.899
	like_2	0.869	0.755				
	like_3	0.844	0.712				

Table 5 HTMT values

	COMP	CUSA	CUSL	LIKE
COMP				
CUSA	0.465 (UB$_{95}$: 0.552)			
CUSL	0.532 (UB$_{95}$: 0.618)	0.755 (UB$_{95}$: 0.809)		
LIKE	0.780 (UB$_{95}$: 0.843)	0.577 (UB$_{95}$: 0.640)	0.737 (UB$_{95}$: 0.803)	

Note: UB$_{95}$: represents the upper bounds of the 95% confidence interval

CUSA does not have a measurement model, which can be assessed using the standard evaluation criteria.

Formative Measurement Model Assessment

The formative measurement model assessment initially focuses on the constructs' convergent validity by conducting a redundancy analysis of each construct (i.e., *ATTR, CSOR, PERF,* and *QUAL*). The redundancy analysis draws on global single items, which summarize the essence each formatively measured construct purports to measure. These single items have been included in the original questionnaire. For example, respondents had to answer the statement, "Please assess to which degree [the company] acts in socially conscious ways," measured on a scale of 1 (not at all) to 7 (extremely). This question can be used as an endogenous single-item construct to validate the formative measurement of corporate social responsibility (*CSOR*). For this purpose, we need to create a new PLS path model for each formatively measured construct that explains the global measure as an endogenous single-item construct as shown in Fig. 7. All the path relationships between the formatively measured construct and its global single-item measure (i.e., 0.874, 0.857, 0.811, and 0.805) are above the critical value of 0.70. We thus conclude that convergent validity of the formatively measured constructs has been established.

Next, we assess whether critical levels of collinearity substantially affect the formative indicator weight estimates. We find that the highest *VIF* value (i.e., 2.269 for the formative indicator *qual_3*) is clearly below the more conservative threshold value of 3, suggesting that collinearity is not at a critical level.

Testing the indicator weights' significance draws on the bootstrapping procedure (10,000 samples, percentile bootstrap confidence intervals, two-tailed testing at the 0.05 significance level). Table 6 shows the resulting 95% percentile confidence intervals. The results show that most of the indicator weights are significant, with the exception of *csor_2, csor_4, qual_2, qual_3,* and *qual_4,* whose indicator weight confidence intervals include the value 0. However, these indicators exhibit statistically significant loadings above the 0.50 threshold, providing support for their absolute contribution to the constructs. In addition, prior research has substantiated the relevance of these indicators for the measurement of the *CSOR* and *QUAL* constructs (Eberl 2010; Sarstedt et al. 2013; Schwaiger 2004). Therefore, we retain the nonsignificant, but relevant, indicators in the formative measurement models.

To summarize, the results of the reflective and formative measurement model assessment suggest that all construct measures exhibit satisfactory levels of

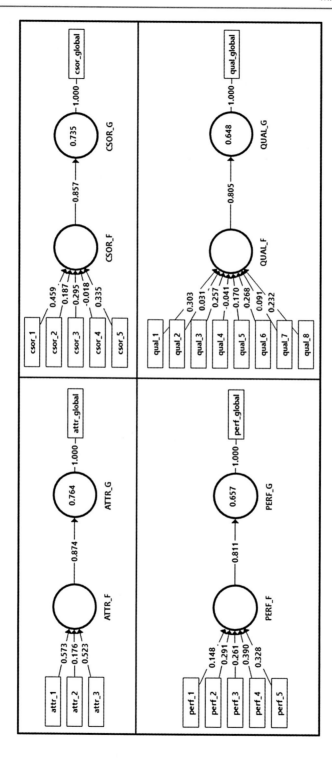

Fig. 7 Redundancy analysis

Table 6 Formative indicator weights and significance testing results

Formative constructs	Formative indicators	Outer weights (outer loadings)	95% confidence interval	Significant ($p < 0.05$)?
ATTR	attr_1	0.414 (0.755)	[0.273, 0.542]	Yes
	attr_2	0.201 (0.506)	[0.067, 0.320]	Yes
	attr_3	0.658 (0.891)	[0.541, 0.777]	Yes
CSOR	csor_1	0.306 (0.771)	[0.126, 0.461]	Yes
	csor_2	0.037 (0.571)	[−0.094, 0.187]	No
	csor_3	0.406 (0.838)	[0.244, 0.552]	Yes
	csor_4	0.080 (0.617)	[−0.070, 0.225]	No
	csor_5	0.416 (0.848)	[0.222, 0.6583]	Yes
PERF	perf_1	0.468 (0.846)	[0.329, 0.594]	Yes
	perf_2	0.177 (0.690)	[0.036, 0.305]	Yes
	perf_3	0.194 (0.573)	[0.092, 0.299]	Yes
	perf_4	0.340 (0.717)	[0.209, 0.475]	Yes
	perf_5	0.199 (0.638)	[0.075, 0.338]	Yes
QUAL	qual_1	0.202 (0.741)	[0.086, 0.309]	Yes
	qual_2	0.041 (0.570)	[−0.051, 0.143]	No
	qual_3	0.106 (0.749)	[−0.009, 0.217]	No
	qual_4	−0.005 (0.664)	[−0.106, 0.112]	No
	qual_5	0.160 (0.787)	[0.053, 0.270]	Yes
	qual_6	0.398 (0.856)	[0.268, 0.509]	Yes
	qual_7	0.229 (0.722)	[0.111, 0.334]	Yes
	qual_8	0.190 (0.627)	[0.066, 0.304]	Yes

reliability and validity. We can therefore proceed with the assessment of the structural model.

Structural Model Assessment

Following the structural model assessment procedure (Fig. 3), we first need to check the structural model for collinearity issues by examining the *VIF* values of all sets of predictor constructs in the model. Most *VIF* values are below the conservative threshold of 3, except for *QUAL* in the regressions of *COMP* and *LIKE* on the four formative predictor constructs. However, as the VIF value (3.487) is very close to 3, we conclude that collinearity among the predictor constructs is not a critical issue in the structural model.

When analyzing the path coefficient estimates of the structural model (Table 7), we start with the key target construct *CUSL* on the right-hand side of the PLS path model (Fig. 6). The construct *CUSA* (0.505) has the strongest effect on *CUSL*, followed by *LIKE* (0.344), while the effect of *COMP* (0.006) is very close to zero. Bootstrapping results substantiate that the effects of *CUSA* and *LIKE* on *CUSL* are significant, while *COMP* does not have a significant effect at the 5% probability of error level. Moreover, *COMP* has a significant, but relatively small effect on *CUSA* (0.146), while the effect of *LIKE* is relatively strong (0.436). We further find that the model explains 56.2% of *CUSL*'s variance (i.e., $R^2 = 0.562$), which is relatively high

Table 7 Path coefficients of the structural model and significance testing results

	Path coefficient	95% confidence interval	Significant ($p < 0.05$)?	f^2 effect size
$ATTR \rightarrow COMP$	0.086	[−0.015, 0.190]	No	0.009
$ATTR \rightarrow LIKE$	0.167	[0.034, 0.297]	Yes	0.030
$COMP \rightarrow CUSA$	0.146	[0.008, 0.270]	Yes	0.018
$COMP \rightarrow CUSL$	0.006	[−0.104, 0.112]	No	<0.001
$CSOR \rightarrow COMP$	0.059	[−0.051, 0.169]	No	0.005
$CSOR \rightarrow LIKE$	0.178	[0.070, 0.278]	Yes	0.035
$CUSA \rightarrow CUSL$	0.505	[0.414, 0.584]	Yes	0.412
$LIKE \rightarrow CUSA$	0.436	[0.321, 0.557]	Yes	0.159
$LIKE \rightarrow CUSL$	0.344	[0.232, 0.457]	Yes	0.138
$PERF \rightarrow COMP$	0.295	[0.167, 0.417]	Yes	0.082
$PERF \rightarrow LIKE$	0.117	[−0.027, 0.250]	No	0.011
$QUAL \rightarrow COMP$	0.430	[0.291, 0.550]	Yes	0.143
$QUAL \rightarrow LIKE$	0.380	[0.272, 0.513]	Yes	0.094

taking into account that the model only considers the effects of customer satisfaction and the rather abstract concept of corporate reputation as predictors of customer loyalty. With a value of 0.292, R^2 of *CUSA* is clearly lower but still satisfactory, considering that only *LIKE* and *COMP* explain customer satisfaction in this model.

When analyzing the key predictors of *LIKE*, which has a substantial R^2 value of 0.558, we find that *QUAL* has the strongest significant effect (0.380), followed by *CSOR* (0.178), and *ATTR* (0.167). *PERF* (0.117) has the weakest effect on *LIKE*, which is not significant at the 5% level (Table 7). Corporate reputation's cognitive dimension *COMP* also has a substantial R^2 value of 0.631. Analyzing this construct's predictors shows that *QUAL* (0.430) and *PERF* (0.295) have the strongest significant effects. On the contrary, the effects of *ATTR* (0.086) and *CSOR* (0.059) on *COMP* are not significant at the 5% level. Analyzing the exogenous constructs' total effects on *CUSL* shows that *QUAL* has the strongest total effect (0.248), followed by *CSOR* (0.105), *ATTR* (0.101), and *PERF* (0.089). These results suggest that companies should focus on marketing activities that positively influence the customers' perception of the quality of their products and services.

Table 7 also shows the f^2 effect sizes. Relatively high f^2 effect sizes occur for the relationships *CUSA* → *CUSA* (0.412), *LIKE* → *CUSA* (0.159), *QUAL* → *COMP* (0.143) and *LIKE* → *CUSL* (0.138). These relationships also have particularly strong path coefficients of 0.30 and higher. Interestingly, the relationship between *QUAL* and *LIKE* has a strong path coefficient of 0.380, but only a weak f^2 effect size of 0.094. All the other f^2 effect sizes in the structural model are weak and, if below 0.02, negligible.

The next step is to assess the model's predictive power by running the PLS$_{predict}$ procedure with ten folds and ten repetitions. The focus is on the model's key target construct *CUSL* and its three indicators *cusl_1*, *cusl_2*, and *cusl_3*. The results in Table 8 show that all three indicators achieve $Q^2_{predict}$ larger than zero, indicating that

Table 8 PLS$_{predict}$ results

	$Q^2_{predict}$	RMSE	
		PLS-SEM	LM
cusl_1	0.260	1.299	1.312
cusl_2	0.234	1.522	1.538
cusl_3	0.142	1.530	1.567

the model outperforms the naïve benchmark (i.e., the training sample means). Analyzing the prediction errors produced by the PLS path model shows their distribution is not highly unsymmetric. Hence, the following analyses focus on the RMSE statistic. The analysis shows thaz the RMSE values produced by the PLS path model are consistently lower than those of the LM benchmark. For example, while the PLS-SEM analysis produces an RMSE value of 1.299 for *cusl_1*, the LM benchmark's RMSE value is 1.312.

The final step involves comparing the original reputation model (Fig. 6) with an alternative, more complex model in which *ATTR*, *CSOR*, *PERF*, and *QUAL* additionally relate to *CUSA* and *CUSL*. As in the PLS$_{predict}$ analysis, the focus is on the key target construct *CUSL*. Computing the BIC for these two models yields a value of −261.602 for the original model and −245.038 for the alternative, more complex model. This result provides empirical support for the original model. Similarly, Liengaard et al. (2021) support the established corporate reputation model using CVPAT when compareing it to an alternative version of this model.

Conclusions

Prior research discussing the benefits and limitations of PLS-SEM or analyzing its performance (e.g., in terms of parameter estimation) has usually not acknowledged that the method takes on a fundamentally different philosophy of measurement compared to factor-based SEM (e.g., Rhemtulla et al. 2020). Rather than assuming a common factor model structure, PLS-SEM draws on composite model logic to represent reflective and formative measurement models. The method linearly combines sets of indicators to form composites that represent the conceptual variables of interest (Lohmöller 1989; Wold 1982). Different from factor-based SEM, which equates constructs and the conceptual variables that they represent (Rigdon et al. 2019), PLS-SEM is an approximation method that inherently recognizes that constructs and conceptual variables are not identical (Rigdon et al. 2017). As Rigdon (2016, p. 19) notes, "common factor proxies cannot be assumed to carry greater significance than composite proxies in regard to the existence or nature of conceptual variables."

PLS-SEM offers a good approximation of common factor models in situations where factor-based SEM (chapter ▸ "Structural Equation Modeling") cannot deliver results due to its methodological limitations in terms of, for example, model complexity, sample size requirements, or inclusion of composite variables in the model (Reinartz et al. 2009; Sarstedt et al. 2016; Willaby et al. 2015). Bentler and Huang's

(2014) PLSe as well as Dijkstra and Henseler's (2015b) PLSc algorithm allow researchers to mimic factor-based SEM results while benefiting from the original PLS-SEM method's flexibility in terms of model specification. Such an analysis assumes, however, that factor-based SEM is the correct estimator that delivers the true results as a benchmark for SEM (Hair et al. 2019a).

Most importantly, PLS-SEM constitutes a causal-predictive approach to SEM, which focuses on establishing the predictive power of a model, whose structure has been derived from theory and logic. PLS-SEM strikes a balance between factor-based SEM, which follows a confirmatory paradigm, and modern machine learning methods, which focus on prediction (Hair and Sarstedt 2021a) by providing a "cognitive path to predictions" (Douglas 2009, p. 454). As Hair and Sarstedt (2021a) note, "we live in a noisy, probabilistic world in which we can at best make imperfect predictions. In such a world, causal explanation reduces the complexity of the world to make it more manageable and understandable." At the same time, solely following the confirmation-only paradigm limits the practical usefulness of research as the 'correct' model does not necessarily exhibit high levels of predictive power.

While standard PLS-SEM analyses provide important insights into the strength and significance of the hypothesized model relationships, more advanced modeling and estimating techniques shed further light on the proposed relationships. Research has brought forward a variety of complementary analysis techniques and procedures, which extend the methodological toolbox of researchers working with the method (e.g., to conduct robustness checks; Sarstedt et al. 2020b). Examples of these methods include the confirmatory tetrad analysis (CTA-PLS), which enables researchers to statistically test if the measurement model operationalization should rather build on effect or composite indicators (Gudergan et al. 2008), and latent class techniques, which allow assessing if unobserved heterogeneity affects the model estimates. Prominent examples of latent class techniques for PLS-SEM include finite mixture partial least squares (Hahn et al. 2002; Sarstedt et al. 2011), PLS genetic algorithm segmentation (Ringle et al. 2014; Ringle et al. 2013), prediction-oriented segmentation (Becker et al. 2013b), iterative reweighted regressions (Schlittgen et al. 2016), and a modified *k*-means clustering approach (Fordellone and Vichi 2020). Further methods to account for heterogeneity in the structural model include the analysis of moderating effects (Memon et al. 2019), and the multigroup analysis (Matthews 2017), including testing for measurement invariance (Henseler et al. 2016b).

Approaches for combing PLS-SEM with the necessary condition analysis (NCA; Richter et al. 2020) and the fuzzy-set qualitative comparative analysis (fsQCA; e.g., Leischnig et al. 2016; Rasoolimanesh et al. 2021), testing nonlinear effects (Hair et al. 2018b), higher-order constructs (Sarstedt et al. 2019), mediation effect (Nitzl et al. 2016), conditional process models (Sarstedt et al. 2020a), and model comparison using CVPAT (Liengaard et al. 2021) and its extensions for predictive model assessment and comparison (Sharma et al. 2021) complement the set of advanced PLS-SEM procedures. A further complementary method, the importance-performance map analysis (IPMA), facilitates richer outcome discussions in that it extends the analysis of total effects in the model by adding a second results dimension to the analysis which incorporates the average values of the latent variables (Ringle and Sarstedt 2016). Finally, Hult et al. (2018) introduced a procedure for handling endogeneity in PLS path models, which occurs when a construct's error term is correlated with the scores of one or more explanatory variables in a partial regression relationship (chapter ▶ "Dealing with Endogeneity: A Nontechnical Guide for Marketing Researchers"). In such a situation, path coefficient estimates become causally uninterpretable, which proves problematic in PLS-SEM analyses that have a strict confirmatory focus. Hair et al. (2018b) provide a more detailed overview and introduction to these complementary techniques for more advanced PLS-SEM analyses. Sarstedt et al. (2020b) discuss a series of robustness tests that draw on advanced modeling and model evaluation techniques.

Cross-References

▶ Dealing with Endogeneity: A Nontechnical Guide for Marketing Researchers
▶ Measuring Customer Satisfaction and Customer Loyalty
▶ Structural Equation Modeling

Acknowledgments This chapter uses the statistical software SmartPLS 3 (https://www.smartpls.com). Ringle acknowledges a financial interest in SmartPLS.

References

Aaker, D. A. (1991). *Managing brand equity: Capitalizing on the value of a brand name.* New York: Free Press.
Aguirre-Urreta, M. I., & Rönkkö, M. (2018). Statistical inference with PLSc using bootstrap confidence intervals. *MIS Quarterly, 42*(3), 1001–1020.
Akter, S., Fosso Wamba, S., & Dewan, S. (2017). Why PLS-SEM is suitable for complex modeling? An empirical illustration in big data analytics quality. *Production Planning & Control, 28*(11–12), 1011–1021.
Albers, S. (2010). PLS and success factor studies in marketing. In V. Esposito Vinzi, W. W. Chin, J. Henseler, & H. Wang (Eds.), *Handbook of partial least squares: Concepts, methods and applications* (Springer handbooks of computational statistics series) (Vol. II, pp. 409–425). Berlin/Heidelberg: Springer.
Ali, F., Rasoolimanesh, S. M., Sarstedt, M., Ringle, C. M., & Ryu, K. (2018). An assessment of the use of partial least squares structural equation modeling (PLS-SEM) in hospitality research. *The International Journal of Contemporary Hospitality Management, 30*(1), 514–538.
Avkiran, N. K., & Ringle, C. M. (Eds.). (2018). *Partial least squares structural equation modeling: Recent advances in banking and finance.* Cham: Springer.
Baumgartner, H., & Homburg, C. (1996). Applications of structural equation modeling in marketing and consumer research: A review. *International Journal of Research in Marketing, 13*(2), 139–161.
Bayonne, E., Marin-Garcia, J. A., & Alfalla-Luque, R. (2020). Partial least squares (PLS) in operations management research: Insights from a systematic literature review. *Journal of Industrial Engineering and Management, 13*(3), 565–597.

Becker, J.-M., & Ismail, I. R. (2016). Accounting for sampling weights in PLS path modeling: Simulations and empirical examples. *European Management Journal, 34*(6), 606–617.
Becker, J.-M., Rai, A., & Rigdon, E. E. (2013a). Predictive validity and formative measurement in structural equation modeling: Embracing practical relevance. In *2013 Proceedings of the International Conference on Information Systems, Milan.*
Becker, J.-M., Rai, A., Ringle, C. M., & Völckner, F. (2013b). Discovering unobserved heterogeneity in structural equation models to avert validity threats. *MIS Quarterly, 37*(3), 665–694.
Bentler, P. M., & Huang, W. (2014). On components, latent variables, PLS and simple methods: Reactions to Rigdon's rethinking of PLS. *Long Range Planning, 47*(3), 138–145.
Bollen, K. A. (1989). *Structural equations with latent variables.* New York: Wiley.
Bollen, K. A. (2002). Latent variables in psychology and the social sciences. *Annual Review of Psychology, 53*(1), 605–634.
Bollen, K. A. (2011). Evaluating effect, composite, and causal indicators in structural equation models. *MIS Quarterly, 35*(2), 359–372.
Bollen, K. A., & Bauldry, S. (2011). Three Cs in measurement models: Causal indicators, composite indicators, and covariates. *Psychological Methods, 16*(3), 265–284.
Bollen, K. A., & Diamantopoulos, A. (2017). In defense of causal–formative indicators: A minority report. *Psychological Methods, 22*(3), 581–596.
Bollen, K. A., & Lennox, R. (1991). Conventional wisdom on measurement: A structural equation perspective. *Psychological Bulletin, 110*(2), 305–314.
Borsboom, D., Mellenbergh, G. J., & van Heerden, J. (2003). The theoretical status of latent variables. *Psychological Review, 110*(2), 203–219.
Burnham, K. P., & Anderson, D. R. (2002). *Model selection and multimodel inference: A practical information-theoretic approach* (2nd ed.). Heidelberg: Springer.
Carlson, K. D., & Herdman, A. O. (2012). Understanding the impact of convergent validity on research results. *Organizational Research Methods, 15*(1), 17–32.
Cenfetelli, R. T., & Bassellier, G. (2009). Interpretation of formative measurement in information systems research. *MIS Quarterly, 33*(4), 689–708.
Cepeda Carrión, G., Cegarra-Navarro, J.-G., & Cillo, V. (2019). Tips to use partial least squares structural equation modelling (PLS-SEM) in knowledge management. *Journal of Knowledge Management, 23*(1), 67–89.
Cheah, J.-H., Sarstedt, M., Ringle, C. M., Ramayah, T., & Ting, H. (2018). Convergent validity assessment of formatively measured constructs in PLS-SEM. *International Journal of Contemporary Hospitality Management, 30*(11), 3192–3210.
Cheah, J.-H., Roldán, J. L., Ciavolino, E., Ting, H., & Ramayah, T. (2020). Sampling weight adjustments in partial least squares structural equation modeling: Guidelines and illustrations. *Total Quality Management & Business Excellence,* forthcoming.
Chin, W. W. (1998). The partial least squares approach to structural equation modeling. In G. A. Marcoulides (Ed.), *Modern methods for business research* (pp. 295–336). Mahwah: Lawrence Erlbaum.
Chin, W. W. (2010). How to write up and report PLS analyses. In V. Esposito Vinzi, W. W. Chin, J. Henseler, & H. Wang (Eds.), *Handbook of partial least squares: Concepts, methods and applications* (Springer handbooks of computational statistics series) (Vol. II, pp. 655–690). Heidelberg: Springer.
Chin, W. W., Marcolin, B. L., & Newsted, P. R. (2003). A partial least squares latent variable modeling approach for measuring interaction effects: Results from a Monte Carlo simulation study and an electronic-mail emotion/adoption study. *Information Systems Research, 14*(2), 189–217.
Chin, W. W., Cheah, J.-H., Liu, Y., Ting, H., Lim, X.-J., & Cham, T. H. (2020). Demystifying the role of causal-predictive modeling using partial least squares structural equation modeling in information systems research. *Industrial Management & Data Systems, 120*(12), 2161–2209.
Cho, G., & Choi, J. Y. (2020). An empirical comparison of generalized structured component analysis and partial least squares path modeling under variance-based structural equation models. *Behaviormetrika, 47,* 243–272.

Cho, G., Hwang, H., Kim, S., Lee, J., Sarstedt, M., & Ringle, C. M. (2021). A comparative study of the predictive power of component-based approaches to structural equation modeling. *Working Paper*.

Chou, C.-P., Bentler, P. M., & Satorra, A. (1991). Scaled test statistics and robust standard errors for non-Normal data in covariance structure analysis: A Monte Carlo study. *British Journal of Mathematical and Statistical Psychology, 44*(2), 347–357.

Cohen, J. (1988). *Statistical power analysis for the behavioral sciences* (2nd ed.). Mahwah: Lawrence Erlbaum.

Cohen, J. (1992). A power primer. *Psychological Bulletin, 112*(1), 155–159.

Danks, N., & Ray, S. (2018). Predictions from partial least squares models. In F. Ali, S. M. Rasoolimanesh, & C. Cobanoglu (Eds.), *Applying partial least squares in tourism and hospitality research* (pp. 35–52). Bingley: Emerald.

Danks, N. P., Sharma, P. N., & Sarstedt, M. (2020). Model selection uncertainty and multimodel inference in partial least squares structural equation modeling (PLS-SEM). *Journal of Business Research, 113*, 13–24.

Diamantopoulos, A. (2006). The error term in formative measurement models: Interpretation and modeling implications. *Journal of Modelling in Management, 1*(1), 7–17.

Diamantopoulos, A. (2011). Incorporating formative measures into covariance-based structural equation models. *MIS Quarterly, 35*(2), 335–358.

Diamantopoulos, A., & Winklhofer, H. M. (2001). Index construction with formative indicators: An alternative to scale development. *Journal of Marketing Research, 38*(2), 269–277.

Diamantopoulos, A., Sarstedt, M., Fuchs, C., Wilczynski, P., & Kaiser, S. (2012). Guidelines for choosing between multi-item and single-item scales for construct measurement: A predictive validity perspective. *Journal of the Academy of Marketing Science, 40*(3), 434–449.

Dijkstra, T. K. (2010). Latent variables and indices: Herman Wold's basic design and partial least squares. In V. Esposito Vinzi, W. W. Chin, J. Henseler, & H. Wang (Eds.), *Handbook of partial least squares: Concepts, methods and applications* (Springer handbooks of computational statistics series) (Vol. II, pp. 23–46). Berlin/Heidelberg: Springer.

Dijkstra, T. K. (2014). PLS' Janus face – Response to professor Rigdon's 'rethinking partial least squares modeling: In praise of simple methods'. *Long Range Planning, 47*(3), 146–153.

Dijkstra, T. K., & Henseler, J. (2015a). Consistent and asymptotically normal PLS estimators for linear structural equations. *Computational Statistics & Data Analysis, 81*, 10–23.

Dijkstra, T. K., & Henseler, J. (2015b). Consistent partial least squares path modeling. *MIS Quarterly, 39*(2), 297–316.

do Valle, P. O., & Assaker, G. (2016). Using partial least squares structural equation modeling in tourism research: A review of past research and recommendations for future applications. *Journal of Travel Research, 55*(6), 695–708.

Douglas, H. E. (2009). Reintroducing prediction to explanation. *Philosophy of Science, 76*(4), 444–463.

Eberl, M. (2010). An application of PLS in multi-group analysis: The need for differentiated corporate-level Marketing in the Mobile Communications Industry. In V. Esposito Vinzi, W. W. Chin, J. Henseler, & H. Wang (Eds.), *Handbook of partial least squares: Concepts, methods and applications* (Springer handbooks of computational statistics series) (Vol. II, pp. 487–514). Berlin/Heidelberg: Springer.

Eberl, M., & Schwaiger, M. (2005). Corporate reputation: Disentangling the effects on financial performance. *European Journal of Marketing, 39*(7/8), 838–854.

Edwards, J. R., & Bagozzi, R. P. (2000). On the nature and direction of relationships between constructs and measures. *Psychological Methods, 5*(2), 155–174.

Esposito Vinzi, V., Chin, W. W., Henseler, J., & Wang, H. (Eds.). (2010). *Handbook of partial least squares: Concepts, methods and applications* (Springer handbooks of computational statistics series) (Vol. II). Heidelberg: Springer.

Evermann, J., & Tate, M. (2016). Assessing the predictive performance of structural equation model estimators. *Journal of Business Research, 69*(10), 4565–4582.

Falk, R. F., & Miller, N. B. (1992). *A primer for soft modeling*. Akron: University of Akron Press.

Fordellone, M., & Vichi, M. (2020). Finding groups in structural equation modeling through the partial least squares algorithm. *Computational Statistics & Data Analysis, 147*, 106957.

Fornell, C. G., & Bookstein, F. L. (1982). Two structural equation models: LISREL and PLS applied to consumer exit-voice theory. *Journal of Marketing Research, 19*(4), 440–452.

Fornell, C. G., Johnson, M. D., Anderson, E. W., Cha, J., & Bryant, B. E. (1996). The American customer satisfaction index: Nature, purpose, and findings. *Journal of Marketing, 60*(4), 7–18.

Franke, G., & Sarstedt, M. (2019). Heuristics versus statistics in discriminant validity testing: A comparison of four procedures. *Internet Research, 29*(3), 430–447.

Garson, G. D. (2016). *Partial least squares regression and structural equation models*. Asheboro: Statistical Associates.

George, D., & Mallery, P. (2019). *IBM SPSS statistics 25 step by step: A simple guide and reference* (15th ed.). New York: Routledge.

Geweke, J., & Meese, R. (1981). Estimating regression models of finite but unknown order. *International Economic Review, 22*(1), 55–70.

Ghasemy, M., Teeroovengadum, V., Becker, J.-M., & Ringle, C. M. (2020). This fast car can move faster: A review of PLS-SEM application in higher education research. *Higher Education, 80*, 1121–1152.

Goodhue, D. L., Lewis, W., & Thompson, R. (2012). Does PLS have advantages for small sample size or non-Normal data? *MIS Quarterly, 36*(3), 981–1001.

Grace, J. B., & Bollen, K. A. (2008). Representing general theoretical concepts in structural equation models: The role of composite variables. *Environmental and Ecological Statistics, 15*(2), 191–213.

Gregor, S. (2006). The nature of theory in information systems. *MIS Quarterly, 30*(3), 611–642.

Gudergan, S. P., Ringle, C. M., Wende, S., & Will, A. (2008). Confirmatory tetrad analysis in PLS path modeling. *Journal of Business Research, 61*(12), 1238–1249.

Haenlein, M., & Kaplan, A. M. (2004). A Beginner's guide to partial least squares analysis. *Understanding Statistics, 3*(4), 283–297.

Hahn, C., Johnson, M. D., Herrmann, A., & Huber, F. (2002). Capturing customer heterogeneity using a finite mixture PLS approach. *Schmalenbach Business Review, 54*(3), 243–269.

Hair, J. F. (2021). Next-generation prediction metrics for composite-based PLS-SEM. *Industrial Management & Data Systems, 121*(1), 5–11.

Hair, J. F., & Sarstedt, M. (2019). Composites vs. factors: Implications for choosing the right SEM method. *Project Management Journal, 50*(6), 1–6.

Hair, J. F., & Sarstedt, M. (2021a). Data, measurement, and causal inferences in machine learning: Opportunities and challenges for marketing. *Journal of Marketing Theory & Practice, 29*(1), 65–77.

Hair, J. F., & Sarstedt, M. (2021b). Explanation plus prediction – The logical focus of project management research. *Project Management Journal*, forthcoming.

Hair, J. F., Ringle, C. M., & Sarstedt, M. (2011). PLS-SEM: Indeed a silver bullet. *Journal of Marketing Theory and Practice, 19*(2), 139–151.

Hair, J. F., Sarstedt, M., Pieper, T. M., & Ringle, C. M. (2012a). The use of partial least squares structural equation modeling in strategic management research: A review of past practices and recommendations for future applications. *Long Range Planning, 45*(5-6), 320–340.

Hair, J. F., Sarstedt, M., Ringle, C. M., & Mena, J. A. (2012b). An assessment of the use of partial least squares structural equation modeling in marketing research. *Journal of the Academy of Marketing Science, 40*(3), 414–433.

Hair, J. F., Ringle, C. M., & Sarstedt, M. (2013). Partial least squares structural equation modeling: Rigorous applications, better results and higher acceptance. *Long Range Planning, 46*(1-2), 1–12.

Hair, J. F., Hollingsworth, C. L., Randolph, A. B., & Chong, A. Y. L. (2017a). An updated and expanded assessment of PLS-SEM in information systems research. *Industrial Management & Data Systems, 117*(3), 442–458.

Hair, J. F., Hult, G. T. M., Ringle, C. M., Sarstedt, M., & Thiele, K. O. (2017b). *Mirror, mirror on the wall: A comparative evaluation of composite-based structural equation modeling methods.* Journal of the Academy of Marketing Science, 45(5), 616–632.

Hair, J. F., Black, W. C., Babin, B. J., & Anderson, R. E. (2018a). *Multivariate data analysis* (8th ed.). Mason: Cengage.

Hair, J. F., Sarstedt, M., Ringle, C. M., & Gudergan, S. P. (2018b). *Advanced issues in partial least squares structural equation modeling (PLS-SEM).* Thousand Oaks: Sage.

Hair, J. F., Risher, J. J., Sarstedt, M., & Ringle, C. M. (2019a). When to use and how to report the results of PLS-SEM. *European Business Review, 31*(1), 2–24.

Hair, J. F., Sarstedt, M., & Ringle, C. M. (2019b). Rethinking some of the rethinking of partial least squares. *European Journal of Marketing, 53*(4), 566–584.

Hair, J. F., Howard, M. C., & Nitzl, C. (2020). Assessing measurement model quality in PLS-SEM using confirmatory composite analysis. *Journal of Business Research, 109*, 101–110.

Hair, J. F., Hult, G. T. M., Ringle, C. M., & Sarstedt, M. (2022). *A primer on partial least squares structural equation modeling (PLS-SEM)* (3rd ed.). Thousand Oaks: Sage.

Helm, S., Eggert, A., & Garnefeld, I. (2010). Modelling the impact of corporate reputation on customer satisfaction and loyalty using PLS. In V. Esposito Vinzi, W. W. Chin, J. Henseler, & H. Wang (Eds.), *Handbook of partial least squares: Concepts, methods and applications* (Springer handbooks of computational statistics series) (Vol. II, pp. 515–534). Heidelberg: Springer.

Henseler, J. (2017). Using variance-based structural equation modeling for empirical advertising research at the Interface of design and behavioral research. *Journal of Advertising, 46*(1), 178–192.

Henseler, J. (2021). *Composite-based structural equation modeling: Analyzing latent and emergent variables.* New York: Guilford Press.

Henseler, J., & Sarstedt, M. (2013). Goodness-of-fit indices for partial least squares path modeling. *Computational Statistics, 28*(2), 565–580.

Henseler, J., & Schuberth, F. (2020). Using confirmatory composite analysis to assess emergent variables in business research. *Journal of Business Research, 120*, 147–156.

Henseler, J., Ringle, C. M., & Sinkovics, R. R. (2009). The use of partial least squares path modeling in international marketing. In R. R. Sinkovics & P. N. Ghauri (Eds.), *Advances in international marketing* (Vol. 20, pp. 277–320). Bingley: Emerald.

Henseler, J., Ringle, C. M., & Sarstedt, M. (2012). Using partial least squares path modeling in international advertising research: Basic concepts and recent issues. In S. Okazaki (Ed.), *Handbook of research in international advertising* (pp. 252–276). Cheltenham: Edward Elgar Publishing.

Henseler, J., Dijkstra, T. K., Sarstedt, M., Ringle, C. M., Diamantopoulos, A., Straub, D. W., Ketchen, D. J., Hair, J. F., Hult, G. T. M., & Calantone, R. J. (2014). Common beliefs and reality about partial least squares: Comments on Rönkkö & Evermann (2013). *Organizational Research Methods, 17*(2), 182–209.

Henseler, J., Ringle, C. M., & Sarstedt, M. (2015). A new criterion for assessing discriminant validity in variance-based structural equation modeling. *Journal of the Academy of Marketing Science, 43*(1), 115–135.

Henseler, J., Hubona, G. S., & Ray, P. A. (2016a). Using PLS path modeling in new technology research: Updated guidelines. *Industrial Management & Data Systems, 116*(1), 2–20.

Henseler, J., Ringle, C. M., & Sarstedt, M. (2016b). Testing measurement invariance of composites using partial least squares. *International Marketing Review, 33*(3), 405–431.

Houston, M. B. (2004). Assessing the validity of secondary data proxies for marketing constructs. *Journal of Business Research, 57*(2), 154–161.

Hui, B. S., & Wold, H. (1982). Consistency and consistency at large of partial least squares estimates. In K. G. Jöreskog & H. Wold (Eds.), *Systems under indirect observation, part II* (pp. 119–130). Amsterdam: North-Holland.

Hult, G. T. M., Hair, J. F., Dorian, P., Ringle, C. M., Sarstedt, M., & Pinkwart, A. (2018). Addressing endogeneity in marketing applications of partial least squares structural equation modeling. *Journal of International Marketing, 26*(3), 1–21.

Hwang, H., Sarstedt, M., Cheah, J.-H., & Ringle, C. M. (2020). A concept analysis of methodological research on composite-based structural equation modeling: Bridging PLSPM and GSCA. *Behaviormetrika, 47*(1), 219–241.

Jöreskog, K. G. (1971). Simultaneous factor analysis in several populations. *Psychometrika, 36*(4), 409–426.

Jöreskog, K. G. (1973). A general method for estimating a linear structural equation system. In A. S. Goldberger & O. D. Duncan (Eds.), *Structural equation models in the social sciences* (pp. 255–284). New York: Seminar Press.

Jöreskog, K. G., & Wold, H. (1982). The ML and PLS techniques for modeling with latent variables: Historical and comparative aspects. In H. Wold & K. G. Jöreskog (Eds.), *Systems under indirect observation, part I* (pp. 263–270). Amsterdam: North-Holland.

Kaufmann, L., & Gaeckler, J. (2015). A structured review of partial least squares in supply chain management research. *Journal of Purchasing and Supply Management, 21*(4), 259–272.

Khan, G., Sarstedt, M., Shiau, W.-L., Hair, J. F., Ringle, C. M., & Fritze, M. (2019). Methodological research on partial least squares structural equation modeling (PLS-SEM): A social network analysis. *Internet Research, 29*(3), 407–429.

Kock, N., & Hadaya, P. (2018). Minimum sample size estimation in PLS-SEM: The inverse square root and gamma-exponential methods. *Information Systems Journal, 28*(1), 227–261.

Latan, H., & Noonan, R. (Eds.). (2017). *Partial least squares structural equation modeling: Basic concepts, methodological issues and applications*. Berlin/Heidelberg: Springer.

Lee, L., Petter, S., Fayard, D., & Robinson, S. (2011). On the use of partial least squares path modeling in accounting research. *International Journal of Accounting Information Systems, 12*(4), 305–328.

Lei, P.-W., & Wu, Q. (2012). Estimation in structural equation modeling. In R. H. Hoyle (Ed.), *Handbook of structural equation modeling* (pp. 164–179). New York: Guilford Press.

Liengaard, B. D., Sharma, P. N., Hult, G. T. M., Jensen, M. B., Sarstedt, M., Hair, J. F., & Ringle, C. M. (2021). Prediction: Coveted, yet forsaken? Introducing a cross-validated predictive ability test in partial least squares path modeling. *Decision Sciences, 52*(2), 362–292.

Leischnig, A., Henneberg, S. C., & Thornton, S. C. (2016). Net versus combinatory effects of firm and industry antecedents of sales growth. *Journal of Business Research, 69*(9), 3576–3583.

Lohmöller, J.-B. (1989). *Latent variable path modeling with partial least squares*. Heidelberg: Physica.

Manley, S. C., Hair, J. F., Williams, R. I., & McDowell, W. C. (2020). Essential new PLS-SEM analysis methods for your entrepreneurship analytical toolbox. *International Entrepreneurship and Management Journal*, forthcoming.

Marcoulides, G. A., & Chin, W. W. (2013). You write, but others read: Common methodological misunderstandings in PLS and related methods. In H. Abdi, W. W. Chin, V. Esposito Vinzi, G. Russolillo, & L. Trinchera (Eds.), *New perspectives in partial least squares and related methods* (Springer proceedings in Mathematics & Statistics) (Vol. 56, pp. 31–64). New York: Springer.

Marcoulides, G. A., & Saunders, C. (2006). Editor's comments: PLS: A silver bullet? *MIS Quarterly, 30*(2), iii–ix.

Marcoulides, G. A., Chin, W. W., & Saunders, C. (2012). When imprecise statistical statements become problematic: A response to Goodhue, Lewis, and Thompson. *MIS Quarterly, 36*(3), 717–728.

Mason, C. H., & Perreault, W. D. (1991). Collinearity, power, and interpretation of multiple regression analysis. *Journal of Marketing Research, 28*(3), 268–280.

Mateos-Aparicio, G. (2011). Partial least squares (PLS) methods: Origins, evolution, and application to social sciences. *Communications in Statistics - Theory and Methods, 40*(13), 2305–2317.

Matthews, L. (2017). Applying multigroup analysis in PLS-SEM: A step-by-step process. In H. Latan & R. Noonan (Eds.), *Partial least squares path modeling: Basic concepts, methodological issues and applications* (pp. 219–243). Cham: Springer.

McDonald, R. P. (1996). Path analysis with composite variables. *Multivariate Behavioral Research, 31*(2), 239–270.

Mehmetoglu, M., & Venturini, S. (2021). *Structural equation modelling with partial least squares using Stata and R*. Boca Raton: CRC Press.

Memon, M. A., Cheah, J. H., Ramayah, H. T., Chuah, F., & Cham, T. H. (2019). Moderation analysis: Issues and guidelines. *Journal of Applied Structural Equation Modeling, 3*(1), i–xi.

Nitzl, C. (2016). The use of partial least squares structural equation modelling (PLS-SEM) in management accounting research: Directions for future theory development. *Journal of Accounting Literature, 37*, 19–35.

Nitzl, C., & Chin, W. W. (2017). The case of partial least squares (PLS) path modeling in managerial accounting. *Journal of Management Control, 28*(2), 137–156.

Nitzl, C., Roldán, J. L., & Cepeda Carrión, G. (2016). Mediation analysis in partial least squares path modeling: Helping researchers discuss more sophisticated models. *Industrial Management & Data Systems, 119*(9), 1849–1864.

Noonan, R., & Wold, H. (1982). PLS path modeling with indirectly observed variables: A comparison of alternative estimates for the latent variable. In K. G. Jöreskog & H. Wold (Eds.), *Systems under indirect observations: Part II* (pp. 75–94). Amsterdam: North-Holland.

Nunnally, J. C., & Bernstein, I. (1994). *Psychometric theory* (3rd ed.). New York: McGraw Hill.

Olsson, U. H., Foss, T., Troye, S. V., & Howell, R. D. (2000). The performance of ML, GLS, and WLS estimation in structural equation modeling under conditions of misspecification and nonnormality. *Structural Equation Modeling: A Multidisciplinary Journal, 7*(4), 557–595.

Peng, D. X., & Lai, F. (2012). Using partial least squares in operations management research: A practical guideline and summary of past research. *Journal of Operations Management, 30*(6), 467–480.

Raithel, S., & Schwaiger, M. (2015). The effects of corporate reputation perceptions of the general public on shareholder value. *Strategic Management Journal, 36*(6), 945–956.

Raithel, S., Sarstedt, M., Scharf, S., & Schwaiger, M. (2012). On the value relevance of customer satisfaction: Multiple drivers and multiple markets. *Journal of the Academy of Marketing Science, 40*(4), 509–525.

Ramayah, T., Cheah, J., Chuah, F., Ting, H., & Memon, M. A. (2016). *Partial least squares structural equation modeling (PLS-SEM) using SmartPLS 3.0: An updated and practical guide to statistical analysis*. Kuala Lumpur: Pearson.

Rasoolimanesh, S. M., Ringle, C. M., Sarstedt, M., & Olya, H. (2021). The combined use of symmetric and asymmetric approaches: Partial least squares-structural equation modeling and fuzzy-set qualitative comparative analysis. *International Journal of Contemporary Hospitality Management*, forthcoming.

Reinartz, W. J., Haenlein, M., & Henseler, J. (2009). An empirical comparison of the efficacy of covariance-based and variance-based SEM. *International Journal of Research in Marketing, 26*(4), 332–344.

Rhemtulla, M., van Bork, R., & Borsboom, D. (2020). Worse than measurement error: Consequences of inappropriate latent variable measurement models. *Psychological Methods, 25*(1), 30–45.

Richter, N. F., Sinkovics, R. R., Ringle, C. M., & Schlägel, C. (2016). A critical look at the use of SEM in international business research. *International Marketing Review, 33*(3), 376–404.

Richter, N. F., Schubring, S., Hauff, S., Ringle, C. M.. & Sarstedt, M. (2020). When predictors of outcomes are necessary: Guidelines for the combined use of PLS-SEM and NCA. *Industrial Management & Data Systems, 120*(12), 2243–2267.

Rigdon, E. E. (2012). Rethinking partial least squares path modeling: In praise of simple methods. *Long Range Planning, 45*(5–6), 341–358.

Rigdon, E. E. (2013). Partial least squares path modeling. In G. R. Hancock & R. O. Mueller (Eds.), *Structural equation modeling. A second course* (2nd ed., pp. 81–116). Charlotte: Information Age Publishing.

Rigdon, E. E. (2016). Choosing PLS path modeling as analytical method in European management research: A realist perspective. *European Management Journal, 34*(6), 598–605.

Rigdon, E. E., Becker, J.-M., Rai, A., Ringle, C. M., Diamantopoulos, A., Karahanna, E., Straub, D., & Dijkstra, T. K. (2014). Conflating antecedents and formative indicators: A comment on Aguirre-Urreta and Marakas. *Information Systems Research, 25*(4), 780–784.

Rigdon, E. E., Sarstedt, M., & Ringle, C. M. (2017). On comparing Results from CB-SEM and PLS-SEM. Five perspectives and five recommendations. *Marketing ZFP–Journal of Research and Management, 39*(3), 4–16.

Rigdon, E. E., Becker, J. M., & Sarstedt, M. (2019). Factor indeterminacy as metrological uncertainty: Implications for advancing psychological measurement. *Multivariate Behavioral Research, 54*(3), 429–443.

Ringle, C. M. (2019). What makes a great textbook? Lessons learned from joe Hair. In B. J. Babin & M. Sarstedt (Eds.), *The great facilitator: Reflections on the contributions of Joseph F. Hair, Jr. to marketing and business research* (pp. 131–150). Cham: Springer.

Ringle, C. M., & Sarstedt, M. (2016). Gain more insight from your PLS-SEM results: The importance-performance map analysis. *Industrial Management & Data Systems, 116*(9), 1865–1886.

Ringle, C. M., Sarstedt, M., & Straub, D. W. (2012). Editor's comments: A critical look at the use of PLS-SEM in MIS quarterly. *MIS Quarterly, 36*(1), iii–xiv.

Ringle, C. M., Sarstedt, M., Schlittgen, R., & Taylor, C. R. (2013). PLS path modeling and evolutionary segmentation. *Journal of Business Research, 66*(9), 1318–1324.

Ringle, C. M., Sarstedt, M., & Schlittgen, R. (2014). Genetic algorithm segmentation in partial least squares structural equation modeling. *OR Spectrum, 36*(1), 251–276.

Ringle, C. M., Wende, S., & Becker, J.-M. (2015). *SmartPLS 3 [computer software]*. Bönningstedt: SmartPLS. Retrieved from https://www.smartpls.com.

Ringle, C. M., Sarstedt, M., Mitchell, R., & Gudergan, S. P. (2020). Partial least squares structural equation modeling in HRM research. *International Journal of Human Resource Management, 31*(12), 1617–1643.

Roldán, J. L., & Sánchez-Franco, M. J. (2012). Variance-based structural equation modeling: Guidelines for using partial least squares in information systems research. In M. Mora, O. Gelman, A. L. Steenkamp, & M. Raisinghani (Eds.), *Research methodologies, innovations and philosophies in software systems engineering and information systems* (pp. 193–221). Hershey: IGI Global.

Russo, D., & Stol, K. J. (2021). PLS-SEM for software engineering research: An introduction and survey. *ACM Computing Surveys, 54*(4), 1–38.

Sarstedt, M. (2019). Der Knacks and a Silver Bullet. In B. J. Babin & M. Sarstedt (Eds.), *The great facilitator: Reflections on the contributions of Joseph F. Hair, Jr. to marketing and business research* (pp. 155–164). Cham: Springer.

Sarstedt, M., & Cheah, J.-H. (2019). Partial least squares structural equation modeling using SmartPLS: A software review. *Journal of Marketing Analytics, 7*(3), 196–202.

Sarstedt, M., & Mooi, E. (2019). *A concise guide to market research: The process, data, and methods using IBM SPSS statistics* (3rd ed.). Berlin/Heidelberg: Springer.

Sarstedt, M., Becker, J.-M., Ringle, C. M., & Schwaiger, M. (2011). Uncovering and treating unobserved heterogeneity with FIMIX-PLS: Which model selection criterion provides an appropriate number of segments? *Schmalenbach Business Review, 63*(1), 34–62.

Sarstedt, M., Wilczynski, P., & Melewar, T. C. (2013). Measuring reputation in global markets – A comparison of reputation measures' convergent and criterion validities. *Journal of World Business, 48*(3), 329–339.

Sarstedt, M., Ringle, C. M., Smith, D., Reams, R., & Hair, J. F. (2014). Partial least squares structural equation modeling (PLS-SEM): A useful tool for family business researchers. *Journal of Family Business Strategy, 5*(1), 105–115.

Sarstedt, M., Hair, J. F., Ringle, C. M., Thiele, K. O., & Gudergan, S. P. (2016). Estimation issues with PLS and CBSEM: Where the bias lies! *Journal of Business Research, 69*(10), 3998–4010.

Sarstedt, M., Hair, J. F., Cheah, J.-H., Becker, J.-M., & Ringle, C. M. (2019). How to specify, estimate, and validate higher-order models. *Australasian Marketing Journal, 27*(3), 197–211.

Sarstedt, M., Hair, J. F., Nitzl, C., Ringle, C. M., & Howard, M. C. (2020a). Beyond a tandem analysis of SEM and PROCESS: Use PLS-SEM for mediation analyses! *International Journal of Market Research, 62*(3), 288–299.

Sarstedt, M., Ringle, C. M., Cheah, J. H., Ting, H., Moisescu, O. I., & Radomir, L. (2020b). Structural model robustness checks in PLS-SEM. *Tourism Economics, 26*(4), 531–554.

Schlittgen, R., Ringle, C. M., Sarstedt, M., & Becker, J.-M. (2016). Segmentation of PLS path models by iterative reweighted regressions. *Journal of Business Research, 69*(10), 4583–4592.

Schloderer, M. P., Sarstedt, M., & Ringle, C. M. (2014). The relevance of reputation in the nonprofit sector: The moderating effect of socio-demographic characteristics. *International Journal of Nonprofit and Voluntary Sector Marketing, 19*(2), 110–126.

Schuberth, F., Henseler, J., & Dijkstra, T. K. (2018). Confirmatory composite analysis. *Frontiers in Psychology, 9*, 2541.

Schwaiger, M. (2004). Components and parameters of corporate reputation: An empirical study. *Schmalenbach Business Review, 56*(1), 46–71.

Schwarz, G. (1978). Estimating the dimension of a model. *The Annals of Statistics, 6*(2), 461–464.

Shah, R., & Goldstein, S. M. (2006). Use of structural equation modeling in operations management research: Looking back and forward. *Journal of Operations Management, 24*(2), 148–169.

Sharma, P. N., Shmueli, G., Sarstedt, M., Danks, N., & Ray S. (2018). Prediction-oriented model selection in partial least squares path modeling. *Decision Sciences*, forthcoming.

Sharma, P. N., Liengaard, B. D., Hair, J. F., Sarstedt, M., & Ringle C. M. (2021). Predictive model assessment and selection in composite-based modeling using PLS-SEM: Extensions and guidelines for using CVPAT. *Working Paper*.

Shmueli, G. (2010). To explain or to predict? *Statistical Science, 25*(3), 289–310.

Shmueli, G., & Koppius, O. R. (2011). Predictive analytics in information systems research. *MIS Quarterly, 35*(3), 553–572.

Shmueli, G., Ray, S., Velasquez Estrada, J. M., & Chatla, S. B. (2016). The elephant in the room: Evaluating the predictive performance of PLS models. *Journal of Business Research, 69*(10), 4552–4564.

Shmueli, G., Sarstedt, M., Hair, J. F., Cheah, J.-H., Ting, H., & Ringle, C. M. (2019). Predictive model assessment in PLS-SEM: Guidelines for using PLSpredict. *European Journal of Marketing, 53*(11), 2322–2347.

Shugan, S. (2009). Relevancy is robust prediction, not alleged realism. *Marketing Science, 28*(5), 991–998.

Stieglitz, S., Linh, D.-X., Bruns, A., & Neuberger, C. (2014). Social media analytics. An interdisciplinary approach and its implications for information systems. *Business and Information Systems Engineering, 6*, 89–96

Streukens, S., & Leroi-Werelds, S. (2016). Bootstrapping and PLS-SEM: A step-by-step guide to get more out of your bootstrap results. *European Management Journal, 34*(6), 618–632.

Tenenhaus, M., Esposito Vinzi, V., Chatelin, Y.-M., & Lauro, C. (2005). PLS path modeling. *Computational Statistics & Data Analysis, 48*(1), 159–205.

Usakli, A., & Kucukergin, K. G. (2018). Using partial least squares structural equation modeling in hospitality and tourism: Do researchers follow practical guidelines? *International Journal of Contemporary Hospitality Management, 30*(11), 3462–3512.

Venkatesh, V., Morris, M. G., Davis, G. B., & Davis, F. D. (2003). User acceptance of information technology: Toward a unified view. *MIS Quarterly, 27*(3), 425–478.

Wagenmakers, E. J., & Farrell, S. (2004). AIC model selection using Akaike weights. *Psychonomic Bulletin & Review, 11*(1), 192–196.

Westland, J. C. (2019). Partial least squares path analysis. In *Structural equation models: From paths to networks* (2nd ed., pp. 17–38). Cham: Springer.

Willaby, H. W., Costa, D. S. J., Burns, B. D., MacCann, C., & Roberts, R. D. (2015). Testing complex models with small sample sizes: A historical overview and empirical demonstration of what partial least squares (PLS) can offer differential psychology. *Personality and Individual Differences, 84*, 73–78.

Wold, H. (1975). Path models with latent variables: The NIPALS approach. In H. M. Blalock, A. Aganbegian, F. M. Borodkin, R. Boudon, & V. Capecchi (Eds.), *Quantitative sociology: International perspectives on mathematical and statistical modeling* (pp. 307–357). New York: Academic.

Wold, H. (1980). Model construction and evaluation when theoretical knowledge is scarce: Theory and application of PLS. In J. Kmenta & J. B. Ramsey (Eds.), *Evaluation of econometric models* (pp. 47–74). New York: Academic.

Wold, H. (1982). Soft modeling: The basic design and some extensions. In K. G. Jöreskog & H. Wold (Eds.), *Systems under indirect observations: Part II* (pp. 1–54). Amsterdam: North-Holland.

Wold, H. (1985). Partial least squares. In S. Kotz & N. L. Johnson (Eds.), *Encyclopedia of statistical sciences* (Vol. 6, pp. 581–591). New York: Wiley.

Wong, K. K. K. (2019). *Mastering partial least squares structural equation modeling (PLS-SEM) with SmartPLS in 38 hours*. Bloomington: iUniverse.

Zeng, N., Liu, Y., Gong, P, Hertogh, M., & König, M. (2021). Do right PLS and do PLS right: A critical review of the application on PLS in construction management reserarch. *Frontiers of Engineering Management*, forthcoming.

Automated Text Analysis

Ashlee Humphreys

Contents

Introduction	634
Foundations of Text Analysis	635
History	635
Approaches to Text Analysis	635
Dictionary-Based Methods	636
Classification Methods	638
Topic Modeling	638
Market Research Applications of Text Analysis	639
Sentiment Analysis	640
Studying Word of Mouth Through Text Analysis	641
Topic Discovery and Creating Positioning Maps from Online Text	642
Measurement of the Organization and Firm Environment	642
Issues in Working with Textual Data	643
Extended Example: Word-Of-Mouth Differences Between Experts and Nonexperts to a Product Launch	644
Purpose	644
Stage 1: Develop a Research Question	645
Stage 2: Data Collection	646
Stage 3: Construct Definition	647
Stage 4: Operationalization	648
Stage 5: Interpretation and Analysis	650
Stage 6: Validation	657
Conclusion and Future Directions	659
Cross-References	659
References	659

A. Humphreys (✉)
Integrated Marketing Communications, Medill School of Journalism, Media, and Integrated Marketing Communications, Northwestern University, Evanston, IL, USA
e-mail: a-humphreys@northwestern.edu

© Springer Nature Switzerland AG 2022
C. Homburg et al. (eds), *Handbook of Market Research*,
https://doi.org/10.1007/978-3-319-57413-4_26

Abstract

The amount of text available for analysis by marketing researchers has grown exponentially in the last two decades. Consumer reviews, message board forums, and social media feeds are just a few sources of data about consumer thought, interaction, and culture. However, written language is filled with complex meaning, ambiguity, and nuance. How can marketing researchers possibly transform this rich linguistic representation into quantifiable data for statistical analysis and modeling? This chapter provides an introduction to text analysis, covering approaches that range from top-down deductive methods to bottom-up inductive methods for text mining. After covering some foundational aspects of text analysis, applications to marketing research such as sentiment analysis, topic modeling, and studying organizational communication are summarized and explored, including a case study of word-of-mouth response to a product launch.

Keywords

Text analysis · computer-assisted text analysis · automated content analysis · content analysis · topic modeling · sentiment analysis · LDA · word-of-mouth

Introduction

Automated or computer-assisted text analysis describes a family of methods for parsing, classifying, and then quantifying textual data for further statistical analysis. Although automated text analysis using computers dates to the 1960s, the rise of digital technology for communicating has created a deluge of textual data for analysis and increased managerial desire to gain insights from text produced by consumers. Platforms like Twitter and Facebook provide a space for consumer-to-consumer discussion of products, brands, and services. Retail sites like Amazon, Best Buy, and Zappos and review sites like CNET and Yelp! host consumer reviews on a nearly endless array of products and services. Particular brand sites like Sephora, Gap, and Brooks Brothers offer social shopping capabilities such as consumer reviews represented by stars and extensive product reviews that detail fit, material, and quality (Stephen and Toubia 2010). This text from consumers, firms, and the media can provide insight into consumer needs and wants, sentiment, market structure, and transmission of word-of-mouth communication.

This chapter presents a high-level overview of methods for conducting text analysis in market research and provides resources for further investigating the methodological details depending on the approach one takes to text analysis.

Foundations of Text Analysis

History

To understand the implementation of automatic analysis, it will help to first review its relation to and its emergence from traditional content analysis. Content analysis is a method used in the social sciences to systematically assess and analyze the content of a message, usually in the form of text. Although traditions of content analysis go as far back as sixteenth-century monastic life, modern content analysis was first proposed by Max Weber (1924) to study the press. Since then, scholars in sociology and communications have used human-coded content analysis to investigate differences in media content, describe trends in communications over time, reveal patterns of organizational or individual attention, and examine attitudes, interests, intentions, or values of an individual or a group (e.g., Berelson 1971; Gamson and Modigliani 1989).

Traditional content analysis was first introduced to consumer behavior with Kassarjian's (1977) outline of the method and was then updated by Kolbe and Burnett (1991) in an attempt to improve reliability and objectivity, focusing primarily on standards for calculating inter-coder agreement (see also Grayson and Rust 2001). In consumer research and marketing, traditional content analysis has been used to analyze trends in magazine advertisements (Belk and Pollay 1985), direct mail (Stevenson and Swayne 1999), newspaper articles (Garrett 1987), and word-of-mouth communication (Moore 2015; Phelps et al. 2004) to name a few. Although automated text analysis can improve the efficiency and reliability of traditional content analysis, it also has limitations. For instance, computerized text analysis can miss subtleties in the text and cannot code finer shades of meaning. While dealing with negation is possible (Jia et al. 2009; Villarroel Ordenes et al. 2017), it remains somewhat analytically onerous.

Automated text analysis is not radically new, but it has become easier to implement since the widespread of adoption of the personal computer. The General Inquirer (Stone 1966) was one of the first computer content-analytic tools used in consumer research (Kranz 1970). Since then, vast strides have been made in automated text analysis. Kranz's (1970) early three-page treatment of computer-assisted content analysis in marketing deals with dictionary creation, but does not address category creation, validity, or measurement decisions. Since then, a variety of approaches have emerged.

Approaches to Text Analysis

In current practice, there are essentially two orientations toward automated text analysis: top-down vs. bottom-up approaches (Boyd and Pennebaker 2015a; Mehl and Gill 2008). The top-down approach counts concepts of interest, identified either through a list of words or through a set of rules. Top-down, also called dictionary-based, methods are deductively or theoretically driven in the sense that researchers use them to look for hypothesized patterns in text from a known set of concepts. Bottom-up approaches, on the other hand, code all concepts present in the text and then look for patterns (Rayson 2009). These approaches can range considerably from methods of supervised learning, where researchers define some preliminary categories and then train the computer to sort documents based on latent differences, to discovery-oriented approaches such as calculating then flagging statistically significant differences between groups of texts (Rayson 2009), or fully automated processes where a computer identifies topics based on word co-occurrence (Lee and Bradlow 2011). In this way, bottom-up approaches to text analysis become similar to data mining approaches. That is, first the researcher looks at all differences in the data and builds conclusions from those differences.

Top-down, dictionary-based methods have been used extensively in social sciences like consumer research (Humphreys and Wang 2018), psychology (Chung and Pennebaker 2013; Mehl and Gill 2008; Pennebaker and King 1999), sociology (Van de Rijt et al. 2013), and political science (Grimmer and Stewart 2013; Lasswell and Leites 1949) due to their ability to translate theoretical constructs into text and the transparency in reporting results and reliabilities. Bottom-up methods, on the other hand, have been used more extensively in engineering, computer science, and marketing science. Marketing strategy has drawn from both approaches, although dictionary-based approaches appear to be more common (Ertimur and Coskuner-Balli 2015; Humphreys 2010; Ludwig et al. 2013; Packard et al. 2014). This chapter briefly covers the fundamentals of each approach before moving to their application in marketing.

Dictionary-Based Methods

Dictionary-based methods for text analysis are based on a predeveloped word list, or dictionary, for counting the occurrence of words in a text. Standardized dictionaries are available for many constructs such as sentiment (e.g., Hutto and Gilbert 2014), marketing-related constructs like authenticity and brand personality (Kovács et al. 2013; Opoku et al. 2006), as well as many standard concepts in psychology (Pennebaker et al. 2001; Snefjella and Kuperman 2015) and other fields like political science (Dunphy et al. 1974; Stone 1966). In addition to using a standard dictionary, many researchers choose to create their own dictionary to fit the specific context, although this should be done only if a standard dictionary is not available.

There are several methods for dictionary creation ranging from inductive to deductive. The most inductive method of dictionary creation is to work from a concordance, or all words in the document listed in terms of frequency and group words according to relevant categories for the research question and hypothesis (Chung and Pennebaker 2013). If the researcher does not know what categories are relevant a priori, qualitative methods of reading and coding the text prior to dictionary development can be used to create a set of relevant concepts and a list of words for their operationalization in text (Humphreys 2010). For example, to study institutional logics pertaining to the Yoga industry in newspaper articles, Ertimur and Coskuner-Balli (2015) first open and then axially code a dataset of newspaper articles and other historical texts. Generally, a random sample of 10–20% of the dataset is sufficient for coding (Humphreys and Wang 2018), but researchers should be mindful of unevenness in data quantity according to category or time period and stratify accordingly (Humphreys 2010). The most deductive method for dictionary creation is to create a wordlist from theoretical concepts or categories. However, one should be mindful of the tendency for researchers and writers to pick more abstract words than are generally present in textual data (Palmquist et al. 2009). For this reason, careful postmeasurement validation is necessary to ensure construct validity. After text is cleaned and stored and the dictionary has been created, researchers use a program like Diction, LIWC, WordStat, or R to execute counts. Data can then be saved and analyzed using a traditional statistical package or, for some packages like Wordstat and R, analyzed within the same package.

After calculating word frequencies, postmeasurement validation should be performed, and for this there are a variety of methods ranging from methods that are iterative with dictionary development to stand-alone calculations of inter-rater reliability. Weber (2005) suggests a saturation procedure whereby researchers pull a sample of 10 or 20 instances of a concept and have a research assistant code them as accurately representing the category (or not). If the rate is below 80%, the dictionary category should be revised until the threshold is met. Pennebaker et al. (2001) recommend a method of validating the dictionary, but not the resulting measurements. Here, three research assistants count a word as being representative of the category or not, and words are retained if two of the three coders agree. If they do not, the word should be dropped from the dictionary. Percentage agreements on dictionary categories can then be calculated and reported, and the general threshold is similar to that for Krippendorf's alpha, above 75%. A final option is to compare the computer-coded results with an extensive set of human-coded results from two or more coders. To do this, one selects a random sample from the dataset (the amount may vary depending on the size of the dataset) and human coders code the text according to the category descriptions, calculating reliability as one would in a traditional content analysis. This can then be compared to the additional "coder" of the computer to produce a similarity score. Although this final method has the advantage of comparison with traditional content analysis, it is not always necessary and in some cases can produce misguided results. Human coders pick up on subtle meanings that computers cannot and likewise computers are able to code concepts consistently and evenly over an entire dataset without omission or bias. For this reason, comparing human to computer coding can in some cases be like comparing apples to oranges.

Dictionary-based analyses have studied a wide range of theoretical concepts such as emotion (Berger and Milkman 2012), construal level (Snefjella and Kuperman 2015), institutional logics (Ertimur and Coskuner-Balli 2015), risk (Humphreys and Thompson 2014), speech acts (Ludwig et al. 2016; Villarroel Ordenes et al. 2017), and framing (Fiss and Hirsch 2005; Humphreys and Latour 2013; Jurafsky et al.

2014). A wide variety of contexts can be explored through dictionary-based analysis such as product and restaurant reviews (Barasch and Berger 2014, Jurafsky et al. 2014; Kovács et al. 2013), tweets (Mogilner et al. 2010), customer service calls (Packard et al. 2014), blogs (Arsel and Bean 2013), and news articles (Humphreys 2010; Humphreys and Thompson 2014).

Classification Methods

Bottom up methods include classification and topic modeling. Classification methods of text analysis are based on categorizing documents into different "types" and then further describing what textual elements best predict the likelihood of being a "type." For example, Tirunillai and Tellis (2012) use classification to train a model to recognize positive versus negative reviews based on star rating. Using a training data set, they use both a Naïve Bayes and a support vector machine (SVM) classifier to find which words predict star rating and then use this information to categorize the entire set of reviews, achieving a precision – meaning their algorithm predicts true positives – 68–85% of the time, depending on the product category. Villarroel Ordenes et al. (2017) further refine measures of sentiment by using both explicit and implicit indicators of emotion to measure sentiment and sentiment strength, also testing their framework on a set of starred reviews from Tripadvisor, Amazon, and Barnes and Noble. Classification models vary in sophistication; accuracy of these approaches varies from 55% to 96% for sentiment, for example (Hutto and Gilbert 2014). In general, considerations for model selection are based on the underlying frequency of occurrence of words that one wants to use to make predictions and the clarity of categories one wants to produce. For instance, SVM classification provides clear, mutually-exclusive categories, while LDA produces probabilistic groupings where it is possible for categories to overlap.

Classification models have been used to study reviews (Tirunillai and Tellis 2012; Van Laer et al. 2017), online forums (Homburg et al. 2015), email (Ludwig et al. 2016), and literary texts (Boyd and Pennebaker 2015b; Plaisant et al. 2006). For example, to measure sentiment of message board posts, Homburg et al. (2015) classify a training dataset of unambiguously positive and negative posts. They then use sentiment as a dependent measure to understand how much firm engagement actually increases positive consumer sentiment, finding that there are diminishing returns to engagement.

Topic Modeling

Topic modeling is an approach that begins by parsing text into discrete words, and then finding recurring patterns in co-occurrence that are statistically unlikely if one assumes that word occurrence is independent. In this way, the analysis identifies categories that may be latently represented by the manifest presence of words, and these word groupings are then labeled to represent meaningful concepts or traits in the data as one would in factor analysis. For example, in a study of hotel reviews, Mankad et al. (2016) use latent Dirichlet allocation (LDA) to identify five topics that occur in users' TripAdvisor comments, identifying amenities, location, transactions, value, and experience as key topics mentioned by reviewers. Latent semantic analysis (LSA), k-means clustering (Lee and Bradlow 2011), probabilistic latent semantic analysis (PLSA), and LDA (Blei et al. 2003) are all methods for topic modeling, with LDA being the most recent and common analytical methods for topic modeling.

LSA is based on the relatively straightforward process of generating a matrix that represents word occurrence (0 for nonoccurrence and 1 for occurrence) and then generating a vector of similarity that represents either the similarity between *documents* (the dot product of the rows) or the similarity between two or more *words* (the dot product of the columns). These vectors can then be reduced using singular value decomposition (SVD) to represent the "topics" that tend to occur across documents. PLSA is a similar process; topics are treated as word distributions based on probability.

LDA is a hierarchical Bayesian model for determining the mixture of topics present in a given document. Like PLSA, it assumes topics are probabilistic distributions of words, except it uses a Dirichlet prior for estimation, which reduces over-fitting. For LDA, one sets the number of topics prior to running the analysis (other methods such as hierarchical Diriclet Process do not need this assumption). Using assumptions that there is a certain probability distribution for the choice of topic, and a certain distribution within that for choice of words to represent that topic, LDA produces a final list of topics (as represented by a list of words in that topic) and probabilities that a given topic is in the document. Although most approaches are word or phrase based, Büschken and Allenby (2016) conduct an LDA analysis using sentences as the unit of analysis and find that this produces results more predictive of rating than word-based LDA. A sentence-based model assumes that all words in the sentence are part of the same topic, which is reasonable, given Grice's maxims of relation and manner (Grice 1975). Büschken and Allenby (2016) use this model to identify topics for Italian restaurants and hotels from reviews on Expedia and we8there.com.

LDA has been used in a wide range of applications (Büschken and Allenby 2016; Tirunillai and Tellis 2014). As with dictionary approaches, postmeasurement validation, in this case using a hold-out sample or other predictive technique (e.g., external DV) is highly advisable. Machines will only read literal meaning, and therefore homonyms and other colloquialisms including sarcasm can be problematic, as they are overly general and overly specific words. Further, careful cleaning and preparation of the text can reduce errors, as textual markers can sometimes be added during data collection (e.g., headers, footers, etc.).

Market Research Applications of Text Analysis

This section discusses ways that text analysis has been incorporated into marketing research. Although potentially useful for many types of sources and research questions, text analysis has been particularly fruitful for representing consumer sentiment, studying word-of-mouth communication, and creating positioning maps from online text, among other uses.

Sentiment Analysis

Many text analytic programs and practitioners claim to measure sentiment, but it is not always clear what goes into this key metric. Before discussing the text analysis of sentiment, it might first to help to discuss what sentiment is and what it is trying to capture. In most marketing contexts, researchers and practitioners are interested in consumer attitude toward a brand, product, or service. Yet attitudes are complex mental structures composed not only of emotion, but also cognitive beliefs and intentions (Fishbein and Ajzen 1972). Further, the importance an attitude for any given product for ultimate purchase and future behavior like loyalty depends to a large degree on context and involvement (Petty and Cacioppo 1979). Further, people may articulate attitudes online that do not fully reflect their underlying attitude, there may be selection bias in the attitudes they choose to articulate, and they may behave differently than the attitudes they espouse. Nonetheless, discourse online, as expressed in sentiment, can reflect some underlying attitude about a brand, product, or service, and importantly can affect the social consensus shared among other consumers. Sentiment has been shown to predict movie sales (Krauss et al. 2008; Mestyán et al. 2013) and stock market returns (Bollen et al. 2011; De Choudhury et al. 2008; Tirunillai and Tellis 2012), although there may be natural biases in nonreporting of null results. Structurally, most approaches seek to classify or measure text as having positive, negative, or sometimes neutral sentiment, and some approaches transform this into net sentiment, subtracting negative words from positive words (e.g., Ludwig et al. 2013; Homburg et al. 2015). Top-down approaches do this using a dictionary or lexicon of words, while bottom-up approaches use some underlying external classification like human coding of a training set or customer ratings to identify the set of words that indicate sentiment.

In addition to valence, sentiment can also have strength and certainty. Previous research has used both explicit, semantic indicators of emotion along with implicit, more pragmatic indicators of emotion such as speech acts (commission, assertion, and direction) to successfully measure strength of sentiment (Villarroel Ordenes et al. 2017). Work has further shown that other types of speech such as demonstratives (Potts and Schwarz 2010) and other pragmatic markers can indicate expressive content, commonly expressed in product reviews (Constant et al. 2009).

Using predeveloped, standardized dictionaries is one of the most reliable ways to measure sentiment across contexts, as these wordlists have been developed and tested on a wide range of textual data, and some have themselves been developed through bottom-up approaches.

VADAR, for example, uses a dictionary with a rule-based approach for measuring sentiment. Specifically, Hutto and Gilbert (2014) use a combination of dictionaries based on previous standardized dictionaries like LIWC and General Inquirer but then also develop five rules that take into account syntax and grammar to measure intensity as well. Bottom-up approaches to measure sentiment produce accuracies ranging from 55% to 96%, depending on the context (Hutto and Gilbert 2014). For example, Tirunillai and Tellis (2012) use star rating to create a classification system for sentiment, with an accuracy rate of 68–85%.

Studying Word of Mouth Through Text Analysis

The primary use of text analysis in marketing research to date has been to study online word-of-mouth communication. Consumers have always shared product information through interpersonal communication (Arndt 1967), and this communication has been shown to be more effective than commercial messages (Brown and Reingen 1987; see also Godes and Mayzlin 2004; Money et al. 1998). And yet while word-of-mouth communication was previously communicated face to face or over the telephone, it is now visible and archived on social shopping sites (Stephen and Toubia 2010), social media (Humphreys 2015), and third-party review sites and platforms. Product reviews on Amazon, hotel reviews on TripAdvisor, and restaurant reviews on Yelp! have all provided marketing insights to better understand the relationship of ratings to sales and stock price (Moe and Schweidel 2014; Schweidel and Moe 2014; Moe and Trusov 2011). For example, Moe and Trusov (2011) find that positive reviews have a direct effect on sales, but this effect is somewhat short-lived because of downward convergence as people post more ratings (i.e., the social dynamics of posts result in reviews becoming relatively more negative over time). Further, positivity can vary depending on platform (Schweidel and Moe 2014; Villarroel Ordenes et al. 2017).

Word of mouth online can be represented by measuring valence, volume, and variance (Godes and Mayzlin 2004). Volume and variance are relatively compatible with existing modeling measures, as volume can be aggregated and variance can be measured through start ratings or other user input. Valence, while partially captured by star measures, is perhaps best measured by sentiment, which requires text analysis as a method for converting the unstructured data of linguistic description into data that can be incorporated into quantitative models. There is also, it should be noted, a wide range of linguistic properties and semantic content beyond valence that usefully informs marketing research (Humphreys and Wang 2018). For instance, Kovács et al. (2013) show that restaurants have higher ratings if reviewers mention authenticity in their reviews, even when controlling for restaurant quality.

The role of emotion in the spread of word of mouth is one key topic. In a study of sharing news articles, Berger and Milkman (2012) find that positive emotion increases virality, but so too does the presence of intense negative emotion like anger or anxiety in the article. Effects of the sender and speech context have also been investigated through text analysis using pronouns. Using a standard dictionary for first-person personal pronouns ("I," "me"), Packard and Wooten (2013) find that consumers self-enhance more in word of mouth to signal knowledge about a particular domain. Consumers have also been shown to engage in self-presentation by sharing fewer negative emotions when broadcasting to a large audience versus narrowcasting to a smaller one (Barasch and Berger 2014). When evaluating a product like a movie, consumers are more likely to use pronouns referring to themselves when expressing views about taste vs. their views about quality (Spiller and Belogolova 2016).

Topic Discovery and Creating Positioning Maps from Online Text

Text analysis can be used to create positioning maps for brands, companies, or products and to visualize market structure based on attributes within a particular category. Bottom-up methods such as LDA, LSA, and similar methods like k-means clustering are used to group words in a text (like reviews) into attributes or brands based on common co-occurrence. For example, to create a visualization of market structure for cameras from a set of reviews on Epinions.com, Lee and Bradlow (2011) first extract phrases related to particular attributes (e.g., battery life, photo quality) and then use k-means clustering to group phrases based on their similarity (calculated as cosine similarity between vectors of words). They then go on to show that this kind of analysis reveals attributes mentioned by and important to consumers, but absent from expert reviews such as size, design, and screen brightness. Similarly, using text data from diabetes forums, Netzer et al. (2012) find several side effects commonly mentioned on the forum, but absent from a site like WebMD (e.g., weight gain, kidney problems).

Topic-based models are compatible with psychological theories such as spreading activation in semantic memory (Collins and Loftus 1975). For instance, based on the idea that people talk about brands together that are related in semantic memory, Netzer et al. (2012) produce a perceptual map for car brands using reviews from Edmunds.com and compare that to results from perceptual maps based on more typical survey and brand-switching based on sales approaches. In doing so, they find several notable differences between the results based on text analysis versus those based on sales or survey data. For instance, based on the sales data, Korean brands of cars are not associated with the Japanese brands. However, based on the textual data, these brands are grouped together. This suggests that while text analysis can capture cognitive associations, these may not necessarily translate into behavior such as brand switching (Table 1).

Measurement of the Organization and Firm Environment

Finally, text analysis can be used to measure organizational attention through the analysis of shareholder reports, press releases, and other marketing communication. These studies are primarily based on dictionary-based analysis, and often create dictionaries rather than using standardized dictionaries to fit the industry or original context and research question. For example, scholars have developed dictionaries to study the changes in CSR language over time to reveal differences in developing countries (Gandolfo et al. 2016). In an analysis of annual reports, Lee et al. (2004) find that companies that issued internal reasons for negative events had higher stock

Table 1 Types of text analysis

Type of text analysis	Materials	Theoretical areas	Software/ methods	Relevant examples
Dictionary-based	Reviews, tweets, online forums, news articles, press releases, annual reports	Sentiment/emotion, psychological mindset (e.g., construal level), brand attention and brand value, legitimacy/corporate image, customer service	LIWC, WordStat, Diction	Humphreys (2010), Berger and Milkman (2012), Packard et al. (2018)
Classification	Reviews, online forums, literary texts, tweets, email	Sentiment, deception, product attributes, market structure	SVM, Naïve Bayes, k-nearest neighbor, neural networks, WordStat	Homburg et al. (2015), Van Laer et al. (2018), Tirunillai and Tellis (2012)
Topic modeling	Product or service reviews, online forums	Product attributes, positioning, market structure, customer needs	LDA, LSA, PLSA, K-means clustering, R, WordStat	Netzer et al. (2012), Lee and Bradlow (2006), Buschken and Allenby (2016)

prices a year after the event, suggesting that organizations who attribute blame to firm-controlled factors appear more in control than those who do not and therefore have more favorable impressions from investors. Interactions between firm employees or agents can also be better understood. For example, Ludwig et al. (2016) develop a method for detecting deception in sales emails. They find that deceivers are more likely to use elaborate, superfluous descriptions, and less self-referencing, quickly taking on the linguistic style of their intralocular.

Firm environment can also be captured through measuring media such as newspapers, magazines, and trade publications. For example, Humphreys (2010) shows that changes in the institutional and cultural environment enabled the legitimation of the casino gambling industry in the United States. Humphreys and Thompson (2014) study the environment of risk perceptions following two crises – the Exxon and BP oils spills – and find that the media narratives serve to contain risk perceptions following these disasters. Ertimur and Coskuner-Balli (Ertimur and Coskuner-Balli 2015) trace how the Yoga industry shifted over time, developing distinct institutional logics that impacted branding and positioning within the industry.

Issues in Working with Textual Data

Although language provides a window into many areas of consumer thought and market strategy, there are several issues to consider when analyzing text. Language rarely, if ever, follows patterns of normal distribution (Zipf 1932). For instance, functional words like "a," "he," and "there" make up about 40% of all language in normal usage. Common words like nouns and verbs make up another 59%, and only a small fraction of those common words will usually be relevant to the research question. Textual data are often left-skewed (lots of zeros), documents often contain different numbers of words, and the words of interest are often too infrequently or too frequently occurring to make meaningful comparisons. For these reasons, after word frequency has been calculated, researchers will often transform the data prior to statistical analysis. Further, many test such as ANOVA would not be appropriate due to the non-normal distribution of the data.

Text is therefore almost always represented as a percentage of words in the document (e.g., Ludwig et al. 2013), and log transformation to account for skewedness is often commonly employed (Netzer et al. 2012), although there are several possible transformations used (Manning et al. 2008). Tf*idf is a measure often used to account for the term frequency, standardized by the overall frequency of a word in the dataset as a whole (see Salton and McGill 1983 for details in calculating tf*idf, with attendant options for transformation).

Traditional methods for measuring co-occurrence such as Pearson correlation can be problematic due to the large number of zeros in a dataset (Netzer et al. 2012). For this reason, researchers will often use cosine similarity or Jaccard distance to compare words and documents. A series of robustness checks using multiple methods to calculate co-occurrence is often necessary to ensure that results do not occur simply due to infrequently or too-frequently occurring words (Monroe et al. 2009; Netzer et al. 2012). For example, if a word like "him" is very common, it is likely to co-occur with more words than an infrequent word like "airbag." And yet, the word "airbag" may be more diagnostic of the concept safety than a personal pronoun like "him" even though detecting the co-occurrence will be more likely. Because data are not normally distributed, statistical tests such as the Mann-Whitney test, which tests for significance in rankings rather than absolute number, can serve as a replacement for ANOVA.

Extended Example: Word-Of-Mouth Differences Between Experts and Nonexperts to a Product Launch

Purpose

This section presents a sample text analysis as an illustration of top-down, dictionary-based methods according to the six stages (Table 2) (Reprinted from the Web Appendix to Humphreys and Wang (2018), Automated Text Analysis for Consumer Research, *Journal of Consumer Research, 44*(6), 1 (April), 1274–1306, with permission from Oxford University Press.). Automated text analysis is appropriate for tracking systematic trends in language over time and making comparisons between groups of texts. To illustrate a top-down approach to text analysis, this section presents a short study of consumer response to the product launch of an mp3 player/wireless device, the Apple iTouch. This case has been selected because it

Table 2 Stages of automated content analysis

Stages of automated content analysis (dictionary-based analysis)	
Stage	Elements of stage
1. Identify a research question	Select a research topic and a question within that topic
2. Data collection	Identify sources of information Online databases or newspapers Digital converters for printed text Web scraping for internet data Archival materials Field interviews
2a. Data cleaning	Organize the file structure Spell check, if applicable Eliminate problematic characters or words
3. Construct definition	Qualitatively analyze a subsample of the data Create a word list for each concept Have human coders check and refine dictionary Preliminarily implement dictionary to check for false positives and false negatives

4. Operationalization	Conduct computer analysis to compute the raw data
	Make measurement decisions based on the research question:
	  Percent of all words
	  Percent of words within the time period or category
	  Percent of all coded words
	  Binary ("about" or "not about" a topic)

5. Interpretation and analysis	Make unit of analysis decisions: By article, year, decade
	Comparison by genre, speaker, etc.
	Choose the appropriate statistical method for the research question:
	  Analysis of variance (ANOVA)
	  Regression analysis
	  Multidimensional scaling
	  Correlational analysis

6. Validation	Pull a subsample and have coded by a research assistant or researcher Calculate Krippendorf's alpha or a hit/miss rate

can be used to illustrate both comparison between groups and change over time and because it is relatively agnostic regarding theoretical framework. One could study word-of-mouth communication from a psychological, sociological, anthropological, or marketing strategy point of view (c.f. Godes and Mayzlin 2004; Kozinets 2010; Phelps et al. 2004; Winer 2009).

Stage 1: Develop a Research Question

This study proposes a specific, strategic research question: After a product launch, do experts respond differently from nonexperts? Further, how does word-of-mouth response change in expert versus nonexpert groups as the product diffuses? Word of mouth from experts can be particularly influential in product adoption, so it is important to know how their views may change over time and in comparison with nonexpert groups. The context chosen for this study, the launch of the Apple iTouch, is a good case to study because both the product category and the criteria for evaluating the product were ambiguous at the time of launch.

Stage 2: Data Collection

Data. Data were collected from two websites, Amazon.com and CNET.com. Consumer comments from Amazon were used to reflect a nonexpert or mixed consumer response, while user comments from CNET were used to measure expert response. Amazon is a website that sells everything from books to toys and has a broad audience. CNET, on the other hand, is a website dedicated exclusively to technology and is likely to have posters with greater expertise. Archival data also suggests that there are differences among visitors to the two sites.

According to Quantcast estimates (Quantcast 2010a, CNET Monthly Traffic (Estimated)) (www.quantcast.com/cnet), users to CNET.com are predominantly male and likely to visit websites like majorgeeks.com and read PC World. Amazon users, on the other hand, represent a broader demographic. They are more evenly divided between men and women (48/52), are more likely to have kids, and, visit websites like buy.com (Quantcast 2010b, Amazon monthly traffic (estimated)) (www.quantcast.com/amazon.com). Data were collected on November 2009.

Data were collected with the help of a research assistant from Amazon.com and CNET.com from September 5, 2007 to November 6, 2009. Keyword search for "iPod Touch" was used to gather all customer reviews available for the product at the time of analysis. Reviews for multiple versions of the device (first and second generation) were included and segmented in the analysis according to release date. The first-generation iPod Touch was released on September 5, 2007, and the second-generation was released on September 9, 2008.

Data were scraped from the internet, stored in a spreadsheet, and segmented by post. The comment date, poster name, rating, location of the poster, and the text of the comment itself were all stored as separate variables. Two levels of analysis were chosen. The most basic level of analysis is at the comment level. Each comment was coded for its content so that correlations between the content of that post and the date, poster experience, and location could be assessed. The second level of analysis is the group level, between Amazon and CNET. Comparisons can thus be made between expert and nonexpert groups based on the assumption that Amazon posters are nonexperts or a mix of experts and nonexperts, while dedicated members of the CNET community have more expertise. Lastly, because the time variable exists in the dataset, it will also be possible to periodize the data. This may be relevant in assessing the effects of different product launches (e.g., first- vs. second-generation iPods) on the textual content of posts. About 204 posts were collected from Amazon and 269 posts were collected from CNET, yielding a sample size high enough to make statistical comparisons between groups.

After a file structure was created, data were cleaned by running a spell check on all entries. Slang words (e.g., "kinda") were replaced with their proper counterparts. Text was scanned for problematic words. For example, "touch" appeared with greater frequency than usual because it was used to refer to the product, not to the sense. For that reason, "touch" was replaced with a noncodable character like "TTT" so that it would not be counted in the haptic category used in the standard dictionary.

Stage 3: Construct Definition

Work in information processing suggests that experts process information differently from novices (Alba and Hutchinson 1987). In general, experts view products more cognitively, evaluating product attributes over benefits or uses (Maheswaran and Sternthal 1990; Maheswaran et al. 1996; Sujan 1985). While novices use only stereotypical information, experts use both attribute information and stereotypical cues (Maheswaran 1994). Experts are able to assimilate categorical ambiguity, which means one would expect for them to adjust to an ambiguous product more quickly than nonexperts (Meyers-Levy and Tybout 1989). They also tend to approach judgment in an abstract, higher level construal than nonexperts (Hong and Sternthal 2010).

From previous research, several working hypotheses can be developed. The strategic comparison we wish to make is about how experts versus nonexperts evaluate the product and whether or not this changes over time. First, one might expect that experts would use more cognitive language and that they would more critically evaluate the device.

H1: Experts will use more cognitive language than novices.

Secondly, one would also expect that experts would attend to features of the device, but nonexperts would attend more to uses of the device (Maheswaran et al. 1996). Note that this is based on the necessary assumption that users discuss or verbally elaborate on what draws their mental attention, which is reasonable according to previous research (Carley 1997).

H2: Experts will discuss features more than nonexperts.

H3: Nonexperts will discuss benefits and uses more than experts.

Thirdly, over time, one might predict that experts would be able to assimilate ambiguous product attributes while nonexperts would not. Because experts can more easily process ambiguous category information and because they have a higher construal level, one would predict that they would like this ambiguous product more than novices and would learn to assimilate the ambiguous information. For example, in this case, the capacity of the device makes it hard to categorize (cell phone vs. mp3 player). One would expect that experts would more quickly understand this ambiguity and that over time their elaboration on this feature would decrease.

H4: Experts will talk about ambiguous attributes (e.g., capacity) less over time, while nonexperts will continue to discuss ambiguous attributes.Lastly, previous research suggests that these differences in focus, experts on features and nonexperts on benefits, would differentially influence product ratings. That is, ratings for nonexperts will depend on evaluation of benefits such as entertainment, but expert ratings would be influenced more by features.

H5: Ratings will be driven by benefits for nonexperts.
H6: Ratings will be driven by features by experts.

These are only a few of the many potential hypotheses that could be explored in an analysis of online word-of-mouth communication. One could equally explore the cultural framing of new technologies (Giesler 2008) or the co-production of brand communications by seeding product reviews with bloggers (Kozinets 2010). The question posed here – do experts respond differently to new products than nonexperts over time? – is meant to be illustrative of what can be done with automated text analysis rather than a rigorous test of the psychological properties of expertise.

In this illustrative example, the key constructs in examining H1 through H6 are known: expert and nonexperts, cognitive expressions, affect, product features, and benefits. We therefore proceed with a top-down approach. Operationalization for some of the constructs – cognitive and affective language – is available through a standardized measure (LIWC; Pennebaker et al. 2001), and we can therefore use a standardized dictionary for their operationalization. However, some constructs such as features and benefits are context-specific, and a custom dictionary will be necessary for operationalization. In addition, there may be other characteristics that distinguish experts from nonexperts. We will therefore also perform a bottom-up approach of classification.

Stage 4: Operationalization

For this analysis, the standard LIWC dictionary developed by Pennebaker et al. (2001) was used in addition to a custom dictionary. Table 3 presents the categories used from both the standardized and the custom dictionaries. The standard dictionary includes categories for personal pronouns such as "I," parts of speech such as adjectives, psychometrically pretested categories such as positive and negative emotion, and content-related categories such as leisure, family, and friend-related language.

A custom dictionary was also developed to identify categories specific to the product word-of-mouth data analyzed here. Ten comments from each website were selected and open coded, with the researcher blind to the site from which they came. Then, ten more comments from each website were selected and codes were added until saturation was reached (Weber 2005). In all, the subsample required to develop the custom dictionary was 60 comments, 30 from each website, about 11% of all comments. Fourteen categories were created, each containing six words on average.

The qualitative analysis of comments revealed posters tended to talk about the product in terms of features or aesthetics. Dictionary categories were therefore created for words associated with features (e.g., GPS, camera, hard drive, battery) and for aesthetics (e.g., sharp, clean, sexy, sleek). Posters also had recurring concerns about the capacity of the device, the cost of the product, and reported problems they experienced using the product. Categories were created for each of these concerns. Because there might be some researcher-driven interest in product uses and because posters frequently mentioned entertainment and work-related uses, categories were created for each type of use. Categories of "big" versus "small" were included because previous theorization in sociology has suggested that the success of the iPod comes from its offerings of excess – large screen, excess capacity, etc. (Sennett 2006). Two categories were created to count when competitive products were mentioned, either within the Apple brand or outside of it.

The dictionary categories were validated by three coders who suggested words for inclusion and exclusion. Percent agreements between coders on each dictionary category can be found in Table 3. Average agreement was 90%. Text files were run

Table 3 Standard and custom dictionaries

Category	Abbv	Words	No. of words	Alpha*
Social processes	Social	Mate, talk, they, child	455	97%
Affective processes	Affect	Happy, cried, abandon	915	97%
Positive emotion	Posemo	Love, nice, sweet	406	97%
Negative emotion	Negemo	Hurt, ugly, nasty	499	97%
Cognitive processes	Cogmech	Cause, know, ought	730	97%
Past tense	Past	Went, ran, had	145	94%
Present tense	Present	Is, does, hear	169	91%
Future tense	Future	Will, gonna	48	75%
Discrepancy	Discrep	Should, would, could	76	80%
Exclusive	Excl	But, without, exclude	17	67%
Perceptual processes	Percept	Observing, heard, feeling	273	96%
Relativity	Relativ	Area, bend, exit, stop	638	98%
Space	Space	Down, in, thin	220	96%
Time	Time	End, until, season	239	94%
Work	Work	Job, majors, xerox	327	91%
Aesthetics	Aesth	Sleek, cool, shiny, perfect	9	83%
Capacity	Cap	Capacity, space, storage	7	93%
Cost	Cost	Price, cost, dollars	6	100%
Big	Big	Large, huge, full	5	83%
Problems	Prob	Bugs, crash, freeze	7	100%
Competitors	Comp	Zune, Microsoft, Archos	4	67%
Apple	Apple	Nano, iPod, iPhone	4	100%
Entertainment	Ent	Music, video, fun	9	85%
Job	Job	Work, commute, conference	9	100%
Connectability	Connect	Wifi, internet, web	9	95%
Features	Feat	GPS, camera, battery	5	87%
Love	Love	Amazing, best, love	7	100%
Small	Small	Empty, small, tiny	4	100%
Expertise	Expert	Jailbreak, jailbroke, keynote	4	67%

*Alpha is the percent agreement of three coders on dictionary words in the category

through the LIWC program, first using the standard dictionary, then using the custom dictionary. A spreadsheet was created from three sets of data: (1) the comment data collected directly from the website (e.g., date of post, rating of product), (2) the computer output from the standard dictionary, and (3) the output from the custom dictionary.

Validation. Once rough findings were gleaned, the coding was validated. Twenty instances from each category were pulled from the dataset and categorized. "Hits" and "false hits" were then calculated. This yielded an average hit rate of 85% and a "false hit" rate of 15%. The least accurate category was aesthetics, with a hit rate of 70% and a false hit rate of 30%. The most accurate category was "small," which had a hit rate of 95% and a false hit rate of 5%.

Stage 5: Interpretation and Analysis

Overall, the findings indicate that there are systematic differences between the way experts and nonexperts interpret the new device. As with most textual data, there are many potential variables and measures of interest. The standard LIWC dictionary contains 61 categories, and in the dataset studied here, 28 of these categories were significantly different among text from the three websites. We will report some of the most notable differences, including those needed to test the hypotheses.

Comparison between groups. First, we assessed differences among the two groups of comments. This was done by comparing differences in the percent of words coded in each category between groups using the Mann-Whitney test due to the skewed distribution of the data. Tables 4 and 5 show the differences by category. With the standard dictionary, several important differences between the word of mouth of nonexperts and experts can be discerned.

First, experts use more cognitive words ($M_{cog|CNET} = 16.57$, $M_{cog|Amazon} = 15.64$, Mann-Whitney $U = 30,562$, $z = 2.12$ $p < 0.05$) than nonexperts, but they also use more affective (both positive and negative) language ($M_{affect|CNET} = 7.3$ vs. $M_{affect|Amazon} = 6.53$, $U = 30,581$, $z = 2.14$, $p < 0.05$) as well. The finding that experts evaluate the product cognitively is congruent with previous research (Maheswaran et al. 1996), and the highly affective tone indicates that they are likely more involved in product evaluation (Kelting and Duhacheck 2009). However, CNET posters use more negation ($M_{neg|CNET} = 2.47$, $M_{neg|Amazon} = 1.74$, $U = 34,487$, $z = 4.81$, $p < 0.001$). Together with the presence of cognitive language, this indicates that they may be doing more critical evaluation. The first hypothesis was therefore supported.

Secondly, nonexperts focus on distal rather than proximate uses, while experts focus on device-related issues like features. Nonexperts on Amazon use more distal social, time-, family-related language (e.g., $M_{social|Amazon} = 5.55$ vs. $M_{scoial|NET} = 4.23$, $U = 22,259.5$, $z = -3.52$, $p < 0.001$ and $M_{time|Amazon} = 5.65$, $M_{time|CNET} = 3.89$, $U = 18,527$ $z = -6.01$, $p < 0.001$). Experts on CNET, on the other hand, focus on features ($M_{features|CNET} = 0.61$ vs. $M_{features|Amazon} = 0.41$, $U = 30,012.5$, $z = 2.10$, $p < 0.05$) and capacity ($M_{connect|CNET} = 1.08$ vs. $M_{connect|Amazon} = 0.756$, $U = 35,819$, $z = 6.14$, $p < 0.001$), but also on aesthetics

Table 4 Amazon vs. CNET differences in means, standard dictionary

	Amazon	CNET
WC	160.99	149.11
Social***	5.55	4.23
Affect†	6.53	7.20
Posemo	5.50	5.94
Negemo	1.10	1.31
Cogmech*	15.64	16.57
Past***	3.58	2.13
Present	8.91	9.22
Future*	0.76	1.01
Certain	1.66	1.87
Excl**	2.68	3.20
Percept***	3.34	4.86
Relativ***	11.26	9.53
Space*	4.06	4.64
Time***	5.65	3.89
Work	2.08	1.92
Achieve	2.24	2.58
Leisure†	3.28	3.80

†$p < 0.10$
*$p < 0.05$
**$p < 0.01$
***$p < 0.001$

Table 5 Differences in means, custom dictionary

	Amazon	CNET
Aesthetics***	0.168	0.833
Capacity***	0.538	1.408
Cost*	0.384	0.641
Big**	0.070	0.178
Problems†	0.286	0.165
Competitors	0.080	0.104
Apple*	1.461	1.927
Entertainment**	1.377	1.838
Job†	0.164	0.087
Connect*	0.756	1.075
Features†	0.413	0.606
Love***	0.746	1.470
Small*	0.054	0.135
Expert*	0.009	0.028

†$p < 0.10$
*$p < 0.05$
**$p < 0.01$
***$p < 0.001$

($M_{aesth|CNET} = 0.833$ vs. $M_{aesth|Amazon} = 0.168$, $U = 33{,}518$, $z = 5.02$, $p < 0.001$). Experts discussed aesthetics about eight times more than the mixed group on Amazon. These differences indicate that, in general, experts focus on the device itself while nonexperts focus on uses. This lends convergent evidence to support to H2 and H3.

One other finding not specified by the hypotheses is notable. Nonexperts use more past-oriented language ($M_{past|Amazon} = 3.58$ vs. $M_{past|CNET} = 2.13$, $U = 21{,}289$, $z = -4.20$, $p < 0.001$), while expert posters use more future-oriented language ($M_{future|CNET} = 1.01$, $M_{future|Amazon} = 0.76$, $U = 31{,}446$, $z = 2.83$, $p < 0.01$). This suggests that experts might frame the innovation in the future while nonexperts focus on the past. Recent research suggests experts and novices differ in temporal construal (Hong and Sternthal 2010). Experts focus on the far future while novices focus on the near future. The results here provide convergent evidence that supports previous research and suggests a further hypothesis – that novices focus on past-related information – for future experimental research (Table 6).

In an extended analysis, adding a third group could help the researcher draw more rigorous conclusions through techniques of analytic induction (Mahoney 2003; Mill 1843). That is, if an alternative explanation is possible, the researcher could include a comparison set to rule out the alternative explanation. For example, one might propose that the difference in "cost" discourse is because Amazon.com users make less money than CNET users, on average, and are therefore more concerned about price. One could then include an expert website where the users are known to have a lower income than the posters on Amazon to address this explanation. If the same results are found, this would rule out the alternative hypothesis.

Trends over time. Because the product studied here is an innovation, the change of comments over time as the product diffuses is of interest. Time was analyzed first as a continuous variable in a correlation analysis and then as a discrete variable in ordinary least squares regression analyses, where the release of the first and second generation of iTouch marked each period.

A correlation analysis was used to analyze time as a continuous variable (Table 7). We find that affect increases over time in the expert group, which indicates that group becomes more involved ($r_{(affect,\ Date|CNET)} = 0.144$, $p < 0.01$). Experts become less concerned with capacity ($r_{(capacity,\ Date|CNET)} = -0.203$ $p < 0.01$) while Amazon users do not change in their concern for capacity. This indicates that experts learn something about the product category: the limited capacity was initially a shock to reviewers, as it was unorthodox for an mp3 player. But, over time, experts learned that this new category segment – mp3 wireless devices – did not offer as much memory. This supports Hypothesis 4 (Fig. 1).

Besides the correlation analysis, we also did ordinary least square linear regression analyses to analyze whether reviewers' expressions changed over time (Table 8). We created a binary variable, which is set to "1″" if the review is posted after the second generation of iTouch is released, and "0″" if the review is for the first generation of iTouch. To account for asymmetry in their distributions due to non-normality, we log-transformed the term frequency measurements of affect and capacity, our variables of interest. The results from the OLS analyses are congruent

Table 6 Correlation table, Amazon vs. CNET

Correlations

Statistics = Pearson correlation

	Site	Rating	Date	Affect	Posemo	Negemo	Aesth	Capacity	Ent	Connect	Feat	Love	Big	Small
Rating	Amazon	1	0.009	0.282[a]	0.387[a]	−0.200[a]	0.061	0.064	0.216[a]	0.002	0.128	0.273[a]	0.015	−0.024
	CNET	1	−0.012	0.095	0.319[a]	−0.433[a]	0.024	−0.058	0.044	0.145[b]	−0.118	0.373[a]	0.091	−0.053
Date	Amazon	0.009	1	−0.087	−0.046	−0.118	−0.082	0.013	0.073	0.008	−0.040	0.022	−0.156[b]	−0.095
	CNET	−0.012	1	0.144[b]	0.145[b]	0.011	−0.009	−0.203[a]	0.114	0.127[b]	−0.102	−0.006	−0.106	−0.001
Affect	Amazon	0.282[a]	−0.087	1	0.910[a]	0.350[a]	−0.049	−0.098	−0.043	−0.187[a]	0.049	0.450[a]	−0.001	−0.036
	CNET	0.095	0.144[b]	1	0.865[a]	0.263[a]	0.367[a]	−0.036	0.111	0.036	0.108	0.411[a]	−0.096	0.034
Posemo	Amazon	0.387[a]	−0.046	0.910[a]	1	−0.056	0.005	−0.052	0.032	−0.164[b]	0.064	0.473[a]	0.006	−0.015
	CNET	0.319[a]	0.145[b]	0.865[a]	1	−0.253[a]	0.409[a]	−0.019	0.156[b]	0.106	0.104	0.514[a]	−0.038	−0.056
Negemo	Amazon	−0.200[a]	−0.118	0.350[a]	−0.056	1	−0.117	−0.140[b]	−0.194[a]	−0.104	−0.030	−0.013	0.026	−0.050
	CNET	−0.433[a]	0.011	0.263[a]	−0.253[a]	1	−0.086	−0.026	−0.087	−0.139[b]	0.000	−0.205[a]	−0.119	0.167[a]
Aesth	Amazon	0.061	−0.082	−0.049	0.005	−0.117	1	0.131	−0.019	0.016	0.005	−0.055	0.126	0.003
	CNET	0.024	−0.009	0.367[a]	0.409[a]	−0.086	1	−0.025	0.040	−0.052	0.291[a]	0.015	−0.072	−0.053
Capacity	Amazon	0.064	0.013	−0.098	−0.052	−0.140[b]	0.131	1	0.055	0.052	−0.044	−0.010	−0.046	0.144[b]
	CNET	−0.058	−0.203[a]	−0.036	−0.019	−0.026	−0.025	1	0.079	−0.177[a]	−0.079	−0.048	−0.025	0.020
Ent	Amazon	0.216[a]	0.073	−0.043	0.032	−0.194[a]	−0.019	0.055	1	0.139[b]	−0.022	−0.061	0.069	0.063

(continued)

Table 6 (continued)

Correlations

Connect	CNET	0.044	0.114	0.111	0.156[b]	−0.087	0.040	0.079	1	0.023	−0.141[b]	0.072	0.055	−0.012
	Amazon	0.002	0.008	−0.187[a]	−0.164[b]	−0.104	0.016	0.052	0.139[b]	1	0.007	−0.055	−0.077	−0.009
Feat	CNET	0.145[b]	0.127[b]	0.036	0.106	−0.139[b]	−0.052	−0.177[a]	0.023	1	0.008	0.139[b]	0.038	−0.056
	Amazon	0.128	−0.040	0.049	0.064	−0.030	0.005	−0.044	−0.022	0.007	1	0.000	−0.019	−0.024
Love	CNET	−0.118	−0.102	0.108	0.104	0.000	0.291[a]	−0.079	−0.141[b]	0.008	1	−0.086	−0.045	−0.096
	Amazon	0.273[a]	0.022	0.450[a]	0.473[a]	−0.013	−0.055	−0.010	−0.061	−0.055	0.000	1	−0.016	−0.048
Big	CNET	0.373[a]	−0.006	0.411[a]	0.514[a]	−0.205[a]	0.015	−0.048	0.072	0.139[b]	−0.086	1	0.078	0.044
	Amazon	0.015	−0.156[b]	−0.001	0.006	0.026	0.126	−0.046	0.069	−0.077	−0.019	−0.016	1	0.055
Small	CNET	0.091	−0.106	−0.096	−0.038	−0.119	−0.072	−0.025	0.055	0.038	−0.045	0.078	1	0.059
	Amazon	−0.024	−0.095	−0.036	−0.015	−0.050	0.003	0.144[b]	0.063	−0.009	−0.024	−0.048	0.055	1
	CNET	−0.053	−0.001	0.034	−0.056	0.167[a]	−0.053	0.020	−0.012	−0.056	−0.096	0.044	0.059	1

[a]Correlation is significant at the 0.01 level (2-tailed)
[b]Correlation is significant at the 0.05 level (2-tailed)

Table 7 OLS regression coefficient estimates. Affect and capacity by time and Amazon vs. CNET

Dependent variable		B	Std. error
ln(capacity)	(Intercept)***	0.275	0.058
	Is 2nd Gen	0.024	0.081
	Is CNET***	0.407	0.069
	Is 2nd Gen × CNET***	−0.546	0.158
ln(affect)	(Intercept)***	1.916	0.048
	Is 2nd Gen	−0.043	0.068
	Is CNET	0.063	0.057
	Is 2nd Gen × CNET*	0.275	0.132

p < 0.10
*p < 0.05
**p < 0.01
***p < 0.001

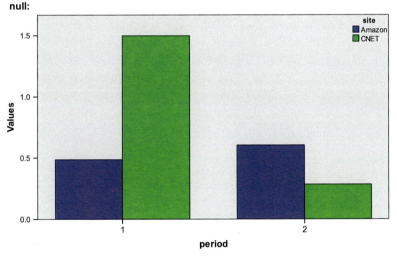

Fig. 1 Mean number of capacity words by site and time period

with the correlation analysis. We observe that in general expert reviewers discussed capacity more than nonexperts ($\hat{\beta} = 0.407$, p < 0.001). However, as predicted by Hypothesis 4, such discussions decreased after the release of the second-generation iPod ($\hat{\beta} = -0.546$, p < 0.001).

Affect also changes differentially in each group (Fig. 2). The OLS analysis (Table 7) shows that in the first time-period, affective language is roughly equivalent, but experts on CNET use more affective language in the second time-period than they do in the first time-period ($\hat{\beta} = 0.275$, p < 0.05). In short, site and period have a positive interactive effect on affective expressions. These are just two examples of

Table 8 Regression coefficients: predictors of product rating for experts vs. nonexperts

Coefficients							
Site	Category	Unstandardized coefficients		Standardized coefficients		t	Sig.
		B	Std. error	Beta			
Amazon	(constant)	3.839	0.137			27.932	0.000
	Aesthetics	0.145	0.175	0.058		0.833	0.406
	Capacity	0.064	0.087	0.051		0.732	0.465
	Problems	−0.015	0.086	−0.012		−0.174	0.862
	Entertainment	**0.150**	**0.047**	**0.221**		**3.178**	**0.002**
	Connect	−0.035	0.073	−0.033		−0.476	0.635
	Features	**0.174**	**0.088**	**0.136**		**1.972**	**0.050**
CNET	(constant)	3.799	0.144			26.373	0.000
	Aesthetics	0.031	0.031	0.062		0.978	0.329
	Capacity	−0.029	0.042	−0.043		−0.697	0.486
	Problems	−0.290	0.195	−0.091		−1.484	0.139
	Entertainment	0.011	0.040	0.017		0.277	0.782
	Connect	**0.100**	**0.049**	**0.128**		**2.062**	**0.040**
	Features	**−0.126**	**0.059**	**−0.137**		**−2.138**	**0.033**

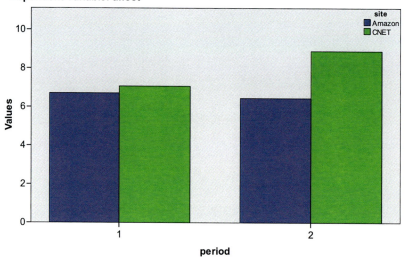

Fig. 2 Mean number of affect words by site and time period

how automated content analysis can be used to assess changes in word-of-mouth communication.

Regression with ratings. Now that relationships between semantic elements in the text have been discerned, their relationship to other, nonsemantic variables is of interest. For example, what factors impact ratings for experts vs. nonexperts? To test the impact of discourse on rating, an OLS regression was run with rating as the dependent variable and the discursive categories as the independent variables. Several discursive variables were significant predictors of ratings overall ($F_{Amazon} = 2.55$, $p < 0.05$; $F_{CNET} = 2.30$, $p < 0.05$). Results are shown in Table 8. These reveal that the ratings of nonexperts were influenced by entertainment and features, while the ratings of experts were affected by connectability and by the (negative) evaluation of the features. This provides support for H5 and H6. However, they also indicate a more complicated relationship. Features are correlated with both expert and nonexpert ratings. However, for nonexperts, features are positively correlated with ratings while for experts, they are negatively correlated. Problems and cost, although much discussed in the posts, appeared to have little effect on ratings. The unimportance of cost may be explained by the fact that the ratings data are nonbehavioral, that is, most posters had already purchased the device.

Stage 6: Validation

The previous analyses revealed there were systematic differences in the number of words used between experts and nonexperts. To assess construct validity, we used a triangulation approach to explore the relationships between the concepts through a correlation analysis of word association within comment (Table 7). This means that we are looking for how the dictionary categories occur together within one post. To assess construct validity of affect, we included another operationalization of affect, star rating, in the correlational analysis. We calculated Pearson correlations for all categories in the set and compared them with cosine similarities. Both tables produced directionally similar results, and here we report Pearson correlations, as it accounts for both presence and absence of collocation. First, a few expected correlations between categories were checked. For both sites, positive emotion is correlated with rating ($r_{(posem,\ rating)} = 0.335$, $p < 0.01$), as one would expect. Negative emotion is negatively correlated with positive emotion ($r_{(negemo, posemo)} = -0.348$, $p < 0.01$). More can be learned, however, by comparing word association in expert versus nonexpert groups.

In general, nonexperts use positive language alongside distal uses for the iPod such as work and family ($r_{(work, posem|Amazon)} = 0.243$, $p < 0.01$ and $r_{(family,\ posemo|Amazon)} = 0.190$, $p < 0.01$). For the non-experts, negative emotion is correlated with problems, as one would expect ($r_{(problems, negem|Amazon)} = .470$). For experts, positive emotion occurs alongside aesthetics ($r_{(aesth, posem|CNET)} = 0.409$, $p < 0.01$). For experts, there is also a positive correlation between Apple and love ($r_{(Apple,\ love|}$

$_\text{CNET)} = 0.203$, p < 0.01) that does not exist for nonexperts. These correlations indicate that aesthetics are viewed positively by experts and that they are involved with not only the device but the brand as well. Cosine similarities produce directionally similar results.

Secondly, features are interpreted differentially between the two groups. Novices interpret some features using standards of other categories (like an mp3 player), while experts are more willing to judge them relative to the standards for a new category. For example, from the correlation between small and capacity among the nonexpert group ($r_\text{(capacity,small|Amazon)} = 0.144$, p < 0.01), one can conclude that posters feel the capacity is too small. No such correlation exists for experts. This could be because the iTouch is a product without a known category. Experts can interpret size for this ambiguous product, but novices are uncertain about what capacity is appropriate for the device. These are just a few of the findings that can be gleaned using a correlation Table. A full spatial analysis might compare the network of meanings in the Amazon group to the network of meanings in the CNET group.

For the binary logistic classification, k-fold cross-validation was performed, and per convention, we set $k = 10$. The resulting comparisons between predicted values based on our model and the real values show that overall the model is 80.13% accurate (95% accuracy confidence interval $= [0.7624, 0.8363]$). Table 9 shows the confusion matrix.

In sum, the automated text analysis presented here shows that that experts evaluate new products in a systematically different way from nonexperts. Using comparison between groups, we show that experts evaluate products by focusing on features while nonexperts focus on the uses and benefits of the devices. Using correlation analysis, we find that experts associate aesthetics with positive emotion while nonexperts associate positive emotion with uses of the device and negative emotion with problems. Further, the correlation analysis provides some validation for the method of automated content analysis by demonstrating the correlation between positive emotion and ratings, a variable used in previous studies of online word-of-mouth communication (Godes and Mayzlin 2004, 2009). We find that, over time, experts focus less on problematic features like capacity and speak more affectively about the product. A regression analysis of the elements of discourse on ratings demonstrates that ratings for experts are driven by features, while ratings by nonexperts are better predicted by both features and the amount of talk about entertainment, a benefit. Note that, like field research, these findings make sense in convergence with previous findings from experimental data and provide ecological validity to previous findings obtained in laboratory settings. These are not meant to be a rigorous test of expertise,

Table 9 Confusion matrix from tenfold cross-validation. Accuracy $= 0.8013$. p-Value [accuracy $>$ no information rate] $= < 2e\text{-}16$

Prediction		Expert	Not expert
	Expert	237	62
	Not expert	32	142

but rather an illustration of the way in which text analysis can provide convergent evidence that is meaningful to consumer researchers.

Conclusion and Future Directions

Developments in text analysis have opened a large and fascinating arena for marketing research. Theoretically, marketing research can now incorporate linguistic theory to understand consumer attitudes, interaction, and culture (Humphreys and Wang 2018). While most approaches have focused on analyzing word frequencies, a vast world of looking at text structure at higher, conversational levels remain open. For example, understanding where a word like "great" falls within the text itself (early, middle, or late in a sentence or paragraph) may shed light on the importance of the word in predicting, for example, consumer sentiment. Drawing inferences on the sentence or paragraph level may yield more meaningful results in some contexts (Büschken and Allenby 2016). Lastly, pragmatics, the area of linguistic research aimed at understanding the effect of context on word meaning may help marketing researchers capture more about the nature of consumer communication online.

Practically, incorporating this kind of data allows researchers and managers to integrate the abundance of textual data with existing and growing datasets of behavioral data collected online or through devices. And yet one must be aware of the many limitations of using machines to interpret a human language that has developed socially in face-to-face contexts over 100,000 years. Text analysis can often be used to gather information about top-line patterns of attention or relatively wrote patterns of interaction, but capturing the subtly of human communication remains allusive to machines. Further, due to the ambiguity of language, careful and transparent analysis and interpretation are required at each step of text analysis, from cleaning textual markers that may be misleading to correctly interpreting correlations and differences. Despite these challenges, marketing researchers have clearly shown the theoretical, practical, and managerial insight that can be distilled through the seemingly simple process of counting words.

Cross-References

- ▶ Return on Media Models
- ▶ Social Network Analysis

References

Alba, J. W., & Hutchinson, J. W. (1987). Dimensions of consumer expertise. *Journal of Consumer Research, 13*(4), 411–454.

Arndt, J. (1967). Role of product-related conversations in the diffusion of a new product. *Journal of Marketing Research, 4*, 291–295.

Arsel, Z., & Bean, J. (2013). Taste regimes and market-mediated practice. *Journal of Consumer Research, 39*(5), 899–917.

Arvidsson, A., & Caliandro, A. (2016). Brand public. *Journal of Consumer Research, 42*(5), 727–748.

Barasch, A., & Berger, J. (2014). Broadcasting and narrowcasting: How audience size affects what people share. *Journal of Marketing Research, 51*(3), 286–299.

Belk, R. W., & Pollay, R. W. (1985). Images of ourselves: The good life in twentieth century advertising. *Journal of Consumer Research, 11*(4), 887.

Berelson, B. (1971). *Content analysis in communication research*. New York: Hafner.

Berger, J., & Milkman, K. L. (2012). What makes online content viral? *Journal of Marketing Research, 49*(2), 192–205.

Blei, David M., Andrew Y. Ng, & Michael I. Jordan. (2003). Latent dirichlet allocation. *Journal of machine Learning research 3*, 993–1022.

Bollen, J., Mao, H., & Zeng, X. (2011). Twitter mood predicts the stock market. *Journal of Computer Science, 2*(1), 1–8.

Boyd, R. L., & Pennebaker, J. W. (2015a). Away with words. In *Consumer psychology in a social media world* (p. 222). Abingdon: Routledge.

Boyd, R. L., & Pennebaker, J. W. (2015b). Did Shakespeare write double falsehood? Identifying individuals by creating psychological signatures with text analysis. *Psychological Science, 26*(5), 570–582.

Brown, J. J., & Reingen, P. H. (1987). Social ties and word-of-mouth referral behavior. *Journal of Consumer Research, 14*(3), 350–362.

Büschken, J., & Allenby, G. M. (2016). Sentence-based text analysis for customer reviews. *Marketing Science, 35*(6), 953–975.

Carley, K. (1997). Network text analysis: The network position of concepts. In C. W. Roberts (Ed.), *Text analysis for the social sciences: Methods for drawing statistical inferences from texts and transcripts*. Mahwah: Lawrence Erlbaum.

Chung, C. K., & Pennebaker, J. W. (2013). Counting little words in Big Data. In *Social cognition and communication* (p. 25). New York: Psychology Press.

Collins, A. M., & Loftus, E. F. (1975). A spreading-activation theory of semantic processing. *Psychological Review, 82*(6), 407.

Constant, N., Davis, C., Potts, C., & Schwarz, F. (2009). The pragmatics of expressive content: Evidence from large corpora. *Sprache und Datenverarbeitung, 33*(1–2), 5–21.

De Choudhury M., Sundaram H., John A., & Seligmann D. D. (2008). Can blog communication dynamics be correlated with stock market activity? In *Proceedings of the nineteenth ACM conference on hypertext and hypermedia*, ACM, pp. 55–60

Duhachek, Adam, and Katie Kelting. (2009). Coping repertoire: Integrating a new conceptualization of coping with transactional theory. *Journal of Consumer Psychology 19*(3), 473–485.

Dunphy, D. M., Bullard, C.G., & Crossing, E.E.M. (1974). Validation of the general inquirer Harvard Iv Dictionary. Paper presented at the 1974 Pisa conference on content analysis, Pisa, Italy.

Ertimur, B., & Coskuner-Balli, G. (2015). Navigating the institutional logics of markets: Implications for strategic brand management. *Journal of Marketing, 79*(2), 40–61.

Fishbein, M., & Ajzen, I. (1972). Attitudes and opinions. *Annual Review of Psychology, 23*(1), 487–544.

Fiss, P. C., & Hirsch, P. M. (2005). The discourse of globalization: Framing and sensemaking of an emerging concept. *American Sociological Review, 70*(1)., 24p.

Gamson, W. A., & Modigliani, A. (1989). Media discourse and public opinion on nuclear power: A constructionist approach. *The American Journal of Sociology, 95*(1), 1–37.

Gandolfo, A., Tuan, A., Corciolani, M., & Dalli, D. (2016). What do emerging economy firms actually disclose in their CSR reports? A longitudinal analysis. In *CSR-HR Project (Corporate Social Responsibility and Human Rights Project). Research Grant of University of Pisa (PRA_2015_0082)*.

Garrett, D. E. (1987). The effectiveness of marketing policy boycotts: Environmental opposition to marketing. *Journal of Marketing, 51*(2), 46–57.

Giesler, M. (2008). Conflict and compromise: drama in marketplace evolution. *Journal of Consumer Research, 34*(6), 739–753.

Godes, D., & Mayzlin, D. (2004). Using online conversations to study word-of-mouth communication. *Marketing Science, 23*(4), 545–560.

Godes, D., & Mayzlin, D. (2009). Firm-created word-of-mouth communication: Evidence from a field test. *Marketing Science, 28*(4), 721–739.

Grayson, K., & Rust, R. (2001). Interrater reliability assessment in content analysis. *Journal of Consumer Psychology, 10*(1/2), 71–73.

Grice, H. P. (1975). *Logic and Conversation*. Syntax and Semantics, vol.3 edited by P. Cole and J. Morgan, Academic Press. Reprinted as ch.2 of Grice 1989, 22–40.

Grimmer, J., & Stewart, B. M. (2013). Text as data: The promise and pitfalls of automatic content analysis methods for political texts. *Political Analysis, 21*(3), 267–297.

Homburg, C., Ehm, L., & Artz, M. (2015). Measuring and managing consumer sentiment in an online community environment. *Journal of Marketing Research, 52*(5), 629–641.

Hong, J., & Sternthal, B. (2010). The effects of consumer prior knowledge and processing strategies on judgments. *Journal of Marketing Research, 47*(2), 301–311.

Humphreys, A. (2010). Megamarketing: The creation of markets as a social process. *Journal of Marketing, 74*(2), 1–19.

Humphreys, A., & Latour, K. A. (2013). Framing the game: Assessing the impact of cultural representations on consumer perceptions of legitimacy. *Journal of Consumer Research, 40*(4), 773–795.

Humphreys, A., & Thompson, C. J. (2014). Branding disaster: Reestablishing trust through the ideological containment of systemic risk anxieties. *Journal of Consumer Research, 41*(4), 877–910.

Humphreys, A. (2015). *Social media: Enduring principles*. New York/Oxford: Oxford University Press.

Humphreys, A., & Wang, R. J.-H. (2018). Automated text analysis for consumer research. *Journal of Consumer Research, 44*(6), 1274–1306. https://doi.org/10.1093/jcr/ucx104

Hutto, C. J., & Gilbert, E. (2014). Vader: A parsimonious rule-based model for sentiment analysis of social media text. In *Eighth international AAAI conference on weblogs and social media*.

Jia, L., Clement, Y., & Meng, W. (2009). The effect of negation on sentiment analysis and retrieval effectiveness. In *Proceedings of the 18th ACM conference on information and knowledge management*: ACM, pp. 1827–1830.

Jurafsky, D., Chahuneau, V., Routledge, B. R., & Smith, N. A. (2014). Narrative framing of consumer sentiment in online restaurant reviews. *First Monday, 19*(4). https://doi.org/10.5210/fm.v19i4.4944.

Kassarjian, H. H. (1977). Content analysis in consumer research. *Journal of Consumer Research, 4*(1), 8–19.

Kolbe, R. H., & Burnett, M. S. (1991). Content-analysis research: An examination of applications with directives for improving research reliability and objectivity. *Journal of Consumer Research, 18*(2), 243–250.

Kovács, B., Carroll, G. R., & Lehman, D. W. (2013). Authenticity and consumer value ratings: Empirical tests from the restaurant domain. *Organization Science, 25*(2), 458–478.

Kozinets, R. V. (2010). Networked narratives: Understanding word-of-mouth marketing in online communities. *Journal of Marketing, 74*(2), 71–89.

Kranz, P. (1970). Content analysis by word group. *Journal of Marketing Research, 7*(3), 377–380.

Krauss, J., Nann, S., Simon, D., Gloor, P. A., & Fischbach, K. (2008). Predicting movie success and academy awards through sentiment and social network analysis. In *ECIS*, pp. 2026–2037.

Lasswell, H. D., & Leites, N. (1949). *Language of politics; studies in quantitative semantics*. New York: G. W. Stewart.

Lee, F., Peterson, C., & Tiedens, L. Z. (2004). Mea culpa: Predicting stock prices from organizational attributions. *Personality and Social Psychology Bulletin, 30*(12), 1636–1649.
Lee, T. Y., & Bradlow, E. T. (2011). Automated marketing research using online customer reviews. *Journal of Marketing Research, 48*(5), 881–894.
Ludwig, S., Ko, d. R., Friedman, M., Brüggen, E. C., Wetzels, M., & Pfann, G. (2013). More than words: The influence of affective content and linguistic style matches in online reviews on conversion rates. *Journal of Marketing, 77*(1), 87–103.
Ludwig, S., Van Laer, T., De Ruyter, K., & Friedman, M. (2016). Untangling a web of lies: Exploring automated detection of deception in computer-mediated communication. *Journal of Management Information Systems, 33*(2), 511–541.
Maheswaran, D., & Sternthal, B. (1990). The effects of knowledge, motivation, and type of message on ad processing and product judgments. *Journal of Consumer Research, 17*(1), 66–73.
Maheswaran, D. (1994). Country of origin as a stereotype: Effects of consumer expertise and attribute strength on product evaluations. *Journal of Consumer Research, 21*(2), 354–365.
Maheswaran, D., Sternthal, B., & Gurhan, Z. (1996). Acquisition and impact of consumer expertise. *Journal of Consumer Psychology, 5*(2), 115.
Mahoney, J. (2003). Strategies of causal assessment in comparative historical analysis. In J. Mahoney & D. Rueschemeyer (Eds.), *Comparative historical analysis in the social sciences*. Cambridge, UK/New York: Cambridge University Press. pp. xix, 444.
Mankad, S., Han, H. S., Goh, J., & Gavirneni, S. (2016). Understanding online hotel reviews through automated text analysis. *Service Science, 8*(2), 124–138.
Mehl, M. R., & Gill, A. J. (2008). Automatic text analysis. In S. D. G. J. A. Johnson (Ed.), *Advanced methods for behavioral research on the internet*. Washington, DC: American Psychological Association.
Mestyán, M., Yasseri, T., & Kertész, J. (2013). Early prediction of movie box office success based on Wikipedia activity big data. *PLoS One, 8*(8), e71226.
Meyers-Levy, J., & Tybout, A. M. (1989). Schema congruity as a basis for product evaluation. *Journal of Consumer Research, 16*(1), 39–54.
Mill, J. S. (1843). *A system of logic, ratiocinative and inductive: Being a connected view of the principles of evidence, and methods of scientific investigation*. London: J.W. Parker.
Moe, Wendy W., and Michael Trusov. (2011). The value of social dynamics in online product ratings forums. *Journal of Marketing Research 48*(3), 444–456.
Moe, W. W., & Schweidel, D. A. (2014). *Social media intelligence*. Cambridge, UK/New York: Cambridge University Press.
Mogilner, C., Kamvar, S. D., & Aaker, J. (2010). The shifting meaning of happiness. *Social Psychological and Personality Science, 2*(4), 395–402.
Money, R. B., Gilly, M. C., & Graham, J. L. (1998). Explorations of national culture and word-of-mouth referral behavior in the purchase of industrial services in the United States and Japan. *Journal of Marketing, 62*, 76–87.
Monroe, B. L., Colaresi, M. P., & Quinn, K. M. (2009). Fightin' words: Lexical feature selection and evaluation for identifying the content of political conflict. *Political Analysis, 16*(4), 372–403.
Moore, S. G. (2015). Attitude predictability and helpfulness in online reviews: The role of explained actions and reactions. *Journal of Consumer Research, 42*(1), 30–44.
Netzer, O., Feldman, R., Goldenberg, J., & Fresko, M. (2012). Mine your own business: Market-structure surveillance through text mining. *Marketing Science, 31*(3), 521–543.
Opoku, R., Abratt, R., & Pitt, L. (2006). Communicating brand personality: Are the websites doing the talking for the top South African business schools? *Journal of Brand Management, 14*(1–2), 20–39.
Packard, G., Moore, S. G., & McFerran, B. (2014). How can "I" help "you"? The impact of personal pronoun use in customer-firm agent interactions. MSI report, pp. 14–110.
Packard, G. M., & Wooten, D. B. (2013). Compensatory knowledge signaling in consumer word-of-mouth. *Journal of Consumer Psychology 23*(4), 434–450.

Palmquist, M. E., Carley, K., & Dale, T. (2009). Analyzing maps of literary and non-literary texts. In K. Krippendorff & M. A. Bock (Eds.), *The content analysis reader* (pp. 4120–4415). Thousand Oaks: Sage.

Pennebaker, J. W., Francis, M. E., & Booth, R. J. (2001). *Linguistic inquiry and word count: Liwc 2001* (Vol. 71). Mahway: Lawrence Erlbaum Associates.

Pennebaker, J. W., & King, L. A. (1999). Linguistic styles: Language use as an individual difference. *Journal of Personality and Social Psychology, 77*(6)., 17p.

Petty, R. E., & Cacioppo, J. T. (1979). Issue involvement can increase or decrease persuasion by enhancing message-relevant cognitive responses. *Journal of Personality and Social Psychology, 37*(10), 1915.

Phelps, J. E., Lewis, R., Mobilio, L., Perry, D., & Raman, N. (2004). Viral marketing or electronic word-of-mouth advertising: Examining consumer responses and motivations to pass along email. *Journal of Advertising Research, 44*(4), 333–348.

Plaisant, C., Rose, J., Bei, Y., Auvil, L., Kirschenbaum, M. G., Smith, M. N., Clement T., & Lord G. (2006). Exploring erotics in emily Dickinson's correspondence with text mining and visual interfaces. In *Proceedings of the 6th ACM/IEEE-CS joint conference on digital libraries*, ACM, pp. 141–150.

Potts, C., & Schwarz, F. (2010). Affective 'this'. *Linguistic Issues in Language Technology, 3*(5), 1–30.

Quantcast. (2010a) Cnet monthly traffic (estimated). (www.quantcast.com/cnet.com).

Quantcast. (2010b). Amazon monthly traffic (estimated). (www.quantcast.com/amazon.com).

Rayson, P. (2009). Wmatrix: A web-based corpus processing environment. Edited by C. Department, Lancaster University, UK.

Salton, Gerard, and Michael J. McGill. (1983). Introduction to modern information retrieval McGraw-Hill. New York.

Schweidel, D. A., & Moe, W. W. (2014). Listening in on social media: A joint model of sentiment and venue format choice. *Journal of Marketing Research, 51*(4), 387–402.

Sennett, R. (2006). *The culture of the new capitalism*. New Haven: Yale University Press.

Snefjella, B., & Kuperman, V. (2015). Concreteness and psychological distance in natural language use. *Psychological Science, 26*(9), 1449–1460.

Spiller, S. A., & Belogolova, L. (2016). On consumer beliefs about quality and taste. *Journal of Consumer Research, 43*(6), 970–991.

Stephen, A. T., & Toubia, O. (2010). Deriving value from social commerce networks. *Journal of Marketing Research, 47*(2), 215–228.

Stevenson, T. H., & Swayne, L. E. (1999). The portrayal of African-Americans in business-to-business direct mail: A benchmark study. *Journal of Advertising, 28*(3), 25–35.

Stone, P. J. (1966). *The general inquirer; a computer approach to content analysis*. Cambridge: MIT Press.

Sujan, M. (1985). Consumer knowledge: Effects on evaluation strategies mediating consumer judgments. *Journal of Consumer Research, 12*(1), 31–46.

Tirunillai, S., & Tellis, G. J. (2012). Does chatter really matter? Dynamics of user-generated content and stock performance. *Marketing Science, 31*(2), 198–215.

Tirunillai, S., & Tellis, G. J. (2014). Mining marketing meaning from online chatter: Strategic brand analysis of big data using latent Dirichlet allocation. *Journal of Marketing Research, 51*(4), 463–479.

Van de Rijt, A., Shor, E., Ward, C., & Skiena, S. (2013). Only 15 minutes? The social stratification of fame in printed media. *American Sociological Review, 78*(2), 266–289.

Van Laer, T., Escalas J. E., Ludwig S., & Van den Hende E. A. (2017). What happens in Vegas stays on TripAdvisor? Computerized text analysis of narrativity in online consumer reviews.

Ordenes, V., Francisco, S. L., Ko, D. R., Grewal, D., & Wetzels, M. (2017). Unveiling what is written in the stars: Analyzing explicit, implicit, and discourse patterns of sentiment in social media. *Journal of Consumer Research, 43*(6), 875–894.

Weber, K. (2005). A toolkit for analyzing corporate cultural toolkits. *Poetics, 33*(3/4), 26p.

Weber, M. (1924). Towards a sociology of the press. Paper presented at the first congress of sociologists, Frankfurt.

Winer, R. S. (2009). New communications approaches in marketing: Issues and research directions. *Journal of Interactive Marketing, 23*(2), 108–117. https://doi.org/10.1016/j.intmar.2009.02.004.

Zipf, G. K. (1932). *Selected studies of the principle of relative frequency in language.* Cambridge, MA: Harvard University Press.

Image Analytics in Marketing

Daria Dzyabura, Siham El Kihal, and Renana Peres

Contents

Introduction	666
Top Research Questions by Area Using Image Analytics	669
Product Design	670
Advertising	671
Branding	672
Online Shopping Experience	674
Consumer Perspective	675
Data: Consumer Vs. Firm Images	675
Consumer-Generated Images	676
Firm-Generated Images	679
Methods	681
Feature Extraction	681
Model Training	683
Model Evaluation and Validation	684
Model Application	685
Integrating It All Together	685
Conclusion	688
Cross-References	689
References	689

D. Dzyabura
New Economic School and Moscow School of Management SKOLKOVO, Moscow, Russia
e-mail: ddzyabura@nes.ru

S. El Kihal (✉)
Frankfurt School of Finance and Management, Frankfurt, Germany
e-mail: s.elkihal@fs.de

R. Peres
School of Business Administration, Hebrew University of Jerusalem, Jerusalem, Israel
e-mail: renana.peres@mail.huji.ac.il

Abstract

Recent technical advances and the rise of digital platforms enhanced consumers' abilities to take and share images and led to a tremendous increase in the importance of visual communication. The abundance of visual data, together with the development of image processing tools and advanced modeling techniques, provides unique opportunities for marketing researchers, in both academia and practice, to study the relationship between consumers and firms in depth and to generate insights which can be generalized across a variety of people and contexts.

However, with the opportunity come challenges. Specifically, researchers interested in using image analytics for marketing are faced with a triple challenge: (1) To which type of research questions can image analytics add insights that cannot be obtained otherwise? (2) Which visual data should be used to answer the research questions, and (3) which method is the right one?

In this chapter, the authors provide a guidance on how to formulate a worthy research question, select the appropriate data source, and apply the right method of analysis. They first identify five relevant areas in marketing that would benefit greatly from image analytics. They then discuss different types of visual data and explain their merits and drawbacks. Finally, they describe methodological approaches to analyzing visual data and discuss issues such as feature extraction, model training, evaluation, and validation as well as application to a marketing problem.

Keywords

Image analytics · Visual information · Image processing · Image tagging · Firm images · Consumer images · Feature extraction · Deep neural networks · High-level features · Low-level features · Human-coded features · Color histograms · Gabor filters

Introduction

"The drawing shows me at one glance what might be spread over ten pages in a book."

Ivan S. Turgenev, Fathers and Sons, 1862.

In the past two decades, images have been playing an increasing role in the marketing arena. Social media outlets have become more image rich, new versions of mobile phones have enhanced ability to take, store, and share photos, and storage and communication infrastructures have become more accessible. These processes have immensely increased the significance of images in consumer life in general, and in marketing in particular.

Images have always been an important part of firms' marketing efforts. Visuals convey a sense of proximity and closeness, and thus, are able to represent objects better than words (Amit et al. 2009). Relative to text, visual information was found to be better processed and better remembered by humans (MacInnis and Price 1987). Therefore, many of the components of product design, packaging, brand elements, advertising, and design of shopping outlets, use visuals.

These visuals impact consumer response and purchase. For example, Raghubir and Greenleaf (2006) found that certain geometrical ratio of rectangular packaging and print ads influence consumers' relative preferences and purchase intentions. Meyers-Levy and Zhu (2008) showed that various visual elements of store design, such as architecture, freestanding in-store structures, display surfaces, type and arrangement of display cases, mirror orientation, and artwork, relate to consumers' choice and shopping behaviors.

In marketing communications, images are dominant in brands' paid media, such as print, outdoor, and television advertising. Over time, the proportion of pictorial content in a typical magazine ad has grown, while the proportion of text has been gradually shrinking (McQuarrie 2008). A higher proportion of pictorial content in an ad is more efficient in attracting attention (Pieters and Wedel 2004), and is associated with more positive attitude toward the ad (Radach et al. 2003) and with a better memory of the advertised brand (Wedel and Pieters 2000). The layout of the ad, and the size and color combination of its elements have a strong impact on consumers' perceptions and attitudes toward the ad as well as the brand (Janiszewski 1998; Wedel and Pieters 2014; Cho et al. 2008). For example, studies have found that ads containing colors with lighter shade (high "value" in color theory terms) lead to greater liking of the ad. This effect is mediated by stronger feelings of relaxation induced by higher value colors. Higher levels of chroma (a color dimension that relates to the intensity of the color) induce feelings of excitement, which in turn also increase the likeability of the ad (Gorn et al. 1997). Finally, upward looking angles are aligned with perception of potency while photos taken from a downward looking angle were found to lead to a more detailed recall of the brand (Peracchio and Meyers-Levy 2005).

In addition to product design and marketing communications, images are prominently used in marketing research. Consumers express their thoughts, perceptions, and emotions through images. Images have been demonstrated to successfully disrupt people's well-rehearsed narratives and reflect authentic thoughts and deep metaphors. For this reason, visual research methods often better reflect emotions, cultural practices, and attitudes compared to verbal methods (Reavey 2012). Qualitative visual methods are used to arrange brand associations on a map (John et al. 2006), to create brand collages (Zaltman and Coulter 1995; Zaltman and Zaltman 2008), and to elicit brand associations. Other studies used lab experiments (Peracchio and Meyers-Levy 2005) or user-generated digital content (Liu et al. 2017; Klostermann et al. 2018; Pavlov and Mizik 2019; Dzyabura and Peres 2021) to create visual representation of brand associations and connect them with brand characteristics.

The development of digital platforms has further increased the role of images in consumers' lives. Pictures became an important part of brands' owned media – websites, apps, and social media outlets, as well as of brands' earned media – that is, brand content posted by users on social media. Industry reports indicate that 74% of the content generated by firms contains some form of visual elements, including photos, illustrations, videos, and data visualization (Venngage 2020). Much of the visual activity happens through social media outlets: every minute 136,000 photos are uploaded to Facebook. Every day five Million photos are uploaded to Instagram, added to its corpus of 50 billion photos, which are viewed and receive 3.5 billion likes per day by Instagram's one billion users (ibid.). Consumers use images to communicate with each other and share their experiences, feelings, and impressions. Brands use visual data to learn about consumers' needs and perceptions, to create and communicate value, to shape consumers' attitudes and drive them into action. This ongoing activity has created a rich, dynamic, and vibrant visual ecosystem, which provides a fertile ground for marketing research and marketing activity.

The abundance of visual data, together with the development of image processing tools and advanced modeling techniques, provides unique opportunities for marketing researchers, in both academia and practice, to study the relationship between consumers and firms in depth and to generate insights which can be generalized across a variety of people and contexts.

However, with the opportunity come challenges. Specifically, researchers interested in using image analytics for marketing are faced with a triple challenge. First is the formulation of the research question. Since working with visuals requires elaborate data collection and elaborate analysis, one should identify a research question to which image analytics can add insights that are difficult to obtain in other, more conventional ways.

The second challenge is the choice of data. Visual data sources include user-generated content on brands' web pages (e.g., comments on the brand's Facebook page), data from consumer interactions with other consumers (e.g., one's own Instagram), firm-generated content, general photo repositories (e.g., Flickr), visual product presentation in shopping outlets (eBay, Airbnb), or directly elicited visuals (e.g., online collages). Each of these data sources has its own merits as well as limitations and sometimes, once the research question has been identified, the right data source needs to be carefully chosen. Sometimes, none of the existing data sources contains all the information of interest and the researcher must find ways to combine several sources or supplement the dataset with additional data collection.

The third challenge is the choice of method – most methods used in image analytics were developed in engineering and computer science and were not necessarily optimized for marketing questions. Therefore, using image analytics in marketing requires tailoring existing methods to better fit the data and the research question, or developing new methods altogether.

These three challenges are not independent of each other – the data and method need to be congruent with the research question. For example, a research which seeks to elicit brand associations (Dzyabura and Peres 2021) will need to use interpretable features (such as objects in the pictures), rather than low-level image patterns, and consequently can use image tagging methods and tag-based classifiers to extract high-level features. On the other hand, forecasting the success of a brand based on consumer reviews (Zhang and Luo 2019) has more freedom in choosing the features, but requires showing that pictorial content contains information which cannot be retrieved by a straightforward sentiment or content analysis of the review text. Finding the right combination of research question, data source, and method is the key to producing meaningful image analytics research in marketing.

Our goal in this chapter is to provide guidance as to how to approach this triple challenge: formulate a worthy research question, select the appropriate data source, and apply the right method of analysis. We start by identifying research questions in five areas that would greatly benefit from using image analytics. We then discuss the different types of visual data including firm-generated and user-generated data and explain their merits and limitations. While data sources constantly change, we suggest guidelines for their characterization and evaluation. We further describe the methodological approaches to analyzing visual data, discussing issues such as feature extraction, model training, classification, and deep learning. We conclude with a decision matrix which can be used as a tool to assist in matching the data and method to the problem at hand. To provide the novice researcher with a gateway to start implementing the ideas, we provide a hands-on tutorial (available on https://github.com/dariasil/image_tutorial), which contains code implementation of several fundamental image analytics tasks and explanations on the required software tools and libraries. We hope that the set of research questions, data sources, richness of methods, code and examples, and guidelines as to how to bring them all together, will help marketing researchers to maximize the tremendous potential of image analytics methods in order to expand the understanding of important research problems and gain meaningful, valuable insights for the benefit of the field.

Top Research Questions by Area Using Image Analytics

The rapid evolution of the visual ecosystem has created unprecedented opportunities to obtain new perspectives on enduring marketing questions. At the same time, it also evoked a large number of new managerial decisions and consumer behaviors which need to be studied. We are just beginning to scratch the surface of this fascinating realm. We outline below the five major areas in marketing that have been most affected by this ecosystem and offer, within each of them, a set of research questions that could lead the further research using image analytics. These questions are summarized in Fig. 1.

Fig. 1 Summary of future research questions for image analytics in marketing

Product Design

In many product categories, design is a dominant factor in consumer choices (Bloch 1995; Rubera 2015). Firms use product design and aesthetics to differentiate themselves (Crilly et al. 2004) and to strategically position their brand among competitors (Keller 2003).

Research has demonstrated how specific elements of product and package design impact consumer perception (Greenleaf and Raghubir 2008). Studies of product aesthetics are mostly focused on one or several specific visual aspects of a design, such as characteristic lines, silhouettes, ornamentation, color, or texture (Orsborn et al. 2009; Eisenman et al. 2016; Chan et al. 2018). Image analytics, on the other hand, allows taking a more holistic view and study the joint, synergetic effect of the overall product design to customer decision or product performance. It also makes it possible to automatically compare a large number of designs and derive quantitative insights and predictions.

Characterizing Designs: How Can Designs Be Characterized Above and Beyond Their Specific Visual Elements?

Images can be used to classify and characterize product designs without the need to break them down into specific predefined visual elements. Such classification can help to:

1. Measure similarity and differences between designs. Specifically, quantify the distance of a focal design from the "average" design, to evaluate how unique the focal design is. This distance could be used to construct a metric measuring design differentiation and design innovativeness.
2. Map designs to brand perceptual dimensions. For example, whether a car design looks family friendly, or a shoe looks rugged, or a sofa looks modern.
3. Match the product design to the customer's personal style. Such matching can be used to identify and assemble the products to recommend to customers (see stitchfix.com).
4. Creating new designs. Models of image analytics can be used to augment the creative process of product design by suggesting novel and unexpected combinations of existing design elements. Algorithms of generative adversarial networks (GAN) that use computer vision to assist in the process of product design. Burnap et al. (2019) demonstrate how image analytic algorithms of GAN to generate models of cars for the design team to consider.

Quantifying the Value of Designs: How Can We Assess and Predict Consumer Attitudes Toward Various Product Designs?

Traditionally, demand models are based on quantifiable product attributes (e.g., miles per gallon, battery life, screen size, brand name, safety rating, price). The design of a product, that is, its overall appearance, vibes, emotion, and symbolism, is hard to be decomposed into quantifiable product attributes, yet they are critical factors in consumer choice. When a model is estimated using only these traditional functional attributes, these design characteristics end up in the error term.

Image analytics can improve the accuracy of such models by incorporating product images alongside the traditional characteristics in the demand model. For example, they can incorporate information about the success of previous designs in order to forecast various aspects of demand such as product liking, purchase in different channels, product returns or word-of-mouth. Combining image analytics with traditional models requires the development of new models and estimation methods. Specifically, the challenge is to retain the interpretability and un-biasness of some of the traditional coefficients such as price.

Advertising

Image analytics opens new possibilities for taking a systematic, quantitative approach to selecting, adjusting, and optimizing the visual composition of print and video advertisements.

Assessing Ad Creativity: How Can Print and Video Advertisements Be Rated According to Their Level of Creativity? What Are the Combinations of Visual Elements That Make an Ad Perceived as Creative?

Creativity is an important property of advertising messages that is associated with ad recall and effectiveness (Ang et al. 2007). It is sometimes defined as being composed of two factors: divergence and relevance. Divergence is the originality of the ad, and relevance is the extent to which at least some ad or brand elements are meaningful or valuable to the consumer (Smith et al. 2007).

Identifying the visual qualities which construct creativity is challenging. Therefore, creativity of visual ads is typically evaluated by human judges, using research tools such as surveys (Yang and Smith 2009; Sheinin et al. 2011), creativity awards (Lehnert et al. 2014), or crowdsourcing platforms (Kireyev et al. 2020).

Image analytics can allow for automated and scalable assessment of ad creativity. This can be done, for example, by comparing the focal ads to award winning ads, or to a corpus of candidate ads. Toubia and Netzer (2017) developed a prototypicality-based measure of text creativity. Based on their approach, a similar measure can also be constructed for images, either over predefined attributes or as a self-emergent arrangement of the visual space.

Linking Visuals to Emotional and Cognitive Effects: What Visuals Should Be Included in an Ad in Order to Achieve a Desired Outcome? What Objects, Colors, Shades, or Visual Structures Can Be Used to Spark Laughter, Fear, Urgency, Attention, Long-Term Recall, or Other Effects?

Image analytics could address these questions by taking large repositories of photos and their corresponding consumer reactions, and identifying images with certain emotional and cognitive effects.

Initial steps in this direction were taken by Rietveld et al. (2020), who extracted emotional information (i.e., arousal and valence levels) from Instagram photos of different brands and combined them with text analysis to predict customer engagement with the brand. However, there is need for further research in order to achieve a more complete visual-emotional-cognitive mapping.

Monetizing the Value of Images: What Is the Value of Images in Various Stages of the Customer Journey?

For the first time, differential effectiveness of visuals throughout the purchase funnel can be quantified by image analytics. Specifically:

1. Which visual features are most appropriate for various stages of the purchase funnel – what visuals get consumers' attention? Enhance awareness? Increase consideration, liking, and purchase intentions?
2. Which visuals should a firm present to customers at various stages in the customer life cycle? For example, are different images effective for customer acquisition vs. repeat purchase, upgrade, development, and retention?
3. How should visual features in ads be priced? Image analytics could revolutionize the way ads are priced. While media outlets are priced according to their reach, creative advertising is priced based on the effort invested and the reputation of the creative team. Quantifying the value of various visual components of an ad can lead to a differential pricing scheme. For example, measuring the relative value of a face in an ad versus a white space, or scenery, enables value-based pricing of ad creatives.

Branding

Images play a key role in consumer brand perception, recall, and associations (Peracchio and Meyers-Levy 1994, 2005). Image analytics opens new opportunities for brands to execute their desired positioning through visuals, manage their brand portfolio, and foster brand collaborations.

Visual Brand Representation: What Is the Visual Representation of Brand Associations? How Does It Align with Brand Characteristics? What Is the Role of the Visual Brand Elements and Brand Communications in Shaping Brand Perception and Associations?

A recently proposed tool to explore the visual representation of brand perception and elicit brand associations was described in the work of Dzyabura and Peres (2021). They developed a platform for eliciting brand associations through creating and analyzing online collages of images and showed how these collages can be used to retrieve a visual representation of brand associations and to connect it to brand personality and brand equity metrics. Such approaches have the potential to address many additional questions relating to the nature of these associations, their dynamics over time, their representation in brand communications, and their connection to various brand metrics.

Every brand has a unique set of visual brand elements (logo, colors, fonts, etc.) created by designers in collaboration with brand managers. These brand elements reflect the brand positioning, foster the desired associations and differentiate the brand from its competitors. Through image analytics, marketing scholars and brand managers can evaluate to what extent a proposed design achieves these goals (Dew et al. 2019).

Brand Hierarchy: What Are the Optimal Relationships Between the Visual Elements of Brands in a Brand Portfolio?

Sub-brands within a brand hierarchy require identities which are distinct from one another and yet convey the identity of the master brand. Brands vary in the extent the master brand dominates these sub-brand identities. For example, Fig. 2 shows the brand hierarchy of FedEx and Gillette. For FedEx, the master brand visual elements are clearly dominant, while for Gillette, the sub-brands have distinct visual elements of their own with the master brand being represented to a much lesser degree.

Image analytics can assist in achieving the desired balance between these two extremes. First, image analytics methods can be used to measure the level of visual coherence within the brand hierarchy. Second, it identifies the visual elements that create the perception of similarity. Third, it can connect the overall visuals of the hierarchy to brand performance metrics.

Brand Strategic Collaborations: When Brands Collaborate with Each Other, What Is the Right Mix of Their Visual Elements Which Will Ensure that Both Brands Are Fairly Represented?

Creating a visual identity for a collaboration of brands is often challenging and complicated for the collaborating parties to agree which visual elements should be taken from each brand and how to combine them together. Consider, for example, the two designs of the joint Philadelphia-Milka brand illustrated in Fig. 3. Design A contains more Milka colors, but a larger Philadelphia logo than Design B. Do they manage to achieve parity? Image analytics can help address such dilemma by evaluation to what extent a proposed design represents the desired collaborative identity.

Source: FedEx (2020)

Fig. 2 Examples of the brand hierarchies of FedEx and Gillette

Fig. 3 Comparison of collaborative design packages with different mix of visual elements

Online Shopping Experience

Image analytics can help firms make better decisions with respect to physical store design and the visual elements of online shopping outlets.

The Role of Visuals in Online Product Display: How Does the Composition of Visual Elements, Objects, Size, Background, and Relative Location Impact the Search, Click, and Purchase Propensity?

When photographing a shirt for the online shop, the retailer has numerous options as to how to present the item: folded neatly on a flat surface, laying more carelessly, hanging against the wall, worn by a model, photographed against a solid color background, in an outdoor or indoor location, etc. All these factors influence consumer reactions and expectations from the product.

For example, Zhang et al. (2019) demonstrate that the photographic properties of homes displayed on Airbnb, such as diagonal dominance and rule of thirds, influence demand. Li et al. (2019a, b) show, on the same platform, that the order and layout in which the photos are presented also influence demand. Peng et al. (2020) show that the facial attractiveness of hosts on such rental platforms also influences the occupancy of these homes. More research is needed to explore a larger variety of situations, context, product categories, and consumer behaviors and understand their underlying mechanisms.

The Role of Visuals in Ecommerce Website Design: How Do the Visual Components of an Ecommerce Website Contribute to Profitability?

Designing an ecommerce website is a visual challenge. Designers must make decisions on the sizes and colors of the items that are displayed on the website (e.g., product images or buttons) and create a design that helps users to search for products, explore assortments, get inspired, and discover new products. At the same time, the items should be presented in a way that will match their brand identity. This raises several practical questions which can be answered by employing image analytics methods:

1. How do images change/affect consumers' propensity to keep searching on the website? How does this propensity change at different stages of the search process?
2. How to create more personalized website layouts? For example, Hauser et al. (2009, 2014) use a multi-armed bandit approach that balances exploration and exploitation to automatically match the look-and-feel of the website to customers' cognitive styles.

Consumer Perspective

Studies have shown that consumers use photos to express emotions and attitudes as well as to document their experiences (Van House et al. 2005). This usage has greatly increased with the abundance of mobile phone cameras, storage space, and sharing apps. While traditionally photos were taken on special occasions, people have moved to continuously documenting and sharing their daily routines.

Uncovering Consumer Attitudes: What Are the Hidden Consumer Traits and Attitudes That Can Be Revealed Through Images and Go Beyond the Standard Metrics?

The rich body of consumer-generated photos can be used by researchers to gain a deeper understanding of the consumer experience, to profile and characterize a wide range of experiences, and, in addition, to segment consumers based on dimensions that could not be revealed otherwise.

For example, photos taken by consumers (either posted on social media or collected directly through mobile diaries) can show what is the actual choice set that consumers face when walking around the supermarket; what their environment looks like when sitting in a restaurant; what food brands are served at the same meal; what is their personal style and how it relates to the brands they buy, etc.

Data: Consumer Vs. Firm Images

Once the research question has been formulated, constructing the appropriate data is the next key step. A good dataset for image analysis should satisfy the following criteria: First, it should capture the specific constructs being studied. In many cases this involves the combination of images and additional data. For example, photos that users post on restaurant reviews and the corresponding restaurant financial performance (Zhang and Luo 2019), or photos of Airbnb properties accompanied by property price, location, history, and host characteristics (Zhang et al. 2019, 2021; Li et al. 2019a, b).

Second, the dataset should be large enough to allow drawing insights. The state-of-the-art deep neural network models are trained on the ImageNet dataset, a freely available dataset which contains over 1.2 million images, organized into one thousand categories (http://image-net.org/). In marketing such big sizes are rare, but the datasets still have to contain thousands of images for researchers to be able to draw meaningful insights. Third, the dataset should contain minimal biases that could interfere with the main constructs. For example, using user-generated content to understand brand perception should be done carefully, since the sample is not controlled, and since users often post strategically to signal something about themselves (rather than about the brand) to their peers.

Below we describe the main data sources for image analytics in marketing, as summarized in Fig. 4. As illustrated in the figure, the data sources can be classified into consumer-generated images and firm-generated images.

Consumer-Generated Images

Consumer images include all the images created by consumers for different purposes: as a part of their own documentation of experiences and memories, for the purpose of sharing with other consumers, and for sharing with firms. They can be retrieved by researchers either through mining Internet and social media outlets, or directly elicited through surveys, diaries, panels, and collage making tasks.

Images from Internet and Social Media

Consumers increasingly share images on social media platforms such as Instagram or Facebook, and also on review platforms such as Yelp or Booking.com. For example, both Rietveld et al. (2020) and Liu et al. (2020) use Instagram images to monitor how brands are portrayed by consumers, and compare their perception to firm-generated visuals. Zhang and Luo (2019) use consumer-posted images on Yelp as a leading indicator of restaurant survival. They show that photos are more predictive of restaurant survival than reviews. Jalali and Papatla (2016) use brand images posted by users on Instagram to see how the color composition of the photo

Fig. 4 Sources for image data in Marketing

influences its click-through rate, when a photo is curated by the website of the brand. They found that click-rates are higher for photos that include higher proportions of green and lower proportions of red and cyan. They also found that photos with higher click-rates are characterized by higher chroma of red and blue. Klostermann et al. (2018) use brand-related Instagram posts to derive insights on how consumers think and feel about a brand (McDonald's) in different brand-related situations.

The appeal of Internet and social media as sources of consumer-generated images is that they are abundant, free, unaided, and cover a broad range of topics. However, for many relevant research questions, these data will not capture the constructs of interest. First, social media data are available for only certain categories and brands: while the brand Nike generates a lot of social media commentary, finding social media posts on other brands such as Colgate, is difficult. Second, it is difficult to control the characteristics of the content contributors. For example, users who have a stronger relationship with the brand (Labrecque 2014), or hold a particularly strong positive or negative opinion, may contribute more than those who have only mild opinions (Lovett et al. 2013). Finally, it is important to carefully interpret the content, since consumers' posts may serve a self-signaling or other purpose (Han et al. 2010).

Social media resources are also valuable in constructing the visual representation of concepts. In many cases the images are tagged and labeled by the users, and these tags can be used as a means of describing the content of the picture. This labeling goes beyond object detection. It can be used to interpret the visual representation of emotions (e.g., happiness), abstract characteristics (e.g., glamorous), and general concepts (e.g., big-city life). For example, several researchers have used Flickr to gather an annotated dataset of images (e.g., Dhar et al. 2011; McAuley and Leskovec 2012; Zhang et al. 2012; Dzyabura and Peres 2021). Flickr lends itself well to gathering an annotated image dataset, because it provides a search engine that returns the most relevant images for a keyword. The search is based on text labels provided by users, image content, and clickstream data (Stadlen 2015). An image ranked at the top for a particular query has often been validated by tens of thousands of users who clicked on the image, reflecting a large population consensus regarding a strong association between the image and the query term.

Directly Elicited Images

Another approach for retrieving visual data from consumers is direct elicitation, namely, asking respondents to provide, create, rate, or choose images according to certain criteria.

Elicitation can go in one of two directions – one is presenting the respondents with an image and asking them to indicate the properties of interest in this image. For example, does the image look fun (Liu et al. 2020), does a clothing item in an image has asymmetry (Dzyabura et al. 2020), does a logo look modern (Dew et al. 2019), etc. Typically, several human judges are required to rank each image. Management of such tasks can be done using commercially available software tools such as Amazon MTurk or Appen.

The other direction is to provide respondents with a concept (a brand, an emotion, a mood, etc.) and ask them to select or create the images that best represent this concept to them. Such a technique is used by Dzyabura and Peres (2021) who developed a brand visual elicitation platform that allows firms to ask consumers to create collages of images that they associate with a brand. Collage making is a projective technique that has long been used for qualitative research by psychologists (Koll et al. 2010) and brand researchers (Zaltman and Coulter 1995; Zaltman and Zaltman 2008). Typically, participants select images representing the concept in focus, and then explain to the moderator why they chose these images. Dzyabura and Peres (2021) have used image analytics to transform this task into a quantitative market research method. Using online data collection, image processing, and machine learning techniques, collage making now allows researchers to retrieve a large number of images for any concept of interest, over a large number of respondents. Figure 5 describes examples of collages (with some verbal descriptions) created using this method for the brand Starbucks.

Another useful method to directly elicit visuals from consumers is mobile diaries. Mobile diaries are a trending tool to collect repeated self-reports about experiences. They have been used as a research tool in variety of domains including psychology, geography, health, medicine (e.g., Hektner et al. 2007; Heinonen et al. 2012; Hensel et al. 2012; Hofmann and Patel 2015), marketing practice, and recently also by academic researchers (Lovett and Peres 2018). In mobile diary visual studies, respondents are usually asked to take photos of certain experiences – for example, photograph what they see on the shelf, windows of

Fig. 5 Examples for four collages for the brand Starbucks, created by four different respondents, with verbal descriptions. (Source: Dzyabura and Peres (2021))

stores they stop by, or the content of their refrigerator. These data can be later analyzed to create a data-driven representation of consumer stimuli, choice set, environment, and experience.

Note that data sources can be combined. For example, directly elicited data can be used to validate conclusions derived from social media, to provide insights on the underlying mechanisms, or complement the social media-generated data with interpretable features. For example, Hartmann et al. (2021) complement data from Twitter and Instagram with results from a lab experiment to show that the mechanism behind higher click-through rates of brand selfies (images of consumers holding a branded product, but face not showed in the frame) is that brand selfies induce more self-related thoughts. Peng et al. (2020) use surveys to elaborate on the mechanism behind the U-shaped relationship between facial attractiveness of the seller and product sales.

Firm-Generated Images

Firms continuously create visuals as part of their marketing efforts. Data originating from firms come in different formats such as visual brand elements (logo, colors, fonts etc.), product images on online stores, images used in advertising, and the firm's social media outlets. All these provide rich data for visual research. Unlike consumer-generated images, firm-generated images are typically curated and created by professional teams to meet the firm positioning goals. Thus, they constitute a visual representation of the firm strategy and can be used to study market structure and competitive landscape. The reactions to these images by consumers can, in turn, be used to study consumer response to various marketing actions. We list below several main sources for firm-generated data.

Product Images on Retail Websites

Retail websites are a great source for product images, since they contain many products from various vendors. The images are typically of good quality, focused on the product itself, and often capture the product from various angles. Many retail sites also require standardization of the images. For example, the shoe retail website Zappos.com photographs all shoes in the same way: from seven angles, against a solid white background. The uniformity makes it easier for image processing algorithms to focus on the product image. Retail sites typically provide other relevant product information such as price, materials, size, manufacturer, and brand, which can complement the analysis.

The challenge with using image data from retail websites is that they often lack data on many dependent variables of interest, such as clicks, likes, purchases, profitability, product returns, and repeat purchase rates. Answering research questions regarding these variables requires collaboration with the firm. For example, Dzyabura et al. (2020) used product images from an apparel retailer's online shop and collaborate with the firm to obtain information on the corresponding products' online and offline purchases and product return rates. They found that incorporating the image in the prediction model in addition to the nonvisual attributes (e.g., price, category, season, size) greatly improved its accuracy.

Some multi-vendor retail platforms such as Alibaba, eBay, Airbnb, and Amazon provide consumer reviews and information about the product popularity, which can serve as a proxy for some of these variables. Zhang et al. (2021), for example, use property images posted by Airbnb hosts and combine it with the occupancy rate of the property.

Images on the Firm Social Media Pages

The social media pages of firms are also a rich source of image data. They contain, in addition to the products themselves, other components of the firm's visual representation – endorsers, users and usage scenarios, print and video ads, brand elements, sceneries, locations, activities, and all the visuals curated by the firms to create and enhance its brand associations. These data can be used to study the competitive landscape by identifying differences and similarities between the visual representation of competing brands, as well as between the brand self-representation and consumer perceptions of the firm. Unlike the retail sites, social media outlets also contain more dependent variables, such as consumer likes, shares, reactions, and comments. For example, Li and Xie (2020) used photos of major airlines and sport utility vehicle brands collected from Twitter and Instagram, and measured the engagement they created through retweets and likes. One of their findings is that the presence of a human face and the fit between the image and the textual content of the post can induce higher user engagement on Twitter but not on Instagram.

The Firm Brand Communications

Researchers can use visual elements of brands of interest in order to explore questions related to brand associations and brand image. This often requires the research team to assemble their own dataset. For example, Dew et al. (2019) assembled a dataset consisting of logos, textual description of firms, industry labels, and brand personality rating of 706 major brands. Then they used image analytics to explore the visual elements of logos they assembled and show how they can be used to create new brand identities and spark ideation.

Advertising Databases

Advertising visuals are continuously being generated by firms, displayed in social media outlets, websites, magazines, TV channels, and billboards. Interestingly, central repositories of advertising images are hard to find. Studies on advertising design effectiveness are mostly behavioral (Wedel and Pieters 2008) and use specific manipulations to test theories. A notable exception is the paper of Pieters et al. (2007), who used data from advertisements by several chains of grocery retailers in the Netherlands to measure the relative importance of the pictorial content in the ad in getting consumer attention.

Large-scale advertising image data across multiple firms, if assembled, could be used to study aspects of parity and differentiation between similar offerings and explore how the competitive landscape is reflected in the visual space. Combined with brand perception, consumer responses, and advertising expenditure, these data can be used to study advertising effectiveness and provide guidance for the optimal design for an ad. Such data repositories are already available in many domains such as fashion (Xiao et al. 2017), autonomous driving (Caesar et al. 2020), and medical imaging. A common general repository is ImageNet, a public dataset of 1.2 million images labeled by humans, which was used to train many state-of-the-art models (e.g., Krizhevsky et al. 2017). A joint data collection effort in advertising could lead to many new and impactful insights on the visual aspects of advertisements.

Methods

Marketing researchers who study visual data have an unprecedented opportunity of access to state-of-the-art methods and analysis techniques. These methods are rapidly improving due to the increased computational power and ongoing efforts of the machine-learning community to broaden the scope of the analysis tools and make them publicly available and user-friendly. An image analytic process is typically composed of the four stages: feature extraction, model training, model evaluation and validation, and model application to the marketing problem.

Feature Extraction

The first step of the image analytics process is determining what feature space to work in. A key challenge of working with images is that the raw input elements – the pixels that make up the images – are not suitable features. A single pixel in isolation does not lend itself to meaningful interpretation. Compared to text, for example, this challenge is particularly pronounced. In text, the basic unit of analysis is words, which carry a meaning, a positive or negative valence, and can be grouped by topic. Pixels, on the other hand, have none of these properties. Therefore, a critical step in any modeling of image data is generating features which will provide a meaningful representation of the images.

There are multiple approaches to feature generation. One is predefined feature extraction. Researchers have developed a variety of predefined features. Perhaps the simplest are **color** histograms, which capture the distribution of the color composition of the image. Such histograms are created by discretizing the colors in the image into bins, based on a color space, and counting the number of image pixels in each bin. The most common color spaces are RGB (red, green, blue) and HSV (hue, saturation, value). Another dimension of interest is **shape**, where the features are line directions, corners, and curves. A third common property is **texture** – defining the repeating patterns in the image, such as line and color intensity. Texture is most commonly measured by a Gabor filter, which detects repeating frequencies of color in certain parts of the image. For videos, Li et al. (2019b) add a dynamic component by defining a measure of visual variation, calculated by decomposing a video into a number of static frames and then computing the visual distance between consecutive frames.

The role of the feature extraction step has been revolutionized with the development of deep neural networks (NN). In an NN, the feature selection and the model training are done simultaneously, so the network automatically extracts the features that are optimal for the specific research problem. For example, it would extract different features for determining whether there is a pedestrian or a traffic light in an image, versus determining whether an image appears fun or serious. A deep NN does such simultaneous training by applying several "layers" of nonlinear transformations on the raw pixel data. The outputs of each transformation serve as the features, or predictor variables, for the next layer. Through multiple layers of such transformations, the network extracts higher- and higher-level representations of the data, allowing the final layer to easily classify the data. For example, lower layers of a deep-learning model may extract edges and textures, whereas higher layers detect motifs, object parts, and complete objects (Goodfellow et al. 2016). The final layer maps the resulting features onto the target variables with a classification function.

There are many neural network architectures that are used in different applications that differ in the types of functions captured by their nodes, their depth, data flow, etc. – together, these make up the network architecture. The networks that work best for image analytics problems are Convolutional Neural Networks, or ConvNets. ConvNets are characterized by the first several layers of the network being *convolutional layers*: each neuron applies a particular transformation to a small part of the image. Rather than applying a transformation to the entire image, it processes small "batches" of the image separately, to detect shapes and edges in different parts of the image. Two commonly used ConvNet architectures are ResNet and VGG19.

Feature extraction using deep NN almost always results in higher predictive accuracy than human-coded features. However, it has two major caveats. One is that the features are not interpretable – they are complex nonlinear transformations of pixels, which have no meaning on their own. While this is not a disadvantage if the main task is prediction, it is, if interpretable insights are desired. For example, interpretability is important if the goal is to understand what people associate with a brand (Klostermann et al. 2018; Dzyabura and Peres 2021), what kind of image content gets most engagement on social media (Li and Xie 2020), to give recommendations for photographing a home for rent on Airbnb (Zhang et al. 2019), or to create a promotional video for a project in a crowd funding platform (Li et al. 2019b). In such cases, the modeling must be done on interpretable features. One way to obtain them is by using tagging software or a tagged dataset from sources such as Flickr, in order to identify the objects, activities, sceneries, and themes presented in the image. Thus, the image is described by a set of words or tags, which serve as the features, and the image analysis task is transformed into a text analysis task. This opens a wide range of options for the analysis: using word embeddings, various dictionaries such as LIWC, sentiment analysis techniques, and topic modeling (chapter ▶ "Automated Text Analysis").

The other caveat is that training a deep neural network from scratch is extremely challenging: it requires a very large annotated dataset, massive memory and computational power, and complex engineering. Additionally, a lot of modeling choices, such as the number, type, and order of layers, how much regularization to use, and learning rate, are made through trial and error. To simplify the training stage, most deep learning applications in marketing use *transfer learning*: rather than designing and training a new neural network for every task, they use a network that has already been trained by someone else for a different purpose. The reasoning behind it is that knowledge gained from performing one task can be used to perform another. For example, knowledge gained from recognizing image aesthetics could be applied to forecast product demand or recognize brand perceptual attributes (Bengio et al. 2011; Bengio 2012).

The transfer can be done either by taking the final layers of the trained network as is, or by fine tuning the trained NN. Dzyabura et al. (2020) took the first approach – they used the second-to-last pre-output of ResNet, which is trained on the ImageNet data, as features in a random forest model to predict the return rates of clothing items.

The fine tuning approach does train the NN, but instead of initializing the model parameters with random numbers, the model is initialized with parameters learned from another NN. The idea is similar to using an informed prior in Bayesian estimation. Relative to training the model from scratch, fine tuning significantly increases model performance and avoids overfitting (Donahue et al. 2014; Girshick et al. 2014; Yosinski et al. 2014). Li et al. (2019a, b) employ fine tuning by using ResNet50 to train their model and learn picture quality and room type (e.g., bedroom, bathroom) for images from Airbnb postings. The resulting features are used to predict occupancy rates of the properties. Interestingly, Zhang et al. (2019) also predict image quality on Airbnb, but they use a different pretrained model, VGG16 (Simonyan and Zisserman 2015), also pretrained on ImageNet. The paper uses the results to explain the decision-making process of the hosts who use pictures of lower quality even when a high-quality option is free and available.

Model Training

Regardless of what approach was chosen for feature extraction, the resulting feature space for an image problem will be very large, often larger than the number of observations. Standard statistical methods which assume linear models and estimate their coefficients cannot be applied. The large number of coefficients makes it impossible to identify every single coefficient without bias. Therefore, researchers apply machine learning methods which are tailored for working in very large feature spaces.

Many image analytics problems can be formulated as a *supervised classification task* – determining whether an image belongs to one or multiple predefined categories or classes. For example, in Liu et al. (2020), image classification is used to determine whether an image exhibits a brand perceptual attribute: does the image look fun? rugged healthy? glamorous? A classifier is trained on an annotated dataset of images labeled with the desired classes, that is, images that are known to belong or not to belong to the classes (e.g., images which are glamorous and not glamorous). As explained in "Product Design," the annotated datasets can be taken from publicly available sources, company data, or collected by the researchers. After training, the classifier can assign a class to a new, unlabeled image.

Some research problems do not involve classifying images into predefined categories. Instead, the researcher is looking to identify patterns in the data – such as recurring objects, colors, shapes, and themes. This is most commonly done by representing the images in a feature space (either using predefined features or with deep neural networks), and then using *unsupervised methods* (e.g., clustering using K-means or nearest neighbors) to group them together (Dew et al. 2019; Peng et al. 2020; chapter ▶ "Cluster Analysis in Marketing Research"). If the feature extraction is based on tagging, then one could use unsupervised methods for text analysis – such as topic modeling (Dew et al. 2019; Nanne et al. 2020; Peng et al. 2020). In some cases, the image analytic task aims at creating novel combinations of existing patterns, for example – to create new designs of the product, using generative models (Burnap et al. 2019), or predicting "design gaps" in a certain market (Burnap and Hauser 2018).

Model Evaluation and Validation

Once the model has been trained, it is important to evaluate and validate it. Evaluation establishes its performance and validation ensures that the output obtained from the images measures the construct of interest.

A proper evaluation is done by testing the model performance on a different sample than the one it was trained on. In most machine learning algorithms, a portion of the sample is held out and used to test the model. This out-of-sample test is important since the large size of the feature space can easily lead to overfitting. This is only true for supervised learning. For unsupervised learning, model accuracy is hard to evaluate, because there is no specific independent target variable.

Validation depends greatly on the nature of the task. Basically, validation ensures that the model was successful in capturing the construct it intended to measure. For example, if the analysis was done to assess how happy a face is, the results should be validated by testing that faces that were identified as happy are indeed perceived as happy by people. Validation is particularly challenging and particularly important in the unsupervised case. Since predictive accuracy cannot be shown, how can one prove that one clustering is better than another clustering, or that the identified patterns are true? For example, Dzyabura and Peres (2021), used images to extract brand associations from collages of images created by users. They used two layers of validation to demonstrate that the extracted associations are the correct ones: users were first asked to match extracted associations to a collage, and second, to guess the brand based on the associations. Dew et al. (2019) built a model to predict the visual features of a logo based on the verbal descriptions of the brand from the company website, and validated it by taking the brand ShakeShack, using the model to predict the visual elements of its logo and comparing it against the existing logo. Peng et al. (2020) studied face attractiveness and whether it can predict product sales in ecommerce platforms. After extracting facial features, they validated the model using a group of coders that were asked to rank the attractiveness of the faces. In Zhang and Luo (2019), user-posted images were used to predict survival of restaurants. In such tasks, when looking at the examples the algorithm misclassified, one can notice which types of restaurant the classifier fails, and add information accordingly. In addition, by calculating the proportion of mistakes of each type, we can have a better understanding of the precision rate that is possible.

Model Application

The final step of the analysis is applying the model to the research problem, whether it be computing a brand metric (Liu et al. 2020), forecasting demand (Peng et al. 2020), or optimizing the visual communication (Li and Xie 2020; Li et al. 2019b). This stage is important, since in marketing, clustering or classifying images is rarely the end goal. The images are a manifestation of a more fundamental underlying construct, and their analysis is typically an intermediate step in deriving meaningful insights with respect to this construct and its relationship with perceptual, behavioral, and economic variables.

Integrating It All Together

Image analytics could very easily go wrong. The researcher is faced with numerous data sources, code packages, constantly improving methods, and pre-trained models. All of these open a broad range of research opportunities, yet they often create confusion as to the right choice of the model components. Specifically, the researcher has to carefully match the research problem, data, and method. This is a challenging task: the data, although very rich, might not contain the variables of interest; the model might be good in classifying images but incapable of yielding interpretable insights; the data can suffer from various biases and confounds, such as user strategic posting and self-signaling. Many failures in image analytics tasks are caused by incorrect matching between the various components, leading to none, or even worse – misleading insights.

To ensure an optimal match between the research question, data, and method in order to produce the highest quality analytics with meaningful insights, the researcher should ask herself two questions: first, whether or not there is a single dependent variable that is the crux of the research question. Such a variable could be demand (Zhang et al. 2019, 2021), crowdfunding success (Li et al. 2019b; Peng et al. 2020), business survival (Zhang and Luo 2019), ad recall (Rosbergen et al. 1997), or product return rates (Dzyabura et al. 2020). Second, whether interpretability of the features is important for the task. That is, do the desired insights involve interpretation of specific elements of the image? The answers to these questions determine the appropriate methods and data type. They can be described in the following 2×2 matrix presented in Fig. 6.

Most computer vision tasks fall into the ***top right quadrant*** of the matrix: there is a specific target variable of interest and interpretation of the features is not necessary. This is the quadrant where most engineering computer vision problems belong. A typical computer vision task is to identify, for instance for a self-driving car, whether an image contains a pedestrian or a traffic light. A good algorithm for such problems is engineered to detect the objects of interest with a low probability of error. It does not need to be able to say what about the picture forms a pedestrian. The set of methods in this quadrant are by definition supervised, and are typically based on deep neural networks.

Thanks to the rapid growth and development of the computer vision field, research questions in marketing that fall into this quadrant have a rich and constantly improving set of methods to choose from. The choice of method depends on the nature of the problem. Nanne et al. (2020) compared different computer vision algorithms to monitor user-generated content, and found that they have different strengths: Google Cloud Vision is more accurate in object detection, whereas Clarifai provides more useful labels to interpret the portrayal of a brand and YOLOV2 did not prove to be useful to analyze visual brand-related UGC. This should be taken into account when conducting the analysis, and one might need to use several methods and assess their performance for the specific research problem.

In order to apply these methods, the researcher needs to obtain good data from a reliable source. The image data must be annotated with the target variable and it must be very large: contain thousands of annotated images in the training set. In marketing, this is often challenging to accomplish. Most brands, for example, do not

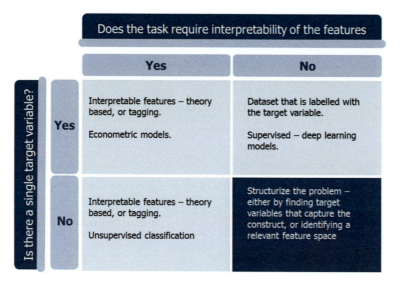

Fig. 6 A classification matrix for combining data, features, and image analytic model

produce thousands of images. To get a large enough dataset, one may need to pool data across multiple brands or over time, risking introducing noise to the data.

Unlike engineering, many marketing questions do involve some sort of interpretation of the image characteristics and their relationship with the target variable. For example, in the case of forecasting demand based on product images, one likely wants to know what it is about the product or the way it was photographed that leads to high or low demand. Such cases belong to the *top left quadrant*. In this quadrant, one faces a tradeoff, because the most accurate predictive models are not based on interpretable features. Once one introduces a constraint on the types of features, predictive accuracy will be compromised.

One way in which interpretable features can be generated is using image tagging software which extracts the image content and produces a list of the objects, sceneries, activities, moods, and other themes in the image (Klostermann et al. 2018; Rietveld et al. 2020; Nanne et al. 2020). Another way is to apply domain expertise to identify the relevant features. In photography, these may be diagonal dominance and rule of thirds (Zhang et al. 2019); in apparel, these may be types of prints, graphics, collar type, sleeve length, symmetry or metallic details (Vilnai-Yavetz and Tifferet 2015). These can be extracted using either machine learning classifiers or using human judges. Once the features were extracted, one can use econometric methods, such as regression, to obtain insights as to how they relate to the target variable.

If both interpretable insights and accurate predictions are important, the analysis should include both: a deep learning model trained to optimize the features and the model for maximum predictive accuracy, and regression analyses over interpretable features. For example, Dzyabura et al. (2020) use deep learned features to predict the return rate of a product based on its image. Then, they have four independent judges manually label the images with respect to industry standard design elements such as symmetry, pattern (solid, floral, striped, geometric/abstract), and additional details (text, metallic/sequin, graphic, lace). The authors then analyze which of these are associated with higher return rates in a regression.

The *bottom left quadrant* comprises situations in which there are no dependent variables of interest. Instead, we ask an open-ended question such as – how is a brand perceived by consumers? How do consumers use the product? What visual features of logos are associated with what brand perceptions?

These questions often require the combined use of interpretable features with unsupervised learning algorithms. The features create a meaningful and managerially relevant space, into which all the relevant observations can be mapped. The unsupervised algorithms, in turn, detect patterns and identify data-driven classifications in this space. For example, Dew et al. (2019) use features taken from theories of logo semantics to form a "visual dictionary" that describes logos in a way that is meaningful to designers (e.g., the amount of white space, corners, and edges). They then use a probabilistic modeling framework to flexibly capture the linkages between the brand descriptions, logo features, industry labels, and brand personality metrics. Dzyabura and Peres (2021) used tagging to identify image content, and then use unsupervised topic modeling to reveal latent topics. Klostermann et al. (2018) tag objects and situations using object detection software, and then employ unsupervised clustering algorithms to form associative networks connecting image content to consumer sentiment. The resulting map of associations is informative for brand management, communications, and monitoring the response of consumers to new products and features.

Finally, questions that belong to the ***bottom right quadrant*** do not have a specific target variable and do not require interpretability of the features. This quadrant is challenging since it applies structure neither to the features nor to the dependent variable. In order to impose structure on these problems one might consult with domain experts to identify either some relevant dependent variables that are of interest to managers or a set of features that represent the space in a meaningful way.

Conclusion

In the past two decades, major technological advances and the popularity of digital platforms made taking and sharing images a crucial part of consumers' daily lives. In addition to the abundance of visual data, image processing tools and advances in modeling techniques created unprecedented opportunities to obtain new perspectives on important marketing questions. We are now able to study new phenomena, investigate the relationship between consumers and firms and obtain insights that would have been difficult or impossible to obtain otherwise.

Using image analytics to generate insights is not trivial though. Researchers are faced with different sources of data, various analysis techniques, and continuously improving methods. In order to benefit from implementing image analytics in solving relevant marketing problems, matching a good research question with the right visual data and appropriate method comes with many challenges. However, once the researcher is able to surmount these challenges, many marketing areas can benefit from image analytics to gain new insights. In the area of **Product Design**, researchers can for example explore how to characterize designs above and beyond their specific elements. Moreover, they can use image analytics to quantify the value of designs by incorporating product images in traditional consumer demand models. In the area of **Advertising**, image analytics can allow for a holistic quantitative approach to selecting, adjusting, and optimizing the visual composition of print and video advertisements. In **Branding**, image analytics opens new perspectives for firms to strategically position their brands, manage their brand portfolio, and identify new collaborations. Image analytics can also help firms make well-grounded decisions to enhance consumers' **Online Shopping Experience** by identifying the role of visuals in ecommerce websites for example. Finally, from a **Consumer Perspective**, image analytics has the potential to reveal through images more about consumers than we knew so far. For example, firms can understand how consumers see brands, how they think about consumption, and how they perceive and evaluate their environments.

Cross-References

▶ Automated Text Analysis
▶ Cluster Analysis in Marketing Research

References

Amit, E., Algom, D., & Trope, Y. (2009). Distance-dependent processing of pictures and words. *Journal of Experimental Psychology: General, 138*(3), 400.

Ang, S. H., Lee, Y. H., & Leong, S. M. (2007). The ad creativity cube: Conceptualization and initial validation. *Journal of the Academy of Marketing Science, 35*(2), 220–232.

Bengio, Y. (2012). Deep learning of representations for unsupervised and transfer learning. In I. Guyon, G. Dror, V. Lemaire, G. Taylor, & D. Silver (Eds.), *Proceedings o the ICML workshop unsupervised transfer learn* (pp. 17–36). Bellevue.

Bengio, Y., Bergeron, A., Boulanger-Lewandowski, N., Breuel, T., Chherawala, Y., Cisse, M., & Erhan, D. (2011). Deep learners benefit more from out-of-distribution examples. In G. Gordon, D. Dunson, & D. Miroslav (Eds.), *Proceedings of the 14th international conference artificial intelligence statist* (pp. 164–172). Fort Lauderdale, FL.

Bloch, P. H. (1995). Seeking the ideal form: Product design and consumer response. *Journal of Marketing, 59*(3), 16–29.

Burnap, A., & Hauser, J. (2018). Predicting "design gaps" in the market: Deep consumer choice models under probabilistic design constraints. *arXiv preprint arXiv*, 1812.11067.

Burnap A., Hauser, J., & Timoshenko A. (2019). *Design and evaluation of product aesthetics: A human-machine hybrid approach*. Available at SSRN 3421771.

Caesar, H., Bankiti, V., Lang, A. H., Vora, S., Liong, V. E., Xu, Q., Krishnan, A., Pan, Y., Baldan, G., & Beijbom, O. (2020). NuScenes: A multimodal dataset for autonomous driving. In *Proceedings of the IEEE/CVF conference on computer vision and pattern recognition* (pp. 11621–11631).

Chan, T. H., Mihm, J., & Sosa, M. E. (2018). On styles in product design: An analysis of US design patents. *Management Science, 64*(3), 1230–1249.

Cho, H., Schwarz, N., & Song, H. (2008). Images and preferences: A feelings-as-information analysis. In M. Wedel & R. Pieters (Eds.), *Visual marketing: From attention to action* (pp. 259–276). New York: Lawrence Erlbaum Associates.

Crilly, N., Moultrie, J., & Clarkson, P. J. (2004). Seeing things: Consumer response to the visual domain in product design. *Design Studies, 25*(6), 547–577.

Dew, R., Ansari, A., & Toubia, O. (2019). *Letting logos speak: Leveraging multiview representation learning for data-driven logo design*. Available at SSRN 3406857.

Dhar, S., Ordonez, V., & Berg, T. L. (2011, June). High level describable attributes for predicting aesthetics and interestingness. In *CVPR 2011* (pp. 1657–1664). IEEE.

Donahue, J., Jia, Y., Vinyals, O., Hoffman, J., Zhang, N., Tzeng, E., & Darrell, T. (2014, January). Decaf: A deep convolutional activation feature for generic visual recognition. In *International conference on machine learning* (pp. 647–655).

Dzyabura, D., & Peres, R. (2021). Visual elicitation of brand perception. *Journal of Marketing*, forthcoming.

Dzyabura, D., El Kihal, S., Ibragimov, M., & Hauser J. (2020). *Leveraging the power of images in managing product return rates*. Available at SSRN 3209307.

Eisenman, M., Frenkel, M., & Wasserman, V. (2016). Toward a theory of effective aesthetic communication. In *Academy of management proceedings* (Vol. 2016, p. 12822). Briarcliff Manor: Academy of Management.

Girshick, R., Donahue, J., Darrell, T., & Malik, J. (2014). Rich feature hierarchies for accurate object detection and semantic segmentation. In *Proceedings of the IEEE conference on computer vision and pattern recognition* (pp. 580–587).

Goodfellow, I., Bengio, Y., Courville, A., & Bengio, Y. (2016). *Deep learning* (Vol. 1, No. 2). Cambridge: MIT Press.

Gorn, G. J., Chattopadhyay, A., Yi, T., & Dahl, D. W. (1997). Effects of color as an executional cue in advertising: They're in the shade. *Management Science, 43*(10), 1387–1400.

Greenleaf, E., & Raghubir, P. (2008). Geometry in the marketplace. In M. Wedel & R. Pieters (Eds.), *Visual marketing: From attention to action* (pp. 113–143). New York: Lawrence Erlbaum Associates.

Han, Y. J., Nunes, J. C., & Drèze, X. (2010). Signaling status with luxury goods: The role of brand prominence. *Journal of Marketing, 74*(4), 15–30.

Hartmann, J., Heitmann, M., Schamp, C., & Netzer, O. (2021) The Power of brand selfies. *Journal of Marketing Research, 58*(6), 1159–1177. https://doi.org/10.1177/00222437211037258

Hauser, J. R., Urban, G. L., Liberali, G., & Braun, M. (2009). Website morphing. *Marketing Science, 28*(2), 202–223.

Hauser, J. R., Liberali, G., & Urban, G. L. (2014). Website morphing 2.0: Switching costs, partial exposure, random exit, and when to morph. *Management Science, 60*(6), 1594–1616.

Heinonen, R., Luoto, R., Lindfors, P., & Nygård, C. H. (2012). Usability and feasibility of mobile phone diaries in an experimental physical exercise study. *Telemedicine and e-Health, 18*(2), 115–119.

Hektner, J. M., Schmidt, J. A., & Csikszentmihalyi, M. (2007). *Experience sampling method: Measuring the quality of everyday life*. Thousand Oaks: Sage Publications, Inc.

Hensel, D. J., Fortenberry, J. D., Harezlak, J., & Craig, D. (2012). The feasibility of cell phone based electronic diaries for STI/HIV research. *BMC Medical Research Methodology, 12*(75), 1–12.

Hofmann, W., & Patel, P. V. (2015). Survey signal a convenient solution for experience sampling research using participants' own smartphones. *Social Science Computer Review, 33*(2), 235–253.

Jalali, N. Y., & Papatla, P. (2016). The palette that stands out: Color compositions of online curated visual UGC that attracts higher consumer interaction. *Quantitative Marketing and Economics, 14*(4), 353–384.

Janiszewski, C. (1998). The influence of display characteristics on visual exploratory search behavior. *Journal of Consumer Research, 25*(3), 290–301.

John, D. R., Loken, B., Kim, K., & Monga, A. B. (2006). Brand concept maps: A methodology for identifying brand association networks. *Journal of Marketing Research, 43*(4), 549–563.

Keller, K. L. (2003). Brand synthesis: The multidimensionality of brand knowledge. *Journal of Consumer Research, 29*(4), 595–600.

Kireyev, P., Timoshenko, A., & Yang, C. L. (2020). *Scaling human effort in idea screening and content evaluation*. INSEAD Working Paper No. 2020/42/MKT, HEC Paris Research Paper No. MKG-2020-1384, Available at SSRN: https://ssrn.com/abstract=3685882 or https://doi.org/10.2139/ssrn.3685882

Klostermann, J., Plumeyer, A., Böger, D., & Decker, R. (2018). Extracting brand information from social networks: Integrating image, text, and social tagging data. *International Journal of Research in Marketing, 35*(4), 538–556.

Koll, O., Von Wallpach, S., & Kreuzer, M. (2010). Multi-method research on consumer–brand associations: Comparing free associations, storytelling, and collages. *Psychology & Marketing, 27*(6), 584–602.

Krizhevsky, A., Sutskever, I., & Hinton, G. E. (2017). Imagenet classification with deep convolutional neural networks. *Communications of the ACM, 60*(6), 84–90.

Labrecque, L. I. (2014). Fostering consumer–brand relationships in social media environments: The role of Parasocial interaction. *Journal of Interactive Marketing, 28*(2), 134–148.

Lehnert, K., Till, B. D., & Ospina, J. M. (2014). Advertising creativity: The role of divergence versus meaningfulness. *Journal of Advertising, 43*(3), 274–285.

Li, Y., & Xie, Y. (2020). Is a picture worth a thousand words? An empirical study of image content and social media engagement. *Journal of Marketing Research, 57*(1), 1–19.

Li, H., Simchi-Levi, D., Wu, M. X., & Zhu, W. (2019a). *Estimating and exploiting the impact of photo layout in sharing economy.* Available at SSRN.

Li, X., Shi, M., & Wang, X. S. (2019b). Video mining: Measuring visual information using automatic methods. *International Journal of Research in Marketing, 36*(2), 216–231.

Liu, X., Burns, A. C., & Hou, Y. (2017). An investigation of brand-related user-generated content on Twitter. *Journal of Advertising, 46*(2), 236–247.

Liu, L., Dzyabura, D., & Mizik, N. (2020). Visual listening in: Extracting brand image portrayed on social media. *Marketing Science, 39*(4), 669–686.

Lovett, M. J., & Peres, R. (2018). Mobile diaries – Benchmark against metered measurements: An empirical investigation. *International Journal of Research in Marketing, 35*(2), 224–241.

Lovett, M. J., Peres, R., & Shachar, R. (2013). On brands and word of mouth. *Journal of Marketing Research, 50*(4), 427–444.

MacInnis, D. J., & Price, L. L. (1987). The role of imagery in information processing: Review and extensions. *Journal of Consumer Research, 13*(4), 473–491.

McAuley, J., & Leskovec, J. (2012, October). Image labeling on a network: Using social-network metadata for image classification. In *European conference on computer vision* (pp. 828–841). Berlin/Heidelberg: Springer.

McQuarrie, E. F. (2008). Differentiating the pictorial element in advertising – A rhetorical perspective. In M. Wedel & R. Pieters (Eds.), *Visual marketing: From attention to action* (pp. 91–112). New York: Psychology Press.

Meyers-Levy, J., & Zhu, R. (2008). Perhaps the store made you purchase it: Toward an understanding of structural aspects of indoor shopping environment. In M. Wedel & R. Pieters (Eds.), *Visual marketing: From attention to action* (pp. 193–224). New York: Psychology Press.

Nanne, A. J., Antheunis, M. L., van der Lee, C. G., Postma, E. O., Wubben, S., & van Noort, G. (2020). The use of computer vision to analyze brand-related user generated image content. *Journal of Interactive Marketing, 50*, 156–167.

Orsborn, S., Cagan, J., & Boatwright, P. (2009). Quantifying aesthetic form preference in a utility function. *Journal of Mechanical Design, 131*(6), 061001.

Pavlov, E., & Mizik, N. (2019). *Increasing consumer engagement with firm-generated social media content: The role of images and words.* Working Paper, University of Washington.

Peng, L., Cui, G., Chung, Y., & Zheng, W. (2020). The faces of success: Beauty and ugliness premiums in e-commerce platforms. *Journal of Marketing, 84*(4), 67–85.

Peracchio, L. A., & Meyers-Levy, J. (1994). How ambiguous cropped objects in ad photos can affect product evaluations. *Journal of Consumer Research, 21*(1), 190–204.

Peracchio, L. A., & Meyers-Levy, J. (2005). Using stylistic properties of ad pictures to communicate with consumers. *Journal of Consumer Research, 32*(1), 29–40.

Pieters, R., & Wedel, M. (2004). Attention capture and transfer in advertising: Brand, pictorial, and text-size effects. *Journal of Marketing, 68*(2), 36–50.

Pieters, R., Wedel, M., & Zhang, J. (2007). Optimal feature advertising design under competitive clutter. *Management Science, 53*(11), 1815–1828.

Radach, R., Lemmer, S., Vorstius, C., Heller, D., & Radach, K. (2003). Eye movements in the processing of print advertisements. In R. Radach & H. Deubel (Eds.), *The mind's eye* (pp. 609–632). Amsterdam: Elsevier Science Publishers.

Raghubir, P., & Greenleaf, E. A. (2006). Ratios in proportion: What should the shape of the package be? *Journal of Marketing, 70*(2), 95–107.

Reavey, P. (Ed.). (2012). *Visual methods in psychology: Using and interpreting images in qualitative research.* Routledge. London.

Rietveld, R., van Dolen, W., Mazloom, M., & Worring, M. (2020). What you feel, is what you like influence of message appeals on customer engagement on Instagram. *Journal of Interactive Marketing, 49*, 20–53.

Rosbergen, E., Pieters, R., & Wedel, M. (1997). Visual attention to advertising: A segment-level analysis. *Journal of Consumer Research, 24*(3), 305–314.

Rubera, G. (2015). Design innovativeness and product sales' evolution. *Marketing Science, 34*(1), 98–115.

Sheinin, D. A., Varki, S., & Ashley, C. (2011). The differential effect of ad novelty and message usefulness on brand judgments. *Journal of Advertising, 40*(3), 5–18.

Simonyan, K., & Zisserman, A. (2015). Very deep convolutional networks for large-scale image recognition. In Proceedings of *International Conference on Learning Representations (ICLR)*. Available at https://arxiv.org/abs/1409.1556

Smith, R. E., MacKenzie, S. B., Yang, X., Buchholz, L. M., & Darley, W. K. (2007). Modeling the determinants and effects of creativity in advertising. *Marketing Science, 26*(6), 819–833.

Stadlen, A. (2015). *Find every photo with Flickr's new unified search experience*. Available at https://blog.flickr.net/en/2015/05/07/flickr-unified-search/

Toubia, O., & Netzer, O. (2017). Idea generation, creativity, and prototypicality. *Marketing Science, 36*(1), 1–20.

Van House, N., Davis, M., Ames, M., Finn, M., & Viswanathan, V. (2005). The uses of personal networked digital imaging: An empirical study of cameraphone photos and sharing. In *CHI'05 extended abstracts on human factors in computing systems* (pp. 1853–1856). ACM.

Venngage. (2020). *14 Visual content marketing statistics to know for 2020*. Available at https://venngage.com/blog/visual-content-marketing-statistics/

Vilnai-Yavetz, I., & Tifferet, S. (2015). A picture is worth a thousand words: Segmenting consumers by Facebook profile images. *Journal of Interactive Marketing, 32*, 53–69.

Wedel, M., & Pieters, R. (2000). Eye fixations on advertisements and memory for brands: A model and findings. *Marketing Science, 19*(4), 297–312.

Wedel, M., & Pieters, R. (2008). A review of eye-tracking research in marketing. *Review of Marketing Research, 4*(2008), 123–147.

Wedel, M., & Pieters, R. (2014). *Looking at vision* (p. 2014). Abingdon: Routledge.

Xiao, H., Rasul, K., & Vollgraf, R. (2017). Fashion-MNIST: A novel image dataset for benchmarking machine learning algorithms. *arXiv preprint arXiv*, 3.

Yang, X., & Smith, R. E. (2009). Beyond attention effects: Modeling the persuasive and emotional effects of advertising creativity. *Marketing Science, 28*(5), 935–949.

Yosinski, J., Clune, J., Bengio, Y., & Lipson, H. (2014). How transferable are features in deep neural networks? In *Advances in neural information processing systems* (pp. 3320–3328). Available at https://arxiv.org/abs/1411.1792

Zaltman, G., & Coulter, R. H. (1995). Seeing the voice of the customer: Metaphor-based advertising research. *Journal of Advertising Research, 35*(4), 35–51.

Zaltman, G., & Zaltman, L. H. (2008). *Marketing metaphoria: What deep metaphors reveal about the minds of consumers*. Boston: Harvard Business Press.

Zhang, M., & Luo, L. (2019). *Can User-posted photos serve as a leading indicator of restaurant survival? Evidence from Yelp*. Available at SSRN 3108288.

Zhang, H., Korayem, M., You, E., & Crandall, D. J. (2012). Beyond co-occurrence: Discovering and visualizing tag relationships from geo-spatial and temporal similarities. In *Proceedings of the fifth ACM international conference on web search and data mining* (pp. 33–42). Available at https://doi.org/10.1145/2124295.2124302

Zhang, S., Mehta, N., Singh, P. V., & Srinivasan, K. (2019). *Can lower-quality images lead to greater demand on AirBnB?* Technical report, working paper, Carnegie Mellon University.

Zhang, S., Lee, D., Singh, P. V., & Srinivasan, K. (2021) "What makes a good image? Airbnb demand analytics leveraging interpretable image features". *Management Science*. Forthcoming.

Social Network Analysis

Hans Risselada and Jeroen van den Ochtend

Contents

Introduction	694
The Relevance of Network Analyses for Marketing Purposes	695
Network Metrics	697
Network	698
Basic Notation	698
Actor Level	699
Tie Level	701
Network Level	702
Network Data and Sampling Methods	703
Data Collection	703
Network Sampling	706
Social Network Analysis in R	707
Data	707
Calculating Actor Level Metrics	709
Calculating Tie Level Metrics	710
Modeling Social Contagion	712
A Word of Caution	713
Conclusion	715
Cross-References	715
References	715

Abstract

The increased awareness about the presence of social effects in consumer networks has inspired marketers to better understand and address the needs of their consumers through network analyses. In this chapter we consider network

H. Risselada (✉)
University of Groningen, Groningen, The Netherlands
e-mail: h.risselada@rug.nl

J. van den Ochtend (✉)
University of Zürich, Zürich, Switzerland
e-mail: jeroen.vandenochtend@business.uzh.ch

analyses as a set of techniques which allows researchers to analyze how the social structure of relationships around consumers affects their attitudes and behavior, and vice versa, how attitudes and behavior may affect the social structure. We focus on the types of network analyses that are currently most prominent within the field of marketing. We provide basic network theory and notation with references to key publications in the field. We also provide suggestions for software (packages) and useful functions including code snippets to support researchers and practitioners in setting up their first social network analyses. At the end of the chapter we discuss several more advanced network analysis methods and list several resources that might be useful to the interested reader.

Keywords

Social Networks · Social Influence · Social Contagion · Network Analysis · Consumer Networks

Introduction

While marketers have shifted from mass marketing techniques to personalized marketing strategies in which the focus lies on the individual consumer, a broad stream of literature in the social sciences has shown that consumers do not operate as separate entities. That is, consumers typically affect other consumers with their behavior and at the same time are themselves affected by the behavior of others. For example, Bikhchandani et al. (1992) show that consumers are likely to conform to the behavior of other consumers in order to reduce the risk associated with a commercial decision. This behavior is based on the presumption that the majority must be right. Another example is provided by Burnkrant and Cousineau (1975) who provide experimental evidence that consumers perceive products as more favorable after they observed other consumers evaluating the product positively. Thus, it has been known for decades that ignoring social effects prevents marketers from fully understanding consumers' behavior and leads to missed marketing opportunities. Fortunately, the increasing availability of consumer network data creates a widespread opportunity for marketers to fully realize the potential of marketing campaigns that incorporate social effects to better address the consumers' needs. This chapter provides both scholars and practitioners with fundamental information on social network analyses and allows them to get their first hands-on experience in estimating social effects from observational data.

In this chapter, we consider social network analysis as a set of techniques, which allows researchers to analyze how the social structure of relationships around consumers affects their behavior and attitudes, and vice versa, how behavior and attitudes may affect the social structure. That is, marketers can leverage network data in several ways. On the one hand, social networks among consumers facilitate the working of social influence. For example, networks facilitate the diffusion of information and therefore, observing the social network of consumers allows marketers to strategically spread information about new products or services through word-of-mouth mechanisms (e.g., Peres et al. 2010). Not only do consumers regularly become aware of new products or competing offers through their peers, they also consider their peers to be the most trustful source of information (Nielsen 2015). As a result, consumer behavior is influenced by information provided by their social network on a daily basis. On the other hand, observing the behavior and attitudes of a consumer's social network can reveal latent information about the consumer her/himself (e.g., Goel and Goldstein 2014). For example, little is known about a consumer before acquisition. However, consumers tend to be part of a network that consists of individuals with similar preferences and characteristics, a phenomenon called homophily (Aral et al. 2009). Hence, when data about the consumer of interest is not directly available, data about their already acquired peers can provide a solution. Similarly, consumers' decisions to adopt or defect can inform marketers about the propensity of connected consumers to adopt or defect as well (e.g., Nitzan and Libai 2011; Landsman and Nitzan 2020). In summary, with the right network data and analyses, marketers are able to (1) identify consumers that can either be acquired or should be actively retained based on the behavior of their peers, and (2) try to acquire or retain these consumers by leveraging social effects within their personal network. Of course, the possibilities that network analysis provides to marketers are much broader, and the rapidly expanding research stream on social influence continuously provides additional insights about the relevance and usability of social effects among consumers, e.g., by integrating consumers' influence in their customer lifetime value (Kumar et al. 2010) or by identifying the most influential consumers (Goldenberg et al. 2009). The goal of this chapter is to provide a comprehensive overview of marketing insights that can be generated from network data, and to summarize and illustrate the most common methods to generate these insights. In the next section, we briefly discuss how network analyses can benefit both marketing researchers and practitioners. Subsequently, we discuss the most important components and metrics of network data. Next, we illustrate the suitability of various types of data and sampling methods for network analyses. After this, we will illustrate how to derive the network metrics and apply some of the discussed network analyses on a publicly available dataset. We will conclude with a few words on more advanced network analysis methods and list several resources that might be useful to the reader.

The Relevance of Network Analyses for Marketing Purposes

Network analysis enables marketers to derive a broad range of customer insights. We start with a brief overview of two broad research fields within the social sciences and marketing in particular: (1) social influence, which includes the study of the underlying social mechanisms and (2) the role of influencers, which includes the study of consumer network characteristics at an aggregated and individual level. These types of network analyses are broadly researched and applied in practice and will be the main focus throughout the chapter. However, network analyses can serve a much broader set of marketing purposes. We refer to Valente (2012) for a brief overview of possible network interventions that can be used to accelerate behavioral change.

The first question marketers might ask themselves is how relevant social influence is for their customer acquisition, development, and retention processes. While the presence of social influence among consumers has been acknowledged for decades, the role of social influence can fiercely vary depending on the type of consumer decision and the underlying mechanism of social influence. First, *social normative pressure*, i.e., the discomfort a consumer might experience if they don't own a product their peers purchased, is typically high for products and services that are displayed to a broad audience (Burnkrant and Cousineau 1975). For example, peer groups can easily observe whether their members conform to the established fashion norms and praise those who do or reprimand those who don't. On the contrary, this social mechanism might be less relevant for brands that offer services and products that are consumed in a private setting or that are not strongly associated with consumer identity (Iyengar et al. 2015). For example, it is ambiguous to establish social norms on the use of household products because it is difficult to observe compliance and praise/reprimand accordingly. Second, the presence of *social learning*, i.e., gathering information from the decisions and experiences of peers, is typically strong for consumer decisions that involve high risk, while it will be much weaker for decisions that involve little investment and commitment (Iyengar et al. 2015). For example, consumers interested in the services of a telecom provider generally commit to a long-term contract and therefore reduce the decision risk by gathering information from their social environment (Nitzan and Libai 2011; Haenlein 2013). on the other hand it is unlikely to find strong social effects for purchase decisions of cheap consumer goods, as consumers can learn from their own experiences against low informational costs. Third, there are some other less common social influence mechanisms that are context-specific. For example, *network effects* cause an increase in product/service value with an increase in adoption rate, e.g., the value of online social platforms increases with the number of users (imagine being the only Twitter user, it would get boring quite fast). Further, *competitive concerns* cause influence among firms, as failing to adopt new innovations that are adopted by the competition can lead to competitive disadvantages (Van den Bulte and Lilien 2001).

Thus, the relevance of social influence varies between industries, brands, and the type of consumer decision, e.g., adoption versus repurchases (Hahn et al. 1994). Self-evidently, marketing tools like influencer marketing, brand ambassadors, and referral campaigns will be much more efficient when there is a sufficient level of social influence among the target consumers. Therefore, studying the presence and nature of social influence in the relevant context is a critical step in the development of a successful social network strategy. We will discuss different measures of social influence and provide an example of the identification of social influence on a publicly available dataset later on in the chapter.

When social influence is present, a first step toward leveraging these social mechanisms is to understand the role of hubs, also commonly referred to as influencers or opinion leaders. Typically, within a network, there are certain consumers that exert a greater influence (e.g., Goldenberg et al. 2009). First, these consumers might have a higher level of persuasiveness because they are considered experts, because they represent a desirable image, or because of a combination of both. As it is sometimes ambiguous to identify these features from pure network data, additional survey data can provide a solution (Iyengar et al. 2011). Second, consumers might exert a greater influence because of their reach. Obviously, a consumer with many connections can spread information quicker to a broad audience than consumers with a small number of connections (Hinz et al. 2011). However, besides the number of connections, a consumer's position within a network is at least as important (Burt 2004; Granovetter 1983). Consumers that are connected to other well-connected consumers can help to spread information even faster. Understanding the role that such consumers play in the working of social effects gives marketers valuable insights about whom to target first with their marketing campaigns.

Even in the absence of social influence, network analyses can be used to generate valuable consumer insights. For example, it is well known that consumers that are more alike tend to be clustered within a network (Aral et al. 2009). As such, different clusters within the network might differ in preferences, in behavior, or in their attitude toward the brand (chapter ▶ "Market Segmentation" in this Handbook). Identifying the value and preferences of consumers within a cluster reveals information about the potential to acquire the consumer and helps to predict whether the consumer will have a high customer lifetime value (chapter ▶ "Modeling Customer Lifetime Value, Retention, and Churn" in this Handbook; Haenlein and Libai 2013). Further, identifying the overall attitude of a network segment is especially important for managers that seek to manage positive and negative word-of-mouth on social media channels (Homburg et al. 2015). However, while on the one hand homophily can be an important driver of social influence, the clustering of preferences and attitudes within a network also causes severe challenges in the identification of social influence. We will highlight these benefits and challenges further throughout the chapter. Next, we will first introduce some basic network metrics that help marketers to better understand the network that they aim to analyze.

Network Metrics

A social network is made up of two components, i.e., actors and ties. A social network is defined as the set of actors and the ties between them. As terminology differs across research disciplines, actors are also referred to as individuals, nodes, vertices, agents, players, and in the marketing field typically as consumers. Commonly used alternatives to the term tie are dyad, link, edge, and relationship. We will use these terms interchangeably throughout this chapter.

Social networks are a subset of all possible networks and have the unique characteristic that the actors are human beings. Examples of other networks are infrastructure networks (e.g., actors: train stations, ties: railroads) or the Internet (e.g., actors: websites, ties: links). This observation illustrates the interdisciplinary nature of the social network field. Theories and models to guide the use of social network analysis in marketing could come from a broad set of research fields, such as logistics (i.e., understanding the flow of products through infrastructure networks), computer science (i.e., understanding information flow and the ranking of search results on the Internet), sociology (i.e., fundamental theories on social interactions), and medicine (i.e., understanding the spread of viruses through a population) among others.

We distinguish two types of social network analysis, namely, the analysis of the evolution of the structure of a network and the analysis of behavior and information flow within an existing network. In this chapter, we focus on the latter, because it facilitates the discussion of basic network characteristics and analyses. There is an interesting body of literature on the evolution of networks (e.g., Snijders et al. 2010) which is beyond the scope of this chapter as most of the marketing studies have used static networks only.

Network

A first step in social network analysis is describing a social network by means of simple metrics. We can measure networks at three different levels, the actor level, the tie level, and the network level. These metrics provide information on characteristics of the actors, ties, and the network as a whole, respectively. They enable marketers to get a first impression of which consumers might be influential and which relationships are likely to be crucial for the diffusion of innovations. In the following paragraphs, we introduce basic network notation and a selection of network metrics, their formulas and corresponding examples on how to calculate and interpret these metrics. We provide only a selection, because the complete set of metrics described in the literature is large and once the intuition on this type of metrics is clear, it should be easy to find and calculate the metric that is particularly relevant to answer a specific research question.

Basic Notation

We use notation that is widely used by others, e.g., Jackson (2010). We define a set of actors: $N = \{1,...,i,...,j,...,n\}$ and a $n \times n$ matrix A where each element of this matrix, A_{ij}, represents a tie between actors i and j. In the simplest case, A is a binary matrix where $A_{ij} = 1$ if there is a tie between actors i and j, and $A_{ij} = 0$ otherwise. We refer to A_{ij} as an adjacency matrix. Instead of just the presence or absence of a tie, it is also possible to indicate the strength of the tie between two actors by any real number for A_{ij}. We then refer to this matrix as a weight matrix. In both cases, we denote the resulting network or graph as (N, A). To illustrate several metrics, we use an example network, Fig. 1a, based on the adjacency matrix in Fig. 1b. We assume that the distance between all adjacent pairs is 1.

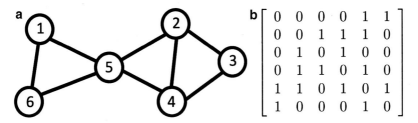

Fig. 1 (a) Example network, (b) Adjacency matrix of the example network

Actor Level

We start our discussion on metrics at the actor level. These metrics capture individual characteristics and therefore complement the set of consumer-level variables typically used in marketing, such as socio-demographic or service usage data. These so-called centrality measures each relate to a particular role of an individual in the network, such as influencer or information broker. Marketers can use this additional individual level information to enrich their customer segmentations and prediction models for behaviors such as product adoption and churn.

Degree Centrality

The most basic and most commonly used centrality measure is degree centrality. It is simply the number of ties an actor has, for example, the number of friends on Facebook or the number of connections on LinkedIn. Those with an extremely high degree centrality are called (social) hubs and are generally seen as influential individuals.

To calculate degree centrality one only accounts for the presence or absence of a tie and ignores the potential direction of the relationship. However, in many real networks, relationships are generally asymmetric or only go in one direction. For example, on Twitter you may be a follower of person j (the tie goes in the direction from i to person j, $i \rightarrow j$), but person j may not be following you (there is no tie going back from person j to i). Undirected ties are graphically represented by either a line i-j or double arrows $i \rightleftarrows j$. An undirected network is formalized by a symmetric adjacency matrix while a directed network is formalized by an asymmetric adjacency matrix. To account for this directionality, we use the metrics in-degree centrality and out-degree centrality. In-degree centrality measures the number of incoming ties and out-degree measures the number of outgoing ties.

Assuming an undirected network in which $A_{ij} = A_{ji}$ for all i and j, you calculate degree centrality of actor i, $d_i(A)$, as:

$$d_i(A) = \#\{\ j : A_{ij} = 1\}$$

In the case of a directed network, we define in-degree centrality, $d_{i,in}$, and out-degree, $d_{i,out}$, as follows:

$$d_{i,in}(A) = \#\{ j : A_{ji} = 1 \}$$

$$d_{i,out}(A) = \#\{ j : A_{ij} = 1 \}$$

Some authors divide this measure by the maximum number of ties $(n-1)$ to obtain values between 0 and 1. This standardization accounts for the size of the network and facilitates comparison of degree centralities across networks. The standardized version is most insightful in small networks where having ties to all other actors would be feasible, e.g., a class in school or a sports club, and you would observe values in the entire (0, 1) range. Table 1 shows the degree centralities of our example network.

Betweenness Centrality

The second, slightly more complex centrality measure that we discuss is betweenness centrality. This measure is based on the number of times an actor occurs on the shortest path between any pair of actors in a network. To calculate betweenness centrality, you first need to determine the shortest paths between all possible pairs of actors and then count how many times an actor appears on each of these paths. The difficulty here is that there may be multiple shortest paths and an actor might be on none, some, or all of these shortest paths.

A high betweenness centrality implies that a large amount of information flows "through" an actor on its way from sender to receiver. This gives the actor a high level of influence over which and how much information to pass on through the network and thus provides the actor with brokerage power (Burt 2004).

We define the number of shortest paths between actors j and k as $P(kj)$ and the number of shortest paths between j and k that go through actor i as $P_i(kj)$. Then, the ratio $P_i(kj)/P(kj)$ indicates how crucial actor i is in the relationship between actors j and k. The betweenness centrality of actor i is as follows:

$$BC_i = \Sigma_{k \neq j, i \text{ not in } \{k,j\}} P_i(kj)/P(kj)$$

Some authors divide this measure by the total number of pairs of actors $(n-1)(n-2)/2$ to obtain average values. The latter would facilitate comparison across networks, but other than that the measures are equally useful. Table 1 shows the betweenness centralities of our example network.

Table 1 Actor level metrics of our example network

Actor	Degree centrality	Betweenness centrality	Closeness centrality	Eigenvector centrality
1	2	0	1.8	0.54
2	3	1.5	1.4	0.88
3	2	0	2	0.62
4	3	1.5	1.4	0.88
5	4	6	1.2	1.00
6	2	0	1.8	0.54

Closeness Centrality

Closeness centrality is the average distance between an actor and all other actors in the network. Distance could reflect the number of steps between two actors (1: friend, 2: friend of a friend, etc.), or it could be a weighted version of the number of steps by, for example, tie strength. It indicates quite literally how close everyone else in the network is to an actor and thus how much effort it would take to reach all others. Using the length of the shortest path $l(i,j)$ between actor i and any other actor j, the closeness centrality of actor i is:

$$CC_i = \Sigma_{j \neq i} l(i,j)/(n-1)$$

Some authors take the inverse of this metric such that higher values of closeness centrality correspond to shorter paths and thus increased closeness. Which one to choose is a matter of conceptual preference and/or convention in a research domain. Table 1 shows the degree centralities of our example network.

Eigenvector Centrality

The previous three metrics reflect how central an actor is directly based on the actor's characteristics. Eigenvector centrality on the other hand is more complex and indirect in that it reflects how central an actor is based on how central or well-connected the actor's neighbors are. This metric builds on the notion that an actor can be considered central even if she/he only has a limited number of connections (i.e., low degree centrality) when these actors in turn are well-connected. Calculating this metric by hand is rather complex, because it is self-referential: the eigenvector centrality of actor i partly depends on the eigenvector centrality of his/her neighboring actor j, but the eigenvector centrality of this actor j again depends partly on the eigenvector centrality of actor i. Table 1 shows the eigenvector centralities of our example network.

Tie Level

We now move to the metrics on tie level. We distinguish two types of tie level characteristics, (1) those that measure a characteristic of the tie itself (e.g., strength or direction) and (2) those that measure similarities and differences between the two actors forming the tie (e.g., homophily). These tie characteristics provide a lot of information in addition to the actor level variables. They capture the social context in which the actor operates and allow you to put the actor characteristics in perspective. For example, for contagion purposes it might matter whether a female consumer is mainly connected to other males or females and whether her ties with others are generally strong or weak.

Tie Strength

Measuring tie strength is less straightforward than measuring the actor characteristics from the previous section. Following Granovetter, we define tie strength as "a combination of the amount of time, the emotional intensity, the intimacy (mutual confiding), and the reciprocal services which characterize the tie" (Granovetter 1973, p. 1361). The challenge is how to operationalize this definition, because many social network datasets lack information on one or several of the dimensions from the definition. Most papers in the marketing literature use a proxy for tie strength based on interaction intensity, see Table 2.

Homophily

Homophily refers to the phenomenon that we tend to form relationships with others that are in some way similar to us. A well-known expression for this phenomenon is "birds of a feather flock together" (McPherson et al. 2001). When analyzing social network data, homophily is important to take into account, because otherwise observed similarities in behavior of connected individuals might erroneously be attributed to social influence or contagion (Aral et al. 2009; Manski 2000). The reason for this is that connected individuals tend to be similar and similar individuals with similar preferences tend to behave similarly regardless of any social influence occurring between them. Only after adjusting your analysis for homophily one can infer the impact of social influence properly.

Network Level

Metrics on the network level provide information on the network as a whole. They provide the context in which the lower level (actor, tie) action takes place. The role of these network level metrics is similar to the role of descriptive statistics for cross-sectional data: it gives you a good first impression of the information contained in the data at a glimpse.

Size

The most basic network level metric is the size of the network, i.e., the number of actors. Like the sample size in cross-sectional data, it is an important metric to report as it helps to calculate all other lower-level network metrics.

Table 2 Operationalizations of tie strength

Data source	Papers	Tie strength measure
Call detail records (telecom)	Haenlein (2013) Meyners et al. (2017) Nitzan and Libai (2011) Onnela et al. (2007) Risselada et al. (2014)	Aggregated duration of calls between users A and B over a reciprocated tie (relative to an actor's total calling duration).
Direct messaging network	Aral et al. (2009)	Number/fraction of exchanged messages.

Density

Network density reflects the proportion all existing ties in a network to all possible ties in a network. It is closely related to the actor level variable degree centrality discussed above. You calculate the density of a network by dividing the average degree centrality of all actors by $(n-1)$, with n the number of actors in the network. It tells you how much of the network potential is actually used.

Degree Distribution

The degree distribution of a network is the relative frequency of actors with a certain degree. The distribution is therefore not a metric but rather a feature of a social network. Many social networks have a degree distribution which is highly skewed, where many actors have only a few ties, and only a few actors have many ties. This phenomenon is caused by preferential attachment, i.e., actors typically want to connect to popular (high-degree) actors. A common term for networks with such properties is scale-free networks. On the contrary, when the degree distribution follows a normal distribution, the network is said to be random, i.e., the likelihood that actors connect is independent of their degree. See Barabasi and Bonabeau (2003) and Broido and Clauset (2019) for more information about the properties of common real-world networks.

Network Data and Sampling Methods

Scaling down to networks that are relevant for marketers, there are still numerous networks that differ substantially in the nature of ties and actors, and the structure of the network. Networks that are often analyzed in marketing include product networks (for recommendation systems), networks of companies (for B2B marketing), organizational networks (for social influence among employees), and market networks (for buyer–seller relationships). As before, we focus on networks of consumers, as this is the most common network type in marketing research and practice. A large collection of different types of networks is provided by the Colorado Index of Complex Networks (https://icon.colorado.edu/).

Data Collection

To gather insights in consumer networks, there are multiple data solutions. Table 3 illustrates the types of online and offline network data and their benefits and disadvantages. A solution that is as straightforward as it is effective is the use of geographic proximity (Wuyts et al. 2011; Meyners et al. 2017). Naturally, consumers that live close to each other tend to interact with each other. In addition, local social influence effects can be quite strong due to the high level of perceived similarity between consumers that live in the same area (i.e., perceived homophily). For example, Nam et al. (2010) estimate the effect of social influence on

Table 3 Types of network data with selection of papers

Type of network data	Benefits	Disadvantages	Examples within the marketing literature
Geographic proximity	Easy to obtain data Highly scalable	Low accuracy No information about the individual ties No detailed information about homophily	Bell and Song (2007) Nam et al. (2010) Choi et al. (2010)
Survey data	High accuracy Complete network Tie-strength info Information about nature of relationship Detailed information about homophily	Hard to obtain data Not highly scalable Self-report bias	Iyengar et al. (2011) Iyengar et al. (2015) Nair et al. (2010)
CDR data	High accuracy Highly scalable Tie-strength info Some information about homophily	Privacy issues No information about nature of relationship	Nitzan and Libai (2011) Onnela et al. (2007) Risselada et al. (2014)
Social network platform	Medium hard to obtain data Highly scalable Tie-strength info Detailed information about homophily Information about WOM content	Limited data access through APIs Strong sampling bias dependent on type of platform	Ma et al. (2015) Trusov et al. (2009) Trusov et al. (2010) Aral and Walker (2014) Valsesia et al. (2020)
Instant messenger	Highly scalable Tie-strength info	Hard to obtain data Little information about nature of relationship	Aral et al. (2009)
Community networks	High accuracy Detailed information about homophily Information about WOM content	Only information about current customers	Zhang and Godes (2018) Park et al. (2018)

the adoption of a video-on-demand service by measuring how local quality differences drive the adoption within the same geographical area. The benefit of geographical data is that it is relatively easy and cheap to obtain for a large group of consumers. However, the data is often an imperfect representation of the true network and does not allow for detailed information about the ties, such as tie strength and homophily. A second method that requires more effort is the use of surveys (chapter ▶ "Crafting Survey Research: A Systematic Process for Conducting Survey Research" in this Handbook). The benefit of survey data is that one can measure the more detailed tie attributes such as tie-strength and homophily. For example, Iyengar et al. (2015) are able to distinguish individuals that are seen as experts from individuals that are seen as discussion partners. Besides the high costs of collecting data, researchers should be aware of possible self-report biases. For example, friendships are not always reciprocal, and the number of friends or the own social status can be overestimated (Wuyts et al. 2011; Haenlein 2013). To generate a connected network from survey data, one can engage in snowball sampling or the so-called referral chain sampling (Ebbes et al. 2016; Reingen and Kernan 1986). This type of sampling refers to a specific type of survey distribution, in which the surveyed consumers forward the questionnaire to his/her connections. As such, one can obtain a network in which each node is connected with the entire network. A third technique that is widely applied in marketing is to leverage third party data of a telecom provider. The so-called "call detail records" (CDR) data contains all phone calls of the customers of the telecom company. Based on these calls, one can derive the relevant network of the customer. For example, Nitzan and Libai (2011) identify the effect of social influence on churn behavior from such a dataset. Studies show that such networks accurately represent offline networks (Eagle et al. 2009). Features such as the weight of a tie can be estimated by taking the frequency and the duration of calls into account (Risselada et al. 2014). However, little information about the nature of the relationship is known (e.g., friends or colleagues?) and the rising privacy regulations make it more difficult to obtain CDR data. A fourth method is to analyze the network from a social network platform such as Twitter or LinkedIn. Often such data can be gathered through an API provided by the platform and gives a good indication of the individuals network, see https://developer.twitter.com/en/docs for APIs that can be used to download data from Twitter and see https://www.linkedin.com/developers/ for APIs that can be used to download data from LinkedIn. When the platform also tracks features such as individual messaging, or interactions with user-generated content, one can use these as tie strength measures. In addition, these platforms often gather demographic and behavioral data of their users, which allows for precise homophily measures between the nodes. An example of the use of such data is the study by Valsesia et al. (2020), which shows that the number of out-degree ties, conditional on the number of in-degree ties, has a negative effect on the perceived and actual influence of social media users. Similar data can be derived from online communication tools, such as networks based on e-mail traffic or online message services. While the true nature of the ties is often unobserved in such networks, they are able to provide a sufficient proxy for the offline network of consumers. However, not every online network is a representation of the offline network. Typically, the boundary between friends and strangers deteriorates when moving from an offline to an online network. Nevertheless, online networks are highly relevant for marketers as consumers can be influenced by both close friends as well as by acquaintances or complete strangers (Zhang et al. 2015). Finally, other typical online networks are community networks. Firms create community networks to foster shared consumption experiences, collaboration, or competition between their customers. In addition, it provides their customers with a single point of concentration information about the products or services of a firm. For example, analyzing the network of an online gaming community, Park et al. (2018) identify a positive effect of social contagion on users' spending behavior.

Network Sampling

Consumer networks can include millions of nodes and the square number of ties resulting in large and complex data. As such, to map out and analyze the entire network is a computationally expensive task. Even though some of the techniques to model networks discussed later on are scalable, many methods are limited in their capacity and require a lot of computational power. To reduce the size and complexity of the network, researchers can apply several sampling techniques. These techniques differ in their ability to recover the different network characteristics. As such, their suitability depends on the goal of the researchers.

When the goal of the analyses is to identify the impact of social influence on consumer behavior at an individual level, researchers can rely on random sampling. To measure social influence, the data needs to include (1) the behavior of an individual node, (2) the nodes that are connected to the focal node, and (3) the behavior of the connected nodes. As such, the overall network structure is less relevant, and the interest focuses mainly on the ego-network, i.,. the focal actor ("ego") and the nodes that are directly connected to the actor (e.g., Risselada et al. 2014; Nitzan and Libai 2011; Haenlein 2013). Such direct connections are typically referred to as first-degree neighbors. Scholars that are interested in social influence across multiple nodes or on a global level can expand the ego-network to include second- or higher-degree neighbors. Figure 2 illustrates the relevant ego network versus the complete network.

As soon as marketers are interested in social influence at the global level or want to predict the results of possible marketing initiatives that leverage social influence, network sampling techniques are required. To derive a representative sample of the network, it is important to recover important network characteristics such as betweenness and closeness centrality, and the degree distribution. This can be achieved through the so-called subgraph sampling methods. These methods differ

Fig. 2 Ego network (gray = ego) versus complete network

from the random sampling described above. In the procedure of collecting data from ego-networks, we first select a group of random nodes and subsequently select their links. In subgraph sampling, we sample the nodes and links jointly. There are four widely applied network sampling methods to derive a subgraph from a population network, i.e., the random sampling method, the snowball method, the random walk method, and the forest fire method. To illustrate the different methods, we define a population network as G = (V, E), with the set of actors V = $\{v_1, \ldots, v_N\}$ and the set ties E = $\{(v_i, v_j)\}$. We define a subgraph of G as G* = (V*, E*), where the sampled actor set and tie set of graph G* are V* $\subseteq$ V and E* $\subseteq$ E. In the case of random sampling, we take a random selection of actors, V*, and then include all ties between the actors, E*, to build the subgraph G* = (V*, E*). For snowball sampling, we start with selecting one actor, v_1*, then select all neighbors, v_2*, and select all their unselected neighbors, v_3*, up to v_k*, until we've reached a large enough set of actors V*$\{v_1$*, ..., v_k*$\}$. In the case of the random walk method, we only select one neighbor at random from the entire set of unselected neighbors. In the case of the forest fire method, we select a certain percentage (i.e., the burn rate) of the remaining unselected neighbors at random for each round. Ebbes et al. (2016) compare the performance of all methods and conclude that (1) forest-fire sampling with a burn-rate around 50% should be used in research on local influence, as this method is best in recovering the degree distribution of the graph, and (2) the random walk method or forest-fire sampling with a low burn-rate (e.g., 20%) should be used for research on influence at a network level as it is best in retrieving the centrality measures.

Social Network Analysis in R

In this section, we illustrate how to calculate the metrics discussed above and how to estimate a basic model to quantify social influence. The main package we use for the network-related analyses is the *igraph* package (Csardi and Nepusz 2006) in R (R Core Team 2018). This package is also available for Python.

Data

We use the classic Coleman's Drug Adoption dataset "Innovation among Physicians," which is publicly available in the *spatialprobit* R-package (Wilhelm and de Matos 2015). You can find a detailed description of the dataset in the package by typing? CKM in the R console after loading the *spatialprobit* package.

```
> library(spatialprobit) #load the spatialprobit package
> ?CKM #this calls for the help on the CKM dataset
```

The dataset contains information on 246 physicians in four cities and was collected in 1966. Table 4 shows the variables we use in our examples.

To be able to work with the dataset, you need to load it in R.

Table 4 Variable names and descriptions as given in the *spatialprobit* package

Variable name	Description
city	a numeric vector; City: 1 Peoria, 2 Bloomington, 3 Quincy, 4 Galesburg
adoption. date	an ordered factor with levels November, 1953; December, 1953; January, 1954; February, 1954; March, 1954; April, 1954; May, 1954; June, 1954; July, 1954; August, 1954; September, 1954; October, 1954; November, 1954; December, 1954; December/January, 1954/1955; January/February, 1955; February, 1955; no prescriptions found; no prescription data obtained
med_sch_yr	Years in practice
friends	friends
community	Time in the community
specialty	Medical specialty

```
> data(CKM) #load the dataset
```

We use the data tables format in R to make the data manipulation and coding as easy as possible. See https://cran.r-project.org/web/packages/data.table/vignettes/datatable-intro.html for more information regarding the data table format and the *data.table* package (Dowle and Srinivasan 2019).

```
> library(data.table) #load the data.table package
> CKM <- as.data.table(CKM) #make CKM a data.table object
> CKM[,date := as.numeric(adoption.date)] #change the variable
type of adoption.date to numeric for ease of analysis
```

We add a new variable called id to have a clear identifier for all individuals in the dataset.

```
> CKM[,id := 1:.N] #assign IDs to all individuals in the dataset
```

Now we are all set to create the network. Here we use an adjacency matrix approach where each element of the matrix simply indicates absence (0) or presence (1) of a tie. In this example, we base the adjacency matrix on three matrices for which the original authors collected data by means of a sociometric approach. The three relevant questions were "When you need information or advice about questions of therapy where do you usually turn?", "Who are the three or four physicians with whom you most often find yourself discussing cases or therapy in the course of an ordinary week – last week for instance?", and "Would you tell me the first names of your three friends whom you see most often socially?." These three questions resulted in an advice matrix (A1), a discussion matrix (A2), and a friend matrix (A3), respectively. For illustrative purposes, we combine the three matrices in a unique adjency matrix A4 by setting its elements to 1 if it was 1 in A1, A2, or A3.

```
> A4 <- A1 + A2 + A3 #add up the advice, discussion, and friend
matrices
```

```
> A4[A4 > 0] <- 1 #create a binary adjacency matrix
> library(igraph) #load the igraph package
> medinnovNetw <- graph_from_adjacency_matrix(A4) #create the
network
```

To get a first impression of the network you can use the *plot* function to generate a simple network plot. This will only provide useful output for smaller networks. Large networks will be messy or even unreadable. Visualizing large and complex networks requires specialized software, e.g., Gephi (https://gephi.org).

Calculating Actor Level Metrics

Figure 3 shows that the network is not fully connected. It consists of several disconnected clusters. For illustrative purposes we will use the largest cluster and calculate the actor level metrics discussed above. The reason for this is that a metric

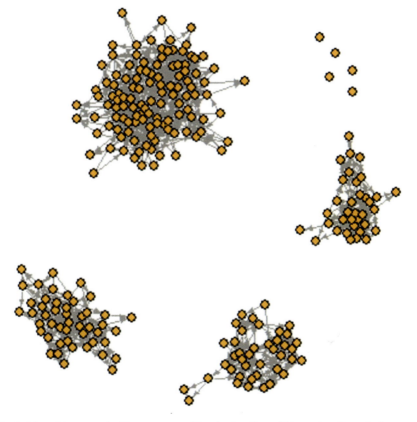

Fig. 3 Plot of the network. (Notes: generated by plot (medinnovNetw,vertex.size = 5,edge.arrow. size = 0.3,vertex.label = ""))

like closeness centrality cannot be calculated for disconnected parts of the network, because the distance between two actors in different clusters would be infinite.

```
> medinnovNetw.components <- clusters(medinnovNetw) #identify the
clusters in the network; the largest cluster consists of 117 actors
> medinnovNetw.components.graphs <- decompose.graph(medinnovNetw)
#decompose the network into separate clusters; each cluster is an
element in a list
> medinnovNetw.subgraph1 <- as.undirected(medinnovNetw.
components.graphs[[1]]) #we store the largest cluster as an
undirected network for illustrative purposes
> gorder(medinnovNetw.subgraph1) #check whether the subgraph is
indeed the one with 117 vertices
```

Now that we have our new network, we can easily calculate all network metrics using standard functions in the *igraph* package. We show the code here and provide summary statistics in Table 5.

```
> subgraph1.degree.centrality <- degree(medinnovNetw.subgraph1)
> subgraph1.betweenness.centrality <- betweenness(medinnovNetw.
subgraph1)
> summary(subgraph1.closeness.centrality)
> subgraph1.eigenvector.centrality <- eigen_centrality
(medinnovNetw.subgraph1)#the first element of this list contains the
centralities
```

Calculating Tie Level Metrics

We now switch back to using the complete dataset. Most papers using communication-based network data, for example, call detail records or online social network data, use interaction intensity as a proxy for tie strength. However, the dataset that we use here is not based on communication, but on survey responses and the network is based on sociometric questions related to advice, discussion, and friendship. We used the binary adjacency matrices to construct the network and we can use the weight matrices derived from the adjacency matrices (and included as W1, W2, and W3 in the CKM data) as our tie strength measure. The weight matrices are just the normalized versions of the adjacency matrices. For example, if physician 1 indicated

Table 5 Descriptive statistics of the actor level metrics

Actor level metric	Mean	S.D.	Min.	Max.
Degree centrality	7.966	4.026	2.000	26.000
Betweenness centrality	91.880	99.114	0.000	717.120
Closeness centrality	0.003	0.0003	0.003	0.004
Eigenvector centrality	0.262	0.153	0.031	1.000

7 friends, the weight of each of those friends would be 1/7. The implicit assumption here would be that the more friends you have, the weaker the tie per friend.

The variables in the dataset that we use to calculate homophily are the city (*city*), years in practice (*med_sch_yr*), time in the community (*community*), and medical specialty (*specialty*). Before we can perform these calculations, we need to prepare the data. Note that we continue with the adjacency matrix A4 that we created earlier.

```
> dimnames(A4) <- list(as.character(CKM$id),as.character(CKM$id))
> g <- graph_from_adjacency_matrix(A4)
> g.list <- data.table(get.edgelist(g)) #this returns a data table
with all edges (relationships)
> friends <- g.list[,list(id=as.numeric(V1),friend=as.numeric
(V2))] #set names
> friends <- rbind(friends,friends[,list(id=friend,friend=id)])
#the original data is directed, but here we make an edgelist for an
undirected graph
> friends <- merge(friends,
+                  CKM[,list(friend=id,
+                            d.adopt=date,
+                            f.city=city,
+                            f.med_sch_yr=med_sch_yr,
+                            f.community=community,
+                            f.specialty=specialty)],
+                  by="friend") #we add the adoption dates and the
variables we need to calculate homophily later for the friends
> friends[,f.adopt := 1]
> friends[d.adopt > 17,f.adopt := 0] #in these two steps we create
an adoption dummy and set it equal to zero when the adoption month
is larger than 17 (i.e. the end of the observation period)
> friends2 <- merge(friends,
+                   CKM[,list(id =id,
+                             id.city=city,
+                             id.med_sch_yr=med_sch_yr,
+                             id.community=community,
+                             id.specialty=specialty)],
+                   by="id") #we add the variables we need to calculate
homophily later for the ids
> setkey(friends,id) #we create a key to sort the data and speed up
the data manipulation
```

To check whether we got the desired results we use the head() function to display the first few rows of the dataframe, see Fig. 4. In the table friends2 we see the

```
> head(friends2)
   id friend d.adopt f.city f.med_sch_yr f.community f.specialty f.adopt id.city id.med_sch_yr id.community id.specialty
1:  1      8       3      1            4           5           1       1       1             2            6            3
2:  1     58       4      1            2           6           4       1       1             2            6            3
3:  1     78       1      1            3           5           3       1       1             2            6            3
4:  1     87      19      1            6           2           4       0       1             2            6            3
5:  1     90      19      1            2           3           4       0       1             2            6            3
6:  1    110      20      1            9           2           4       0       1             2            6            3
```

Fig. 4 The result of head(friends2)

two physician identifiers (*id, friend*) forming a tie, the adoption date (*d.adopt*) and dummy (*f.adopt*) of the friend, and the variables we use for the homophily calculation of both id and friend.

We can now calculate the homophily variable in two steps. First, we create a new variable per dimension attaching a weight of ¼ when id and friend have the same value for that dimension. We add the conditions that end with "! = 9" to exclude the cases where the respondent indicated "no answer," because two individuals not answering does not make them more similar. In the second step we add all the weights to get a homophily score per id, the variable *HOMOPH*.

```
> friends3 <- friends2 %>%
+   mutate(
+     city.hom = ifelse(id.city == f.city, 1/4, 0),
+     med_sch_yr.hom = ifelse(id.med_sch_yr == f.med_sch_yr & id.med_sch_yr != 9, 1/4, 0),
+     community.hom = ifelse(id.community == f.community & id.community != 9, 1/4, 0),
+     specialty.hom = ifelse(id.specialty == f.specialty & id.specialty != 9, 1/4, 0),
+     HOMOPH = city.hom + med_sch_yr.hom + community.hom + specialty.hom
+   )
```

Modeling Social Contagion

Assessing the relationship between the adoption by the id and the adoption(s) by his/her friend(s) is our main objective here. We start by creating a clean version of the original CKM dataset.

```
> CKM <- CKM[date < 19] #remove all missing values on adoption (date == 19 or 20)
> CKM[,adoption := 1] #we create an adoption dummy
> CKM[date == 18,adoption := 0] #set it to 0 if id did not adopt (date == 18)
> CKM <- CKM[discuss != 9 & friends != 9] #remove if no answer on friends or discussion
```

Then we create a panel dataset with a unique row per id-month combination. The last month per id is the month in which the id adopted (i.e., adoption = 1). If id did not adopt at all during the observation period the maximum number of rows is 17 where adoption = 0 for all rows. The time-independent covariates are the same in every row per id. Figure 5 below shows the top of the created panel dataset CKM. panel.

```
> CKM.panel <- CKM[,list(month=seq(from=1,to=17,by=1)),by=id]
> CKM.panel <- merge(CKM.panel,CKM[,list(id,date,jours,patients, med_sch_yr,specialty)],all.x=T,by="id")
```

Social Network Analysis

id	month	date	jours	patients	med_sch_yr	specialty	adoption
1	1	1	8	5	2	3	1
2	1	12	4	4	6	1	0
2	2	12	4	4	6	1	0
2	3	12	4	4	6	1	0
2	4	12	4	4	6	1	0
2	5	12	4	4	6	1	0

Fig. 5 First six rows of the CKM.panel dataset

```
> CKM.panel[,adoption := 0]
> CKM.panel[date == month, adoption := 1]
> CKM.panel <- CKM.panel[month <= date]
```

We need to create another dataset based on the friends dataset we created earlier in order to be able to link the adoptions by friends to the adoption by id in a certain month. The code below sums up the number of adoptions (`f.adopt = sum(f.adopt)`) per id-date (`by = c("id","d.adopt")`) combination and stores this in a new dataset called friends.adopt.

```
> friends.adopt <- friends[,list(f.adopt=sum(f.adopt)),by=c
("id","d.adopt")]
> setnames(friends.adopt,"d.adopt","month")
```

We can now merge the friends.adopt dataset with the CKM.panel to obtain the analysis set.

```
> CKM.panel <- merge(CKM.panel,friends.adopt,all.x=T,by=c
("id","month"))
> CKM.panel[is.na(f.adopt),f.adopt := 0]
> CKM.panel[,c.adopt := cumsum(f.adopt),by=id]
```

Our social contagion model simply regresses adoption by the id in a certain month to the number of adoptions of friends until and including that month (chapter ▶ "Regression Analysis" in this Handbook). Figure 6 shows the results. The parameter of the social influence variable is positive and significant ($\beta = 0.367, p < 0.001$), which implies that the likelihood of adoption by an individual is greater when the number of friends who already adopted is larger.

A Word of Caution

To identify social influence is not an easy task. For example, the model above is fairly simple and misses many important variables. To increase the causal evidence, we could include the homophily variable (HOMOPH) that we created earlier in our social contagion model. One way to do this is by using the homophily variable as a

```
> summary(glm(adoption ~ f.adopt ,data=CKM.panel,family=binomial("cloglog")))

Call:
glm(formula = adoption ~ f.adopt, family = binomial("cloglog"),
    data = CKM.panel)

Deviance Residuals:
    Min      1Q   Median      3Q     Max
-1.1429  -0.4567  -0.4567  -0.4567  2.1505

Coefficients:
            Estimate Std. Error z value Pr(>|z|)
(Intercept)  -2.2607     0.1195 -18.920  < 2e-16 ***
f.adopt       0.3670     0.1089   3.368 0.000757 ***
---
Signif. codes:  0 '***' 0.001 '**' 0.01 '*' 0.05 '.' 0.1 ' ' 1

(Dispersion parameter for binomial family taken to be 1)

    Null deviance: 595.09  on 831  degrees of freedom
Residual deviance: 585.13  on 830  degrees of freedom
AIC: 589.13
```

Fig. 6 R code and estimation results of our social contagion model

weight for the adoptions (e.g., Risselada et al. 2014). Another refinement would be to take the recency of adoptions into account where adoptions of more than a certain number of periods ago would no longer contribute to the social influence variable. Alternatively, one could use a stock variable approach which is commonly for advertising expenditures in sales response models. Further, scholars have shown that controlling for marketing initiatives removes the evidence of social influence that we found in the dataset above (van den Bulte and Lilien 2001).

However, when analyzing social influence based on network data, there are three additional challenges that can lead to a biased estimate of social influence, i.e., simultaneity, external shocks, and homophily (Manski 2000). Simultaneity or reflection arises when two consumers influence each other simultaneously. When this is the case, it remains unclear whether the actor is influenced by her/his connections, or whether the connections are influenced by the actor. To avoid a bias due to simultaneity, scholars can use a lagged variable of social influence. That is, the behavior of connections in the past can influence the current behavior of the actor, but not vice versa. External shocks refer to a change in the environmental conditions that can influence the behavior of consumers that are connected at the same time. For example, changes at a geographical local level might impact the behavior of multiple connected consumers. Finally, there is the issue of homophily. While we can use similarity measures based on observed characteristics to capture homophily and even use it as moderator of social influence, it is likely that we do not observe all relevant characteristics. That is, there are latent variables, such as unobserved consumer preferences, that both drive the network formation as well as the behavior of interest.

As such, observed clustered behavior within a network might not be the cause of social influence, but rather a result of the clustered unobserved preferences. Several solutions to this problem have been proposed, such as propensity score matching on observed variables (Aral et al. 2009), the use of fixed effects with longitudinal data (Park et al. 2018), the use of instrumental variables (Aral and Nicolaides 2017), or the use of specific network models such as the latent space model (Davin et al. 2013) or the spatial error model (Ansari et al. 2011). Currently, the problem of homophily and the mentioned solutions are still subject to an ongoing discussion (Shalizi and Thomas 2011). Both, the issue of external shocks and homophily are similar to the endogeneity problem caused by omitted variables (chapter ▶ "Dealing with Endogeneity: A Nontechnical Guide for Marketing Researchers" in this Handbook).

Conclusion

While the existence of social influence among consumers has been studied for decades, the increasing availability of network data and the tools to analyze these allows marketers to better understand and address consumers' needs. However, collecting and analyzing network data brings new challenges to marketing researchers and practitioners. In this chapter we provide basic network theory and notation with references to key publications in the field. We also provide suggestions for software (packages) and useful functions including code snippets to support you in preparing and running your first social network analyses. Our aim was neither to provide a complete literature overview nor was it the aim to go into the most advanced social contagion models. We hope that this chapter is a good starting point for those willing to discover the exciting social network domain.

Cross-References

- ▶ Crafting Survey Research: A Systematic Process for Conducting Survey Research
- ▶ Dealing with Endogeneity: A Nontechnical Guide for Marketing Researchers
- ▶ Market Segmentation
- ▶ Modeling Customer Lifetime Value, Retention, and Churn
- ▶ Regression Analysis

References

Ansari, A., Koenigsberg, O., & Stahl, F. (2011). Modeling multiple relationships in social networks. *Journal of Marketing Research, 48*(4), 713–728.

Aral, S., & Nicolaides, C. (2017). Exercise contagion in a global social network. *Nature Communications, 8*(1), 1–8.

Aral, S., & Walker, D. (2014). Tie strength, embeddedness, and social influence: A large-scale networked experiment. *Management Science, 60*(6), 1352–1370.

Aral, S., Muchnik, L., & Sundararajan, A. (2009). Distinguishing influence-based contagion from homophily-driven diffusion in dynamic networks. *Proceedings of the National Academy of Sciences, 106*(51), 21544–21549.

Barabási, A. L., & Bonabeau, E. (2003). Scale-free networks. *Scientific American, 288*(5), 60–69.

Bell, D. R., & Song, S. (2007). Neighborhood effects and trial on the internet: Evidence from online grocery retailing. *Quantitative Marketing and Economics, 5*(4), 361–400.

Bikhchandani, S., Hirshleifer, D., & Welch, I. (1992). A theory of fads, fashion, custom, and cultural change as informational cascades. *Journal of Political Economy, 100*(5), 992–1026.

Broido, A. D., & Clauset, A. (2019). Scale-free networks are rare. *Nature Communications, 10*(1), 1–10.

Burnkrant, R. E., & Cousineau, A. (1975). Informational and normative social influence in buyer behavior. *Journal of Consumer Research, 2*(3), 206–215.

Burt, R. S. (2004). Structural holes and good ideas. *American Journal of Sociology, 110*(2), 349–399.

Choi, J., Hui, S. K., & Bell, D. R. (2010). Spatiotemporal analysis of imitation behavior across new buyers at an online grocery retailer. *Journal of Marketing Research, 47*(1), 75–89.

Csardi, G., & Nepusz, T. (2006). The igraph software package for complex network research. *InterJournal, Complex Systems, 1695*(5), 1–9.

Davin, J. P., Gupta, S., & Piskorski, M. J. (2013). Separating homophily and peer influence with latent space. Available at SSRN 2373273.

Dowle, M., & Srinivasan, A. (2019). data.table: Extension of `data.frame`. R package version 1.12.6. https://CRAN.R-project.org/package=data.table

Eagle, N., Pentland, A. S., & Lazer, D. (2009). Inferring friendship network structure by using mobile phone data. *Proceedings of the National Academy of Sciences, 106*(36), 15274–15278.

Ebbes, P., Huang, Z., & Rangaswamy, A. (2016). Sampling designs for recovering local and global characteristics of social networks. *International Journal of Research in Marketing, 33*(3), 578–599.

Goel, S., & Goldstein, D. G. (2014). Predicting individual behavior with social networks. *Marketing Science, 33*(1), 82–93.

Goldenberg, J., Han, S., Lehmann, D. R., & Hong, J. W. (2009). The role of hubs in the adoption process. *Journal of Marketing, 73*(2), 1–13.

Granovetter, M. (1973). The strength of weak ties. *American Journal of Sociology, 78*(6), 1360–1380.

Granovetter, M. (1983). The strength of weak ties: A network theory revisited. *Sociological Theory, 1*, 201–233.

Haenlein, M. (2013). Social interactions in customer churn decisions: The impact of relationship directionality. *International Journal of Research in Marketing, 30*(3), 236–248.

Haenlein, M., & Libai, B. (2013). Targeting revenue leaders for a new product. *Journal of Marketing, 77*(3), 65–80.

Hahn, M., Park, S., Krishnamurthi, L., & Zoltners, A. A. (1994). Analysis of new product diffusion using a four-segment trial-repeat model. *Marketing Science, 13*(3), 224–247.

Hinz, O., Skiera, B., Barrot, C., & Becker, J. U. (2011). Seeding strategies for viral marketing: An empirical comparison. *Journal of Marketing, 75*(6), 55–71.

Homburg, C., Ehm, L., & Artz, M. (2015). Measuring and managing consumer sentiment in an online community environment. *Journal of Marketing Research, 52*(5), 629–641.

Iyengar, R., Van den Bulte, C., & Valente, T. W. (2011). Rejoinder – Further reflections on studying social influence in new product diffusion. *Marketing Science, 30*(2), 230–232.

Iyengar, R., Van Den Bulte, C., & Lee, J. Y. (2015). Social contagion in new product trial and repeat. *Marketing Science, 34*(3), 408–429.

Jackson, M. O. (2010). *Social and economic networks*. Princeton: Princeton university press.

Kumar, V., Aksoy, L., Donkers, B., Venkatesan, R., Wiesel, T., & Tillmanns, S. (2010). Undervalued or overvalued customers: Capturing total customer engagement value. *Journal of Service Research, 13*(3), 297–310.

Landsman, V., & Nitzan, I. (2020). Cross-decision social effects in product adoption and defection decisions. *International Journal of Research in Marketing, 37*(2), 213–235.

Ma, L., Sun, B., & Kekre, S. (2015). The squeaky wheel gets the grease – An empirical analysis of customer voice and firm intervention on twitter. *Marketing Science, 34*(5), 627–645.

Manski, C. F. (2000). Economic analysis of social interactions. *Journal of Economic Perspectives, 14*(3), 115–136.

McPherson, M., Smith-Lovin, L., & Cook, J. M. (2001). Birds of a feather: Homophily in social networks. *Annual Review of Sociology, 27*(1), 415–444.

Meyners, J., Barrot, C., Becker, J. U., & Goldenberg, J. (2017). The role of mere closeness: How geographic proximity affects social influence. *Journal of Marketing, 81*(5), 49–66.

Nair, H., Manchanda, P., & Bhatia, T. (2010). Asymmetric social interactions in physician prescription behavior: The role of opinion leaders. *Journal of Marketing Research, 47*(5), 883–895.

Nam, S., Manchanda, P., & Chintagunta, P. K. (2010). The effect of signal quality and contiguous word of mouth on customer acquisition for a video-on-demand service. *Marketing Science, 29*(4), 690–700.

Nielsen. (2015). Global trust in advertising. Available online at http://www.nielsen.com/us/en/insights/reports/2015/global-trust-in-advertising-2015.html. Updated on 09-28-2015, checked on 5/3/2017.

Nitzan, I., & Libai, B. (2011). Social effects on customer retention. *Journal of Marketing, 75*(6), 24–38.

Onnela, J.-P., Saramäki, J., Hyvönen, J., Szabó, G., Lazer, D., Kaski, K., et al. (2007). Structure and tie strengths in mobile communication networks. *Proceedings of the National Academy of Sciences, 104*(18), 7332–7336.

Park, E., Rishika, R., Janakiraman, R., Houston, M. B., & Yoo, B. (2018). Social dollars in online communities: The effect of product, user, and network characteristics. *Journal of Marketing, 82*(1), 93–114.

Peres, R., Muller, E., & Mahajan, V. (2010). Innovation diffusion and new product growth models: A critical review and research directions. *International Journal of Research in Marketing, 27*(2), 91–106.

R Core Team. (2018). R: A language and environment for statistical computing. R Foundation for Statistical Computing, Vienna. https://www.R-project.org/

Reingen, P. H., & Kernan, J. B. (1986). Analysis of referral networks in marketing: Methods and illustration. *Journal of Marketing Research, 23*(4), 370–378.

Risselada, H., Verhoef, P. C., & Bijmolt, T. H. A. (2014). Dynamic effects of social influence and direct marketing on the adoption of high-technology products. *Journal of Marketing, 78*(2), 52–68.

Shalizi, C. R., & Thomas, A. C. (2011). Homophily and contagion are generically confounded in observational social network studies. *Sociological Methods & Research, 40*(2), 211–239.

Snijders, T. A. B., van de Bunt, G. G., & Steglich, C. E. G. (2010). Introduction to stochastic actor-based models for network dynamics. *Social Networks, 32*(1), 44–60.

Trusov, M., Bucklin, R. E., & Pauwels, K. H. (2009). Effects of word-of-mouth versus traditional marketing: Findings from an internet social networking site. *Journal of Marketing, 73*(5), 90–102.

Trusov, M., Bodapati, A. V., & Bucklin, R. E. (2010). Determining influential users in internet social networks. *Journal of Marketing Research, 47*(4), 643–658.

Valente, T. W. (2012). Network interventions. *Science, 337*(6090), 49–53.

Valsesia, F., Proserpio, D., & Nunes, J. C. (2020). The positive effect of not following others on social media. *Journal of Marketing Research*. forthcoming.

Van den Bulte, C., & Lilien, G. L. (2001). Medical innovation revisited: Social contagion versus marketing effort. *American Journal of Sociology, 106*(5), 1409–1435.

Wilhelm, S., & de Matos, M. G. (2015). spatialprobit: Spatial Probit Models. R package version 0.9–11. https://CRAN.R-project.org/package=spatialprobit.

Wuyts, S. H. K., Dekimpe, M. G., Gijsbrechts, E., & Pieters, F. G. M. R. (2011). *The connected customer: The changing nature of consumer and business markets*. Routledge.

Zhang, Y., & Godes, D. (2018). Learning from online social ties. *Marketing Science, 37*(3), 425–444.

Zhang, J., Liu, Y., & Chen, Y. (2015). Social learning in networks of friends versus strangers. *Marketing Science, 34*(4), 573–589.

Bayesian Models

Thomas Otter

Contents

Introduction: Why Use Bayesian Models?	720
Bayesian Essentials	722
Bayesian Estimation	731
Examples of Posterior Distributions in Closed Form	732
Posterior Distributions Not in Closed Form	736
Model comparison	761
Numerical Illustrations	765
A Brief Note on Software Implementation	765
A Hierarchical Bayesian Multinomial Logit Model	766
Mediation Analysis: A Case for Bayesian Model Comparisons	769
Conclusion	771
Cross-References	771
Appendix	772
MCMC for Binomial Probit Without Data Augmentation	772
HB-Logit Example	776
References	778

Abstract

Bayesian models have become a mainstay in the tool set for marketing research in academia and industry practice. In this chapter, I discuss the advantages the Bayesian approach offers to researchers in marketing, the essential building blocks of a Bayesian model, Bayesian model comparison, and useful algorithmic approaches to fully Bayesian estimation. I show how to achieve feasible Bayesian inference to support marketing decisions under uncertainty using the Gibbs sampler, the Metropolis Hastings algorithm, and point to more recent developments – specifically the no-U-turn implementation of Hamiltonian Monte Carlo sampling available in Stan. The emphasis is on the development of an

T. Otter (✉)
Goethe University Frankfurt am Main, Frankfurt am Main, Germany
e-mail: otter@marketing.uni-frankfurt.de

appreciation of Bayesian inference techniques supported by references to implementations in the open source software R, and not on the discussion of individual models. The goal is to encourage researchers to formulate new, more complete, and useful prior structures that can be updated with data for better marketing decision support.

Keywords

Marketing decision-making · Bayesian inference · Gibbs sampling · Metropolis Hastings · Hamiltonian Monte Carlo · R · bayesm · Stan

Introduction: Why Use Bayesian Models?

Bayesian models have gained popularity over the past 30 years both among academics in marketing and marketing research practitioners. There are several reasons for this popularity. First, many marketing problems involve data in the form of relatively short panels but with many observational units (large N, small T). Each observational unit, e.g., a respondent, a customer, or a store supplies only a limited amount of data, but there are many observational units in the data set. In the vast majority of these applications, decision makers know a priori that observational units are heterogeneous in their underlying, at least partially unobserved characteristics that generated the data. And the successful marketing of differentiated goods that involves market segmentation, targeting and positioning requires measures of heterogeneity in the population of observational units. Estimating separate, independent models for each observational unit results in unreliable estimates, and in many applications, individual level time series are too sparse for individual level maximum likelihood estimates to be defined. Hierarchical Bayes models offer a convenient and practical solution to this problem.

Second, the overwhelming majority of marketing data sets involve so-called limited dependent variables, e.g., choices, ratings, rankings, or generally dependent variables that have strongly noncontinuous features. Although a number of non-Bayesian estimators are available for models with such dependent variables (see e.g., Amemiya 1985; Long 1997), the assessment of statistical uncertainty in estimates relies on large sample asymptotic arguments. In marketing, large samples that allow for inference based on asymptotic arguments are the exception, even in an era where big data has become a ubiquitous buzzword. Big data, by definition, involves large data sets. However, the size of the data set usually does not translate into more statistical information about individual target parameters. Big data are always "big" because of their dimensionality spanning across, e.g., tens of thousands of customers, products, and time points, and include a myriad of potentially useful conditioning arguments. The dimensionality of the data at the very source of its size, or "bigness," regularly translates into similarly high-dimensional models and estimation problems, such that the amount of statistical information about individual target parameters is small yet again. Bayesian models allow for coherent inference even in small samples, or more generally in situations where there is little data-based information about individual parameters. Moreover, a number of relatively simple yet powerful computational algorithms facilitate the estimation of limited dependent variable models.

Third, in marketing, inference about model parameters or more generally about different models, i.e., the statistical assessment of the likely mechanisms that bring about consumers' and competitors' behaviors in a market is usually not an end in itself but input to the decisions of marketing managers in companies. The likely benefit from various alternatives for, e.g., product design, product line composition, pricing, or advertising schedules can be expressed as a function of a model and its parameters. However, knowledge of model parameters and generally the model that generated the observed market behaviors will never be perfect. Bayesian modeling facilitates the accurate incorporation of any remaining uncertainty about the mechanism behind observed market behaviors in managerial decisions.

Fourth, computational resources become more powerful and affordable every year, facilitating the estimation of ever more realistic and thus complex models in academic and industry applications. In addition, freely available software such as, e.g., the R-package bayesm (see Rossi et al. 2005) makes a collection of Bayesian models useful for marketing applications readily accessible (The latest version of bayesm is written for speed using the R-package Rcpp (Eddelbuettel and François 2011; Eddelbuettel 2013). The last complete version mostly written in plain R is version 2.2–5. The R-files are available from the CRAN-archives and often a useful start when developing your own routines). In fact, one reason for the popularity of Bayesian modeling among market research practitioners has been the adoption of hierarchical Bayes models for inference by companies like Sawtooth software (Orme 2017) that revolutionized how market research consultants approach the analysis of, for example, choice-based conjoint experiments. Finally, Stan (Carpenter et al. 2017) appears as a big step towards freeing creative modeling from having to invest substantial amounts of time in the development of efficient Bayesian estimation routines.

Fifth, because Bayesian estimation is simply the exact reverse of the data generating process (DGP), it is naturally attractive to researchers that are interested in the development and the empirical test of their own marketing models. Some researchers view the need to specify a complete DGP as a drawback. The argument is that theory never is precise enough to do so, and that this requirement leads to arbitrary choices that unduly impact the inference for quantities the data are more or less directly informative about. The Bayesian response to this criticism is to specify highly flexible DGPs in instances where theory is lacking. This strategy is facilitated by algorithms that adaptively determine a reasonable dimensionality of a flexibly formulated model. This determination is based on statistical evidence that potentially favors a lower dimensional, simpler model and not just fails to reject that model as in classical hypothesis testing.

All that said, it usually still takes longer to estimate a fully Bayesian model than it takes to compute maximum likelihood estimates, in case they exist. I have also heard people "complain" about the amount of information contained in large samples from posterior distributions as produced by modern numerical Bayesian inference tools (Compared to a collection of maximum likelihood estimates and their standard errors). However, it seems natural to wait somewhat longer for a more complete answer to a decision problem. And many interesting decision problems cannot be properly addressed based on a collection of maximum likelihood estimates (should they even exist) and especially upon realizing that their standard errors cannot be reliably estimated with the data at hand.

Bayesian Essentials

A Bayesian model consists of a likelihood function $p\,(\mathbf{y}|\boldsymbol{\theta})$ that fully specifies the probability of the data $\mathbf{y}$ given parameters $\boldsymbol{\theta}$, i.e., the process that generates the data for known parameters. In fact, if the researcher only wants to work with one likelihood function, is not interested in comparing across different mechanisms that may have generated the data, any function that is proportional to $p\,(\mathbf{y}|\boldsymbol{\theta})$ will do, i.e., all functions that differ from $p\,(\mathbf{y}|\boldsymbol{\theta})$ only by an arbitrary positive constant c are likelihood functions, $\ell(\mathbf{y}|\,\boldsymbol{\theta}) \equiv c \cdot p(\mathbf{y}|\boldsymbol{\theta})$. We will revisit this point later. A simple example is the linear regression model $y_i = \mathbf{x}_i'\boldsymbol{\beta} + \varepsilon_i$, $\varepsilon_i \sim iid\,\mathcal{N}\left(0, \sigma_\varepsilon^2\right)$ that implies the following likelihood for the data $p\left(\mathbf{y}|\boldsymbol{\beta}, \sigma_\varepsilon^2\right) = \prod_{i=1}^{N} \mathcal{N}\left(y_i|\,\mathbf{x}_i'\boldsymbol{\beta}, \sigma_\varepsilon^2\right)$.

The second component of a Bayesian model is a prior distribution for the parameters indexing the likelihood $p(\boldsymbol{\theta})$. The notation $p(\boldsymbol{\theta})$ means "the density p evaluated at the value $\boldsymbol{\theta}$." Further, defining the prior distribution as $p(\boldsymbol{\theta})$ implies that $\boldsymbol{\theta} \sim p$, i.e., that $\boldsymbol{\theta}$ is (a priori) distributed according to density p, or simply is p-distributed. The notation $p(\boldsymbol{\theta})$ is short-hand because it omits the (subjective prior) parameters indexing the prior distribution. For example, in an application the statement that the prior is a multivariate normal distribution is incomplete. We need to add the information about the prior mean and variance, e.g., $p(\boldsymbol{\theta}) = \mathcal{N}\left(\boldsymbol{\theta}|\boldsymbol{\theta}^0, \boldsymbol{\Sigma}^0\right)$, where $\mathcal{N}\left(\boldsymbol{\theta}|\boldsymbol{\theta}^0, \boldsymbol{\Sigma}^0\right)$ is the multivariate normal distribution with mean $\boldsymbol{\theta}^0$ and variance-covariance $\boldsymbol{\Sigma}^0$ evaluated at $\boldsymbol{\theta}$. The multivariate normal density can be evaluated in R using the command dmvn from the R-package mvnfast (Fasiolo 2016) or the command dmvnorm from R-package mvtnorm (Genz et al. 2018). Both commands support computations on the log-scale which are *essential* for numerical accuracy. For example, a log-likelihood value of -2000 can only be numerically distinguished from a log-likelihood value of, say, -2050 on the log-scale, because both likelihoods, i.e., exp(-2000) and exp(-2050) evaluate to an "exact" machine zero at currently available machine accuracies.

The need to specify prior distributions for Bayesian analysis is often viewed as a drawback of the Bayesian approach. There are several aspects to the specification and the role of the prior distribution in a Bayesian model. First, as suggested by the name, the prior distribution is the formal vehicle to bring prior substantive knowledge to bear on the analysis. And it is sometimes overlooked by critics of the Bayesian approach that such knowledge is already required when specifying the likelihood function. Second, from a purely technical point of view, prior distributions improve the statistical properties of estimators derived from the model (see e.g., Robert 1994, p. 75).

In the regression example, a useful way to probe into prior knowledge is to think about expected changes in y_i as a function of changes in $\mathbf{x_i}$. Unless the substantive domain the data originates from is unknown, it is extremely likely that the analyst will have some substantive idea about the DGP that should be used in the formulation of prior distributions. In the event where the analysis is a follow-up on previous statistical analyses in the same or a related domain, the choice of prior can build on these results. An example would be market research companies that more or less continuously study demand in a set of markets.

With the specification of a prior distribution, the analyst expresses his beliefs about what parameter values are more likely than other parameter values and by how much, based on his existing substantive understanding of the DGP. If the analyst specifies a prior such that parameters in a relatively small subset of the parameter space are much more likely than other parameters, the prior is usually referred to as an *informative* prior. The most extreme case of an informative prior is a distribution that concentrates all its mass on a singular parameter value. Such a prior is called *degenerate*. Degenerate priors constrain parameters to take particular values known a priori. Conversely, the prior is *weakly informative* or *diffuse* if there is no discernible concentration of prior mass on subsets of the parameter space. However, unless the parameter space is bounded in all directions as, e.g., in the case of a parameter measuring a probability, it is impossible to put exactly equal prior weight on all parameter values without violating the requirement that the prior needs to be in the form of a probability density function (A function $p(\boldsymbol{\theta})$ is a probability density function if $\int p(\boldsymbol{\theta}) d\boldsymbol{\theta} = 1$). Priors that fulfill this requirement are also referred to as *proper* priors and priors that do not are *improper* or literally *noninformative*. Finally, if the prior puts zero mass on subsets of the parameter space, e.g., zero mass on positive price coefficients in a demand model, it is called a *constrained* prior.

Bayesian models then apply Bayes' theorem to derive the posterior distribution of model parameters given the data:

$$p(\boldsymbol{\theta}|\mathbf{y}) = \frac{p(\mathbf{y}|\boldsymbol{\theta})\ p(\boldsymbol{\theta})}{\int p(\mathbf{y}|\boldsymbol{\theta})\ p(\boldsymbol{\theta})\ d\boldsymbol{\theta}} = \frac{p(\mathbf{y},\boldsymbol{\theta})}{p(\mathbf{y})} \tag{1}$$

Equation 1 identifies the goal of a Bayesian model as to make probability statements about quantities of interest, $\boldsymbol{\theta}$. More specifically, a Bayesian model extracts information in the data $\mathbf{y}$ via the likelihood function $p(\mathbf{y}|\boldsymbol{\theta})$ to update prior knowledge about these quantities summarized in the prior distribution $p(\boldsymbol{\theta})$. The updated knowledge is then used to compare among marketing actions a with payoffs that depend on $\boldsymbol{\theta}$. If we define the loss from an action a given $\boldsymbol{\theta}$ as $\mathcal{L}(a, \boldsymbol{\theta})$ the optimal Bayes action minimizes the posterior expected loss:

$$\mathcal{L}(a|\mathbf{y}) = \int \mathcal{L}(a,\boldsymbol{\theta})\ p(\boldsymbol{\theta}|\mathbf{y})\ d\boldsymbol{\theta} \tag{2}$$

In marketing applications, the loss usually does not directly depend on θ but on the implied data $\hat{\mathbf{y}}$, usually some manifestation of demand, i.e., $\mathcal{L}(a,\theta) = \int \mathcal{L}(a,\hat{\mathbf{y}}) p(\hat{\mathbf{y}}|\theta,a)\, d\hat{\mathbf{y}}$. The notation $p(\hat{\mathbf{y}}|\theta,a)$ covers the relevant case where the actions under investigation are conditioning arguments to the DGP. A well-known example is finding the coupon strategy that maximizes net revenues, i.e., minimizes the loss defined as negative net revenues in Rossi et al. (1996).

The denominator in Eq. 1, $p(\mathbf{y})$, is known as the marginal likelihood of the data $\mathbf{y}$ or the normalizing constant of the posterior distribution $p(\theta|\mathbf{y})$. As we will see in section "Bayesian Estimation," knowledge of this quantity is not required for Bayesian inference given a particular model. However, statements about quantities of interest θ in probability form require that $0 < p(\mathbf{y}) < \infty$. Only if this condition is met, the posterior $p(\theta|\mathbf{y})$ will be in the form of a probability density functions, i.e., $\int p(\theta|\mathbf{y})d\theta = 1$.

In addition, the marginal likelihood of the data is $p(\mathbf{y})$ needed for the comparison across different models for the *same* data where models may be arbitrarily different in terms of the likelihood function, the prior distribution or both. In fact, based on the marginal likelihood of the data given a particular model $\mathcal{M}$, i.e., $p(\mathbf{y}|\mathcal{M})$, the decision theoretic framework in Eq. 2 can be extended to cover decisions about the DGP itself, and to take uncertainty about the data generating model into account when choosing a marketing action. The optimal action given a set of possible data generating models $\mathcal{M}_1, \ldots, \mathcal{M}_K$ and the data minimizes

$$\mathcal{L}(a|\mathbf{y}, \mathcal{M}_1, \ldots, \mathcal{M}_K) = \sum_k p(\mathbf{y}|\mathcal{M}_k) \Pr(\mathcal{M}_k) \int \mathcal{L}(a,\theta) p(\theta|\mathbf{y}, \mathcal{M}_k) d\theta \quad (3)$$

where $\Pr(\mathcal{M}_k)$ is the subjective prior probability that model k is the true model that is often chosen to be $1/K$ in the absence of better knowledge. A marketing application following this general idea is presented in Montgomery and Bradlow (1999).

The fundamental appeal of being able to make probability statements about quantities of interest θ is the seamless integration with decision-making based on the expected utility from a set of possible actions. Note that the posterior expected loss in Eq. 2 will only usefully distinguish between different actions a if the posterior $p(\theta|\mathbf{y})$ integrates to 1, i.e., is a valid probability density function. It should be recognized that a *proper* prior distribution $p(\theta)$ essentially guarantees that we can make these probability statements, independent of any data deficiencies that may be present. A Bayesian model therefore quantifies how much the data, through the likelihood, add to our prior understanding of a DGP by comparing the prior distribution $p(\theta)$ to the posterior distribution $p(\theta|\mathbf{y})$. This is different from the classical question what models or model parameters the data can identify.

Consider the following illustrative example. Let us assume that someone measured the preferences for various credit cards on a linear, continuous scale. The cards vary in terms of brand: Mastercard, Visa, Discover; interest rate on outstanding balances: 18%, 15%, 12%; annual fee: no annual fee, $10, $20; and finally the credit limit: $1000, $2500, $5000. The researcher has preference measures for the following eight cards in Table 1, where "1 s" indicate which attribute levels are present.

Dummy coding using the brand Mastercard, 18% interest, no annual fee and a credit limit of $1000 as base lines, and adding a constant, we obtain the matrix corresponding to the linear regression model $y_i = \beta_0 + x_{1,i}\beta_1 + \ldots + x_{8,i}\beta_8 + \varepsilon_i, \varepsilon_i \sim \mathcal{N}(0, \sigma_\varepsilon^2)$ for cards $i = 1, \ldots, 8$ in Table 2.

It is easy to verify that the overall nine β-coefficients in this model are not jointly likelihood identified, because there are only eight observations. This can be viewed as toy example of the increasingly common situation, where the number of (potential) explanatory variables exceeds the number of observations, including big data that owe their size to the number of variables in addition to the number of observations (are "broader" than "long"). In such data sets, a purely data-based distinction between connections from explanatory variables to the dependent variable is no longer possible, even if all explanatory variables come from independent processes a priori.

Inspecting the bivariate correlations between covariates in Table 2 that are depicted in Table 3, we can see that these correlations are not too strong, individually. However, we also see that no two design columns are perfectly orthogonal. I further

Table 1 Credit card Designmatrix

	Brand			Interest			Annual fee			Credit limit		
#	Master	Visa	Discover	18%	15%	12%	$0	$10	$20	$1000	$2500	$5000
1	1	0	0	1	0	0	1	0	0	1	0	0
2	1	0	0	0	0	1	0	0	1	0	0	1
3	0	1	0	1	0	0	0	1	0	0	0	1
4	0	0	1	1	0	0	0	0	1	0	1	0
5	0	0	1	0	0	1	0	1	0	1	0	0
6	0	0	1	0	1	0	1	0	0	0	0	1
7	0	1	0	0	0	1	1	0	0	1	0
8	1	0	0	0	1	0	0	1	0	0	1	0

Table 2 Credit card Modelmatrix

		Brand		Interest		Annual fee		Credit limit	
	Constant	Visa	Discover	15%	12%	$10	$20	$2500	$5000
#	x_0	x_1	x_2	x_3	x_4	x_5	x_6	x_7	x_8
1	1	0	0	0	0	0	0	0	0
2	1	0	0	0	1	0	1	0	1
3	1	1	0	0	0	1	0	0	1
4	1	0	1	0	0	0	1	1	0
5	1	0	1	0	1	1	0	0	0
6	1	0	1	1	0	0	0	0	1
7	1	1	0	0	1	0	0	1	0
8	1	0	0	1	0	1	0	1	0

investigate the model in Table 2 using regression analysis. Specifically, I regress each column in Table 2 (excluding the constant) on the remaining columns. Every one of these eight regression results in a perfect prediction because we have $9 - 1 = 8$ predictors and 8 observations, each. The rows in Table 4 report the coefficients from regressing the covariate indicated by the row name on the remaining seven covariates in addition to a constant. A dash indicates that the covariate indicated by the column label in Table 4 is the dependent variable. The "NAs" result from perfect predictions of the covariates "Discover," "12% interest rate," and "$10 annual fee" before including the covariate "$5,000 credit limit" as predictor.

For example, the last line of Table 4 implies the following deterministic equation from regressing the covariate "$5,000 credit limit" on the remaining covariates in Table 2: $x_8 = 0 + 1x_1 + 0x_2 + 1x_3 + 0x_4 + 0x_5 + 1x_6 - 1x_7$. The contrasts x_1, x_3, and x_6 involving "Visa," "15% interest," and "$20 annual fee" are therefore positively confounded with the contrast involving "$5,000 credit limit," and this latter contrast is negatively confounded with the contrast x_7 involving "$2,500 credit limit."

Now, what are the implications for modeling the variation in the preference measures y as a function of covariates? In order to arrive at a likelihood-identified regression model, we need to reduce the number of covariates (the number of columns in Table 2) such that the resulting **X**-matrix is of full column rank, and the inverse of **X′X** is well defined. As a general rule, we can always throw out covariates that are independent of *all* covariates we would like to keep in the model,

Table 3 Correlations between design columns

	Visa	Discover	15%	12%	$10	$20	$2500	$5000
Visa	1							
Discover	−0.45	1						
15%	−0.33	0.15	1					
12%	0.15	−0.07	−0.45	1				
$10	0.15	−0.07	0.15	−0.07	1			
$20	−0.33	0.15	−0.33	0.15	−0.45	1		
$2500	0.15	−0.07	0.15	−0.07	−0.07	0.15	1	
$5000	0.15	−0.07	0.15	−0.07	−0.07	0.15	−0.6	1

Table 4 Design column dependence – regression analysis

	Constant	Visa	Discover	15%	12%	$10	$20	$2500	$5000
Visa	0	–	0	−1	0	0	−1	1	1
Discover	0.5	−0.5	–	0	0	0	0	0	NA
15%	0	−1	0	–	0	0	−1	1	1
12%	0.5	0	0	0	–	0	0	0	NA
$10	0.5	0	0	0	0	–	−0.5	0	NA
$20	0	−1	0	−1	0	0	–	1	1
$2500	0	1	0	1	0	0	1	–	−1
$5000	0	1	0	1	0	0	1	−1	–

without biasing our inference for the influence of the latter. Throwing out such covariates, at worst, increases the unexplained variance. In this example, no covariate fulfills this criterion by the mere fact that we have too many covariates to choose from, relative to the number of observations.

As a second general rule, we can eliminate covariates from the model which we strongly believe (know a priori) to have no (direct) effect on the dependent variable. We can do so regardless of how such covariates are related to covariates we would like to keep in the model, for unbiased inference about the influence of the latter.

However, if we eliminate a covariate that actually has a direct effect on the dependent variable that is *not* independent of all covariates we would like to keep in the model, the resulting inference will be biased. For example, whatever the true preference contribution of "$5,000 credit limit" relative to the baseline of only "$1,000 credit limit," the coefficients associated with "Visa," "15% interest," and "$20 annual fee" will be biased upward by this amount, and the coefficient associated with "$2,500 credit limit" will be biased downward by the same amount upon deleting column x_8 ("$5,000 credit limit") for identification in this example. Also, note that the confounds identified here are not automatically resolved upon collecting more data. In fact, even an infinite number of observations from the model in Table 2 will exhibit the same problem. What is required for improved data based identification is not only more but also "different" data, i.e., data generated by **X**-configurations different from those in Table 2. However, more data will necessarily be "suitably different" if the processes that generate the covariates are independent, at least conditionally.

In this particular example, there is no obvious choice of covariates that could be omitted based on strong prior beliefs that their direct effect is equal to zero. In fact, a prior understanding of preferences for credit cards would suggest that all covariates likely causally relate to the observed preferences for the different cards. Thus, any likelihood identified model obtained by omitting covariates from Table 2 is likely to yield substantially biased inferences regarding the influence of covariates retained in the model.

At this point, it is useful to relate likelihood-identification by omitting covariates to the formulation of a prior. In a sense, omitting covariates to achieve likelihood-identification corresponds to a degenerate prior concentrated on zero for the effects of omitted covariates, coupled with an improper prior for the effects of covariates retained in the model. In contrast, a Bayesian model for this data defined through a proper prior over *all* observed covariates expresses the belief that these covariates contributed *causally* independently to the observed preferences, with some prior uncertainty about the size of the individual contributions.

From the perspective of different (implied) priors, I believe that essentially nobody would prefer one of the many possible likelihood identified models in this example to the Bayesian model that keeps with the prior causal structure. Mutilating the prior causal structure to overcome data deficiencies and to achieve likelihood-identification (and more generally statistical efficiency) does not seem to be a generally useful strategy. Obviously, one often can (and should) try to obtain more informative data. However, completely discounting the information in only partially informative data seems to be a wasteful strategy.

Importantly, a prior that expresses the belief in invariant structural aspects of the data generating process will eventually translate into accurate posterior measures of the strength of structural relationships, once more likelihood information becomes available. A model (or prior structure) that is formulated in response to observed data deficiencies will not. Thus, the findings from such a model are generally not useful as prior input to future analysis of data from the same process, be it informative, or again deficient per se, potentially in a different way. We will revisit this topic when we discuss and numerically illustrate hierarchical Bayesian models that manage to extract information about the distribution of parameters from a collection of likelihoods that individually fail likelihood-identification (a collection of "deficient" data sets).

A big intellectual step is thus to acknowledge the limits of a perspective that literally asks "for the data to speak." The decisions that go into "making the data speak," be it in the form of simple summaries or complicated (likelihood identified) models, always involve prior knowledge. In this context, trading beliefs about an underlying structure for the ability to relate parameters to well-determined functions of the data only regularly voids the thus identified parameters from the meaning sought by the analyst in the first place. In contrast, updating a structurally intact prior with deficient data preserves the structural interpretation of parameters, at the expense of "purely" data-based identification (I put "purely" in quotes, because the decision about how to arrive at a model that can be identified only based on the data at hand always involves subjective, i.e., non-data based prior knowledge).

Now back to our example. When passed to R's lm-function, for example, lm automatically deletes the last column from the model for a model that just identifies the remaining β-coefficients. This model computes eight parameters from eight observations and thus trivially fits the data perfectly. Because of the perfect fit of every member of the class of just identified models, the data cannot distinguish among models in this class. However, as mentioned earlier, prior knowledge strongly suggests that no likelihood-identified model obtained by deleting covariates makes much structural sense in this example.

For illustration, I simulate 1000 data sets using the model matrix in Table 2, a coefficient vector $\beta = (4,2,0,1,1.5,-1,-1.5,2,3)$, and $\sigma_\varepsilon^2 = 1$. For each data set, I estimate the regression model in Table 2 dropping column x_8 for identification which corresponds to the default in R's lm-function. I also estimate a fully conjugate (Conjugacy refers to mathematical properties of a prior in combination with a particular likelihood function. So-called conjugate priors result in posteriors of the same distributional form as the prior. For example, a normal prior is the conjugate prior for the parameters in a normal likelihood with known variance, i.e., a likelihood that implies (conditionally) normally distributed data) Bayesian regression model with conditional prior $\beta \sim \mathcal{N}\left(\mathbf{0}, \mathbf{I}\sigma_\varepsilon^2 100\right)$ and without dropping any columns from Table 2 using the routine runireg in the R-package bayesm (Rossi et al. 2005) (The marginal prior for σ_ε^2. is inverse Gamma with 3 degrees of freedom and scale equal to the observed variance of **y** in each data set, i.e., the default in the R-package bayesm).

Table 5 reports the data generating true β-values, the mean of the OLS- and Bayes-estimates across 1000 data replications, as well as the corresponding standard deviations. The comparison between the data generating values and the mean of the

Table 5 Sampling experiment

	True values	OLS Mean	OLS Standard deviation	Bayes Mean	Bayes Standard deviation
Constant	4.0	3.96	0.91	3.95	0.88
Visa	2.0	5.04	1.29	2.72	0.53
Discover	0.0	0.01	0.70	0.01	0.69
15%	1.0	4.02	1.33	1.70	0.54
12%	1.5	1.49	0.68	1.49	0.66
$10	−1.0	−1.00	0.70	−0.98	0.68
$20	−1.5	1.53	1.31	−0.77	0.55
$2500	2.0	−0.98	0.68	1.33	0.38
$5000	3.0	**0**	–	2.31	0.42

OLS-estimates clearly illustrates the bias analyzed theoretically earlier. The coefficients associated with "Visa," "15% interest," and "$20 annual fee" are biased upwards by about a value of 3 which corresponds to the data generating preference contribution of $x_8 = 1$, i.e., "$5,000 credit limit" which was dropped from estimation for identification. The coefficient associated with "$2,500 credit limit" is biased downward by the same amount. Taking into account the standard deviations in parentheses, these biases appear to be statistically significant, despite the small samples of eight observations. In contrast, the mean of the Bayes-estimates for the same coefficients is much closer to the data generating values. In addition, the standard deviations show that especially the parameters affected by bias in the OLS-regression are estimated with more statistical precision in the Bayesian model.

The main difference between the classical OLS approach and the Bayesian approach here are the assumptions that enable the extraction of information from the data. While classical estimation requires prior information about how to reduce the dimensionality of the inferential problem to deliver estimates, the Bayesian approach allows us to retain the original dimensionality at the expense of assumptions that make regression parameters outside of some range very unlikely. In applications where the form and thus the dimensionality of the likelihood function derive from causal reasoning, i.e., theory, the Bayesian approach thus facilitates inference without having to compromise on what is the core of existing beliefs about the DGP in response to data deficiencies.

The rapidly developing field of machine learning provides alternative approaches to flexibly "regularize" a likelihood function (see e.g., Hastie et al. 2001). On a formal level, the regularization techniques employed in machine learning can be re-expressed as prior assumptions about parameters or likely model structures. And while the machine learning approach may have advantages in applications where the analyst has minimal to no prior knowledge about the DGP, the Bayesian approach excels when such knowledge is available.

The prior employed in our illustrative example certainly is closer to a common sense understanding of preferences for credit cards than the model implied by deleting x_8 ("$5,000 credit limit"), or any other likelihood-identified model obtained by deleting covariates in this example. However, it is still in the spirit of regularization without much attention to details and incidentally essentially corresponds to a ridge-regression approach (Hoerl and Kennard 1970).

To illustrate further, Fig. 1 depicts the joint posterior of coefficients associated with "Visa" and "$5,000 credit limit" obtained from one of the 1000 simulated data sets. It illustrates a strong one-to-one trade-off between the "Visa" and "$5000 credit limit" coefficients (compare the 45-degree downward sloping solid line through the origin). When the draw of the "Visa"-coefficient suggests an exceedingly positive preference for Visa relative to the baseline brand Mastercard, the "$5,000 credit limit "-coefficient suggests a pronounced distaste for the $5000 credit limit relative to the baseline, and vice versa. Without the prior, this distribution would collapse to a line with equal support for all coefficients from $(\beta_{Visa} = -\infty, \beta_{\$5,000} = \infty)$ to $(\beta_{Visa} = \infty, \beta_{\$5,000} = -\infty)$, and consequently zero support for any finite set of coefficients. This line is the graphical analogue to nonidentifiability. The prior essentially allows for point identification by concentrating posterior support away from the endpoints $(-\infty, \infty)$ and $(\infty, -\infty)$. I believe that essentially everybody would view this as a reasonable assumption after pondering combinations of, say "infinite" preference for Visa with "infinite" distaste for a credit limit of $5000.

A more elaborate prior could, for example, harness the (weak) prior preference ordering of the levels of interest rate, annual fee, and credit limit, or specific knowledge about the person rating the credit cards (see e.g., Allenby et al. 1995).

Finally, many marketing applications such as, for example, conjoint experiments or the analysis of scanner panel data are characterized by a collection of small data sets that individually are similarly problematic as the one corresponding to Table 2. In such settings, so-called hierarchical Bayes models are useful. Hierarchical Bayes

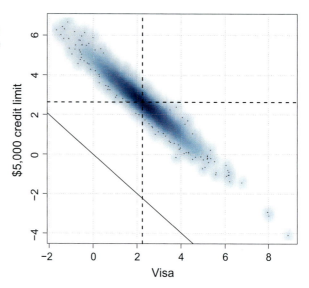

Fig. 1 Posterior correlation of the "Visa" and the "$5,000 credit limit" coefficient in one simulated data set

models learn the form of the prior to apply to each individual data set from the collection of data sets. In a hierarchical model, the prior that regularizes each individual level likelihood is therefore itself an object of statistical inference (see e.g., Lenk et al. 1996).

Even in settings where a data set formally identifies the parameters in a likelihood function Bayes theorem (Eq. 1) implies that the prior distribution will "bias away" the posterior from the information in the data. At least in small samples or generally in the context of data that does not contain much information about target parameters, the optimal Bayes action (see Eq. 2) may thus be different from the action that only conditions on likelihood information. And often analysts trained in classical frequentist statistics point out that an objective assessment of, for example, the statistical relevance of a parameter is no longer possible once a subjectively formulated prior enters the inferential procedure.

This criticism is certainly valid. However, the quest for objective inference comes at the price of not being able to use some data sets at all, or only subject to assumptions that likely are less defensible or further removed from a common understanding of the DGP than can be incorporated in a prior distribution. Furthermore, when only finite amounts of data are available, the frequentist assessment of statistical uncertainty in estimates or about models often relies on large sample asymptotic arguments in all but simple linear models. Large sample asymptotic arguments are certainly objective but may or may not hold in a particular application that has to rely on finite data.

Finally, the posterior distribution from priors that have positive support over the entire support of the parameter space as defined by the likelihood function, i.e., are neither degenerate or constrained, will converge to the maximum likelihood estimate as the data become more and more informative. In this sense, priors that are neither degenerate nor constrained result in large sample consistent inferences.

Bayesian Estimation

For the purpose of inference given a particular Bayesian model, knowledge of the marginal likelihood $p(\mathbf{y})$ is not required, because as long as $p(\mathbf{y})$ is finite and positive, we have

$$p(\boldsymbol{\theta}|\mathbf{y}) \propto p(\mathbf{y}|\boldsymbol{\theta})p(\boldsymbol{\theta}) \qquad (4)$$

i.e., the posterior distribution is proportional to the product of the likelihood times the prior. This proportionality follows from elementary probability calculus upon recognizing that the product of likelihood times the prior defines the joint density of the data $\mathbf{y}$ and parameters $\boldsymbol{\theta}$, i.e., the conditional distribution of $\boldsymbol{\theta}$ given the data $\mathbf{y}$ is proportional to the joint distribution of parameters and the data.

Another way to appreciate this proportionality is to think about the graphical representation of the posterior distribution of a scalar parameter. It is obvious that the linear scaling of the y-axis in this graph does not matter for *relative* probability statements of the form $p\,(\theta_i|\mathbf{y})\,/p\,(\theta_j|\mathbf{y})$, because any finite multiplicative constant would cancel from this ratio. For the same reason, posterior Bayesian inference given a model is invariant to rescaling the likelihood, the prior, or both by multiplicative constants. Similarly, the *relative* expected loss from two actions a_k and a_l given a particular model $\mathcal{L}\,(a_k|\mathbf{y})/\,\mathcal{L}\,(a_l|\mathbf{y})$ does not depend on multiplicative constants. However, to compute the expected loss in Eq. 2, we need absolute probability statements about $\boldsymbol{\theta}$, i.e., we need to normalize the product $c_1p\,(\mathbf{y}|\boldsymbol{\theta})$ $c_2\,p(\boldsymbol{\theta})$, where c_1 and c_2 are arbitrary positive "rescaling" constants.

I first discuss two examples where it is relatively obvious how to compute the normalizing constant $\int c_1 p(\mathbf{y}|\,\boldsymbol{\theta})\,c_2\,p(\boldsymbol{\theta})\,d(\boldsymbol{\theta})$ in closed form. When the normalizing constant is available in closed form, the posterior $p(\boldsymbol{\theta}|\mathbf{y})$ will usually be in the form of a known distribution. For known distributions, random number generators are implemented as part of statistical programming languages such as, for example, R or can be easily constructed. Based on $r = 1, \ldots, R$ draws from such a random number generator, we can approximate the posterior expected loss in Eq. 2 to an arbitrary degree of precision and for arbitrarily complicated nonlinear loss-functions as

$$\mathcal{L}(a|\mathbf{y}) \approx \frac{1}{R}\sum_{r=1}^{R}\mathcal{L}(a,\boldsymbol{\theta}^r), \quad \boldsymbol{\theta}^r \sim p(\boldsymbol{\theta}|\mathbf{y}), \tag{5}$$

because $\lim_{R\to\infty}\frac{1}{R}\sum_{r=1}^{R}\mathcal{L}(a,\boldsymbol{\theta}^r) = \int \mathcal{L}(a,\boldsymbol{\theta})p(\boldsymbol{\theta}|\mathbf{y})\,d\boldsymbol{\theta}$ by the law of large numbers provided that $\mathcal{L}\,(a|\,\mathbf{y})$ is known to be finite (Compare this to the definition of the (posterior) mean, i.e., $\int \boldsymbol{\theta} p(\boldsymbol{\theta}|\mathbf{y})d\boldsymbol{\theta}$ and its estimator from a sample $\boldsymbol{\theta}^1, \ldots, \boldsymbol{\theta}^r, \ldots, \boldsymbol{\theta}^R$, i.e., $\frac{1}{R}\sum_{r=1}^{R}\boldsymbol{\theta}^r$). This condition will always hold if the loss function evaluates to finite values over the definitional range of $\boldsymbol{\theta}$, formally $-\infty < \min_{\boldsymbol{\theta}}(\mathcal{L}(a,\boldsymbol{\theta})) \leq \max_{\boldsymbol{\theta}}(\mathcal{L}(a,\boldsymbol{\theta})) < \infty$, or more generally if nonfinite $\mathcal{L}(a,\boldsymbol{\theta})$ is an event of probability measure zero.

I then move to models where the posterior distribution cannot be computed in closed form and introduce Gibbs sampling facilitated by data augmentation and the Metropolis-Hastings algorithm as solutions to Bayesian inference in this case.

Examples of Posterior Distributions in Closed Form

Beta-binomial model. Consider a Bernoulli experiment that yields identically, independently (*iid*) distributed observations y_i taking one of two values, say "1" and "0" with probabilities θ and $1 - \theta$. Repeating the Bernoulli experiment n times results in $s = \sum_{i=1}^{n} y_i$ "1 s" and $n - \sum_{i=1}^{n} y_i$ "0 s". The probability of observing s in n trials given θ is then

$$p(s|n,\theta) = \binom{n}{s}\theta^s(1-\theta)^{n-s} = \frac{\Gamma(n+1)}{\Gamma(s+1)\Gamma(n-s+1)}\theta^s(1-\theta)^{n-s} \tag{6}$$

where Γ is the Gamma-function (The relation $\Gamma(n + 1) = n!$ provides some useful intuition for the Gamma-function).

As we will see, a convenient prior for the unobserved $p(y_i = 1) = \theta$ is in the form of a Beta density:

$$p(\theta|a,b) = \frac{\Gamma(a+b)}{\Gamma(a)\Gamma(b)} \theta^{a-1}(1-\theta)^{b-1} \tag{7}$$

The parameters a and b can be interpreted as the number of "1 s" and "0 s" in a hypothetical prior experiment and serve to express prior beliefs about θ. However, all real valued $a,b > 0$ result in proper priors for the probability θ over its definitional range, i.e., $\int_0^1 p(\theta|a,b)\,d\theta = 1$. For example, setting both a and b equal to 1 yields the uniform density over the unit interval expressing the absence of prior knowledge about what θ-values are more likely than others. Setting a and b equal to the same value larger than 1 yields a density that in the limit of $a, b \to \infty$ degenerates to a point mass at 0.5, which corresponds to various degrees of prior belief strength about θ being equal to 0.5. The mean and mode of the Beta density are given by $a/(a+b)$ and $(a-1)/(a+b-2)$. Therefore, $a > b$ ($a < b$) expresses prior beliefs that $\theta > 0.5$ ($\theta < 0.5$). Finally, for $0 < a, b < 1$, the Beta density takes a bathtub shape that piles up mass at the borders of the parameter space 0 and 1.

Conditional on the data $y_1, \ldots, y_n$, the binomial coefficient that forms the first factor in Eq. 6 is a fixed constant. Similarly, the normalizing constant of the Beta density, i.e., the first factor on the right hand side of Eq. 7 is fixed for a given choice of a,b.

Defining $c_1 = (\Gamma(n+1))^{-1}\Gamma(s+1)\Gamma(n-s+1)$ and $c_2 = (\Gamma(a+b))^{-1}\Gamma(a)\Gamma(b)$ and making use of the proportionality in Eq. 4, we thus have

$$p(\theta|a,b,s,n) \propto c_1 p(s|n,\theta) c_2 p(\theta|a,b)$$
$$\propto \theta^s (1-\theta)^{n-s} \theta^{a-1}(1-\theta)^{b-1} = \theta^{s+a-1}(1-\theta)^{n-s+b-1} \tag{8}$$

Comparing the rightmost expression in Eqs. 8 to 7, we see that this product is in the form of a (non-normalized) Beta density with parameters $\tilde{a} = s+a$ and $\tilde{b} = n-s+b$, and therefore

$$p(\theta|a,b,s,n) = \frac{\Gamma(\tilde{a}+\tilde{b})}{\Gamma(\tilde{a})\Gamma(\tilde{b})} \theta^{\tilde{a}-1}(1-\theta)^{\tilde{b}-1} \tag{9}$$

The fact that the posterior distribution in Eq. 9 is of the same known distributional from as the Beta-prior makes the Beta-prior very convenient in the context of a binomial likelihood function. Technically, the Beta-prior is the conjugate prior to the binomial likelihood.

Moving from Eqs. 6 and 7 to Eq. 8 we dropped all multiplicative constants from the likelihood and the prior that do not depend on θ and then normalized the result from Eq. 8 to arrive at Eq. 9. As discussed following Eq. 4 above, we can do so for the purpose of inference given a particular model that consists of a specific likelihood function and prior. I will address the role of these model-specific constants in the context of formal comparisons between different models further below.

Finally, a useful exercise for first time acquaintances with Bayesian inference is to simulate binomial data, for example, using R's `binom` command, or simply by making up n and s, and then simulate from the posterior in Eq. 9 using R's `rbeta` command for different specifications of a and b. Observe how the posterior changes as you use more or less (informative) data and more or less informative priors.

Another intellectually useful exercise is to think about different finite amounts of Bernoulli data that either consists of only "1 s" (or only "0 s"). Clearly, the maximum-likelihood estimate of the data generating probability is one (zero) in this case, and a purely data-based assessment of uncertainty in this estimate is impossible. A question at the core of statistical decision theory then is the following: Is a decision maker better off taking the maximum likelihood probability estimate of one (zero) for granted, or should he rather base his decisions on a proper posterior distribution? (Obtained using a proper prior distribution with positive support over the uniform interval.) A general answer to this question, which we will not attempt to prove here, is that any proper prior will translate into better decisions than taking the maximum likelihood estimate for granted. The only exception is the case where prior knowledge itself implies a deterministic process.

Normal-Normal model. The second example is a normal regression likelihood with a known observation error variance coupled with a normal prior for the regression coefficients. This example is of limited direct practical value. However, it showcases another important conjugate relationship. Moreover, this model serves as a useful building block for Bayesian inference in the binomial probit model discussed later, and numerous other models. Consider the following regression model and implied likelihood function

$$y_i = \mathbf{x}_i'\boldsymbol{\beta} + \varepsilon_i \quad \varepsilon_i \sim iid\mathcal{N}(0,1)$$
$$p(y_1,\ldots,y_n) = \frac{1}{\sqrt{2\pi}} \prod_{i=1}^{n} \exp\left(-\frac{1}{2}\left(y_i - \mathbf{x}_i'\boldsymbol{\beta}\right)^2\right), \quad (10)$$

and a multivariate normal prior distribution for the k regression coefficients corresponding to the entries in $\mathbf{x}_i$, i.e.,

$$p(\boldsymbol{\beta}|\boldsymbol{\beta}^0,\boldsymbol{\Sigma}^0) = (2\pi)^{-k/2}|\boldsymbol{\Sigma}^0|^{-1/2}\exp\left(-\frac{1}{2}(\boldsymbol{\beta}-\boldsymbol{\beta}^0)'(\boldsymbol{\Sigma}^0)^{-1}(\boldsymbol{\beta}-\boldsymbol{\beta}^0)\right). \quad (11)$$

Defining $\mathbf{y} = (y_1,\ldots,y_n)'$ and $\mathbf{X} = (\mathbf{x}_1,\ldots,\mathbf{x}_n)'$ the posterior distribution is then proportional to (see Eq. 4):

$$\begin{aligned}p(\boldsymbol{\beta}|\mathbf{y},\boldsymbol{\beta}^0,\boldsymbol{\Sigma}^0) &\propto \exp\left(-\frac{1}{2}(\boldsymbol{\beta}-\boldsymbol{\beta}^0)'(\boldsymbol{\Sigma}^0)^{-1}(\boldsymbol{\beta}-\boldsymbol{\beta}^0)\right)\prod_{i=1}^{n}\exp\left(-\frac{1}{2}\left(y_i-\mathbf{x}_i'\boldsymbol{\beta}\right)^2\right) \\ &\propto \exp\left(-\frac{1}{2}(\boldsymbol{\beta}-\tilde{\boldsymbol{\beta}})'\left(\mathbf{X}'\mathbf{X}+(\boldsymbol{\Sigma}^0)^{-1}\right)(\boldsymbol{\beta}-\tilde{\boldsymbol{\beta}})\right)\exp\left(-\frac{\tilde{s}}{2}\right) \\ &\propto \exp\left(-\frac{1}{2}(\boldsymbol{\beta}-\tilde{\boldsymbol{\beta}})'\left(\mathbf{X}'\mathbf{X}+(\boldsymbol{\Sigma}^0)^{-1}\right)(\boldsymbol{\beta}-\tilde{\boldsymbol{\beta}})\right),\end{aligned}$$
$$(12)$$

where

$$\tilde{\beta} = \left(X'X + \left(\Sigma^0\right)^{-1}\right)^{-1} \left(X'y + \left(\Sigma^0\right)^{-1} \beta^0\right) \tag{13}$$

$$\tilde{s} = (y - X'\tilde{\beta})'(y - X'\tilde{\beta}) + (\tilde{\beta} - \beta^0)'\left(\Sigma^0\right)^{-1}(\tilde{\beta} - \beta^0) \tag{14}$$

See Rossi et al. (2005) or Zellner (1971) for the details of the transformations in Eq. 12 and note that the posterior mean $\tilde{\beta}$ in Eq. 13 will converge to the ordinary least squares or maximum likelihood estimate as the sample size (the information in the data) increases, for all nondegenerate prior settings (i.e., $|\Sigma^0| > 0$). Smaller (larger) variances in Σ^0 put more (less) prior weight behind the prior guess β^0. For a well-defined ordinary least squares estimate $\hat{\beta}$ (a well-defined inverse of $X'X$), we can write Eq. 13 as

$$\tilde{\beta} = \left(X'X + \left(\Sigma^0\right)^{-1}\right)^{-1} \left(X'X(X'X)^{-1}X'y + \left(\Sigma^0\right)^{-1} \beta^0\right)$$

$$= \tilde{\beta} = \left(X'X + \left(\Sigma^0\right)^{-1}\right)^{-1} \left(X'X\hat{\beta} + \left(\Sigma^0\right)^{-1} \beta^0\right)$$

which illustrates that the posterior mean $\tilde{\beta}$ is a weighted convex combination of the ordinary least squares or maximum likelihood estimate $\hat{\beta}$ and the prior mean β^0, where the weights are information from the data in $X'X$ and the amount of prior information $(\Sigma^0)^{-1}$, respectively. Thus, the posterior mean will be somewhere "in between" the ordinary least squares estimate and the prior mean.

When combining the normal likelihood (Eq. 10) with the normal prior (Eq. 11) in Eq. 12, we dropped the multiplicative constants $\frac{1}{\sqrt{2\pi}}$ and $(2\pi)^{-k/2}|\Sigma^0|^{-1/2}$ from the likelihood and the prior, respectively. Again, this is fine as long we are only interested in inference given this specific model. Upon recognizing that the last line of Eq. 12 is the so-called kernel of a multivariate normal distribution (the kernel of a distribution drops all factors that do not directly depend on both unobserved parameters and the data or variables the distribution is for) and thus using

$$\int \exp\left(-\frac{1}{2}(\beta - \tilde{\beta})'\left(X'X + \left(\Sigma^0\right)^{-1}\right)(\beta - \tilde{\beta})\right) d\beta =$$

$$= (2\pi)^{k/2} \left|X'X + \left(\Sigma^0\right)^{-1}\right|^{-1/2} \tag{15}$$

we obtain the joint posterior distribution of the k regression coefficients in closed form:

$$p(\beta|y, \beta^0, \Sigma^0) = (2\pi)^{-k/2} \left|X'X + \left(\Sigma^0\right)^{-1}\right|^{1/2} \exp\left(-\frac{1}{2}(\beta - \tilde{\beta})'\left(X'X + \left(\Sigma^0\right)^{-1}\right)(\beta - \tilde{\beta})\right)$$

$$= \mathcal{N}\left(\beta|\tilde{\beta}, \left(X'X + \left(\Sigma^0\right)^{-1}\right)^{-1}\right) \tag{16}$$

We can directly sample from this distribution using, for example, the command rmvnorm in the R-package mvtnorm (Genz et al. 2018) or the faster version rmvn available in the R-package mvnfast (Fasiolo 2016). The bayesm (Rossi et al. 2005) routine corresponding to this model is breg.

Posterior Distributions Not in Closed Form

Next, I discuss the model defined by the combination of a binomial probit likelihood and a multivariate normal prior for the regression coefficients (see Eq. 11). Bayesian inference for this model is relatively much more challenging than for the two models discussed already because the normalizing constant of the posterior distribution is not available in closed form. The binomial probit likelihood is, similar to the binomial likelihood in Eq. 6, a DGP for independently distributed observations y_i taking one of two values, say "1" and "0". The probit likelihood defines the probability of observing $y_i = 1$ as a function of covariates $\mathbf{x}_i$ and (probit-)regression parameters $\boldsymbol{\beta}$ as follows:

$$p(y_i = 1|\boldsymbol{\beta}) = \Phi(\mathbf{x}_i'\boldsymbol{\beta}) = \int_{-\infty}^{\mathbf{x}_i'\boldsymbol{\beta}} \mathcal{N}(z|0,1)\,dz \qquad (17)$$

$$p(y_i = 0|\boldsymbol{\beta}) = \Phi(-\mathbf{x}_i'\boldsymbol{\beta}) = \int_{\mathbf{x}_i'\boldsymbol{\beta}}^{\infty} \mathcal{N}(z|0,1)\,dz \qquad (18)$$

Thus, observations $\mathbf{y} = (y_1, \ldots, y_n)'$ are not identically distributed but provide information about $\boldsymbol{\beta}$ exchangeably. "Exchangeably" essentially means that we don't need to keep track of the order or sequence of the data for proper inference. Exchangeability here is a consequence of conditional independence given the data generating parameters and observed covariates (see e.g., Bernardo and Smith 2001), conditional on covariates $\mathbf{X} = (\mathbf{x}_1, \ldots, \mathbf{x}_n)'$. The data $\mathbf{y}$ then have probit likelihood:

$$\begin{aligned} p(\mathbf{y}|\boldsymbol{\beta}) &= \prod_{i=1}^{n} \left(\Phi(\mathbf{x}_i'\boldsymbol{\beta})\right)^{y_i} \left(\Phi(-\mathbf{x}_i'\boldsymbol{\beta})\right)^{1-y_i} \\ &= \prod_{i=1}^{n} \left(\int_{-\infty}^{\mathbf{x}_i'\boldsymbol{\beta}} \mathcal{N}(z|0,1)\,dz\right)^{y_i} \left(\int_{\mathbf{x}_i'\boldsymbol{\beta}}^{\infty} \mathcal{N}(z|0,1)\,dz\right)^{1-y_i} \end{aligned} \qquad (19)$$

By Eq. 4, the posterior distribution of $\boldsymbol{\beta}$ is proportional to:

$$p(\boldsymbol{\beta}|\mathbf{y},\boldsymbol{\beta}^0,\boldsymbol{\Sigma}^0) \propto \exp\left(-\frac{1}{2}(\boldsymbol{\beta}-\boldsymbol{\beta}^0)'(\boldsymbol{\Sigma}^0)^{-1}(\boldsymbol{\beta}-\boldsymbol{\beta}^0)\right) \prod_{i=1}^{n} \left(\Phi(\mathbf{x}_i'\boldsymbol{\beta})\right)^{y_i} \left(\Phi(-\mathbf{x}_i'\boldsymbol{\beta})\right)^{1-y_i} \qquad (20)$$

As already mentioned, the normalizing constant of the right hand side in Eq. 20 cannot be computed in closed form and we thus cannot derive the posterior distribution directly, unlike in the previous examples. I will introduce Gibbs sampling as one solution to Bayesian inference in this model. To this end, an alternative interpretation of the probit likelihood suggested by the integral on the right hand side of Eq. 17 will be useful. Taking advantage of the symmetry of the normal distribution, we can rewrite:

$$p(y_i = 1|\beta) = \int_{-\infty}^{x'_i\beta} \mathcal{N}(z|0,1)dz = \int_0^{\infty} \mathcal{N}(z|x'_i\beta,1)dz \qquad (21)$$

$$p(y_i = 0|\beta) = \int_{x'_i\beta}^{\infty} \mathcal{N}(z|0,1)dz = \int_{-\infty}^0 \mathcal{N}(z|x'_i\beta,1)dz \qquad (22)$$

and interpret the binomial probit model as a random utility model in which latent utilities z_i are independently normally distributed with means $x'_i\beta$ and standard deviations equal to 1. A latent utility draw z_i from $\mathcal{N}(x'_i\beta,1)$ larger than 0 generates an observed $y_i = 1$ and a draw smaller than 0 an observed $y_i = 0$, i.e., $y_i = \mathbf{1}(z_i > 0)$. This is exactly equivalent to generating a y-observation using the probability in Eq. 21 as the parameter of a Bernoulli distribution (Draw a random uniform number u from the interval [0, 1], e.g., using `runif (1)` in R and compare to the probability in Eq. 21. Set $y_i = 1$ ($y_i = 0$) when u is smaller (larger) than this probability or use the R-command `rbinom`) because, e.g., $\lim_{R \to \infty} \frac{1}{R} \sum_{r=1}^{R} \mathbf{1}(z^r > 0) = E_z \mathbf{1}(z > 0) = \int_0^{\infty} \mathcal{N}(z|x'\beta,1)\,dz$.

If we had access to the latent utilities $\mathbf{z} = (z_1, \ldots, z_n)'$ that generated the observed binomial data $\mathbf{y} = (y_1, \ldots, y_n)'$, we could comfortably rely on the closed form results in Eq. 16 for Bayesian inference. Conditional on the data generating $\mathbf{z}$, we would in fact learn more about the regressions coefficients than we ever could from the corresponding $\mathbf{y}$.

Conversely, if we knew the regression coefficients β that generated the data, we could make an informed guess about the corresponding data generating $\mathbf{z}$. Based on the $\mathbf{y}$-data, we know that $\mathbf{z}$ that correspond to observed 1's must have been larger than zero and those corresponding to observed 0's smaller than zero. Based on β and the random utility interpretation of the probit likelihood, we know that the z_i came independently from $\mathcal{N}(x'_i\beta,1)$. Putting these insights together, we arrive at the following conditional distribution for a z_i corresponding to observed $y_i = 1$, and that for a z_j corresponding to observed $y_j = 0$ given β:

$$p(z_i|\beta,y_i = 1) = \frac{\mathcal{N}(z_i|x'_i\beta,1)\,\mathbf{1}(z_i > 0)}{\int_0^{\infty} \mathcal{N}(z|x'_i\beta,1)dz} = \mathcal{TN}(z_i|x'_i\beta,1,0,\infty) \qquad (23)$$

$$p(z_j|\beta,y_j = 0) = \frac{\mathcal{N}(z_j|x'_j\beta,1)\mathbf{1}(z_j < 0)}{\int_{-\infty}^0 \mathcal{N}(z|x'_j\beta,1)\,dz} = \mathcal{TN}(z_j|x'_j\beta,1,-\infty,0) \qquad (24)$$

Here $\mathbf{1}(\cdot)$ is an indicator function that evaluates to one it its argument is true and else to zero, and $\mathcal{TN}(a,b,c,d)$ is short for a normal distribution with mean a, variance

b, truncated below c, and above d. We can simulate from these distributions using a trick known as the inverse CDF-transformation (see e.g., Rossi et al. 2005), or rely on the command `rtruncnorm` in the R-package `truncnorm` (Mersmann et al. 2018) which builds on Geweke (1991).

Based on the results in Eq. 16 the conditional distribution of β given the $\mathbf{z}$ and the $\mathbf{y}$ is:

$$p(\beta|\mathbf{z},\mathbf{y},\beta^0,\Sigma^0) = p(\beta|\mathbf{z},\beta^0,\Sigma^0) = \mathcal{N}\left(\tilde{\beta},\left(\mathbf{X}'\mathbf{X} + (\Sigma^0)^{-1}\right)^{-1}\right), \qquad (25)$$

where

$$\tilde{\beta} = \left(\mathbf{X}'\mathbf{X} + (\Sigma^0)^{-1}\right)^{-1}\left(\mathbf{X}'\mathbf{z} + (\Sigma^0)^{-1}\beta^0\right) \qquad (26)$$

Note that once we condition on the $\mathbf{z}$ in Eq. 25, the $\mathbf{y}$ are no longer required as conditioning argument. A particular set of $\mathbf{z}$ transmits all the information, and in fact more information than contained in the $\mathbf{y}$, to β (I will discuss general rules for the derivation of conditional distributions later and for now concentrate on what can be achieved based on conditional distributions).

Gibbs sampler. Our goal is thus to derive the marginal posterior distribution $p(\beta|\mathbf{y},\beta^0,\Sigma^0)$ that is free from the extra, but virtual information about β that comes with each particular set of $\mathbf{z}$ we may condition on in Eq. 25. However, as we already know, this posterior is not available in closed form. A convenient solution to this problem is the Gibbs sampler. The Gibbs sampler allows us to generate draws from $p(\beta,\mathbf{z}|\mathbf{y},\beta^0,\Sigma^0)$ based on knowledge of $p(\mathbf{z}|\mathbf{y},\beta) = \prod_{i=1}^{n} p(z_i|\beta,y_i)$ and $p(\beta|\mathbf{z},\beta^0,\Sigma^0)$, i.e., conditional distributions only. Once we have draws from $p(\beta,\mathbf{z}|\mathbf{y},\beta^0,\Sigma^0)$, each draw of β in that sample is a draw from our target distribution $p(\beta|\mathbf{y},\beta^0,\Sigma^0)$ (Recall that the joint distribution $p(\beta,\mathbf{z}|\mathbf{y},\beta^0,\Sigma^0)$ can be decomposed into the product of the marginal distribution $p(\beta|\mathbf{y},\beta^0,\Sigma^0)$ and the conditional distribution $p(\mathbf{z}|\mathbf{y},\beta)$ by elementary probability calculus. If we have access to a sample from the joint distribution, drawing a β with no regard to the companion $\mathbf{z}$ and then looking at the companion $\mathbf{z}$ in the sample is equivalent to drawing from $p(\beta|\mathbf{y},\beta^0,\Sigma^0)$ and then from $p(\mathbf{z}|\mathbf{y},\beta)$).

The Gibbs sampler is an application of the fact that the joint distribution $p(\beta,\mathbf{z}|\mathbf{y},\beta^0,\Sigma^0)$ is uniquely determined by corresponding complete sets of conditional distributions (Besag 1974). The correspondence between the conditional distributions $p(\beta|\mathbf{z},\beta^0,\Sigma^0)$ and $p(\mathbf{z}|\mathbf{y},\beta)$ and the joint posterior distribution is illustrated in Eq. 27 which is an instance of the Hammersley-Clifford theorem. For clarity of notation, I abbreviate the subjective prior parameters β^0,Σ^0 to "•" in the following.

$$\begin{aligned} p(\beta,\mathbf{z}|\mathbf{y},\bullet) &= p(\beta|\mathbf{z},\bullet)p(\mathbf{z}|\mathbf{y},\bullet) \\ &= p(\beta|\mathbf{z},\bullet)\left(\int \frac{p(\beta|\mathbf{z},\bullet)}{p(\mathbf{z}|\mathbf{y},\beta)}d\beta\right)^{-1} \end{aligned} \qquad (27)$$

Proof:

$$p(\mathbf{z}|\mathbf{y},\beta)p(\beta|\mathbf{y},\bullet) = p(\beta|\mathbf{z},\bullet)p(\mathbf{z}|\mathbf{y},\bullet)$$

$$\frac{p(\beta|\mathbf{y},\bullet)}{p(\mathbf{z}|\mathbf{y},\bullet)} = \frac{p(\beta|\mathbf{z},\bullet)}{p(\mathbf{z}|\mathbf{y},\beta)}$$

$$\int \frac{p(\beta|\mathbf{y},\bullet)}{p(\mathbf{z}|\mathbf{y},\bullet)} d\beta = \int \frac{p(\beta|\mathbf{z},\bullet)}{p(\mathbf{z}|\mathbf{y},\beta)} d\beta \qquad (28)$$

$$\frac{1}{p(\mathbf{z}|\mathbf{y},\bullet)} = \int \frac{p(\beta|\mathbf{z},\bullet)}{p(\mathbf{z}|\mathbf{y},\beta)} d\beta$$

Based on $r = 1, \ldots, R$ draws from $p(\beta|\mathbf{z},\bullet)$, we can therefore estimate the *marginal* distribution:

$$p(\mathbf{z}|\mathbf{y}) = \left(\int \frac{p(\beta|\mathbf{z},\bullet)}{p(\mathbf{z}|\mathbf{y},\beta)} d\beta \right)^{-1} \approx \left(\frac{1}{R} \sum_{r=1}^{R} \frac{1}{p(\mathbf{z}|\mathbf{y},\beta^r)} \right)^{-1} \qquad (29)$$

and thus compute the *joint* distribution $p(\beta,\mathbf{z}|\mathbf{y},\bullet)$ based on only knowledge of the *conditional* distributions $p(\mathbf{z}|\mathbf{y},\beta)$ and $p(\beta|\mathbf{z},\bullet)$. The Gibbs sampler which builds on this fundamental relationship proceeds as follows:

1. Based on a starting value for β draw $\mathbf{z}$ from $p(\mathbf{z}|\mathbf{y},\beta)$ as given in Eqs. 23 and 24.
2. Use the most recent draw of $\mathbf{z}$ as conditioning argument in $p(\beta|\mathbf{z},\bullet)$ (Eq. 25) and draw a new β.
3. Use the most recent draw of β as conditioning argument in $p(\mathbf{z}|\mathbf{y},\beta)$ (Eqs. 23 and 24) and draw new $\mathbf{z}$.
4. Return to step 2, until completing R cycles through step 2 and step 3, and then stop.

Each completed cycle through steps 2 and 3 delivers a pair $(\beta, \mathbf{z})^r$ where $r = 1, \ldots, R$ indexes the cycle or iteration number of the Gibbs-sampler. Under rather general conditions for the conditional distributions involved, these pairs will represent draws from the joint distribution after some initial iterations, and independent of the choice of starting value. The initial iterations serve to "make the Gibbs sampler forget" the arbitrary starting value in step 1 above. This is often referred to as the "burn-in" period of the Gibbs-sampler. Intuitively, the choice of starting value does not matter, because the Gibbs sampler will forget it, no matter which value was chosen (However, the choice of starting value may influence how many iterations it takes before the Gibbs sampler converges, i.e., delivers pairs $(\beta, \mathbf{z})^r$ in proportion to their joint posterior density in a finite sample of R draws. Another practical concern for the choice of starting values is the numerical stability of the techniques used to draw from the conditional distributions).

Steps 2 and 3 above are often referred to as "blocks of the sampler." Note that step 2 itself consists of n-subblocks that each draw from the conditional distribution of a particular z_i. However, because all z_i are conditionally independent, i.e., $p(\mathbf{z}|\mathbf{y},\boldsymbol{\beta}) = \prod_{i=1}^{n} p(z_i|\boldsymbol{\beta}, y_i)$ (see Eqs. 23 and 24), step 2 effectively draws from the joint conditional posterior distribution of z. Similarly, step 3 draws from the joint conditional posterior distribution of all elements in $\boldsymbol{\beta}$.

To further strengthen the intuition for the Gibbs sampler, it is useful to think about each iteration as an exploration of the joint distribution in some neighborhood defined by the respective conditioning arguments. By the notion of sampling and updating of conditioning arguments, the Gibbs sampler is, however, not going to stay in this neighborhood but will move away from it and eventually return.

Each time it returns to some fixed neighborhood of $\boldsymbol{\beta}$-values, for example, it will do so from a different constellation of z. Returns from z-constellations that are closer to this $\boldsymbol{\beta}$-neighborhood in the sense of Eqs. 25 and 26 will occur more often than returns from z-constellations that are further away. Thus, looking at pairs $(\boldsymbol{\beta}, \mathbf{z})^r$ in this neighborhood, it is impossible to distinguish between moves "from $\boldsymbol{\beta}$ to z" and moves "from z to $\boldsymbol{\beta}$," and this will be true of every $\boldsymbol{\beta}$-neighborhood and z-neighborhood supported by the posterior distribution. In addition, by successively sampling from conditional distributions which are, by definition, proportional to the joint distribution, the Gibbs sampler is going to spend relatively more (fewer) iterations in areas of higher (lower) density under the joint distribution.

In other words, successive pairs $(\boldsymbol{\beta}, \mathbf{z})^1, \ldots, (\boldsymbol{\beta}, \mathbf{z})^r, \ldots, (\boldsymbol{\beta}, \mathbf{z})^R$ produced by iterations of the Gibbs sampler are locally dependent in the sense that pairs produced in successive iterations are more similar to each other than pairs produced further apart from each other, where distance is measured in iteration counts of the Gibbs sampler. However, all pairs provide exchangeable information about the joint posterior distribution. We can therefore use the output from the Gibbs sampler to approximate posterior expected loss (see Eq. 5) and any aspect of the posterior distribution we may be interested in by the corresponding expectation using the Gibbs output. For example, the posterior probability that a particular regression coefficient is larger than zero, i.e., $P(\beta_k > 0|\mathbf{y}, \cdot) = \int_0^\infty p(\beta_k|\mathbf{y}, \cdot)$ would be estimated from the Gibbs output as $\frac{1}{R} \sum_{r=1}^{R} \mathbf{1}\left(\beta_k^r > 0\right)$ Note that we control the degree of accuracy of these approximations by the length of the Gibbs sample R.

The particular Gibbs sampler described here is implemented as routine `rbprobitGibbs` in the R-package `bayesm` (Rossi et al. 2005) and dates back to Albert and Chib (1993). The routine comes with an example that illustrates input and output (Another `bayesm` routine, `rbiNormGibbs`, nicely illustrates how the Gibbs sampler explores a two-dimensional joint distribution by successively sampling from the corresponding two conditional distributions).

Data augmentation. In this application of the Gibbs sampler, the interest really is on the marginal posterior distribution of probit regression coefficients, i.e., $p(\boldsymbol{\beta}|\mathbf{y}, \cdot)$, and Gibbs sampling from the joint posterior distribution of $\boldsymbol{\beta}$ and z is just a means to obtaining the marginal distribution of interest. Drawing from $p(\mathbf{z}|\mathbf{y}, \boldsymbol{\beta})$ is therefore referred to as "data augmentation" in the literature. Data augmentation often helps transform Bayesian inference problems that involve "unknown" distributions, i.e., distributions without a normalizing constant in closed form, into problems that only involve sampling from distributions with known normalizing constants through conditioning. Canonical examples for the successful application of this technique are the multinomial probit model (McCulloch and Rossi 1994), the multivariate probit model Edwards and Allenby (2003), mixture models (see e.g., Allenby et al. 1998; Frühwirth-Schnatter et al. 2004; Lenk and DeSarbo 2000; Otter et al. 2004), and hierarchical models in general.

From the perspective of Gibbs sampling, there is no distinction between (unobserved) aspects of the data, unobserved parameters, or any unobservable we can derive a conditional distribution for, within the confines of the Bayesian model under investigation. However, before one gets too excited about the possibilities of *inference* about any unobservable, it is useful to reflect about how much we can learn about β and $\mathbf{z}$ from the data in this example.

While it is possible to attain perfect posterior knowledge about β in this model in the limit of an infinitely large sample, it is impossible to ever learn the particular set of $\mathbf{z}$'s that generated the data. This information is lost forever when moving from the data generating $\mathbf{z}$ to the observed $\mathbf{y}$ based on the indicator function $y_i = \mathbf{1}(z_i > 0)$. We have one observation y_i to learn about each z_i. This observation only set identifies z_i, i.e., indicates if $z_i < 0$ or $z_i > 0$. In addition $\mathcal{N}(\mathbf{x}'_i\beta, 1)$ which can be viewed as a hierarchical prior for the z_i cannot degenerate, i.e., cannot deliver a perfect prediction by the definition of the probit likelihood. Any finite valued $\mathbf{x}'_i\beta$ allows for $y_i = 1$ and $y_i = 0$, even if one of the two outcomes is extremely unlikely.

As such, we are severely limited in what we can learn about the data generating $\mathbf{z}$ no matter how many probit observations become available or what subjective prior parameters β^0 and Σ^0 we use. Thus, it is generally useful to distinguish between unobservables that can be consistently estimated in a particular model and unobservables that cannot, before further using the output from the Gibbs sampler. Here "consistently" means that we can think of amounts of data, i.e., likelihood information, or a subjective prior setting that translates into a degenerate posterior distribution which concentrates all its mass in one point. For example, it would be foolish to believe that using the posterior distribution of $\mathbf{z}$ could somehow further improve decisions informed by the data $\mathbf{y}$ and the model at hand, which depend on $p(\beta|\mathbf{y})$, only.

Blocking. One could replace step 2 in the Gibbs sampler above by a Gibbs cycle through the full conditional distributions of each element β_k. in β, i.e., $p(\beta_k \mid \beta_{-k}, \mathbf{z}, \bullet)$, where β_{-k} is short for all but the k-th element (These conditional densities are easily derived from the joint conditional normal distribution in Eq. 16 using linear regression theory).

Because any corresponding complete set of conditional distributions uniquely determines the joint distribution, this alternative sampler again delivers draws from the *same* joint posterior distribution $p(\beta, \mathbf{z}|\mathbf{y}, \bullet)$. However, the local dependence between successive pairs $(\beta, \mathbf{z})^1, \ldots, (\beta, \mathbf{z})^r, \ldots, (\beta, \mathbf{z})^R$ produced by iterations of this alternative Gibbs sampler is relatively higher. This is because two successive cycles through $p(\beta_k|\beta_{-k}, \mathbf{z}, \bullet)$ for all k-elements deliver draws of β that are more similar in expectation than two draws from $p(\beta|\mathbf{z}, \bullet)$, which are independently distributed.

Replacing a cycle like that through $p\left(\beta_k \mid \beta_{-k}, \mathbf{z}, \cdot\right)$ for all k-elements by a direct draw from the corresponding conditional joint distribution, in this case $p\left(\beta | \mathbf{z}, \beta^0, \Sigma^0\right)$, in a Gibbs sampler is referred to as "blocking," or "grouping" (e.g., Chen et al. 2000). In general, blocked Gibbs samplers deliver more additional information about the posterior distribution per incremental iteration than unblocked samplers, which is intuitive considering direct *iid*-sampling from the joint posterior distribution as the theoretical limit of blocking. As such, blocked samplers also deliver pairs $(\beta, \mathbf{z})'$ in proportion to their joint posterior density in a finite sample based on fewer iterations, converge faster from arbitrary starting values.

Another technical aspect is the order in which to successively draw from the blocks of a Gibbs sampler. The theory of Gibbs sampling implies that the order does not matter and in fact a random ordering is easiest to motivate theoretically (see e.g., Roberts 1996, p. 51). However, in our particular example, repeated draws from step 2, i.e., $p(\beta|\mathbf{z}, \cdot)$, or step 3, i.e., $p(\mathbf{z}|\mathbf{y}, \beta)$, without switching to the respective other block in between are a perfect waste of time because these draws are conditionally *iid*. Furthermore, randomly switching to step 2 before updating *all* elements of $\mathbf{z}$ in step 3 is inefficient because step 2 pools information across all $\mathbf{z}$. The updated pooled information is then "redistributed" across all $\mathbf{z}$ when drawing from $p(\mathbf{z}|\mathbf{y}, \beta)$ in step 3.

Conditional posterior distributions. Next I show how to derive the full conditional distributions that define the Gibbs sampler for the probit model above (see also Gilks 1996). Recall that by specifying a prior distribution and a likelihood function, we implicitly specify the joint distribution of unobservables and the data (see Eq. 1). Starting from the joint distribution of the data and unobservables in our example, i.e.,

$$p\left(\mathbf{y}, \mathbf{z}, \beta | \beta^0, \Sigma^0\right) = p\left(y_1, \ldots, y_n, z_1, \ldots, z_n, \beta_1, \ldots, \beta_K | \beta^0, \Sigma^0\right)$$

we can derive any conditional distribution of interest using elementary probability calculus. Omitting the conditioning arguments β^0 and Σ^0 for clarity of notation we have for example

$$p(z_1|y_1,\ldots,y_n,z_2,\ldots,z_n,\beta_1,\ldots,\beta_K) = \frac{p(y_1,\ldots,y_n,z_1,\ldots,z_n,\beta_1,\ldots,\beta_K)}{\int p(y_1,\ldots,y_n,z_1,\ldots,z_n,\beta_1,\ldots,\beta_K)\,dz_1} \qquad (30)$$

which does not look simple or useful yet. However, based on an understanding of how the model operates as a DGP, we can greatly simplify this expression. It is in this sense that Bayesian inference exactly reverses the steps that we believe generated the data.

Recall the latent utility interpretation of the probit likelihood function. Given β, latent utilities $\mathbf{z}$ are generated independently from $\mathcal{N}(\mathbf{X}\beta, \mathbf{I}_n) = \prod_{i=1}^N \mathcal{N}(\mathbf{x}_i'\beta, 1)$. Then the signs of the elements in $\mathbf{z}$ independently determine the data $\mathbf{y}$ according to indicator functions $y_i = \mathbf{1}(z_i > 0)$ for all $i = 1, \ldots, n$. Based on this understanding of the conditional independence relationships in the DGP, we can rewrite and simplify Eq. 30 as follows:

$$
\begin{aligned}
&p(z_1|y_1,\ldots,y_n,z_2,\ldots,z_n,\beta_1,\ldots,\beta_K)\\
&= \frac{p(\beta_1,\ldots\beta_K)\prod_{i=1}^n p(y_i|z_i)p(z_i|\beta_1,\ldots,\beta_K)}{\int p(\beta_1,\ldots,\beta_K)\prod_{i=1}^n p(y_i|z_i)p(z_i|\beta_1,\ldots,\beta_K)dz_1}\\
&= \frac{p(\beta_1,\ldots,\beta_K)\prod_{i=2}^n p(y_i|z_i)p(z_i|\beta_1,\ldots,\beta_K)p(y_1|z_1)p(z_1|\beta_1,\ldots,\beta_K)}{p(\beta_1,\ldots,\beta_K)\prod_{i=2}^n p(y_i|z_i)p(z_i|\beta_1,\ldots,\beta_K)\int p(y_1|z_1)p(z_1|\beta_1,\ldots,\beta_K)dz_1}\\
&= \frac{p(y_1|z_1)p(z_1|\beta_1,\ldots,\beta_K)}{\int p(y_1|z_1)p(z_1|\beta_1,\ldots,\beta_K)dz_1} = \frac{p(y_1|z_1)p(z_1|\beta_1,\ldots,\beta_K)}{p(y_1|\beta_1,\ldots,\beta_K)}\\
&\propto p(y_1|z_1)p(z_1|\beta_1,\ldots,\beta_K) \propto p(z_1|y_1,\beta_1,\ldots,\beta_K)
\end{aligned}
$$
(31)

The last line in Eq. 31 follows from the fact that both y_1 and $\beta_1,\ldots,\beta_K$ are conditioning arguments, i.e., fixed (for the moment). A useful interpretation of the final result, and in fact a way to derive the result almost instantly, is that the (conditional) posterior of z_1 is proportional to the "likelihood" of z_1 i.e., $p(y_1|z_1) = \mathbf{1}(z_i > 0)^{y_1}\mathbf{1}(z_i < 0)^{1-y_i}$ times a "prior probability" of z_1, i.e., $p(z_1|\beta_1,\ldots,\beta_K) = \mathcal{N}(z_1|\mathbf{x}_1'\boldsymbol{\beta})$. In other words, the (conditional) posterior is proportional to the probability of everything that directly depends on z_1, i.e., the probability of z_1's "children," times the probability of z_1 given everything z_1 directly depends on, i.e., z_1's "parents." (The terminology "children" and "parents" is owed to the representation of joint distributions and their conditional independence relationships in the form of directed acyclic graphs (see e.g., Pearl 2009, p. 12))

Using the same logic, we can derive the full conditional density of, e.g., the first element in $\boldsymbol{\beta}$:

$$
\begin{aligned}
&p(\beta_1|y_1,\ldots,y_n,z_1,\ldots,z_n,\beta_2,\ldots,\beta_K)\\
&= \frac{p(\beta_1,\ldots,\beta_K)\prod_{i=1}^n p(y_i|z_i)p(z_i|\beta_1,\ldots,\beta_K)}{\int p(\beta_1,\ldots,\beta_K)\prod_{i=1}^n p(y_i|z_i)p(z_i|\beta_1,\ldots,\beta_K)d\beta_1}\\
&= \frac{p(\beta_2,\ldots,\beta_K)\prod_{i=1}^n p(y_i|z_i)p(\beta_1|\beta_2,\ldots,\beta_K)\prod_{i=1}^n p(z_i|\beta_1,\ldots,\beta_K)}{p(\beta_2,\ldots,\beta_K)\prod_{i=1}^n p(y_i|z_i)\int p(\beta_1|\beta_2,\ldots,\beta_K)\prod_{i=1}^n p(z_i|\beta_1,\ldots,\beta_K)d\beta_1}\\
&= \frac{p(\beta_1|\beta_2,\ldots,\beta_K)\prod_{i=1}^n p(z_i|\beta_1,\ldots,\beta_K)}{\int p(\beta_1|\beta_2,\ldots,\beta_K)\prod_{i=1}^n p(z_i|\beta_1,\ldots,\beta_K)d\beta_1}\\
&= \frac{p(\beta_1|\beta_2,\ldots,\beta_K)\prod_{i=1}^n p(z_i|\beta_1,\ldots,\beta_K)}{\prod_{i=1}^n p(z_i|\beta_2,\ldots,\beta_K)}\\
&\propto p(\beta_1|\beta_2,\ldots,\beta_K)\prod_{i=1}^n p(z_i|\beta_1,\ldots,\beta_K) \propto p(\beta_1|z_1,\ldots,z_n,\beta_2,\ldots,\beta_K)
\end{aligned}
$$
(32)

Therefore, the full conditional posterior of β_1 does not depend on the observed data $\mathbf{y}$, conditional on $\mathbf{z}$. Again we find that the conditional posterior is proportional to the product of the (conditional) prior $p(\beta_1|\beta_2,\ldots,\beta_K)$ times the "likelihood," i.e., the probability of everything that directly depends on β_1 in the DGP, i.e., $\prod_{i=1}^{n} p(z_i|\beta_1,\ldots,\beta_K)$. Note both factors in this product involve normal distributions, and drawing all elements of $\boldsymbol{\beta}$ jointly from $p(\beta_1,\ldots,\beta_K|z_n,\ldots,z_n)$, as in Eq. 25 is simple if the joint prior distribution of $\boldsymbol{\beta}$ is multivariate normal.

Bayesian prediction. We just saw that in a Bayesian model conditional posterior distributions derive from the joint density of the data and the parameters defined by the Bayesian model, i.e., the combination of a likelihood function with a prior distribution for its parameters. Now consider the problem of making predictions from the perspective of expanding this joint density to include the unobserved data response y^u. In the context of our exemplary Bayesian model, we move from $p(\mathbf{y},\mathbf{z},\boldsymbol{\beta})$ to $p(y^u,z^u,\mathbf{y},\mathbf{z},\boldsymbol{\beta})$ noting that the former is obtained from the latter by integration with respect to (y^u,z^u).

$$p(y^u,z^u|y_1,\ldots,y_n,z_1,\ldots,z_n,\beta_1,\ldots,\beta_K)$$
$$= \frac{p(\beta_1,\ldots,\beta_K)\prod_{i=1}^{n} p(y_i|z_i)p(z_i|\beta_1,\ldots,\beta_K)p(y^u|z^u)p(z^u|\beta_1,\ldots,\beta_K)}{\int p(\beta_1,\ldots,\beta_K)\prod_{i=1}^{n} p(y_i|z_i)p(z_i|\beta_1,\ldots,\beta_K)p(y^u|z^u)p(z^u|\beta_1,\ldots,\beta_K)d(y^u,z^u)}$$
$$= \frac{p(y^u|z^u)p(z^u|\beta_1,\ldots,\beta_K)}{\int p(y^u|z^u)p(z^u|\beta_1,\ldots,\beta_K)d(y^u,z^u)}$$
$$= p(y^u|z^u)p(z^u|\beta_1,\ldots,\beta_K) \tag{33}$$

For predicting a pair y^u, z^u conditional on $\boldsymbol{\beta}$, we are thus back at data generation, i.e., get a draw z^u from $\mathcal{N}(z^u|(\mathbf{x}^u)'\boldsymbol{\beta})$ and determine y^u according to the sign of z^u. The predictive probability $p(y^u=1|\boldsymbol{\beta})$ can be simulated as $\frac{1}{R}\sum_{r=1}^{R}\mathbf{1}((z^u)^r>0)$ or computed using Eq. 17.

However, predictions conditional on a particular value of $\boldsymbol{\beta}$ are rarely of interest or relevant because, with finite data and nondegenerate priors, $\boldsymbol{\beta}$ will only be known up to a posterior distribution. As a consequence, $p(y^u,\mathbf{y},\boldsymbol{\beta}) \neq p(y^u,\mathbf{y})$ where the latter is defined as $\int p(y^u,\mathbf{y},\boldsymbol{\beta})d\boldsymbol{\beta}$ which in turn is defined as $\int p(y^u,z^u,\mathbf{y},\mathbf{z},\boldsymbol{\beta})d(z^u,\mathbf{z},\boldsymbol{\beta})$. The corresponding predictive probability marginalized with respect to latent utility z^u and parameters $\boldsymbol{\beta}$, i.e., $p(y^u=1|\mathbf{y})$ can be simulated as:

$$p(y^u=1|\mathbf{y}) \approx \frac{1}{R}\sum_{r=1}^{R}\mathbf{1}((z^u)^r>0), \quad (z^u)^r \sim \mathcal{N}(z^u|(\mathbf{x}^u)'\beta^r) \tag{34}$$

or more efficiently as:

$$p(y^u=1|\mathbf{y}) \approx \frac{1}{R}\sum_{r=1}^{R}\Phi((\mathbf{x}^u)'\beta^r) \tag{35}$$

in the sense that the approximation to $p(y^u = 1|y)$ in Eq. 35 delivers the same accuracy as that in Eq. 34 based on relatively smaller R. The sample $(\beta^1, \ldots, \beta^R)$ to be averaged over is obtained by Gibbs sampling from the posterior distribution $p(\beta|y)$. Note that because of the nonlinearity of the probit likelihood, $p(y^u = 1|y) \neq p\left(y^u = 1|\hat{\beta}\right)$ where $\hat{\beta}$ is some point estimate. Specifically, probabilities larger (smaller) than 0.5 will be over- (under-) estimated if posterior uncertainty in β is ignored.

To better appreciate this generally important point, it is useful to simulate probit data following the example given with the rbprobitGibbs routine in the R-package bayesm, to sample from the corresponding posterior using rbprobitGibbs, and then to simulate and compare predictions for different $\mathbf{x}^u$ as explained above. For a comparison with predictions at a frequentist point, estimate the R-command glm(..., family=binomial(link="probit"),...) is useful.

Conditional posterior distributions in hierarchical models. Hierarchical models estimate a distribution of response coefficients, e.g., $\{\beta_i\}_{i=1}^N \sim p(\{\beta_i\}_{i=1}^N|\tau)$ from a collection of $i = 1, \ldots, N$ time series $\mathbf{Y} = (\mathbf{y}_1, \ldots, \mathbf{y}_N)'$ where $\mathbf{y}_i = (y_{i,1}, \ldots y_{i,t}, \ldots y_{i,T_i})'$. $P(\{\beta_i\}_{i=1}^N|\tau)$ forms a *hierarchical* prior distribution. The difference to a purely subjective prior distribution is that the sample of time series observations contains likelihood information about parameters τ that index the hierarchical prior. In other words, upon placing a subjective prior distribution on τ, the likelihood information contained in the collection of time series will update this prior distribution to the posterior distribution $p(\tau|\mathbf{Y})$.

It should be noted that in these models, marginal posteriors for individual level coefficients, i.e., $p(\beta_i|\mathbf{Y})$ will be biased or "shrunk" towards the hierarchical prior distribution for T_i relatively small or, more precisely, limited individual level likelihood information in $p(\mathbf{y}_i|\beta_i)$ relative to the information about β_i in the hierarchical prior. And it is precisely this situation that motivates the use of hierarchical models in the first place.

However, parameters τ indexing the hierarchical prior can be estimated consistently, and in many marketing applications where the behavior of the particular consumers in the estimation sample is just a means to learning about optimal actions in the population these consumers belong to, $p(\tau|\mathbf{Y})$ is the main target of inference.

The currently popular algorithms for Bayesian inference in a hierarchical model take advantage of the following decomposition of the joint distribution of the data and the parameters which is characteristic, if not definitive of a hierarchical model:

$$p(\mathbf{Y}, \{\beta_i\}_{i=1}^N, \tau) = p(\mathbf{Y}| \{\beta_i\}_{i=1}^N) p(\{\beta_i\}_{i=1}^N|\tau) p(\tau) \tag{36}$$

An important consequence of this decomposition is that, by the rules developed earlier, the conditional posterior distribution of τ does not involve the data $\mathbf{Y}$ as conditioning argument:

$$p(\tau|\mathbf{Y}, \{\beta_i\}_{i=1}^N) = p(\tau| \{\beta_i\}_{i=1}^N) \propto p(\{\beta_i\}_{i=1}^N|\tau) p(\tau) \tag{37}$$

For many popular and useful choices of $p(\tau)$, Eq. 37 results in a conjugate update, i.e., a conditional distribution in the form of known distribution we can directly sample from. Perhaps the most prominent example is the model that takes $p(\{\boldsymbol{\beta}_i\}_{i=1}^N|\tau) = \prod_{i=1}^N \mathcal{N}(\boldsymbol{\beta}_i, \overline{\boldsymbol{\beta}}, \mathbf{V}_\beta)$ and uses a so-called Normal-Inverse Wishart prior for $p(\overline{\boldsymbol{\beta}}, \mathbf{V}_\beta)$ that is sometimes rather confusingly referred to as "the H (ierarchical)B(ayes)-model." Examples are the routines `rhierBinLogit`, `rhierLinearModel`, `rhierMnlRwMixture`, and `rhierNegbinRw`, in the R-package `bayesm` (Rossi et al. 2005) that implement this hierarchical prior (or its finite mixture generalization in the case of `rhierMnlRwMixture`) for collections of time series of binomial logit, linear, multinomial logit, and negative binomial observations, respectively.

One interpretation of this approach towards inference for the parameters in the hierarchical prior is that it relies on the so-called random effects $\{\boldsymbol{\beta}_i\}_{i=1}^N$ as augmented data, similar to the augmentation of latent utilities in the probit model discussed earlier. Different authors have argued that this approach may be suboptimal depending on the amount of likelihood information at the individual level and the amount of unobserved heterogeneity in $(\boldsymbol{\beta}_1, \ldots, \boldsymbol{\beta}_N)$ (see e.g., Chib and Carlin 1999; Frühwirth-Schnatter et al. 2004). However, practical alternative approaches that apply beyond the special case of conditionally normal individual level likelihood functions coupled with a (conditionally) normal hierarchical prior have yet to be developed.

In the common situation where $p(\mathbf{Y}|\{\boldsymbol{\beta}_i\}_{i=1}^N) = \prod_{i=1}^N p(\mathbf{y}_i|\boldsymbol{\beta}_i)$ and similarly $p(\{\boldsymbol{\beta}_i\}_{i=1}^N|\tau) = \prod_{i=1}^N p(\boldsymbol{\beta}_i|\tau)$, we obtain the following conditional posterior distribution for $\boldsymbol{\beta}_i$.

$$p(\boldsymbol{\beta}_i|\mathbf{y}_i, \tau) \propto p(\mathbf{y}_i|\boldsymbol{\beta}_i) p(\boldsymbol{\beta}_i|\tau) \tag{38}$$

$p(\boldsymbol{\beta}_i|\tau)$ acts as a usually rather informative prior for $\boldsymbol{\beta}_i$ here. However, as already discussed τ is not subjectively set but estimated from the data.

For many individual level likelihood functions of interest in marketing, and perhaps most prominently so for the multinomial logit likelihood, the product on the right hand side of Eq. 38 does not translate into a known distribution. A solution to generating draws from distributions with unknown normalizing constants, the Metropolis-Hastings algorithm is discussed next. Finally, if sampling from the distribution in Eq. 38 is computationally expensive, the combination of Eqs. 37 and 38 suggests scope for parallel sampling from the latter for $i = 1, \ldots, N$ and then feeding back the updated $(\boldsymbol{\beta}_1, \ldots, \boldsymbol{\beta}_N)$ as conditioning arguments into Eq. 37 and so on.

Metropolis-Hastings. The Gibbs sampler solves the problem posed by a (joint) posterior distribution with unknown normalizing constant if there is a corresponding set of conditional posterior distributions with known normalizing constants. The Gibbs sampler is extremely powerful and in some sense universal if one is content with approximations to the posterior on a discrete grid (Ritter and Tanner 1992). However, a general technique to sample from distributions with unknown normalizing constants known as the Metropolis-Hastings (MH) algorithm further substantially facilitates real world applications of Bayesian inference. A practically important example in marketing is Bayesian inference for models defined by type-I extreme value error (T1EV) likelihoods, e.g., logit-models, coupled with normal prior distributions for the (regression) coefficients in the likelihood.

The MH-sampler generates a *dependent* sample from some posterior $p(\theta|y)$ according to the following transition rule:

$$\alpha = min\left(1, \frac{p(\mathbf{y}|\theta^*)p(\theta^*)q(\theta^r)}{p(\mathbf{y}|\theta^r)p(\theta^r)q(\theta^*)}\right), \quad \theta^* \sim q \tag{39}$$

$$p(\theta^{r+1}|\mathbf{y},\theta^r) = \begin{cases} \alpha & \theta^{r+1} = \theta^* \\ 1-\alpha & \theta^{r+1} = \theta^r \end{cases} \tag{40}$$

On iteration r, the MH-sampler thus transitions from the current "state" or parameter value θ^r to a new state θ^* with probability α. With probability $1 - \alpha$, the current state at iteration $r + 1$ equals that at iteration r, i.e., $\theta^{r+1} = \theta^r$ (Compute α according in Eq. 39, preferably on the log-scale, exponentiate, and compare the result to a draw u from a standard uniform distribution. If $u < \alpha$ move to θ^*, else stay at θ^r, to obtain θ^{r+1}). The so-called candidate value or state θ^* is sampled from the known "candidate generating" or "proposal" density q. Note that the unknown normalizing constant $p(\mathbf{y}) = \int p(\mathbf{y}|\theta)p(\theta)d\theta$ cancels from Eq. 39.

A remarkable property of this transition rule is that it defines a Markov chain or process with invariant or stationary distribution equal to the posterior distribution $p(\theta|\mathbf{y})$. (A Markov process is a stochastic process in which the future, i.e., the $(r + 1)$-th value only depends on the value attained in the r-th iteration. All values taken before at the $(r - 1)$-th, $(r - 2)$-th, and so on iteration are irrelevant for predicting or generating the $(r + 1)$-th value.) In practice, this implies that subject to rather weak conditions for the proposal density q, repeated application of the transition rule in Eq. 40 eventually delivers draws from the posterior distribution of the model under investigation, independent of the choice of initial or starting value $\theta^{r=0}$. In other words, after discarding, say the first b values $\theta^1, \ldots, \theta^r, \ldots, \theta^b$ generated by b applications of Eq. 40 starting from θ^0, we can use the remaining $R - b$ draws as a representative sample of the posterior distribution.

To better appreciate this point, define the parameter space countably such that we can replace integration by summing over (a potentially infinite number of) countable sets (This is a technicality to avoid measure theoretic complications associated with events "of probability measure zero," and without loss of generality. The event that a continuous parameter takes a particular value, for example, is an event of probability measure zero because any ε-environment around that value – no matter how small – contains uncountably infinitely many values), and consider a condition known as "detailed balance":

$$p(\theta_i|\mathbf{y})q(\theta_j)\alpha(\theta_i \to \theta_j) = p(\theta_j|\mathbf{y})q(\theta_i)\alpha(\theta_j \to \theta_i)$$
$$p(\theta_i|\mathbf{y})q(\theta_j) \times \min\left(1, \frac{p(\mathbf{y}|\theta_j)p(\theta_j)q(\theta_i)}{p(\mathbf{y}|\theta_i)p(\theta_i)q(\theta_j)}\right) = p(\theta_j|\mathbf{y})q(\theta_i) \times \min\left(1, \frac{p(\mathbf{y}|\theta_i)p(\theta_i)q(\theta_j)}{p(\mathbf{y}|\theta_j)p(\theta_j)q(\theta_i)}\right) \quad (41)$$
$$\min(p(\theta_i|\mathbf{y})q(\theta_j), p(\theta_j|\mathbf{y})q(\theta_i)) = \min(p(\theta_j|\mathbf{y})q(\theta_i), p(\theta_i|\mathbf{y})q(\theta_j))$$

where the last line establishes that the first two equalities hold. Now rewrite the first line of Eq. 41 as follows:

$$\frac{p(\theta_i|\mathbf{y})}{p(\theta_j|\mathbf{y})} = \frac{q(\theta_i)\alpha(\theta_j \to \theta_i)}{q(\theta_j)\alpha(\theta_i \to \theta_j)} \quad (42)$$

Equation 42 makes apparent that the probability of proposing and accepting the move from θ_j to θ_i relative to the probability of proposing and accepting the reverse move in the MH algorithm is equal to the ratio of posterior probabilities of the respective target values. Because Eq. 42 holds for all $\theta_i, \theta_j \in \Theta$ where Θ is the parameter space defined by the model under investigation, we have:

$$\sum_{\theta_i} \frac{p(\theta_i|\mathbf{y})}{p(\theta_j|\mathbf{y})} = \sum_{\theta_i} \frac{q(\theta_i)\alpha(\theta_j \to \theta_i)}{q(\theta_j)\alpha(\theta_i \to \theta_j)}$$
$$p(\theta_j|\mathbf{y}) = \left(\sum_{\theta_i} \frac{q(\theta_i)\alpha(\theta_j \to \theta_i)}{q(\theta_j)\alpha(\theta_i \to \theta_j)}\right)^{-1} \quad (43)$$
$$\sum_{\theta_j} p(\theta_j|\mathbf{y}) = \sum_{\theta_j} \left(\sum_{\theta_i} \frac{q(\theta_i)\alpha(\theta_j \to \theta_i)}{q(\theta_j)\alpha(\theta_i \to \theta_j)}\right)^{-1}$$
$$= 1$$

Equation 43 makes intuitive that the collection of moves away from θ_j and moves returning to θ_j by the MH sampler eventually represent the posterior support for θ_j and, because this holds for all values θ_j, the entire posterior support. The "eventual" part of this statement comes from the fact that we may start off the sampler at a parameter value $\theta_j = \theta^0$ in a region of the parameter space Θ with extremely small posterior probability, i.e., in some extreme tail of the posterior distribution. As the MH sampler perhaps very slowly navigates the posterior, i.e., using many iterations depending on the proposal density q, moving into regions of the parameter space with higher posterior support, the draws along the path to that region over-represent the posterior support for these draws in any finite MH sample. This explains why the first b-iterations of the MH sampler that deliver the sequence $\theta^1, \ldots, \theta^r, \ldots, \theta^b$ from the arbitrary initial starting value θ^0 need to be discarded as burn-in for the sequence $\theta^{b+1}, \ldots, \theta^{b+r}, \ldots, \theta^R$ to be representative of the posterior distribution.

Convergence. Unfortunately, there is no simultaneously practical and reliable way to assess the length of the burn-in sample b. I strongly recommend that users of so-called Monte-Carlo-Markov-Chain (MCMC) techniques that encompass the Gibbs sampler, the MH sampler, as well as collections and combinations, these techniques always take the time to check the convergence behavior of a particular algorithm using simulated data, no matter if the algorithm was designed by someone else or is being newly developed, coded from scratch. In this process, three additional advantages emerge from working with simulated data. First, it forces the researcher to be absolutely clear about his understanding of the data generating process. Second, it delivers an understanding of what informative and less informative data are. Third, it helps with assessing the influence of subjective prior choices.

The investigation of convergence behavior relies on time-series plots of posterior quantities of interest where "time" is measured in iterations of the MCMC sampler. We want these time series plots to look stationary, at least after projecting to the loss from different actions. In other words, at least times series plots of $\mathcal{L}(a, \theta^r)$ need to have converged to stationary sequences over the first b iterations of the sampler. Obviously, the series of $\mathcal{L}(a, \theta^r)$ will converge if the series of parameter draws θ^r converges. However, it sometimes may be easier to assess convergence in $\mathcal{L}(a, \theta^r)$ than in θ^r because the latter often is a high-dimensional object in applied work. In addition, strong posterior dependence between elements of the parameter vector θ may mask convergence to a stable predictive distribution. Interesting examples are "fundamentally over-parameterized" models in the sense that even an infinite amount of data only likelihood-identifies lower dimensional projections of the parameters (see e.g., McCulloch and Rossi 1994; Edwards and Allenby 2003; Wachtel and Otter 2013) (As discussed in section "Bayesian Essentials" above, a proper prior distribution effectively guarantees that the posterior distribution is proper, independent of what can be identified from the likelihood). However, strong posterior dependence between elements of θ^r is not limited to fundamentally over-parameterized models.

If a MCMC explores the posterior distribution quickly ("mixes well"), it will yield a representative sample of the posterior distribution in fewer iterations than a MCMC that explores the posterior distribution more slowly ("does not mix well"). The mixing-behavior of a MCMC has implications for the required length of the burn-in sample b. If a chain mixes well, we can choose vastly different starting values and we will quickly lose the ability to distinguish among chains that use different starting values based on summaries of draws. The information in the draws from the posterior all chains converge to will swamp the initial differences between chains. Reliable formal tests of convergence implemented in the R-package CODA (Plummer et al. 2006), for example, build on this idea. However, when a chain mixes well, the researcher will (almost always) see this when exploring the posterior sample generated by the MCMC graphically. And because chains that mix well converge quickly, this limits the need for formal testing. In applied work, it thus is a priority to make sure that the MCMC employed mixes well. This brings us back to the role of simulated data in the development and testing of numerically intensive inference routines such as MCMC. I will give practical examples further below.

Construction of proposal densities The proposal density q needs to be known in the sense that we need to generate draws from it. In general, we also need to be able to evaluate the proposal density, i.e., to compute $q(\theta)$ when computing α in Eq. 39. However, normalizing constants can be omitted because they cancel from the ratio in α. The best proposal density possible is the posterior distribution itself. Setting $q(\theta) = p(\theta|\mathbf{y})$ the acceptance probability α becomes

$$\begin{aligned}\alpha &= min\left(1, \frac{p(\mathbf{y}|\theta^*)p(\theta^*)p(\theta^r|\mathbf{y})}{p(\mathbf{y}|\theta^r)p(\theta^r)p(\theta^*|\mathbf{y})}\right) \quad \theta^* \sim p(\theta|\mathbf{y}) \\ &= min\left(1, \frac{p(\mathbf{y}|\theta^*)p(\theta^*)p(\mathbf{y}|\theta^r)p(\theta^r)p(\mathbf{y})}{p(\mathbf{y}|\theta^r)p(\theta^r)p(\mathbf{y}|\theta^*)p(\theta^*)p(\mathbf{y})}\right) \\ &= min\left(1, \frac{p(\mathbf{y})}{p(\mathbf{y})}\right) \\ &= 1\end{aligned} \quad (44)$$

However, the reason for using the MH sampler in the first place is that we cannot directly sample from the posterior distribution (Note that one can think of the Gibbs sampler as a cycle through MH steps with conditional proposal densities equal to the conditional posterior distributions). Nevertheless, it is sometimes possible to construct proposal densities as close approximations to the posterior distributions. An example is the routine rmnlIndepMetrop in the R-package bayesm (Rossi et al. 2005) that uses a normal approximation to the likelihood to construct a multivariate t-distributed proposal centered at a penalized maximum likelihood estimate.

An obvious requirement for the proposal density is that the parameter set over which the proposal density q has positive support Θ_q is equal to, or a superset of the parameter set over which the posterior distribution has positive support, i.e., $\Theta_{p(\theta|\mathbf{y})} \subseteq \Theta_q$. If the proposal density q is such that parameter values that have positive support under the posterior distribution can never be reached, an MH sampler using this proposal density cannot possibly deliver draws that are representative of the posterior distribution.

Conversely, if the proposal density extends beyond the support of the posterior, i.e., $\Theta_{p(\theta|\mathbf{y})} \subset \Theta_q$, proposals to move into a region of the parameter space that is not supported under the posterior will simply be rejected. The corresponding acceptance probability α is equal to zero (see Eq. 39).

A related, less obvious but nevertheless practically important requirement for the proposal density is that it should have more mass in its tails relative to the posterior distribution. The reason is that a concentrated proposal density may effectively fail to navigate the entire posterior distribution in a way similar to a proposal that is only defined over a subset of the parameters space. A tricky aspect of thin tailed proposal densities, and concentrated in an area where the posterior distribution is relatively flat, is that time series plots of any finite number of MH draws may fail to indicate that the sampler has not converged, i.e., the plots may indicate convergence over a range of parameters that is not representative of the entire posterior distribution.

A simple recipe to specifying a proposal that necessarily has more mass in the tails relative to the posterior distribution is to define q as a random walk (RW), i.e., $\theta^* = \theta^r + \epsilon$ with $q(\epsilon)$ defined such that $q(\epsilon) = q(-\epsilon)$ for all $\theta^* \subset \Theta_q$. This recipe works for continuous and discrete distributions, and both for multivariate and univariate posterior distributions, in principle. Based on a RW proposal, the MH acceptance probability α simplifies to

$$\begin{aligned} \alpha &= \min\left(1, \frac{p(\mathbf{y}|\boldsymbol{\theta}^*)p(\boldsymbol{\theta}^*)q(\boldsymbol{\theta}^r)}{p(\mathbf{y}|\boldsymbol{\theta}^r)p(\boldsymbol{\theta}^r)q(\boldsymbol{\theta}^*)}\right), \boldsymbol{\theta}^* = \boldsymbol{\theta}^r + \boldsymbol{\epsilon}, \boldsymbol{\epsilon} \sim q \\ &= \min\left(1, \frac{p(\mathbf{y}|\boldsymbol{\theta}^r + \boldsymbol{\epsilon})p(\boldsymbol{\theta}^r + \boldsymbol{\epsilon})q(\boldsymbol{\theta}^* - \boldsymbol{\theta}^r)}{p(\mathbf{y}|\boldsymbol{\theta}^* - \boldsymbol{\epsilon})p(\boldsymbol{\theta}^* - \boldsymbol{\epsilon})q(\boldsymbol{\theta}^r - \boldsymbol{\theta}^*)}\right) \\ &= \min\left(1, \frac{p(\mathbf{y}|\boldsymbol{\theta}^r + \boldsymbol{\epsilon})p(\boldsymbol{\theta}^r + \boldsymbol{\epsilon})q(\boldsymbol{\epsilon})}{p(\mathbf{y}|\boldsymbol{\theta}^* - \boldsymbol{\epsilon})p(\boldsymbol{\theta}^* - \boldsymbol{\epsilon})q(-\boldsymbol{\epsilon})}\right) \\ &= \min\left(1, \frac{p(\mathbf{y}|\boldsymbol{\theta}^*)p(\boldsymbol{\theta}^*)}{p(\mathbf{y}|\boldsymbol{\theta}^r)p(\boldsymbol{\theta}^r)}\right) \end{aligned} \tag{45}$$

However, in many applications, the dimensionality of the parameter space is too large for a RW proposal that attempts to move all parameters simultaneously in one "big" MH step to work well. Conditional independence relationships in the DGP can be exploited to break one big MH step into a collection of MH steps of smaller dimensionality following the same logic that we used earlier to decompose the joint posterior distribution into a set of more manageable conditional posterior distributions for the Gibbs sampler.

In fact, the MH sampler delivers draws from conditional posterior distributions automatically if we propose to only change an individual element of the parameter vector, say θ_k:

$$\begin{aligned} \alpha &= \min\left(1, \frac{p(\mathbf{y}|\boldsymbol{\theta}^r_{-k}, \theta^*_k)p(\boldsymbol{\theta}^r_{-k}, \theta^*_k)q(\boldsymbol{\theta}^r)}{p(\mathbf{y}|\boldsymbol{\theta}^r)p(\boldsymbol{\theta}^r)q(\boldsymbol{\theta}^r_{-k}, \theta^*_k)}\right), \quad \theta^*_k \sim q(\theta_k|\boldsymbol{\theta}_{-k}) \\ &= \min\left(1, \frac{p(\theta^*_k|\mathbf{y}, \boldsymbol{\theta}^r_{-k})q(\theta^r_k|\boldsymbol{\theta}^r_{-k})q(\boldsymbol{\theta}^r_{-k})}{p(\theta_k|\mathbf{y}, \boldsymbol{\theta}^r_{-k})q(\theta^*_k|\boldsymbol{\theta}^r_{-k})q(\boldsymbol{\theta}^r_{-k})}\right) \\ &= \min\left(1, \frac{p(\theta^*_k|\mathbf{y}, \boldsymbol{\theta}^r_{-k})q(\theta^r_k|\boldsymbol{\theta}^r_{-k})}{p(\theta_k|\mathbf{y}, \boldsymbol{\theta}^r_{-k})q(\theta^*_k|\boldsymbol{\theta}^r_{-k})}\right) \end{aligned} \tag{46}$$

The second line in Eq. 46 follows from the application of Bayes' theorem (see Eq. 1 and note that normalizing constants $\int p(\mathbf{y}|\boldsymbol{\theta}^r_{-k}, \theta_k)p(\boldsymbol{\theta}^r_{-k}, \theta_k)\,d\theta_k$ cancel) and the decomposition of the joint proposal density into a conditional times a marginal. However, it is wasteful not to exploit conditional independence relationships that often vastly simplify the computation of the ratio in Eq. 46 for particular conditional posterior distributions (see e.g., the conditional posterior distribution in Eq. 31).

Moreover, unobservables that are conditionally independent a posteriori should always be drawn in separate MH steps, upon introducing the respective conditioning argument. It would be wasteful to constrain the sampler to either accept a joint move of all these unobservables to the respective candidate values or to reject the entire move and to repeat all respective values from iteration r. The conditional posterior $p(\mathbf{z}|\mathbf{y}, \boldsymbol{\beta}) = \prod_{i=1}^{n} p(z_i|\boldsymbol{\beta}, y_i)$ discussed earlier in the context of the binomial probit likelihood serves as an example.

The practical advantage of working with full conditional distributions as the basis for MH-RW sampling is that the proposal densities $q_k(\epsilon)$ are univariate. As a consequence, we only need to determine the concentration of these distributions around $\epsilon_k = 0$, which corresponds to $\theta_k^* = \theta_k^r$. When attempting to make multivariate proposals with the goal to move more than one element of the parameter vector in one step, a simple multivariate RW proposal of the form $q(\boldsymbol{\epsilon}) = \prod_{k=1}^{K} q(\epsilon_k)$ may suggest moves into directions with minimal support under the posterior which will result in $\boldsymbol{\theta}^{r+1} = \boldsymbol{\theta}^r$ for many iterations. Thus, setting up an MCMC as a repeated cycle through conditional MH steps facilitates the definition of suitable proposal densities. This is analogous to conditioning leading to known distributions in the Gibbs sampler, which can be viewed as a special case of MH sampling (see Eq. 44).

For continuous parameters the default choice for $q_k(\epsilon)$ is $N(0, \sigma_k^2)$ where the parameter σ_k^2 is subject to "tuning" by the analyst. For an integer parameter $\epsilon = (\eta + 1) s$ could be used, where η is distributed Poisson with tuning parameter λ, and s takes values from $\{-1,1\}$ with probability 0.5 (For strictly categorical parameters with no ordering among their values, the notion of a random walk is not defined. However, because of the finite prior support of such parameters, it is possible to use discrete uniform proposal distributions. Because all values have the same probability under a uniform distribution, the proposal distributions again cancel from the ratio in the acceptance probability α).

The tuning parameter implicitly specifies an average size of ϵ and thus an average distance between θ_k^* and θ_k^r (also known as the step-size of the proposal distribution), ϵ small in absolute value result in θ_k^* close to θ_k^r that are more likely accepted, i.e., $\theta_k^{r+1} = \theta_k^*$ than ϵ large in absolute value that will more likely result in $\theta_k^{r+1} = \theta_k^r$ when applying Eq. 40. If the number of total iterations R to run the MH sampler were of no concern, any setting of the tuning parameters that results in nondegenerate $q_k(\epsilon)$ would result in valid posterior inferences based on applications of Eq. 40.

However, both ϵ that are too small on average and ϵ that are too large on average will result in MH samplers that require a larger number of total iterations R to deliver the same *amount* of information about the posterior distribution than "optimally sized" ϵ. The situation is analogous to studying a population based on sampling. Larger samples result in more reliable inference and some sampling techniques result in higher statistical efficiency than others based on the same number of observations. Here, the population is the posterior distribution, the proposal density plays the role of the sampling plan, and importantly the sample size R is under our control, within the limits set by computational speed and time.

When the tuning parameter is set such that ϵ is too small on average, the MH sampler will explore the posterior in local neighborhoods extensively and navigate the entire posterior over many, many small steps creating "large swings" such that time series plots look like those of financial indices that can move into one direction for extended periods of times, in this case potentially for tens of thousands of iterations. The consequence is that the chain may appear as if it does not converge to a stationary distribution at all.

When the tuning parameter is set such that ϵ is too large on average, the chain will remain at the same value for many iterations and may fail to move at all, i.e., never accept to set $\theta_k^{r+1} = \theta_k^*$. However, if it at least moves sometimes, such a chain will arrive at a region of relatively large posterior support in large jumps and tend to stay there. In that sense, ϵ that are too large – provided that the chain moves at all – are the lesser evil. However, any reliable statements about posterior uncertainty based on a finite number of MH draws require decently tuned proposal densities. In practice, some experimentation is required that again is supported by the analysis of simulated data.

To illustrate, I simulated 500 observations from a binomial-probit model with data generating parameter vector $\beta = (-3, 2, 4)$. The first coefficient is an intercept and the remaining two are slope coefficients for two randomly uniformly distributed covariates (see the Appendix for the corresponding R-script). The script calls a simple, stylized RW-MH-sampler for a binomial probit model coupled with a multivariate normal prior for the probit coefficients implemented in plain R (see the function rbprobitRWMetropolis in the Appendix).

I ran the MCMC for 200,000 iterations using a weakly informative prior and initializing the chain at $\beta^{r=0} = (0,0,0)$. Fig. 2 shows MCMC-traces of β for four different $q(\epsilon) = \prod_{k=1}^K N(0, \sigma_k^2)$, i.e., $\sigma_k = 0.001$, $\sigma_k = 0.005$, $\sigma_k = 0.2$, and finally $\sigma_k = 3$ for all $k = 1,2,3$. These step-sizes translate into average acceptance rates α of RW-proposals of 99%, 97%, 25%, and 0.05% (see Eq. 45). The black, red, and green MCMC-traces correspond to the first, second, and third element of the parameter vector, respectively.

The top-left plot in Fig. 2 depicts the MCMCs that use the smallest step-size investigated here. It presents an example of an MCMC-trace from a sampler that has not converged to delivering samples from the posterior distribution. All three traces exhibit a trend away from zero over the entire course of the 200,000 iterations the sampler was run. Looking at the y-axis, we see that the individual traces are nowhere near the data generating values and reflective of the starting values, even in the last iteration. In an application to real data, we would not now what the data generating parameter values are to compare. However, upon seeing something similar to the top-left plot, we would conclude that the sampler has not converged to a stationary distribution yet. Thus, summaries of the full set or any subset of the 200,000 draws in the top-left plot do not represent the posterior distribution.

The traces in the top-right plot are with a step-size σ_k that is five times larger than that in the top-left plot. We see that the three traces appear to converge to stationarity around iteration 50,000 or so, and we could use summaries of the last 150,000 draws to learn about the posterior distribution. With an even larger $\sigma_k = 0.2$, convergence to the stationary distribution is much quicker (see the bottom-left plot). Finally, when we use $\sigma_k = 3$, the largest MH step-size investigated here, we see that the MCMC relatively quickly jumps into the neighborhood of the data generating β, but sticks to the same parameter value, often for thousands of iterations.

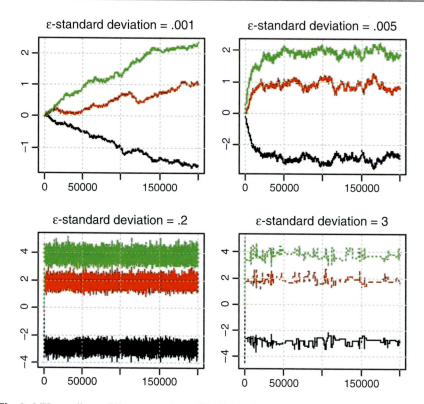

Fig. 2 MH-sampling – different step-sizes, 200,000 iterations

From theory we have that all four MCMC chains investigated here will eventually represent the posterior distribution $p(\beta|\mathbf{y})$ equally well, when run for an infinite number of iterations. The concept of an infinite number of iterations is not helpful in practice. However, to illustrate convergence of traces even with poorly tuned MH-steps, I ran each chain for 400,000 more iterations. Figure 3 depicts MCMC-traces obtained by stringing together the first 200,000 iterations from Fig. 2 with the subsequent 400,000 for a total of 600,000 iterations. It can be seen that all four MH-samplers converge eventually, even the sampler that uses $\sigma_k = 0.001$.

However, convergence of the MCMC to its stationary distribution is a necessary but not a sufficient criterion for high-quality inferences about the posterior distribution based on any finite sample of MCMC draws. To illustrate this point, Fig. 4 zooms into the last 50,000 iterations of the 600,000 total iterations from each sampler. Intuitively, the collection of draws in the bottom-left contain most information about the posterior, followed by that in the top-right. It is harder to order the collection of draws in the top-left and the bottom-right according to their information content by visual inspection.

Table 6 summarizes the traces depicted in Fig. 4 numerically, i.e., the last 50,000 draws from each chain. We see reasonable agreement between the chains operating with step-sizes of 0.005, 0.02, and 3 in terms of posterior means. However, the

Bayesian Models

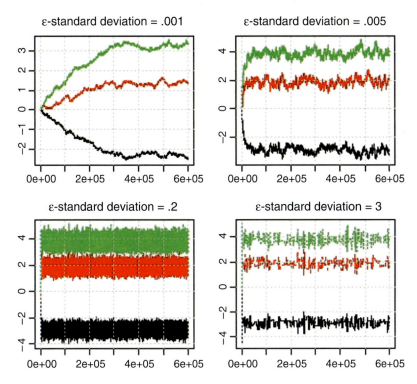

Fig. 3 MH-sampling – different step-sizes, 600,000 iterations

chains with step-sizes of 0.005 and 3 underestimate the posterior standard deviations relative to that with a step-size of 0.2 based on the last 50,000 draws (The posterior standard deviations of MCMC draws measure the posterior uncertainty in the knowledge about the parameters to be estimated. The analogy to frequentist standard errors applies. However, while reasonable estimates of frequentist standard errors maybe hard to come by in finite samples, posterior standard deviations are well defined automatically by virtue of using proper priors. In addition, based on a sample from the posterior distribution, posterior standard deviations of functions of parameters are easily computed as the standard deviation of functional values computed at each draw from the posterior). The chain with step-size 0.001, which required about 350,000 draws to converge to stationarity (see the top-left plot in Fig. 3), results in different means and dramatically smaller posterior standard deviations when looking at the last 50,000 draws.

Table 7 reports analogous summaries, but now based on the last 250,000 draws (compare Fig. 3). Based on these five times larger samples from the posterior, we see reasonable agreement between chains with step-sizes 0.005, 0.2, and 3 both in terms of posterior means and posterior standard deviations. This again illustrates that MCMC will "always work," if we only run the chains for long enough. However, it also illustrates that some MCMCs deliver more information about the posterior holding the number of iterations fixed than others, and that a valid MCMC chain can be practically useless if it explores the posterior too slowly.

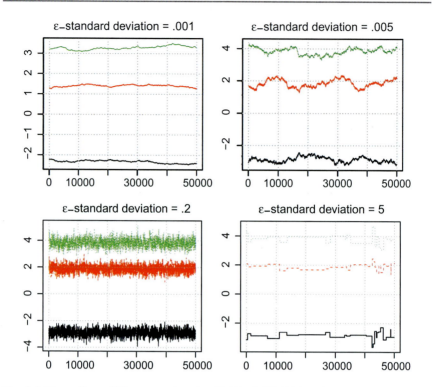

Fig. 4 MH-sampling – different step-sizes, last 50,000 of 600,000 iterations

Table 6 Posterior means and standard deviations from the last 50,000 iterations

	Mean			Standard deviation		
Step-size	β_0	β_1	β_2	β_0	β_1	β_2
0.001	−2.32	1.41	3.28	0.06	0.05	0.09
0.005	−2.86	1.85	3.84	0.16	0.25	0.21
0.2	−2.89	1.89	3.83	0.24	0.26	0.30
0.3	−2.85	1.87	3.82	0.17	0.18	0.25

Table 7 Posterior means and standard deviations from the last 250,000 iterations

	Mean			Standard deviation		
Step-size	β_0	β_1	β_2	β_0	β_1	β_2
0.001	−2.28	1.34	3.23	0.10	0.10	0.13
0.005	−2.92	1.90	3.89	0.23	0.27	0.29
0.2	−2.88	1.88	3.83	0.24	0.26	0.30
3	−2.90	1.94	3.82	0.23	0.23	0.32

Finally, I illustrate the notion of exploring the posterior distribution more quickly (more efficiently) and more slowly (less efficiently) by comparing the RW-MH-chains with step-sizes 0.005, 0.2, and 3 to each other, and to posterior draws from the Gibbs-sampler that relies on data-augmentation discussed earlier (rbprobitGibbs in the

R-package bayesm). I focus on the first slope coefficient (the red trace in the figures above), and compute means and standard deviations from batches of 1000 consecutive draws starting from iteration 50,001 until iteration 600,000. The histograms in Figs. 5 and 6 summarize the resulting distributions of 550 (= (600,000–50,000)/1000) batch means and batch standard deviations for RW-MH-chains with step-sizes 0.005, 0.2, and 3 and the Gibbs-sampler.

Assuming the true posterior standard deviation (from a hypothetical infinite run of the MCMC) to be about 0.26 (see Table 7), we would expect the batch means to be distributed normally around the true mean with standard deviation $.26/\sqrt{1000} \approx .008$ simply because we cannot learn the exact mean of a non-degenerate posterior distribution from a finite sample. This translates into a 5-σ interval around the mean with a length of about 0.08. Any excess variation in batch means is evidence of the inefficiency of the employed sampling technologies relative to a hypothetical *iid*-sampler. From the *x*-axes in Fig. 5, we can see that batch means are distributed much more widely. Intuitively, a single 1000-iterations batch from each of the MCMCs is less informative about the posterior (more likely to summarize information from only parts of the posterior) than 1000 draws from a hypothetical *iid*-sampler. In addition, if someone had to bet on the inference from a randomly

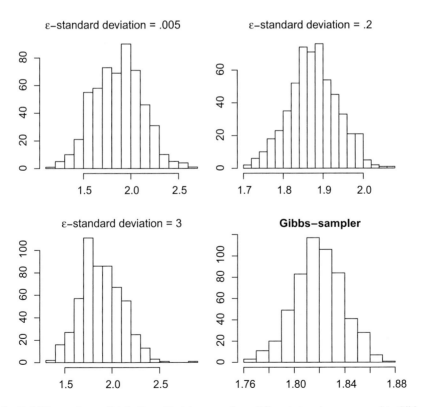

Fig. 5 MH-sampling – distribution of batch means from different step-sizes compared to Gibbs-sampling

drawn single batch, he would prefer a draw from the Gibbs-sampler (in the bottom-right), followed by a draw from the RW-MH-sampler with step-size 0.2 (in the top-right). The decision between step-sizes 0.005 and 3 is less clear. However, from the wider distribution of batch means, it is obvious that MCMCs with these step-sizes explore the posterior less efficiently.

Finally, the batch standard deviations in Fig. 6 again identify the Gibbs-sampler as most efficient, followed by the RW-MH-chain with step-size 0.2. A randomly drawn batch of 1000 consecutive draws from these samplers is likely to yield a posterior standard deviation close to the posterior standard deviation estimated from all $600{,}000 - 50{,}000 = 550{,}000$ draws. In addition, the top-left plot in Fig. 6 demonstrates that each and every single 1000 consecutive iterations batch from the chain with step-size 0.005 substantially underestimates the posterior standard deviation. In contrast, the chain with the (too) large step-size of 3 often suggests no posterior uncertainty at all – when no proposal is accepted in the batch – but does not uniformly underestimate the posterior standard deviation. This again suggests that chains with step-sizes that are too small are potentially more misleading than chains with step-sizes that are too large.

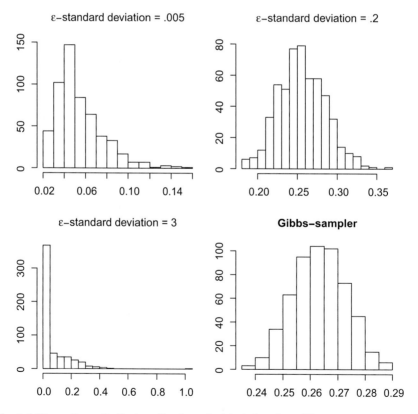

Fig. 6 MH-sampling – distribution of batch standard deviations from different step-sizes compared to Gibbs-sampling

The examples discussed here nicely showcase that the emphasis in applied work should be on using, devising sampling schemes that mix well, before even considering the formal assessment of convergence. In a sense, it is almost always obvious from a graphical inspection of MCMC-trace plots whether a sampler that mixes well has converged or not.

For first time acquaintances with MH sampling I suggest the following additional coding exercises to develop an intuition for MH-sampling based on personal experience:

1. Change the function `rbprobitRWMetropolis` in the Appendix to cycling through MH-steps that update individual elements of the parameter vector one at a time from their conditional posterior distributions. Experiment with tuning RW-proposals for each element of the parameter vector independently.
2. Obtain a copy of the "plain R" version of `rbprobitGibbs` (version 2.2–5 of `bayesm` available from the CRAN-archives), replace the part that generates latent utilities z in line 141 with RW-MH steps, and verify with simulated data that this new algorithm works. The setup is generally interesting, because it is a toy version of a hierarchical model with MH-updates at the lower level and conjugate updates of parameters that form the hierarchical prior.
3. Modify this sampler such that you propose candidate values z_i^* from their (hierarchical) prior distribution $\mathcal{N}(\mathbf{x}_i'\boldsymbol{\beta},1)$. Note that the proposal and the prior distribution will cancel from the ratio in the MH-acceptance probability α. You will likely see that this sampler does not converge to a posterior distribution $p(\boldsymbol{\beta}|\mathbf{y})$ anywhere near the data generating values, even though the time series of $\boldsymbol{\beta}^1, \ldots, \boldsymbol{\beta}^r, \ldots, \boldsymbol{\beta}^R$ suggests immediate convergence and superior mixing! This is an example of the drawbacks of a (collection of) proposal densities that do not have enough mass in their tails.

Recent developments. An important recent development in the context of making numerically intensive Bayesian analysis more practical is the No U-turn Sampler (NUTS) by Hoffman and Gelman (2014) which is a self-tuning Hamiltonian-Monte-Carlo sampler (see e.g., Neal 2011). This technique has been implemented in `Stan` (Carpenter et al. 2017) which interfaces with many popular software environments including `R`, `Python`, `Matlab`, and `Stata`, for example.

The basic principle of Hamiltonian-Monte-Carlo (HMC) is to leverage Hamiltonian dynamics for a more effective exploration of the posterior. In physics, Hamiltonian dynamics describe the change in location and momentum of an object by differential equations. The solutions to the differential equations yield the location and the momentum of an object at any particular point in time.

In HMC, the locations correspond to value of the q-element parameter vector to be estimated. Each location is associated with a potential energy and the statistical analogue is the negative of log-posterior evaluated these values (Thus, the posterior mode is the point of lowest potential energy we would gravitate to in the absence of "extra" kinetic energy that enables movements away from this point). The analogue to the momentum comes from expanding the parameter space by p additional parameters (where $p = q$), the negative log-density of which is the statistical analogue of kinetic energy (Thus, again the mode of this density is the point (the momentum vector) with the lowest kinetic energy). Usually, these additional parameters are assumed to be standard normally distributed. However, it should be noted that the p additional parameters and their density are purely technical devices to complete the Hamiltonian. Similarly, proposal distributions in the context of MH-sampling are technical devices to accomplish MH-sampling.

The algorithm first draws a p-element "momentum" vector from standard normal distributions. The momentum vector both defines the direction of the movement away from the current location (parameter value), and the maximum distance that can be realized, as explained next. HMC obeys the principle that the total energy, i.e., the sum of the potential and the kinetic energy is constant in the closed system described by the Hamiltonian, when deriving a new location (and a new momentum) at any point in time (see Eq. 2.12 in Neal 2011). Here time refers to some arbitrary time point after the onset of the momentum that generates a movement away from the current location.

The location-change is a function of the change in kinetic energy and the momentum-change a function of the change in potential energy. Note that the change in potential energy corresponds to the gradient of the negative log-posterior, and the change in kinetic energy to the gradient of the negative log-density of auxiliary momentum variables respectively, in statistical applications. If the differential equations describing the change in position and momentum could be solved exactly, one could solve for the location that is furthest away from the current location that can be reached in the direction of the current draw of the momentum, given its associated kinetic energy, define this as the new location, draw a new momentum vector, and so on.

It is useful to contemplate how such a procedure would explore the posterior. With a fixed distribution of momentum vectors (and corresponding kinetic energies), it would tend to move away more slowly from a pronounced posterior mode, i.e., in smaller steps in expectation, because of the steep increase in potential energy (defined as the negative of the log-posterior) around this mode. Here, the expectation is with respect to the fixed distribution of momentum vectors (and corresponding kinetic energies). Only outlying momentum vectors would supply sufficient kinetic energy to move far into directions of (much) higher potential energy. Conversely, it would tend to move more quickly, i.e., in larger steps in expectation, through areas of high-potential energy (small values of the log-posterior), and in the direction of low potential energy, in expectation. It is therefore somewhat intuitive that such a procedure would result in direct draws from the posterior that could represent the posterior effectively based on a relatively small number of draws. In contrast to RW-MH-sampling, the distance between two successive draws from this procedure would automatically reflect the concentration of the posterior at every value of the parameter space.

However, in practice, the solutions to the differential equations defining the Hamiltonian dynamics need to be approximated in discretized time. Again, time here refers to the time after the onset of the momentum that generates a movement away from the current location, i.e., the current parameter value. A discrete approximation that can be tuned to high accuracy (relative to the exact solution) is leapfrog integration. At each iteration of the HMC, L leapfrog steps that each correspond to a discrete time step of length ϵ are performed. Ideally, the number of steps L and the length of each step ϵ are chosen so that the new location (a new parameter value) is as far away as possible from the current parameter value, given the current draw of the p-element momentum vector and its associated kinetic energy, while keeping the approximation error low. Any remaining approximation error is controlled in a MH-step that compares the value of the Hamiltonian at the new position and the momentum at this position to the value of the Hamiltonian at the old position and the momentum vector that initiated the movement to the new position (In other words, the potential energy at the new location and the (remaining) kinetic energy are compared to the potential energy at the old location and the kinetic energy that brought about the movement to the new location). By the law of conservation of energy in the closed system described by the Hamiltonian, the Hamiltonian would evaluate to the same value if the discrete time approximation were exact.

NUTS automatically tunes L, ϵ, and additional parameters that rescale the kinetic energy in different dimensions of the log-posterior to arrive at a highly effective HMC-sampler that does not normally require user intervention. Thus, the researcher can fully concentrate on specifying the model, i.e., the likelihood and the pior, knowing that high quality numerical inference from the implied posterior is available through NUTS. A limitation is that the gradient of the log-posterior needs to be defined, which excludes discrete variables as direct objects of inference. However, in many models, discrete latent variables are introduced as augmented data, such as in models defining a discrete mixture of distributions. In these cases, NUTS could be used to sample from the posterior marginalized with respect to discrete latent variables. Based on the marginal posterior, the posterior distribution of discrete latent variables can be easily derived.

To numerically illustrate the performance of NUTS, I revisit the binomial probit example discussed earlier. I run the NUTS implemented in `Stan` for 600,000 iterations and compute 550 batch means and batch standard deviations of the first slope coefficient (the red trace in Figs. 2 to 4) from the last 550,000 iterations (see Fig. 7). A comparison between Fig. 7 and Figs. 5 and 6 shows that a randomly drawn batch of 1000 consecutive iterations from NUTS is likely to be a better representation of the posterior than a randomly drawn batch of 1000 consecutive iterations from the samplers discussed earlier, including the Gibbs-sampler. However, it should be noted that each NUTS-iteration is more computationally intensive than one iteration of the MH-sampler investigated. The computational intensity of Gibbs-sampling relative to NUTS in this model depends on the sample size, where larger samples are likely to favor NUTS because of the need to augment latent utilities for all observations when Gibbs-sampling.

Model comparison

In the introduction, I mentioned the possibility of determining the dimensionality of a flexibly formulated model using the Bayesian approach. I also alluded to the possibility of making comparisons across different models for the *same* data, where models may arbitrarily differ in terms of likelihood functions, prior

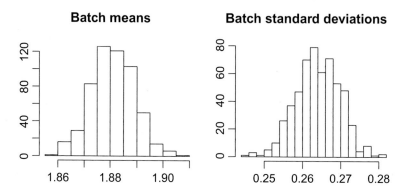

Fig. 7 No U-Turn-sampling – distribution of batch means and batch standard deviations

specifications, or both. Here, I will briefly describe the basic principles to this end. Specifically, I will show how the Bayesian approach can deliver consistent evidence for a more parsimonious model. As usual, consistency means convergence to the data generating truth as the sample size increases (When the set of models compared does not contain the model that in fact corresponds to the data generating truth, consistency means convergence to the model that is closest to the data generating truth in a predictive sense).

This contrasts with the classical frequentist approach, where we can only "fail to reject" relatively simpler descriptions of the world, i.e., more parsimonious theories and models in comparison to more complex models. I personally see this as a drawback of the classical frequentist approach because theory aimed at understanding the underlying causal mechanisms of observed associations generally thrives on establishing that particular (direct) causal effects do not exist.

The Bayesian approach towards comparing between two or more alternative models builds – as one may expect – on Bayes' theorem. Consider a set of models $\mathcal{M}_1, \ldots, \mathcal{M}_K$ formulated for the same observed data $\mathbf{y}$. Note that this encompasses the possibility that models use different sets of covariates, different likelihood functions, different priors, or may be calibrated including additional or even different data $\mathbf{y}'$, as long as they define a predictive density for the *same* $\mathbf{y}$ (For example, Otter et al. (2011) show how to derive a marginal likelihood for demand data in a model that specifies a joint density for supply side variables (that enter the demand model as conditioning arguments) and demand data). Bayesian model comparisons then rest on the posterior probabilities of a model given the (focal) data (Eq. 47).

$$\Pr(\mathcal{M}_j|\mathbf{y}) = \frac{p(\mathbf{y}|\mathcal{M}_j)\Pr(\mathcal{M}_j)}{\sum_{k=1}^{K} p(\mathbf{y}|\mathcal{M}_k)\Pr(\mathcal{M}_k)} \quad (47)$$

Here $\Pr(\mathcal{M}_k)$ is the subjective prior probability that model k is the true model which is often chosen to be $1/K$ in the absence of better knowledge, and $p(\mathbf{y}|\mathcal{M}_K)$ is the so-called marginal likelihood of the data given model k defined as $\int p_k(\mathbf{y}|\boldsymbol{\theta}) p_k(\boldsymbol{\theta})\, d\boldsymbol{\theta}$. The subscript k indicates that the likelihood and the prior and thus the "content" of θ can be model dependent. If $\Pr(\mathcal{M}_k)$ can be reduced to one and the same constant for all models under consideration, this constant can obviously be ignored in Eq. 47. Then, the comparison between any two models k and j in the set can be based on so-called Bayes' factors, defined as ratios of marginal likelihoods (Eq. 47).

$$BF_{k,j} = \frac{p(\mathbf{y}|\mathcal{M}_k)}{p(\mathbf{y}|\mathcal{M}_j)} \qquad (48)$$

By convention, Bayes Factors larger 3 count as weak but sufficient evidence in favor of the model in the numerator; Bayes Factors larger 20 count as strong evidence (Kass and Raftery 1995). I will comment more on this convention later.

For example, it would be perfectly alright to compare model k with marginal likelihood $\int p_k(\mathbf{y}|\theta)p_k(\theta)d\theta$ to a model j that introduces observed conditioning arguments (predictors, covariates) $\mathbf{X}$, i.e., $\int p_j(\mathbf{y}|\mathbf{X},\theta)p_j(\theta)d\theta$, or to include model i that uses additional data $\mathbf{y}'$ for calibration in the comparison, based on $\int p_i(\mathbf{y}|\theta)p_i(\theta|\mathbf{y}')d\theta$ (However, note that $\int p_i(\mathbf{y},\mathbf{y}'|\theta)p_i(\theta)d\theta \neq \int p_i(\mathbf{y}|\theta)p_i(\theta|\mathbf{y}')d\theta$. The former is a marginal likelihood for the data $(\mathbf{y}, \mathbf{y}')$ and not for the data $\mathbf{y}$. Marginal likelihoods for different models can only be directly compared as long as they pertain to the *same* data). A useful intuition for marginal likelihoods is that they reduce radically different, per se incomparable "stories" about what may have generated the data to densities for the data, which are directly comparable in the same way as we can compare predictions for the *same* event completely independent of the considerations that gave rise to the prediction.

However, we still need to establish the intuition for how Bayesian model comparisons can possibly consistently support the more parsimonious model. I will do this by returning to the regression example from Eq. 10. Recall that we were able to derive the posterior distribution analytically in this example (see Eq. 16). Exploiting this fact, we obtain an analytical expression for the marginal likelihood of the data under this model as follows:

$$\begin{aligned} p(\mathbf{y}|\beta^0, \Sigma^0) &= \frac{p(\mathbf{y}|\beta)p(\beta|\beta^0,\Sigma^0)}{p(\beta|\mathbf{y},\beta^0,\Sigma^0)} \\ &= \frac{\frac{1}{\sqrt{2\pi}}\prod_{i=1}^{n}\exp\left(-\frac{1}{2}(y_i - \mathbf{x}_i'\beta)^2\right)(2\pi)^{-k/2}|\Sigma^0|^{-1/2}\exp\left(-\frac{1}{2}(\beta-\beta^0)'(\Sigma^0)^{-1}(\beta-\beta^0)\right)}{(2\pi)^{-k/2}\left|\mathbf{X}'\mathbf{X} + (\Sigma^0)^{-1}\right|^{1/2}\exp\left(-\frac{1}{2}(\beta-\tilde{\beta})'\left(\mathbf{X}'\mathbf{X}+(\Sigma^0)^{-1}\right)(\beta-\tilde{\beta})\right)} \\ &= |\Sigma^0|^{-1/2}\left|\mathbf{X}'\mathbf{X} + (\Sigma^0)^{-1}\right|^{-1/2}\exp\left(\frac{-\tilde{s}}{2}\right) \end{aligned}$$

(49)

Here, we exploited the fact $p(\mathbf{y}|\beta^0, \Sigma^0)p(\beta|\mathbf{y},\beta^0,\Sigma^0) = p(\mathbf{y}|\beta)p(\beta|\beta^0,\Sigma^0)$, by elementary rules of probability. Also note that with the intent to eventually compare across models defined by different likelihoods and priors, we kept track of all normalizing constants that we conveniently ignored before, when deriving the posterior distribution in Eq. 16. Specifically, we previously ignored the factors

$1/\sqrt{2\pi}$ and $(2\pi)^{-k/2}|\Sigma^0|^{-1/2}$ in the likelihood $p(\mathbf{y}|\boldsymbol{\beta})$ and the prior $p(\boldsymbol{\beta}|\boldsymbol{\beta}^0, \Sigma^0)$, respectively.

Recall that $\tilde{s}$ in the last line of Eq. 49 is a deterministic function of the subjective prior parameters $\boldsymbol{\beta}^0$, Σ^0, and the data $\mathbf{y}$ (see Eq. 14). For all nondegenerate prior choices, $\tilde{s}$ is going to be dominated by the term $(\mathbf{y} - \mathbf{X}'\tilde{\boldsymbol{\beta}})'(\mathbf{y} - \mathbf{X}'\tilde{\boldsymbol{\beta}})$, where $\tilde{\boldsymbol{\beta}}$ converges to the maximum likelihood or ordinary least squares estimate as more data become available (assuming regular $\mathbf{X}$).

Now consider the comparison between two models. Model $\mathcal{M}_0$ happens to employ the p-column $\mathbf{X}$-matrix that collects all covariates that systematically influenced $\mathbf{y}$, when the data was generated – the true model. Model $\mathcal{M}_1$ uses a model matrix that features the same p covariates in $\mathbf{X}$ plus s additional covariates in $\mathbf{X}^s$ that did not contribute to the variation in $\mathbf{y}$, when the data was generated. The Bayes' factor $BF_{0,1}$ is then:

$$BF_{0,1} = \frac{p(\mathbf{y}|\mathcal{M}_0)}{p(\mathbf{y}|\mathcal{M}_1)}$$

$$= \frac{\left|\Sigma_0^0\right|^{-1/2}\left|\mathbf{X}'\mathbf{X} + \left(\Sigma_0^0\right)^{-1}\right|^{-1/2}\exp\left(\frac{-\tilde{s}_0}{2}\right)}{\left|\Sigma_1^0\right|^{-1/2}\left|(\mathbf{X},\mathbf{X}^s)'(\mathbf{X},\mathbf{X}^s) + \left(\Sigma_1^0\right)^{-1}\right|^{-1/2}\exp\left(\frac{-\tilde{s}_1}{2}\right)} \quad (50)$$

where Σ_0^0 and Σ_1^0 are of dimension $p \times p$ and $(p+s) \times (p+s)$, respectively. In the limit of more and more data, $\tilde{s}_0$ and $\tilde{s}_1$ will converge to the same value, as the data determine that the elements in $\tilde{\boldsymbol{\beta}}_1$ that correspond to $\mathbf{X}^s$ are equal to zero. Then, the limit of the ratio in Eq. 50 only depends on:

$$(|(\mathbf{X},\mathbf{X}^s)'(\mathbf{X},\mathbf{X}^s) \| \mathbf{X}'\mathbf{X}|^{-1})^{1/2}$$
$$= (n^{p+s}|n^{-1}(\mathbf{X},\mathbf{X}^s)'(\mathbf{X},\mathbf{X}^s) \| n^{-1}\mathbf{X}'\mathbf{X}|^{-1}n^{-p})^{1/2}$$
$$\approx n^{s/2}$$

which is easily seen to converge to infinity in the limit of more and more data (larger n), for regular $(\mathbf{X},\mathbf{X}^S)$ (The expressions $n^{-1}(\mathbf{X},\mathbf{X}^S)'(\mathbf{X},\mathbf{X}^S)$ and $n^{-1}\mathbf{X}'\mathbf{X}$ define covariance matrices that will converge to fixed matrices in the sample size n for covariates with finite variance). Thus, the Bayes' factor can in fact produce infinitely strong evidence for the more parsimonious model, if it is the data generating mechanism.

If in contrast $\mathcal{M}_1$ were the true model, or just closer to the truth in this case, the coefficients in $\tilde{\boldsymbol{\beta}}_1$ that correspond to $\mathbf{X}^s$ do not converge to zero. As a consequence, $\tilde{s}_0$ would grow faster in n than $\tilde{s}_1$, and $SF_{0,1}$ would converge to zero (Note that $\exp\left(\frac{-\tilde{s}_0+\tilde{s}_1}{2}\right) = \exp\left(n\frac{-\tilde{s}_0/n+\tilde{s}_1/n}{2}\right)$ converges to zero faster than $n^{s/2}$ grows because of the exponential function, where $-\tilde{s}_0/n + \tilde{s}_1/n$ converges to the true difference in average squared errors between $\mathcal{M}_1$ and $\mathcal{M}_0$). Thus, the Bayes' factor can both produce increasing evidence for the more parsimonious model, when the constraints imposed by this model hold exactly, and increasing evidence against it, when they do not (consider $BF_{1,0}$ instead of $BF_{0,1}$ in this case) (In this case, the conventional classifications of weak and strong evidence in favor of the model in the numerator of the Bayes' factor often align with the usual cut-off values for rejecting a more constrained model based on p-values). In contrast, p-values can reliably reject a parsimonious model but are incapable of producing increasing evidence for such a model. By construction, the probability of rejecting a true, more parsimonious model in favor of a larger, over-parameterized model is equal to the chosen significance level data in repeated applications of the frequentist testing procedure, and independent of the sample size (the amount of information in the data).

Numerical Illustrations

A Brief Note on Software Implementation

Researcher interested in adopting the Bayesian approach nowadays have quite some choice regarding different software and available implementations of the Bayesian approach. More recently, established products for data analysis such as SPSS, STATA, or SAS have started to include options for Bayesian estimation of well established "standard" statistical models such as ANOVA and generalized linear regression models (Advanced users can certainly use these tools to estimate "their own" models too, and STATA specifically emphasizes this possibility). In contrast, WINBUGS is an example of an attempt to automate Bayesian inference, with the idea that the user should be able to exclusively concentrate on the specification of a model – likely outside of the set of "standard" statistical models implemented elsewhere – aided by a graphical user interface.

Much if not the vast majority of "Bayesian-papers" published in marketing to this day have relied on coding up the model and the (invariably) MCMC-routine to perform Bayesian inference "from scratch," starting with some example code and taking advantage of components that repeat themselves across different models, e.g., conditionally conjugate updating of parameters indexing hierarchical priors. The programming languages used in this context include compiled languages such as C or Fortran, and interpreted languages such as Matlab, R, and Gauss. Here, the former are by construction less interactive when coding and the latter slower in the execution of code "that works." Recently, Rcpp (Eddelbuettel and François 2011; Eddelbuettel 2013) emerged as an extremely useful compromise between the speed of compiled and the coder-friendliness of interpreted languages.

I am currently relying heavily on Rcpp in my own research. However, I view the advent of the No U-turn Sampler (NUTS) by Hoffman and Gelman (2014) as implemented in Stan (Carpenter et al. 2017) as a major breakthrough towards the goal of focusing on the specification of innovative models (almost) exclusively.

A Hierarchical Bayesian Multinomial Logit Model

At least in marketing, no treatment of Bayesian modeling would be complete without illustrating the benefits from a hierarchical Bayesian model in the context of large N, small T data. I consider the stylized case of multinomial logit choice from choice sets with two inside alternatives, say brands A and B, and an outside option with expected utility normalized to zero. The utility of the two inside alternatives stems, in addition to alternative specific constants, from a uniformly distributed covariate x, i.e., $U_{Ait} = \beta_{Ai} + \beta_i x_{Ait} + \varepsilon_{Ait}$ and $U_{Bit} = \beta_{Bi} + \beta_i x_{Bit} + \varepsilon_{Bit}$. Here, $i = 1, \ldots, N$ indexes heterogeneous individuals and $t = 1, \ldots, T$ choice occasions. Population preferences are distributed according to:

$$\beta_i = \begin{pmatrix} \beta_{Ai} \\ \beta_{Bi} \\ \beta \end{pmatrix} \sim \mathcal{N}\left(\begin{bmatrix} .3 \\ -2 \\ -1 \end{bmatrix}, \begin{bmatrix} 3 & -2.99 & 0 \\ -2.99 & 3 & 0 \\ 0 & 0 & .1 \end{bmatrix} \right)$$

Thus, brand A is slightly preferred to the outside good on average, whereas brand B is less attractive than the outside good to the average consumer in this market. However, there is a fair amount of heterogeneity in brand preferences in this market. For example, about 12.4% of consumers in this market prefer brand B to the outside good and around 43% prefer the outside good to brand A at $x = 0$. Moreover, consumers that have an above average preference for brand A are likely to have a below average preference for brand B in this market, as per the strongly negatively correlated brand coefficients in the population ($\rho = -.997$). The tastes for the covariate x are relatively more homogenous and only consumers in the extreme tail of the preference distribution exhibit a higher preference for larger values of x in this population. I simulate $N=2,000$ individuals from this population and have each individual make $T = 5$ choices from complete sets that randomly vary in the x-values for brands A and B, both across $t = 1,\ldots,T$ and $i = 1,\ldots,N$. I use this data to calibrate a Bayesian hierarchical MNL-model. I rely on the default subjective prior distributions implemented in bayesm's estimation routine rhierMnlRwMixture and run this RW-MH-sampler with automatic tuning of proposal densities for 100,000 iterations saving every 10th draw (in *bayesm* : R $=$ 100, 000, keep $=$ 10). The complete posterior is a 6009-dimensional object (3 means plus 3 variances plus 2 covariances plus 2000 times 3 individual level random effects). Because of the high dimensionality of the posterior, saving every draw from a long MCMC run can easily produce an object that taxes a computer's RAM heavily. Saving every keep-th draw increases the information content in a posterior sample limited by a computer's RAM. For a maximum number of draws than can be saved, we can increase the number of MCMC-iterations R , when we simultaneously increase the number of iterations between parameters to be saved (*keep* $-$ 1). The information content in the resulting sample is increased because saved draws separated by *keep* $-$ 1 MCMC iterations will tend to be more independent from each other, replicate less of the information contained the preceding draw saved.

Figure 8 exhibits individual level posteriors for individuals 3, 99, and 2000 in our simulated panel data. For this purpose, I use the last 9000 draws of the 10,000 draws I saved. The three rows in Fig. 8 correspond to β_A, β_B, and β, respectively. Each

Bayesian Models

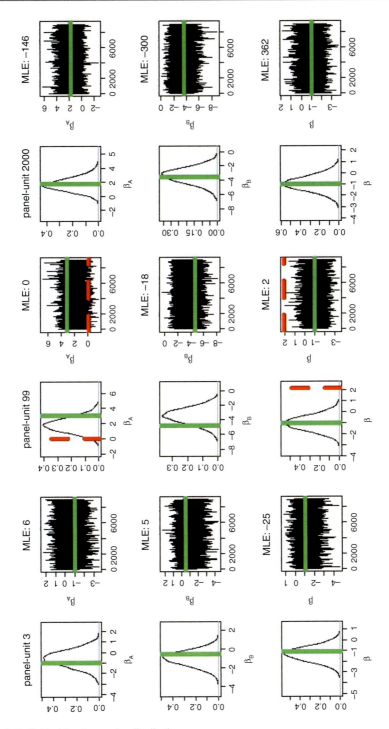

Fig. 8 Individual level posterior distributions

individual's posterior is depicted in two different ways in two adjacent columns of Fig. 8, each. The first column summarizes marginal posterior densities using density plots obtained by Gaussian-kernel-smoothing. The second column shows the MCMC-trace plot of draws underlying the density plots in the respective first column. Green solid bars indicate data generating parameter values. Red-dashed bars indicate individual level maximum likelihood estimates obtained from numerical maximization of the likelihood function using the R-function `optim` (I report numerical estimates regardless of the existence of a finite maximum likelihood estimate given the 5 choices from a specific individual and the corresponding design matrices). If no red-dashed bar is showing, this indicates that the maximum likelihood estimate falls outside of the range of parameter values plotted. To still give an impression of maximum likelihood estimates, the MCMC-trace plots in the respective second columns have the maximum likelihood estimates in the title.

Looking at the maximum likelihood estimates and comparing them to the green bars, we can see that they are extremely inaccurate. Clearly, individual level posterior inference benefits tremendously from the information in the hierarchical prior distribution that the model learns by pooling information across the 2000 consumers in our simulated short panel.

Finally, Fig. 9 illustrates how the hierarchical Bayesian MNL-model recovers the joint distribution of preferences for brands A and B in the population of consumers. We recognize the strongly negative relationship between preferences for brands A and B in the population (However, the posterior mean correlation of -0.88 (0.037) overestimates the data generating correlation of -0.997, which can be traced back to the finite information in the data available for calibration and the subjective priors for population level parameters employed here. See the documentation of `rhierMnlRwMixture` for details). Thus, if a particular individual level likelihood is only informative about the preference for brand A (B), the corresponding preference

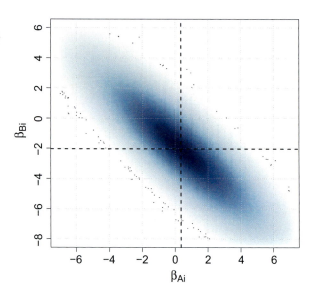

Fig. 9 Joint posterior distribution of $\{\beta_{Ai}\}$ and $\{\beta_{Ai}\}$

for brand B (A) can be inferred rather accurately from the hierarchical prior distribution. Dashed lines in Fig. 9 indicate posterior population means, that nicely recover the data generating values from the information in all $N \times T$ choice observations. The code to replicate this illustration is again available in the Appendix.

Note that we estimated the model that was used to generate the data here. In applications, it is very likely that some or all subjective choices that go into the formulation of the model result in systematic differences from the data generating mechanism, including the choice of the hierarchical prior distribution that was (implicitly) chosen to be multivariate normal in this illustration. However, it is also clear that even misspecified hierarchical prior distributions can strike a beneficial bias-variance trade-off in applications where individual level maximum likelihood estimates are extremely noisy or may not exist at all. In fact, this bias-variance trade-off is at the source of the inroads Bayesian hierarchical models have made into applications in marketing. For a discussion of how to imbue hierarchical prior distributions with subjective knowledge about ordinal relationships, see Pachali et al. (2018).

Mediation Analysis: A Case for Bayesian Model Comparisons

In this section, we borrow from Otter et al. (2018). Mediation analysis has developed in psychology, as a tool to empirically establish the process by which an experimental manipulation brings about its effect on the dependent variable of interest. An important distinction in this context is that between full and partial mediation at a causal theory level. I will not discuss the related model specification questions here but focus on the fact that if an experimentally manipulated cause X and a measured consequence Y become independent when conditioned on a measured mediator M, evidence for (full) mediation is established (This is because conditional independence would only result in very particular essentially zero probability circumstances from models where full mediation is not the causal mechanism at work. Results that do not establish some form of conditional independence, which are often interpreted as "partial mediation," actually are ambiguous with regarding their interpretation (Otter et al. 2018)). The original test for mediation proposed by Baron and Kenny (1986) builds on the connection between full mediation and conditional independence and tests conditional mean independence. Their test rests on the following set of regression equations, where t's denote intercepts (see also Fig. 10).

Fig. 10 Mediation according to Baron and Kenny (Baron and Kenny 1986)

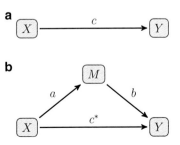

$$Y_i = t_1 + cX_i + \varepsilon_{Y,i} \tag{51}$$

$$M_i = t_2 + aX_i + \varepsilon_{M,i} \tag{52}$$

$$Y_i = t_3 + c^*X_i + bM_i + \varepsilon^*_{Y,i} \tag{53}$$

The first equation regresses Y on the randomly assigned experimental variable X. A statistically significant coefficient c establishes empirical support for the total effect from X to Y (see Fig. 10, Panel a). Because of random assignment of X, the coefficient c necessarily measures a causal effect. The second equation regresses M on X. A statistically significant coefficient a establishes empirical support for the effect from X to M that is again causal by experimental design. The third equation regresses Y on randomly assigned X and on observed M. Finding that the effect from X on Y vanishes, when conditioned on M (i.e., that there is no direct effect c^*), unequivocally establishes (full) mediation as the causal data generating model (see Fig. 10, Panel b) (In the limit of an infinite amount of data, the estimate of c^* will only converge to exactly zero under full mediation. The only alternative process that yields $c^* = 0$ in the limit features M as a joint cause of X and Y without another connection between X and Y. This process is ruled out a priori, when X is experimentally manipulated). Usually, empirical support for the hypothesis of $c^* = 0$ is established based on p-values larger than some subjectively chosen significance level. An obvious drawback of this approach is that p-values, by construction, fail to measure the strength of empirical support for conditional independence, which in turn establishes full mediation. Based on p-values, we can only "fail to reject" the null-hypothesis.

Next, I illustrate the differences between the classical and the Bayesian approach in the context of $c^* = 0$ using a sampling experiment. I thus consider the case of full mediation as DGP. Accordingly, I set $t_2 = t_3 = 1$, $a = 4$, $c^* = 0$, $b = 0.5$, and $\sigma_M = \sigma_{Y^*} = 1$ in Eqs. 52 and 53 and generate artificial data sets of different sizes: $N_1 = 50$, $N_2 = 200$, as well as $N_3 = 2000$ (X_i is drawn from a uniform distribution for each $i \in, \ldots, N\}$). I conduct 1000 replications for each data set size and compute Bayes' factors defined as ratios of marginal likelihoods of the model $\mathcal{M}_0 : Y_i = t_3 + bM_i + \varepsilon^*_{Y,i}$ and the model $\mathcal{M}_1 : Y_i = t_3 + c^*X_i + bM_i + \varepsilon^*_{Y,i}$. Note that the former is more restricted than the latter and implies that the coefficient c^* is equal to zero in the latter model (see Otter et al. (2018) for the computational details and R-scripts).

Table 8 illustrates the distribution of estimated Bayes Factors over the 1000 simulation replications testing the hypothesis of $c^* = 0$. The results in Table 8 verify that the Bayes Factor correctly favors $\mathcal{M}_0$ over $\mathcal{M}_1$ for the vast majority of sampling replications. Importantly, this table also illustrates that the Bayes Factor provides increasingly stronger evidence for $\mathcal{M}_0$ (i.e., $c^* = 0$) as the sample size increases.

The classical testing framework based on p-values fails to measure the strength of evidence in favor of $c^* = 0$. In line with how they are defined, p-values are uniformly distributed over sampling replications in the interval of (0,1) (see Table 9). The probability of observing a p-value smaller than the specified significance level is

Table 8 Distribution of Bayes' factors in simulation

	Pr(BF) > 3	Pr(BF) > 20	Pr(BF) > 100
$N = 50$	0.94	0.04	0.00
$N = 200$	0.97	0.71	0.00
$N = 2000$	0.99	0.93	0.43

Table 9 Distribution of p-values in simulation

	Pr(p-value) > 0.01	Pr(p-value) > 0.05	Pr(p-value) > 0.10
$N = 50$	0.99	0.96	0.90
$N = 200$	0.99	0.96	0.90
$N = 2000$	0.99	0.96	0.90

equal to this level, and independent of the sample size, when the null-hypothesis is actually true. In contrast, the probability of obtaining a Bayes Factor larger than 20 in support of $c^* = 0$ increases in the sample size and, for example, approaches one for $N = 2000$ (see Table 8).

Thus, when the data generating process implies conditional independence ($c^* = 0$), the Bayesian approach is the superior measure of empirical evidence for this process, compared to the approach based on p-values.

Conclusion

Writing a chapter like this, one certainly involves many trade-offs. I have chosen to emphasize general principles of Bayesian decision-making and inference in the hope of interesting and exciting readers that have an inclination towards quantitative methodology and are serious about improving marketing decisions. The promise from a deeper appreciation of the Bayesian paradigm, both in terms of its foundations in (optimal) decision-making and in terms of its computational approaches are better tailored quantitative approaches that can be developed and implemented as required by a new decision problem, or for the purpose of extracting (additional) knowledge from a new data source.

A drawback of this orientation is that the plethora of existing models that are usefully implemented in a fully Bayesian estimation framework, including common place prior distributions, are not even enumerated in this chapter. However, I believe that the full appreciation of individual, concrete applications requires a more general understanding of the Bayesian paradigm. Once this understanding develops, that for different individual models follows naturally.

Cross-References

▶ Finite Mixture Models
▶ Fusion Modeling

▶ Multilevel Modeling
▶ Panel Data Analysis: A Non-technical Introduction for Marketing Researchers

Acknowledgments I would like to thank Anocha Aribarg, Albert Bemmaor, Joachim Büschken, Arash Laghaie, anonymous reviewers, the editors, and participants in my class on "Bayesian Modeling for Marketing" helpful comments and feedback. All remaining errors are obviously mine.

Appendix

MCMC for Binomial Probit Without Data Augmentation

Simulate data, call MCMC routine, plot MCMC-traces. This R-script sources a RW-MH-sampler for the binomial probit model (see teh following script), simulates probit data, and runs the code with different step-sizes (standard deviations of ϵ).

```
# may need to install these packages first
library ( bayesm )
library ( latex2exp )

# needs to be in R's working directory
source (' rbprobitRWMetropolis .r')

# function to simulate from binary probit
simbprobit = function (X, beta ) {
y= ifelse ((X%*% beta + rnorm ( nrow (X))) <0 ,0 ,1)
list (X=X,y=y, beta = beta )
}

nobs =500 # number of simulated observations
X= cbind ( rep (1, nobs ), runif ( nobs ), runif ( nobs ))
beta =c( -3 ,2 ,4) # data generating parameters
nvar = ncol (X)
simout = simbprobit (X, beta )

# probit responses
y= simout $y

R =200000 # length of MCMC sample

# data list to passed to MCMC routine
Data = list (X= simout $X,y= simout $y)

Mcmc = list (R=R, keep =1)

# prior mean set to zero, prior variances set to 100
Prior = list ( betabar = double ( nvar ),A= diag ( rep (.01, nvar )))

out _1= rbprobitRWMetropolis ( Data =Data, Mcmc =Mcmc,
```

Bayesian Models

```
Prior =Prior, stepsize =.001)
out _2= rbprobitRWMetropolis ( Data =Data, Mcmc =Mcmc,
Prior =Prior, stepsize =.005)
out _3= rbprobitRWMetropolis ( Data =Data, Mcmc =Mcmc,
Prior =Prior, stepsize =.8)
out _4= rbprobitRWMetropolis ( Data =Data, Mcmc =Mcmc,
Prior =Prior, stepsize =3)

windows ()
par ( mfrow =c (2,2))
matplot ( out _1$ betadraw, type ='l',xlab = ", ylab = ",
main = TeX ('$\cr epsilon $-standard deviation =.001 ')); grid ()
matplot ( out _2$ betadraw, type ='l',xlab = ", ylab = ",
main = TeX ('$\cr epsilon $-standard deviation =.005 ')); grid ()
matplot ( out _3$ betadraw, type ='l',xlab = ", ylab = ",
main = TeX ('$\cr epsilon $-standard deviation =.8 ')); grid ()
matplot ( out _4$ betadraw, type ='l',xlab = ", ylab = ",
main = TeX ('$\cr epsilon $-standard deviation =3')); grid ()
```

MCMC function. The following function implements a simple RW-MH-sampler for the binomial probit model coupled with a multivariate normal prior. All regression parameters are updated simultaneously in one MH-step.

```
rbprobitRWMetropolis <- function (Data, Prior, Mcmc, stepsize )
{
require ( bayesm )
# because of the use of lndMnv to evaluate the log - density of a ...
# ... multivariate normal distribution
y = Data $y
nvar = ncol (X)
nobs = length (y)
betabar = Prior $ betabar
A = Prior $A
R = Mcmc $R
keep = Mcmc $ keep

betadraw = matrix ( double ( floor (R/ keep ) * nvar ), ncol = nvar )
loglike = double ( floor (R/ keep ))
beta = c( rep (0, nvar ))

priorcov = chol2inv ( chol (A))
rootp = chol ( priorcov )
rootpi = backsolve (rootp, diag ( nvar ))

# intialize log - likelihood at starting value
oldloglike =
```

```
sum ( pnorm (0, (X%*% beta )[ as. logical (y)], 1, log .p= TRUE ))+
sum ( pnorm (0, (-X%*% beta )[!as. logical (y)], 1, log .p= TRUE ))
# compute non - normalized log - posterior at starting value
oldlpost = oldloglike + lndMvn (beta, betabar, rootpi)
naccept = 0
for ( rep in 1:R) {
betac = beta + rnorm ( nvar )* stepsize # random walk proposal
# compute probit log - likelihood at proposed value
cloglike =
sum ( pnorm (0, -(X%*% betac )[ as. logical (y)], 1, log .p= TRUE ))+
sum ( pnorm (0, (X%*% betac )[!as. logical (y)], 1, log .p= TRUE ))
# compute non - normalized log - posterior at proposed value
clpost = cloglike + lndMvn (betac, betabar, rootpi )
# compute log - ratio of non - normalized posterior at proposed ...
# ... and old value
ldiff — clpost - oldlpost
alpha = min (1, exp ( ldiff )) # acceptance probability
if ( alpha < 1) {
unif = runif (1)
}
else {
unif = 0
}
if ( unif <= alpha ) {
beta = betac
oldloglike = cloglike
oldlpost = clpost
naccept = naccept + 1
}
if ( rep %% keep == 0) {
mkeep = rep / keep
betadraw [mkeep, ] = beta
loglike [ mkeep ] = oldloglike
}
}
# betadraw is the matrix containing draws from the posterior
# rateaccept is the relative frequency of accpeting proposed moves ...
# ... from oldbeta to betac
# loglike is the log - likelihood ...
# ... evaluated at the current MCMC state ( beta )
return ( list ( betadraw = betadraw, mkeep =mkeep,
```

```
rateaccept = naccept /R, loglike = loglike ))
}
```

Stan probit definition file. This file that is called as `StanProbit.stan` by the R-script immediately below defines a binomial probit model with a multivariate normal prior for `Stan`. According to the model, the data are independently Bernoulli distributed with probabilities implied by the probit-link, parameters, and covariates.

```
data {
int N; // number of observations
int K; // number of covariates
int < lower =0, upper =1> y[N]; // information
matrix [N,K] X; // design matrix
}
parameters {
vector [K] beta ; // beta coefficients
}
model {
vector [N] mu;
beta ~ normal (0, 100);
mu = X* beta ;
for (n in 1:N) mu[n] = Phi (mu[n ]);

y ~ bernoulli (mu );
}
```

Calling Stan from R to estimate a binomial probit model. This R-script calls `Stan` to sample from the posterior of the binomial probit model coupled with a multivariate normal prior defined in the file above.

```
# may need to install the rstan package first
require ( rstan ) # load the rstan package
# see sripts above for nobs, nvar, simout objects
prob _ data = list (N=nobs ,K=nvar ,X= simout $X,y=as. vector ( simout $y))
rstan _ options ( auto _ write = TRUE )
options (mc. cores = parallel :: detectCores ())
stanfit _ probit = stan ( file =" StanProbit . stan ",data = prob _ data,
pars = c(" beta "), chains = 1,
iter = 600000, warmup = 1000)

# Make draws available for posterior analysis in R
out _ StanProbit = extract ( stanfit _ probit )
```

HB-Logit Example

This code generates MNL-data from a hierarchical model, estimates an HB-logit model, and compares selected individual level posteriors to the corresponding maximum likelihood estimates.

```
genXy <- function (betai ,p,T){
## generate multinomial logit choices
# alternative specific constants
# ... this assumes p=3 ( two inside brands, one outside choice )
X= kronecker ( rep (1,T), matrix (c(1 ,0 ,0 ,0 ,1 ,0) , ncol =(
length ( betai ) -1)))
# add the continuous covariate
X= cbind (X, runif (T*p))
index = seq (p,p*T,p)
X[index ,]=0 # outside good
Xbeta =t( matrix (X%*%betai , nrow =p))
index = cbind (1:T, max . col ( Xbeta ))
maxl = Xbeta [ index ]
logsumel = log ( rowSums ( exp (Xbeta - maxl ))) + maxl
logprob = matrix (Xbeta - logsumel , nrow =T)
y= double (T)
for (t in 1:T){
y[t]= sum ( cumsum ( exp ( logprob [t ,])) < runif (1))+1  ## draw
from the CDF of probs
}
return ( list (y=y,X=X))
}

p=3 # number of alterantives in each choice set
T=5 # number of repeated measurements, i.e., choice sets or choices

# generate panel data for MCMC analysis
N =2000 # number of individuals in the panel

# population mean preference
betap =c(.3 , -2 , -1)

# variance - covariance of preferences in the population
Vbeta = matrix (c(3 , -2.99 ,0 , -2.99 ,3 ,0 ,0 ,0 ,.1) , ncol =3)
# just for demonstration to make sure we all get ...
# ... the same result date and results
set . seed (66)
# draw individual specific preferences from MVNormal distribution
betai = betap +t( chol ( Vbeta ))%*% matrix ( rnorm (N* length (
betap )), ncol =N)
lgtdata <- vector (" list ", N)
```

```
T=5 # number of choices per individual
betaMLE = betai
betaMLE [ , ]=0

for (i in 1:N){
outgen = genXy ( betai [,i],p,T)
# For Bayesian analysis using rhierMnlRwMixture ...
# ... you need to organize your data in list format as ...
# ... in the command line below
# y :: vector of choice outcomes of length T or ...
# ... T_i in case different panel units provide different numbers of choices
# X :: A (p*T) rows x length ( beta [,i]) columns model matrix ;
# the first ( second ) p rows correspond to the first ( second ) choice set, and so on.
# Each alternative is represented by one row in X.
# The numbers in y point to which 'row ' was chosen from a particular choice set
lgtdata [[i ]]= list (y= outgen [[1]], X= outgen [[2]])
out = optim ( par = betai [,i], fn=llMNL, gr=NULL, y= outgen [[1]], X= outgen [[2]], p=p, hessian = FALSE, control = list ( fnscale = -1))
betaMLE [,i]= out $ par # collect MLE estimates
}

# load the bayesm package into the workspace
# (if this gives you an error, ...
# ... you need to install the package first )
library ( bayesm )
# run the Bayesian hierarchical model
outMCMC = rhierMnlRwMixture ( Data = list (p=p, lgtdata = lgtdata ),
Prior = list ( ncomp =1), Mcmc = list (R =100000, keep =10))

# posterior of individual specific coefficients
betaimc = outMCMC $ betadraw

index =1001:10000

# may need to install this first
library ( latex2exp )

M=c (3 ,99 ,2000) # plot betai posterior for consumers in M
jpeg ( filename =" ILposteriors880 . jpg ", quality = 100 , width = 880 , height = 480)
# windows ()
par ( mfcol =c( length ( betap ), length (M)* 2))
```

```
for (i in M){
plot ( density ( betaimc [i ,1, index ]),
xlab = TeX ('$\cr beta _{A}$'), ylab = " ", main = paste ("panel -
unit ", i))
abline (v= betai [1,i], col ='green ', lwd =5, lty =1 )
abline (v= betaMLE [1,i], col ='red ', lwd =5, lty =2 )
plot ( density ( betaimc [i ,2, index ]),
xlab = TeX ('$\cr beta _{B}$'), ylab = " ", main =" ")
abline (v= betai [2,i], col ='green ', lwd =5, lty =1 )
abline (v= betaMLE [2,i], col ='red ', lwd =5, lty =2 )
plot ( density ( betaimc [i ,3, index ]),
xlab = TeX ('$\cr beta $'), ylab = " ", main =" ")
abline (v= betai [3,i], col ='green ', lwd =5, lty =1 )
abline (v= betaMLE [3,i], col ='red ', lwd =5, lty =2 )

plot ( betaimc [i ,1, index ], type ='l',
xlab =" ", ylab = TeX ('$\cr beta _{A}$'), main = paste (" MLE :
 ", round ( betaMLE [1,i ])))
abline (h= betai [1,i], col ='green ', lwd =5, lty =1 )
abline (h= betaMLE [1,i], col ='red ', lwd =5, lty =2 )
plot ( betaimc [i ,2, index ], type ='l',
xlab =" ", ylab = TeX ('$\cr beta _{B}$'), main = paste (" MLE :
 ", round ( betaMLE [2,i ])))
abline (h= betai [2,i], col ='green ', lwd =5, lty =1 )
abline (h= betaMLE [2,i], col ='red ', lwd =5, lty =2 )
plot ( betaimc [i ,3, index ], type ='l',
xlab =" ", ylab = TeX ('$\cr beta $'), main = paste (" MLE : ",
round ( betaMLE [3,i ])))
abline (h= betai [3,i], col ='green ', lwd =5, lty =1 )
abline (h= betaMLE [3,i], col ='red ', lwd =5, lty =2 )
}
```

References

Albert, J. H., & Chib, S. (1993). Bayesian analysis of binary and polychotomous response data. *Journal of the American Statistical Association, 88*(422), 669–679. http://www.jstor.org/stable/2290350

Allenby, G. M., Arora, N., & Ginter, J. L. (1995). Incorporating prior knowledge into the analysis of conjoint studies. *Journal of Marketing Research, 32*(2), 152–162. http://www.jstor.org/stable/3152044

Allenby, G. M., Arora, N., & Ginter, J. L. (1998). On the heterogeneity of demand. *Journal of Marketing Research, 35*(3), 384–389. http://www.jstor.org/stable/3152035

Amemiya, T. (1985). *Advanced econometrics*. Cambridge, MA: Harvard University Press.

Baron, R. M., & Kenny, D. A. (1986). The moderator–mediator variable distinction in social psychological research: Conceptual, strategic, and statistical considerations. *Journal of Personality and Social Psychology, 51*, 1173–1182. https://doi.org/10.1037/0022-3514.51.6.1173.

Bernardo, J. M., & Smith, A. F. M. (2001). Bayesian theory. *Measurement Science and Technology, 12*(2), 221. http://stacks.iop.org/0957-0233/12/i=2/a=702.

Besag, J. (1974). Spatial interaction and the statistical analysis of lattice systems. *Journal of the Royal Statistical Society. Series B (Methodological), 36*(2), 192–236. http://www.jstor.org/stable/2984812

Carpenter, B., Gelman, A., Hoffman, M., Lee, D., Goodrich, B., Betancourt, M., Brubaker, M., Guo, J., Li, P., & Riddell, A. (2017). Stan: A probabilistic programming language. *Journal of Statistical Software, Articles, 76*(1), 1–32. https://doi.org/10.18637/jss.v076.i01. https://www.jstatsoft.org/v076/i01.

Chen, M.-H., Shao, Q.-M., & Ibrahim, J. G. (2000). *Monte Carlo methods in Bayesian computation*. New York: Springer. http://gateway.library.qut.edu.au/login?url=http://link.springer.com/openurl?genre=book&isbn=978-1-4612-1276-8.

Chib, S., & Carlin, B. P. (1999). On MCMC sampling in hierarchical longitudinal models. *Statistics and Computing, 9*(1), 17–26. https://doi.org/10.1023/A:1008853808677.

Eddelbuettel, D. (2013). *Seamless R and C++ integration with Repp*. New York: Springer.

Eddelbuettel, D., & François, R. (2011). Repp: Seamless R and C++ integration. *Journal of Statistical Software, 40*(8), 1–18. https://doi.org/10.18637/jss.v040.i08. http://www.jstatsoft.org/v40/i08/

Edwards, Y. D., & Allenby, G. M. (2003). Multivariate analysis of multiple response data. *Journal of Marketing Research, 40*(3), 321–334. https://doi.org/10.1509/jmkr.40.3.321.19233.

Fasiolo, M. (2016). *An introduction to mvnfast. R package version 0.1.6*. https://CRAN.R-project.org/package=mvnfast

Frühwirth-Schnatter, S., Tüchler, R., & Otter, T. (2004). Bayesian analysis of the heterogeneity model. *Journal of Business & Economic Statistics, 22*(1), 2–15. https://doi.org/10.1198/073500103288619331.

Genz, A., Bretz, F., Miwa, T., Mi, X., Leisch, F., Scheipl, F., & Hothorn, T. (2018). *mvtnorm: Multivariate normal and t distributions*. https://CRAN.R-project.org/package=mvtnorm. R package version 1.0-8.

Geweke, John. (1991). Efficient simulation from the multivariate normal and student-t distributions subject to linear constraints and the evaluation of constraint probabilities. In: E. M. Keramidas (Ed.), *Computing Science and Statistics: Proceedings of the 23rd Symposium on the Interface*, pp. 571–578.

Gilks, W. R. (1996). Full conditional distributions. In S. (Sylvia) Richardson, D. J Spiegelhalter, & W. R. (Walter R.) Gilks (Eds.), *Markov chain Monte Carlo in practice* (pp. 75–88). London/Melbourne: Chapman & Hall.

Hastie, T., Tibshirani, R., & Friedman, J. H. (2001). *The elements of statistical learning: data mining, inference, and prediction*. New York: Springer.

Hoerl, A. E., & Kennard, R. W. (1970). Ridge regression: Biased estimation for nonorthogonal problems. *Technometrics, 12*(1), 55–67. https://doi.org/10.1080/00401706.1970.10488634.

Hoffman, M. D., & Gelman, A. (2014). The no-U-turn sampler: Adaptively setting path lengths in Hamiltonian Monte Carlo. *Journal of Machine Learning Research, 15*, 1593–1623. http://jmlr.org/papers/v15/hoffman14a.html.

Kass, R. E., & Raftery, A. E. (1995). Bayes factors. *Journal of the American Statistical Association, 90*(430), 773–795. https://doi.org/10.1080/01621459.1995.10476572.

Lenk, P. J., & DeSarbo, W. S. (2000). Bayesian inference for finite mixtures of generalized linear models with random effects. *Psychometrika, 65*(1), 93–119. https://doi.org/10.1007/BF02294188.

Lenk, P. J., DeSarbo, W. S., Green, P. E., & Young, M. R. (1996). Hierarchical Bayes conjoint analysis: Recovery of partworth heterogeneity from reduced experimental designs. *Marketing Science, 15*(2), 173–191. https://doi.org/10.1287/mksc.15.2.173.

Long, J. S. (1997). *Regression models for categorical and limited dependent variables*. Thousand Oaks: Sage Publications. https://uk.sagepub.com/en-gb/eur/regression-models-for-categorical-and-limited-dependent-variables/book6071.

McCulloch, R., & Rossi, P. (1994). An exact likelihood analysis of the multinomial probit model. *Journal of Econometrics, 64*(1–2), 207–240. https://EconPapers.repec.org/RePEc:eee:econom:v:64:y:1994:i:1-2:p:207-240.

Mersmann, O., Trautmann, H., Steuer, D., & Bornkamp, B. (2018). *truncnorm: Truncated normal distribution*. https://CRAN.R-project.org/package=truncnorm. R package version 1.0-8

Montgomery, A. L., & Bradlow, E. T. (1999). Why analyst overconfidence about the functional form of demand models can lead to overpricing. *Marketing Science, 18*(4), 569–583. http://www.jstor.org/stable/193243

Neal, R. M. (2011). MCMC using Hamiltonian dynamics. In S. Brooks, A. Gelman, G. L. Jones, & X-L. Meng (Eds.), *Handbook of Markov chain Monte Carlo* (Chap. 5). Chapman & Hall/CRC. http://arxiv.org/abs/1206.1901

Orme, B. (2017). *The CBC system for choice-based conjoint analysis*. Technical Report. https://sawtoothsoftware.com/download/techpap/cbctech.pdf

Otter, T., Tüchler, R., & Frühwirth-Schnatter, S. (2004). Capturing consumer heterogeneity in metric conjoint analysis using Bayesian mixture models. *International Journal of Research in Marketing, 21*(3), 285–297. https://doi.org/10.1016/j.ijresmar.2003.11.002. http://www.sciencedirect.com/science/article/pii/S0167811604000308

Otter, T., Gilbride, T. J., & Allenby, G. M. (2011). Testing models of strategic behavior characterized by conditional likelihoods. *Marketing Science, 30*(4), 686–701. http://www.jstor.org/stable/23012019

Otter, T., Pachali, M. J., Mayer, S., & Landwehr, J. R. (2018). Causal inference using mediation analysis or instrumental variables – Full mediation in the absence of conditional independence. *Marketing ZFP, 40*(2), 41–57. https://doi.org/10.15358/0344-1369-2018-2-41.

Pachali, M. J., Kurz, P., & Otter, T. (2018). *How to generalize from a hierarchical model?* Technical Report. https://ssrn.com/abstract=3018670

Pearl, J. (2009). *Causality: Models, reasoning and inference* (2nd ed.). New York: Cambridge University Press.

Plummer, M., Best, N., Cowles, K., & Vines, K. (2006). Coda: Convergence diagnosis and output analysis for MCMC. *R News, 6*(1), 7–11. https://journal.r-project.org/archive/.

Ritter, C., & Tanner, M. A. (1992). Facilitating the Gibbs sampler: The Gibbs stopper and the Griddy-Gibbs sampler. *Journal of the American Statistical Association, 87*(419), 861–868. https://doi.org/10.1080/01621459.1992.10475289.

Robert, C. P. (1994). *The Bayesian choice: a decision-theoretic motivation*. New York: Springer.

Roberts, G. O. (1996). Markov chain concepts related to sampling algorithms. In S. (Sylvia) Richardson, D. J. Spiegelhalter, & W. R. (Walter R.) Gilks (Eds.), *Markov chain Monte Carlo in practice* (pp. 45–58). London/Melbourne: Chapman & Hall.

Rossi, P. E., McCulloch, R. E., & Allenby, G. M. (1996). The value of purchase history data in target marketing. *Marketing Science, 15*(4), 321–340. https://doi.org/10.1287/mksc.15.4.321.

Rossi, P. E., Allenby, G. M., & McCulloch, R. E. (2005). *Bayesian statistics and marketing*. Chichester: Wiley.

Wachtel, S., & Otter, T. (2013). Successive sample selection and its relevance for management decisions. *Marketing Science, 32*(1), 170–185. https://doi.org/10.1287/mksc.1120.0754.

Zellner, A. (1971). *An introduction to Bayesian inference in econometrics*. New York: Wiley.

Choice-Based Conjoint Analysis

Felix Eggers, Henrik Sattler, Thorsten Teichert, and Franziska Völckner

Contents

Introduction	782
Model	787
Utility Model	787
Choice Model	791
Procedure for Conducting Discrete Choice Experiments	791
Identification of Attributes and Attribute Levels	791
Creating the Experimental Design	793
Implementation into Questionnaire	796
Estimation	799
Advanced Estimation Techniques	808
Outlook	813
Appendix: R Code	813
References	816

Abstract

Conjoint analysis is one of the most popular methods to measure preferences of individuals or groups. It determines, for instance, the degree how much consumers like or value specific products, which then leads to a purchase decision. In particular, the method discovers the utilities that (product) attributes add to the

---

F. Eggers
University of Groningen, Groningen, The Netherlands
e-mail: f.eggers@rug.nl

H. Sattler · T. Teichert
University of Hamburg, Hamburg, Germany
e-mail: henrik.sattler@uni-hamburg.de; thorsten.teichert@uni-hamburg.de

F. Völckner (✉)
Department of Marketing and Brand Management, University of Cologne, Köln, Germany
e-mail: voelckner@wiso.uni-koeln.de

© Springer Nature Switzerland AG 2022
C. Homburg et al. (eds), *Handbook of Market Research*,
https://doi.org/10.1007/978-3-319-57413-4_23

overall utility of a product (or stimuli). Conjoint analysis has emerged from the traditional rating- or ranking-based method in marketing to a general experimental method to study individual's discrete choice behavior with the choice-based conjoint variant. It is therefore not limited to classical applications in marketing, such as new product development, pricing, branding, or market simulations, but can be applied to study research questions from related disciplines, for instance, how marketing managers choose their ad campaign, how managers select internationalization options, why consumers engage in or react to social media, etc. This chapter describes comprehensively the "state-of-the-art" of conjoint analysis and choice-based conjoint experiments and related estimation procedures.

Keywords

Preference measurement · Choice experiments · Conjoint analysis · Conjoint measurement · Tradeoff analysis · Choice-based conjoint · Adaptive conjoint · Utility function · New product development · Revealed preference · Incentive-aligned mechanisms · Willingness-to-pay · Market simulation

Introduction

Assume that an electronics company wants to enter the market for ebook readers. The company has already developed a working prototype with the basic functionality. However, consumers did not yet consider buying this specific product according to a survey, but continue to buy a (more expensive) competitor's product instead. The manufacturer therefore would like to know which attributes of an ebook reader are valued by consumers and which specific attributes they need to improve. Given limited budgets, they can only modify their product in one or two attributes, depending on the manufacturing costs, so that they need to reveal which attributes are most important. Moreover, they would like to know how price-sensitive consumers are and how much they are willing to spend for an ebook reader. Finally, they also need an estimate of the achievable market share to reach the final decision if they should market their product or not.

These questions and related ones can be addressed with preference measurement. The aim of preference measurement is to discover the degree how much consumers like or value (i.e., derive a utility from) specific products, which then leads to a purchase decision. Conjoint analysis, as one of the most popular methods within preference measurement, assumes that products are attribute bundles. Accordingly, an ebook reader is considered as a bundle of screen technology, screen size, screen resolution, storage size, brand name, price, etc. The method tries to discover the utilities that each attribute (and attribute level, respectively) adds to the overall utility of the product by systematically varying specific levels of the attribute. It is a decompositional method, meaning that it elicits consumers' overall utilities for experimentally varied product concepts and then decomposes the overall utility into the attributes' utilities (so-called "partworth utilities" or just "partworths") via statistical procedures. In line with this description, the American Marketing

Association (2015) defines conjoint analysis as a "statistical technique in which respondents' utilities or valuations of attributes are inferred from the preferences they express for various combinations of these attributes."

As a result, conjoint analysis provides researchers with a utility function that translates the specific attribute levels of a product into consumers' preferences. This utility function serves multiple purposes; it can explain consumers' actual purchase decisions and predict their choices given changes to the product configuration, i.e., modification of attributes. In this regard, it is the basis for a multitude of relevant marketing applications, for example:

- New product development and innovation, e.g., which product concept will be preferred by consumers? (e.g., Page and Rosenbaum 1992; Urban and Hauser 1993)
- Pricing, e.g., how much are consumers willing to pay and how much are improvements in products attributes allowed to cost? (e.g., Miller et al. 2011)
- Branding, e.g., how much value can be attributed to the brand of a product? (e.g., Sattler 2005)
- Market segmentation, e.g., are there different market segments that differ in terms of certain preferred product attributes? (e.g., Teichert 2001b)
- Market scenarios, e.g., what is the effect of a new product entry on the market shares of the incumbents? (e.g., Burmester et al. 2016)

Conjoint analysis is not limited to applications in marketing, but can be generally applied when individuals need to make a decision regarding multiattributive objects. It is also a popular method in other areas, such as transportation (e.g., Hensher 1994), litigation (e.g., Eggers et al. 2016), agriculture (e.g., Lusk and Schroeder 2004), or health economics (e.g., De Bekker-Grob et al. 2012). Due to its broad area of applications, conjoint analysis has advanced to a widely respected method since its introduction into marketing in the 1970s. Overviews of its popularity can be found in Green and Srinivasan (1978, 1990) as well as in empirical studies conducted, for example, by Wittink et al. (1994), Voeth (1999), Sattler (2006), and Orme (2016).

Conjoint methods differ in terms of how the overall utilities are elicited. Traditional approaches use ratings of single product concepts (rating-based conjoint), ratings of pairs of products, or rankings of a selection of products (ranking-based conjoint). Currently, the most popular conjoint approach with over 80% of applications (Orme 2016) is based on choices among several product concepts, i.e., choice-based conjoint (CBC; also termed discrete choice experiments; Haaijer and Wedel 2003; Louviere and Woodworth 1983). Using choices as the dependent variable has become popular because they mimic consumers' behavior when they are making purchase decisions.

Continuing the example case mentioned above, assume that the manufacturer of the ebook reader is currently producing a black ebook reader with a 6-in. E Ink display and 4 GB storage. They are exploring different options to improve their product, e.g., identified via qualitative research or pretests: (1) increasing the storage from 4 GB to 8 GB, (2) increasing the screen size from 6 to 7 in., or (3) changing the

Table 1 List of potential ebook readers (2^3 design)

Concept	Storage (GB)	Screen size (in.)	Color
1	4	6	Black
2	4	7	Black
3	4	6	White
4	4	7	White
5	8	6	Black
6	8	7	Black
7	8	6	White
8	8	7	White

case color from black to white. Accordingly, there are (2^3) eight different options they could potentially offer, resulting from the different combination of attribute levels (Table 1).

Although one could assume that more storage is better so that 8 GB models are preferred to 4 GB models, this is not necessarily true for screen size since consumers might either value a small (and less bulky) product or a larger (and more readable) screen. There is also no a priori preference order for color. Hence, it is not known beforehand which option would be the most preferred one. Moreover, it might not be profitable to offer an 8 GB model if the increase in preference, and therefore demand, is only marginal and does not justify the additional manufacturing costs. Thus, conjoint analysis is a suitable method to solve this decision problem.

Traditional conjoint analysis (e.g., rating-based conjoint) would present each of the products in Table 1 to a consumer in a survey and ask for his/her preference, e.g., on a rating scale from 0 ("not at all preferred") to 10 ("very much preferred"). The partworth utilities for the attribute levels can then be derived by using the ratings as a dependent variable in a regression model in which the attribute levels serve as independent variables (e.g., as dummy variables). Although ratings can be considered an acceptable manifestation of preferences, they do not mimic consumers behavior in the marketplace. Moreover, it is often questionable how the ratings can be translated into actual choices (Teichert 2001a).

These issues are among the reasons why CBC approaches have become popular. They offer respondents a selection of product alternatives in a choice set (also called "choice task") and ask for their most preferred option (Fig. 1). This procedure is repeated across multiple sequential choice sets, each presenting alternatives that are systematically varied by an experimental design. The decisions within a choice set often require a trade-off between attributes. For example, if a consumer prefers larger screens (as in option 1 in Fig. 1) and more storage (as in option 2), she/he needs to determine how important each of these attributes really is in order to reach a decision between option 1 and option 2, while also considering color. These decisions increase the realism of the tasks as trade-off decisions are very often required in the marketplace, e.g., when a higher quality is offered for a higher price. Another element that increases the realism of CBC is that it is possible to include a so-called no-choice option (also termed "none option" or "outside good"), which can be

	Option 1	Option 2	Option 3
Which of these ebook readers do you prefer?			
Please assume that these two options do not differ in terms of other attributes, i.e., both option have a self-lit E Ink display with 758x1024 pixels resolution, WiFi, and 3 weeks battery life. They both support multiple formats (PDF, EPUB) and connect to major book distributors.			
Storage:	4 GB	8 GB	I would not buy any of these
Screen size:	7 inch	6 inch	
Color:	White	Black	
	○	○	○

Fig. 1 Exemplary choice set of a CBC experiment

chosen if none of the alternatives are acceptable. In this example, the no-choice option could also be termed, e.g., "With these options I would keep reading books on paper," so that a threshold can be identified which indicates the utility that is needed to make consumers switch from traditional books to an ebook reader.

The higher degree of realism of CBC experiments leads to the expectation that CBC exhibits a higher validity compared to traditional, metric conjoint analysis. However, not all studies find significantly better results for CBC compared to traditional conjoint analysis, although the direction of the effects is as expected (Chakraborty et al. 2002; Elrod et al. 1992; Moore 2004; Moore et al. 1998; Vriens et al. 1998). A disadvantage of CBC experiments is that choices among alternatives are nominal and generate less information than, e.g., rating each alternative separately. Therefore, CBC requires collecting a multitude of sequential choice sets, which might invoke respondent fatigue and could serve as an explanation for those findings in which CBC is not predicting significantly better than rating or ranking-based conjoint.

The traditional conjoint approaches (e.g., rating and ranking-based conjoint) and CBC can be classified as static because they do not adapt to the responses that the consumer has given in the survey. To make the information collection more efficient, adaptive procedures dynamically adjust to the preferences of the respondents. They are typically based on a hybrid approach that combines a decompositional and a compositional method. Compositional approaches (e.g., the self explicated method) ask respondents directly about their preference for attribute levels and the relative importance of the attributes, e.g., via rating scales (Srinivasan and Park 1997). This input can then be used as a first estimate of the consumer's preferences in order to show product concepts in the conjoint procedure that are meaningful to the individual respondent or that generate most information about the respondent's preferences. The rating-based Adaptive Conjoint Analysis (ACA, Johnson 1987) and Adaptive CBC (ACBC, Sawtooth 2014) follow this idea. Other adaptive approaches from the machine learning literature dynamically anticipate each respondent's utility based on previous answers, i.e., either ratings (Toubia et al. 2003) or choices (Toubia et al. 2004, 2007). Hybrid individualized two-level CBC (HIT-CBC, Eggers and Sattler 2009) uses a compositional approach in order to ask for the best and worst levels for each attribute and adjusts the CBC part to these two extreme levels only. Thus, it can be seen as a compositional approach in which the attribute importance is derived by a conjoint experiment.

In newer conjoint analysis approaches, respondents interact with each other, following the principles of barter markets (Ding et al. 2009), auctions (Park et al. 2008), or poker games (Toubia et al. 2012). Preferences can then be inferred from these transactions. Figure 2 summarizes the evolution of conjoint analysis approaches.

It should be noted that the above-mentioned example of ebook reader attributes is a very simple case that is used for illustration only. Typically, conjoint studies apply more complex scenarios with more attributes, including price, and additional levels per attribute. Therefore, as an extended example, we will introduce additional attribute levels and a fourth attribute: price. The list of attributes and levels for the extended example is given in Table 2. Because of the popularity of CBC approaches, the remaining chapters will focus on these approaches.

- **Static**
    - Rating-/Ranking-based Conjoint　　　　　　　　　　(Srinivasan/Rao 1971)
    - Choice-based Conjoint (CBC)　　　　　　　　(Louviere/Woodworth 1983)

- **Adaptive**
    - Adaptive Conjoint Analysis　　　　　　　　　　　　　(Johnson 1987)
    - Adaptive CBC　　　　　　　　　　　　　　　　　　(Sawtooth 2014)
    - Fast Polyhedral Adaptive Conjoint　　　　　(Toubia et al. 2003, 2007)
    - Hybrid Individualized Two-Level CBC　　　　　　(Eggers/Sattler 2009)

- **Interactive**
    - Upgrading Auctions　　　　　　　　　　　　　　(Park/Ding/Rao 2008)
    - Barter Markets　　　　　　　　　　　　　　(Ding/Park/Bradlow 2009)
    - Conjoint Poker　　　　　　　　　　　　　　　　(Toubia et al. 2012)

Fig. 2 Evolution of conjoint analysis approaches

Table 2 Attributes and levels for the extended example

Attribute	Level 1	Level 2	Level 3	Level 4
Storage	4 GB	8 GB	16 GB	n.a.
Screen size	5 in.	6 in.	7 in.	n.a.
Color	Black	White	Silver	n.a.
Price	€79	€99	€119	€139

Model

Conjoint applications assume a (purchase) decision model in which consumer preferences, i.e., utilities, are the central element of the choice process. The assumption is that specific product attributes determine the individual utility evaluations and these, in turn, form the basis for the observed choice behavior (Fig. 3). This requires two interdependent models: a utility model and a choice model, which translates utilities into multinomial choices.

The literature on preference measurement or conjoint-related literature is often equivocal in their terminology. Throughout this chapter, we will use the following terminology (with alternative formulations noted in parentheses): We measure the utility (= preference, need, liking, worth, value) of a consumer (= respondent, individual, subject) for a specific product or service (= alternative, stimulus, object, option, profile) that consists of different attributes (= factors, dimensions), each having specific attribute levels (= characteristics, features).

Utility Model

The basis for the utility model in a choice context is random utility theory (RUT), which states that the overall utility U of consumer c for a product i is a latent construct that includes a systematic component V and an error component e, i.e., $U_{ci} = V_{ci} + e_{ci}$ (McFadden 1981; Walker and Ben-Akiva 2002). The stochastic error term catches all effects that are not accounted for and can include, e.g., respondent fatigue, omitted variables, biases in the data collection, or unaccounted heterogeneity (Louviere and Woodworth 1983).

The theory assumes that a consumer chooses the product from a set of alternatives that exhibits the highest utility. Since the overall utility is influenced by a stochastic component, it is only possible to state a probability that this consumer would choose the product. Consequently, the probability p that a consumer chooses product i from a set of products $S = \{i, j\}$ is (Train 2009):

$$p_i = p(U_i > U_j) = p(V_i - V_j > e_j - e_i) \qquad (1)$$

According to Eq. (1) a consumer is more likely to choose product *i* if the utility of *i* is larger than the utility of *j*. This requires that there is a positive residual from the difference in systematic utilities and that this residual exceeds the influence of error. Consequently, only differences in product attributes are considered, e.g., if consumers need to choose between two ebook readers and both devices are black then

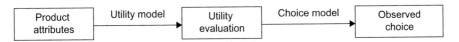

Fig. 3 Elements of a purchase decision model

color does not affect the decision. Generally, any constant value can be added to the utility functions and it will not affect the outcome, which is why choice-based utilities are interval-scaled and choice models do not have a general regression constant (constants, if any, need to be alternative-specific).

The systematic utility V represents the function that translates the product attributes and their levels into partworth utilities. The estimated utility V_i for a product i with N attributes can be divided into two subfunctions ψ and f_n as follows (Teichert 2001a):

$$V_i = \Psi[f_1(v_{1i}), f_2(v_{2i}), \ldots, f_N(v_{Ni})] \quad (2)$$

with

v_{ni}: Partworth utility of attribute n in product i, $n = 1, 2, \ldots, N$
f_n: Evaluation function of attribute n, $n = 1, 2, \ldots, N$
ψ: Function to combine partworth utilities across attributes

Evaluation Function for Attribute Levels

The function f_n in Eq. 2 describes how levels of attribute n are evaluated. The basic idea is that at least one attribute level represents the ideal point for the consumer (or at least the most preferred level from the available attribute levels). Differences to this ideal point lead to a loss in utility. Figure 4 depicts three potential functional forms.

The vector model assumes that increasing (decreasing) the attribute level leads to a proportional positive (negative) effect in utility. Hence, the ideal point is positive (negative) infinity. This model would be appropriate when assuming, e.g., that increasing the screen size of an ebook reader from 5 to 6 in. leads to the same positive utility difference as upgrading the screen from 6 to 7 in. The vector model uses the actual numeric values of the attributes and just one utility parameter to represent the partworth utility:

$$v_{in} = \beta_n * X_{inm} \quad (3)$$

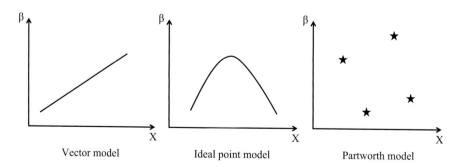

Fig. 4 Alternative functional forms for the evaluation of attribute levels

with,

v_{in}: partworth utility for attribute n in product i
β_n: utility vector for attribute n
X_{inm}: numeric value of level m of attribute n in product i

The ideal point model does not assume a linear slope of the utility function as the vector model but assumes diminishing (or increasing) marginal utilities. For example, although consumers might in general prefer larger screens for an ebook reader, very large sizes will become impractical so that utilities will decrease again when increasing the size from an (individually perceived) ideal point further. Likewise, when an ebook reader already has a very large storage, it can be expected that increasing the storage further leads to a diminishing marginal utility for the consumer. The ideal point model thus considers not only the numeric value of the attribute level, e.g., its screen size, but also its squared term:

$$v_{in} = \beta_{n1} * X_{inm} + \beta_{n2} * X^2_{inm} \qquad (4)$$

with,

v_{in}: partworth utility for attribute n in product i
β_{n1}: utility vector for attribute n
β_{n2}: utility vector for the squared value of attribute n
X_{inm}: numeric value of level m of attribute n in product i

The partworth model estimates separate partworth utilities for each level of the attribute, i.e., there is no assumed functional relationship between the attribute levels. This model is required for qualitative, nominal attributes, e.g., color, but can also be applied to quantitative, numeric attributes. If the choice sets include a no-choice option, this option is also represented by a separate partworth that measures the attractiveness of not choosing any of the alternatives. The partworth model is typically based on dummy-coding (or effect-coding) techniques, which requires $M-1$ variables to represent an attribute with M levels:

$$v_{in} = \sum_{m=1}^{M-1} \beta_{nm} * X_{inm} \qquad (5)$$

with,

v_{in}: partworth utility for attribute n in product i
β_{nm}: partworth utility for level m of attribute n
X_{inm}: dummy variable with value 1 if product i features level m of attribute n, otherwise 0

Regarding the number of parameters that these models require for the estimation, the vector model is the most parsimonious as it only uses one parameter per attribute.

The ideal point model is based on two parameters. The partworth model requires setting one attribute level as the reference level, which is left out of the estimation so that it requires $M - 1$ parameters.

The partworth model can be considered conservative since it does not require a prior specification or theory about the slope of the partworth utility function. If more than two attribute levels are present, it uses the most number of parameters and therefore provides the best model fit (by sacrificing degrees of freedom). It is therefore not surprising that the partworth model is predominantly used in conjoint analysis and is partly also considered as a constitutive element (Shocker and Srinivasan 1973).

Function to Combine Partworth Utilities Across Attributes

The function ψ in Eq. 2 determines how to combine partworth utilities across attributes. Conjoint analysis assumes a compensatory utility model. In a linear additive utility model, the overall systematic utility V_i of a product i is the sum of the partworth utilities v_{in} of its attributes $n = 1, \ldots, N$:

$$V_i = \sum_{n=1}^{N} v_{in} \tag{6}$$

Complex functions can be modeled as extension to this base model, e.g., interaction effects between attributes. Interaction effects occur when the utility evaluation of one attribute level depends on the level of another attribute. For example, consumers might prefer a white color for ebook readers with large screens but black for readers with smaller screens.

Interaction effects can be modeled as additional effects in the linear additive base model by including separate partworth utilities for the cross product of two attributes. The overall utility for a product is then represented as the sum of the partworth utilities of both the main effects and the interaction effects:

$$V_i = \sum_{n=1}^{N} v_{in} + \sum_{m=1}^{M-1} \sum_{m'=1}^{M'-1} \beta_{nm,n'm'}^{IA} * X_{inm} * X_{in'm'} \tag{7}$$

with,

$\beta_{nm;n'm'}^{IA}$: Interaction effect between level m of attribute n and level m' of attribute n'; $m = 1, 2, \ldots, M$; $m' = 1, 2, \ldots, M'$

$X_{inm}; X_{in'm'}$: Dummy variable with value 1 if product i features level m (m') of attribute n (n'), otherwise 0

Interaction effects increase the complexity of a model. For this reason, they are predominantly added if theory or prior assumptions about them exist. However, being able to measure interaction effects with conjoint analysis is a major advantage compared to other survey techniques, e.g., compositional approaches.

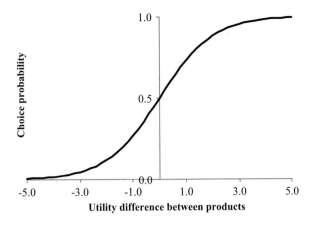

Fig. 5 S-shaped function of the multinomial logit model

Choice Model

Choice models can be differentiated according to the assumptions about the stochastic error component (see Train 2009 for an overview). In most applications, the error is assumed to be independent and identically distributed (iid) as extreme value type, i.e., Gumbel. This assumption leads to a logistic distribution of the differences of error terms and the multinomial logit (MNL) model (McFadden 1981; Hensher and Johnson 1981; Louviere et al. 2000). Accordingly, choosing an object i from a choice set with S alternatives is represented by the MNL model in terms of choice probabilities p:

$$p(i|S) = \frac{\exp(V_i)}{\sum_{j \in S} \exp(V_j)} \qquad (8)$$

The MNL model results in an S-shaped relationship between utility difference and choice probability (Fig. 5).

An alternative to the Gumbel distribution is the assumption of a normal distribution of the error term, which results in a multinomial probit model (Haaijer et al. 1998). The probit model requires multiple integrals and complex estimation procedures. Because of the compact form of the logit function (see Eq. 8), the MNL model is predominantly applied in CBC analyses (Haaijer and Wedel 2003).

Procedure for Conducting Discrete Choice Experiments

Identification of Attributes and Attribute Levels

The prerequisite – and most relevant step – for conducting conjoint analyses is to identify the relevant determinants of consumers' choices, i.e., product attributes and their levels. The selection of attributes and levels should reflect the products on the marketplace and should affect consumers' preferences. Otherwise, the validity of the model can be questioned. In general, the selection of attributes has to fulfill the following requirements (Green and Srinivasan 1978, 1990; Orme 2002):

- Attributes should be relevant, i.e., they should influence consumers' utility. In order to identify relevant attributes qualitative surveys, e.g., focus groups or depth interviews can be used.
- Attributes should discriminate, i.e., they should be able to differentiate between the competitive offerings on the marketplace.
- The number of attributes should be manageable. CBC experiments typically use less than seven attributes. Using more attributes greatly increases the complexity of the experimental design and requires high cognitive capabilities of the respondents.
- Attributes should not be interrelated, i.e., they should measure independent aspects of the product. If attributes are interrelated, then certain combinations might be highly unrealistic and confusing to the respondents. However, if, e.g., higher storages typically go along with higher prices, it is possible to consider these attributes as independent and analyze "what-if" scenarios. It should be noted that this requirement does not preclude potential interaction effects, i.e., although the attributes are independent, it does not mean that the preferences for them are as well.

After setting the attributes, their levels need to be determined. Regarding the type and number of levels, the following requirements should be considered (Green and Srinivasan 1978, 1990; Orme 2002; Teichert 2001a):

- The levels should span a range that is larger than in reality, but not substantially, in order to be able to cover potential future scenarios.
- Levels that have an ambiguous meaning should be avoided. For example, instead of using levels "large" and "small" for screen size, it is better to use specific values because they are free from interpretation. Moreover, specific values allow using a vector or ideal point model for estimation.
- The number of levels should be kept low because the complexity of the experimental design will increase exponentially with more levels. Consider the example in Table 1 with $2^3 = 8$ combinations. If three levels per attribute were used instead there are already $3^3 = 27$ potential options. Conjoint experiments can consider complex designs, however, most applications use an average of three to four levels per attribute.
- When setting the number of attribute levels, it should also be considered if the linearity or nonlinearity of the utility function (e.g., an ideal point model) should be tested, which then requires at least three levels. For testing interaction effects, it would be preferable (but not required) to use just two levels in order to keep the number of interaction effect parameters low.
- The number of levels should be balanced across attributes. Otherwise, the number-of-levels effect can occur, which leads to an artificially higher relevance of attributes that have more levels (Eggers and Sattler 2009; Verlegh et al. 2002).

- Levels should be generally acceptable. Unacceptable levels would otherwise invalidate the assumed compensatory utility model.
- Attribute levels are assumed to be mutually exclusive. For example, if an attribute "extra features" is added to the ebook reader setup with the levels "waterproof" and "integrated music player," the reader can only have one of these levels. If it is also interesting for the researcher to analyze preferences for both features in combination, this combination should be added as a separate level (an alternative would be to define each extra as a separate attribute with the levels "yes" and "no").

Creating the Experimental Design

The experimental design determines which combinations of attribute levels are presented to the respondent as stimuli (factorial design) and how these stimuli are allocated to choice sets (choice design). It represents the independent variable matrix for the analysis. To estimate the main effects of the attributes – and potentially interaction effects between them – the experimental design needs to make sure that these effects can be identified.

Criteria to evaluate the efficiency of an experimental design are (Huber and Zwerina 1996):

- Balance, i.e., each attribute level is presented an equal number of times
- Orthogonality, i.e., attribute levels are uncorrelated
- Minimal overlap, i.e., alternatives within a choice set are maximally different
- Utility balance, i.e., alternatives within a choice set should be equally attractive so that there should not be dominated or dominating alternatives

Balance and orthogonality refer to the factorial design, while minimal overlap and utility balance relate to the choice design.

Factorial Design

The set of all potential stimuli, i.e., every combination of attribute levels, leads to a full factorial. With N attributes and M_1 levels for attribute 1, M_2 levels of attribute 2, and M_N levels of attribute N, the size of the full factorial consists of all permutations $M_1 * M_2 * \ldots * M_N$. Table 1 shows a full factorial of the 2^3 design. Full factorials are always balanced, i.e., the attribute levels occur an equal number of times (here, four times), and orthogonal, i.e., each pair of attribute levels is balanced (here, each pair occurs twice).

A full factorial is only required if all main effects and all potential interaction effects should be estimated. The 2^3 design with three binary attributes A, B, C allows to estimate the three main effects, the three two-factor interaction effects (A*B, A*C, B*C), as well as the three-factor interaction (A*B*C). This is demonstrated in Table 2, in which the attribute levels are effect-coded (first level = 1, second level = -1). The interaction levels result from multiplying the levels of the underlying main effect attributes. As can be seen, the resulting interaction levels are not identical to any other column, i.e., are independent, and are also balanced and orthogonal so that they can be identified.

Since the full factorial increases exponentially when more attributes and/or more attribute levels are added, its size quickly becomes hard to handle in an experimental survey. For example, the extended example with three three-level attributes and one four-level attribute consists of $3^3 * 4 = 108$ potential alternatives. Moreover, very often three-factor interaction effects can be neglected and not all two-factor interaction effects may be required. In general, smaller factorials, i.e., fractional factorials, still allow estimating main effects and selected interaction effects (Addelman 1962).

The idea of creating a fractional factorial design is demonstrated with an example. Consider that a fourth binary attribute D would be added to the simple example in Table 3. The full factorial would then increase to $2^4 = 16$ stimuli. A fractional design assumes that at least one of the interaction effects between the attributes A, B, and C would be zero so that it can be replaced with the main effect of D, e.g., $D = A*B$, i.e., each level of the interaction between A and B becomes the new level of D. The fractional factorial then consists of the 8 entries in Table 2 and columns A, B, C, as well as $D = AB$. The factorial was reduced to 8 stimuli, i.e., by 50% compared to the full factorial. Nevertheless, it is still able to identify all main effects, i.e., the design is still balanced and orthogonal. As a downside, however, the interaction effect between A and B cannot be estimated as it is confounded with the main effect of D.

Fractional factorials are documented for the most common experimental designs (e.g., Sloan 2015) or can be generated via software (e.g., SAS or SPSS). The efficiency of the fractional design can be tested easily by checking the correlation matrix of all assumed main and interaction effects. If there are no or only minor correlations, then the design is orthogonal and the parameters can be identified without bias.

For traditional rating- or ranking-based conjoint procedures, it is sufficient to evaluate the factorial design. CBC methods require an additional step of allocating alternatives of the factorial design to specific choice sets, i.e., to evaluate the choice design.

Table 3 Main and interaction effects of a full factorial 2^3 design

Stimulus	Main effect			Interaction effects			
	A	B	C	AB	AC	BC	ABC
1	−1	−1	−1	1	1	1	−1
2	−1	−1	1	1	−1	−1	1
3	−1	1	−1	−1	1	−1	1
4	−1	1	1	−1	−1	1	−1
5	1	−1	−1	−1	−1	1	1
6	1	−1	1	−1	1	−1	−1
7	1	1	−1	1	−1	−1	−1
8	1	1	1	1	1	1	1

Choice Design

Choice experiments require that the factorial is subdivided into choice sets with a selection of alternatives. Creating an optimal choice design involves complex algorithms based on combinatorics. For example, even with the simple example and a 2^3 full factorial, there are $\binom{8}{2} = 28$ different choice sets with two alternatives. The complexity increases with the size of the factorial, e.g., in the extended example there would be $\binom{108}{3} = 205{,}156$ potential choice sets of size three. The challenge lies in selecting those choice sets that provide the most information about the respondents' preferences. The efficiency criteria minimal overlap and utility balance help reducing the size of the list of potential choice sets (Huber and Zwerina 1996).

Minimal overlap requires that the alternatives within a choice set are maximally different, i.e., have different attribute levels (Sawtooth 1999). It is based on the idea that an attribute that exhibits the same level for each alternative within a set does not affect the choice (see Eq. 1). A choice design with minimal overlap can be created for the simple example when the first four entries in the full factorial in Table 1 are coupled with their fold-over, i.e., opposite level. Accordingly, concept 1 (4 GB, 6 in., black) would be coupled with concept 8 (8 GB, 7 in., white) to create one choice set; concept 2 would be coupled with concept 7, etc., so that in total four choice sets with minimal overlap are created.

The idea of selecting choice sets that are utility balanced is that alternatives are allocated to a choice set that are equally attractive (Huber and Zwerina 1996). Contrarily, a choice set that features a dominating or dominated alternative provides no new knowledge since the choice can be anticipated. However, dominating alternatives can only be identified if there is a priori knowledge about the respondents' preference structure or if respondents' preferences are anticipated during the experiment with adaptive conjoint approaches (see above).

Because of the complexity of creating an optimal choice design, computer algorithms are recommended. For example, SAS or Sawtooth offer algorithms to create optimal choice designs and analyze their efficiency.

Decision Parameters

Relevant decision parameters for the experimental design also concern the number of stimuli per choice set and the number of choice sets.

Each choice task should be manageable for the respondent, which favors showing only a few alternatives per set (Batsell and Louviere 1991). On the other hand, more alternatives increase the information of each choice. Therefore, two to five stimuli per choice set are most common (Meissner et al. 2016). Using eye-tracking data, Meissner et al. (2016) show that the number of alternatives also affects search patterns. It is therefore advisable to use a choice set size that is similar to the typical size of a consideration set when consumers make purchase decisions. In product categories in which consumers frequently have to choose from a multitude of alternatives, e.g., toothpaste in supermarkets, choice sets could also include a larger number of alternatives (Hartmann 2004). The selection of the number of alternatives should also consider the number of attribute levels since using a number of alternatives that is a subset of the number of levels provides statistical benefits (Zeithammer and Lenk 2009).

Apart from the number of alternatives per choice set, the number of choice sets needs to be considered when selecting an optimal design. More choice sets lead to a higher reliability of the parameters. However, from a consumer perspective, more choice sets induce fatigue so that respondents tend to make more errors or even switch their decision strategy, e.g., focusing more on the price attribute (Johnson and Orme 1996), which is counterproductive. Consistently, results concerning the predictive validity depending on the number of choice sets indicate that the marginal benefit of additional choice sets declines (Sattler et al. 2004; Teichert 2001a). A review of articles published in the *Journal of Marketing Research* between 2000 and 2017 shows that most researchers make a compromise between statistical reliability and consumer fatigue so that most applications (14 out of 42) have used 11–15 sets. Slightly fewer studies (13 out of 42) have used ten sets or less. The number of applications decreases with more choice sets, i.e., nine studies used 16–20 choice sets, five applications 21–25 sets, and one study more than 25.

Implementation into Questionnaire

The implementation of the CBC experiment into a questionnaire requires decisions regarding the presentation of stimuli, integration of a no-choice option, collecting additional choices per choice set, applying incentive alignment mechanisms, and adding holdout choice sets.

Presentation of Stimuli

Most CBC interviews are computer-based since they facilitate handling complex experimental designs. Moreover, having more than two alternatives per choice set puts high cognitive burden on respondents, e.g., when described via telephone interviews. Computer-based interviews are beneficial because they allow implementing attribute levels or overall stimuli as multimedia information. Instead of using text only it is possible to depict the size of the ebook reader screens as a pictogram or to show actual ebook readers in different colors. When certain functionalities, e.g., page-turn effects, are included as attributes, these could be showcased with instructional videos (e.g., following the idea of information acceleration, Urban et al. 1996). Eggers et al. (2016) demonstrate that the more realistic the experiment can be made compared to what consumers see in the marketplace, i.e., investing in "craft," the higher is the validity of the results, which might also change the managerial implications from the results compared to studies that rely on defaults, e.g., text-only descriptions of the stimuli.

No-Choice Option

An advantage of CBC experiments compared to metric (rating or ranking-based) conjoint analyses is that respondents can indicate that they prefer none of the presented alternative. This none (or no-choice) option increases the realism since it does not force a decision if the alternatives are unacceptable so that consumers would not buy any of them or switch stores in reality (Haaijer et al. 2001). Recent approaches suggest asking for the no-choice option separately, i.e., sequentially after each choice set ("dual response none"; Brazell et al. 2006). In the dual response procedure respondents are first asked to select the most preferred option (excluding no-choice) in a forced-choice task and, sequentially, whether they would purchase the selected product concept in a second step (Brazell et al. 2006; Wlömert and Eggers 2016).

This procedure allows observing the preferred alternative even if it is not acceptable to be purchased. At the same time, consumers have no possibility to opt out of difficult decisions. Moreover, Wlömert and Eggers (2016) show that the increased salience of the no-choice option leads to more realistic predictions of adoption shares.

The no-choice option plays a central role when calculating (absolute) willingness-to-pay (see section "Market Simulations"). Implications from these analyses are limited if consumers show extreme response behavior and never or always choose the none option. To avoid these extremes, Gensler et al. (2012) present an adaptive approach that dynamically adjusts the price levels downwards whenever the respondent selected the no-choice option and upwards whenever the respondent selected an alternative. Schlereth and Skiera (2016) address this issue by proposing a separated adaptive dual response (SADR) procedure. They adjust the dual response procedure so that the forced choice and purchase question are not presented within the same task but are separated into sequential blocks. Presenting the block of forced choices first allows them to approximate the utility of the alternatives and adaptively select fewer, but more informative alternatives (not necessariliy the alternatives selected in the forced choices) in the purchase questions thereafter.

Collecting Additional Choices per Choice Set

Recently, it was suggested to ask not only for the best option but also for the worst option in a so-called best-worst scaling (or MaxDiff) approach (Louviere et al. 2015; Sawtooth 2013). By assuming that worst choices are reversed best choices, both decisions measure the same construct, i.e., preferences. Stated differently, if β_{nb} represents the partworth utility for attribute n based on best choices and β_{nw} is the partworth utility for the same attribute based on worst choices then it can be assumed that $\beta_{nb} = -\beta_{nw}$. The choices can then be used to make the estimation more reliable since twice as many observations exist. Collecting more choices per set is not limited to best and worst decisions only. More choices can be used as separate dependent variables in order to explore different aspects of consumers' preferences. An additional choice can be, e.g., "Which of these ebook readers would you buy for your partner?" which might explore consumers' gift giving behavior. In a study by Kraus et al. (2015), the authors collected additional choices per set to analyze managers' perception of risk and success of different internationalization strategies.

Figure 6 shows an example of a choice set that includes best and worst choices and a dual response no-choice option.

	Option 1	Option 2	Option 3
Storage:	4 GB	8 GB	16 GB
Screen size:	6 inch	7 inch	5 inch
Color:	Silver	Black	White
Prize:	€99	€119	€139
Best option:	○	○	○
Worst option:	○	○	○

Which of these ebook readers is your most preferred option and which option is the least attractive?

Please assume that these options do not differ in terms of other attributes, i.e., all options have a self-lit E Ink display with 758x1024 pixels resolution, WiFi, and 3 weeks battery life. They support multiple formats (PDF, EPUB) and connect to major book distributors.

Would you actually buy your most preferred option if it was available?
○ Yes
○ No

Fig. 6 Choice set with best and worst choices and dual response no-choice option

Incentive Alignment

Ding et al. (2005) introduced incentive alignment mechanisms to conjoint analysis. The basic idea of incentive-aligned (IA) mechanisms is to attenuate hypothetical bias by influencing the type of reward that is provided to respondents. Specifically, the reward is linked to the preferences the respondent expresses during the data collection.

Ding et al. (2005) implemented the IA mechanism by rewarding the respondent with the alternative that she/he selected in a randomly selected choice task (including the no-choice option). In this way, each choice might constitute the potential reward so that respondents are motivated to answer truthfully. If the study features a price attribute, then respondents are required to actually purchase the product for the price shown. Payment is typically achieved by providing the respondents with a budget. If the respondent selected the no-choice option, she/he gets the full budget as a monetary reward. If she/he selected a product for a price €X, she/he will get the actual product plus the remaining change (i.e., initial budget minus €X).

Ding (2007) proposed an alternative IA approach in which respondents are informed before completing the choice tasks that their choices will be used to infer their willingness-to-pay (WTP) for one specific product concept (see sections "Willingness-to-Pay" and "Market Simulations" for details about calculating WTP). Under this WTP-based mechanism, incentive alignment is achieved by obliging participants to purchase this specific product concept at a randomly drawn price if this random price is less or equal to the WTP inferred from the CBC experiment. This approach integrates the incentive compatible Becker-Degroot-Marschak (BDM) auction procedure (Becker et al. 1964, see also Wertenbroch and Skiera 2002) with CBC analysis. Ding (2007) shows theoretically that truthful answers constitute the Bayesian Nash equilibrium for participants in such applications as long as the respondents do not know the configuration of the product that is used as a reward prior to the study.

Dong et al. (2010) introduced and validated a third variant of IA conjoint experiments which involves predicting a rank ordering of the possible rewards based on estimated preferences. Eventually, the reward that is predicted to be ranked first is given to the respondent. Again, respondents are motivated to answer truthfully and keep the impact of error small in order to be rewarded with their most preferred product.

It has been shown that incentive-aligned (IA) data collection procedures substantially increase the predictive performance of conjoint choice experiments compared with traditional CBC analysis (Ding 2007; Ding et al. 2005; Dong et al. 2010) so that their application is recommended. However, one drawback of incentive alignment is that their application is limited to contexts where at least one concept of the research object can be rewarded after the experiment. This may not be feasible in many instances, for example, when the research object is an innovative product and not yet available on the market.

Holdout Choice Sets

A holdout choice set is a choice task that mimics a regular choice set but that is not used in the estimation. The answers given in the holdout choice set provide a benchmark for the (internal) predictive validity of the estimation results. The better the preference estimates are able to predict the actual choices made in the holdout sets the higher the predictive validity. Validity can be assessed with different measures. The hit rate compares on an individual level if the predicted most preferred alternative based on the estimates equals the alternative actually chosen in the holdout set, i.e., a hit meaning a correct prediction. The hit rate is then the mean value across all respondents. The mean absolute error (MAE), as an alternative measure among others, considers the absolute differences between predicted and actual choice shares for each alternative in the holdout set (e.g., Moore et al. 1998).

Estimation

Since choices from choice sets typically do not provide enough information to estimate reliable utilities at the individual level, they require some level of aggregation (see Frischknecht et al. 2014 for an alternative approach). The estimation procedure described here is based on the maximum likelihood procedure. It aggregates all choices from all respondents and produces one set of utilities that represent all consumers, i.e., it neglects consumer heterogeneity (see section "Advanced Estimation Techniques" for advanced estimation procedures without this assumption).

We will use the MNL model for describing the estimation in more detail. The estimates are based on the extended ebook reader example. The (simulated) data are based on 200 respondents who answered 10 choice sets, each showing three product alternatives plus a no-choice option.

Coding

The estimation of partworth utilities requires transforming the attribute levels according to a dummy (or effect) coding technique. When applying a partworth utility model to an attribute with M levels, M − 1 dummy-coded variables are needed to represent this attribute in the estimation. Each variable represents one attribute level and can take the values 1 or 0 depending on whether the attribute level was shown or not. The Mth attribute level (or any other level) is left out since it can be expressed as a linear combination of the other variables and cannot be estimated separately. The partworth utility of this reference level is set to 0. The partworth utilities of the remaining attribute levels need to be interpreted in relation to this level. Thus, it matters for the interpretation which level represents the reference.

Conjoint experiments are frequently coded using effect-coding. Effect-coded variables (Louviere et al. 2000), as an alternative to dummy-coding, are zero-centered so that the sum of partworth utilities across all levels of the attribute is zero, i.e., positive partworth utilities indicate higher preferences for that level compared to the average partworth utility across all levels of the attribute. Therefore, positive or negative values do not necessarily mean that these levels are perceived as positive or negative on an absolute level but only compared to the mean of the levels that were included in the experimental design. The reference level, which is left out of the estimation, can be recovered by calculating the partworth utility that is needed so that the average across all utilities is zero. Effect-coding therefore provides a partworth utility value for each attribute level, and it is irrelevant which level is set as the reference.

Effect-coding can be accomplished by setting the reference level to −1, instead of 0 as in dummy coding. Table 4 shows an example of effect-coding two attributes with M = 3 and M = 4 levels. Figure 7 shows an excerpt of the first two choice sets from the ebook reader dataset. In this dataset, each alternative (indicated by Alt_id) is represented by one row such that four rows represent one choice set (indicated by Set_id). The none option is included as one of the alternatives, which is represented by the None variable. The columns in dark grey show the numeric values for screen size, storage, and price, and text information for color. Effect-coding (columns in light grey) needs two parameters each for the attributes storage, screen size, and color, and three parameters for the effect-coded prices. This means that a partworth model requires ten parameters in total, i.e., nine parameters for the effect-coded variables and one variable for the none option (here, dummy coded). The column Selected is a dummy coded variable that shows which alternative was chosen in each choice set. It serves as the dependent variable in the estimation model.

Table 4 Effect-coding of attribute levels

Level	Effect-coded variables for M = 3		Effect-coded variables for M = 4		
	X_1	X_2	X_1	X_2	X_3
1	1	0	1	0	0
2	0	1	0	1	0
3	−1	−1	0	0	1
4			−1	−1	−1

Resp_id	Set_id	Alt_id	Selected	None	Storage	Screen. size	Color	Price	Storage_4GB	Storage_8GB	Screen. size_5inch	Screen. size_6inch	Color_black	Color_white	Price_79	Price_99	Price_119
1	1	1	0	0	4	7	Silver	119	1	0	-1	-1	-1	-1	0	0	1
1	1	2	1	0	16	5	White	79	-1	-1	1	0	0	1	1	0	0
1	1	3	0	0	8	6	Black	99	0	1	0	1	1	0	0	1	0
1	1	4	0	1	0	0	0	0	0	0	0	0	0	0	0	0	0
1	2	1	0	0	8	5	Silver	139	0	1	1	0	-1	-1	-1	-1	-1
1	2	2	0	0	16	6	White	79	-1	-1	0	1	0	1	1	0	0
1	2	3	0	0	4	7	Black	119	1	0	-1	-1	1	0	0	0	1
1	2	4	1	1	0	0	0	0	0	0	0	0	0	0	0	0	0

Fig. 7 Excerpt from the ebook reader dataset

Maximum Likelihood Estimation

Applying OLS procedures for the estimation is not appropriate because CBC analyses provide nominal data. The estimation of the MNL model therefore relies on maximum likelihood procedures. In aggregate-level analyses, all respondents are pooled to estimate one set of partworth utilities for the entire sample (Louviere and Woodworth 1983; Sawtooth 1999).

The maximum likelihood procedure aims at finding the set of partworth utilities that best represents the observed choices. The likelihood function L results from multiplying the MNL probabilities as shown in Eq. (8) across all choice sets $t = 1, 2, \ldots, T$ and – in the aggregate-level estimation – across all respondents $c = 1, 2, \ldots, C$ (Louviere et al. 2000):

$$L = \prod_c^C \prod_t^T p(i_{tc} | S_{tc}) \qquad (9)$$

with,

i_{tc} = chosen alternative in choice set t by respondent c
S_{tc} = alternatives in choice set t presented to respondent c

The parameters can be found by maximizing the function subject to the partworth utilities, i.e., $\frac{\partial L}{\partial \beta} = 0$.

The likelihood function lies in the interval [0, 1] and expresses the aggreggate probability to observe the choice data given the set of estimated partworth utilities. However, the minimum of zero is only a theoretical value as choosing randomly between the choice options, i.e., assuming that all betas are zero, would yield a probability of 1/S, with S being the number of alternatives in the choice set. For example, choosing randomly between three ebook readers and the no-choice option would give a probability of 1/4 that the choice matches the respondents preferred option. The lowest logical value of the likelihood function is therefore $(1/S)^{\wedge}(T*C)$. Since this value is very close to zero, the optimization of the function is typically based on the logarithm, i.e., log-likelihood function (Louviere et al. 2000). The lowest value, and the benchmark to assess the model fit, then is $T*C*\log(1/S)$, e.g., for the ebook reader case with 10 choice sets with four alternatives and 200 respondents: $10*200*\log(1/4) = -2772.6$. The estimation model should exceed this value significantly, i.e., have a log-likelihood value that is less negative (closer to zero), because otherwise the partworth utilities would not predict choices better than a random, NULL model.

Estimating the partworth utilities based on the ebook reader example yields a log-likelihood value of -2277.8. To test if the difference in log-likelihood between the NULL model and the estimated model is significant, a likelihood ratio test can be applied. The test statistic is $\chi^2 = 2 * (LL_1 - LL_0)$, with LL_1 representing the log-likelihood of the estimated model and LL_0 the log-likelihood value of the NULL model. This test statistic is distributed χ-squared with degrees of freedom (df) equal to the difference in the number of parameters between both models. In this case, χ^2 is

$2 * (-2277.8 - (-2772.6)) = 989.6$, with df $= 10$. This test is highly significant ($p < 0.001$), i.e., the estimated model predicts significantly better than the NULL model.

Another measure to assess the goodness of fit is the Pseudo-R^2 or McFadden's $R^2 = 1 - (LL_1/LL_0)$. For the ebook reader example, it is: $R^2 = 1 - (-2277.8/-2772.6) = 0.178$. McFadden's R^2 can be adjusted according to the number of parameters, i.e., $1 - ((LL_1 - npar)/LL_0)$, with npar being the number of parameters. This R^2 value has a different interpretation than in linear regression models. Typically, values exceeding 0.2–0.4 are considered acceptable. Although the ebook reader model is significantly different from the NULL model, its fit relative to this benchmark is not exceeding the threshold of 0.2. A potential explanation for this low fit is that consumers likely have heterogeneous preferences, e.g., towards screen size or color, which are not acknowledged in the aggregate model and therefore increase the error term.

The estimated partworth utilities are depicted in Table 5 (see "Appendix" for the corresponding R code). The partworth utilities for the attribute levels are effect-coded, which can be seen by checking that the sum across the betas is zero. The betas for storage and price show face validity as increasing the storage (price) yields higher (lower) utilities. There is no such trend regarding screen size as 6-in. models have the highest utility, followed by 5-in. models and 7-in. screens. White ebook readers are more preferred than black and silver models.

The no-choice option was dummy coded in this case, with "no-choice" equal to one and "not the no-choice" equal to zero. As can be seen, not choosing one of the

Table 5 Estimated partworth utilities based on the aggregate-level model

Attributes	Beta	Standard error	t-value	Attribute importance
Storage				21.6%
4 GB	−0.389	0.042	−9.323	
8 GB	−0.051	0.039	−1.322	
16 GB	0.440	0.036	12.143	
Screen size				22.0%
5 in.	−0.049	0.039	−1.274	
6 in.	0.446	0.036	12.352	
7 in.	−0.397	0.042	−9.528	
Color				12.5%
Black	−0.002	0.038	−0.059	
White	0.240	0.037	6.547	
Silver	−0.238	0.040	−5.952	
Price				43.9%
€79	0.840	0.045	18.502	
€99	0.286	0.047	6.103	
€119	−0.284	0.053	−5.416	
€139	−0.842	0.063	−13.447	
No-choice				
	−0.532	0.069	−7.749	

ebook readers shows a negative partworth utility so that on average (i.e., with all attributes at their mean utility of zero), choosing one of the ebook readers provides a higher utility and is therefore more likely than choosing none.

The partworth utilities can be transformed to be more accessible for managerial use compared to the rather abstract units of utility. Three transformations shall be elaborated subsequently: relative attribute importances, willingness-to-pay measures, and calculation of purchase probabilities within market simulations.

Relative Attribute Importance

The attribute importance w_n of an attribute n can be calculated based on the relative range of the partworth utilities, i.e., the difference between the most and least preferred attribute levels related to the sum of ranges across all attributes:

$$w_n = \frac{\max(\beta_n) - \min(\beta_n)}{\sum_{i=1}^{N} (\max(\beta_i) - \min(\beta_i))} \quad (10)$$

For example, storage exhibits a range of 0.829 (=0.440 − (−0.389)). The sum of all attribute ranges is 3.832. The relative importance of storage is therefore 0.829/3.832 = 21.6%. The attribute importance serves as a first indicator which attribute is most influential in affecting respondents' choices. However, these attribute importances only consider the extremes of the partworth utilities and not the intermediate levels. Moreover, the importances can only be interpreted in the context of the selected attributes and levels. Additionally, the attribute importance has to be evaluated in the context of the ability to discriminate between market offerings (Bauer et al. 1996). For example, most ebook readers on the market are 6-in. models. Although the attribute is the second most important based on the range of partworth utilities, it is less managerially relevant since most manufacturers are already offering the most preferred size so that using this attribute level does not help to differentiate from the competitors.

Willingness-to-Pay

The willingness-to-pay (WTP) transformation is based on the idea to analyze how much utility is lost (gained) when the price increases (decreases) and to relate this utility difference to the partworth utility of an attribute level. As a result, the partworth utilities for nonprice attributes can be expressed in monetary terms (Orme 2001).

The WTP calculation requires a vector model for the price attribute, which means that these analyses are only meaningful if the price function is indeed linear. The WTP for level m of attribute n can then be derived by dividing the partworth utility for the specific attribute level by the value of the price vector:

$$WTP_{nm} = \frac{\beta_{nm}}{\beta_p} \quad (11)$$

Choice-Based Conjoint Analysis

with,

β_{nm}: partworth utility for level m of attribute n
β_p: utility vector for the price attribute

The estimate for the price vector in the ebook reader example is -0.028, i.e., if price increases by one Euro utility drops by 0.028 units (see Table 6 below). The WTP values for the color attribute can then be calculated as $0.240/-0.028 = €-8.57$

Table 6 Estimation results of alternative modeling approaches

Attributes	Partworth model	Vector model for storage and price	Ideal point model for screen size	Interaction effect between screen size and color
Log-likelihood	−2277.8	−2278.3	−2278.3	−2273.3
Storage				
4 GB	−0.389			
8 GB	−0.051			
16 GB	0.440			
(linear)		0.067	0.067	0.067
Screen size				
5 in.	−0.049	−0.050		−0.044
6 in.	0.446	0.446		0.454
7 in.	−0.397	−0.396		−0.410
(linear)			7.854	
(squared)			−0.669	
Color				
Black	−0.002	−0.003	−0.003	−0.015
White	0.240	0.240	0.240	0.255
Silver	−0.238	−0.237	−0.237	−0.240
Price				
€79	0.840			
€99	0.286			
€119	−0.284			
€139	−0.842			
(linear)		−0.028	−0.028	−0.028
No-choice	−0.532	−2.965	19.632	−2.984
Screen size × color				
5 in. × black				−0.123
6 in. × black				0.173
7 in. × black				−0.051
5 in. × white				0.018
6 in. × white				−0.164
7 in. × white				0.146

for the color white, €0.07 for black, and €8.50 for silver. The interpretation of these values is that if an ebook reader is not available in, e.g., the preferred color white consumers would accept this drawback only if the price of the reader was, on average, at least €8.57 cheaper. In this case, the negative utility difference of a nonwhite reader is balanced with the positive utility difference of a cheaper price. Vice versa, a consumer would accept paying €8.57 more for a white ebook reader, on average. The least preferred color is silver and consumers would be willing to spend €17.07 for upgrading from a silver ebook reader to a white product. The WTP values can therefore be interpreted directly in terms of consumers' *incremental* willingness to pay for differences in attribute levels. Note, however, that the interpretation needs to consider the differences in signs, i.e., attribute levels with positive utilities have a negative WTP and vice versa.

Market Simulations

The most common ebook readers on the market, e.g., the Amazon Kindle, currently feature 4 GB storage, a 6-in. screen, in the color black for €139. To see how likely it is that consumers buy this product or no ebook reader at all, purchase probabilities can be calculated by applying the MNL function (Eq. 8). These calculations require the specification of a market scenario. A scenario consists of assumptions about the products that are available on the market, i.e., about S, which could include multiple products. In this example, we assume that there are two options, the above-mentioned ebook reader and the no-choice option. On the basis of the aggregate-level estimates, the overall utility of the ebook reader is $V_i = -0.389$ (4 GB) + 0.446 (6 in.) − 0.002 (black) − 0.842 (€139) = −0.787. The utility of the no-choice option is $V_j = -0.532$, i.e., consumers are more likely to buy no ebook reader compared to the one available. The purchase probability for the reader can be calculated by applying Eq. (8):

$$p(i|S) = \frac{\exp(-0.787)}{(\exp(-0.787) + \exp(-0.532))} = 0.437$$

That is, the probability that the sample buys the ebook reader is 43.7%. Market simulations then offer the possibility to see how the market will react if the product configuration is changed. If, e.g., the storage is increased to 8 GB, the overall utility increases to $V_i = -0.449$ and the purchase probability to 0.521. Thus, this modification would be sufficient to make consumers more likely to buy an ebook reader compared to not buying one. Purchase probabilities can be increased further by changing the color to white or reducing the price. These simulations therefore allow detecting promising product modifications. Moreover, a company that wants to enter the market can identify attractive product concepts and assess their effect on purchase probabilities given a specific market scenario that could also consider competitor products. Sophisticated simulation procedures also consider optimal competitive reactions and resulting Nash equilibria (Allenby et al. 2014).

Changing the price in a market simulation, ceteris paribus, allows creating a demand function. In the example above, the purchase probability for the ebook

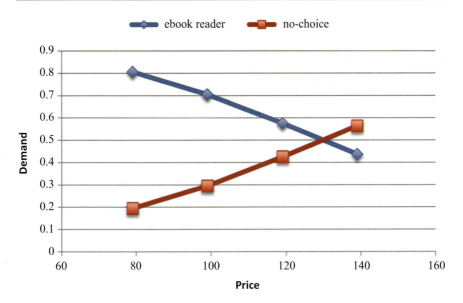

Fig. 8 Demand function for the ebook reader example

reader for €139 is 0.437. Systematically reducing the price increases the probabilities to 0.575 for €119, 0.705 for €99, and 0.806 for €79. The resulting demand function is depicted in Fig. 8. This function can be used to analyze the price elasticity or constitutes an alternative way to calculate WTP. In this example, the price that makes consumers indifferent between choosing the ebook reader and the no-choice option can be taken as the consumers' *absolute* WTP, in this case €130.

The purchase probabilities are frequently interpreted in terms of market shares. Interpreting the predicted probabilities as market shares is ambitious because they have to meet several assumptions (Orme and Johnson 2006). Specifically, probabilities are closer to market shares:

(a) The more the experiment resembles reality, i.e., all attributes and levels that affect buyers need to be accounted for and all competitors are included in the market scenario (assumptions that are not met in this example).
(b) The more the real market environment matches the experiment, i.e., all offers are available, e.g., the products are equally distributed, consumers are aware of the available offers, and there are no switching costs between the offers.

Furthermore, predictions are closer the less consumers' choices are influenced by errors that are introduced by the CBC experiment. It has been shown that incentive alignment is a suitable procedure to accomplish more valid answers so that predictions are closer to market shares (Wlömert and Eggers 2016). Moreover, it is often beneficial to consider heterogeneity among consumers via advanced estimation techniques.

Modeling Alternatives

Table 6 depicts the estimation results of alternative modeling approaches. Next to the partworth model interpreted above, it also shows an approach that uses a vector model for storage and price, i.e., that uses their numeric values instead of its effect codes. It can be seen that the model fit changes only marginally as the difference in log-likelihood is only −0.5, despite using three parameters less. According to a likelihood ratio test this difference is not significant (p = 0.793), i.e., this vector model achieves the same fit, while being more parsimonious. The vector model shows that utility increases linearly by 0.067 with every additional GB storage and decreases by −0.028 with every Euro more in purchase price. As the attributes are orthogonal, the other estimates remain largely unaffected. Only the estimate of the no-choice option changes substantially because the numeric values of storage and price are not zero-centered, unlike using effect-coding. This shift does not affect the implications, however.

The third model shown in Table 6 demonstrates the estimation of an ideal-point model for screen size. It requires two parameters, one for the linear effect and one for the squared term. Its model fit is therefore identical to the model in which screen size is represented by a partworth model, which also uses two parameters. The utility for screen size is given by the function $v_{screensize} = 7.854 * screensize - 0.669 * screensize^2$. Accordingly, the ideal point can be calculated as $\partial v/\partial screensize = 7.854 - 2 * 0.669 * screensize = 0$, which shows a maximum at 5.87 in.

Finally, the last column of Table 6 adds an interaction effect between the attributes screen size and color. Screen size and color are both represented by two parameters so that 2 * 2 additional parameters are required. Adding these four parameters significantly increases the model fit (p = 0.039), i.e., there is an interaction between these two attributes. Accordingly, consumers prefer a black ebook reader in 6 in. and a white version in 7 in.

Advanced Estimation Techniques

The assumption of aggregate-level analyses that consumers are all identical is usually too restrictive. Considering consumer heterogeneity with advanced estimation techniques is therefore beneficial in reducing the error term. Finite mixture (latent class) procedures assume that the sample consists of distinct segments and estimates different utilities for these segments. Continuous mixture (hierarchical Bayes) models are able to estimate individual-level partworth utilities by assuming that the utilities are drawn from a common distribution, e.g., normal distribution. As a result, partworth utilities are generated for each segment or each individual. These values can subsequently be interpreted analogously to the procedures described in sections "Relative Attribute Importance," "Willingness-to-Pay," and "Market Simulations."

Segment-Level Estimation

Segment-level estimation procedures, i.e., latent class estimation, are assuming that a finite number of (homogeneous) segments can represent the heterogeneity of the respondents in the sample. A segment-level perspective is also in line with discovering market segments with distinct preferences that are an attractive target group for a company's market offerings (i.e., following the segmentation, targeting, and positioning approach).

There are two general approaches for segmentation. The first approach determines segments based on socio-demographic data, e.g., separating males and females and estimating aggregate-level preferences for each of these segments. This a priori segmentation, however, is usually not able to detect segments that reflect systematically different preferences towards the attribute levels. The second approach, i.e., the latent class procedure, aims at finding segments that differ in their choice behavior and estimates segment-specific partworth utilities. These segments are latent, i.e., each respondent belongs to the segments with a certain probability (DeSarbo et al. 1995). If a consumer differs in his/her choice behavior from the partworth utilities of the respective segment, this is reflected by a lower probability to belong to this segment (Teichert 2001b).

Before the estimation starts, the researcher needs to define a specific number of segments. In a first step of an iterative-recursive procedure, the segment-specific partworth utilities for the given number of segments are estimated via maximizing the likelihood function. Afterwards, the utility functions are evaluated given the individual respondent's choices in order to allocate the respondents probabilistically to the segments. This results in posterior probabilities of segment membership based on conditional probabilities according to Bayes' rule (DeSarbo et al. 1995). These calculated probabilities form the basis for the iterative process of re-estimating segment-specific utilities. This loop is repeated until only minor changes in the probabilistic allocation of respondents to segments are observed (Sawtooth 2004).

The iterative-recursive process should be repeated for several numbers of segments. The "optimal" number of segments is not determined by the algorithm and has to be based on information criteria, e.g., AIC, BIC, or CAIC (Wedel and Kamakura 2000; Sawtooth 2004). Moreover, a measure of entropy should be inspected, which reflects the accuracy of the segmentation. It is based on the posterior membership probabilities of the respondents. The entropy can exhibit values in the interval [0, 1] and values close to "1" indicate that the segments are well separated, i.e., respondents can be allocated to one of the segments with almost certainty (DeSarbo et al. 1995).

By weighing the segment-level estimates with the membership probability, individual level estimation can be calculated. However, these values lie in the convex hull of the segment-specific utilities so that it is questionable if they can represent individual-level data well (Wedel et al. 1999). Applying the hierarchical Bayes procedures is more appropriate to estimate individual-level preferences (see next chapter).

Table 7 Segment-level estimates

Attributes	Segment 1	Segment 2	Segment 3
Relative segment size	0.592	0.249	0.158
Storage			
4 GB	−0.323	−0.544	−1.195
8 GB	−0.102	0.122	−0.091
16 GB	0.425	0.422	1.286
Screen size			
5 in.	−0.243	0.815	−0.945
6 in.	0.859	0.011	0.108
7 in.	−0.616	−0.826	0.837
Color			
Black	0.302	−0.593	−0.067
White	−0.240	1.246	0.259
Silver	−0.062	−0.653	−0.192
Price			
€79	1.009	0.920	1.423
€99	0.425	0.411	−0.195
€119	−0.318	−0.250	−0.542
€139	−1.116	−1.081	−0.686
No-choice			
	0.118	−2.383	−0.876

Applying the latent class estimation procedure with three segments to the ebook reader case results in a log-likelihood value of −2056.6, i.e., an acceptable McFadden's R^2 of 0.258. The entropy value of 0.948 shows a good separation between the segments. The segment-specific partworth utilities are depicted in Table 7 (not showing standard errors and t-values for better readability).

Based on the membership probabilities, segment 1 is the largest segment with about 60% of the respondents. Segment 2 includes a quarter of the sample and segment 3 follows in size with about 15%. As in the aggregate-level case, the estimates for storage and price show face validity for each segment. Moreover, the segmentation is able to discover segments that prefer smaller screens (segment 2) and larger screens (segment 3). The color white is preferred by segments 2 and 3, however, not by segment 1 that prefers black ebook readers. Finally, segment 1 shows a positive value for the no-choice option, which reflects that this segment is more likely to choose no ebook reader compared to the other segments.

Note that in the aggregate-level analysis 6-in. screens and the color white are preferred by the sample. The conclusion to launch this kind of ebook reader would have been suboptimal as none of the segments prefer this product, i.e., segment 1 prefers 6-in. screens but not the color white, and segment 2 and 3 prefer white but smaller or larger screens.

Individual-Level Estimation

An estimation of individual-level partworth utilities with the MNL model is possible with the hierarchical Bayes (HB) procedure. The idea of the procedure is that the aggregate sample is used to determine the distribution of partworth utilities. The distribution then serves as a basis to draw conditional estimates for each individual given the respondent's choice data. The HB model therefore consists of two coupled layers (Lindley and Smith 1972). The first model layer describes the choice probabilities given the individual partworth utilities, i.e., the MNL model (Eq. 8). The second layer relates the respondents' partworth utilities to each other by assuming a multivariate (normal) distribution of the utilities with unknown mean (Arora et al. 1998).

The model parameters can then be estimated in an iterative process, e.g., with the Metropolis-Hasting algorithm (Chen et al. 2000). Figure 9 depicts the sequence of the HB procedure.

The researcher first needs to specify the type and parameters of the distribution of the utilities. Based on the distribution and the observed choice data, estimates for the individual partworth utilities are drawn in an iterative recursive process. These utilities, in turn, affect the parameters of the distribution, which then serves as a basis to draw a new set of individual-level partworth utilities in a next iteration. This process runs for a large number of iterations, e.g., 20,000, until the parameters converge. Typically, the first set of individual-level utilities draws is discarded as "burn-in" (Sawtooth 2000). The second set of individual-level draws can be used to make inferences about consumer preferences (Allenby et al. 1995).

Figure 10 shows the distribution of individual-level partworth utilities of the ebook reader dataset as boxplots. The mean and median values are plausible and in

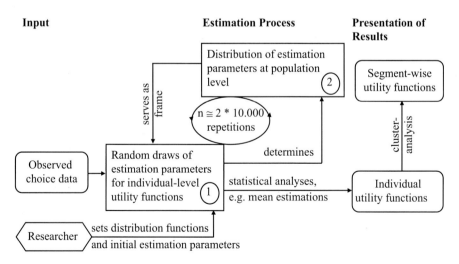

Fig. 9 HB estimation procedures (Teichert 2001b)

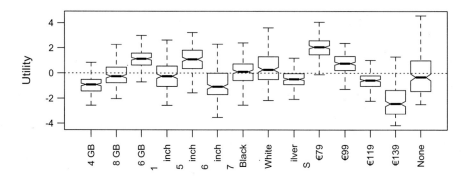

		Mean	Standard deviation
Storage			
	4 GB	-0.960	0.749
	8 GB	-0.173	0.820
	16 GB	1.134	0.731
Screen size			
	5 inch	-0.187	1.210
	6 inch	1.067	0.921
	7 inch	-0.880	1.151
Color			
	Black	0.026	0.990
	White	0.445	1.260
	Silver	-0.472	0.668
Price			
	€79	2.030	0.804
	€99	0.739	0.736
	€119	-0.565	0.663
	€139	-2.204	1.275
No-choice			
		-0.088	1.593

Fig. 10 Boxplots of partworth utilities and summary statistics for individual-level preferences

line with the aggregate-level model. The distribution and the standard deviation across the respondents' utilities indicate those attributes and attribute levels that exhibit a larger amount of heterogeneous preferences, e.g., screen size, the color white, the highest price, or the no-choice option.

Outlook

Conjoint analysis has emerged from the traditional rating- or ranking-based method in marketing to a general experimental method to study individual's discrete choice behavior with the choice-based conjoint variant. It is therefore not limited to classical applications in marketing, such as new product development, but can be applied to study research questions from related disciplines, e.g., how marketing managers choose their ad campaign, how managers select internationalization options, why consumers engage in or react to social media, etc.

This chapter aims at providing the necessary terminology of conjoint analysis and the requirements to conduct and interpret discrete choice experiments. It also lays the foundation to understand more sophisticated methods and models.

Given the large scope of discrete choice experiments, this attempt is also limited. CBC taps into general theories of how individuals (or groups) choose. These are vast theoretical and empirical grounds, which we cannot cover in detail in this chapter. Understanding CBC models requires not only knowledge of the statistical properties but also understanding behavioral aspects and biases, such as context effects (e.g., compromise, attraction, similarity effects) or trade-off aversion. While knowledge about these aspects is important when running discrete choice experiments, CBC can likewise be used to identify these effects, e.g., by incorporating context effects (Rooderkerk et al. 2011) or by measuring price-quality heuristics (Rao and Sattler 2003).

Although CBC is well developed and documented, many areas are still under research, ranging from, e.g., optimal experimental designs, incentive alignment procedures, to estimation techniques. It will therefore remain an active research area with numerous managerial applications in marketing in the future.

Appendix: R Code

The R code and dataset that correspond to the ebook reader example and estimated models can be found at: http://www.preferencelab.com/data/CBC.R. The estimation uses the mlogit package (Croissant 2012), which needs to be installed first. A less documented version of the R code can be found below (# indicates a comment):

```
# load the library to estimate multinomial choice models.
library(mlogit)

# load (simulated) data about ebook readers
cbc <- read.csv(url("http://www.preferencelab.com/data/
Ebook_Reader.csv"))

# convert data for mlogit
cbc <- mlogit.data(cbc, choice="Selected", shape="long", alt.
var="Alt_id", id.var = "Resp_id")
```

```
### calculate models ###

### partworth model ###
ml1 <- mlogit(Selected ~ Storage_4GB + Storage_8GB +
  Screen.size_5inch + Screen.size_6inch +
  Color_black + Color_white +
  Price_79 + Price_99 + Price_119 +
  None | 0, cbc)
summary(ml1)

# recover reference level estimates (effect-coding)

# Storage_16GB
-(coef(ml1)["Storage_4GB"] + coef(ml1)["Storage_8GB"])

# Screen.size_7inch
-(coef(ml1)["Screen.size_5inch"] + coef(ml1)["Screen.size_6inch"])

# Color_silver
-(coef(ml1)["Color_black"] + coef(ml1)["Color_white"])

# Price_139
-(coef(ml1)["Price_79"] + coef(ml1)["Price_99"] + coef(ml1)
["Price_119"])

# standard errors of the effects are given by the
# square root of the diagonal elements of the
# variance-covariance matrix
covMatrix <- vcov(ml1)
sqrt(diag(covMatrix))

# with effect-coding, the standard error of the reference
# level needs to consider the off-diagonal elements of the
# corresponding attribute levels

# Std. Error Storage_16GB
sqrt(sum(covMatrix[1:2, 1:2]))

# Std. Error Screen.size_7inch
sqrt(sum(covMatrix[3:4, 3:4]))

# Std. Error Color_silver
sqrt(sum(covMatrix[5:6, 5:6]))

# Std. Error Price_139
sqrt(sum(covMatrix[7:9, 7:9]))
```

Vector model
Storage and Price follow a linear trend. Replacing
parameters leads to a more parsimonious model.

```
ml2 <- mlogit(Selected ~ Storage +
 Screen.size_5inch + Screen.size_6inch +
 Color_black + Color_white +
 Price +
 None | 0, cbc)
summary(ml2)

# likelihood ratio test
lrtest(ml2, ml1)

# incremental willingness-to-pay for storage
coef(ml2)["Storage"]/coef(ml2)["Price"]

# WTP to upgrade from a black to a white ebook reader
(coef(ml2)["Color_white"] - coef(ml2)["Color_black"])/coef(ml2)
["Price"]
```

Vector model for screen size has sig. worse fit
```
ml3 <- mlogit(Selected ~ Storage + Screen.size + Color_black +
 Color_white + Price + None | 0, cbc)
summary(ml3)

lrtest(ml3, ml2)
```

Testing an ideal point model for screen size
```
ml4 <- mlogit(Selected ~ Storage +
 Screen.size + I(Screen.size**2) +
 Color_black + Color_white +
 Price +
 None | 0, cbc)
summary(ml4)

# same model fit because no differences in df
lrtest(ml4, ml2)
```

Adding interactions between screen size and color
```
ml5 <- mlogit(Selected ~ Storage +
 Screen.size_5inch + Screen.size_6inch +
 Color_black + Color_white +
 Price +
 Screen.size_5inch * Color_black +
 Screen.size_6inch * Color_black +
```

```
Screen.size_5inch * Color_white +
Screen.size_6inch * Color_white +
None| 0, cbc)
summary(ml5)

# likelihood ratio test
lrtest(ml2, ml5)
```

References

Addelman, S. (1962). Orthogonal main-effect plans for asymmetrical factorial experiments. *Technometrics, 4*(1), 21–46.
Allenby, G. M., Arora, N., & Ginter, J. L. (1995). Incorporating prior knowledge into the analysis of conjoint studies. *Journal of Marketing Research, 32*(2), 152–162.
Allenby, G. M., Brazell, J. D., Howell, J. R., & Rossi, P. E. (2014). Economic valuation of product features. *Quantitative Marketing and Economics, 12*(4), 421–456.
American Marketing Association. (2015). American Marketing Association AMA. https://www.ama.org/resources/Pages/Dictionary.aspx. Accessed 15 Nov 2015.
Arora, N., Allenby, G. M., & Ginter, J. L. (1998). A hierarchical Bayes model of primary and secondary demand. *Marketing Science, 17*(1), 29–44.
Batsell, R. R., & Louviere, J. J. (1991). Experimental analysis of choice. *Marketing Letters, 2*(3), 199–214.
Bauer, H., Herrmann, A., & Homberg, F. (1996). *Analyse der Kundenwünsche zur Gestaltung eines Gebrauchsgutes mit Hilfe der Conjoint Analyse.* Universität Mannheim, Lehrstuhl für ABWL und Marketing II, Working Paper Nr. 110.
Becker, G. M., Degroot, M. H., & Marschak, J. (1964). Measuring utility by a single-response sequential method. *Behavioral Science, 9*(3), 226–232.
Brazell, J. D., Diener, C. G., Karniouchina, E., Moore, W. L., Séverin, V., & Uldry, P.-F. (2006). The no-choice option and dual response choice designs. *Marketing Letters, 17*(4), 255–268.
Burmester, A., Eggers, F., Clement, M., & Prostka, T. (2016). Accepting or fighting unlicensed usage – Can firms reduce unlicensed usage by optimizing their timing and pricing strategies? *International Journal of Research in Marketing, 33*(2), 434–356.
Chakraborty, G., Ball, D., Gaeth, G. J., & Jun, S. (2002). The ability of ratings and choice conjoint to predict market shares – A Monte Carlo simulation. *Journal of Business Research, 55*(3), 237–249.
Chen, M.-H., Shao, Q.-M., & Ibrahim, J. G. (2000). *Monte Carlo methods in Bayesian computation.* New York: Springer Series in Statistics.
Croissant, Y. (2012). Estimation of multinomial logit models in R: The mlogit packages. *R package version 0.2-2.* http://cran.r-project.org/web/packages/mlogit/vignettes/mlogit.pdf.
De Bekker-Grob, E. W., Ryan, M., & Gerard, K. (2012). Discrete choice experiments in the health economics: A review of the literature. *Health Economics, 21*(2), 145–172.
DeSarbo, W. S., Ramaswamy, V., & Cohen, S. (1995). Market segmentation with choice-based conjoint analysis. *Marketing Letters, 6*(2), 137–147.
Ding, M. (2007). An incentive-aligned mechanism for conjoint analysis. *Journal of Marketing Research, 44*(2), 214–223.
Ding, M., Grewal, R., & Liechty, J. (2005). Incentive-aligned conjoint analysis. *Journal of Marketing Research, 42*(2), 67–82.
Ding, M., Park, Y.-H., & Bradlow, E. T. (2009). Barter markets for conjoint analysis. *Management Science, 55*(6), 1003–1017.

Dong, S., Ding, M., & Huber, J. (2010). A simple mechanism to incentive-align conjoint experiments. *International Journal of Research in Marketing, 27*(1), 25–32.

Eggers, F., & Sattler, H. (2009). Hybrid individualized two-level choice-based conjoint (HIT-CBC): A new method for measuring preference structures with many attribute levels. *International Journal of Research in Marketing, 26*(2), 108–118.

Eggers, F., Hauser J. R., & Selove, M. (2016). The effects of incentive alignment, realistic images, video instructions, and ceteris paribus instructions on willingness to pay and price equilibria. *Proceedings of the Sawtooth Software conference*, 1–18 September.

Elrod, T., Louviere, J. J., & Davey, K. S. (1992). An empirical comparison of ratings-based and choice-based conjoint models. *Journal of Marketing Research, 29*(3), 368–377.

Frischknecht, B., Eckert, C., Geweke, J., & Louviere, J. J. (2014). A simple method for estimating preference parameters for individuals. *International Journal of Research in Marketing, 31*(1), 35–48.

Gensler, S., Hinz, O., Skiera, B., & Theysohn, S. (2012). Willingness-to-pay estimation with choice-based conjoint analysis: Addressing extreme response behavior with individually adapted designs. *European Journal of Operational Research, 219*(2), 368–378.

Green, P. E., & Srinivasan, V. (1978). Conjoint analysis in consumer research: Issues and outlook. *Journal of Consumer Research, 5*, 103–123.

Green, P. E., & Srinivasan, V. (1990). Conjoint analysis in marketing: New developments with implications for research and practice. *Journal of Marketing, 54*, 3–19.

Haaijer, R., & Wedel, M. (2003). Conjoint experiments. general characteristics and alternative model specifications. In A. Gustafsson, A. Herrmann, & F. Huber (Eds.), *Conjoint measurement: Methods and applications* (3rd ed., pp. 371–412). Berlin: Springer.

Haaijer, R., Wedel, M., Vriens, M., & Wansbek, T. (1998). Utility covariances and context effects in conjoint MNP models. *Marketing Science, 17*(3), 236–252.

Haaijer, R., Kamakura, W. A., & Wedel, M. (2001). The "no-choice" alternative to conjoint choice experiments. *International Journal of Market Research, 43*(1), 93–106.

Hartmann, A. (2004). *Kaufentscheidungsprognose auf Basis von Befragungen. Modelle, Verfahren und Beurteilungskriterien*. Wiesbaden: Gabler.

Hensher, D. A. (1994). Stated preference analysis of travel choices: The state of practice. *Transportation, 21*(2), 107–133.

Hensher, D. A., & Johnson, L. W. (1981). *Applied discrete choice modelling*. New York: Wiley.

Huber, J., & Zwerina, K. (1996). The importance of utility balance in efficient choice designs. *Journal of Marketing Research, 33*(3), 307–317.

Johnson, R. M. (1987). Adaptive conjoint analysis. In *Sawtooth software conference proceedings*. Ketchum: Sawtooth Software.

Johnson, R. M., & Orme, B. K. (1996). *How many questions should you ask in choice-based conjoint studies?* (Sawtooth software research paper series). Sequim: Sawtooth Software.

Kraus, S., Ambos, T. C., Eggers, F., & Cesinger, B. (2015). Distance and perceptions of risk in internationalization decisions. *Journal of Business Research, 68*(7), 1501–1505.

Lindley, D. V., & Smith, A. F. (1972). Bayes estimates for the linear models. *Journal of the Royal Statistical Society, Series B, 34*(1), 1–41.

Louviere, J. J., & Woodworth, G. (1983). Design and analysis of simulated consumer choice or allocation experiments. An approach based on aggregated data. *Journal of Marketing Research, 20*(4), 350–367.

Louviere, J. J., Hensher, D. A., & Swait, J. D. (2000). *Stated choice methods. Analysis and application*. Cambridge: Cambridge University Press.

Louviere, J. J., Flynn, T. N., & Marley, A. A. J. (2015). *Best-worst scaling: Theory, methods, and applications*. Cambridge: Cambridge University Press.

Lusk, J. L., & Schroeder, T. C. (2004). Are choice experiments incentive compatible? A test with quality differentiated beef steaks. *American Journal of Agricultural Economics, 86*(2), 467–482.

McFadden, D. (1981). Econometric models of probabilistic choice. In C. Manski & D. McFadden (Eds.), *Structural analysis of discrete data* (pp. 198–272). Cambridge: MIT-Press.

Meissner, M. Oppewal, H., & Huber, J. (2016). How many options? Behavioral responses to two versus five alternatives per choice. *Proceedings of the Sawtooth Software conference*, 1–18 September.

Miller, K. M., Hofstetter, R., Krohmer, H., & Zhang, Z. J. (2011). How should Consumers' willingness to pay be measured? An empirical comparison of state-of-the-art approaches. *Journal of Marketing Research, 48*(1), 172–184.

Moore, W. L. (2004). A cross-validity comparison of rating-based and choice-based conjoint analysis models. *International Journal of Research in Marketing, 21*(3), 299–312.

Moore, W. L., Gray-Lee, J., & Louviere, J. J. (1998). A cross-validity comparison of conjoint analysis and choice models at different levels of aggregation. *Marketing Letters, 9*(2), 195–207.

Orme, B. (2001). *Assessing the monetary value of attribute levels with conjoint analysis: Warnings and suggestions* (Sawtooth software research paper series). Sequim: Sawtooth Software.

Orme, B. (2002). *Formulating attributes and levels in conjoint analysis* (Sawtooth software research paper series). Sequim: Sawtooth Software.

Orme, B. K. (2016). *Results of the 2017 Sawtooth Software User Survey.* https://www.sawtoothsoftware.com/about-us/news-and-events/news/1693-results-of-2016-sawtooth-software-user-survey.

Orme, B., & Johnson, R.M. (2006). *External effect adjustments in conjoint analysis* (Sawtooth software research paper series). Sequim: Sawtooth Software.

Page, A. L., & Rosenbaum, H. F. (1992). Developing an effective concept testing program for consumer durables. *Journal of Product Innovation Management, 9*, 267–277.

Park, Y.-H., Ding, M., & Rao, V. R. (2008). Eliciting preference for complex products: A web-based upgrading method. *Journal of Marketing Research, 45*(5), 562–574.

Rao, V. R., & Sattler, H. (2003). Measurement of price effects with conjoint analysis: Separating informational and allocative effects of price. In *Conjoint Measurement* (pp. 47–66). Berlin/Heidelberg: Springer.

Rooderkerk, R. P., Van Heerde, H. J., & Bijmolt, T. H. (2011). Incorporating context effects into a choice model. *Journal of Marketing Research, 48*(4), 767–780.

Sattler, H. (2005). Markenbewertung: State-of-the-Art. *Zeitschrift für Betriebswirtschaft, 2*, 33–57.

Sattler, H. (2006). Methoden zur Messung von Präferenzen für Innovationen. *Zeitschrift für Betriebswirtschaftliche Forschung, 54*(6), 154–176.

Sattler, H., Hartmann, A., & Kröger, S. (2004). Number of tasks in choice-based conjoint analysis. *Conference proceedings of the 33rd EMAC conference.* Murcia.

Sawtooth (1999). *The choice-based conjoint (CBC) technical paper* (Sawtooth software technical paper series). Sequim: Sawtooth Software.

Sawtooth. (2000). *The CBC/HB system for hierarchical Bayes estimation version 4.0* (Sawtooth software technical paper series). Sequim: Sawtooth Software.

Sawtooth. (2004). *The CBC latent class technical paper (version 3)* (Sawtooth software technical paper series). Sequim: Sawtooth Software.

Sawtooth. (2013). *The MaxDiff system – Technical paper* (Sawtooth software technical paper series). Orem: Sawtooth Software.

Sawtooth. (2014). *ACBC – Technical paper* (Sawtooth software technical paper series). Orem: Sawtooth Software.

Schlereth, C., & Skiera, B. (2016). Two new features in discrete choice experiments to improve willingness-to-pay estimation that result in SDR and SADR: Separated (adaptive) dual response. *Management Science, 63*(3), 829–842.

Shocker, A. D., & Srinivasan, V. (1973). Linear programming techniques for multidimensional analysis of preference. *Psychometrika*, 337–369.

Sloan, N. J. A. (2015). A library of orthogonal arrays. http://neilsloane.com/oadir/. Accessed 15 Nov 2015.

Srinivasan, V., & Park, C. S. (1997). Surprising robustness of the self-explicated approach to customer preference structure measurement. *Journal of Marketing Research, 34*(2), 286–291.

Teichert, T. (2001a). *Nutzenschätzung in Conjoint-Analysen: Theoretische Fundierung und empirische Aussagekraft*. Wiesbaden: Springer.
Teichert, T. (2001b). Nutzenermittlung in wahlbasierten Conjoint-Analysen. Ein Vergleich zwischen Latent-Class- und hierarchischem Bayes-Verfahren. *Zeitschrift für Betriebswirtschaftliche Forschung, 53*(8), 798–822.
Toubia, O., Simester, D. I., Hauser, J. R., & Dahan, E. (2003). Fast polyhedral adaptive conjoint estimation. *Marketing Science, 22*(3), 273–303.
Toubia, O., Hauser, J. R., & Simester, D. I. (2004). Polyhedral methods for adaptive choice-based conjoint analysis. *Journal of Marketing Research, 41*, 116–131.
Toubia, O., Hauser, J., & Garcia, R. (2007). Probabilistic polyhedral methods for adaptive choice-based conjoint analysis: Theory and application. *Marketing Science, 26*(5), 596–610.
Toubia, O., de Jong, M. G., Stieger, D., & Füller, J. (2012). Measuring consumer preferences using conjoint poker. *Marketing Science, 31*(1), 138–156.
Train, K. (2009). *Discrete choice models with simulation* (2nd ed.). Cambridge: Cambridge University Press.
Urban, G. L., & Hauser, J. R. (1993). *Design and marketing of new products* (2nd ed.). Englewood Cliffs: Prentice Hall.
Urban, G. L., Weinberg, B. D., & Hauser, J. R. (1996). Premarket forecasting of really-new products. *Journal of Marketing, 60*(1), 47–60.
Verlegh, P. W. J., Schifferstein, H. N. J., & Wittink, D. R. (2002). Range and number-of-levels in derived and stated measures of attribute importance. *Marketing Letters, 13*(1), 41–52.
Voeth, M. (1999). 25 Jahre conjointanalytische Forschung in Deutschland. *Zeitschrift für Betriebswirtschaft*, Ergänzungsheft 2, 153–176.
Vriens, M., Oppewal, H., & Wedel, M. (1998). Rating-based versus choice-based latent class conjoint models – An empirical comparison. *Journal of the Market Research Society, 40*(3), 237–248.
Walker, J., & Ben-Akiva, M. (2002). Generalized random utility model. *Mathematical Social Sciences, 43*(3), 303–343.
Wedel, M., & Kamakura, W. A. (2000). *Market segmentation. conceptual and methodological foundations* (2nd ed.). Boston: Springer.
Wedel, M., Kamakura, W. A., Arora, N., Bemmaor, A., Chiang, J., Elrod, T., Johnson, R. M., Lenk, P., Neslin, S., & Poulsen, C. S. (1999). Discrete and continuous representations of unobserved heterogeneity in choice modeling. *Marketing Letters, 10*(3), 219–232.
Wertenbroch, K., & Skiera, B. (2002). Measuring consumers' willingness to pay at the point of purchase. *Journal of Marketing Research, 39*(2), 228–241.
Wittink, D. R., Vriens, M., & Burhenne, W. (1994). Commercial use of conjoint analysis in Europe: Results and critical reflections. *International Journal of Research in Marketing, 11*, 41–52.
Wlömert, N., & Eggers, F. (2016). Predicting new service adoption with conjoint analysis: External validity of BDM-based incentive-aligned and dual-response choice designs. *Marketing Letters, 27*(1), 195–210.
Zeithammer, R., & Lenk, P. (2009). Statistical benefits of choices from subsets. *Journal of Marketing Research, 46*(6), 816–831.

Exploiting Data from Field Experiments

Martin Artz and Hannes Doering

Contents

Introduction	822
Motivation	822
Field Experiments	825
Difference-in-Differences Method	828
Introduction	828
Core Area of Application	830
Critical Assumptions	832
Application in Goldfarb and Tucker (2011)	834
Regression Discontinuity Designs	835
Introduction	835
Core Area of Application	838
Critical Assumptions	839
Application in Flammer (2015)	840
Instrumental Variables	841
Introduction	841
Core Area of Application	845
Critical Assumptions	846
Application in Bennedsen et al. (2007)	848
Application of Methods in Standard Software	849
Conclusions	853
Cross-References	854
References	854

Abstract

This chapter gives an introduction on how to exploit data from field experiments and aims to provide an intuitive understanding for managers and researchers alike. We outline the relevance and hurdles in identifying causal effects compared to observing purely correlational associations in studies which take place in the

M. Artz (✉) · H. Doering
School of Business and Economics, University of Münster, Münster, Germany
e-mail: martin.artz@wiwi.uni-muenster.de; hannes.doering@wiwi.uni-muenster.de

real world. We further provide a framework to classify different kinds of field experiments, such as quasi field experiments and natural field experiments. The core of this chapter focuses on giving an understanding of three standard econometric methods to exploit data from field experiments: difference-in-differences, regression discontinuity, and instrumental variables. For each method, we provide an intuitive understanding of the core features and its critical assumptions. We complement those explanations with an in-depth look at one practical application of each method in a field experiment setting and with a variety of practical examples from recently published research. Lastly, we provide a brief overview on how to implement each method in standard software packages such as STATA, R, and SPSS.

Keywords

Field experiment · Quasi experiment · Natural experiment · Causality · Causal inference · Difference-in-differences · Regression discontinuity · Instrumental variable

Introduction

"There is two ways to get fired from Harrah's: Stealing from the company or failing to include a proper control group in your business experiment." (Gary Loveman, economist and former CEO of Harrah's Entertainment)

Motivation

Suppose a fashion retailer decides to place a specific jeans brand right at the stores' entrance in order to temporarily increase in-store sales. For the weeks following the rearrangement, the retailer observes an increase in sales for this jeans brand. Clearly, this entrance placement co-moves with an increase in sales. Nevertheless, the question remains whether the rearrangement has caused the sales to increase or whether the increase is due to a long list of alternative reasons. For instance, in the weeks after the rearrangement, customer preferences for this particular brand could have changed or competitors offering the same brand could have increased prices. A co-movement between the two factors – change in placement and increase in sales – is easy to observe, but claiming causality between those two factors is difficult.

Suppose now, the fashion retailer offers free shipping for all orders. Subsequently, the amount of orders and the value per order in the fashion retailer's online store increase. Again, some action (i.e., the free shipping offer) is linked to some outcome. And again, one has to be cautious to credibly claim that this action indeed caused the outcome. Maybe the retailer simultaneously launched an advertising campaign, a competitor filed for bankruptcy or some of the brick-and-mortar stores were temporarily closed for renovations. All those events may interfere with the free shipping offer and also potentially co-move with sales. So, top management of this retail chain will once again raise the question: Which of those events caused the increase in sales? Has it been particularly one of these actions, the interplay of various actions, or some (unobserved) events which ultimately caused the increase in online sales?

As these rather simple examples demonstrate, managers and researchers are typically interested in causal relationships to improve the quality of business decisions. *"However, data reveal only associations, which are a combination of causal and non-causal (i.e., spurious) components"* (Keele 2015, p. 102). In order to separate those two components and establish a clear causal path between an action and a particular observable outcome, three general conditions have to be fulfilled (Kenny 1979):

- The cause has to precede the outcome, that is, the cause must occur before the effect temporarily. In the fashion retailer examples, the change in placement of jeans in the store or the free shipping offer occurred before any increase in sales had been observed.
- Cause and effect have to co-move, that is, changes in the cause must be accompanied by changes in the effect. In the fashion retailer examples, this has been the case. After each initiative (i.e., the change in placement or the free shipping initiative), the retailer observed a co-movement between the initiative and sales. Standard measures often used in business practice and in academic research are contingency tables or various forms of correlation coefficients such as Pearson or Spearman (Spearman 1904). These statistical performance measures suggest a weaker or stronger existence of a (linear) co-movement between two variables as well as whether the co-movement is negative or positive.
- The relation between presumed cause and effect cannot be explained by alternative reasons. Stated differently, the new placement or the free shipping initiative is supposed to be the sole driver of any observed sales outcome. However, excluding alternative explanations with certainty has demonstrated to be difficult in both fashion retailer examples and is indeed often the most difficult hurdle to establish causality. A potential way out of this dilemma is drawing conclusions from data generated via a controlled experimental design. Since such data is generated under controlled conditions, external influences can be fully eliminated via the design of the experiment.

In management practice, *field* experiments – experiments that take place in real-world environments instead of laboratory settings – have gained much importance in the last years. As an illustration, the solid line in Fig. 1 depicts the number of search results for the term "field experiment" for the abstract of academic, peer-reviewed business publications for the past 20 years. In practice, online business models are able to vary treatments (i.e., design of marketing campaigns, product offers, or price discounts) between randomized customer groups (i.e., A/B testing) and offline business models try new initiatives in some business units before rolling them out through the whole corporation (i.e., pilot studies). In any case, an experiment requires two stages: a design stage before the experiment is implemented, including,

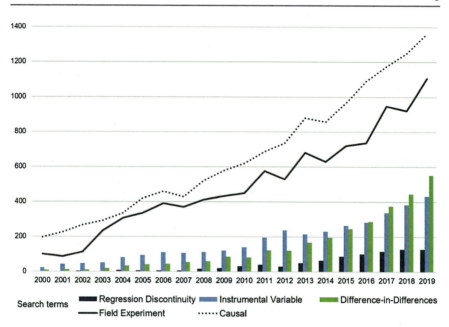

Fig. 1 Yearly number of academic, peer-reviewed publications in business and economics (via *EBSCOhost Business Source Premier*) for which the respective search term is mentioned in the article's abstract (own illustration)

for instance, the selection of the initiative as well as the number and randomization of groups, and an examination stage after the experiment took place to analyze the data which had been generated.

This chapter focuses on the second part. Its objective is to present, describe, and explain different methods to analyze data generated by field experiments, thus focusing on the examination stage after the experiment took place. Further, it follows the approach of giving the interested reader an intuitive understanding of the standard methods to analyze data from field experiments, often at the cost of a detailed statistical discussion. We refer the reader to Angrist and Pischke (2009), Antonakis et al. (2010), Verbeek (2008), and Wooldridge (2012) for a more detailed discussion of statistical and econometric methods. Further, each section will provide literature relevant to each method for the interested reader. For a detailed introduction on how to design and execute a (field) experiment, we refer to Bornemann and Hattula (chapter ▶ "Experiments in Market Research") as well as Valli et al. (chapter ▶ "Field Experiments") in this handbook.

The chapter is structured as follows: Section two clarifies the term field experiment. Sections three, four, and five refer to three core methodologies to analyze data generated by a field experiment such as the difference-in-differences methodology (section "Difference-in-Differences Method"), a regression discontinuity design (section "Regression Discontinuity Designs"), and an instrumental variable approach (section "Instrumental Variables"). Section "Application of Methods in Standard Software" provides an overview of how these three methods are implemented in standard software packages such as STATA, R, and SPSS and provides a selection of data sets that are suitable for one own's replication efforts for each method. The last section concludes this chapter.

Field Experiments

The understanding and interpretation of what constitutes a field experiment and where to draw the line to similar and more distinct research designs widely varies among researchers and practitioners. Among all groups, it seems universally accepted that an experiment represents a study design which requires at minimum two different groups that are equal along each characteristic except for the fact that one gets access to a treatment (i.e., the treatment group), while the other does not (i.e., the control group). Often, this treatment is also called an intervention or manipulation in an experiment. Any observed outcome differences are only due to this intervention, guaranteed via a rigorous design that fulfills the conditions of causality.

Turning to the more specific case of *field* experiments, definitions and interpretations of the term vary. Harrison and List (2004) interpret the term *field* as any experimental intervention which includes a treatment that is related to the real world, independent of whether the experiment takes place inside or outside of the laboratory. In their taxonomy, for example, inviting managers to perform job-related tasks in a laboratory would constitute a field experiment. Other authors refer to field experiments as experiments that take place outside the laboratory environment. For instance, Lourenço (2019) defines field experiments as experiments which take place in the natural environment of the subjects, where researchers are in control of the random assignment of treatment and where subjects "*are not aware that they are part of an experiment*" (Lourenço 2019, p. 2). Contrarily, Harrison and List (2004) would refer to those experiments as "natural field experiments" (Harrison and List 2004, p. 1014). Notably, these definitions also include field experiments that are not designed and implemented by firms, but by other institutions (e.g., regulatory or governmental institutions), or occur as natural events (e.g., extreme weather events).

Beyond these differences in academic contributions, practitioners use additional terms to describe certain types of field experiments in different settings and business models. The term *A/B testing* is often used when referring to field experiments in online environments, meaning that, for example, one randomly selected group of customers is presented with packaging design A and another group is presented with packaging design B for an otherwise identical product (Goldfarb and Tucker 2014). In traditional market research, the term *pilot test* describes a setting where a product is only offered to a selected group of customers, often in one store whose customer base reflects a representative set of all customers.

Given these differences in terminology and definitions, we suggest a broader classification including all possible types of field experiments conducted in business practice and research. Figure 2 characterizes four different types of field experiments in a two-by-two matrix along the dimensions of *Control over*

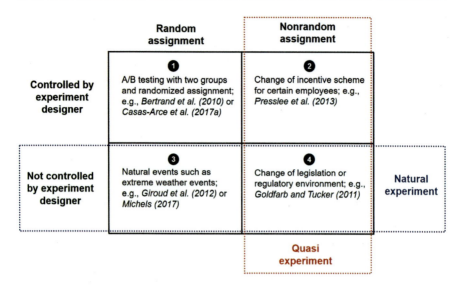

Fig. 2 Classification of field experiments (own illustration)

Treatment and *Randomness of Assignment* borrowing the terminology of Shadish et al. (2002):

- *Control over Treatment* describes the researcher's ability to design and have full control over the type of treatment and the selection of subjects and circumstances. Here, we differentiate between controlled and not controlled by experiment designer. In the fashion retailer example, management is able to decide where and when to place the jeans brand and whether other promotions are conducted simultaneously. However, sometimes the treatment is outside of the designer's control and is either determined by exogenous conditions (i.e., natural weather events) or by executives at higher decision-making levels (i.e., regulatory or governmental institutions). These exogenous interventions are often simply called "shocks" (Atanasov and Black 2016). We classify such designs as natural field experiments.
- *Randomness of Assignment* describes whether the experimental design classifies subjects randomly (or not) to the treatment and the control group. Here, we differentiate between random and nonrandom assignment. In the fashion retailer example, the firm could randomly offer the free shipping option to some online shop visitors (i.e., the treatment group) but not to others (i.e., the control group). Although a nonrandom allocation may not represent a rigorous experimental design, this type of experiment plays a significant role in research and practice (Shadish et al. 2002). We classify such designs as quasi field experiments.

Along those two dimensions, we differentiate four types of field experiments:

- Quadrant 1 (controlled by designer, random assignment) characterizes field experiments which satisfy the definition of Lourenço (2019). Here, the designer is able to select the treatment and can randomize this treatment across subjects. An example for such a field experiment is Casas-Arce et al. (2017a). For this field experiment, the authors collaborate with an insurance company and randomize the frequency and level of detail of customer satisfaction reports provided to independent contractors. Consequently, they can observe and measure performance improvements for the different contractor groups and report a causal link between the frequency and detail of reports and performance. Another example is Bertrand et al. (2010) who partner with a consumer lender in South Africa to randomly vary different aspects of advertising content to existing customers. The authors can clearly identify that particular aspects of the advertising content affect lending demand of various customer groups.

- Quadrant 2 (controlled by designer, nonrandom assignment) constitutes experiments in which the designer can select the treatment but the assignment of the treatment to subjects itself is not random. Often, the collaborating partner (i.e., a firm or regulatory body) does not allow for true random assignment as it would be favored to establish causality. For example, Presslee et al. (2013) are able to select different cash and intangible rewards given to employees of a call center for a limited time span. The authors observe the employees' behavior with regard to chosen goal difficulty, goal commitment, and, ultimately, performance. Nevertheless, the call center firm decided which group of employees received which treatment and did so on the basis of the geographic location of its call centers. Due to the lack of complete randomization, Presslee et al. (2013) point out that their setup represents a quasi field experiment.
- Quadrant 3 (not controlled by designer, random assignment) consists of those experiments for which the treatment is assigned randomly but not at the designer's control, that is, the designer does not administer the random assignment by herself. Rather, the random treatment is occurring due to exogenous causes such as extreme weather events. Those events may be floods, wild fires, hurricanes, or heavy snowfall affecting one group of subjects differently than others. For example, Giroud et al. (2012) exploit unexpected snowfall in the Austrian Alps for their natural experiment in the domain of finance research, and Michels (2017) exploits events of floods and hurricanes in the domain of financial accounting research. In a marketing context, Shriver et al. (2013) use the plausibly random variation in wind speeds on Swiss surf spots to explain the generation of content in an online social network for wind surfers. In general, the pure randomness of weather events may be discussed for some instances, either with regard to self-selection into areas of particular weather conditions or with regard to systematic climate changes; this discussion is yet beyond the scope of this more general introduction.
- Finally, quadrant 4 (not controlled by designer, nonrandom assignment) consists of those experiments in which the designer neither is in full control of the treatment nor is the treatment randomly assigned to subjects. Both limitations with regard to a rigorous experimental design may be present because the collaborating partner is either not willing or not able to give up full control. Especially regulatory bodies such as the European Central Bank or national tax authorities have their own, distinct statutes and agendas when deciding for

specific policy changes and are hesitant to implement policies "at random." This strongly limits the designer's ability to conduct an ideal field experiment and limits the opportunity to study certain questions such as the change in business tax rates across European firms or spikes in prime lending rates for financial institutions at various points in time. Nevertheless, some interesting research has been conducted around the introduction of or changes in legislation or regulation. For example, Goldfarb and Tucker (2011) exploit the change in privacy regulation in the European Union as a regulatory shock to advertisers and their respective possibility to target customers with advertisement. In this quasi-natural field experiment, the authors are strongly concerned with the limits of their research setting, consequently adding sophisticated statistical analyses to derive causal statements from their results. Thinking in terms of distance from the ideal field experiment, studies in this quadrant are certainly those where approaching causality requires additional (and often complex) statistical analyses and further, partially untestable assumptions to mitigate concerns that other factors might be responsible for the observed effects.

As already indicated, some researchers argue that natural experiments (quadrants three and four) are not rigorous experiments since the designer does not have full control which constitutes a violation of one of the key components of an experiment (Lourenço 2019). Often, this kind of shock-based research relies on an event to happen and requires the event to affect only a certain group of individuals without the primary purpose of exploiting this manipulation for research (Atanasov and Black 2016). Typically, violations of randomization are addressed via supplementary statistical analyses and by carefully considering any interfering factor in order to establish causality. However, despite these concerns, the term experiment is usually not disputed. Conclusively, what distinguishes a field experiment from any other study (potentially also conducted "in the field") is its clear variation through a (quasi) exogenous treatment allowing to derive a causal treatment effect.

The following sections deal with methods of how to analyze data generated by all types of field experiments classified in Fig. 2. Since these methods do not distinguish between the data generating process, we discuss methods that are applicable to all kinds of field experiments. However, it will become apparent that some methods are more suitable for some particular designs. In particular, we now refer to the difference-in-differences method (section "Difference-in-Differences Method"), regression discontinuity designs (section "Regression Discontinuity Designs"), and instrumental variable approach (section "Instrumental Variables").

Difference-in-Differences Method

Introduction

In any study, no matter whether it is conducted in the laboratory or in the field, the researcher compares the observable outcome of the treatment group against the outcome of a control group, that is, the group which is (ideally) identical to the treatment group but does not receive the treatment. As long as treatment and control groups are equal along all characteristics (i.e., when the researcher was able to fully randomize the treatment on a homogeneous group as in quadrant 1), a simple comparison of average outcomes between the two groups is sufficient to derive the average treatment effect (ATE). Unfortunately, for many field experiments, an ideal control group does not exist, is impossible or too costly to observe, or its design would violate ethical or legal boundaries.

To exploit data from field experiments which lack the perfect control group, the difference-in-differences method relaxes the requirements for the control group from being "practically identical" to "showing the same trend," called "parallel" or "common" trends assumption (Antonakis et al. 2010, pp. 1108–1109). In this setup, the control group is not equal to the treatment group along all possible variables but exhibits the same trend over time along the relevant dimensions prior to the treatment (Angrist and Pischke 2009, pp. 169–172). Thus, levels may be different but the distance between those levels stays constant over time. For example, two customer groups exhibit different levels of product purchases (e.g., in terms of order value) but over time both groups' spending increases at the same rate so that the difference in levels remains equal.

Figure 3 illustrates how exploiting this requirement allows to draw causal inferences from nonequal groups within the difference-in-differences design. Before the intervention, the treatment group and the control group are not on the same level (e.g., in terms of number of products purchased or order value) but follow the same trend (i.e., order value increases over time at the same rate for both groups). After the treatment, the level of order value continues to increase at the same rate for the control group. Yet, for the treatment group, the trend has changed and the rate at which the order value increases is greater. In this setup, the desired difference

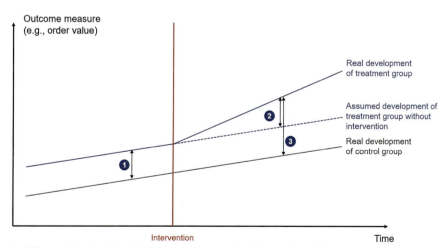

1. Difference before the intervention between treatment and control group (observable)
2. Desired observable effect of the treatment
3. Observable difference between the treatment and control group

Fig. 3 Graphical illustration of difference-in-differences approach (own illustration)

Stylized difference-in-differences regression

Outcome = β_0 + β_1*Treated + β_2*Post + β_3*Treated*Post + ε

Isolation of the treatment effect

	Post = 0	Post = 1	Intertemporal Difference
Treated = 0	β_0	$\beta_0 + \beta_2$	β_2
Treated = 1	$\beta_0 + \beta_1$	$\beta_0 + \beta_1 + \beta_2 + \beta_3$	$\beta_2 + \beta_3$
Cross-Sectional Difference	β_1	$\beta_1 + \beta_3$	β_3

Fig. 4 Isolation of the treatment effect in a stylized difference-in-differences regression (adapted from Wooldridge 2012)

(2) is derived by observing the difference in order value between the two groups after the change (3) and deducting the observed difference in order value between the two groups before the change (1). Thus, the difference-in-differences methodology exploits an intertemporal comparison and a cross-sectional comparison in one design with a "treatment" dummy variable and a "temporal" dummy variable (Wooldridge 2012, pp. 452–455). This results in a two-by-two matrix in which one axis represents the "pre" and "post" period with regard to the timing of the intervention and the other axis represents the "treatment" and "control" units of observation (Goldfarb and Tucker 2014, p. 9). By combining both dimensions, the desired treatment effect can be isolated in β_3 corresponding to the interaction of both dimensions, "treated" and "post," as presented in the stylized regression in Fig. 4.

Core Area of Application

The difference-in-differences methodology exploits two different comparisons within one design: an intertemporal comparison and a cross-sectional comparison. The first comparison is the intertemporal difference within the treatment group; thus, the difference in observation before and after the treatment only for the group which has been affected by the manipulation (Wooldridge 2012, pp. 453–455). While this would satisfy causality condition one (cause precedes the outcome) and allows to observe a co-movement between the observed outcome and the treatment (causality condition two), it would not satisfy causality condition three (absence of other interfering factors) because general time trends or other global shocks are not accounted for. Thus, the observed outcome cannot be considered causal to the treatment. For example, the fashion retailer switches from a fixed-pay scheme ("pre" period) to a commission-based pay scheme ("post" period) for its shop floor personnel and subsequently the performance of the sales people (e.g., revenue per sales person) increases, satisfying causality condition one and two. Yet, condition three is not satisfied because general time trends such as an economic boom or shocks such as a competitor filing for bankruptcy are not incorporated, both of which would affect the sales people's potential to sell products and in turn affects the retailer's revenue.

The second difference constitutes the variation between the treatment and the control group. Here, observable outcomes of treatment and control group are compared for one or more points in time only after the intervention, that is, a cross-sectional difference is exploited. For the fashion retailer, this would mean changing the compensation scheme for its personnel in one store but leaving it as it is at another store and comparing the subsequent performance between the two groups after the change. While it is now possible to incorporate the difference between the two groups (and thus a general time trend) and a co-movement between "compensation scheme" and "sales made" can be observed, this approach neglects the difference between the two groups of sales people which was preexistent before the intervention, that is, working in two different stores (Angrist and Krueger 1999, pp. 1298–1299). Most likely, the two stores had different levels of sales before the change in compensation scheme due to their specific locations, product offerings, or manager's discretion with regard to promotions. Thus, a purely cross-sectional comparison would again fail to meet condition three (exclusion of other factors) and could not establish a causal relationship. In combining both differences, intertemporal and cross-sectional, the difference-in-differences methodology allows to draw causal inferences as long as it fulfills specific conditions (Goldfarb and Tucker 2014, p. 9). We discuss these conditions in the subsequent section in detail when we deal with critical assumptions of the difference-in-differences method.

A specific but important application area for the difference-in-differences methodology is a so-called staggered design. Here, researchers either design their field experiment in a way, or exploit the fact, that the treatment does not occur to all treated individuals or groups at the same time but is introduced step-by-step. Staggered designs are often observed when regulations or legal directives are adopted or firms subsequently roll out a new policy over subjects such as business units, facilities, employee groups, or customers. For example, contrary to an EU Regulation (e.g., the General Data Protection Regulation), an EU Directive has to be adopted into national law in each member state resulting in different adoption dates for a law throughout the EU which allows to observe the effects of the adoption at several points in time. In this setting, a member state belongs to the control group as long as the directive has not yet come into effect and belongs to the treatment group from that moment on when it comes into effect. As more countries adopt the new law, the size of the treatment group grows while the size of the control group shrinks. Such a staggered design is strengthening the case that it is unlikely that another, unobserved factor systematically drives the outcome because the treatment effect is observable for various treatment and control group compositions at various points in time. In this way, concerns regarding the randomness of assignment and control over treatment are mitigated. In this fashion, Heese and Pérez-Calvazos (2020) exploit the introduction of new flight routes between major cities throughout the USA over several years. Similarly, Aghamolla and Li (2018) exploit the staggered introduction of new (and enhanced) debt contract enforcement in India as an opportunity to apply a difference-in-differences design in a natural field experiment.

Some authors also consider event studies as a special application of difference-in-differences designs (Atanasov and Black 2016, p. 219). Event studies generally exploit very short time frames such as a few days before and after the treatment and are common for research in capital markets and stock exchanges where market reaction times are short and prices evolve quickly. In these cases, the intertemporal difference stems from a period before and after an event happens (e.g., the announcement of a CEO leave). The cross-sectional difference stems from the comparison of the stock's performance against the broader market, that is, a market performance index such as the S&P500 or the Dow Jones Industrial Index. For example, in a field experiment in cooperation with Yahoo! Finance, Lawrence et al. (2018) investigate the influence of news coverage on the stock prices of the firms which are covered by the news. Yahoo! Finance randomly gave earnings announcements more or less prominent coverage on its website. Subsequent to this treatment, the authors observe the stock price reaction in a one-day period, comparing the difference in stock price movement and the index movement of the "post" period to the same difference of the "pre" period. In this vain, an event study can also be regarded as an application of a difference-in-differences design.

Critical Assumptions

The most relevant assumption for the difference-in-differences approach is the parallel trends assumption which postulates that the treatment and the control group do not necessarily have to be identical but have to be "very similar" or "comparable" (Antonakis et al. 2010, pp. 1108–1109), showing "similar trends" over time (Angrist and Krueger 1999, p. 1297). The difference between groups with regard to the outcome variable is expected to be stable over time so it can be assumed that they would have continued to stay in parallel had there not been the intervention. This idea follows, yet relaxes, the idea of a counterfactual in any experimental design according to which the control group should be identical to the treatment group to represent the unobservable counterfactual (Atanasov and Black 2016, pp. 218–219). Similar to the inherently unobservable true counterfactual, the assumption of a parallel trend continuing after the treatment ("post" period) cannot be tested empirically. Nevertheless, for any pair of treatment and control group, it can be shown that both groups were moving in parallel prior to the intervention ("pre" period) in order to plausibly state the assumption that this trend would have continued in absence of the intervention (Goldfarb and Tucker 2014, p. 15). In order to assure parallel trends, relevant variables and covariates need to be measured repeatedly at different points in time during the "pre" period. Additional plausible reasoning and supporting data can strengthen that the intervention was an exogenous shock in a way that assignment to treatment was as good as random (Atanasov and Black 2016, pp. 238–241). Gill et al. (2017) use an alternative way to ensure comparability of groups in a setting where buyers in a market could voluntarily self-select into the treatment (i.e., using a business-to-business app). They explicitly model the decision to become part of the treatment via a first-stage selection model, thus correcting statistically for systematic differences between treatment and control group before intervention.

The absence of a single suitable control group that fulfills the parallel trend assumption lead to the development of synthetic controls (Abadie et al. 2010). This method has become popular in economics, marketing, and other disciplines in recent years since it is particularly useful in studying interventions that are implemented at an aggregate level, affecting a small number of large units (such as regions or business units). The synthetic control method is based on the idea that a weighted combination of candidates for a control group provides a more appropriate comparison than a single control group alone. Therefore, the control group is a weighted combination of several control group candidates where the respective weights are the outcome of a prediction model. Based on observable variables, the approach fits the weighted control group to the treatment group before the treatment takes place, thus constructing a hypothetical control, i.e., a synthetic group. In one application, Pattabhiramaiah et al. (2019) require a control group for the readership of the *New York Times* newspaper and are able to compose a weighted average of other newspapers such as the *Washington Post*, the *LA Times*, and the *Chicago Tribune* to study the effects of a paywall introduction on the newspaper's revenue. For further details and application areas of this approach, we refer to Abadie et al. (2010), Abadie (2020), and Acemoglu et al. (2016).

While the parallel trends assumption is basically always addressed in research that employs a difference-in-differences design, many other assumptions are often left implicit (we refer to Atanasov and Black 2016, pp. 237–249 for a thorough review). One of those assumptions addresses the issue that there must not be a second event which has diametrically opposed effects on the treatment and the control group, that is, events to which subjects in the two groups react systematically different based on their group status. Armstrong et al. (2019) explicitly point out three more assumptions with relevance to the difference-in-differences method and provide reasoning to which extent their specific research design meets those assumptions:

- The first additional assumption beyond parallel trends postulates that the treatment status of one unit should not interfere with another unit's outcome. For example, customer A's status (qualified for free shipping) should not affect the amount of money spent by another customer B. This assumption is not testable but has to be analyzed and plausibly argued in each research setting.
- The second additional assumption demands that neither subject in the treatment or in the control group anticipates the intervention or is affected by the treatment prior to the intervention. This assumption might be violated in cases where subjects can voluntarily choose to become part of a group, that is, a customer may decide to purchase an additional item to cross the threshold of the free shipping minimum order amount. Other examples of such violations include changes in accounting rules, voluntary compliance with stricter environmental standards, or customer data protection.
- Finally, the difference-in-differences method implicitly assumes perfect compliance. This means all individuals in the treatment group are in fact treated. In case

of a violation, the method estimates (just) an "intention to treat" effect. This intention to treat effect is more conservative than the treatment on the treated estimation because it is based on a smaller variance within the data set making it harder to detect a statistically significant effect between treatment and control group (see also Gassen and Muhn 2018, pp. 21–22). For the free shipping threshold, it may occur that certain customers may either simply not recognize that free shipping is available or at which threshold they would qualify for the free shipping.

Despite being relevant to difference-in-differences designs in particular, the ideas expressed in these additional assumptions are not exclusive to difference-in-differences models but can be seen as some broader requirements for conducting (field) experiments in general (Lourenço 2019). Most field experiments implicitly consider these assumptions by prohibiting units of observations to interact with each other, so that the treatment is not "diluted." For example, Casas-Arce et al. (2017a) explicitly state that *"information sharing among professionals [treated units] was not common"* and Casas-Arce et al. (2017b) state that the treatment (here: introduction of a simulation software) *"was installed overnight and a memo was sent to branch managers with instructions for its use,"* assuring that the treatment could not have been anticipated.

Application in Goldfarb and Tucker (2011)

Goldfarb and Tucker (2011) use the difference-in-differences method in their study investigating the (potential) impact of a regulatory reform on advertisement effectiveness based on the introduction of an online privacy law in 2004 by the European Union. Before the implementation of the Privacy Regulation, firms had the ability to broadly monitor users' online activities and behaviors and thus were able to specifically target users with advertisement based on their activities. For example, knowing that a user searched the terms "holiday" and "Spain" would lend itself to promoting summer fashion or flights to Madrid. With the introduction of the Privacy Regulation, marketers' possibilities to collect and use such information were severely limited, making it plausible to observe a decline in advertising effectiveness subsequent to the introduction. Goldfarb and Tucker (2011) exploit the change in legislation in a difference-in-differences approach in which they compare advertising effectiveness before and after the change in regulation.

The authors are able to exploit unique data of advertising effectiveness from a repeated survey response study conducted by a research agency between 2000 and 2008 in the EU and the USA. In this survey, the research agency measured ad effectiveness for marketers by randomly showing ads and placebo ads to real online users and subsequently surveying users from both groups with regard to purchase intent of the promoted product. While in itself this (repeated) field experiment already provides the possibility to draw causal inferences on the ad effectiveness, the authors add another dimension, namely time, to measure the change in effectiveness. Hence, the treatment in this design is the implementation of the new privacy regulation. All users who were shown personalized ads belong to the treatment group, while all users who were shown placebo ads belong to the control group (i.e., a cross-sectional comparison). The addition of the time dimension accounts for the difference-in-differences design of this quasi-natural experiment. Effectively, Goldfarb and Tucker (2011) are even able to exploit a so-called triple difference-in-differences design with changes in three different dimensions: the variation over time, the variation between treatment and control group within the EU, and the differences between the EU and the USA. Using the rigorous difference-in-differences design, their results not only suggest that the advertisement effectiveness declined after the Privacy Regulation was put into effect but also that this outcome is a causal result of the introduction of the Privacy Regulation (Goldfarb and Tucker 2011, p. 70).

Table 1 provides an overview of further applications of the difference-in-differences method in business research literature exploiting various settings and exogenous shocks.

Regression Discontinuity Designs

Introduction

As discussed in prior sections, field experiments are building on the critical aspect of random assignment to the treatment. Quasi field experiments lack this requirement due to a nonrandom assignment of the treatment. For example, in the US banking industry, loans were granted without requesting further proof of income or collateral as long as the applicant had a FICO score (US credit rating) of 620 points or more (Keys et al. 2010). Thus, 620 points serve as the threshold for (not) getting a loan without further documentation, that is, for receiving the treatment. Using the cut-off to differentiate between treatment and control group is not per se helpful to establish causality. The problem is that those two groups are not comparable because a credit score is specifically designed to reflect a wide range of indicators, to differentiate credit worthiness levels, and to facilitate credit approval decisions. However, it may be more likely that an applicant scoring 619 is at least very similar to an applicant scoring 621 despite having a (marginally) lower score. Regression discontinuity designs make use of a comparison between subjects in close proximity to a threshold that are likely to be (almost) equal in terms of characteristics else than the treatment.

Figure 5 depicts the regression discontinuity setting. The horizontal axis may depict the credit score of applicants and the vertical axis may depict the likelihood of receiving a loan without further documentation. Instead of showing a continuous, functional relationship between credit score and the need to provide further documentation, the plotted distribution manifests a jump (or step) at the threshold value of 620 points (1). This arbitrary threshold divides the sample into a treatment and control group. The bandwidth (2) describes the range in close proximity to the

Table 1 Literature table for difference-in-differences applications in business research

Author(s), year, journal	Title	Type of field experiment	Dependent variable(s)	Independent variable(s), exogenous treatment	Findings
Amiram, D., Bauer, A. M., Frank, M.M. (2019) *The Accounting Review*	Tax Avoidance at Public Corporations Driven by Shareholder Taxes: Evidence from Changes in Dividend Tax Policy	Quasi-natural field experiment	Corporate tax avoidance measured in spread between statutory and effective tax rate	Change in countries' dividend tax policy triggered by ECJ decisions, dividend payouts, share repurchases, array of financial controls	Average firm affected by an elimination of imputation systems reduces its cash effective tax rate by 5.5%
Ascarza, E., Ebbes, P., Netzer, O., Danielson, M. (2017) *Journal of Marketing Research*	Beyond the Target Customer: Social Effects of Customer Relationship Management Campaigns	Field experiment	Telephone usage (in minutes) and churn rates of customers who are socially connected to the targeted customers	CRM campaign targeted at specific, random telecom providers' customers	CRM campaign targeted at changing the behavior of specific customers transmits through social network, socially connected customers also increase consumption and decrease churn rates
Chen, T., Lin, C. (2018) *Journal of Financial and Quantitative Analysis*	Does Information Asymmetry Affect Corporate Tax Aggressiveness?	Natural field experiment	Five standard measures of tax avoidance (among others: total book-tax difference)	Analyst coverage of firms, closure and mergers of brokers covering firms as exogenous treatment	Firms avoid tax more aggressively after a reduction in analyst coverage
Gill, M., Sridhar, S., Grewal, R. (2017) *Journal of Marketing*	Return on Engagement Initiatives: A Study of a Business-to-Business Mobile App	Field experiment	Return on Engagement Initiatives (RoEI) and Sales Revenues	Customer engagement via a mobile app; adoption of the app as treatment (combined with mitigation of self-selection problems)	Adoption of the app increased revenues by 19.1 to 22.8% and resulted in positive RoEI
Grullon, G., Michenaud, S., Weston, J.P. (2015) *The Review of Financial Studies*	The Real Effects of Short-Selling Constraints	Natural field experiment	Corporate investment, external financing activities, stock price sensitivity	Capital market frictions operationalized as the SEC announcement of removal of short sale restrictions	Increase in short-selling activity causes stock prices to decrease; small firms react to these lower prices by reducing equity issues and investments

Authors	Title	Type	Dependent variable	Independent variable	Findings
Houston, J.F., Lin, C., Liu, S., Wie, L. (2019) *The Accounting Review*	Litigation Risk and Voluntary Disclosure: Evidence from Legal Changes	Quasi-natural field experiment	(Frequency of) Disclosures with regard to financially relevant events	Good/Bad News, three legal decisions with regard to disclosure requirements as plausibly exogenous shocks	Treated firms tend to make fewer (more) management earnings forecasts relative to the control firms when they expect litigation risk to be lower (higher) following the legal event
Huse, C., Koptyug, N. (2017) *Journal of Economics and Management Strategy*	Bailing on the Car that was not Bailed Out: Bounding Consumer Reactions to Financial Distress	Quasi-natural field experiment	Brand's sales	Consumer confidence, financial distress of durable consumer goods manufacturers as exogenous treatment	Significant decrease in the sales of Saab following its filing for insolvency/ restructuring
Gong, S., Zhang, J., Zhao, P., Jiang, X. (2017) *Journal of Marketing Research*	Tweeting as a Marketing Tool: A Field Experiment in the TV Industry	Field experiment	Percentage of channel's audience viewing particular show	Number of firms' tweets and influencers' retweets, number of noncommercial tweets	Company tweets directly increase viewing; influential retweets increase viewing only if the show tweet is informative
Jiang, J., Wang, I., Wang, K. (2019) *The Accounting Review*	Big N Auditors and Audit Quality: New Evidence from Quasi-Experiments	Quasi field experiment	Audit quality measured in financial statement divergence score	Big N auditors' acquisition of Non Big N auditors (and forced switch in auditor for the client)	Treated firms' audit quality improves after switch to Big N auditor
Mochon, D., Johnson, K., Schwartz, J., Ariely, D. (2017) *Journal of Marketing Research*	What Are Likes Worth? A Facebook Page Field Experiment	Field experiment	Customers' online and offline responses to invitation of liking firm's Facebook page	Invitation to like firm's Facebook pages as treatment (randomized subset of existing customers); promotional activities on the page	Acquired (invited) Facebook page likes have a positive effect on offline customer behavior

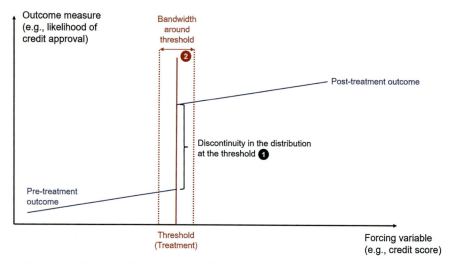

Fig. 5 Graphical illustration of regression discontinuity design (own illustration)

threshold of 620 points for which it is assumed that applicants are reasonably comparable along each dimension despite being above/below the threshold value.

Core Area of Application

Regression discontinuity designs provide an opportunity for causal inference when the assignment to the treatment is unlikely to be random for the whole sample but may be as good as random around a certain threshold. In contrast to a difference-in-differences approach, the regression discontinuity only refers to two different groups and one type of variation: The difference in outcome for the treated group (right of the discontinuity) and the outcome for the control group (left of the discontinuity). The cut-off may be either a cross-sectional difference or an intertemporal difference but cannot be both (as we have seen for the difference-in-differences approach in the previous section).

Antonakis et al. (2010) exemplify this idea in a business context with leadership training for managers, for which the effect on team performance is unclear. In an ideal field experiment, leadership training would be offered to a randomly selected group of managers independent of prior performance. Yet, the firm wants to spend funds as efficiently as possible and wants to prioritize those managers for leadership training who showed lower performance in prior periods. Thus, the firm favors managers for the training who scored below average in their past annual evaluation. While comparing the team performance of all managers below and above the average performance subsequent to the training would not yield satisfactory results, the regression discontinuity approach would compare the teams' performance whose managers were just above and just below the average. The comparison thus is limited to those managers who were just not granted training against those who just received the training. In this fashion, regression discontinuity designs also demonstrate a potential pathway to accommodating a firm's requirement for efficient spending and the requirements for drawing causal inferences.

Critical Assumptions

As it becomes evident, a regression discontinuity design requires a discontinuous function, that is, the treatment should show a plausible, discrete jump in its distribution. Therefore, it becomes critical to assess whether a jump in a distribution originates from an actual discontinuity or instead represents a nonlinear relationship around the threshold. We discuss three potential ways of verifying the plausibility of a suspected discontinuity.

First, it can be assessed whether the jump is plausible via an understanding of the data generation process. In the example of US credit scores and lending decisions, it is obvious that the discontinuity is an arbitrary threshold and that individuals most likely are unable to specifically manipulate their scores to belong to the treatment or control group. A different case is the example of the fashion retailer's free shipping option. Here, the retailer may decide to offer free shipping above an order value of 40 Euro. While this may lead to a discontinuity in the distribution of order values, this design in itself does not qualify for a regression discontinuity approach. Here, shoppers being close to the threshold have the discretion to become part of the treatment group (the group of people receiving free shipping). Due to this self-selection, the treatment neither is exogenously assigned to shoppers nor is it random, and a regression discontinuity analysis will not yield causal inferences (Goldfarb and Tucker 2014, p. 23).

Second, managers and researchers can statistically test whether the comparability assumption holds and whether subjects within a certain bandwidth around the discontinuity are comparable in observable characteristics. For the online shopper example, it could be useful to compare prior order values of the customers left and right of the discontinuity or to compare characteristics such as age or method of payment as proxies for shoppers' socio-economic background. For a more sophisticated test of self-selection and sorting behavior of subjects in regression discontinuity designs, we refer to McCrary (2008).

Third, it is possible to statistically test for different data generating processes and assess whether those are likely to be a valid origin of the observed data. While it is often advised to test whether a higher order polynomial may have generated the perceived discontinuity in the data, Gelman and Imbens (2019) specifically stress the idea to use local higher order polynomials (i.e., a quadratic function) or local linear functions instead of global higher order polynomials (e.g., sixths order) to control for the possibility of continuous data generating processes and to avoid poor or highly sensitive estimations.

Another crucial point in all regression discontinuity designs is the power of statistical tests. On the one hand, the number of observations around the threshold is often small, thus, allowing for the possibility that single extreme values drive findings. From this perspective, a wider bandwidth would be favorable. On the other hand, regression discontinuity designs critically build on the assumption that subjects left and right of the cut-off are comparable along observable and unobservable characteristics. This perspective speaks in favor of a narrow bandwidth around the threshold. Hence, widening the bandwidth around the threshold will decrease the risk of influential outliers due to more observations, yet it will simultaneously corrode the assumption of comparableness between treatment and control group. Therefore, the bandwidth around the discontinuity becomes a critical aspect. A simple and effective way of dealing with this issue is to work with different bandwidths around the threshold value such as $\pm 1\%$, $\pm 2.5\%$, $\pm 5\%$, and $\pm 10\%$ to determine which bandwidth yields the optimal trade-off. Another solution is proposed by Imbens and Kalyanaraman (2012) who suggest to select a bandwidth by minimizing the mean squared error which is an efficient, yet economically less intuitive solution.

Application in Flammer (2015)

Flammer (2015) addresses the question of whether the approval of a Corporate Social Responsibility (CSR) related shareholder proposal is firm value enhancing. She motivates her study by presenting two competing theories. On the one hand, a resource-based view predicts that firms only engage in activities which are value enhancing. On the other hand, agency theory argues that private managerial concerns for reputation may motivate executives in engaging in CSR activities in order to increase personal reputation at the cost of firm value. It should be noted, however, that those two arguments are not mutually exclusive. The design of the field experiment in this paper can more easily explain whether the resource-based view holds because it insufficiently addresses the question of whether the agency explanation holds in this research setting due to the shareholders voting instead of management taking decisions.

To address her research question, Flammer (2015) exploits a discontinuity in the data – a majority vote threshold. She collects data from publicly listed firms in the USA concerning their relative stock market performance (cumulative abnormal returns) as outcome variable and data on all CSR-related shareholder proposals which were put to a vote in the annual shareholder meeting. In case a shareholder proposal met the threshold of "50% plus one vote," it was approved and, thus, regarded as treated. All other proposals that did not pass the majority vote threshold are assigned to the control group. In a second step, she isolates all those proposals which were approved and rejected at a very thin margin (± 5 percentage points around the threshold) and investigates the share price development of those firms subsequent to the shareholder meeting.

As outlined before, it is crucial to provide evidence that the jump in the distribution can be attributed to a discontinuity in the data. The threshold of 50% approval provides plausible grounds. Visual inspection of the distribution of abnormal returns for the vote share bandwidth of 45% to 55% also reveals a jump in the distribution around the approval threshold of 50%. Flammer (2015) further provides statistical evidence that the discontinuity unlikely stems from a higher order polynomial data generating process and therefore provides sufficient indication that she is in fact exploiting a valid discontinuity in the data.

After having provided evidence for the validity of the discontinuity, she also provides evidence regarding the second relevant requirement, the absence of self-selection effects. To ensure that the distribution is as good as random, she first investigates potential preexisting differences in various variables before and after the shareholder meeting. For the full sample, that is, all firms that held a vote on CSR-related proposals, she finds that firms *"that pass a CSR proposal differ significantly from companies that reject it"* (Flammer 2015, p. 2557). This finding supports the idea that passing a CSR proposal is not independent of other firm characteristics. Nevertheless, when only comparing firms which narrowly pass or reject a CSR proposal (i.e., firms within the ±5% bandwidth), these differences disappear, providing plausible evidence that the passage of a CSR proposal is uncorrelated to firm characteristics for this subsample. Unfortunately, the risk remains that the latter result (statistically insignificant differences in the subsample) is partially driven by a smaller sample size when considering only firms at the threshold and therefore has to be considered with caution. Therefore, this evidence is further underscored by a formal approach which tests for the continuity of vote shares in the data set (McCrary 2008).

Employing a regression discontinuity design, Flammer (2015) is able to provide empirical evidence that a firm's CSR engagement is not only positively correlated to its financial performance but that it is likely that engaging in CSR initiatives in fact drives firm value. Her study demonstrates how valid thresholds can be exploited to establish causality in quasi field experiments but also demonstrates the method's limits: Due to the small sample size around the threshold (61 observations), the author cautions against generalizing her findings and suggests additional studies on this issue.

Table 2 provides an overview of further applications of the regression discontinuity method in business research literature exploiting various settings and quasi-random distributions through arbitrary thresholds.

Instrumental Variables

Introduction

While the difference-in-differences method and the regression discontinuity design broadly lend themselves to satisfy causality condition three, the absence of interfering factors, instrumental variables may be used to solve more specific and complex issues. In general, instrumental variables take a special role with regard to field experiments because the method allows to embed an experiment into settings which did not allow for causal inference because the setting did or could not provide a (quasi) exogenous treatment, that is, when the setting was not a field experiment in

Table 2 Literature table for regression discontinuity applications in business research

Author(s), year, journal	Title	Type of field experiment	Dependent variable	Independent variable(s), exogenous treatment and threshold	Findings
Bird, A., Karolyi, S.A. (2019) *The Accounting Review*	Governance and Taxes: Evidence from Regression Discontinuity	Natural field experiment	Tax avoidance measured in effective tax rates (book-tax expense and cash taxes paid)	Institutional ownership variation over time, threshold of (not) being included in Russel 1000 and Russel 2000 index (entering or leaving index)	Increased institutional ownership around Russell index reconstitutions lead to significant decreases in effective tax rates and to increased use of international tax planning
Chang, Y., Hong, H., Liskovich, I. (2015) *The Review of Financial Studies*	Regression Discontinuity and the Price Effects of Stock Market Indexing	Natural field experiment	Stock Price	Inclusion and exclusion in Russel 1000 and Russel 2000 index as treatment/threshold	Additions to the Russell 2000 result in price increases and deletions result in price decreases
Chava, S., Roberts, M.R. (2008) *The Journal of Finance*	How Does Financing Impact Investment? The Role of Debt Covenants	Natural field experiment	Firms' investments (measured in ratio of CAPEX)	Debt covenant violations and subsequent threat of transfer of ownership, violation of the covenant as the arbitrary threshold	Capital investment declines sharply following a financial covenant violation
Chemmanur, T.J., Tian, X. (2018) *Journal of Financial and Quantitative Analysis*	Do Antitakeover Provisions Spur Corporate Innovation? A Regression Discontinuity Analysis	Natural field experiment	Innovation measured in number of patents and citations of patents	Proposals of antitakeover provisions which did (not) pass the shareholders' vote, threshold at 50% of shareholder votes	Positive effect of passage of antitakeover provisions on innovation

Kajüter, P., Klassmann, F., Nienhaus, M. (2019) *The Accounting Review*	The Effect of Mandatory Quarterly Reporting on Firm Value	Quasi-natural field experiment	Firm valuation, cumulative abnormal returns	Exemption from quarterly financial reporting; stock market capitalization threshold at fiscal year end	Five percent decrease in firm value, consistent with theory that mandatory quarterly reporting is a net burden for smaller firms
Narayanan, S., Kalyanam, K. (2015) *Marketing Science*	Position Effects in Search Advertising and their Moderators: A Regression Discontinuity Approach	Quasi-natural field experiment	Click through rates and sales orders	Higher position in Google Search measured as the difference in AdRank	Position effects are stronger when advertiser is smaller; position effects are weaker when keyword phrase has specific brand/product information
Vashishtha, R. (2014) *Journal of Accounting and Economics*	The Role of Bank Monitoring in Borrowers' Discretionary Disclosure: Evidence from Covenant Violations	Natural field experiment	Firms' disclosure measured as likelihood of issuing earnings forecast	Increased bank monitoring of firms (change in governance structure) subsequent to debt covenant violations	Firms reduce disclosure subsequent to change in governance structure (violation of debt covenant)

the first place (Angrist and Krueger 1999, p. 1300). Second, instrumental variables are used whenever simultaneity poses a challenge to causal inference (thus, violation of condition one, cause has to precede the outcome). Third, instrumental variables are employed specifically when unobservable variables not only drive the observed outcome variable but also influence the presumed treatment variable. For example, this could be the case if subjects self-select into the suspected treatment or are noncompliant with the treatment. This influence of other factors on both treatment and outcome variable is often referred to as "endogeneity of the treatment." We refer to Ebbes et al. (chapter ▶ "Dealing with Endogeneity: A Nontechnical Guide for Marketing Researchers") in this handbook, Roberts and Whited (2013), and Angrist et al. (1996) for a more detailed and specific discussion about endogeneity.

Suppose a fashion retailer is aiming to increase its online store revenue by increasing its spending on paid search ads. As it is common, the search platform, such as Google or Yahoo!, charges the fashion retailer for every click on the paid search result that directs a customer to the fashion retailer's online store (pay-per-click model). If the fashion retailer is now interested in the effectiveness of the paid search ads to generate revenues, the retailer would observe that the ad expenses and the online store revenues increase by some factor, for example, for every 1% increase in ad expense, revenues increase by 0.1%. Yet, this simple observation of co-movement would ignore that the consumer's behavior (a click on the ad) both drives the revenues and the expenses alike because the ad expense is not a lump-sum payment (Blake et al. 2015). In this case, instrumental variables are addressing the concern that the treatment cannot be clearly distinguished from other factors which affect the outcome and the treatment itself by "replacing" the original treatment variable with an instrumented variable, that is, an estimated variable based off an instrument. We will present and discuss examples for valid instruments and instrumental variables in the context of field experiments in the following segments.

Before turning to instrumental variables in field experimental settings, it is crucial to understand the mechanics of the instrumental variables approach. An instrument offers exogenous variation which the actual treatment cannot provide (Angrist and Krueger 1999, p. 30). In brief, an instrument is a "third" variable which explains as much variation in the treatment variable as possible but is exogenous to the outcome variable of interest, except for its influence through the treatment. The instrument thus replaces the treatment variable with estimated "cleaned, exogenous" values of the treatment instead of actual values by estimating the treatment variable in the first stage.

This idea is depicted in Fig. 6. The first box shows the original relationship of interest, for example, the effect of education (X) on income after graduation (Y). As the treatment education is endogenous (i.e., future income expectations are likely to influence education choices), an appropriate instrument (Z) is required. This instrument should be valid (i.e., it explains the number of years an individual spends on education) but exogenous (i.e., it is only related to income after graduation via education). Such an instrument could be mandatory school attendance (Angrist and Krueger 1991). In a first step, this instrument is used to estimate (mandatory) years of education ($\hat{X}$) which in turn is used to estimate income after graduation. The terms e and u represent the respective residuals of the performed regression whose potential interrelation may be one reason for unobserved effects in the model.

Exploiting Data from Field Experiments

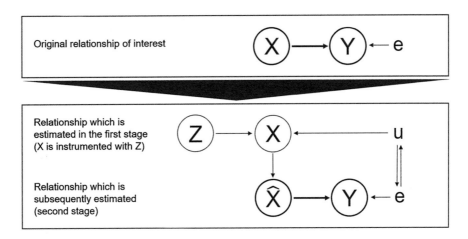

Fig. 6 Graphical illustration of instrumental variables method (own illustration)

Core Area of Application

Instrumental variables are useful in cases in which the main research question does not constitute a field experiment due to the lack of a (quasi) exogenous intervention as described for difference-in-differences settings (Angrist and Krueger 1999, p. 1300; Goldfarb and Tucker 2014, p. 26). Putting it in a more pointed way, the second stage of the instrumental variables design is not an experiment with (quasi) exogenous treatment because if it were, the research question would not require an instrumental variables design in the first place but could be addressed with a comparison of means or possibly a sophisticated difference-in-differences design. In that sense, an instrumental variables approach implements a (quasi) natural field experiment before the original relationship of interest is addressed. Turning to the causality conditions, instrumental variables provide an opportunity to establish causality in cases where either condition one (cause precedes effect) or condition three (absence of interfering factors) is difficult to meet. In other words, in these cases, it is difficult to isolate the effect of the treatment variable from an array of other unobservable factors. This also includes cases in which subjects deliberately decide to become part of the treatment group, that is, when (quasi) random assignment cannot be ensured. Here, instrumental variables have become the standard method to address this problem, developed and driven mostly by research in economics (e.g., Angrist and Krueger 1991). Nevertheless, it has found its way into business research as a result of stronger emphasis on causal inferences.

For any field experiment which can be considered being part of the first quadrant, that is, the designer has full control over the treatment and the treatment is randomized, an instrumental variable approach is generally not necessary because the treatment (i.e., the cause) precedes the outcome by design and ideally there are no unobservable characteristics which influence the treatment and the outcome alike. For natural field experiments or quasi field experiments, the issue of other (un) observable influences becomes of increasing concern as managers or researchers are lacking control over those circumstances. In most cases, potentially interfering factors are nevertheless observable and only affect the outcome but not the treatment and can thus be integrated into the estimation as control variables. For example, Goldfarb and Tucker (2011) employ their difference-in-differences design on the introduction of a new privacy law in the EU but include a range of control variables in their estimation such as age or income of the survey participants. Furthermore, the intervention is quasi exogenously determined by the EU regulatory body. Contrarily, in the case of Giroud et al. (2012), the authors are not able to isolate the effect of an increase in financial leverage from unobserved, opportunistic behavior of the hotels' managers, which they suspect to also influence the outcome variable, the likelihood of bankruptcy. Therefore, the authors resort to an instrument to estimate their treatment variable. Disaggregating their study, the core question of interest does not include an experiment because it lacks the randomized intervention from an external body (experiment's designer or regulatory body). Including an instrumental variable allows the authors to exploit an experimental setting (excessive amount of snowfall) in a first step before addressing the actual research question, making their research design qualify as a quasi-natural field experiment.

Another case can be made for situations in which the assignment to treatment is not random but individuals choose to become part of the treatment group, for example, if firms voluntarily disclose nonfinancial information. In an example of overcoming the problem of voluntary decisions by firms, Ladika and Sautner (2020) investigate the question whether CEOs are likely to scale back investments when they are presented with more short-term incentives. While so-called "accelerated option vesting" by firms is generally regarded as a valid indicator for shortening top management's incentive horizon, doing so is a voluntary decision by the firm. Thus, it is most likely correlated with factors which also drive investment decisions. In that sense, one may also argue that this setting per se does not qualify as a field experiment as the treatment is not exogenously determined. In order to mitigate this concern, Ladika and Sautner (2020) exploit a regulation by the Financial Accounting Standard Board (FASB) which creates a strong incentive for firms to accelerate option vesting. Importantly, this incentive becomes effective quasi-randomly for each firm at different points in time as it is tied to a firm's fiscal year end. Therefore, it can be used as an instrument for actual accelerated option vesting, again "attaching" an experiment to a research question which in itself would not qualify as a field experiment.

Critical Assumptions

Any instrument has to satisfy two fundamental criteria, the relevance condition, and the exclusion restriction (Wooldridge 2012, p. 508):

- According to the relevance condition, the instrument must be informative about the independent (exogenous) variable. For example, in their field experiment, Shriver et al. (2013) investigate the relationship between social ties and the

creation of content in an online social network. As those two concepts are intertwined, it poses a challenge to causality condition one (cause precedes effect). The authors choose wind speeds at the observed surfing locations as their instrument and establish that wind speeds are informative about the blogging behavior of surfers in their online social network. Here, wind speeds higher than the median enable surfing at a specific location and in turn enable surfers to write about their experience on an online platform.
- According to the exclusion restriction, the instrument must be exogenous to the dependent variable. This means that the instrument should only affect the observed outcome variable via the treatment. Again, Shriver et al. (2013) claim that wind speeds in itself should have no direct effect on the likelihood of surfers developing social ties in an online network. Stated differently, above median winds are per se not increasing the likelihood of surfers getting and sending friend requests in their online social network. Wind speeds should affect social ties in the online social network only through the creation of content of past surfing experiences.

Providing evidence that the instrument meets the relevance and exclusion restriction is challenging and statistical tests can at best only strengthen the credibility of the instrument. The relevance of instruments can be tested in the first-stage regression via the respective F-statistic of whether the instruments are jointly significantly different from zero. As a rule of thumb, an F-statistic smaller than 10 for a single treatment variable indicates the presence of a weak instrument, that is, that the chosen instrument is not sufficiently relevant for the relationship of interest. Yet, for certain cases, this rule of thumb may not be sufficient to determine the relevance of the instrument, for example, Lee et al. (2020) demonstrate the insufficiencies of this rule of thumb in many research applications and propose that a more sensible F-statistic value would lie north of 100. For further details on extended testing for an instrument's relevance, we refer to Stock and Yogo (2005) and more recent development for testing an instrument's validity put forth by Sanderson and Windmeijer (2016).

The exclusion restriction is even more difficult to assess because no single, universal statistical test exists to date. Thus, arguing in favor of a valid instrument which satisfies the exclusion restriction requires in-depth knowledge on the domain and a very sound understanding of the data generating process. Therefore, authors often caution their readers against taking results at face value. For instance, Shriver et al. (2013) state that they *"present an IV approach based on wind speeds, which delivers estimates of causal effects under the assumption of exogeneity of these instruments. If these assumptions are violated, the causal interpretation no longer holds."* (Shriver et al. 2013, p. 1430).

Two further assumptions are required to sensibly employ an instrumental variable approach: the independence condition and the monotonicity assumption. The independence condition states that the instrument itself must not suffer from the same property as the variable that is instrumented, namely it must not suffer from endogeneity itself. This condition aligns with the idea of exploiting a field experimental setting in the first stage. Secondly, the monotonicity condition states that the instrument must only have a one directional effect on the treatment variable. Specifically, the instrument may partially not affect certain individuals (e.g., because they effectively withdraw from being treated) but it must not adversely affect the likelihood of being treated (Angrist and Pischke 2009, p. 114). Circling back to Shriver et al. (2013), while wind speed may not affect those surfers who may have had a "rest day" in their schedule or were sick on one of the days in the observation period, above median wind speeds should not decrease the likelihood of surfing for some of the surfers but it should only increase the likelihood for all surfers. This assumption may be questioned, potentially arguing that for some extreme wind speeds, especially beginners may be discouraged from surfing. On the other hand, extreme winds may also encourage content creation for those beginners without an imminent surfing experience, for example, by creating content on the extreme weather conditions. This brief discussion again illustrates the problem of those assumptions being mostly untestable and heavily relying on convincing argumentation and discussions. Nevertheless, meeting all the aforementioned conditions and assumptions paves the way to deriving the local average treatment effect (LATE) in the desired research setting.

Application in Bennedsen et al. (2007)

Bennedsen et al. (2007) pursue the research question whether choosing a family CEO or an external CEO positively affects the financial performance of a family firm. Choosing a CEO from the family has the advantage of insider knowledge and greater alignment between the interests of the owning family and the CEO, which mitigates agency conflicts. In contrast, choosing an outside CEO enables the firm to choose a skilled manager from a larger talent pool. Thus, from a theoretical point of view, both scenarios, a family CEO being more and being less valuable to the firm compared to an outsider, are plausible.

Ideally, researchers have full control over the treatment and could randomly assign a family CEO or an outside CEO to identical family firms and measure their subsequent financial performance. Unsurprisingly, this is not feasible. Similarly, it is not helpful to simply investigate the correlation between "family vs. outsider CEO" on subsequent financial performance of all firms. This analysis would satisfy causality condition one and two but certainly not condition three, the absence of other influencing factors. The problem is that the choice of appointing a CEO from the ranks of the family is endogenous to its performance, that is, some factors influence both the appointment decision and subsequent financial performance. Thus, the research question itself does not constitute a field experiment due to the lack of an exogenous intervention. Therefore, Bennedsen et al. (2007) instrument the choice of appointing a family CEO with a plausibly exogenous variable: the gender of the CEO's first-born child.

The authors gather financial data from privately held Danish firms and match information on whether the CEO's first-born child is male or female. The gender of the first-born is plausibly random and not influenced by their parents, especially as techniques to identify the gender before birth were not widely employed prior to 1980 (Bennedsen et al. 2007, p. 650). Further, the gender of the first-born is plausibly independent of firm's financial performance. While the chance of being born a male is 50%, the rate of family succession within Danish firms is 39% when the first-born is male while it is only 29.4% when the first-born is female (Bennedsen et al. 2007, p. 650). Stated differently, a male first-born has a 32.7% higher likelihood of becoming a CEO in his parents' company than a female first-born. The chosen instrument satisfies both the exclusion restriction (gender being uncorrelated to firm's financial performance) and the relevance condition (gender being informative about CEO appointment choice). As outlined before, an instrumental variable setup critically builds on plausible reasoning and extended empirical tests to demonstrate that the relevance condition and exclusion condition are fulfilled.

Exploiting the instrumental variable in this field experiment, the authors are able to identify a causal relationship between appointing a family CEO and subsequent financial performance. They find that family successions hurt firm performance: in particular, firms with the parting CEO's first child being male demonstrate an average decline in operative return on assets of 0.8 to 1.2 percentage points, statistically significant at the 5% level. Correlational analyses suggest that the negative effect persists, meaning that firms whose performance is relatively weaker subsequent to appointing a family CEO do not catch up to their peers in the 3 years following the CEO succession (Bennedsen et al. 2007, p. 678).

Table 3 provides further applications of the instrumental variables method in business research literature exploiting various settings and treatment variations. As discussed above, applications of instrumental variables in field experimental settings are rather rare as the method is only useful in specific situations which (by construction) are less prevalent in field experiments.

Application of Methods in Standard Software

As the presented methods to exploit data from field experiments have become increasingly more popular and wide-spread as demonstrated in Fig. 1, this has also materialized in their implementation in various standard software solutions. While a manual application of each method is generally possible in STATA, R, and SPSS, especially STATA and R often provide dedicated functions or packages to execute the methods in a more user-friendly, easy-to-handle way. This provides the user with a wide variety of possibilities to apply the methods tailored to the specific question at hand. Table 4 provides an overview of the application of the methods difference-in-differences, regression discontinuity, and instrumental variables in STATA, R, and SPSS.

In order to familiarize oneself with the presented methods, we suggest replicating research findings that build on publicly available data. As this data is often cumbersome to collect and manipulate to the point where an analysis becomes meaningful, the

Table 3 Literature table for instrumental variables applications in business research

Author(s), year, journal	Title	Type of field experiment	Dependent variable	Independent variable(s), instrument	Findings
Bernstein, S. (2015) *The Journal of Finance*	Does Going Public Affect Innovation?	Quasi-natural field experiment	Number of patents, citations of patents, employee turnover	IPO completion, instrumented by likelihood of completion measured in NASDAQ fluctuation subsequent to IPO filing (book building phase)	Quality of internal innovation declines after IP; key innovators leave firm and often found competing companies
Cannon, J.N. (2014) *The Accounting Review*	Determinants of "Sticky Costs": An Analysis of Cost Behavior using United States Air Transportation Industry Data	Quasi-natural field experiment	(Log) Change in available transportation capacity	Change in demand and capacity unit cost change, instrumented by industry-level unit costs and selling price changes	Managers retain idle capacity and lower selling prices to utilize existing capacity when demand falls, but add capacity (rather than raise selling prices) when demand grows
Hui, S.K., Inman, J.J., Huang, Y., Suher, J. (2013) *Journal of Marketing*	The Effect of In-Store Travel Distance on Unplanned Spending: Applications to Mobile Promotion Strategies	Field experiment	Unplanned customer spending	Mobile promotion, in-store path length, instrumented by reference path determined by store layout and shoppers' planned purchases	Increasing path length by 10% increases unplanned spending by about 16.1% ($2.54); relocating physical products may increase unplanned spending by approximately 7%
Luong, H., Moshirian, F., Nguyen, L., Tian, X., Zhang, B. (2017) *Journal of Financial and Quantitative Analysis*	How Do Foreign Institutional Investors Enhance Firm Innovation?	Quasi-natural field experiment	Number of patents, citations of patents	Foreign institutional ownership, instrumented by varying membership in the MSCI All Country World Index foreign institutional ownership has a positive, causal effect on firm innovation	Foreign institutional ownership has a positive, causal effect on firm innovation

Table 4 Application of methods in standard software packages

Method	STATA	R	SPSS statistics
Difference-in-differences	**Manual application** Generate a "post" and a "treated" dummy variable. Generate an interacted variable from "post" and "treated" dummies. Regression with interacted dummy variable. **Package "diff"** *diff*: Estimate treatment effect based on a difference-in-difference method	**Manual application** Generate a "post" and a "treated" dummy variable. Generate an interacted variable from "post" and "treated" dummies. Regression with interacted dummy variable. **No package available**	**Manual application** Generate a "post" and a "treated" dummy variable. Generate an interacted variable from "post" and "treated" dummies. Regression with interacted dummy variable. **No package available**
Regression discontinuity	**Manual application** Create dummy variable for treatment status. Restrict sample to bandwidth around threshold. Regression with independent variable and the treatment status dummy. **Package "rdrobust"** *rdrobust*: Estimate a treatment effect based on regression discontinuity method. *rdbwselect*: Manual selection of the bandwidth around the threshold. *rdplot*: Plot data to depict the discontinuity	**Manual application** Create dummy variable for treatment status. Restrict sample to bandwidth around threshold. Regression with independent variable and the treatment status dummy. **Package "rdd"** *RDestimate*: Estimate a treatment effect based on regression discontinuity method. *IKbandwidth*: Optimal bandwidth according to Imbens-Kalyanaraman. *Plot.RD*: Plot data to depict the discontinuity	**Manual application** Create dummy variable for treatment status. Restrict sample to bandwidth around threshold. Regression with independent variable and the treatment status dummy. **No package available**

(continued)

Table 4 (continued)

Method	STATA	R	SPSS statistics
Instrumental variables	**Manual application** Estimate instrumented independent variable using the chosen instruments as explanatory variables (first stage) Estimate dependent variable using the instrumented independent variable as explanatory variable (second stage) **Built-in solution "ivregress"** *ivregress*: Estimate a treatment effect based on instrumental variables method **Package "ivreg2"** *ivreg2*: Estimate a treatment effect based on instrumental variables method; more sophisticated than "ivregress" **Built-in solution "ivprobit"** *ivprobit*: Estimate a treatment effect based on instrumental variables method with a binary dependent variable	**Manual application** Estimate instrumented independent variable using the chosen instruments as explanatory variables (first stage) Estimate dependent variable using the instrumented independent variable as explanatory variable (second stage) **Package "AER"** *ivreg*: Estimate a treatment effect based on instrumental variables method	**Manual application** Estimate instrumented independent variable using the chosen instruments as explanatory variables (first stage) Estimate dependent variable using the instrumented independent variable as explanatory variable (second stage) **Built-in solution "Two-stage Least Squares"** Select Two-Stage Least Squares from Regression Menu

following papers provide their applied data set ready for any researcher to use and replicate the findings. Furthermore, the authors of those studies also provide their code which provides a useful check for one own's replication efforts. Employing difference-in-differences designs in natural experiments, Calzada and Gil (2020) investigate the role of online news aggregators on news providers, De Silva et al. (2010) research the causal relationship of migration on wages, and Seiler et al. (2017) address the question of whether and how online word of mouth increases demand. Bronzini and Iachini (2014) and Shapiro (2018) are using regression discontinuity approaches; the former investigates whether incentives for R&D are effective and the latter derives causal claims with regard to advertising in the health insurance market. Lastly, instrumental variables approaches are used by Barron et al. (2020) who address the effect of home-sharing on house prices using Airbnb data and by Draca et al. (2011) who aim to disentangle the effect of police presence on crime using the London 2005 terror attacks as an exogeneous event.

Conclusions

Drawing causal inferences instead of purely relying on associations has gained importance in business practice and research in the past 20 years. Traditionally, conducting experiments in the controlled environment of a laboratory with participants who were randomly selected from a certain pool of candidates was the primary method to gain insights into causal relationships. More recently, field experiments have gained relevance for researchers and practitioners alike due to new (online) possibilities for conducting self-designed experiments outside the laboratory. Yet, as field experiments do not provide the same degree of randomization and controllability, exploiting such data in a way which still provides the means to draw causal conclusions requires a set of selected methods. Moreover, it becomes apparent that the farther one parts from the ideal field experiment, namely towards quasi, natural, or quasi-natural field experiments, the more effort and sophistication is likely to be required in analyzing the data. In order to tackle short-comings in a field experiment's design, three methods have become a standard set in business research: difference-in-differences, regression discontinuity, and instrumental variables. The difference-in-differences method lends itself often when treatment and control group(s) are not necessarily equal but are sufficiently similar so that they are affected by the same environmental conditions and, thus, move in parallel with regard to a set of selected variables. The regression discontinuity method becomes useful when one is able to exploit an arbitrary cut-off, a threshold value, which quasi-randomly divides observations into a treatment and control group so that a prerequisite of causal inferences (random assignment to treatment) is restored for a sufficiently large subsample of the data. Finally, the instrumental variables method helps to exploit data in which one may be confronted with self-selection into treatment and control group, if critical influential variables cannot be observed or if simultaneity is likely present. Those issues may be solved by identifying a "third," exogenous, variable which is able to estimate the treatment variable sufficiently well in order to address the present endogeneity problem.

The three methods presented in this chapter can be employed irrespective of the setting, that is, they may serve practitioners when evaluating the introduction of a new product in one or more markets, when analyzing the effect of a new legislation regarding advertising to children or when testing different purchase processes in the firm's online sales channels. This chapter aimed at providing an introduction to the three methods and their respective applications by providing intuitive, nontechnical explanations for each approach on how to exploit data from field experiments. Understanding, generating, and integrating insights from data created by field experiments will become more relevant even despite the growing availability of big data in business research and practice. Big data often only provides insights into correlational relationships potentially providing misleading guidance for decision making, creating the potential of misusing insights from big data, and leading to worse business decisions. Similar to Keele (2015), in a recent Harvard Business Review publication, Zoumpoulis et al. (2015) subsume that carefully conducted and analyzed field experiments can serve as a remedy and as a complement of increasing importance to make sense of purely correlational evidence from big data.

Cross-References

▶ Dealing with Endogeneity: A Nontechnical Guide for Marketing Researchers
▶ Experiments in Market Research
▶ Field Experiments

References

Abadie, A. (2020). Using synthetic controls: Feasibility, data requirements, and methodological aspects. *Journal of Economic Literature*. (forthcoming).

Abadie, A., Diamond, A., & Hainmueller, J. (2010). Synthetic control methods for comparative case studies: Estimating the effect of California's tobacco control program. *Journal of the American Statistical Association, 105*(490), 493–505.

Acemoglu, D., Johnson, S., Kermani, A., Kwak, J., & Mitton, T. (2016). The value of connections in turbulent times: Evidence from the United States. *Journal of Financial Economics, 121*(2), 368–391.

Aghamolla, C., & Li, N. (2018). Debt contract enforcement and conservatism: Evidence from a natural experiment. *Journal of Accounting Research, 56*(5), 1383–1416.

Angrist, J. D., & Krueger, A. B. (1991). Does compulsory school attendance affect schooling and earnings? *Quarterly Journal of Economics, 106*(4), 989–1014.

Angrist, J. D., & Krueger, A. B. (1999). Empirical strategies in labor economics. In O. Ashenfelter & D. Card (Eds.), *Handbook of labor economics* (Vol. 3, pp. 1277–1366). Amsterdam: North-Holland.

Angrist, J. D., & Pischke, J. S. (2009). *Mostly harmless econometrics*. Princeton: Princeton University Press.

Angrist, J. D., Imbens, G. W., & Rubin, D. B. (1996). Identification of causal effects using instrumental variables. *Journal of the American Statistical Association, 91*(434), 444–455.

Antonakis, J., Bendahan, S., Jacquart, P., & Lalive, R. (2010). On making causal claims: A review and recommendations. *The Leadership Quarterly, 21*(1), 1086–1120.

Armstrong, C. S., Glaeser, S., & Huang, S. (2019). *Controllability of risk and the design of incentive-compensation contracts.* Working paper. Available at SSRN 2896147.

Atanasov, V., & Black, B. (2016). Shock-based causal inference in corporate finance and accounting research. *Critical Finance Review, 5*(1), 207–304.

Barron, K., Kung, E., & Prosperpio, D. (2020). The effect of home-sharing on house prices and rents: Evidence from Airbnb. *Marketing Science, 40*(1), 23–47. Data available at: https://services.informs.org/dataset/mksc/download.php?doi=mksc.2020.1227

Bennedsen, M., Nielsen, K. M., Perez-Gonzalez, F., & Wolfenzon, D. (2007). Inside the family firm: The role of families in succession decisions and performance. *The Quarterly Journal of Economics, 122*(2), 647–691.

Bertrand, M., Karlan, D., Mullainathan, S., Shafir, E., & Zinman, J. (2010). What's advertising content worth? Evidence from a consumer credit marketing field experiment. *The Quarterly Journal of Economics, 125*(1), 263–306.

Blake, T., Nosko, C., & Tadelis, S. (2015). Consumer heterogeneity and paid search effectiveness: A large scale field experiment. *Econometrica, 83*(1), 155–174.

Bronzini, R., & Iachini, E. (2014). Are incentives for R&D effective? Evidence from a regression discontinuity approach. *American Economic Journal: Economic Policy, 6*(4), 100–134. Data available at: https://www.aeaweb.org/articles?id=10.1257/pol.6.4.100

Calzada, J., & Gil, R. (2020). What do news aggregators do? Evidence from Google News in Spain and Germany. *Marketing Science, 39*(1), 134–167. Data available at: https://services.informs.org/dataset/mksc/download.php?doi=mksc.2019.1150

Casas-Arce, P., Lourenço, S. M., & Martínez-Jerez, F. (2017a). The performance effect of feedback frequency and detail: Evidence from a field experiment in customer satisfaction. *Journal of Accounting Research, 55*(5), 1051–1088.

Casas-Arce, P., Martínez-Jerez, F., & Narayanan, V. G. (2017b). The impact of forward-looking metrics on employee decision-making: The case of customer lifetime value. *The Accounting Review, 92*(3), 31–56.

De Silva, D. G., McComb, R. P., Moh, Y.-K., Schiller, A. R., & Vargas, A. J. (2010). The effect of migration on wages: Evidence from a natural experiment. *American Economic Review, 100*(2), 321–326. Data available at: https://www.aeaweb.org/articles?id=10.1257/aer.100.2.321

Draca, M., Machin, S., & Witt, R. (2011). Panic on the streets of London: Police, crime and the July 2005 terror attacks. *American Economic Review, 101*(5), 2157–2181. Data available at: https://www.aeaweb.org/articles?id=10.1257/aer.101.5.2157

Flammer, C. (2015). Does corporate social responsibility lead to superior financial performance? A regression discontinuity approach. *Management Science, 61*(11), 2549–2568.

Gassen, J., & Muhn, M. (2018). *Financial transparency of private firms: Evidence from a randomized field experiment.* Working paper. Available at SSRN 3290710.

Gelman, A., & Imbens, G. W. (2019). Why high-order polynomials should not be used in regression discontinuity designs. *Journal of Business and Economic Statistics, 37*(3), 447–456.

Gill, M., Sridhar, S., & Grewal, R. (2017). Return on engagement initiatives: A study of a business-to-business mobile app. *Journal of Marketing, 81*(4), 45–66.

Giroud, X., Mueller, H. M., Stomper, A., & Westerkamp, A. (2012). Snow and leverage. *The Review of Financial Studies, 25*(3), 680–710.

Goldfarb, A., & Tucker, C. E. (2011). Privacy regulation and online advertising. *Management Science, 57*(1), 57–71.

Goldfarb, A., & Tucker, C. E. (2014). *Conducting research with quasi-experiments: A guide for marketers.* Working paper. Available at SSRN 2420920.

Harrison, G. W., & List, J. A. (2004). Field experiments. *Journal of Economic Literature, 42*(4), 1009–1055.

Heese, J., & Pérez-Calvazos, G. (2020). When the boss comes to town: The effect of headquarter's visits on facility-level misconduct. *The Accounting Review, 95*(6), 235–261.

Imbens, G. W., & Kalyanaraman, K. (2012). Optimal bandwidth choice for the regression discontinuity estimator. *The Review of Economic Studies, 79*(3), 933–959.

Keele, L. (2015). The discipline of identification. *PS: Political Science & Politics, 48*(1), 102–106.
Kenny, D. A. (1979). *Correlation and causality*. New York: Wiley-Interscience.
Keys, B. J., Mukherjee, T., Seru, A., & Vig, V. (2010). Did securitization lead to lax screening? Evidence from subprime loans. *The Quarterly Journal of Economics, 125*(1), 307–362.
Ladika, T., & Sautner, Z. (2020). Managerial short-termism and investment: Evidence from accelerated option vesting. *Review of Finance, 24*(2), 305–344.
Lawrence, A., Ryans, J., Sun, E., & Laptev, N. (2018). Earnings announcement promotions: A Yahoo Finance field experiment. *Journal of Accounting and Economics, 66*(2–3), 399–414.
Lee, D. S., McCrary, J., Moreira, M. J., & Porter, J. (2020). Valid t-ratio inference for IV. *ArXiv*, 2010.05058. Available from: http://arxiv.org/abs/2010.05058
Lourenço, S. M. (2019). Field experiments in managerial accounting research. *Foundations and Trends in Accounting, 14*(1), 1–72.
McCrary, J. (2008). Manipulation of the running variable in the regression discontinuity design: A density test. *Journal of Econometrics, 142*(2), 698–714.
Michels, J. (2017). Disclosure versus recognition: Inferences from subsequent events. *Journal of Accounting Research, 55*(1), 3–34.
Pattabhiramaiah, A., Sriram, S., & Manchanda, P. (2019). Paywalls: Monetizing online content. *Journal of Marketing, 83*(2), 19–36.
Presslee, A., Vance, T. W., & Webb, R. A. (2013). The effects of reward type on employee goal setting, goal commitment, and performance. *The Accounting Review, 88*(5), 1805–1831.
Roberts, M. R., & Whited, T. M. (2013). Endogeneity in empirical corporate finance. In G. M. Constantinides, M. Harris, & R. M. Stulz (Eds.), *Handbook of the economics of finance* (Vol. 2 (A), pp. 493–572). Oxford: North Holland.
Sanderson, E., & Windmeijer, F. (2016). A weak instrument F-test in linear IV models with multiple endogenous variables. *Journal of Econometrics, 190*(2), 212–221.
Seiler, S., Yao, S., & Wang, W. (2017). Does online word of mouth increase demand? (and how?) Evidence from a natural experiment. *Marketing Science, 36*(6), 838–861. Data available at: https://services.informs.org/dataset/mksc/download.php?doi=mksc.2017.1045
Shadish, W. R., Cook, T. D., & Campbell, D. T. (2002). *Experimental and quasi-experimental designs for generalized causal inference*. Boston: Houghton Mifflin.
Shapiro, B. T. (2018). Advertising in health insurance markets. *Marketing Science, 39*(3), 587–611. Data available at: https://services.informs.org/dataset/mksc/download.php?doi=mksc.2018.1086
Shriver, S. K., Nair, H. S., & Hofstetter, R. (2013). Social ties and user-generated content: Evidence from an online social network. *Management Science, 59*(6), 1435–1443.
Spearman, C. (1904). The proof and measurement of association between two things. *The American Journal of Psychology, 15*(1), 72–101.
Stock, J. H., & Yogo, M. (2005). Asymptotic distributions of instrumental variables statistics with many instruments. In D. W. K. Andrews & J. H. Stock (Eds.), *Identification and inference for econometric models*. New York: Cambridge University Press.
Verbeek, M. (2008). *A guide to modern econometrics* (3rd ed.). West Sussex: John Wiley & Sons Ltd.
Wooldridge, J. M. (2012). *Introductory econometrics: A modern approach* (4th ed.). Mason: South-Western Cengage.
Zoumpoulis, S., Simester, D., & Evgeniou, T. (2015 November 12). Run field experiments to make sense of your big data. *Harvard Business Review*. Available from: https://hbr.org/2015/11/run-field-experiments-to-make-sense-of-your-big-data. Accessed 15 Sept 2020.

Mediation Analysis in Experimental Research

Nicole Koschate-Fischer and Elisabeth Schwille

Contents

Introduction	858
Conceptual and Statistical Basics of Mediation Analysis	859
The Single Mediator Model	860
Mediation Models Including More Than One Mediator: The Parallel and Serial Multiple Mediator Model	871
Mediation Models Including a Moderator: Conditional Process Models	879
Further Mediation Models	887
Strengthening Causal Inference in Mediation Analysis	891
Strengthening Causal Inference Through Design	891
Strengthening Causal Inference Through the Collection of Further Evidence	893
Strengthening Causal Inference Through Statistical Methods	894
Questions Arising When Implementing Mediation Analysis	894
Sample Size and Power in Mediation Analysis	895
Mean Centering in Conditional Process Analysis	896
Coding of Categorical Independent Variables	897
Regression Analysis Versus Structural Equation Modeling	898
Software Tools for Mediation Analysis	900
Summary	900
Cross-References	901
References	901

Abstract

This chapter introduces the conceptual and statistical basics of mediation analysis in the context of experimental research. Adopting the respective terminology, mediation analysis can be referred to as an array of quantitative methods developed to investigate the causal mechanism(s) through which an independent variable influences a dependent variable. The chapter takes a regression-based

---

N. Koschate-Fischer (✉) · E. Schwille
University of Erlangen-Nuremberg, Nuremberg, Germany
e-mail: nicole.koschate-fischer@fau.de; elisabeth.schwille@fau.de

approach to mediation analysis and focuses on mediation models likely to be tested in experiments (i.e., the single mediator model, parallel and serial multiple mediator models, and conditional process models). Yet, the scope of mediation analysis beyond an experimental setting will also be touched upon. Furthermore, the chapter addresses the question how to strengthen causal inference in mediation analysis through design, the collection of additional evidence, and statistical methods. It closes with a discussion of common topics of relevance when implementing mediation analysis such as sample size and power, mean centering in conditional process analysis, coding of categorical independent variables, advantages and disadvantages of a regression-based approach to mediation analysis, and software options to perform mediation analysis.

Keywords

Mediation analysis · Conditional process analysis · Regression analysis · Bootstrapping · Experiments

Introduction

One focal goal of market research is to gain insight into whether and why marketing stimuli, such as price or advertising, affect consumer behavior. That is, it is not only important to demonstrate the causal effect of a marketing measure on consumer behavior (e.g., through conducting experiments, Koschate-Fischer and Schandelmeier 2014; chapter ▶ "Field Experiments" by Valli et al., this volume), but it is also crucial to understand the causal mechanism(s) through which an effect occurs. A deeper understanding of the "why" or "how" of an effect is often gained through qualitative methods (e.g., focus groups or interviews). This chapter provides an introduction to regression-based mediation analysis, an array of quantitative methods developed to investigate the causal mechanism(s) through which an independent variable influences a dependent variable, which has gained increasing popularity in experimental research in marketing and market research over the last decade (e.g., Cavanaugh 2014; Koschate-Fischer et al. 2012, 2016; Savary et al. 2014; Touré-Tillery and McGill 2015).

The remainder of this chapter is structured as follows: Starting with the most simple mediation model, the single mediator model, the conceptual and statistical principles of mediation analysis are explained. These will then be applied to mediation models including multiple mediating variables (multiple mediator models) as well as a moderating variable (conditional process models). Further mediation models that take into account additional variables, time (longitudinal mediation models), and nested data (multilevel mediation models) are also briefly addressed. Subsequently, an overview is given of how to strengthen causal inference through design, the collection of further evidence, and statistical methods. The chapter closes with a discussion of selected questions arising when implementing mediation analysis.

Conceptual and Statistical Basics of Mediation Analysis

Adopting the terminology from an experimental context, *mediation* refers to a situation in which the effect of an independent variable on a dependent variable is transmitted through an intervening variable, the *mediator* (e.g., MacKinnon et al. 2007b; Preacher 2015; see also Mathieu and Taylor 2006). A mediator is a third variable included in the conceptual framework describing the simple effect of an independent variable on a dependent variable and can conceptually, yet not necessarily statistically (MacKinnon et al. 2000), be distinguished from other third variables: confounding variables, covariates, and moderators (MacKinnon et al. 2007b). *Confounding variables* influence both the independent variable and the dependent variable and, if unaccounted for (i.e., omitted from the model), bias the estimate of the relationship between the independent variable and the dependent variable. In an experimental context, *covariates* (also called concomitant variables) are variables that share variance with the dependent variable and controlling for them improves the estimation of the relationship between the independent variable and the dependent variable (Miller and Chapman 2001). *Moderators* influence the effect of the independent variable on the dependent variable, such that the magnitude or sign of the relationship changes depending on the values of the moderator.

In marketing and market research, mediators are likely to be psychological processes evoked by marketing stimuli affecting consumer judgment and behavior such as brand-, other-, or self-related cognitions and emotions. We agree with MacKinnon (2008) that mediators should be selected a priori based on theoretical considerations and the careful review of existing literature. If such a basis is not available, possible mediators could also be identified through, for example, qualitative interviews, and tested in subsequent quantitative studies. In either case, it is of paramount importance to carefully consider whether the mediator is a variable that can be causally affected by the independent variable and can, in turn, causally affect the dependent variable. Thus, stable consumer traits, such as cultural norms or values, cannot be mediators (unless the mediating variable denotes a change in such relatively stable traits, see Koschate-Fischer et al. 2017) and the mediator and the dependent variable have to be clearly distinguishable from each other (Pieters 2017).

The concepts and analyses described in this chapter will be illustrated with the help of a hypothetical experiment exploring the effect of sales promotions on consumers' positive word-of-mouth (WOM) intentions. Specifically, the experiment investigates whether a "free gift with purchase" promotion (e.g., "Receive a free summer gift with any $10 purchase") increases positive WOM intentions through providing hedonic benefits to consumers (e.g., making the shopping experience more interesting and fun), a research question derived from the benefit congruency framework of sales promotion effectiveness (Chandon et al. 2000), and literature on WOM generation (Berger 2014). The independent variable in this example is manipulated on two levels (small vs. large free gift) and a between-subject design is employed. Hence, there are two experimental groups to which participants are randomly assigned. In both groups, participants read a scenario in which they imagine they are browsing through an online store to buy a T-shirt. The store offers a wide variety of different T-shirts and brands. They encounter a banner on which it says that for each T-shirt of a specific brand bought today, consumers receive a free gift card for a future purchase in the online shop. In the small free gift condition, the banner states that participants will receive a "$2 gift card with every T-shirt," and in the large free gift condition, it states they will receive a "$10 gift card with every T-shirt." Participants are then asked about the hedonic benefits the sales promotion provides them and their willingness to positively talk about and recommend the promoted products by answering questions such as how inclined they are to like social media content referring to the promoted products. Hence, while the independent variable is manipulated, the mediator as well as the dependent variable are measured, which makes the experiment a measurement-of-mediation design (Spencer et al. 2005). Note that, as the experiment itself, the data the following analyses are based upon are hypothetical, i.e., simulated. Hence, the results reported do not allow to draw conclusions as to the ability of free gifts to stipulate positive WOM intentions through increasing hedonic benefits.

The Single Mediator Model

To illustrate the conceptual and statistical idea of mediation analysis, the most simple mediation model, the single mediator model, is described in the following section. It will be extended in later sections of the chapter by including additional mediating (multiple mediator models) and a moderating variable (conditional process models).

Conceptual Description of the Single Mediator Model

To explain the single mediator model, we start with a conceptual diagram (Hayes 2018) showing the simple causal effect of an independent variable X on a dependent variable Y (Fig. 1). In mediation analysis, this relationship is referred to as the *total effect* of X on Y.

In the single mediator model, this basic causal relationship is extended by a mediator M, which is causally located between X and Y (see Fig. 2). By including M, the total effect is split into direct and indirect components: X affects Y indirectly through M (path a and path b). In addition, X also affects Y directly (path c'). Together, path a and path b are referred to as the *indirect effect* of X on Y. The indirect effect indicates the effect of X on Y that is transmitted through M. Path c' denotes the *direct effect* of X on Y, which corresponds to the effect of X on Y that is

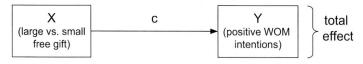

Fig. 1 The conceptual diagram of the total effect of X on Y

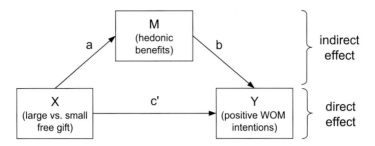

Fig. 2 The conceptual diagram of the single mediator model depicting the direct as well as indirect effect of X on Y

not transmitted through M. The direct effect (path c') differs from the total effect (path c) in that it estimates the effect of X on Y while controlling for the indirect effect of X on Y through M. The total effect, however, denotes the overall effect of X on Y.

Figures 1 and 2 illustrate these concepts with the help of the free gift example introduced above. In this example, the total effect refers to the overall effect of the large (vs. small) free gift on positive WOM intentions without taking into account a possible mediator. The indirect effect denotes the effect of the large (vs. small) free gift on positive WOM intentions that is transmitted through hedonic benefits. It is hypothesized to be positive, because a large (vs. small) free gift provides hedonic benefits to consumers which, in turn, are associated with increased positive WOM intentions. The direct effect denotes the effect of the large (vs. small) free gift on positive WOM intentions which is not transmitted through hedonic benefits.

Statistical Description of the Single Mediator Model

The statistical diagrams (Hayes 2018) for the total effect and the single mediator model are depicted in Fig. 3. The diagrams can be described by a set of linear equations.

The total effect (see panel A in Fig. 3) is quantified by

$$Y = i_y + cX + e_y \tag{1}$$

where i_y denotes the intercept and c the effect of X on Y. The error term of Y is denoted as e_y.

To describe the single mediator model (see panel B in Fig. 3), two equations are necessary, one predicting M and the other predicting Y:

$$M = i_m + aX + e_m \tag{2}$$

$$Y = i_y + bM + c'X + e_y \tag{3}$$

The i parameters in Eqs. 2 and 3 denote the intercepts, a estimates the effect of X on M, b estimates the effect of M on Y controlling for X, and c' estimates the effect of X on Y controlling for M. The error terms are denoted by the e parameters, respectively. Note that i_y as well as e_y in Eqs. 1 and 3 are not equivalent.

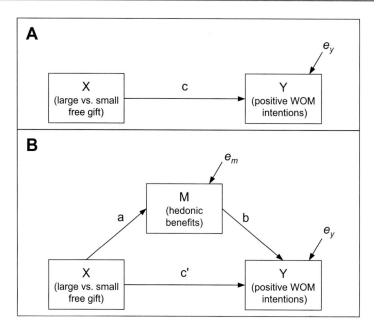

Fig. 3 The statistical diagrams of the total effect of X on Y (panel A), as well as the single mediator model depicting the direct as well as indirect effect of X on Y (panel B)

The indirect effect corresponds to the product of path a and path b, i.e., ab. The total effect equals the sum of the indirect effect and the direct effect (Eq. 4). Hence, the indirect effect can be also expressed as the difference between the total effect and the direct effect (Eq. 5):

$$\text{Total effect}: c = ab + c' \tag{4}$$

$$\text{Indirect effect}: ab = c - c' \tag{5}$$

The effects are usually reported as unstandardized regression coefficients, especially when X is dichotomous (as in the free gift example), as standardized coefficients are not meaningful in this case (Hayes 2018).

In the previously introduced free gift example, X is coded with "0" (small free gift) and "1" (large free gift). Hence, a total effect of $c = 0.218$ denotes that in comparison to a small free gift, a large free gift increases positive WOM intentions by 0.218 units. An indirect effect of $ab = 0.103$ indicates that a large (vs. a small) free gift increases positive WOM intentions by 0.103 units through its effect on hedonic benefits which, in turn, is associated with positive WOM intentions. A direct effect of $c' = 0.115$ shows that controlling for the indirect effect of a large (vs. small) free gift on positive WOM intentions through hedonic benefits, a large (vs. small) free gift increases positive WOM intentions by 0.115 units. As can be seen, the total effect $c = 0.218$ is the sum of the indirect effect $ab = 0.103$ and the direct effect $c' = 0.115$, as $0.103 + 0.115 = 0.218$.

Please note that the direct effect c' does not have to be smaller (i.e., closer to zero) than the total effect c even though the total effect c is the sum of both, the indirect effect ab and the direct effect c'. There are situations when the total effect c is equal in size to the direct effect c' or even smaller, for instance, if M acts as a suppressor (MacKinnon et al. 2000).

Statistical Inference for the Single Mediator Model

Various approaches have been suggested to determine whether or not mediation occurs, that is, whether the indirect effect ab is significantly different from zero (for an overview, see Hayes and Scharkow 2013; MacKinnon et al. 2002). MacKinnon et al. (2002) classify these according to the coefficients tested within the respective approaches: While the *causal steps approach* (Baron and Kenny 1986; Judd and Kenny 1981) establishes mediation through testing whether the individual paths in a mediation model are significantly different from zero, the *difference in coefficients approach* and the *product of coefficients approach* test whether the indirect effect (as indicated by the difference $c-c'$ or the product ab) is different from zero. Each approach will be described subsequently.

The causal steps approach consists of a series of regressions run separately and sequentially in order to demonstrate mediation. Mediation is logically inferred if, first, the total effect c is significant, second, path a is significant, third, path b is significant, and, fourth, the direct effect c' is not significant (Judd and Kenny 1981) or considerably reduced in size as compared to the total effect c (Baron and Kenny 1986).

The causal steps approach has been extraordinarily influential. The paper illustrating it – Baron and Kenny (1986) – is one of the most cited papers in the social sciences. However, it has also been criticized heavily (e.g., Hayes 2009; MacKinnon et al. 2000; Rucker et al. 2011; Shrout and Bolger 2002; Zhao et al. 2010). One major criticism is that the method requires a significant total effect to establish mediation ("an effect to be mediated"). It has been argued that there are situations in which significant mediation occurs even though the total effect of X on Y is not significant. Hence, requiring an effect to be mediated impairs the power of the approach (MacKinnon et al. 2002). Other criticism refers to the fact that testing the individual paths in the mediation model separately is statistically as well as conceptually different from directly testing the indirect effect: Testing the constituent paths answers the question whether they, considered individually, are different from zero. Testing the indirect effect, however, answers the question whether the indirect effect as a whole is different from zero. It might be intuitive to assume that, if the paths comprising the indirect effect are significant, the indirect effect must also be significant. However, this is not necessarily the case. Hence, to establish mediation, the focus should be on testing the indirect effect.

As opposed to the causal-steps approach, the difference in coefficients approach and the product of coefficients approach directly test the indirect effect. While the difference in coefficients approach does so using the right side of Eq. 5, $c-c'$, the product of coefficients approach refers to the left side of Eq. 5, ab. The indirect effect can be tested through computing its standard error which can then be used to create a test statistic or confidence interval. The indirect effect is assumed to be significantly different from zero if the value of the test statistic exceeds some critical value of the normal distribution, or if the confidence interval around the indirect effect excludes zero. The latter approach is based on the following interpretation of a confidence interval: If a study were replicated many times and a confidence interval were computed around the indirect effect in each study, respectively, a large percentage of the confidence intervals obtained (e.g., 95% for a 95% confidence interval) would include the true value of the indirect effect. Hence, if zero is included in a confidence interval around the estimated indirect effect, zero is a fairly plausible value for the true indirect effect. If zero is not included, however, zero is a rather implausible value.

Several different methods have been suggested to estimate the standard error for both expressions, ab as well as $c-c'$ (MacKinnon et al. 2002). The most prominent of those methods is probably the one suggested by Sobel (1982), which is based on the *delta method* and used in the so-called *Sobel test*. With se_a and se_b being the standard errors of the coefficients a and b, respectively, to estimate the standard error of the indirect effect ab, Sobel (1982) suggests the following (first order delta estimator):

$$se_{ab} = \sqrt{a^2 se_b^2 + b^2 se_a^2} \qquad (6)$$

The test statistic Z used in the Sobel test is then

$$Z = \frac{ab}{se_{ab}} \qquad (7)$$

If Z exceeds the critical value of the z-distribution (for a two-sided test and $\alpha = 0.05$, $z_{crit} = \pm 1.96$), the indirect effect ab is assumed to be significantly different from zero. For an overview of other methods to compute standard errors and corresponding test statistics of ab and $c-c'$, see MacKinnon et al. (2002).

The values necessary to compute the Sobel test can be obtained through two ordinary least squares (OLS) regressions fitting the linear equations illustrated in Eqs. 2 and 3. In the free gift example, these regressions yield the following estimates: $a = 0.135$, $b = 0.767$, $se_a = 0.049$, and $se_b = 0.079$. Consequently, se_{ab} can be estimated as $\sqrt{0.135^2 \times 0.079^2 + 0.767^2 \times 0.049^2} = 0.0391$ (see Eq. 6). The test statistic Z is computed as $\frac{0.135 \times 0.767}{0.0391} = 2.650$ (see Eq. 7). As $Z > z_{crit}$ ($z_{crit} = 1.96$), it can be concluded that there is a significant and positive indirect effect of a large (vs. small) free gift on positive WOM intentions through hedonic benefits. That is, as compared to consumers receiving a small free gift, the consumers receiving a large free gift perceive greater hedonic benefits ($a = 0.135$), which, in turn, is associated with increased intentions to positively talk about and recommend the promoted products ($b = 0.767$). Note that one would obtain the same indirect effect if the regression coefficients denoting path a and path b were negative. Hence, although not being the focus when testing ab, the individual path coefficients a and b should by no means be ignored.

One issue with the Sobel test is that inference is based on the assumption that the product of two normally distributed random variables (e.g., regression coefficients) is normally distributed as well. That means, it is assumed that the sampling distribution of the indirect effect ab is normal. However, the sampling distribution of the indirect effect differs from the standard normal distribution with regard to its skewness and kurtosis, especially in small samples (e.g., Bollen and Stine 1990; Kisbu-Sakarya et al. 2014). Hence, relying on the assumption that the sampling distribution of the indirect effect is normal may lead to false conclusions about mediation (MacKinnon et al. 2002, 2004).

Taking this concern into account, MacKinnon and colleagues (e.g., MacKinnon et al. 2007a) developed approaches to compute se_{ab} that are based on the assumption that the indirect effect ab follows the distribution of the product of two normally distributed random variables. Simulation studies show that as compared to the normal theory approach, this *distribution of the product approach* leads to more accurate Type I error rates and higher statistical power to detect a possible indirect effect (MacKinnon et al. 2002), as well as to more precise confidence intervals (MacKinnon et al. 2004). However, the distribution of the product approach is not always easily applicable to more complicated mediation models (Taylor et al. 2008; Preacher and Hayes 2008).

Another set of methods establishes mediation by creating confidence intervals around the indirect effect through resampling (Monte Carlo resampling, Preacher and Selig 2012; jackknife resampling, MacKinnon et al. 2004; bootstrapping, Bollen and Stine 1990). Of these, the presumably most commonly applied method in consumer science is *bootstrapping* (Pieters 2017). The particularly convenient characteristic of bootstrapping is that, unlike the previously presented approaches, it does not require any assumptions to be made about the distribution of the indirect effect, nor does it rely on an estimate of the standard error of the indirect effect. It is a resampling procedure, which means that the distribution of the indirect effect is empirically obtained, that is, obtained from the data itself. To do so, k bootstrap samples ($k_{\min} = 1,000$, Shrout and Bolger 2002; $k_{\max} = 10,000$, Hayes 2018; $k_{\text{recommended}} > 5,000$, Hayes 2018) with N cases each are drawn with replacement from the original dataset (N denotes the original sample size). From each bootstrap sample k, the indirect effect ab_k is estimated. As the bootstrap sample is drawn with replacement (i.e., a participant from the original sample may be selected not at all, once, or multiple times in a bootstrap sample), the individual bootstrap samples will not only differ from the original sample, but also from each other. Consequently, the k estimates of the indirect effect vary. Sorting them from smallest to largest creates a distribution of the indirect effect. This distribution can then be used to compute a confidence interval around the point estimate of ab estimated from the original sample.

Figure 4 depicts such an empirically obtained distribution of the indirect effect from the free gift example. It is based on $k = 5,000$ bootstrap samples. The point estimate for the indirect effect from the original sample is $ab = 0.1035$. Three types of bootstrap confidence intervals are depicted: the percentile bootstrap confidence interval, the bias-corrected bootstrap confidence interval, and the bias-corrected and accelerated bootstrap confidence interval.

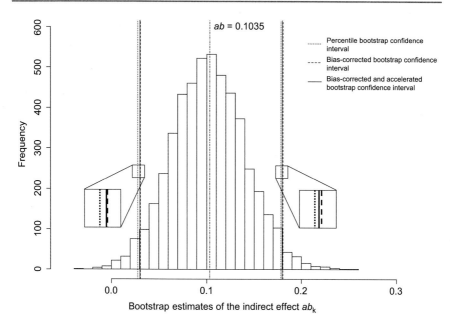

Fig. 4 Distribution of 5000 bootstrap estimates of an indirect effect ($ab = 0.1035$) and the corresponding percentile, bias-corrected, and bias-corrected and accelerated bootstrap confidence intervals (p.bci$_{95\%}$ [0. 0281, 0.1781], bc.bci$_{95\%}$ [0.0310; 0.1805], bca.bci$_{95\%}$ [0.304; 0.1797])

Indicated by the two dotted lines are the lower and upper limits of the percentile bootstrap confidence interval (p.bci), which denotes the values at position $k \times \left(\frac{\alpha}{2}\right)$ (lower limit, ll) and $k \times \left(1 - \frac{\alpha}{2}\right) + 1$ (upper limit, ul). Setting $\alpha = 0.05$, the lower limit of the percentile bootstrap confidence interval (p.bci.ll) corresponds to $5,000 \times \left(\frac{0.05}{2}\right) = 125$, that is, the 125th value in the sorted distribution (p.bci.ll = 0.0281 in Fig. 4); the upper limit of the percentile bootstrap interval (p.bci.ul) corresponds to $5,000 \times \left(1 - \frac{0.05}{2}\right) + 1 = 4,876$, that is, the 4876th value (p.bci.ul = 0.1781 in Fig. 4). Note that due to the skewness of the distribution, bootstrap confidence intervals are usually asymmetric unlike confidence intervals based on the standard normal distribution. As the confidence interval does not include zero (p.bci$_{95\%}$ [0.0281; 0.1781]), zero is not a plausible value for the indirect effect. Hence, the indirect effect is assumed to be significantly different from zero.

In this example, testing the indirect effect with a percentile bootstrap confidence interval leads to the same conclusion as the Sobel test: The effect of the large (vs. small) free gift on positive WOM intentions is significantly mediated by hedonic benefits ($ab = 0.1035$, p.bci$_{95\%}$ [0.0281; 0.1781]). This reflects the notion that although there may be inconsistent results from different approaches to test mediation, they quite frequently agree (Hayes and Scharkow 2013).

As mentioned, Fig. 4 also depicts the bias-corrected bootstrap confidence interval (bc.bci, broken lines) and the bias-corrected and accelerated bootstrap confidence interval (bca.bci, solid lines, Efron 1987). The bias correction adjusts the confidence limits for differences between the point estimate of the indirect effect from the original data set ab and the bootstrap estimates of the indirect effect ab_k (bc.bci$_{95\%}$ [0.0310; 0.1805]). The bias-corrected and accelerated bootstrap confidence interval additionally accounts for the skew of the bootstrapped distribution (bca.bci$_{95\%}$ [0.304; 0.1797]).

The bootstrap approach to mediation analysis has some disadvantages: It requires raw data, which may not always be available. In addition, as the resampling process is random, the limits of the confidence interval may slightly differ when the analysis is repeated. Finally, statistical software has to be set up to perform bootstrapping. However, statistical software generally allows one to save bootstrap estimates for further analysis or to specify a seed to replicate the bootstrap samples. Furthermore, there are an increasing number of software options to perform mediation analysis with bootstrapping.

Most importantly, though, bootstrapping has considerable statistical advantages over normal theory based approaches and the distribution of the product approach: As noted, it makes no assumptions about the sampling distribution of the indirect effect, but empirically determines it through resampling. As a consequence, bootstrap confidence intervals have been shown to be more accurate and perform better with regards to statistical power while maintaining reasonable Type I error rates (Fritz and MacKinnon 2007; Hayes and Scharkow 2013; MacKinnon et al. 2004). The bias-corrected confidence interval has been demonstrated to perform best with regard to power, although somewhat liberally under some conditions (Fritz et al. 2012). Researchers reluctant to take this risk may use the percentile bootstrap confidence interval which is more powerful than the Sobel test, but less liberal than the bias-corrected bootstrap confidence interval. Furthermore, bootstrapping is relatively easy to apply to more complex mediation models (Taylor et al. 2008; Williams and MacKinnon 2008). Hence, in accordance with many others (e.g., Hayes 2018; MacKinnon 2008; Jose 2013), we recommend bootstrapping confidence intervals for testing mediation over normal theory based methods and the distribution of the product approach.

Assumptions of the Single Mediator Model

OLS regression-based mediation analysis relies on assumptions that apply to OLS regression analysis in general (see chapter ▶ "Regression Analysis" by Skiera et al., this volume). Some of these assumptions are particularly crucial in mediation analysis. For instance, it has been shown that measurement error can heavily bias estimates of the indirect effect, especially if it affects the mediator. While this can lead to either overestimation or underestimation of effects in a mediator model, in experimental settings, measurement error affecting the mediator tends to lead to underestimation of the indirect effect (Fritz et al. 2016). Mediation analysis with structural equation modeling accounts for this issue to some degree as it enables measurement error to be estimated (MacKinnon 2008; see also ▶ "Crafting Survey Research: A Systematic Process for Conducting Survey Research," this volume).

Omitting causally relevant variables in mediation analysis can similarly bias the estimate of the indirect effect (see also chapter ▶ "Dealing with Endogeneity: A

Nontechnical Guide for Marketing Researchers" by Ebbes et al., this volume). Pieters (2017) differs between bias as a result of pre- and posttreatment confounding variables. Pretreatment confounding variables are independent of the treatment, that is, the independent variable, but affect the mediator and the dependent variable. One example of pretreatment confounding variables pointed out by Pieters (2017) is common method bias, that is, common variance in the mediator and the dependent variable due to being measured in a similar way or in close proximity to each other. Posttreatment confounding variables are consequences of the treatment and affect the dependent variable. Hence, they are omitted mediators. In experimental studies, the omission of a confounding variable affecting the mediator and the dependent variable likely leads to an overestimation of the indirect effect (Fritz et al. 2016). Pieters (2017) concludes that bias resulting from confounding variables can be addressed through employing different methods to measure the mediator and the dependent variable, the inclusion of possible confounding variables as covariates in the mediation model, the use of advanced statistical methods that account for the influence of unobserved confounding variables on mediation (for an overview, see MacKinnon and Pirlott 2015, see also chapter ▶ "Dealing with Endogeneity: A Nontechnical Guide for Marketing Researchers" by Ebbes et al., this volume), and by running studies in which the mediator is manipulated (for an overview, see Pirlott and MacKinnon 2016).

To address violations of the assumption of homoskedasticity, robust regression analysis (e.g., Hayes and Cai 2007) could be applied which corrects for possible bias in the standard errors of the regression coefficients. However, note that bootstrapping does not rely on estimates of the standard errors of the regression coefficients comprising the indirect effect, but solely on estimates of the regression coefficients which are unaffected by heteroskedasticity (Darlington and Hayes 2017). Hence, the bootstrap approach to testing mediation is generally robust against violations of the assumption of homoskedasticity.

Another assumption in mediation analysis requires that the causal order of variables be correctly specified (i.e., the causal order is assumed to be unidirectional). To test this assumption, it would be necessary to demonstrate that X causes M, which in turn causes Y. The section on causal inference in this chapter will address this issue in greater detail.

Furthermore, it is generally assumed that X and M do not interact to predict Y. Hence, the interaction between X and M is not included in the linear equation predicting Y (see Eq. 3, but see also Fig. 5 for a model including this interaction). That means, neither is the direct effect of X on Y assumed to be affected by M, nor is the effect of M on Y assumed to be affected by X. However, it has been argued that this is not justified and that the interaction between X and M should be estimated in mediation analysis (e.g., Kraemer et al. 2002, 2008; Valeri and VanderWeele 2013), for instance, to test whether mediation differs across levels of X. The questions of when to estimate the interaction term XM in mediation analysis and how to estimate the direct and indirect effects in such a case are addressed by VanderWeele (2015).

Additional assumptions in mediation analysis refer to the correct timing and level of the mediated effect (MacKinnon 2008). Specifically, conclusions based on a

Fig. 5 Conceptual (panel A) and statistical diagram (panel B) of a single mediator model including the interaction between the independent variable X and the mediator M

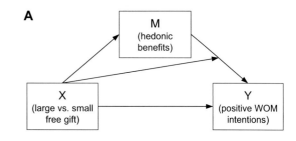

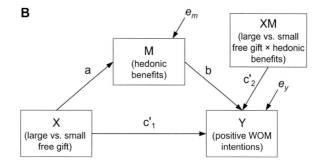

single (as compared to repeated) assessment of X, M, or Y assume that the variables and relationships of interest do not change over time. In addition, inferring mediation without taking into account possible nesting of the data (e.g., consumers nested in geographical locations or repeated measurements nested in one participant) relies on the assumption that mediation is unaffected by such nesting.

Classifying Mediation

Mediation can be classified depending on the significance of the indirect and the direct effect. Zhao et al. (2010) broadly differentiate between *mediation* (if the indirect effect is significant) and *nonmediation* (if the indirect effect is not significant), and further distinguish different types of mediation and nonmediation depending on the significance of the direct effect as well as whether the direct effect and indirect effect have the same sign (see Table 1). Competitive mediation has also been referred to as inconsistent mediation (MacKinnon et al. 2000) or suppression (Shrout and Bolger 2002). Baron and Kenny (1986) refer to complementary mediation as partial mediation and to indirect-only mediation as complete mediation, for which the attributes "perfect" or "full" are also used. According to Zhao et al. (2010), different types of mediations give hints for subsequent theory building. Specifically, complementary and competitive mediation as well as direct-only nonmediation may indicate that a relevant mediator or moderator may have been omitted from the mediation model. However, when drawing theoretical conclusions or classifying mediation based on the significance of the direct effect, note that a nonsignificant direct effect may also be the result of too little power (Rucker et al. 2011). Furthermore, mind that qualitatively classifying mediation as, for example, partial,

Table 1 Classification of mediation according to Zhao et al. (2010)

Classification		1. Is the indirect effect significant?	2. Is the direct effect significant?	3. Do direct and indirect effects have equal signs?
Mediation	Complementary mediation	Yes	Yes	Yes
	Competitive mediation	Yes	Yes	No
	Indirect-only mediation	Yes	No	–
Non-mediation	Direct-only nonmediation	No	Yes	–
	No-effect nonmediation	No	No	–

complete, or competitive, does not allow conclusions to be drawn about the magnitude of an indirect effect.

Effect Size

To quantify mediation, several effect size measures have been proposed with a comprehensive overview provided by Preacher and Kelley (2011). However, none of the measures is without limitations. For instance, effect size measures and their corresponding variance estimates may be inaccurate unless sample size or effect size is large (e.g., $N > 500$, MacKinnon et al. 1995), may not be applicable to specific variable metrics (e.g., exclusively suitable for dichotomous X, Hansen and MacNeal 1996), or may not work in any mediation model more complex than the single mediator model (e.g., Wen and Fan 2015). Hence, we agree with Preacher and Kelley (2011) that, when reported, effect size measures have to be carefully discussed with regard to whether they are bounded (i.e., whether there is an upper and lower limit of possible values of the measure), robust to changes in scales (i.e., standardized) as well as sample size, precise (as indicated by, e.g., a confidence interval), and meaningfully scaled.

Variable Metrics

OLS regression-based mediation analysis can incorporate dichotomous, multi-categorical, or continuous independent variables. A multicategorical independent variable can be included as a set of indicator variables, each representing, for example, a pairwise comparison with a reference group (Hayes and Preacher 2014). Different strategies to create indicator variables will briefly be discussed in the section on coding of categorical independent variables later in the chapter. Including a dichotomous or multicategorical mediator or dependent variable goes beyond what OLS regression-based mediation analysis can accommodate. Yet, the equations presented above can be rewritten for logit models and logistic regressions (Iacobucci 2012; MacKinnon 2008). Note, that in this case, Eq. 5 does not hold anymore, as the difference in coefficients $c-c'$ may be biased due to scale boundedness (MacKinnon and Dwyer 1993). Applying generalized linear models to mediation analysis further allows for the analysis of mediation models with mediators and outcomes taking the form of counts (e.g., VanderWeele and Vansteelandt 2014) or survival rates (e.g., VanderWeele 2015). Additionally, several approaches to incorporate nonnormally distributed but continuous variables into mediation analysis have been described (e.g., Yuan and MacKinnon 2014).

Mediation Models Including More Than One Mediator: The Parallel and Serial Multiple Mediator Model

Some research questions require inclusion of more than one mediator into the conceptual model. It could be of interest, for instance, to pit competing explanations for an effect of X on Y against each other or to test whether an effect of X on Y operates through multiple mechanisms at once. The single mediator model can be extended to include multiple mediators in two different ways: They can be assumed to be causally independent of each other and work in parallel, or form a causal chain from X to Y and operate in serial. The former is referred to as the *parallel multiple mediator model* and will be described next. The latter is referred to as the *serial multiple mediator model* and will be described subsequently. General notes on statistical inference in multiple mediator models are included at the end of this section on mediation models with more than one mediator.

Conceptual Description of the Parallel Multiple Mediator Model

In the parallel multiple mediator model, X is assumed to affect Y through two or more mediators M_i, which are assumed *not* to be causally related (see Fig. 6). Yet, they are also not expected to be completely uncorrelated as they share a common cause. Parallel multiple mediator models are hence particularly suited to disentangle the respective mediating ability of multiple (ideally not too strongly) correlated mediators from each other (Preacher and Hayes 2008).

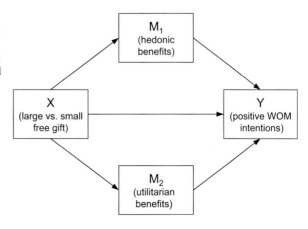

Fig. 6 The conceptual diagram of a parallel multiple mediator model in which the effect of X on Y is transmitted through two mediators M_1 and M_2 operating in parallel

For instance, in the free gift example, it might be of interest to investigate whether the increase in positive WOM intentions in response to the large (vs. small) free gift is solely explained by hedonic benefits or also by utilitarian benefits (e.g., making a purchase decision more efficient because of reduced search costs). In order to investigate these alternative explanations, a second mediator (utilitarian benefits) is added to the previously tested single mediator model, which included hedonic benefits as the only mediator. Furthermore, since it is not assumed that there is a causal relationship between hedonic and utilitarian benefits, the two mediators are hypothesized to act in parallel.

Just like the single mediator model, the parallel multiple mediator model can be separated into indirect and direct components. However, there are multiple indirect components in parallel multiple mediator models, namely, the *specific indirect effects* $a_i b_i$ associated with each mediator M_i, respectively. The crucial characteristic of the specific indirect effect in a multiple mediator model compared to the indirect effect in a single mediator model is that it estimates the specific mediating ability of a mediator while controlling for the remaining specific indirect effects of all other mediators included in the model. Consequently, specific indirect effects are affected by the degree to which the mediators in a parallel multiple mediator model conceptually overlap (i.e., correlate). The specific indirect effects in a parallel multiple mediator model sum up to form the *total indirect effect*, which denotes the ability of a set of mediators to transmit an effect from X on Y. The direct effect denotes the remaining effect of X on Y, controlling for the total indirect effect. Thus, together, the total indirect effect and the direct effect add up to the total effect of X on Y.

Preacher and Hayes (2008) describe several advantages of testing one parallel multiple mediator model instead of multiple single mediator models. First, by testing the total indirect effect, a parallel multiple mediator model allows conclusions to be drawn regarding a set of multiple mediators. Second, disentangling the mediating ability of each mediator enables researchers to identify the specific indirect effect of each mediator as well as to quantitatively compare the specific indirect effects of the different mediators with each other. Third, the parallel multiple mediator model partially accounts for the limitation of the single mediator model with regard to possible bias due to omitted variables.

Statistical Description of the Parallel Multiple Mediator Model

The parallel multiple mediator model with two mediators M_1 and M_2 can be described by the following linear equations predicting M_1, M_2, and Y, respectively (see also Fig. 7):

$$M_1 = i_{m1} + a_1 X + e_{m1} \tag{8}$$

$$M_2 = i_{m2} + a_2 X + e_{m2} \tag{9}$$

$$Y = i_y + b_1 M_1 + b_2 M_2 + c'X + e_y \tag{10}$$

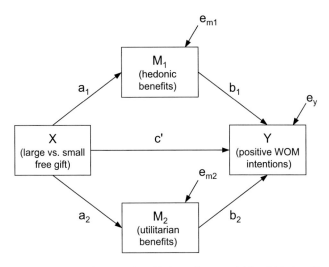

Fig. 7 The statistical diagram of a parallel multiple mediator model in which the effect of X on Y is transmitted through two mediators M_1 and M_2 operating in parallel

The i parameters denote the intercepts and a_i estimates the effect of X on M_i. The coefficient b_1 estimates the effect of M_1 on Y, controlling for X and M_2. Likewise, b_2 estimates the effect of M_2 on Y, controlling for X and M_1. Finally, c' estimates the effect of X on Y, controlling for M_1 and M_2. The error terms are denoted by the respective e parameters. In a parallel multiple mediator model with j mediators, $j + 1$ equations are required to describe the model, one to predict each M_i and one to predict Y.

Analogous to the single mediator model, a specific indirect effect through a mediator M_i is the product of the two unstandardized regression coefficients of path a_i and path b_i, $a_i b_i$. Therefore, in a parallel multiple mediator model with j mediators, there are j specific indirect effects to be estimated. The total indirect effect is the sum of all j specific indirect effects:

$$\text{Total indirect effect} : \sum_{i=1}^{j} (a_i b_i) \qquad (11)$$

The total effect is the sum of the total indirect effect and the direct effect c':

$$\text{Total effect} : c = \sum_{i=1}^{j} (a_i b_i) + c' \qquad (12)$$

Again, the total indirect effect can also be computed by subtracting the direct effect from the total effect as follows:

$$\text{Total indirect effect}: c - c' = \sum_{i=1}^{j}(a_i b_i) \qquad (13)$$

In the parallel multiple mediator model sketched out above, a specific indirect effect through the first mediator (hedonic benefits) of $a_1b_1 = 0.103$ indicates that controlling for the specific indirect effect of the large (vs. small) free gift on positive WOM intentions through utilitarian benefits, the large (vs. small) free gift increases positive WOM intentions through hedonic benefits by 0.103 units. Similarly, a specific indirect effect through the second mediator (utilitarian benefits) of $a_2b_2 = 0.005$ denotes that controlling for the specific indirect effect of the large (vs. small) free gift on positive WOM intentions through hedonic benefits, the large (vs. small) free gift increases positive WOM intentions through utilitarian benefits by 0.005 units. The total indirect effect of $a_1b_1 + a_2b_2 = 0.103 + 0.005 = 0.108$ shows that together, changes in hedonic and utilitarian benefits in response to a large (vs. small) free gift account for a 0.108 unit increase in positive WOM intentions. A direct effect of $c' = 0.110$ indicates that independent of the total indirect effect of the large (vs. small) free gift on positive WOM intentions through hedonic as well as utilitarian benefits, the large (vs. small) free gift increases positive WOM intentions by 0.110 units. As can be seen, the total effect $c = 0.218$ is the sum of the specific indirect effect through the first mediator, $a_1b_1 = 0.103$, the specific indirect effect through the second mediator, $a_2b_2 = 0.005$, and the direct effect $c' = 0.110$, as $0.103 + 0.005 + 0.110 = 0.218$.

Statistical Inference for the Parallel Multiple Mediator Model

Testing for mediation in the parallel multiple mediator model involves testing the total as well as the specific indirect effects. As with the single mediator model, this can be accomplished with the help of bootstrap confidence intervals. There are also other suitable approaches; however, they do not perform as well as the bootstrap approach (Preacher and Hayes 2008; Williams and MacKinnon 2008). Note that specific indirect effects should be investigated irrespective of whether the total indirect effect is significant or not (Preacher and Hayes 2008).

In the free gift example, the bias-corrected bootstrap confidence interval for the specific indirect effect through hedonic benefits lies completely above zero. Hence, the effect is positive and significant ($a_1b_1 = 0.103$, bc.bci$_{95\%}$ [0.029; 0.181]). However, the bias-corrected bootstrap confidence interval for the specific indirect effect through utilitarian benefits straddles zero and is hence not significant ($a_2b_2 = 0.005$, bc.bci$_{95\%}$ [−0.014; 0.029]). The total indirect effect is positive and significant too ($a_1b_1 + a_2b_2 = 0.108$, bc.bci$_{95\%}$ [0.031; 0.189]). That is, as compared to consumers receiving a small free gift, consumers receiving a large free gift perceive greater hedonic benefits ($a_1 = 0.135$), which, in turn, is associated with increased intentions to positively talk about and recommend the promoted products ($b_1 = 0.766$, $a_1b_1 = 0.103$, bc.bci$_{95\%}$ [0.029; 0.181]). Furthermore, hedonic and utilitarian benefits jointly mediate the effect of a large (vs. small) free gift on positive WOM intentions ($a_1b_1 + a_2b_2 = 0.108$, bc.bci$_{95\%}$ [0.031; 0.189]).

In parallel multiple mediator models, it is also possible to address the question of whether specific indirect effects differ from each other. For instance, a researcher may be interested in finding out whether one specific indirect effect is larger than another one. This, too, can be achieved with bootstrapping. The idea is straightforward: If two specific indirect effects a_ib_i and a_jb_j significantly differ from each other, their difference must be different from zero. To test this, the distribution of $a_ib_i - a_jb_j$ is bootstrapped, and a confidence interval is determined. If it excludes zero, the specific indirect effects in question differ significantly from each other. Note, however, that the conclusion that one specific indirect effect is larger than the other can only be drawn if both specific indirect effects compared have the same sign (i.e., are both positive or both negative, Preacher and Hayes 2008). To contrast specific indirect effects with different signs, the difference in absolute values may be determined and tested analogously with the help of a bootstrap confidence interval (Hayes 2018). Furthermore, note that a (specific) indirect effect is scaled in the metrics of X and Y. A change in X by one unit leads to a change in Y through M of ab units. Hence it does not matter whether the same response scales (e.g., 7-point vs. 5-point) are used to assess the respective mediators when comparing two specific indirect effects (Preacher and Hayes 2008).

Conceptual Description of the Serial Multiple Mediator Model

In a serial multiple mediator model, X is assumed to affect Y through two or more mediators M_i. However, in contrast to the parallel multiple mediator model, the mediators in a serial multiple mediator model are hypothesized to form a causal chain (see Fig. 8). Thus, serial multiple mediator models are suitable when a causal chain of mediators is assumed to account for the effect of X on Y. Research investigating serial multiple mediator models may be less common than research on parallel multiple mediator models. Yet, it is frequently possible to assume that mediators are part of a longer causal chain.

In the free gift example, one could hypothesize, for instance, that the effect of a large (vs. small) free gift on positive WOM intentions is in fact the result of an immediate positive emotional response to encountering a sales promotion which is then used as a basis for judging the hedonic benefits provided by the specific promotion. That is, one could argue that a causal chain consisting of, first, a positive emotional response and, second, perceived hedonic benefits, transmits the effect of the large (vs. small) free gift on positive WOM intentions.

As in the case of the parallel multiple mediator model, the serial multiple mediator model can be divided into total and specific indirect and direct components. The total

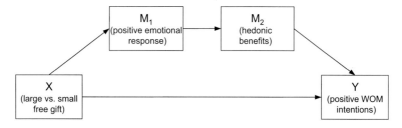

Fig. 8 The conceptual diagram of a serial multiple mediator model in which the effect of X on Y is transmitted through two mediators M_1 and M_2 operating in serial

indirect effect is the sum of the specific indirect effects of X on Y through the respective mediators, considered individually and in sequence (see Fig. 9). The direct effect denotes the remaining effect of X on Y after controlling for the total indirect effect. Together, the direct effect and the total indirect effect add up to the total effect of X on Y.

Statistical Description of the Serial Multiple Mediator Model

Analogous to the previously presented mediation models, the serial multiple mediator model with two mediators M_1 and M_2 (see Fig. 9) can be described by the following linear equations predicting M_1, M_2, and Y:

$$M_1 = i_{m1} + a_1 X + e_{m1} \tag{14}$$

$$M_2 = i_{m2} + a_2 X + d_{21} M_1 + e_{m2} \tag{15}$$

$$Y = i_y + b_1 M_1 + b_2 M_2 + c'X + e_y \tag{16}$$

The i parameters denote the intercepts, a_1 estimates the effect of X on M_1, and a_2 estimates the effect of X on M_2, controlling for the effect of M_1 on M_2 which is captured by d_{21}. The coefficient b_1 denotes the effect of M_1 on Y, controlling for X and M_2. Likewise, b_2 denotes the effect of M_2 on Y, controlling for X and M_1. The coefficient c' estimates the effect of X on Y, controlling for M_1 and M_2. The error terms are denoted by the respective e parameters. Generally, in a serial multiple mediator model with j mediators, there are $j + 1$ equations required to describe the model, one to predict each M_i and one to predict Y.

In a serial multiple mediator model with two mediators, three specific indirect effects are to be estimated, one through each mediator ($a_1 b_1$ and $a_2 b_2$), and one through both mediators ($a_1 d_{21} b_2$). The total indirect effect is the sum of the specific indirect effects:

$$\text{Total indirect effect} : a_1 b_1 + a_2 b_2 + a_1 d_{21} b_2 \tag{17}$$

The total effect is the sum of the total indirect effect and the direct effect c':

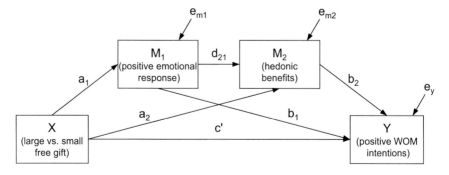

Fig. 9 The statistical diagram of a serial multiple mediator model in which the effect of X on Y is transmitted through two mediators M_1 and M_2 operating in serial

$$\text{Total effect} : c = a_1 b_1 + a_2 b_2 + a_1 d_{21} b_2 + c' \tag{18}$$

Again, the total indirect effect can also be computed by subtracting the direct effect from the total effect:

$$\text{Total indirect effect} : c - c' = a_1 b_1 + a_2 b_2 + a_1 d_{21} b_2 \tag{19}$$

These effects correspond to the following effects from the free gift example: A specific indirect effect through the first mediator (positive emotional response) of $a_1 b_1 = 0.001$ indicates that controlling for all other indirect effects in the model, a large (vs. small) free gift increases positive WOM intentions through a positive emotional response by 0.001 units. Similarly, a specific indirect effect through the second mediator (hedonic benefits) of $a_2 b_2 = 0.067$ denotes that controlling for all other indirect effects in the model, a large (vs. small) free gift increases positive WOM intentions through hedonic benefits by 0.067 units. Finally, a specific indirect effect through both mediators (first, the positive emotional response and then hedonic benefits) of $a_1 d_{21} b_2 = 0.037$ denotes that a large (vs. small) free gift increases positive WOM intentions by 0.037 units sequentially through a positive emotional response which is associated with hedonic benefits which, in turn, is associated with positive WOM intentions. The total indirect effect of $a_1 b_1 + a_2 b_2 + a_1 d_{21} b_2 = 0.105$ shows that together, all three specific indirect effects in the model account for a 0.105 unit increase in positive WOM intentions in response to the large (vs. small) free gift. A direct effect of $c' = 0.114$ indicates that controlling for all specific indirect effects in the model (i.e., the total indirect effect), a large (vs. small) free gift increases positive WOM intentions by 0.114 units. The total effect $c = 0.218$ is the sum of the specific indirect effect through the first mediator (positive emotional response), $a_1 b_1 = 0.001$, the specific indirect effect through the second mediator (hedonic benefits), $a_2 b_2 = 0.067$, the specific indirect effect through both mediators $a_1 d_{21} b_2 = 0.037$, and the direct effect $c' = 0.114$, as $0.001 + 0.067 + 0.037 + 0.114 \approx 0.218$ (the difference is due to rounding).

Hayes (2018) notes that while it is relatively easy to incorporate more than two mediators in a parallel multiple mediator model, the number of specific indirect effects quickly increases in a model with more than two mediators operating in serial. This follows because there is one specific indirect effect through each mediator, one specific indirect effect through each combination of two mediators, one specific indirect effect through each combination of three mediators, and so on. Yet, the same relations apply in such models: The specific indirect effects comprise the total indirect effect and together with the direct effect they sum up to the total effect. Moreover, the total indirect effect can be estimated by subtracting the direct effect from the total effect.

Statistical Inference for the Serial Multiple Mediator Model

As for the parallel multiple mediator model, testing for mediation in the serial multiple mediator model involves testing the total indirect effect as well as the specific indirect effects. Again, there are several suitable methods to do so, yet bootstrap confidence intervals have been demonstrated to perform very well

(Taylor et al. 2008). In addition, as in the case of the parallel multiple mediator model, specific indirect effects should be investigated irrespective of whether or not the total indirect effect is significant (Hayes 2018).

In the free gift example, the results of the analysis are as follows: The bias-corrected bootstrap confidence intervals for the specific indirect effect of the large (vs. small) free gift on positive WOM intentions solely through the positive emotional response as well as the specific indirect effect solely through hedonic benefits include zero, that is, neither of the two effects is significant ($a_1b_1 = 0.001$, bc.bci$_{95\%}$ [−0.043; 0.046], $a_2b_2 = 0.067$, bc.bci$_{95\%}$ [−0.010; 0.145]). However, the specific indirect effect of the large (vs. small) free gift on positive WOM intentions through both mediators sequentially, the positive emotional response and hedonic benefits, is positive and significant ($a_1d_{21}b_2 = 0.037$, bc.bci$_{95\%}$ [0.012; 0.072]). The total indirect effect is positive and significant as well ($a_1b_1 + a_2b_2 + a_1d_{21}b_2 = 0.001 + 0.067 + 0.037 = 0.105$, bc.bci$_{95\%}$ [0.026; 0.192]). That is, as compared to consumers receiving a small free gift, consumers receiving a large free gift show a more positive emotional response to the promotion ($a_1 = 0.199$), which, in turn, is associated with greater perceived hedonic benefits ($d_{21} = 0.241$), and, as a consequence, positive WOM intentions are increased ($b_2 = 0.767$, $a_1d_{21}b_2 = 0.037$, bc.bci$_{95\%}$ [0.012; 0.072]). Furthermore, the positive and significant total indirect effect suggests that a large (vs. small) free gift increases positive WOM intentions through all three specific indirect effects at once ($a_1b_1 + a_2b_2 + a_1d_{21}b_2 = 0.105$, bc.bci$_{95\%}$ [0.026; 0.192]).

Analogous to the parallel multiple mediator model, specific indirect effects can also be contrasted in serial multiple mediator models. The logic is the same and, again, a significant difference between two specific indirect effects can only be interpreted as the one effect being larger than the other one if both specific indirect effects have the same sign. In case they do not, the strength of the two specific indirect effects may be compared by testing the difference between the absolute values of the effects.

How to Interpret Results from Multiple Mediator Models

The crucial difference between a multiple mediator model and a single mediator model lies in the number of mediators included in the model. As a consequence, the interpretation of an "indirect effect" in a multiple mediator model differs from the "indirect effect" in a single mediator model: In a single mediator model, the *indirect effect* denotes the ability of a mediator M to transmit the effect of X on Y. In a multiple mediator model, however, there are multiple indirect components: While a *specific indirect effect* quantifies the unique ability of a mediator M_i to transmit the effect of X on Y taking the specific indirect effects of X on Y through other mediating variables M_j into account, the *total indirect effect* denotes the ability of a set of mediators to transmit the effect of X on Y. These distinctions should be carefully considered when interpreting and comparing results from different single and multiple mediator models (Hayes 2018).

Mediation Models Including a Moderator: Conditional Process Models

The single mediator model can also be extended to include a moderator. Doing so allows to account for the fact that mediation may work differently, for example, for different people or under different circumstances. For instance, it could be of interest in the free gift example to investigate whether the indirect effect of a large (vs. small) free gift on positive WOM intentions through hedonic benefits is the same across consumers differing in their general responsiveness to sales promotions. One might argue that mediation is especially large for consumers that are very deal-prone, that is, overall highly responsive to sales promotions (Lichtenstein et al. 1995), but smaller for consumers that are overall not particularly deal-prone. Moreover, one could hypothesize that as hedonic benefits are more likely to affect consumer judgment if consumers pursue a hedonic consumption motive as compared to a utilitarian consumption motive (Chandon et al. 2000), a large (vs. small) free gift should increase positive WOM intentions through hedonic benefits if the promoted product is associated with a hedonic consumption motive (e.g., a fashionable T-shirt by a high-end brand), but not if it is generally purchased out of utilitarian motives (e.g., a plain T-shirt to wear under a shirt).

Conceptual Description of Conditional Process Models
Mediation models with added moderators can generally be referred to as conditional process models (Hayes 2018), but sometimes, a conceptual distinction is made between *moderated mediation* and *mediated moderation* (e.g., Muller et al. 2005; Preacher et al. 2007). In the prototypical moderated mediation, the research focus lies on whether or not the mediation of X on Y through M is influenced by a moderating variable W, which may affect different paths in the conditional process model. The conceptual diagrams depicted in panel A and B in Fig. 10 are exemplary cases of moderated mediation. Excluding the broken line, panel A shows a conditional process model in which a moderator W affects path a, the effect of X on M. Including the broken line, the model assumes that W also moderates path c', the direct effect of X on Y. These models correspond to the first research question mentioned above, namely, whether the effect of a large (vs. small) free gift on positive WOM intentions through perceived hedonic benefits is affected by consumers' deal proneness, as consumers' deal proneness could be argued to influence the effect of a large (vs. small) free gift on hedonic benefits (i.e., path a and possibly also path c').

Panel B shows a conditional process model in which a moderator V affects path b, the effect of M on Y (excluding the broken line), but also a mediation model in which path c' is additionally affected by V (including the broken line). These models correspond to the second question raised above, namely, whether the effect of a large (vs. small) free gift on positive WOM intentions through hedonic benefits is affected by the consumption motive associated with the promoted product, as this moderator can be hypothesized to influence the effect of hedonic benefits on positive WOM intentions (i.e., path b and possibly also path c').

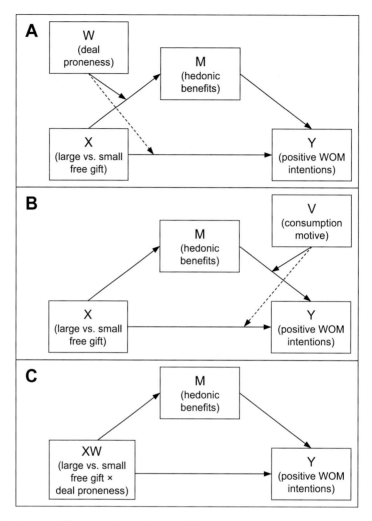

Fig. 10 Conceptual diagrams of exemplary conditional process models. While the model in panel A and panel B are examples of moderated mediation, the model in panel C corresponds to a case of mediated moderation

In the prototypical mediated moderation, the focus lies on whether or not the moderation of an effect of *X* on *Y* by *W* can be explained by a mediator. Thus, in mediated moderation, the effect of an interaction between two variables (i.e., *XW*) on *Y* is transferred through *M* (Hayes 2018). The respective conceptual diagram is depicted in panel C in Fig. 10. This would correspond to the question whether the effect of the interaction between the large (vs. small) free gift and consumers' deal proneness on positive WOM intentions can be explained by hedonic benefits. As it will become clearer in the following section, mediated moderation is a special case of moderated mediation. Hence, mediated moderation can be framed as moderated mediation. Hayes (2018) even argues that mediated moderation should be framed as moderated mediation, as the product between two variables and thus its indirect effect may be difficult to interpret meaningfully.

Just like the previously presented mediation models, a conditional process model can be divided into direct and indirect components which, if qualified by a moderator, are referred to as *conditional indirect effect* and *conditional direct effect*. Together, the (conditional) direct effect and the conditional indirect effect may be added up to the total effect of X on Y.

Statistical Description of Conditional Process Models

In the following section, the three conditional process models depicted in Fig. 10 will be described statistically, starting with the conditional process model depicted in panel A in which a moderator W affects path a (see panel A in Fig. 10 as well as Fig. 11, excluding the broken lines). This conditional process model is described by the following equations:

$$M = i_m + a_1 X + a_2 W + a_3 XW + e_m \tag{20}$$

$$Y = i_y + bM + c'_1 X + e_y \tag{21}$$

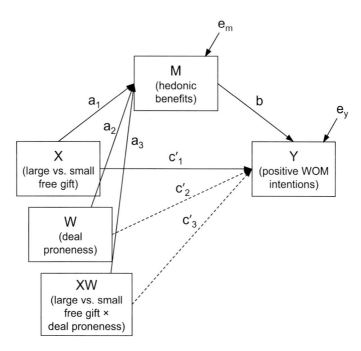

Fig. 11 The statistical diagram of the conditional process model depicted in panel A in Fig. 10 in which a moderator W affects path a (solid lines) as well as path c' (broken lines)

The *i* parameters in Eqs. 20 and 21 denote the intercepts, a_1 estimates the effect of X on M, a_2 the effect of W on M, and a_3 the effect of their interaction XW on M, respectively, controlling for the remaining variables in the equation. The effect of M on Y controlling for X is indicated by b and the effect of X on Y controlling for M is estimated by c'_1. The error terms are denoted by the respective e parameters. If the direct effect is conditional on W as well (see panel A in Fig. 10 as well as Fig. 11, including the broken lines), additional c' parameters would be added to Eq. 21 to denote the partial effects of W and XW on Y resulting in the following equation:

$$Y = i_y + bM + c'_1 X + c'_2 W + c'_3 XW + e_y \tag{22}$$

Irrespective of whether or not a moderator W affects path c', if W moderates path a, the effect of X on M, the conditional indirect effect is denoted as

$$\text{Conditional indirect effect}: \omega_{xw} = (a_1 + a_3 W)b \tag{23}$$

Rewritten as

$$\omega_{xw} = a_1 b + a_3 b W \tag{24}$$

it becomes evident that the conditional indirect effect ω_{xw} is a linear function of the moderator W. That is, there is no single numeric estimate for the conditional indirect effect but many, depending on the value of W.

Hayes (2015) coined the term *index of moderated mediation* for the weight of the moderator $a_3 b$ in Eq. 24 which quantifies the linear dependency of the conditional indirect effect on the moderator W. Specifically, the index of moderated mediation denotes the difference between the conditional indirect effects of participants differing by one unit on the moderator W. Hence, if W is a dichotomous variable indicating two experimental groups and coded with "0" and "1," the index of moderated mediation denotes the difference of the conditional indirect effects in those two groups (Hayes 2015).

The direct effect is denoted by c'_1 if unconditional. If conditional on a moderator W (see broken lines in Fig. 11), it is denoted by

$$\text{Conditional direct effect}: c'_1 + c'_3 W \tag{25}$$

which shows that if the direct effect is moderated by W, the remaining effect of X on Y controlling for the conditional indirect effect varies depending on values of W.

The total effect c is again the sum of the (conditional) direct effect and the conditional indirect effect. If W solely moderates the effect of X on M (Fig. 11, excluding the broken lines), the total effect is denoted by

$$\text{Total effect}: c = \omega_{xw} + c' = (a_1 + a_3 W)b + c' \tag{26}$$

The linear dependency of a conditional indirect effect on a moderator described above is visualized in Fig. 12 which is based on results from the free gift example:

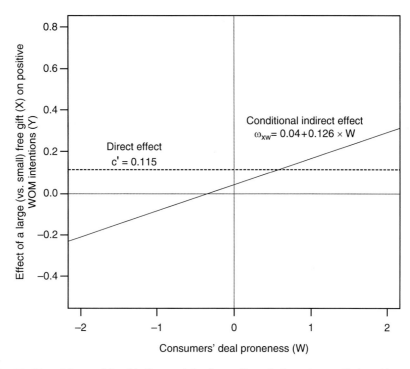

Fig. 12 Plot of the conditional indirect and the direct effect of a large (vs. small) free gift (X) on positive WOM intentions (Y) for different values of consumers' deal proneness (W)

While the y-axis denotes the magnitude of the effect of a large (vs. small) free gift (X) on positive WOM intentions (Y), the x-axis indicates the values of the metric (and mean centered) moderator deal proneness (W). The solid line represents the conditional indirect effect of X on Y through M, which is $\omega_{xw} = a_1 b + a_3 b W = 0.052 \times 0.767 + 0.165 \times 0.767 \times W = 0.040 + 0.126 \times W$ (see also Eq. 24). As the conditional indirect effect ω_{xw} is dependent on W, the slope of the solid line in Fig. 12 is nonzero: The conditional indirect effect of a large (vs. small) free gift on positive WOM intentions through hedonic benefits is descriptively positive for highly deal-prone consumers (e.g., for $W = 2$, $\omega_{xw} = 0.04 + 0.126 \times 2 = 0.292$), but negative for low deal-prone consumers (e.g., for $W = -2$, $\omega_{xw} = 0.04 + 0.126 \times (-2) = -0.212$). The slope of the graph depicting the conditional indirect effect corresponds to the index of moderated mediation, which is $a_3 b = 0.126$.

The broken line in Fig. 12 denotes the direct effect of X on Y which, in contrast to the conditional indirect effect, is not affected by a moderator and denoted by $c' = 0.115$. That means, the direct effect of a large (vs. small) free gift on positive WOM intentions is $c' = 0.115$ for highly deal-prone consumers, but also for low deal-prone consumers. Hence, the broken line is horizontal.

The equations describing a conditional process model in which path b is moderated by V (see panel B in Fig. 10, excluding the broken lines) follow the same principles just applied to the case in which a moderator W affects path a. The conditional process model is described by

$$M = i_m + aX + e_m \tag{27}$$

$$Y = i_y + b_1 M + b_2 V + b_3 MV + c'_1 X + e_y \tag{28}$$

The i parameters denote the intercepts and a estimates the effect of X on M. Controlling for the remaining variables in the equation, the effect of M on Y is estimated by b_1, the effect of V on Y by b_2, the effect of their interaction MV on Y by b_3, and the effect of X on Y by c'_1. The error terms are denoted by the respective e parameters. As Eqs. 27 and 28 show, M is a simple function of X. Y, however, is not only affected by X and M but also by V and by the interaction MV. If the direct effect were conditional on V as well (see panel B in Fig. 10, including the broken line), an additional c' parameter would be added to Eq. 28 to denote the partial effect of XV on Y. The resulting equation would be

$$Y = i_y + b_1 M + b_2 V + b_3 MV + c'_1 X + c'_2 XV + e_y \tag{29}$$

Irrespective of whether or not a moderator V affects path c', if V moderates path b, the effect of M on Y, the conditional indirect effect is denoted as

$$\omega_{mv} = a(b_1 + b_3 V) = ab_1 + ab_3 V \tag{30}$$

In this conditional process model, the index of moderated mediation is indicated by ab_3. The direct effect is again denoted by c'_1 if unconditional, yet, if conditional on the moderator V (see panel C in Fig. 10, including the broken line), it is described by the following equation:

$$\text{Conditional direct effect}: c'_1 + c'_2 V \tag{31}$$

As can be seen from Eqs. 25 and 31 (see also Eqs. 22 and 29 for the interpretation of c'_3 and c'_2, respectively), the equation for the conditional direct effect has the same form irrespective of whether a moderator affects path a and path c' or path b and path c'.

The total effect c is again the sum of the (conditional) direct effect and the conditional indirect effect. If V solely moderates the effect of M on Y, the total effect is denoted by

$$\text{Total effect}: c = \omega_{mv} + c' = a(b_1 + b_3 V) + c' \tag{32}$$

The equations underlying the mediated moderation depicted in panel C in Fig. 10 are the following:

$$M = i_m + a_1 X + a_2 W + a_3 XW + e_m \tag{33}$$

$$Y = i_y + bM + c'_1 X + c'_2 W + c'_3 XW + e_y \tag{34}$$

As can be seen, Eqs. 20 and 33 as well as Eqs. 22 and 34 are identical. That is, mediated moderation as shown in Fig. 10 (panel C) is statistically identical to the case of moderated mediation in which a moderator W affects path a and path c' (Fig. 10, panel A) and corresponds to the statistical model shown in Fig. 11 (including the broken lines). Hence, the same relations apply for mediated moderation as for this case of moderated mediation.

The equations describing other conditional process models (e.g., in which a moderator Z affects path a and path b simultaneously) follow the same general principles applied in the examples outlined above. They can be found in publications by, for example, Edwards and Lambert (2007), Preacher et al. (2007), and Hayes (2018).

Statistical Inference for Conditional Process Models: Conditional Process Analysis

Testing for moderated mediation in conditional process models is somewhat different from testing for mediation in single or multiple mediator models, as no single numerical estimate for "*the* conditional indirect effect" can be tested against zero with the help of a bootstrap confidence interval. Instead, as mentioned above, there are multiple numerical estimates of the conditional indirect effect for different values of the moderator (see Fig. 12), and the question of interest is whether they differ significantly from each other. Different approaches have been introduced to answer this question (e.g., Edwards and Lambert 2007; Fairchild and MacKinnon 2009; Hayes 2015; Muller et al. 2005; Preacher et al. 2007). They can generally be referred to under the term *conditional process analysis* (Hayes 2018).

Earlier approaches (e.g., Muller et al. 2005) implicitly or explicitly rely on the assumption that to establish moderated mediation, one or more paths in the conditional process model need to be significantly moderated. These approaches test moderated mediation, for example, by testing the individual paths in a conditional process model and whether or not they are moderated (Muller et al. 2005) or by extending simple slopes analysis and the Johnson-Neyman technique to determine the significance of the conditional indirect effect at a few (similar to simple slopes analysis) or all (similar to the Johnson-Neyman technique) values of the moderator (Preacher et al. 2007).

It has been pointed out, however, that testing whether a constituent path in the conditional process model is significantly moderated or whether an indirect effect for one or more specific values of the moderator is different from zero is conceptually different from testing whether mediation, that is, the indirect effect, is moderated (Fairchild and MacKinnon 2009; Hayes 2015). In other words, testing moderation of the individual paths in a conditional process model or probing indirect effect for different values of the moderator is useful for descriptive reasons, but it does not address the central question of interest in conditional process analysis.

Addressing this aspect, a further approach to testing moderated mediation is provided by Hayes (2015). He argues that moderated mediation can be demonstrated by testing the index of moderated mediation which, as noted above, corresponds to the weight of the moderator in the equation for the conditional indirect effect (see Eqs. 24 and 30). If the index of moderated mediation is different from zero, the conditional indirect effect significantly varies as a linear function of the moderator. For example, if the index of moderated mediation in the free gift example ($a_3b = 0.126$) is different from zero, it could be concluded that the effect of a large (vs. small) free gift on positive WOM intentions through hedonic benefits is significantly moderated by consumers' deal proneness: The indirect effect would be more positive for highly deal-prone consumers (i.e., consumers that score high on the moderator) as compared to low deal-prone consumers. Specifically, it would be 0.126 units more positive for every unit increase in deal-proneness.

To test the index of moderated mediation, a bootstrap confidence interval can be computed. Hayes (2015) shows that if this confidence interval excludes zero, it can be concluded that any two conditional indirect effects for different values of a moderator (e.g., plus and minus one standard deviation from the mean) significantly differ from each other. In the free gift example, the index of moderated mediation is found to be nonsignificant as the bootstrap confidence interval includes zero ($a_3b = 0.126$, bc.bci$_{95\%}$ [−0.014; 0.284]). Hence, it cannot be concluded that the indirect effect of a large (vs. small) free gift on positive WOM intentions through hedonic benefits is moderated by consumers' deal-proneness.

The shift in focus in conditional process analysis from the moderation of a specific path in earlier approaches (e.g., Muller et al. 2005) to the moderation of the indirect effect in the approach by Hayes (2015) can lead to situations in which significant moderation of the indirect effect is found in the absence of significant moderation of an individual path of the indirect effect, and vice versa. Furthermore, it may happen that the index of moderated mediation is not significant, but there are differences in the significance of conditional indirect effects for different values of the moderator, and vice versa.

Take, for instance, the results from the analysis testing whether the effect of a large (vs. small) free gift on positive WOM intentions through hedonic benefits is dependent on consumers' deal proneness (see Fig. 11): The regression coefficient denoting the moderating effect of W on path a, a_3, is not significant ($a_3 = 0.165$, $p = 0.087$) and neither is the index of moderated mediation, as pointed out above ($a_3b = 0.126$, bc.bci$_{95\%}$ [−0.014; 0.284]). However, a significant indirect effect is found for highly deal-prone consumers (consumers one standard deviation above the mean, $ab_{\text{dealprone+}} = 0.230$, bc.bci$_{95\%}$ [0.056; 0.415]), but not for low deal-prone customers (consumers one standard deviation below the mean, $ab_{\text{dealprone-}} = -0.149$, bc.bci$_{95\%}$ [−0.469; 0.143]). Hence, it cannot be concluded that the effect of a large (vs. small) free gift on hedonic benefits (i.e., path a) is moderated by consumers' deal proneness (a_3 is nonsignificant). Moreover, it cannot be said that the conditional indirect effects of a large (vs. small) free gift on positive WOM intentions through hedonic benefits for differently deal-prone consumers differ from each other (a_3b, the index of moderated mediation is not significant). However, a positive conditional indirect effect of a large (vs. small) free gift on positive WOM intentions through hedonic benefits is found for highly deal-prone consumers ($ab_{\text{dealprone+}}$ is significant), but not for low deal-prone consumers ($ab_{\text{dealprone-}}$ is not significant). In situations like these, we argue that the test corresponding most closely to the specific research question investigated should be given the greatest weight in a researcher's judgment. Furthermore, we emphasize again that moderation of the indirect effect cannot be inferred from the mere observation that mediation occurs for some values of the moderator, but not for others (Hayes 2015).

Variable Metrics

A dichotomous or continuous moderator can easily be incorporated into regression-based mediation analysis. Multicategorical moderators can be included as a set of indicator variables (Hayes 2017), again, each representing a comparison of one category (or a set of categories) to another category (or a set of categories, see, e.g., Darlington and Hayes 2017).

Further Mediation Models

In the following section, further, more complex mediation models are described. These are models with multiple mediators and moderators, and with more than one predictor or outcome. Furthermore, we touch upon mediation analysis for longitudinal and multilevel data. Although these models generally go beyond the scope of a mere introduction to mediation analysis in an experimental context, we address them briefly as they, first, illustrate how the principles applied above can be extended to more complex mediation models and, second, account for assumptions in mediation analysis frequently not considered (omitted variables, timing of mediation, or nested data).

Notably, with some exceptions, the following models go beyond the scope of the OLS regression-based approach to mediation analysis. However, they can be analyzed with the help of other methods (e.g., structural equation modeling, see ▶ "Crafting Survey Research: A Systematic Process for Conducting Survey Research," this volume). Furthermore, it should be emphasized that mediation models do not have to be complex in order to be of scientific value. Rather, the complexity of the model should be determined weighing the principle of parsimony against the premise to include all important causal variables in the model while keeping in mind that bias due to measurement error is a more serious issue in complex mediation models (Cole and Preacher 2014).

Mediation Models with Multiple Mediators and Moderators

Multiple mediator models can also include moderators (see conceptual diagrams in panel A and panel B in Fig. 13 depicting a moderated parallel multiple mediator model and a moderated serial multiple mediator model, respectively). Furthermore, in multiple mediator models with three or more mediators, serial and parallel mediation can be combined (Hayes 2018).

If a conditional process model includes more than one moderator (see panel C and panel D in Fig. 13 for examples), it can be distinguished between the concepts of

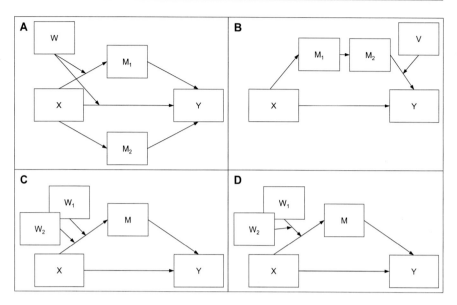

Fig. 13 Conceptual diagrams of mediation models with additional mediators as well as moderators

partial moderated mediation, *conditional moderated mediation*, and *moderated moderated mediation* (Hayes 2017). Partial moderated mediation refers to the question whether a conditional indirect effect of X on Y through M is moderated by a moderator W_1 while a second moderator W_2 affecting the same path is held constant (see panel C in Fig. 13). That is, partial moderated mediation denotes the moderating ability of W_1 independent of W_2. In conditional moderated mediation and moderated moderated mediation, a second moderator W_2 affects the effect of W_1 (see panel D in Fig. 13 for an example). Hence, the moderation of W_1 is dependent on W_2. In this scenario, two questions may be of interest: First, is the conditional indirect effect moderated by W_1 when W_2 takes a specific value? Second, does the moderating ability of W_1 change if W_2 changes? Conditional moderated mediation refers to the first question, that is, whether a conditional indirect effect of X on Y through M is moderated by a moderator W_1 at a specific value of W_2. Moderated moderated mediation addresses the second question, that is, whether the moderation of a conditional indirect effect by a moderator W_1 changes if a second moderator W_2 changes. Details on these concepts, specifically, how to quantify and test them, are discussed by Hayes (2017).

Whether a mediator can be a moderator at the same time is a topic of debate. While some argue that one and the same variable can mediate as well as moderate a relationship between X and Y (e.g., Frazier et al. 2004), others differentiate more (e.g., Kraemer et al. 2002; Kraemer et al. 2008) or less strictly (e.g., Baron and Kenny 1986) between the conceptual definitions of a mediator and a moderator. Without taking a definite stand on the question, we think it is important to be aware of the conceptual and the statistical level of the debate: Differentiating clearly between a moderator and a mediator on a conceptual level does not mean that evidence for a mediating process cannot be provided by testing the significance of interaction effects (e.g., Jacoby and Sassenberg 2011; Kraemer et al. 2002, 2008; Pirlott and MacKinnon 2016; Spencer et al. 2005).

Moreover, while one might consider the same variable as a mediator in one model and as a moderator in another, it is another question to consider a variable simultaneously as mediator and moderator in the same model (Hayes 2018). Pieters (2017), for instance, finds no such model being tested in a review of $N = 138$ papers published in the Journal of Consumer Research between 2014 and 2016, which included $N = 166$ mediation analyses. We contend that one possible reason for the unusualness of models in which a variable acts as a mediator and moderator simultaneously (see Fig. 5 for such a case) is that it may be rather challenging (albeit likely not impossible) to theoretically deduct hypotheses for this situation. Such a model would, for instance, correspond to a hypothesis stating that the direct effect of a large (vs. small) free gift on positive WOM intentions, namely, the effect of a large (vs. small) free gift on positive WOM intentions controlling for the influence of hedonic benefits, is different for consumers perceiving high hedonic benefits from the sales promotion than for consumers perceiving low hedonic benefits from the sales promotion. However, we also see that it is mathematically possible and that researchers test such models (e.g., Kraemer et al. 2002, 2008).

Mediation Models with Multiple Predictors and Outcomes

Mediation models can be extended to include multiple predictor or outcome variables. These more extensive mediation models can be referred to as path analysis (mediation) models (MacKinnon 2008). Including more than one predictor in a mediation model (e.g., by adding covariates to the model or multiple indicator variables in case an independent variable is multicategorical) does not pose much difficulty to OLS regression-based mediation analysis. Each predictor X_i or covariate U_i is assigned a specific effect on M or Y, which is interpreted as the respective ability of X_i or U_i to predict M or Y, controlling for the effects of all other variables affecting M or Y (see Fig. 14).

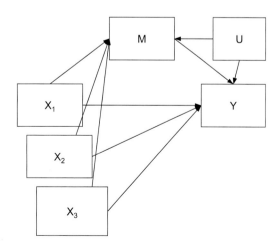

Fig. 14 Conceptual diagram of a mediation model with several predictors X_i as well as a covariate U affecting M and Y

Including more than one outcome in a mediation model generally goes beyond what regression analysis can do, and the use of structural equation modeling becomes necessary to estimate the respective path coefficients (MacKinnon 2008). However, Hayes (2018) points out that, if no relationships between the dependent variables Y_i are modeled, regression analysis can be used to analyze mediation models in which X's effect on multiple Y_i is transmitted through one or more M_i. Then, the estimated indirect effect on Y_i will be the same, regardless of whether the model was fitted simultaneously with structural equation modeling or by a series of separate regressions.

Incorporating Time and Nested Data in Mediation Analysis

Two emerging research fields in mediation analysis are longitudinal mediation analysis and multilevel mediation analysis. Describing them in detail is beyond the scope of this chapter (for overviews, see Preacher 2015 and MacKinnon 2008). However, we briefly address why mediation analysis for longitudinal and multilevel data is relevant.

Development in time is a crucial, albeit often implicit, aspect of mediation analysis: As a cause must precede an effect, time must elapse for X to cause M and for M to cause Y. Cole and Maxwell (2003) argue that mediation analysis based on cross-sectional designs (i.e., designs in which X, M, and Y are measured simultaneously and only once) provide accurate information about a mediation process unfolding over time only under rather limited conditions (see also Maxwell and Cole 2007; Maxwell et al. 2011). Time can be incorporated into mediation analysis through longitudinal designs, that is, repeated measurement of X, M, and Y (MacKinnon 2008; Preacher 2015). An exemplary longitudinal mediation model is depicted in Fig. 15. Longitudinal designs control for error resulting from individual differences and other unobserved variables. However, they are usually affected by common method bias.

Mediation analysis can also accommodate multilevel data, for example, consumers nested in different geographical regions or repeated measurements nested in one participant (Preacher 2015; Tofighi and Thoemmes 2014). An exemplary multilevel mediation model is depicted in Fig. 16. In nested datasets, the assumption

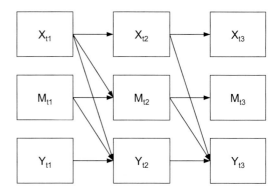

Fig. 15 An exemplary conceptual diagram of a longitudinal mediation model in which X, M, and Y are measured three times (at t_1, t_2, and t_3) and the variables are affected by their hypothesized cause as well as by themselves

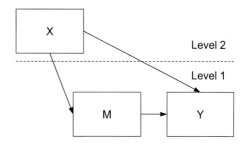

Fig. 16 An exemplary conceptual diagram of a multilevel mediation model in which X is a level-2 variable affecting M and Y which are level-1 variables. This model can be referred to as a 2-1-1 design

of independent error terms is violated (chapter ▶ "Multilevel Modeling" by Wieseke et al., this volume). If this is unaccounted for, that is, if the nesting is ignored, the risk of reporting a nonexistent indirect effect increases.

Strengthening Causal Inference in Mediation Analysis

Inferring causal relationships is the central idea of mediation analysis. Yet, the mere statistical results obtained from mediation analysis do not allow researchers to draw strong conclusions (if any) about the causal relationships between the variables included in the model (e.g., Baron and Kenny 1986; Bollen 1989). According to Cook and Campbell (1979), causality can be inferred when covariation, temporal precedence, and absence of bias due to confounding variables is given. Hence, if a significant indirect effect (i.e., covariation between X, M, and Y) is found based on simultaneously collected and nonexperimental data, alternative models in which the variables are differently ordered could explain the data as well (e.g., Y could precede M, which, in turn, could precede X, or M could precede X as well as Y). The observed relationships could also be a result of bias due to confounding variables. That is, there might be omitted variables causally influencing the variables in a mediation model. Furthermore, the variables assessed for X, M, and Y may only be correlates of the actual causes, mediators and consequences of an effect. Hayes (2018) refers to this as epiphenomenality.

The following section describes how causal inference in mediation analysis can be strengthened through design, the collection of further evidence, and statistical methods. Taken by themselves, none of these methods is sufficient to establish causality. In combination, however, they may strongly support a causal argument. Beyond that, the most crucial method to strengthen causal inference in mediation analysis is to provide strong theoretical support for one's hypotheses tested.

Strengthening Causal Inference Through Design

Causal claims in mediation analysis can be strengthened through experimental methods (Spencer et al. 2005; Stone-Romero and Rosopa 2008). Specifically, randomizing X strengthens causal inference for the effect of X on M, as well as for the total effect of X on Y. This is, first, because X clearly precedes M as well as Y if it is successfully manipulated, and, second, because possible confounding variables are controlled for through the random assignment of participants to different levels of X. Crucially, however, the randomization of X does not allow to causally interpret the effect of M on Y: As participants are not randomly assigned to a "level of M," path b is correlational. Furthermore, as the indirect and the direct effect take path b into account (see Eqs. 3 and 4), neither one of them can be interpreted causally.

Randomizing M has been suggested as a way to strengthen causal inference about the relationship between M and Y, for example, by conducting double randomized experiments (Spencer et al. 2005; Stone-Romero and Rosopa 2008; for an overview of different design approaches to manipulate mediators and mediating effects, see Pirlott and MacKinnon 2016). Double randomized experiments consist of a series of experiments. These are composed, first, of a study randomizing X and measuring M (and Y) and, second, of a study randomizing M and measuring Y (further studies investigating the hypothesized causal effect could be added to probe, e.g., whether Y does not cause M, as hypothesized). Evidently, data collected from a chain of experiments is not analyzed using mediation analysis (but, for instance, through analysis of variance, see chapter ▶ "Analysis of Variance" by Landwehr, this volume).

Establishing the causal chain from X to Y via M through multiple experiments provides strong causal evidence for the hypothesized relationships (Stone-Romero and Rosopa 2008). However, there are several difficulties associated with double randomized experiments (e.g., Bullock et al. 2010; Kenny 2008; MacKinnon 2008; Preacher 2015; Spencer et al. 2005; Stone-Romero and Rosopa 2008). Among other concerns, it has been noted that running double randomized experiments (just like experiments in general, see chapter ▶ "Field Experiments" by Valli et al., this volume) may not always be possible (e.g., because an active manipulation of X or M is not feasible, true randomization cannot be achieved, or a suitable control group cannot be identified) or desirable (e.g., because an active manipulation would be unethical). Furthermore, experimental designs may be somewhat artificial with regard to the operationalization employed (e.g., the manipulation of X or measurement of Y) and the setting chosen (e.g., the laboratory). This may cast doubt on the construct validity of the manipulations and measures, and on the external validity of the results obtained. In addition, double randomization assumes that measuring M (in a study in which X is randomized and M is measured) is equal to manipulating M (in a study in which the effect of M on Y is demonstrated), which may not be the case. Spencer et al. (2005) suggest running double randomized experiments only if the proposed mediating process is easy to manipulate and measure. If this does not apply (e.g., if the mediator is hard to measure but easy to manipulate), Spencer et al. (2005) recommend that other designs be employed.

If (double randomized) experiments cannot be conducted, it may seem reasonable to apply a sequential design to strengthen causal inference in mediation analysis, that is, to measure X, M, and Y on three subsequent points in time and hence "allow" X to "precede" M and M to "precede" Y. However, the logic of a sequential design is problematic as the measurement of a construct is independent of the conceptual timing of a construct: Just because M is measured after X and Y is measured after X and M, one cannot conclude that X precedes M and M precedes Y (Cole and Maywell 2003). As a consequence, a sequential design by itself does not improve causal inference. Besides that, note that the independence of measurement and timing of a construct also implies that, unless the act of measuring Y affects M, Y may just as well be assessed before M without impairing causal inference (Lemmer and Gollwitzer 2017).

Generally, we recommend to apply experimental methods as often as possible while being aware of their limitations in establishing the causal claim that X affects Y through M. Moreover, we encourage readers to run multiple, methodologically diverse studies testing the proposed mediating process as this can compensate for methodological limitations arising when demonstrating mediation only through a single (type of) study. A selective overview of possible strategies to do so is given in the following section.

Strengthening Causal Inference Through the Collection of Further Evidence

Causal inference on mediation can be strengthened through the collection of further evidence after initial support for a proposed mediating process has been found. Specificity designs allow to investigate mediation in greater detail (Preacher 2015), either by isolating the relevant mediator among different possible mediators or by identifying conditions under which mediation is strengthened (enhancement designs) or weakened (blockage design). This can be done through analyzing mediation models with additional mediators or moderators that enhance or block the proposed mediating process (MacKinnon 2008; Pirlott and MacKinnon 2016).

In the free gift example described previously, for instance, testing the parallel multiple mediator model could be interpreted as an attempt to specify the proposed mediator, hedonic benefits. Simultaneously considering two possible mediating variables, hedonic and utilitarian benefits, allows to investigate whether it is specifically hedonic benefits and not consumer benefits more broadly (i.e., including utilitarian benefits) that transmit the effect of the large (vs. small) free gift on positive WOM intentions.

The generalizability of a mediating process can be demonstrated through consistency designs (Preacher 2015), that is, through replications of the initial study in different contexts or employing different conceptually related measures or manipulations (pattern matching, MacKinnon 2008). For instance, a causal claim for the proposed mediation in the free gift example would be strengthened if the effect could be replicated in a study that employs a tangible free gift instead of a gift card.

Further experimental designs to strengthen causal inference in mediation analysis have been suggested by Imai et al. (2013). For instance, strong causal evidence for a proposed mediating process can be provided by employing a parallel design which essentially combines a measurement-of-mediation design (Spencer et al. 2005), that is, a design in which only X is manipulated, but M and Y are measured, with a concurrent double randomization design (Pirlott and MacKinnon 2016) in which both, X and M are simultaneously manipulated and only Y is measured. Furthermore, Preacher (2015) points out that employing a within-subject design, that is, an experiment in which participants are exposed to all levels of X, may be worthwhile to strengthen causal inference, because participants then serve as their own controls by simultaneously being in all experimental groups. Finally, MacKinnon (2008) notes that the mediating process may also be investigated from a qualitative perspective, as the focus in quantitative research may be too much on issues of statistical significance and less on the originally qualitative nature of a research question.

Strengthening Causal Inference Through Statistical Methods

Beyond experimental methods and collecting more data, statistical methods can also contribute to strengthen causal inference in mediation analysis (see also chapter ▶ "Dealing with Endogeneity: A Nontechnical Guide for Marketing Researchers" by Ebbes et al., this volume). Rooted in the potential outcomes framework, a formal (i.e., theoretical) framework which specifies assumptions for causal inference (see chapter ▶ "Field Experiments" by Valli et al., this volume), one group of statistical methods specifically addresses the issue of bias due to omitted confounding variables (for an overview, see Imai et al. 2011; MacKinnon and Pirlott 2015; Preacher 2015). These methods either assess the degree to which results of mediation analysis are affected by possible violations of the assumption that no confounding variable is omitted from the model (through sensitivity analysis, e.g., Imai et al. 2010), or aim to account for the influence of confounding variables (for an overview of different methods, see MacKinnon and Pirlott 2015).

Note that one implicit assumption of these methods is that the causal order of the variables in the mediation model is correctly specified which may not be the case. Importantly, as illustrated by Lemmer and Gollwitzer (2017), testing for a different causal order by comparing the size of indirect effects found in different possible mediation models (e.g., a model assuming that $X \rightarrow M \rightarrow Y$ and a model assuming that $X \rightarrow Y \rightarrow M$) while assuming that the mediation model for which the larger indirect effect is found must be the correct one ("reverse mediation testing"), is unlikely to be a helpful strategy to address this problem. Specifically, Lemmer and Gollwitzer (2017) show that the size of the indirect effect is affected by a factor completely unrelated to the true underlying causal order of the variables in a mediation model, namely, measurement error associated with M and Y. As a consequence, reverse mediation testing is rarely effective, likely ineffective, and potentially misleading (Lemmer and Gollwitzer 2017; see also Thoemmes 2015).

Questions Arising When Implementing Mediation Analysis

In the following, selected questions arising when implementing mediation analysis are addressed. Specifically, an overview of studies investigating required sample size and power in mediation analysis is given, and reasons for mean centering variables in conditional process analysis as well as different coding schemes for categorical independent variables are discussed. Furthermore, limitations of the regression-based approach to mediation analysis are touched on and information is provided as to different software options to perform mediation analysis.

Sample Size and Power in Mediation Analysis

In studies performing mediation analysis, sample size is often too small to achieve sufficient power (Fritz and MacKinnon 2007). Hence, a note on optimal sample size in mediation analysis, that is, the required sample size to detect mediation with a power of $1-\beta = 0.8$, seems warranted. Unfortunately, there is no easy rule of thumb. Overall, however, it has been shown that the effect with the greatest power in a single mediator model is the indirect effect and the power to detect both, the total and the direct effect, tends to be considerably smaller (Kenny and Judd 2014; Rucker et al. 2011).

Optimal sample size in mediation analysis is (sometimes counterintuitively) affected by the inferential approach, the size of the indirect effect and the individual paths, reliability of the measures, and the complexity of the mediation model. For instance, Fritz and MacKinnon (2007) investigate the required sample size to detect an indirect effect in a single mediator model comparing six different inferential approaches. They report that to detect a small indirect effect using a bias-corrected bootstrap confidence interval, the minimal sample size required to achieve a power of $1-\beta = 0.8$ may be well above $N = 400$. If the indirect effect is large, the required sample size drops to approximately $N \geq 40$. The percentile bootstrap confidence interval is somewhat more conservative and, hence, requires slightly larger sample sizes to achieve sufficient power (Fritz and MacKinnon 2007; see also MacKinnon et al. 2004).

Taylor et al. (2008) provide evidence on the performance of different inferential approaches to test the three-path specific indirect effect in a serial multiple mediator model. They find that the bias-corrected bootstrap confidence interval performs well in samples larger than $N = 200$. Yet, Pieters (2017) describes an example in which a sample size of $N = 450$ is necessary to detect a three-path specific indirect effect of $a_1 d_{21} b_2 = 0.02$ with a power of $1-\beta = 0.8$. Thoemmes et al. (2010) point out that in multiple mediator models, the power to detect individual paths and total as well as specific indirect effects can vary considerably. For example, a larger specific indirect effect may be sufficiently powered given a particular sample size, yet a smaller specific indirect effect may be greatly underpowered. Williams and MacKinnon (2008) report that, given a specific sample size, specific indirect effects consisting of three paths are harder to detect than are two-path specific indirect effects.

Fairchild and MacKinnon (2009) report that when performing conditional process analysis, the required sample size to reach a power of $1 - \beta = 0.8$ might be as large as $N = 500$ or even $N = 1,000$, depending on how much variance is explained by the model (the more, the better). These results are in accordance with results reported by Pieters (2017) who found a sample size of $N = 500$ to be needed to demonstrate moderated mediation. Morgan-Lopez and MacKinnon (2006) further show that power to detect mediated moderation is impaired when the direct effect in the model is nonzero and the independent variable and the moderator are correlated.

Hoyle and Kenny (1999) point out that measurement error affecting the mediator can decrease power to detect mediation. Furthermore, they argue that large collinearity between X and M (corresponding to a large effect of X on M in an experimental context) negatively affects power in mediation analysis as it reduces the amount of variance in M that can contribute to predict Y (i.e., path b) and, consequently, the size of the indirect effect.

When data collection is complicated or expensive, sample size will likely be small. Increasing power in mediation analysis without increasing sample size can be achieved by maximizing variance in the independent variable, the mediator, or the dependent variable and by minimizing error variance (Fairchild and MacKinnon 2009; MacKinnon et al. 2013; Fritz et al. 2015). This can be achieved by design (e.g., by ensuring that the experimental manipulation is sufficiently strong), improved measurement (i.e., minimizing measurement error), or statistical methods (e.g., decreasing error through the inclusion of covariates or the use of structural equation modeling). Power could also be increased by using modern missing data techniques instead of listwise deletion of cases (Fritz et al. 2015), or simply by increasing alpha (Fairchild and MacKinnon 2009). However, Fritz et al. (2015) demonstrate that some measures intended to increase power may also have the opposite effect under specific circumstances (e.g., when there is not enough power to detect the effect of a covariate included to reduce error).

Mean Centering in Conditional Process Analysis

In conditional process analysis, it is sometimes recommended to mean center variables composing an interaction term (e.g., Muller et al. 2005). It has been argued that this reduces multicollinearity between the predictors (e.g., X and W) and interaction terms (e.g., XW) in the model, but this argument has been rebutted several times (Dalal and Zickar 2012; Echambadi and Hess 2007; Hayes 2018). However, mean centering variables without a meaningful zero point improves the interpretability of regression coefficients in conditional process analysis (see also chapter ▶ "Regression Analysis" by Skiera et al., this volume).

For instance, earlier, we discussed a conditional process model in which the effect of a large (vs. small) free gift (X) on positive WOM intentions (Y) through hedonic benefits (M) is dependent on consumers' deal proneness (W). Assuming that W only affects path a, the equations describing the model look as follows (see Eqs. 20 and 21): $M = i_m + a_1 X + a_2 W + a_3 XW + e_m$ and $Y = i_y + c'_1 X + bM + e_y$. As the interaction between X and W is included in the model predicting M, the effect of X on M is modeled to depend on W. That is, the effect of X on M changes in value depending on the value of W. The regression coefficient a_1 denoting the effect of X on M must, hence, be tied to a specific value of W and this value is zero. If W is measured on a scale ranging from 1 (not at all deal-prone) to 7 (very deal-prone), zero is not meaningful and, as a consequence, neither is a_1. However, if the moderator is mean centered, zero indicates the mean deal proneness in the sample and a_1 denotes the effect of the large (vs. small) free gift on hedonic benefits for consumers with average deal proneness. Importantly, as interactions are symmetric, the same reasoning applies to the effect of W on M, a_2, which is only meaningful if X has a meaningful zero point.

That is, centering affects the regression coefficients of the variables composing the interaction term. However, it does not affect the regression coefficient associated with the interaction term itself. Hence, to obtain meaningful regression coefficients for variables composing an interaction term, it is important to ensure that these variables have a meaningful zero point. Mean centering is one way of achieving this.

Coding of Categorical Independent Variables

When performing mediation analysis on data gathered in experiments, a coding scheme has to be selected to translate qualitative information about experimental groups into a set of quantitative indicator variables (Hayes and Preacher 2014). The coding scheme determines how the regression coefficients of the indicator variables are interpreted; hence, it should be selected carefully. There is a variety of different coding schemes of which an overview is presented, for example, by Darlington and Hayes (2017). To illustrate how coding affects the interpretation of regression coefficients, and thus, indirect effects, we briefly discuss two common coding schemes, dummy coding and effect coding.

When employing dummy coding (also called treatment coding or indicator coding), each experimental group G_i is compared to a reference group G_R. Accordingly, the regression coefficients associated with dummy coded indicator variables denote the mean difference between one group G_i and G_R, respectively. Dummy coded indicator variables consist of a series of zeros and ones representing these contrasts (see, e.g., Darlington and Hayes 2017). In fact, in all analyses conducted throughout this chapter, X is dummy coded and denoted by a variable taking the value of zero for participants in the small free gift condition and the value of one for participants in the large free gift condition. Consequently, the indirect effect is interpreted as the effect of the large (vs. small) free gift on positive WOM intentions through the respective mediator(s).

Effect coding (also called effects coding or sum coding) differs from dummy coding in that the individual groups G_i are compared to the grand mean, that is, the overall mean of the to-be-predicted variable across all groups. Accordingly, the regression coefficients associated with the indicator variables represent the mean deviation of a group G_i from the grand mean. In the simplest case, an effect coded indicator variable representing two experimental groups takes the values 1 and -1 (for more examples, see, e.g., Darlington and Hayes 2017). For instance, the independent variable from the free gift example could also be denoted by an indicator variable taking the value of 1 for participants in the large free gift condition and the value of -1 for participants in the small free gift condition. In this case, an indirect effect of $ab = 0.051$ indicates that, as compared to the mean positive WOM intentions in the overall sample, a large free gift increases participants positive WOM intentions through hedonic benefits by 0.051 units.

Hair et al. (2006) argue that dummy coding is the most appropriate coding for an experiment in which there is a control group (G_R) that one or more experimental groups (G_i) are to be compared to. More generally, we would argue that whichever coding scheme should be employed depends on the research question investigated and the specific hypotheses to be tested. Notably, results obtained from analysis of variance can be replicated using regression analysis, namely, if the independent variable(s) are effect coded (chapter ▶ "Analysis of Variance" by Landwehr, this volume). This emphasizes the usefulness of regression analysis for analyzing data gathered in experiments.

Regression Analysis Versus Structural Equation Modeling

It was pointed out earlier that the linear equations describing a mediation model can be fitted sequentially with the help of regression analysis or simultaneously using structural equation modeling (SEM, ▶ "Crafting Survey Research: A Systematic Process for Conducting Survey Research," this volume). There is a lively debate about which approach, regression analysis or SEM, is better when it comes to mediation analysis (e.g., James et al. 2006; Iacobucci et al. 2007; Hayes et al. 2017; Pek and Hoyle 2016). Reasonable arguments have been presented for either side referring to conceptual and statistical differences between the two approaches. Ultimately, we leave it up to the reader which approach to take. However, to enable an informed decision, we summarize important differences, shortcomings, and advantages of either approach in the following section.

On a conceptual level, the two approaches differ with regard to their focal mediation paradigm (James et al. 2006). Specifically, as a consequence of traditions specific to either approach, the default mediation model in regression-based mediation analysis assumes that X may directly affect Y even after controlling for M, as this is presumably likely the case in psychological research where the regression-based approach to mediation analysis originated (Baron and Kenny 1986). Within the SEM approach, however, whether or not the direct effect is included in the model depends on a priori considerations specific to the research question. As a consequence, James et al. (2006) argue that the SEM approach is more parsimonious, and hence, more in accordance with scientific principles.

With regards to statistical differences, it is important to consider that SEM encompasses regression analysis, meaning that any model that can be estimated with regression analysis can also be estimated with SEM. However, as mentioned above, the two approaches differ when it comes to fitting a mediation model. Whereas, in the regression-based approach, the equations describing the mediation model are sequentially fitted for each criterion M_i and Y, they are simultaneously fitted in the SEM approach. This has several consequences. First, it has been argued that simultaneously fitting the whole mediation model is closer to the conceptualization of mediation as one process as compared to a causal chain of separate effects (Pek and Hoyle 2016). Second, the SEM approach is more flexible with regards to the complexity of the model fitted. For instance, while it is not possible to fit mediation models including multiple correlated mediators and outcomes with regression analysis (e.g., longitudinal mediation), such models can be analyzed within a SEM framework. At the same time, however, computational tools such as PROCESS, a macro for SPSS and SAS, relying on regression analysis (Hayes 2018) accommodate a variety of mediation models common to experimental research and will, hence, be sufficient in many cases. Third, it is possible in SEM, but not in regression analysis, to assess how well the mediation model fits the data. This allows to evaluate a specific mediation model as well as to compare multiple mediation models to each other. Hayes et al. (2017) argue, however, that information about a mediation model's fit carries little additional insight: First, fit for saturated models, that is, mediation models that include all possible paths, is likely perfect. Moreover, slightly different mediation models may fit equally well. Finally, testing the significance of specific coefficients is likely to carry more weight in a researcher's judgment than information about fit, as hypotheses generally refer to such specific coefficients (e.g., the index of moderated mediation or a specific indirect effect in a multiple mediator model).

Furthermore, while regression analysis is based on the assumption that latent constructs can be inferred from measured variables without measurement error, SEM estimates measurement error by statistically differentiating between manifest, that is, measured variables and latent variables. Provided that all assumptions underlying the estimation of latent variables are met, this accounts for the unreliability of measured variables. However, Pek and Hoyle (2016) note that there is a bias-efficiency trade-off to adding latent variables to a mediation model, as their inclusion to the model (just as the inclusion of manifest variables) makes it necessary to estimate more parameters which, all else being equal, may reduce the power of the analysis. Another issue with latent variables arises in conditional process analysis as the benefits of accounting for measurement error have to be weighed against considerable methodological uncertainty associated with estimating interactions between latent variables (Hayes et al. 2017).

Finally, Hayes et al. (2017) point out that SEM software may have more sophisticated options to deal with missing data than more basic statistical software. Furthermore, Hayes (2018) notes that with small samples, which are common in experimental research, SEM programs may be slightly biased as their standard errors may be underestimated in such conditions. However, Iacobucci et al. (2007) show that SEM performs well with samples as small as $N = 30$.

Overall, though, Hayes (2018) sees little justification in the general claim that SEM is the better approach to mediation analysis than regression analysis. Assuming that both approaches are suitable to analyze a mediation model, he argues that differences observed in the results from regressions and SEM (e.g., estimates of coefficients or boundaries of bootstrap confidence intervals) are indicative of computational characteristics of a specific SEM software rather than an actual difference between both methods in their ability to reveal mediation.

Software Tools for Mediation Analysis

An increasing variety of software tools enable commonly used statistic programs such as SPSS, SAS, or R to perform mediation analysis. For instance, *PROCESS*, the previously mentioned macro for SPSS and SAS (www.processmacro.org, Hayes 2018), allows researchers to analyze a considerable range of mediation models combining several inferential methods within the regression-based approach: *PROCESS* performs the causal steps procedure, runs the Sobel test, and computes different bootstrap confidence intervals. Other macros for SPSS and SAS allow to incorporate nonlinear effects in the mediation model (*MEDCURVE*, Hayes and Preacher 2010), perform mediation analysis in studies employing a two-condition within-subject design (*MEMORE*, Montoya and Hayes 2017), and use the distribution of the product approach to test the indirect effect (*PRODCLIN*, MacKinnon et al. 2007b). Many common SEM software options compute bootstrap confidence intervals for the indirect effect as well (e.g., Mplus, Muthén and Muthén 1998). With the help of so-called packages (i.e., shared code), general statistical software such as R can also be used for rather basic as well as advanced mediation analysis (e.g., *lavaan*, Rosseel 2012; *MBESS*, Kelley 2007; *mediation*, Tingley et al. 2014; *RMediation*, Tofighi and MacKinnon 2011; *psych*, Revelle 2016).

After having collected and analyzed the data, the next step is to report the results of one's mediation analysis. Excellent recommendations on how to do so comprehensively, comprehensibly, and convincingly are given, for example, by Hayes (2018) and Pieters (2017).

Summary

This chapter provides a regression-based introduction to mediation analysis with an emphasis on mediation analysis in an experimental context. Hence, the focus lies on the description and analysis of selected mediation models common to experimental research (the single mediator model, parallel and serial multiple mediator models, and conditional process models), while more complex mediation models are just briefly discussed. The chapter further addresses the question of how to strengthen causal inference in mediation analysis through design, the collection of additional data, and statistical methods, and closes with a discussion of topics frequently arising when implementing mediation analysis.

However, this chapter only represents a partial survey of the impressive progress made in mediation analysis over the last decade. Furthermore, many research questions in mediation analysis remain unsatisfactorily answered (for a recent summary, see Preacher 2015). Hence, we highly encourage readers to use the literature cited here as a starting point for further literature search. For instance, readers interested in a more detailed illustration of regression-based mediation analysis may refer to Hayes (2018), while readers coming from a structural equation background may find more information from MacKinnon (2008). Finally, an illustration of recent developments in mediation analysis with a special emphasis on how to strengthen causal inference in mediation analysis is given by VanderWeele (2015).

Cross-References

- ▶ Analysis of Variance
- ▶ Dealing with Endogeneity: A Nontechnical Guide for Marketing Researchers
- ▶ Field Experiments
- ▶ Multilevel Modeling
- ▶ Regression Analysis
- ▶ Structural Equation Modeling

References

Baron, R. M., & Kenny, D. A. (1986). The moderator-mediator variable distinction in social psychological research: Conceptual, strategic, and statistical considerations. *Journal of Personality and Social Psychology, 51*(6), 1173–1182.

Berger, J. (2014). Word of mouth and interpersonal communication: A review and directions for future research. *Journal of Consumer Psychology, 24*(4), 586–607.

Bollen, K. A. (1989). *Structural equations with latent variables*. New York: Wiley.

Bollen, K. A., & Stine, R. (1990). Direct and indirect effects: Classical and bootstrap estimates of variability. *Sociological Methodology, 20*(1), 115–140.

Bullock, J. G., Green, D. P., & Ha, S. E. (2010). Yes, but what's the mechanism? (Don't expect an easy answer). *Journal of Personality and Social Psychology, 98*(4), 550–558.

Cavanaugh, L. A. (2014). Because I (don't) deserve it: How relationship reminders and deservingness influence consumer indulgence. *Journal of Marketing Research, 51*(2), 218–232.

Chandon, P., Wansink, B., & Laurent, G. (2000). A benefit congruency framework of sales promotion effectiveness. *Journal of Marketing, 64*(4), 65–81.

Cole, D. A., & Maxwell, S. E. (2003). Testing mediational models with longitudinal data: Questions and tips in the use of structural equation modeling. *Journal of Abnormal Psychology, 112*(4), 558–577.

Cole, D. A., & Preacher, K. J. (2014). Manifest variable path analysis: Potentially serious and misleading consequences due to uncorrected measurement error. *Psychological Methods, 19*(2), 300–315.

Cook, T. D., & Campbell, D. T. (1979). *Quasi-experimentation: Design and analysis for field settings*. Boston: Houghton Mifflin.

Dalal, D. K., & Zickar, M. J. (2012). Some common myths about centering predictor variables in moderated multiple regression and polynomial regression. *Organizational Research Methods, 15*(3), 339–362.

Darlington, R. B., & Hayes, A. F. (2017). *Regression analysis and linear models: Concepts, applications, and implementation*. New York: Guilford Press.

Echambadi, R., & Hess, J. D. (2007). Mean-centering does not alleviate collinearity problems in moderated multiple regression models. *Marketing Science, 26*(3), 438–445.

Edwards, J. R., & Lambert, L. S. (2007). Methods for integrating moderation and mediation: A general analytical framework using moderated path analysis. *Psychological Methods, 12*(1), 1–22.

Efron, B. (1987). Better bootstrap confidence intervals. *Journal of the American Statistical Association, 82*(397), 171–185.

Fairchild, A. J., & MacKinnon, D. P. (2009). A general model for testing mediation and moderation effects. *Prevention Science, 10*(2), 87–99.

Frazier, P., Tix, A. P., & Barron, K. E. (2004). Testing moderator and mediator effects in counseling psychology research. *Journal of Counseling Psychology, 51*(1), 115–134.

Fritz, M. S., & MacKinnon, D. P. (2007). Required sample size to detect the mediated effect. *Psychological Science, 18*(3), 233–239.

Fritz, M. S., Taylor, A. B., & MacKinnon, D. P. (2012). Explanation of two anomalous results in statistical mediation analysis. *Multivariate Behavioral Research, 47*(1), 61–87.

Fritz, M. S., Cox, M. G., & MacKinnon, D. P. (2015). Increasing statistical power in mediation models without increasing sample size. *Evaluation & the Health Professions, 38*(3), 343–366.

Fritz, M. S., Kenny, D. A., & MacKinnon, D. P. (2016). The combined effects of measurement error and omitting confounders in the single-mediator model. *Multivariate Behavioral Research, 51*(5), 681–697.

Hair, J. F., Black, W. C., Babin, B. J., Anderson, R. E., & Tatham, R. L. (2006). *Multivariate data analysis*. Upper Saddle River: Pearson Prentice Hall.

Hansen, W. B., & McNeal, R. B. (1996). The law of maximum expected potential effect: Constraints placed on program effectiveness by mediator relationships. *Health Education Research, 11*(4), 501–507.

Hayes, A. F. (2009). Beyond Baron and Kenny: Statistical mediation analysis in the new millennium. *Communication Monographs, 76*(4), 408–420.

Hayes, A. F. (2018). *Introduction to mediation, moderation, and conditional process analysis: A regression-based approach*. New York: Guilford Press.

Hayes, A. F. (2015). An index and test of linear moderated mediation. *Multivariate Behavioral Research, 50*(1), 1–22.

Hayes, A. F. (2017). Partial, conditional, and moderated moderated mediation: Quantification, inference, and interpretation. *Communication Monographs*. https://doi.org/10.1080/03637751-2017-1352100.

Hayes, A. F., & Cai, L. (2007). Using heteroskedasticity-consistent standard error estimators in OLS regression: An introduction and software implementation. *Behavior Research Methods, 39*(4), 709–722.

Hayes, A. F., & Preacher, K. J. (2010). Quantifying and testing indirect effects in simple mediation models when the constituent paths are nonlinear. *Multivariate Behavioral Research, 45*(4), 627–660.

Hayes, A. F., & Preacher, K. J. (2014). Statistical mediation analysis with a multicategorical independent variable. *British Journal of Mathematical and Statistical Psychology, 67*(3), 451–470.

Hayes, A. F., & Scharkow, M. (2013). The relative trustworthiness of inferential tests of the indirect effect in statistical mediation analysis does method really matter? *Psychological Science, 24*(10), 1918–1927.

Hayes, A. F., Montoya, A. K., & Rockwood, N. J. (2017). The analysis of mechanisms and their contingencies: PROCESS versus structural equation modeling. *Australasian Marketing Journal, 25*(1), 76–81.

Hoyle, R. H., & Kenny, D. A. (1999). Sample size, reliability, and tests of statistical mediation. In R. H. Hoyle (Ed.), *Statistical strategies for small sample research* (pp. 195–222). Thousand Oaks: Sage.

Iacobucci, D. (2012). Mediation analysis and categorical variables: The final frontier. *Journal of Consumer Psychology, 22*(4), 582–594.

Iacobucci, D., Saldanha, N., & Deng, X. (2007). A meditation on mediation: Evidence that structural equations models perform better than regressions. *Journal of Consumer Psychology, 17*(2), 139–153.

Imai, K., Keele, L., & Tingley, D. (2010). A general approach to causal mediation analysis. *Psychological Methods, 15*(4), 309–334.

Imai, K., Keele, L., Tingley, D., & Yamamoto, T. (2011). Unpacking the black box of causality: Learning about causal mechanisms from experimental and observational studies. *American Political Science Review, 105*(4), 765–789.

Imai, K., Tingley, D., & Yamamoto, T. (2013). Experimental designs for identifying causal mechanisms. *Journal of the Royal Statistical Society: Series A (Statistics in Society), 176*(1), 5–51.

Jacoby, J., & Sassenberg, K. (2011). Interactions do not only tell us when, but can also tell us how: Testing process hypotheses by interaction. *European Journal of Social Psychology, 41*(2), 180–190.

James, L. R., Mulaik, S. A., & Brett, J. M. (2006). A tale of two methods. *Organizational Research Methods, 9*(2), 233–244.

Jose, P. E. (2013). *Doing statistical mediation and moderation*. New York: Guilford Press.

Judd, C. M., & Kenny, D. A. (1981). Process analysis estimating mediation in treatment evaluations. *Evaluation Review, 5*(5), 602–619.

Kelley, K. (2007). Methods for the behavioral, educational, and social sciences: An R package. *Behavior Research Methods, 39*(4), 979–984.

Kenny, D. A. (2008). Reflections on mediation. *Organizational Research Methods, 11*(2), 353–358.

Kenny, D. A., & Judd, C. M. (2014). Power anomalies in testing mediation. *Psychological Science, 25*(2), 334–339.

Kisbu-Sakarya, Y., MacKinnon, D. P., & Miočević, M. (2014). The distribution of the product explains normal theory mediation confidence interval estimation. *Multivariate Behavioral Research, 49*(3), 261–268.

Koschate-Fischer, N., & Schandelmeier, S. (2014). A guideline for designing experimental studies in marketing research and a critical discussion of selected problem areas. *Journal of Business Economics, 84*(6), 793–826.

Koschate-Fischer, N., Stefan, I. V., & Hoyer, W. D. (2012). Willingness to pay for cause-related marketing: The impact of donation amount and moderating effects. *Journal of Marketing Research, 49*(6), 910–927.

Koschate-Fischer, N., Huber, I. V., & Hoyer, W. D. (2016). When will price increases associated with company donations to charity be perceived as fair? *Journal of the Academy of Marketing Science, 44*(5), 608–626.

Koschate-Fischer, N., Hoyer, W. D., Stokburger-Sauer, N. E., & Engling, J. (2017). Do life events always lead to change in purchase? The mediating role of change in consumer innovativeness, the variety seeking tendency, and price consciousness. *Journal of the Academy of Marketing Science*. https://doi.org/10.1007/s11747-017-0548-3.

Kraemer, H. C., Wilson, G. T., Fairburn, C. G., & Agras, W. S. (2002). Mediators and moderators of treatment effects in randomized clinical trials. *Archives of General Psychiatry, 59*(10), 877–883.

Kraemer, H. C., Kiernan, M., Essex, M., & Kupfer, D. J. (2008). How and why criteria defining moderators and mediators differ between the Baron & Kenny and MacArthur approaches. *Health Psychology, 27*(2S), 101–108.

Lemmer, G., & Gollwitzer, M. (2017). The "true" indirect effect won't (always) stand up: When and why reverse mediation testing fails. *Journal of Experimental Social Psychology, 69*, 144–149.

Lichtenstein, D. R., Netemeyer, R. G., & Burton, S. (1995). Assessing the domain specificity of deal proneness: A field study. *Journal of Consumer Research, 22*(3), 314–326.

MacKinnon, D. P. (2008). *Introduction to statistical mediation analysis*. New York: Routledge.

MacKinnon, D. P., & Dwyer, J. H. (1993). Estimating mediated effects in prevention studies. *Evaluation Review, 17*(2), 144–158.

MacKinnon, D. P., & Pirlott, A. G. (2015). Statistical approaches for enhancing causal interpretation of the M to Y relation in mediation analysis. *Personality and Social Psychology Review, 19*(1), 30–43.

MacKinnon, D. P., Warsi, G., & Dwyer, J. H. (1995). A simulation study of mediated effect measures. *Multivariate Behavioral Research, 30*(1), 41–62.

MacKinnon, D. P., Krull, J. L., & Lockwood, C. M. (2000). Equivalence of the mediation, confounding and suppression effect. *Prevention Science, 1*(4), 173–181.

MacKinnon, D. P., Lockwood, C. M., Hoffman, J. M., West, S. G., & Sheets, V. (2002). A comparison of methods to test mediation and other intervening variable effects. *Psychological Methods, 7*(1), 83–104.

MacKinnon, D. P., Lockwood, C. M., & Williams, J. (2004). Confidence limits for the indirect effect: Distribution of the product and resampling methods. *Multivariate Behavioral Research, 39*(1), 99–128.

MacKinnon, D. P., Fritz, M. S., Williams, J., & Lockwood, C. M. (2007a). Distribution of the product confidence limits for the indirect effect: Program PRODCLIN. *Behavior Research Methods, 39*(3), 384–389.

MacKinnon, D. P., Fairchild, A. J., & Fritz, M. S. (2007b). Mediation analysis. *Annual Review of Psychology, 58*, 593–614.

MacKinnon, D. P., Kisbu-Sakarya, Y., & Gottschall, A. C. (2013). Developments in mediation analysis. In T. D. Little (Ed.), *The Oxford handbook of quantitative methods in psychology: Volume 2: Statistical analysis* (pp. 338–360). New York: Oxford University Press.

Mathieu, J. E., & Taylor, S. R. (2006). Clarifying conditions and decision points for mediational type inferences in organizational behavior. *Journal of Organizational Behavior, 27*(8), 1031–1056.

Maxwell, S. E., & Cole, D. A. (2007). Bias in cross-sectional analyses of longitudinal mediation. *Psychological Methods, 12*(1), 23–44.

Maxwell, S. E., Cole, D. A., & Mitchell, M. A. (2011). Bias in cross-sectional analyses of longitudinal mediation: Partial and complete mediation under an autoregressive model. *Multivariate Behavioral Research, 46*(5), 816–841.

Miller, G. A., & Chapman, J. P. (2001). Misunderstanding analysis of covariance. *Journal of Abnormal Psychology, 110*(1), 40–48.

Montoya, A. K., & Hayes, A. F. (2017). Two condition within-participant statistical mediation analysis: A path-analytic framework. *Psychological Methods, 22*(1), 6–27.

Morgan-Lopez, A. A., & MacKinnon, D. P. (2006). Demonstration and evaluation of a method for assessing mediated moderation. *Behavior Research Methods, 38*(1), 77–87.

Muller, D., Judd, C. M., & Yzerbyt, V. Y. (2005). When moderation is mediated and mediation is moderated. *Journal of Personality and Social Psychology, 89*(6), 852–863.

Muthén, L. K., & Muthén, L. (1998). *Mplus [computer software]*. Los Angeles: Muthén & Muthén.

Pek, J., & Hoyle, R. H. (2016). On the (in) validity of tests of simple mediation: Threats and solutions. *Social and Personality Psychology Compass, 10*(3), 150–163.

Pieters, R. (2017). Meaningful mediation analysis: Plausible causal inference and informative communication. *Journal of Consumer Research, 44*(3), 692–716.

Pirlott, A. G., & MacKinnon, D. P. (2016). Design approaches to experimental mediation. *Journal of Experimental Social Psychology, 66*, 29–38.

Preacher, K. J. (2015). Advances in mediation analysis: A survey and synthesis of new developments. *Annual Review of Psychology, 66*(1), 825–852.

Preacher, K. J., & Hayes, A. F. (2008). Asymptotic and resampling strategies for assessing and comparing indirect effects in multiple mediator models. *Behavior Research Methods, 40*(3), 879–891.

Preacher, K. J., & Kelley, K. (2011). Effect size measures for mediation models: Quantitative strategies for communicating indirect effects. *Psychological Methods, 16*(2), 93–115.

Preacher, K. J., & Selig, J. P. (2012). Advantages of Monte Carlo confidence intervals for indirect effects. *Communication Methods and Measures, 6*(2), 77–98.

Preacher, K. J., Rucker, D. D., & Hayes, A. F. (2007). Addressing moderated mediation hypotheses: Theory, methods, and prescriptions. *Multivariate Behavioral Research, 42*(1), 185–227.

Revelle, W. (2016). psych: Procedures for psychological, psychometric, and personality research (Version 1.6.12). http://personality-project.org/r, http://personality-project.org/r/psych-manual. pdf. Accessed 24 July 2017.

Rosseel, Y. (2012). Lavaan: An R package for structural equation modeling. *Journal of Statistical Software, 48*(2), 1–36.

Rucker, D. D., Preacher, K. J., Tormala, Z. L., & Petty, R. E. (2011). Mediation analysis in social psychology: Current practices and new recommendations. *Social and Personality Psychology Compass, 5*(6), 359–371.

Savary, J., Goldsmith, K., & Dhar, R. (2014). Giving against the odds: When tempting alternatives increase willingness to donate. *Journal of Marketing Research, 52*(1), 27–38.

Shrout, P. E., & Bolger, N. (2002). Mediation in experimental and nonexperimental studies: New procedures and recommendations. *Psychological Methods, 7*(4), 422–445.

Sobel, M. E. (1982). Asymptotic confidence intervals for indirect effects in structural equation models. *Sociological Methodology, 13*, 290–312.

Spencer, S. J., Zanna, M. P., & Fong, G. T. (2005). Establishing a causal chain: Why experiments are often more effective than mediational analyses in examining psychological processes. *Journal of Personality and Social Psychology, 89*(6), 845–851.

Stone-Romero, E. F., & Rosopa, P. J. (2008). The relative validity of inferences about mediation as a function of research design characteristics. *Organizational Research Methods, 11*(2), 326–352.

Taylor, A. B., MacKinnon, D. P., & Tein, J.-Y. (2008). Tests of the three-path mediated effect. *Organizational Research Methods, 11*(2), 241–269.

Thoemmes, F. (2015). Reversing arrows in mediation models does not distinguish plausible models. *Basic and Applied Social Psychology, 37*(4), 226–234.

Thoemmes, F., MacKinnon, D. P., & Reiser, M. R. (2010). Power analysis for complex mediational designs using Monte Carlo methods. *Structural Equation Modeling, 17*(3), 510–534.

Tingley, D., Yamamoto, T., Hirose, K., Keele, L., & Imai, K. (2014). Mediation: R package for causal mediation analysis. *Journal of Statistical Software, 59*(5), 1–38.

Tofighi, D., & MacKinnon, D. P. (2011). RMediation: An R package for mediation analysis confidence intervals. *Behavior Research Methods, 43*(3), 692–700.

Tofighi, D., & Thoemmes, F. (2014). Single-level and multilevel mediation analysis. *The Journal of Early Adolescence, 34*(1), 93–119.

Touré-Tillery, M., & McGill, A. L. (2015). Who or what to believe: Trust and the differential persuasiveness of human and anthropomorphized messengers. *Journal of Marketing, 79*(4), 94–110.

Valeri, L., & VanderWeele, T. J. (2013). Mediation analysis allowing for exposure-mediator interactions and causal interpretation: Theoretical assumptions and implementation with SAS and SPSS macros. *Psychological Methods, 18*(2), 137–150.

VanderWeele, T. J. (2015). *Explanation in causal inference: Methods for mediation and interaction.* New York: Oxford University Press.

VanderWeele, T. J., & Vansteelandt, S. (2014). Mediation analysis with multiple mediators. *Epidemiologic Methods, 2*(1), 95–115.

Wen, Z., & Fan, X. (2015). Monotonicity of effect sizes: Questioning kappa-squared as mediation effect size measure. *Psychological Methods, 20*(2), 193–203.

Williams, J., & MacKinnon, D. P. (2008). Resampling and distribution of the product methods for testing indirect effects in complex models. *Structural Equation Modeling: A Multidisciplinary Journal, 15*(1), 23–51.

Yuan, Y., & MacKinnon, D. P. (2014). Robust mediation analysis based on median regression. *Psychological Methods, 19*(1), 1–20.

Zhao, X., Lynch, J. G., & Chen, Q. (2010). Reconsidering Baron and Kenny: Myths and truths about mediation analysis. *Journal of Consumer Research, 37*(2), 197–206.

Part III
Applications

Measuring Customer Satisfaction and Customer Loyalty

Sebastian Hohenberg and Wayne Taylor

Contents

Introduction	910
Conceptual Background	911
The Relationship of Customer Satisfaction and Loyalty	911
Conceptualizing Customer Satisfaction and Loyalty	913
Measuring Customer Satisfaction	915
Survey Scales	915
Other Measurement Approaches	919
Measuring Customer Loyalty	921
Overview	921
Loyalty Intentions	922
Loyalty Behavior	925
The Future of Managing Customer Satisfaction and Loyalty	932
Concluding Remarks	933
References	934

Abstract

Measuring customer satisfaction and customer loyalty represents a key challenge for firms. In response, researchers and practitioners have developed a plethora of options on how to assess these phenomena. However, existing measurement approaches differ substantially with regard to their complexity, sophistication, and information quality. Furthermore, guidance is scarce on how firms can leverage and combine these approaches to implement a state-of-the-art satisfaction and loyalty measurement system. This chapter attempts to address this vacancy. The authors first define and conceptualize customer satisfaction

---

S. Hohenberg (✉)
McCombs School of Business, The University of Texas, Austin, TX, USA
e-mail: Sebastian.Hohenberg@mccombs.utexas.edu

W. Taylor
Cox School of Business, Southern Methodist University, Dallas, TX, USA
e-mail: wjtaylor@smu.edu

© Springer Nature Switzerland AG 2022
C. Homburg et al. (eds), *Handbook of Market Research*,
https://doi.org/10.1007/978-3-319-57413-4_30

and customer loyalty. Next, the authors provide an overview of the different operationalization and measurement approaches that companies face when designing a customer satisfaction and loyalty measurement system. The authors also discuss some of the common modeling challenges associated with measuring loyalty, namely, dealing with self-selection bias. Finally, the authors project what the future holds in this area.

Keywords

Customer satisfaction · Customer loyalty · Measurement · Conceptualization · Operationalization · Scales · Loyalty programs

Introduction

Customer satisfaction and customer loyalty are key constructs in marketing management (Anderson et al. 1994; Howard and Sheth 1969). Due to their importance, research provides rich insights regarding their nature as well as regarding the determinants and consequences of both phenomena (Palmatier et al. 2006). Moreover, empirical evidence indicates that marketing managers conceive customer satisfaction and loyalty as important success factors (Aksoy 2013). Studies by Bain and Company (2013) and Anderson (2010) identify customer satisfaction and loyalty as top strategic priorities for firms. Furthermore, empirical results show that increasingly volatile customer and competitor behaviors in a digitalized economy will further increase the relevance of systematically managing customer satisfaction and loyalty in the upcoming years (Ernst and Young 2011; Reeves and Deimler 2011). Brooke (2016) recently summarized these issues: "the initial transaction between buyer and seller is but a prologue to the overall concern of marketing. Few businesses can be sure their customers will continue to engage with them (...). We live in an age of disruption" (p. 30).

For successfully managing customer satisfaction and loyalty, the basic requirement is the effective assessment of these constructs (Peterson and Wilson 1992; Watson et al. 2015). However, as Hayes (2008) points out, conceptualizing and measuring customer satisfaction and loyalty represent strong managerial challenges, especially for three main reasons. First, there is a wide range of different assessment approaches. Yet, evidence indicates that the existing conceptualizations and measurement approaches substantially differ with regard to their complexity, sophistication, and information quality (Fornell et al. 1996; Morgeson et al. 2011; Sheth 1970). Second, new marketing trends and technologies, such as Big Data or social media, provide various novel opportunities for marketers to gain insights on customer attitudes and behaviors (Homburg et al. 2015; Kozinets et al. 2010; Weinberg et al. 2015). These novel opportunities may have relevance for assessing customer satisfaction and loyalty in certain contexts. Third, empirical proof shows that the suitability of novel and existing customer satisfaction and loyalty approaches may substantially vary according to the specific application field and the consequences of mis-measurement may be severe (Aksoy 2013; Hayes 2008). For instance, companies may mis-target customers based on an incorrect measurement, that is, dedicating resources to customers who don't need attention (e.g., those that are already satisfied and loyal or those that are a "lost case" for the firm) or failing to dedicate resources to key customers (e.g., customers who the firm is at risk of losing due to declining satisfaction).

Thus, given the lack of overviews, evaluations, and application guidelines of the different traditional and novel tools and measurement approaches, many firms struggle to design appropriate measurement systems for their particular needs and contexts (Hayes 2008). Against this background, this chapter introduces the reader to the constructs of customer satisfaction and loyalty. Moreover, actionable approaches and tools to measure customer satisfaction and loyalty information are described. Specifically, this chapter addresses the following questions:

- How can firms conceptualize customer satisfaction and customer loyalty?
- How can firms measure customer satisfaction?
- How can firms measure customer loyalty?

This chapter answers these questions across six sections. In this first section we have introduced the relationship between satisfaction and customer loyalty. The second section continues this discussion and explores the conceptual background of each construct. The third and fourth sections outline the common methods in which firms measure both satisfaction and customer loyalty. For satisfaction we discuss surveys, focus groups, and complaint analyses, and for customer loyalty we highlight surveys and databases, with additional attention to loyalty programs. We recognize that there are additional methods for measuring customer satisfaction and loyalty (e.g., social media) and that methods can apply to both topics (e.g., some databases can be used to gain insights on customer satisfaction). However, in the interest of brevity, we focus on the primary methods used within each subject in addition to the nuances of using each method for a given subject. The fifth section emphasizes the recent trends and future directions in measuring satisfaction and customer loyalty. Finally, the sixth section concludes.

Conceptual Background

The Relationship of Customer Satisfaction and Loyalty

Research has extensively analyzed customer satisfaction, customer loyalty, their relationship, as well as potential antecedents and consequences (see Palmatier et al. (2006) for an overview). Customer *satisfaction* is generally referred to as a postconsumption evaluation of perceived quality relative to prepurchase expectations about quality (Homburg et al. 2005, p. 85). In contrast, customer *loyalty* is defined as "a collection of attitudes aligned with a series of purchase behaviors that systematically favor one entity over competing entities" (Watson et al. 2015, p. 804). See section "Conceptualizing Customer Satisfaction and Loyalty" for a more detailed conceptualization of both constructs.

As prior investigators have pointed out, the existing knowledge on customer satisfaction and loyalty can be summarized along the "Customer Relationship Management (CRM)-Outcome Chain" (Anderson and Mittal 2000; Kumar and Reinartz 2012). More precisely, according to the CRM-Outcome Chain, firms' marketing activities provoke customers' psychological states (i.e., attitudes) as well as other loyalty reasons, which, in turn, result in diverse loyalty intentions and actual behaviors, eventually manifesting in economic outcomes (cf. Fig. 1). For instance, a firm's investment in a customer loyalty program (i.e., a marketing activity) may enhance customers' satisfaction (i.e., an attitude), which drives their loyalty intentions and is likely to result in additional future sales (e.g., actual loyalty behavior in terms of repurchases or cross-buying) and economic company success.

Thus, as shown by the CRM-Outcome Chain, customer satisfaction represents an important antecedent of customer loyalty. However, as the CRM-Outcome Chain also indicates, an increase in customer satisfaction does not necessarily result in a (equal) gain of customer loyalty (Anderson 1996; Woodruff et al. 1983). This is due to two main reasons. First, there are other factors besides customer satisfaction that can influence customer loyalty, for instance, other psychological states (e.g., trust, commitment), loyalty incentives (e.g., rewards for repurchases or cross-buying), contractual obligations (e.g., due to a legal contract, the customer must stay within a given relationship), technical causes (e.g., the customer depends on a system of a given provider), and economical causes (e.g., changing the supplier is relatively costly due to existing rebates or bonuses) (Hayes 2008; Kumar and Reinartz 2012; Watson et al. 2015). A meta-analysis has therefore found that customer satisfaction explains less than 25% of the variance of components of customer loyalty (Szymanski and Henard 2001). Second, the magnitude of the customer satisfaction-customer loyalty relationship is likely to depend on various situational and

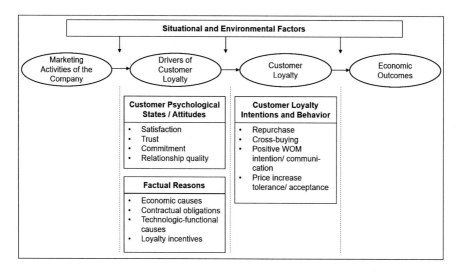

Fig. 1 CRM-Outcome Chain. (Adapted from Kumar and Reinartz 2012; Watson et al. 2015)

environmental factors (Aksoy 2013; Larivière et al. 2016; Shankar et al. 2003). For example, Bolton (1998) found that customer satisfaction is positively related to customer loyalty, yet the strength of this relationship depends on other factors, such as the level of satisfaction or the length of the prior customer-firm relationship. Similarly, Anderson et al. (2004) find the customer satisfaction-loyalty relationship is significantly weaker under high competition.

As a result of potential competing antecedents and various contingent conditions, Kumar et al. (2013) conclude in their review of the customer satisfaction–loyalty relationship: "the customer satisfaction–loyalty main effect is indeed weak and that customer satisfaction, by itself, can hardly change customer loyalty in a significant way. In fact, the systematic presence of moderators, mediators, and other predictors of loyalty introduce a high variability in the findings, thus reducing the role of satisfaction" (p. 247). In line with this point of view, rich evidence today indicates that even very satisfied customers can deflect. For instance, Reichheld (1996) finds that more than 60% of satisfied customers may actually switch their providers. Likewise, evidence indicates that only about half of the households with service problems would remain loyal, even if their problems were satisfactorily resolved (Chandrashekaran et al. 2007). These results emphasize that, in order to achieve sustainably high sales success with the existing customer base, firms need to systematically assess and manage customers' loyalty as well as their satisfaction levels (Luo and Homburg 2007; Rust and Zahorik 1993). In embracing this comprehensive view, this chapter focuses in the following on the conceptualization and measurement of both, customer satisfaction and customer loyalty.

Conceptualizing Customer Satisfaction and Loyalty

To conceptualize customer satisfaction, prior research has distinguished (1) a transaction-specific perspective and (2) a cumulative perspective (Anderson et al. 1994). The former perspective conceives customer satisfaction as the buyer's cognitive state, resulting from the evaluation of being adequately rewarded for a particular sacrifice she has undergone (Churchill Jr. and Surprenant, 1982; Howard and Sheth 1969; Oliver 1981). In contrast, the latter perspective comprehends customer satisfaction as the cognitive state resulting from the evaluations of the entire interactions with a firm over time (Hunt 1977; Verhoef 2003). Hence, the transaction-specific and the cumulative perspective provide a highly similar understanding of customer satisfaction that essentially differs with regard to the reference object (i.e., a single transaction versus the entire relationship).

Thus, by drawing on both of these perspectives, this study conceptualizes customer satisfaction as the result of a cognitive process during which the customer compares her prior expectations regarding the product's performance with the actually perceived performance (Gupta and Zeithaml 2006). This conceptualization builds on the "Confirmation-Disconfirmation Paradigm" (Oliver 1980). According to this paradigm (cf. Fig. 2), customers compare the perceived performance of the product or service to an expected performance standard (e.g., based on prior experiences or desires) (Halstead 1999). If the customer perceives the actual performance as higher (equal) relative to her expectations, the expectations will be positively discontinued (confirmed), thus resulting in customer satisfaction. In contrast, if the expected performance is greater than the actually perceived performance, customers will experience a negative discontinuation of their expectations, which results in dissatisfaction (McCollough et al. 2000).

The conceptualization of customer loyalty is more complicated. Although customer loyalty has been in the focus of marketing research and practice for a long time (Oliver 1999), there is no consensus among researchers on how to define customer loyalty (Aksoy 2013; Kumar and Reinartz 2012; McAlexander et al. 2003). Yet, most prior studies agree that customer loyalty is a complex, multidimensional construct.

More precisely, prior research has often conceptualized customer loyalty by differentiating two theoretical elements, i.e., loyalty (future) intentions and the (current) loyalty behavior (McAlexander et al. 2002; Oliver 1999; Watson et al. 2015). Furthermore, as Fig. 3 shows, these theoretical elements have both been defined in terms of four dimensions (i.e., repurchase, cross-buying, positive WOM/recommendation, and price increase acceptance/tolerance). Recent empirical

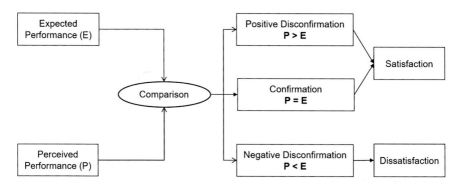

Fig. 2 Conceptualization of customer satisfaction: the Confirmation-Disconfirmation Paradigm. (Adapted from Boshoff 1997)

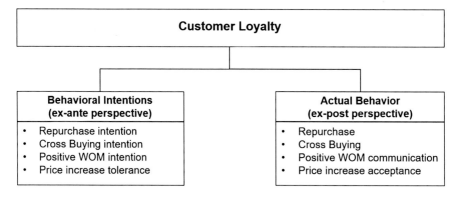

Fig. 3 Conceptualization of Customer Loyalty. (Adapted from Bruhn 2016)

findings showing that loyal customers in many situations tend to pay less, not more, illustrate the relevance of conceptualizing customer loyalty via multiple dimensions and differentiating between intentions and actual behavior, instead of merely looking at repurchase-related variables (see Umashankar et al. (2017) or Wieseke et al. (2014) for detailed overviews).

Measuring Customer Satisfaction

Customer satisfaction can be measured in a variety of ways (Homburg and Fuerst 2010). Due to several advantages in terms of flexibility and comprehensiveness, most academics and practitioners today measure customers' satisfaction through surveys, using and adapting established scales (Hayes 2008; Zairi 2000). Against this background, we discuss in this section how customer satisfaction can be assessed via scales in surveys and then review alternative approaches which can improve upon traditional customer satisfaction scales.

Survey Scales

As previously outlined, there are two conceptual perspectives to customer satisfaction that differ with respect to their reference object: the transaction-specific perspective focuses on individual transactions, whereas the cumulative perspective centers on the entire relationship. Research has shown that customer satisfaction can be operationalized according to both perspectives in surveys which have resulted in the creation of a variety of scales (Hayes 2008; Peterson and Wilson 1992). In the following, we will provide an overview of the leading customer satisfaction scales and present guidelines of how to adapt and choose between them.

Adopting a transaction-specific perspective, Oliver (1980) developed one of the first multi-item customer satisfaction scales. As Table 1 shows, this scale encompasses six reflective items, which have been used and adapted at various times in the marketing literature. For instance, Bearden and Teel (1983) adapted Oliver's (1980) six items to their research context, and then, due to problems with the scale's psychometric properties, reduced the scale to four main items. More recently, Homburg et al. (2005) and Homburg et al. (2006) drew on Oliver (1980) and Bearden and Teel (1983) to measure customers' satisfaction with a specific transaction with 4 items on an 11-point Likert scale. Moreover, various recent measurements of a transaction-specific customer satisfaction in marketing research use further reduced, adapted, and more efficient forms of the Oliver (1980) scale; some even draw on single-item scales (e.g., Chandrashekaran et al. 2007).

Adopting a cumulative perspective, Cannon and Perreault Jr. (1999) provided a multi-item customer satisfaction scale measuring the satisfaction with the entire relationship (see Table 1). This scale was further developed by Homburg and Stock (2004) and Homburg et al. (2011). In synthesizing this literature analysis, findings reveal that customers' satisfaction with a particular transaction and satisfaction with the entire relationship are generally measured with a multi-item

Table 1 Examples of leading customer satisfaction scales

Authors (year)	Reference object	Type of scale	Items (item reliabilities, if specified)	Other psychometric properties
Oliver (1980)	Transaction	Not specified	I am satisfied with my decision to get or not to get a flu shot If I had it to do all over again, I would feel differently about the flu shot program (R∗) My choice to get or not to get a flu shot was a wise one I feel bad about my decision concerning the flu shot (R∗) I think that I did the right thing when I decided to get or not to get the flu shot I am not happy that I did what I did about the flu shot (R∗)	CA = 0.82
Homburg et al. (2005)	Transaction	11-point Likert scale	All in all, I would be satisfied with this restaurant [experience] The restaurant [experience] would meet my expectations The earlier scenario compares to an ideal restaurant experience Overall, how satisfied would you be with the restaurant visit just described?	CR = 0.98 (study 1) CA > 0.94 (study 2)
Cannon and Perreault (1999)	Relationship	7-point Likert scale	Our firm regrets the decision to do business with this supplier (R∗) (0.50) Overall, we are very satisfied with this supplier (0.80) We are very pleased with what this supplier does for us (0.87) Our firm is not completely happy with this supplier (R∗) (0.59) If we had to do it all over again, we would still choose to use this supplier (0.59)	CA = 0.84 AVE = 0.67
Homburg and Stock (2004)	Relationship	5-point Likert scale	We are very pleased with the products and services that this company delivers (0.74) We enjoy collaborating with this company (0.71) On an overall basis, our experience with this company has been positive (0.84) This company is first choice for us for the purchase of these products and services (0.53) On an overall basis, we are satisfied with this company (0.85)	CA = 0.91 CR = 0.92 AVE = 0.55

(continued)

Table 1 (continued)

Authors (year)	Reference object	Type of scale	Items (item reliabilities, if specified)	Other psychometric properties
Homburg et al. (2011)	Relationship	7-point Likert scale	We are very pleased with the products and services of company X (0.61) We intensively enjoy collaborating with company X (0.76) On an overall basis, our experience with company X has been very positive (0.85) On an overall basis, we are very satisfied with this company (0.92)	CA = N/A CR = 0.94 AVE = 0.78
Fuerst (2012)	Relationship	7-point semantic differential	How satisfied are you with firm XYZ? How advantageous do you consider the relationship with firm XYZ? How well does firm XYZ fulfill your expectations?	N/A

Note: R∗ = reverse coded; N/A = not available

reflective Likert scale with an uneven amount of scale points (e.g., seven scale points ranging from "strongly disagree" to "strongly agree"). The scales provided in Table 1 can serve as a source for item selection, but the items obviously need to be adapted to the specific transaction of interest. See Jarvis et al. (2003) for guidance of how to choose between uneven and even scale points and select the exact number of scale points in different situations, and Bergkvist and Rossiter (2007) for potential problems and advantages of single-item scales ("Design and Process of Survey Research").

In addition, previous work across the two conceptual perspectives often recommends measuring customer satisfaction at two different levels: the overall level and the detailed level (Churchill Jr. and Surprenant 1982; Homburg and Fuerst 2010; Rust and Zahorik 1993). This recommendation is because an entity (e.g., a transaction or an overall relationship) and customers' satisfaction with it may encompass various aspects. Hence, knowledge regarding which of the single aspects account for how much of the overall satisfaction score may provide actionable implications for enhancing customers' future satisfaction levels (Hayes 2008).

For instance, according to the cumulative perspective, customer satisfaction at the overall level may refer to the customer's total satisfaction with the entire customer-firm relationship. (Note that customer satisfaction could also be measured at different levels according to the transaction-specific perspective. For instance, the overall level could relate to the satisfaction with the entire transaction (e.g., "how satisfied are you with the purchase of the new iPad overall?") and the detailed level could refer to the functionalities of the product (e.g., the features and the usability) or the purchase process (e.g., consulting by the sales rep, payment modes, financing options, etc.).) As Table 1 shows, overall customer satisfaction is typically measured on a Likert scale with four to five reflective items. Due to the reflective nature of the items, a customer's satisfaction with the overall customer-firm relationship is specified as the average of all chosen scale items (see chapter ▶ "Crafting Survey Research: A Systematic Process for Conducting Survey Research" by Klarmann and Homburg in this handbook for details). In aggregating the overall-level satisfaction of all survey participants, firms can compute the customer satisfaction index (i.e., the average overall customer satisfaction). To enhance the comparability of customer satisfaction indices between different satisfaction measurements, it is recommended to keep the items measuring overall-level customer satisfaction as consistent as possible across measurements and time. Moreover, as previous work has pointed out, firms may choose to rescale customer satisfaction indices to a scale ranging from 0 to 100 to facilitate interpretation and discussion of results (Fuerst 2012; Griffin et al. 1995).

Customer satisfaction at the detailed level in this example refers to the customer's satisfaction with specific performance aspects of the firm (e.g., customer service, complaint handling, or satisfaction with a product) (also see Grigoroudis and Siskos 2009; Rust and Zahorik 1993). Customer satisfaction at the detailed level could also be assessed via reflective multi-item scales (which could lead to a higher validity and reliability of the assessment). However, many customer satisfaction measurements interested in assessing the detailed level draw on single items to ensure parsimony of the measurement and to increase response rates (Fuerst 2012; Hayes 2008). Similar to the overall level, customers' satisfaction with each performance aspects can be aggregated across all survey participants once the individual responses are collected. Comparing the overall customer satisfaction index with the indices of the detailed performance aspects may provide important explanations for the level of the customer satisfaction index and, potentially, indicate first levers for improving the customer satisfaction index in the future (Diamantopoulos 2011; Rust and Zahorik 1993; Homburg and Klarmann 2012).

Measuring customer satisfaction at the detailed level can be conducted in two steps (Fuerst 2012). In the first step, firms should carefully analyze their offerings and identify all major functionalities that may influence the customers' satisfaction in order to design a comprehensive measurement (Griffin et al. 1995; Homburg and Klarmann 2012; Rust and Zahorik 1993). The relevant functionalities may vary substantially according to the product type, the industry, or company-specific factors (Homburg and Fuerst 2010). For example, a limousine transportation service provider might want to assess the quality and response time of the service center, punctuality of service delivery, as well as integrity and commitment of the drivers, whereas a car manufacturer might rather put emphasis on product quality, brand reputation, and satisfaction with after sales service. In the second step, firms should then specify all determinants of the identified functionalities. For instance, if the aforementioned car manufacturer has identified product quality, brand reputation, and after sales service as the critical functionalities, the manufacturer now needs to specify the drivers of these functionalities (e.g., for the functionality after sales service: speed of service, behavior of service personal, possibilities to complain, and quality of service results). Figure 4 demonstrates how customer satisfaction can be operationalized at an overall level and the detailed level, using a different example of a private bank.

Finally, in addition to assessing the level of customer satisfaction, it is a focal aim of customer satisfaction measurements to identify the most critical drivers of customer satisfaction (Morgan et al. 2005). As Gustafsson and Johnson (2004) show, a customer satisfaction measurement encompassing the overall and detailed level can be easily used to make this identification. Figure 5 summarizes one of the advanced methods to conduct such an evaluation: structural equation modeling (see also Gustafsson and Johnson (2004) and Homburg and Klarmann (2012) for more details and overviews of alternative methods). As this figure further indicates, by using structural equation modeling, firms can receive insights regarding the strength of the satisfaction drivers by looking at the standardized path coefficients (see the chapter "▶ Structural Equation Modeling" by Hans Baumgartner and Bert Weijters in this handbook for details).

Other Measurement Approaches

As prior work has demonstrated, there are various other approaches to assess customer satisfaction (Brandt and Reffett 1989; Bruhn 2003; Van Doorn and Verhoef

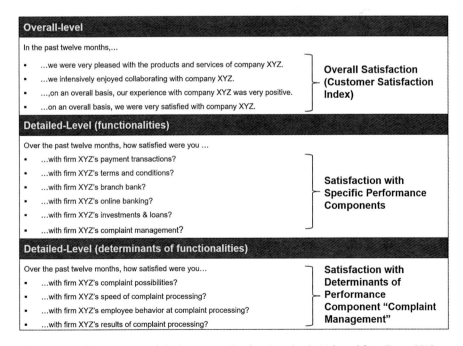

Fig. 4 Measuring customer satisfaction – example of a private bank. (Adapted from Fuerst 2012, p. 134 ff)

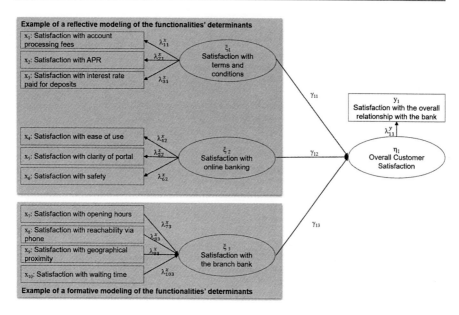

Fig. 5 Simplified structural equation model for determining the strength of satisfaction drivers. (Adapted from Homburg and Klarmann 2012, p. 204)

2008). The following paragraphs will focus on two of the most popular measurement approaches: complaint analysis and focus groups (see Bruhn (2003) for the depiction of further and more rare methods). However, because these approaches generally relate to a specific event or transaction (McCollough et al. 2000; Smith and Bolton 1998), these approaches have various disadvantages as compared to the above-described direct satisfaction ratings via survey scales, e.g., in terms of measuring customer satisfaction comprehensively. Thus, firms generally amend their customer satisfaction surveys with these approaches and use results from the complaint analysis and focus groups for a selective improvement of their offerings (Fuerst 2012).

Prior work has shown that customer suggestions and complaints can be a valuable implicit source for analyzing the underlying factors that determine customer satisfaction levels (Homburg and Fuerst 2005; Singh and Pandya 1991). For instance, if a firm receives many complaints concerning the availability of its call center, it may start to systematically analyze the complaints and the performance data of the call center in order to detect and ultimately eliminate the underlying cause of the problem. Likewise, if a company receives an increased amount of suggestions regarding the functionalities of their products, these suggestions may provide valuable information on how to improve the products' handling in the future, adding to the future satisfaction of customers. An advantage of analyzing customer suggestions and complaints is that the company can utilize existing data to get insights on latent problems that affect customer interactions (Grigoroudis and Siskos (2009); see also Homburg and Fuerst (2005) for a detailed discussion of complaints in the context of customer satisfaction and customer loyalty). However, a major drawback of this method is that usually only a few customers actually complain and, thus, various existing deficits may not become obvious with this method (Richins 1983). Thus, we recommend that firms use the systematic analysis of customer suggestions and complaints in addition to the above-described direct customer satisfaction measurement via scales.

Moreover, firms can use focus groups or other more qualitative research approaches to gain more detailed insights into the underlying reasons for (the lack of) customer satisfaction. More precisely, such qualitative approaches focus on specific customer experiences (i.e., incidents), such as the contact with the service helpdesk of the firm, being advised by a salesperson, or using the product for the first time (Bruhn 2003). Firms can employ the critical incident technique in order to analyze these decisive moments in the customer-firm relationship: these incidents constitute deviations from the customers' "business-as-usual" mindset, which might affect their evaluation of entire business relationship (Gremler 2004; Van Doorn and Verhoef 2008). However, as the incident-related approaches focus on one specific touch point or transaction with the firm, they can hardly be used to assess the cumulative or overall satisfaction (Brandt and Reffett 1989; Bruhn 2003). Thus, in line with recommendations in the methodological research (Davis et al. 2011), we recommend that firms utilize focus groups in addition to customer satisfaction surveys to gain additional in-depth insights on selected issues.

Measuring Customer Loyalty

Overview

As shown in section "Conceptual Background" above, customer loyalty is generally conceptualized as encompassing two theoretical elements (i.e., loyalty intentions and actual loyalty behaviors). Moreover, both theoretical elements can be operationalized alongside four dimensions: repurchase, cross-buying, positive WOM/recommendation, and price increase acceptance/tolerance. The researcher can use both objective data – e.g., from the company's CRM system – and subjective data – e.g., from customer surveys – in order to gather information on customer loyalty. However, assessing actual loyalty behavior in surveys is problematic, because, as Sheppard et al. (1988) demonstrate, stated behavioral intentions are often a weak predictor of actual behavior (e.g., due to unexpected events and factors of the social environment). Thus, prior research recommends focusing on objective data to assess customers' actual loyalty behavior (Hayes 2008; Kumar and Shah 2004; Peters et al. 2010). Moreover, prior work also recommends to focus on subjective data (e.g., surveys) to assess loyalty intentions, because these intentions are latent and subjective in nature (Hayes 2008). In adopting this view, we created Fig. 6, which provides an overview of the operationalization of attitudinal and

Dimension	Behavioral Intentions (surveys)	Actual Behavior (databases)
Repurchase	In how far... ...are you planning to buy the product/service from firm XYZ again? ...are you intending to stay customer at firm XYZ? ...are you planning to increase the share of products/services purchased from firm XYZ?	• Repurchase rate • Share of wallet • Larger cart
Cross-buying	In how far... ...are you planning to buy additional/other products/services from firm XYZ? ...is it an option for you to buy product categories/service categories from firm XYZ?	• Range of product categories purchased • Dollar amount spent on additional product categories
Positive WOM intention/communication	In how far... ...are you intending to recommend firm XYZ to your business partners? ...will you recommend firm XYZ to your acquaintances and friends?	• Number of referrals • Valence of referrals
Price Increase Tolerance/Acceptance	• Would you tolerate a 2/5/10/20 percent price increase and still buy products/services from firm XYZ? • By how much could the prices of firm XYZ increase such that you would still buy from it in the future?	• Number of customers leaving/staying at the firm after a 2/5/10/20 percent price increase • Number of discount requests • Number of pricing complaints

Fig. 6 Measuring customer loyalty intentions and behavior. (Adapted from Homburg and Fuerst 2010)

behavioral customer loyalty. In the following section, we discuss approaches to measuring customer loyalty in greater detail.

Loyalty Intentions

Firms should employ subjective approaches to derive insights with respect to customers' loyalty intentions (Watson et al. 2015). This recommendation is because subjective approaches are particularly suitable to uncover latent constructs and underlying subjective factors (Hayes 2008; Klarmann 2008). Similar to measuring customer satisfaction, there are two different approaches to measuring customer loyalty intentions in surveys (see Table 2). First, there is the aggregated approach, which tries to assess the overall customer loyalty with up to five or more reflective items (e.g., Watson et al. 2015). Applications of the aggregated approach assess the customer's loyalty intentions through indicators that essentially target the same underlying latent loyalty construct (i.e., collection of attitudes aligned with a series of purchase behaviors that systematically favor one entity over competing entities). Second, as also shown in Table 2, there is the disaggregated approach. This approach builds more directly on the above-described conceptualization of customer loyalty via multiple dimensions. Scales following this approach therefore aim to assess customer loyalty intentions for each of its disaggregated dimensions. For instance, Homburg et al. (2011) focus on three dimensions of the customer loyalty concept and measure each dimension via two items.

Table 2 Examples of leading customer loyalty intention scales

Authors (year)	Approach of scale	Type of scale	Items (item reliabilities, if specified)	Other properties
Brakus et al. (2009)	Overall loyalty	7-point Likert scale	In the future, I will be loyal to this brand I will buy this brand again This brand will be my first choice in the future I will not buy other brands if this brand is available at the store I will recommend this brand to others	N/A
Watson et al. (2015)	Overall loyalty	N/A	I prefer [target] over competitors I enjoy doing business with [target] I consider [target] my first preference I have a positive attitude toward [target] I really like [target]	N/A
Zeithaml et al. (1996)	Loyalty dimensions	7-point likelihood scale	Say positive things about XYZ to other people Recommend XYZ to someone who seeks your advice Encourage friends and relatives to do business with XYZ Consider XYZ your first choice to buy services Do more business with XYZ in the next few years Do less business with XYZ in the next few years (R) Take some of your business to a competitor that offers better Continue to do business with XYZ if its prices increase somewhat Pay a higher price than competitors charge for the benefits you currently receive from XYZ Switch to a competitor if you experience a problem with XYZ's service Complain to other customers if you experience a problem with XYZ's service Complain to external agencies, such as the Better Business Bureau, if you experience a problem with XYZ's service Complain to XYZ's employees if you experience a problem with XYZ's service	N/A
Homburg et al. (2011)	Loyalty dimensions	7-point Likert scale	**Customer intentions to repurchase** We consider company X as our first choice for the purchase of	CR = 0.81 AVE = 0.60

(continued)

Table 2 (continued)

Authors (year)	Approach of scale	Type of scale	Items (item reliabilities, if specified)	Other properties
			such products and services (0.49) We intend to stay loyal to company X (0.71) **Customer intentions to increase share of wallet** We intend to do more business with company X in the future (0.77) We intend to additionally purchase other products and services from company X in the future (0.51) **Customer word of mouth** We recommend company X to other people (e.g., customers, business partners, friends) (0.64) We say positive things about company X to other people (e.g., customers, business partners, friends) (0.82)	
Homburg and Fuerst (2010)	Loyalty dimensions	7-point semantic differential	**Repurchase.** In how far… …are you planning to buy the product/service from firm XYZ again? …are you intending to stay customer at firm XYZ? …are you planning to increase the share of products/services purchased from firm XYZ? **Cross-buying.** In how far… …are you planning to buy additional/other products/services from firm XYZ? …is it an option for you to buy product categories/service categories from firm XYZ? **Recommendation.** In how far… …are you intending to recommend firm XYZ to your business partners? …will you recommend firm XYZ to your acquaintances and friends? **Price increase acceptance/ tolerance** Would you tolerate a 2/5/10/20 percent price increase and still buy products/services from firm XYZ? By how much could the prices of firm XYZ increase such that you would still buy from it in the future?	N/A

Note: (R) = reverse coded; N/A = not available

As an alternative to customer loyalty scales, many companies today have adopted the so-called Net Promoter Score (Reichheld 2003). As Keiningham et al. (2007) explain, the "Net Promoter is a metric derived from survey responses to a recommend likelihood question. Respondents who provide a rating of 9–10 are classified as 'promoters': respondents who provide a rating of 6 or lower are classified as 'detractors.' Net Promoter is calculated by subtracting the proportion of a firm's detractors from its proportion of promoters (i.e., Net Promoter = promoters − detractors)" (p. 39). Although the Net Promoter Score is widely spread in practice and appears to be intuitive and efficient, research results regarding the Net Promoter Score are mixed (Keiningham et al. 2007; Morgan and Rego 2006). For instance, in their extensive analysis of various customer loyalty measures, Keiningham et al. (2007) find "no support for the claim that Net Promoter is the single most reliable indicator of a company's ability to grow" (p. 45). Hence, we warn firms to exclusively rely on the Net Promoter Score for assessing their customers' loyalty but instead recommend to integrate it as one component to their measurement system (e.g., as an alternative measure for the recommendation facet of loyalty).

Finally, previous research indicates that customers' loyalty intentions and customers' satisfaction levels are usually assessed within the same survey. Figure 7 provides an overview of decisions that need to be taken when designing a customer survey with sections on satisfaction and loyalty. See the chapter ▶ "Crafting Survey Research: A Systematic Process for Conducting Survey Research" by Vomberg and Klarmann in this handbook for more detailed guidance on the design, process, and evaluation of customer surveys. For interesting application examples of customer satisfaction and loyalty surveys, see Hayes (2008).

Loyalty Behavior

As prior research shows, firms should generally employ objective approaches to measure customer loyalty behavior (Peters et al. 2010; Mellens et al. 1996; Kumar and Shah 2004). This tendency is because the objective approaches draw on directly observable numbers that are not biased due to subjective perceptions, incomplete memory of events, or unexpected events (McNeal 1969; Sheppard et al. 1988). Thus, the objective approaches allow a more valid, reliable, and timely assessment of actual customer behavior (Mellens et al. 1996). Due to the increasing availability of objective data (e.g., from CRM systems), the objective loyalty measurement approaches have gained importance for firms over the past couple of years (Sarstedt and Mooi 2019). Hence, firms can use such data nowadays to gain insights on most of the different dimensions of customer loyalty behavior (i.e., repurchase, cross-buying, price increase acceptance, and positive WOM behavior) by developing and monitoring appropriate key performance indicators (KPIs). In the following, we first explain how firms can use several general databases to generate information on customer loyalty behavior before we discuss loyalty programs, which are for many companies the most valuable data source for loyalty behavior information.

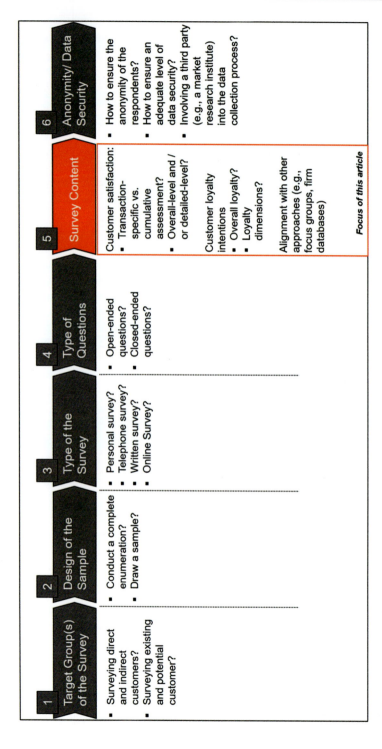

Fig. 7 Overview of decisions and process of a customer satisfaction and loyalty survey

General Databases

As prior work has pointed out, there are two types of objective measurement approaches which differ according to the orientation of the data source (i.e., internal objective and external objective approaches) (Fuerst 2012; Homburg and Fuerst 2010). While the former draw on company-internal data sources (such as CRM systems, central contact management databases, or ERP systems), the latter approaches exploit company-external data sources (such as external panel data). Internal objective approaches provide especially valuable information on actual customer loyalty behavior, since they generally capture individual customer behavior and therefore allow for very detailed and precise evaluations (Sarstedt and Mooi 2019). Thus, these approaches can be used to gain transparency on three of the four behavioral dimensions of customer loyalty (i.e., repurchase behavior, cross-buying behavior, and price increase acceptance). Moreover, depending on the CRM system configuration, firms may also be able to gain first insights regarding the fourth behavioral loyalty dimension (i.e., positive WOM communication), e.g., by monitoring the proportion of new customers that came through recommendations of existing customers. Figure 8 illustrates how firms can derive meaningful KPIs for the different dimensions of customer loyalty behavior by utilizing various objective data sources (e.g., CRM data, central contact management data, or scanner data).

In addition, firms may want to amend the internal objective techniques by external objective techniques to gain more nuanced and comprehensive insights in all customer loyalty behavior dimensions. There are two different kinds of external data that have relevance for the measurement of customer loyalty behavior: panel data (Sarstedt and Mooi 2019) and social media data (Ma et al. 2015). First, when using panel data, firms usually generate information at an aggregated level, such as the market, segment, or company level. This aggregated information on customer

Dimension to be Measured:	Repurchase Behavior	Cross-Buying Behavior	Price Increase Acceptance	Positive WOM Communication
Key Question:	How many customers do actually buy again?	How many of the existing customers start buying from other sales units?	Are the customers willing to continue buying from the firm despite price increases?	How likely is it that a customer recommends the firm to family/ friends/ acquaintances?
Name of KPI:	Repurchase Rate	Cross Buying Extent	Price Elasticity of Demand	Recommendation extent
Definition of KPI:	Number of Repurchases / Number of Initial Purchases	• Number of sales units a customer buys from • Dollar amount a customer spends in additional sales units	(dQ / Q) / (dP / P)	• Amount of recommendations • Positive WOM score
Data Source:	e.g., Scanner Data, Loyalty Program Data, further Data from the CRM Tool of the Sales Department, Social Media, or Panel Data			

Fig. 8 KPIs to measure actual loyalty behavior

loyalty behavior can be valuable. For instance, firms can use this information as benchmarks for their more specific analyses or to detect general trends and tendencies (Fornell et al. 1996). Most panel data with relevance for measuring customer loyalty are collected by the leading market research agencies (e.g., Nielsen, GfK) and need to be purchased. Second, to gain further insights on customer loyalty behavior, such as on product or brand level, firms can use social media analyses. More precisely, firms can employ a social media crawler (e.g., Brandwatch, Social Crawlytics, spirm3r, or PromptCloud) to retrieve all relevant discussions as entries from various social media, such as blogs, communities (e.g., Twitter, Facebook), business networks (e.g., LinkedIn, XING), photo sharing (e.g., Instagram, Flickr), as well as products and services reviews (e.g., Amazon.com). The social media crawler is able to deliver the relevant social media entries on a regular basis (e.g., weekly or monthly) such that firms can systematically evaluate these entries to gain further insights on the recommendation behavior of their customers, at an aggregated level or a more disaggregated level depending on the abilities of the hired social media crawler. See Fig. 9 for an example of automatic outputs of a social media crawler (e.g., daily mentions, author profession, and brand sentiment). These automatic outputs do not provide direct results on customer loyalty. Instead, to gain more direct insights on customer loyalty behavior, more sophisticated text analysis tools (e.g., dictionaries or machine learning algorithms) need to be employed (see chapter ▶ "Automated Text Analysis" by Humphreys in this handbook for more details on text analysis). As Fig. 9 also indicates, with adequate methods, such as sentiment analysis (Homburg et al. 2015), firms could even gain objective insights on customers' attitudes, such as satisfaction and loyalty intentions.

Loyalty Programs

Overview of loyalty programs One of the most common ways that firms measure customer loyalty behavior is through their loyalty programs. Since their beginnings with airlines in the early 1980s, loyalty programs (LPs) as marketers know them today have seen a tremendous increase in participation rates and are now prevalent in a variety of industries. At their core, LPs offer consumers rewards in exchange for providing firms with detailed transaction data to be used to develop marketing strategies that are designed to optimize customer engagement with the firm. Given their importance in measuring loyalty behavior, we briefly review the design and modeling issues associated with loyalty programs.

The design of loyalty programs encompasses five key components: (1) membership requirements, (2) program structure, (3) point structure, (4) reward structure, and (5) program communication (Breugelmans et al. 2015). These components are common to all types of LPs, but the variations in program design across firms are immense. Of the five components, reward structure has been given the most attention in the marketing literature. Currently, there are two types of rewards schemes in loyalty programs: customer tier and frequency based. Customer-tier LPs, which are popular in the airline, hotel, and casino industry, group customers into segments according to their actual or potential purchase volume or profitability, with higher tiers receiving some form of preferential treatment (Blattberg et al. 2008; Kumar and

Measuring Customer Satisfaction and Customer Loyalty

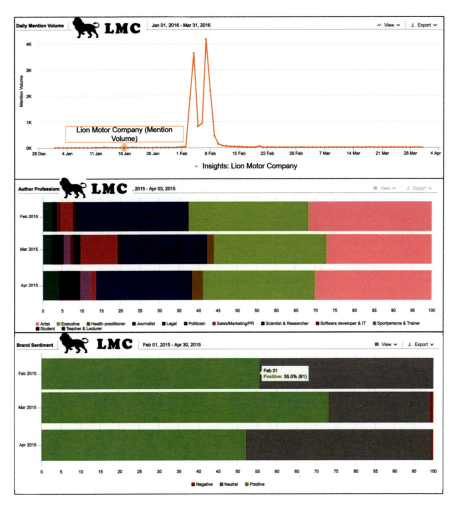

Fig. 9 Example report from a social media crawler. (Fictitious example based on a sample output provided by Brandwatch)

Shah 2004). In frequency-based LPs, customers earn rewards as a function of purchase volume.

In spite of the popularity of loyalty programs, their effectiveness has long been subject to debate. This debate has centered on the costs of giving discounts and perks to the loyal customers, as well as the costs of administering the program itself, and whether these costs are justified by increases in spending by those customers. Loyalty programs have the potential to increase profits by increasing switching costs for existing customers, stealing business from rivals, or through second-degree price discrimination. They may also indirectly increase profits by increasing customers perceptions of the firm, by generating customer data that can be used for targeted promotions or CRM, or by exploiting agency issues such as flights booked by business travelers and paid for by their employers (Roehm et al. 2002; Dreze and Nunes 2008; Verhoef 2003; Shugan 2005). Empirical studies of whether loyalty programs actually do increase profits have found mixed results. Verhoef (2003) finds that the effects are positive but very small, DeWulf et al. (2001) find no support for positive effects of direct mail, Shugan (2005) finds that firms gain short-term revenue at the expense of longer-term reward payments, and Hartmann and Viard (2008) find no evidence that loyalty programs create switching costs. For a more complete review on loyalty programs, see Bijmolt et al. (2011); Liu and Yang (2009); and McCall and Voorhees (2010). Regardless of the profit impact, one clear advantage of loyalty programs is that it allows firms to objectively track and monitor customer interactions with the firm.

Challenges in measuring customer loyalty through loyalty programs As discussed earlier, conceptualizing and measuring customer loyalty can be challenging. In this section, we review the common modeling issues encountered when attempting to measure customer loyalty behavior using an LP and discuss some of the common solutions where applicable. Broadly, these issues can be categorized as follows: endogeneity, complexity, and attribution.

From a modeling perspective, endogeneity is likely the most prevalent issue in measuring customer loyalty. At a high level, it must be recognized that the design of the LP itself is not a random outcome. While this is technically an endogeneity issue, it tends to be abstracted away in most research. In addition, while endogeneity related to price or targeted marketing decisions is a concern, these are relatively simple for a firm to address through randomized experiments. For a detailed discussion of endogeneity issues, see the chapter ▶ "Dealing with Endogeneity: A Nontechnical Guide for Marketing Researchers" by Ebbes, Papies, and van Heerde in this handbook.

A more challenging, and common, scenario to address is when a firm attempts to measure customer loyalty behavior by assessing customer engagement with the loyalty program. This endogeneity issue stems from the fact that customers self-select into loyalty programs, which can lead to biased estimates of LP effectiveness. For example, if a firm compares spending behavior between customers who are enrolled in the loyalty program with those who are not, they will likely find that spending is higher from those who are enrolled. While this difference may be caused by the program itself, the more likely explanation is simply that customers who spend more with the firm are more likely to benefit from the LP and hence are more likely to enroll. A less obvious example is when a firm observes spending for the same customer both before and after joining the loyalty program. Here the firm may be tempted to conclude that changes in spend for each individual eliminate the endogeneity issue. However, again we have a selection issue: it is possible that customers joined the LP due to *anticipated* changes in spend. This will again lead to biased estimates of LP effectiveness.

A common approach to correct selection bias is to employ a Heckman two-stage correction method (Heckman 1979). In the classic bivariate selection problem, we have the following:

$$y_1^* = X_1\beta_1 + \varepsilon_1$$
$$y_2^* = X_2\beta_2 + \varepsilon_2$$

where y_2^* is the outcome of interest (e.g., customer spending) and is only observed if $y_1^* > 0$ (e.g., whether the customer decides to enroll in the LP). The stars indicate that these are latent variables – for example, a firm may not observe customer-level spending unless they are enrolled in the loyalty program. Problems arise in estimating β_2 if there is a nonzero correlation between ε_1 and ε_2.

Under this specification, it can be shown that when

$$\begin{bmatrix} \varepsilon_1 \\ \varepsilon_2 \end{bmatrix} \sim N\begin{pmatrix} 1 & \rho \\ \rho & 1 \end{pmatrix}$$

we have

$$\mathbb{E}[y_2 | y_1^* > 0] = X_2\beta_2 + \rho\lambda(X_1\beta_1)$$

where $\lambda(z) = \phi(z)/\Phi(z)$, or the inverse Mills ratio. Clearly, failure to account for any nonzero correlation ρ will result in a biased estimate of β_2.

To correct this bias, Heckman's two-step estimator first runs a probit regression of y_1 onto $X_1\beta_1$ to get $\widehat{\beta}_1$ in the first step and then runs an OLS of y_2 on $X_2\beta_2 + \rho\lambda\left(X_1\widehat{\beta}\right)$ in the second stage. The estimated coefficient of the inverse Mills ratio, $\widehat{\rho}$, may indicate whether or not sample selection correction is needed (so long as certain model assumptions are met). For more details on model assumptions, estimation, and interpreting the two-step estimator coefficients, see Heckman (1979) and Certo et al. (2016).

Building on this model, later research found that more flexible control functions could be implemented. For example, rather than use the inverse Mills ratio, instead include higher-order polynomials of $\widehat{\beta}_1$. The intuition is that the flexible function will essentially replicate the inverse Mills ratio without the need for a probit in the first stage. See Ahn and Powell (1993) for more details or Ellickson and Misra (2012) for a recent application.

Besides endogeneity, another challenge in the analysis of loyalty program effectiveness is the complexity of the environment in which LPs typically operate. Analysts must recognize that LPs have numerous moving components, each which may influence customer loyalty, for example, the mere offering of a LP, the design of the rewards structure regardless of customer earnings and redemption activity (e.g., a relatively complicated versus simple tier or earnings structure), or strategic reactions from competition (Breugelmans et al. 2015). These are only a few of many potential issues that arise when attempting to model and quantify the effectiveness of a loyalty program and how it influences customer loyalty. Typically, researchers circumvent these challenges by either (1) conducting field experiments to isolate the causal effect of interest, (2) identify a natural experiment in situations where a field experiment is infeasible, or (3) specify a structural model and use economic theory to identify the casual effect of interest.

Related to the complexities distinct to the LP itself is that of attribution among other firm activities. Loyalty programs do not manage customer engagement in a vacuum. Multiple touchpoints make it difficult to pin down exactly what is driving customer engagement, whether it be billboards, TV, print or radio advertising, or the LP itself. It is still not clear the extent to which the LP design interacts with these other components, and more work is needed in this area. These difficult attribution issues have not yet been solved and are only beginning to receive serious attention in research. For a short discussion of current work in this area, see Ascarza et al. (2017). If implemented properly, loyalty programs can be a powerful tool for firms to increase customer engagement with a firm. However, firms must carefully balance the costs of its implementation and management against the potential gains from additional customer information and more refined targeting abilities.

The Future of Managing Customer Satisfaction and Loyalty

The practice of measuring and managing customer satisfaction and loyalty is in a constant state of change (with "satisfaction" and "loyalty" now often referred to using the more general term "customer engagement"). However, these changes have occurred at an increasingly rapid pace, in part because the degree to which a firm can manage the customer engagement process is very much dependent on computational technology (e.g., processing speed, data storage costs, along with the labor to extract and analyze the data, to name a few).

These changes are most visible in the speed, customization, and rate in which customer satisfaction and loyalty is managed. For example, some firms are moving away from static marketing campaigns and ad hoc analyses in favor of systematic, real-time evaluation and tuning of the engagement process (see Schwartz et al. 2017; Hauser et al. 2009). Part of this has been driven by the speed and ease in which firms can customize offers, conduct A/B testing, and in general customize the customer's experience with the firm.

Related, there has been a growing interest in applying machine learning methods to solve marketing problems. Even though machine learning has been around for decades, their use has accelerated in tandem with increases in computational power. A byproduct is that there has been, to some extent, a shift that emphasizes scalability and predictive accuracy in customer behavior rather than understanding causality of marginal effects. However, there has been strong interest in understanding how machine learning can work with econometrics (e.g., Athey 2018) or as a way to augment traditional marketing analyses (Ascarza 2018; Liu and Toubia 2018). In addition, some of the machine learning methods have allowed managers to deal with ultrafine, unstructured data such as text (e.g., social media content, as previously discussed) or voice (such as reviews or call center recordings) which would be cumbersome to process using traditional methods. Although it is a general consensus today that the potential of these methods for assessing customer satisfaction and loyalty is very high, researchers are still in the early phase of determining how best to use these powerful tools and to the boundaries of their limitations.

Given the current environment, what does the future hold? It is not unreasonable to expect continued computation performance increases to drive much of the innovations in marketing and the customer engagement process. We are still a long way from optimizing a customer's lifetime marketing activity, which evolves over time and may be a function of competitor reactions. Relatively, there has been increased attention to how the sequence of outcomes itself influences customer engagement (e.g., reinforcement learning). It is simply a matter of time before even the most complex interactions can be modeled and processed fast enough to be of use to both practitioners and academics.

The key for marketing managers is to not allow advances in technology cloud the primary objective of increasing customer satisfaction and loyalty. Firms should implement technology to augment the customer relationship, rather than force the relationship process around current limitations in technology. More generally, a firm should avoid imposing any part of their management structure onto the relationship process (e.g., sending a customer complaint to a different department simply because that is how the organization is structured). As the field of customer engagement advances, the one unchanging factor is that the customers' experience is of paramount importance.

Concluding Remarks

Customer satisfaction and customer loyalty represent key constructs in marketing research and management. The measurement of customer satisfaction and loyalty is the basic requirement of a successful satisfaction and loyalty management. However, as there is a lack of transparency and guidance regarding the different traditional and novel measurement approaches, many firms currently struggle to identify the most appropriate tools and approaches for their particular situation. Against this background, this chapter has aimed at answering the following research questions: (1) How can firms conceptualize customer satisfaction and customer loyalty? (2) How can firms measure customer satisfaction? (3) How can firms measure customer loyalty?

To address these questions, this chapter has first summarized how customer satisfaction and customer loyalty are generally conceptualized and operationalized. Next, this chapter has outlined various important approaches and issues that relate to the measurement of customer satisfaction and loyalty on the basis of the previously introduced conceptual background. The chapter also discussed the current state and future of measuring both customer satisfaction and loyalty as a function of advances in technology and growing competitive pressure.

There is strong evidence that firms will need to focus on customer satisfaction and loyalty management with even greater emphasis in the upcoming years. Firms should continually reevaluate their approaches and tools for measuring customer satisfaction and loyalty and update when needed. Challenging your firm's current measurement approaches using the ideas and tools presented in this chapter may serve as a first step toward implementing such a continuous improvement process.

References

Ahn, H., & Powell, J. L. (1993). Semiparametric estimation of censored selection models with a nonparametric selection mechanism. *Journal of Econometrics, 58*(1–2), 3–29.

Aksoy, L. (2013). How do you measure what you can't define? The current state of loyalty measurement and management. *Journal of Service Management, 24*(4), 356–381.

Anderson, E. W. (1996). Customer satisfaction and price tolerance. *Marketing Letters, 7*(3), 265–274.

Anderson. (2010). Meng marketing trends report 2010.

Anderson, E. W., & Mittal, V. (2000). Strengthening the satisfaction-profit chain. *Journal of Service Research, 3*(2), 107–120.

Anderson, E. W., Fornell, C., & Lehmann, D. R. (1994). Customer satisfaction, market share, and profitability: Findings from Sweden. *Journal of Marketing, 58*(3), 53–66.

Anderson, E. W., Fornell, C., & Mazvancheryl, S. K. (2004). Customer satisfaction and shareholder value. *Journal of Marketing, 68*(4), 172–185.

Ascarza, E. (2018). Retention futility: Targeting high-risk customers might be ineffective. *Journal of Marketing Research, 55*(1), 80–98.

Ascarza, E., Fader, P. S., & Hardie, B. G. (2017). Marketing models for the customer-centric firm. In *Handbook of marketing decision models* (pp. 297–329). New York: Springer.

Athey, S. (2018). The impact of machine learning on economics. In *The economics of artificial intelligence: An agenda*. Chicago: University of Chicago Press.

Brakus, J. J., Schmitt, B. H., & Zarantonello, L. (2009). Brand experience: what is it? How is it measured? Does it affect loyalty?. *Journal of Marketing, 73*(3), 52–68.

Bain & Company (2013). Management Tools & Trends 2013. http://www.bain.de/Images/BAIN_BRIEF_Management_Tools_%26_Trends_2013.pdf. Accessed 25 July 2016.

Bearden, W. O., & Teel, J. E. (1983). Selected determinants of consumer satisfaction and complaint reports. *Journal of Marketing Research, 20*(1), 21–28.

Bergkvist, L., & Rossiter, J. R. (2007). The predictive validity of multiple-item versus single-item measures of the same constructs. *Journal of Marketing Research, 44*(2), 175–184.

Bijmolt, T. H., Dorotic, M., Verhoef, P. C., et al. (2011). Loyalty programs: Generalizations on their adoption, effectiveness and design. *Foundations and Trends® in Marketing, 5*(4), 197–258.

Blattberg, R., Kim, B., & Neslin, S. (2008). *Database Marketing: Analyzing and Managing Customers*. New York: Springer.

Bolton, R. N. (1998). A dynamic model of the duration of the customer's relationship with a continuous service provider: The role of satisfaction. *Marketing Science, 17*(1), 45–65.

Boshoff, C. (1997). An experimental study of service recovery options. *International Journal of Service Industry Management, 8*(2), 110–130.

Brandt, D. R., & Reffett, K. L. (1989). Focusing on customer problems to improve service quality. *Journal of Services Marketing, 3*(4), 5–14.

Breugelmans, E., Bijmolt, T. H., Zhang, J., Basso, L. J., Dorotic, M., Kopalle, R., Minnema, A., Mijnlieff, W. J., & Wünderlich, N. V. (2015). Advancing research on loyalty programs: A future research agenda. *Marketing Letters, 26*(2), 127–139.

Brooke. (2016). Rewards, returns, and ringside seats. *Marketing News, 50*(6), 28–35.

Bruhn, M. (2003). *Relationship marketing: Management of customer relationships*. Harlow: Pearson Education.

Bruhn, M. (2016). *Kundenorientierung: Bausteine fuer ein exzellentes Customer Relationship Management (CRM)* (Vol. 50950). München: CHE Beck.

Cannon, J. P., & Perreault, W. D., Jr. (1999). Buyer-seller relationships in business markets. *Journal of Marketing Research, 36*(4), 439–460.

Certo, S. T., Busenbark, J. R., Woo, H.-s., & Semadeni, M. (2016). Sample selection bias and heckman models in strategic management research. *Strategic Management Journal, 37*(13), 2639–2657.

Chandrashekaran, M., Rotte, K., Tax, S. S., & Grewal, R. (2007). Satisfaction strength and customer loyalty. *Journal of Marketing Research, 44*(1), 153–163.

Churchill, G. A., Jr., & Surprenant, C. (1982). An investigation into the determinants of customer satisfaction. *Journal of Marketing Research, 19*(4), 491–504.

Davis, D. F., Golicic, S. L., & Boerstler, C. N. (2011). Benefits and challenges of conducting multiple methods research in marketing. *Journal of the Academy of Marketing Science, 39*(3), 467–479.

DeWulf, K., Odekerken-Schrôder, G., & Iacobucci, D. (2001). Investments in consumer relationships: A cross-country and cross-industry exploration. *Journal of Marketing, 65*(4), 33–50.

Diamantopoulos, A. (2011). Incorporating formative measures into covariance-based structural equation models. *MIS Quarterly, 35*, 335–358.

Dreze, X., & Nunes, J. C. (2008). Feeling superior: The impact of loyalty program structure on consumers' perceptions of status. *Journal of Consumer Research, 35*(6), 890–905.

Ernst & Young (2011). The digitisation of everything: How organizations must adapt to changing consumer behaviour, available at: http://www.ey.com/Publication/vwLUAssets/The_digitisation_of_everything_-_How_organisations_must_adapt_to_changing_consumer_behaviour/$FILE/EY_Digitisation_of_everything.pdf. Retrieved on 25 Jul 2016.

Ellickson, P. B., & Misra, S. (2012). Enriching interactions: Incorporating outcome data into static discrete games. *Quantitative Marketing and Economics, 10*(1), 1–26.

Fornell, C., Johnson, M. D., Anderson, E. W., Cha, J., & Bryant, B. E. (1996). The American customer satisfaction index: Nature, purpose, and findings. *Journal of Marketing, 60*(4), 7–18.

Fuerst, A. (2012). Verfahren zur Messung der Kundenzufriedenheit im Ueberblick. *Kundenzufriedenheit: Konzepte–Methoden–Erfahrungen, 8*, 123–154.

Gremler, D. D. (2004). The critical incident technique in service research. *Journal of Service Research, 7*(l), 65–89.

Griffin, A., Gleason, G., Preiss, R., & Shevenaugh, D. (1995). Best practice for customer satisfaction in manufacturing firms. *MIT Sloan Management Review, 36*(2), 87.

Grigoroudis, E., & Siskos, Y. (2009). *Customer satisfaction evaluation: Methods for measuring and implementing service quality* (Vol. 139). Springer Science & Business Media.

Gupta, S., & Zeithaml, V. (2006). Customer metrics and their impact on financial performance. *Marketing Science, 25*(6), 718–739.

Gustafsson, A., & Johnson, M. D. (2004). Determining attribute importance in a service satisfaction model. *Journal of Service Research, 7*(2), 124–141.

Halstead, D. (1999). The use of comparison standards in customer satisfaction research and management: A review and proposed typology. *Journal of Marketing Theory and Practice, 7*(3), 13–26.

Hartmann, W., & Viard, B. (2008). Do frequency reward programs create switching costs? A dynamic structural analysis of demand in a reward program. *Quantitative Marketing and Economics, 6*(2), 109–137.

Hauser, J. R., Urban, G. L., Liberali, G., & Braun, M. (2009). Website morphing. *Marketing Science, 28*(2), 202–223.

Hayes, B. E. (2008). *Measuring customer satisfaction and loyalty: Survey design, use, and statistical analysis methods*. ASQ Quality Press.

Heckman, J. J. (1979). Sample selection bias as a specification error. *Econometrica, 47*(1), 153–161.

Homburg, C., & Fuerst, A. (2005). How organizational complaint handling drives customer loyalty: An analysis of the mechanistic and the organic approach. *Journal of Marketing, 69*(3), 95–114.

Homburg, C., Fürst, A. (2010). Überblick über die Messung von Kundenzufriedenheit und Kundenbindung. In M. Bruhn & C. Homburg (Eds.), Handbuch Kundenbindungsmanagement (pp. 599–634). Wiesbaden: Gabler.

Homburg, C, & Klarmann, M. (2012). Die indirekte Wichtigkeitsbestimmung im Rahmen von Kundenzufriedenheitsuntersuchungen: Probleme und Loesungsansaetze. In C. Homburg

(Eds.), Handbuch Kundenzufriedenheit: Konzepte - Methoden - Erfahrungen. Wiesbaden: Gabler.

Homburg, C., & Stock, R. M. (2004). The link between salespeoples job satisfaction and customer satisfaction in a business-to-business context: A dyadic analysis. *Journal of the Academy of Marketing Science, 32*(2), 144.

Homburg, C., Koschate, N., & Hoyer, W. D. (2005). Do satisfied customers really pay more? A study of the relationship between customer satisfaction and willingness to pay. *Journal of Marketing, 69*(2), 84–96.

Homburg, C., Koschate, N., & Hoyer, W. D. (2006). The role of cognition and affect in the formation of customer satisfaction: A dynamic perspective. *Journal of Marketing, 70*(3), 21–31.

Homburg, C., Mueller, M., & Klarmann, M. (2011). When should the customer really be king? On the optimum level of salesperson customer orientation in sales encounters. *Journal of Marketing, 75*(2), 55–74.

Homburg, C., Ehm, L., & Artz, M. (2015). Measuring and managing consumer sentiment in an online community environment. *Journal of Marketing Research, 52*(5), 629–641.

Howard, J. A. & Sheth, J. N. (1969). The theory of buyer behavior. New York: John Wiley and Sons.

Hunt, H. K. (1977). *Conceptualization and measurement of consumer satisfaction and dissatisfaction* (pp. 77–103). Cambridge, MA: Marketing Science Institute.

Jarvis, C. B., MacKenzie, S. B., & Podsakoff, P. M. (2003). A critical review of construct indicators and measurement model misspecification in marketing and consumer research. *Journal of Consumer Research, 30*(2), 199–218.

Keiningham, T. L., Cooil, B., Andreassen, T. W., & Aksoy, L. (2007). A longitudinal examination of net promoter and firm revenue growth. *Journal of Marketing, 71*(3), 39–51.

Klarmann, M. (2008). *Methodische Problemfelder der Erfolgsfaktorenforschung: Bestandsaufnahme und Empirische Analysen.* Ph.D. thesis.

Kozinets, R. V., De Valck, K., Wojnicki, A. C., & Wilner, S. J. (2010). Networked narratives: Understanding word-of-mouth marketing in online communities. *Journal of Marketing, 74*(2), 71–89.

Kumar, V., & Reinartz, W. (2012). *Customer relationship management: Concept, strategy, and tools.* Berlin: Springer Science & Business Media.

Kumar, V., & Shah, D. (2004). Building and sustaining profitable customer loyalty for the 21st century. *Journal of Retailing, 80*(4), 317–329.

Kumar, V., Dalla Pozza, I., & Ganesh, J. (2013). Revisiting the satisfaction–loyalty relationship: Empirical generalizations and directions for future research. *Journal of Retailing, 89*(3), 246–262.

Larivière, B., Keiningham, T. L., Aksoy, L., Yalgin, A., Morgeson, F. V., III, & Mithas, S. (2016). Modeling heterogeneity in the satisfaction, loyalty intention, and shareholder value linkage: A cross-industry analysis at the customer and firm levels. *Journal of Marketing Research, 53*(1), 91–109.

Liu, J., & Toubia, O. (2018). A semantic approach for estimating consumer content preferences from online search queries. *Marketing Science, 37*(6), 930–952.

Liu, Y., & Yang, R. (2009). Competing loyalty programs: Impact of market saturation, market share, and category expandability. *Journal of Marketing, 73*(1), 93–108.

Luo, X., & Homburg, C. (2007). Neglected outcomes of customer satisfaction. *Journal of Marketing, 71*(2), 133–149.

Ma, L., Sun, B., & Kekre, S. (2015). The squeaky wheel gets the grease - an empirical analysis of customer voice and firm intervention on twitter. *Marketing Science, 34*(5), 627–645.

McAlexander, J. H., Schouten, J. W., & Koenig, H. F. (2002). Building brand community. *Journal of Marketing, 66*(l), 38–54.

McAlexander, J. H., Kim, S. K., & Roberts, S. D. (2003). Loyalty: The influences of satisfaction and brand community integration. *Journal of Marketing Theory and Practice, 11*(4), 1–11.

McCall, M., & Voorhees, C. (2010). The drivers of loyalty program success: An organizing framework and research agenda. *Cornell Hospitality Quarterly, 51*(1), 35–52.

McCollough, M. A., Berry, L. L., & Yadav, M. S. (2000). An empirical investigation of customer satisfaction after service failure and recovery. *Journal of Service Research, 3*(2), 121–137.

McNeal, J. U. (1969). Consumer satisfaction-measure of marketing effectiveness. *MSU Business Topics-Michigan State University, 17*(3), 31–35.

Mellens, M., Dekimpe, M., & Steenkamp, J. (1996). A review of brand-loyalty measures in marketing. *Tijdschrift voor economic en management, 4*, 507–533.

Morgan, N. A., & Rego, L. L. (2006). The value of different customer satisfaction and loyalty metrics in predicting business performance. *Marketing Science, 25*(5), 426–439.

Morgan, N. A., Anderson, E. W., & Mittal, V. (2005). Understanding firms customer satisfaction information usage. *Journal of Marketing, 69*(3), 131–151.

Morgeson, F. V., Mithas, S., Keiningham, T. L., & Aksoy, L. (2011). An investigation of the cross-national determinants of customer satisfaction. *Journal of the Academy of Marketing Science, 39*(2), 198–215.

Oliver, R. L. (1980). A cognitive model of the antecedents and consequences of satisfaction decisions. *Journal of Marketing Research, 17*(4), 460–469.

Oliver, R. L. (1981). Measurement and evaluation of satisfaction processes in retail settings. *Journal of Retailing, 57*, 25.

Oliver, R. L. (1999). Whence consumer loyalty? *Journal of Marketing, 63*(4_suppl 1), 33–44.

Palmatier, R. W., Dant, R. P., Grewal, D., & Evans, K. R. (2006). Factors influencing the effectiveness of relationship marketing: A meta-analysis. *Journal of Marketing, 70*(4), 136–153.

Peters, L. D., Pressey, A. D., & Greenberg, P. (2010). The impact of CRM 2.0 on customer insight. *Journal of Business and Industrial Marketing, 25*, 410.

Peterson, R. A., & Wilson, W. R. (1992). Measuring customer satisfaction: Fact and artifact. *Journal of the Academy of Marketing Science, 20*(1), 61.

Reeves, M., & Deimler, M. (2011). Adaptability: The new competitive advantage. *Harvard Business Review, 89*(4), 134–141.

Reichheld, F. F. (1996). Learning from customer defections. *Harvard Business Review, 74*, 56–69.

Reichheld, F. F. (2003). The one number you need to grow. *Harvard Business Review, 81*(12), 46–55.

Richins, M. L. (1983). Negative word-of-mouth by dissatisfied consumers: A pilot study. *Journal of Marketing, 47*(1), 68–78.

Roehm, M., Pullins, E., & Jr, H. R. (2002). Designing loyalty-building programs for packaged goods brands. *Journal of Marketing Research, 39*(2), 202–213.

Rust, R. T., & Zahorik, A. J. (1993). Customer satisfaction, customer retention, and market share. *Journal of Retailing, 69*(2), 193–215.

Sarstedt, M., Mooi, E., (2019). A concise guide to market research: The process, data, and methods using IBM SPSS Statistics (3rd edition). Springer

Schwartz, E. M., Bradlow, E. T., & Fader, R. S. (2017). Customer acquisition via display advertising using multi-armed bandit experiments. *Marketing Science, 36*(4), 500–522.

Shankar, V., Smith, A. K., & Rangaswamy, A. (2003). Customer satisfaction and loyalty in online and offline environments. *International Journal of Research in Marketing, 20*(2), 153–175.

Sheppard, B. H., Hartwick, J., & Warshaw, P. R. (1988). The theory of reasoned action: A meta-analysis of past research with recommendations for modifications and future research. *Journal of Consumer Research, 15*(3), 325–343.

Sheth, J. N. (1970). Measurement of multidimensional brand loyalty of a consumer. *Journal of Marketing Research, 7*(3), 348–354.

Shugan, S. (2005). Brand loyalty programs: Are they shams? *Marketing Science, 24*(2), 185–193.

Singh, J., & Pandya, S. (1991). Exploring the effects of consumers' dissatisfaction level on complaint behaviours. *European Journal of Marketing, 25*(9), 7–21.

Smith, A. K., & Bolton, R. N. (1998). An experimental investigation of customer reactions to service failure and recovery encounters: Paradox or peril? *Journal of Service Research, 1*(1), 65–81.

Szymanski, D. M., & Henard, D. H. (2001). Customer satisfaction: A meta-analysis of the empirical evidence. *Journal of the Academy of Marketing Science, 29*(l), 16–35.

Umashankar, N., Bhagwat, Y., & Kumar, V. (2017). Do loyal customers really pay more for services? *Journal of the Academy of Marketing Science, 45*(6), 807–826.

Van Doorn, J., & Verhoef, P. C. (2008). Critical incidents and the impact of satisfaction on customer share. *Journal of Marketing, 72*(4), 123–142.

Verhoef, P. (2003). Understanding the effect of customer relationship management efforts on customer retention and customer share development. *Journal of Marketing, 67*(4), 30–45.

Watson, G. F., Beck, J. T., Henderson, C. M., & Palmatier, R. W. (2015). Building, measuring, and profiting from customer loyalty. *Journal of the Academy of Marketing Science, 43*(6), 790–825.

Weinberg, B. D., Milne, G. R., Andonova, Y. G., & Hajjat, F. M. (2015). Internet of things: Convenience vs. privacy and secrecy. *Business Horizons, 58*(l), 615–624.

Wieseke, J., Alavi, S., & Habel, J. (2014). Willing to pay more, eager to pay less: The role of customer loyalty in price negotiations. *Journal of Marketing, 78*(6), 17–37.

Woodruff, R. B., Cadotte, E. R., & Jenkins, R. L. (1983). Modeling consumer satisfaction processes using experience-based norms. *Journal of Marketing Research, 20*(3), 296–304.

Zairi, M. (2000). Managing customer satisfaction: A best practice perspective. *The TQM Magazine, 12*(6), 389–394.

Market Segmentation

Tobias Schlager and Markus Christen

Contents

Introduction to the Concept	940
Market Segmentation: Key Considerations	942
Heterogeneity and Homogeneity	942
Segment-of-One	942
Concluding Thoughts	943
Market Segmentation: Process	943
Step 1: Characterizing the Ideal Market Segment	944
Step 2: Determining the Segmentation Criteria	945
Step 3: Collecting and Evaluating Data	948
Step 4: Forming Segments	951
Step 5: Evaluating the Final Segment Solution	957
Step 6: Implementing the Market Segmentation	960
Conclusions and Managerial Implications	962
Cross-References	964
References	965

Abstract

Market segmentation describes the practice of grouping consumers that are alike concerning specific characteristics. The idea is that firms can better identify and target attractive segments and customize marketing actions for each segment. Equally important, segmentation allows firms to avoid consumers that are unprofitable or otherwise incompatible with its marketing strategy. Like other marketing concepts, market segmentation has changed over the years with increasing globalization and digitalization. But the concept of market segmentation has been and will continue to be one of the key concepts in marketing practice. In this chapter, we define market segmentation along with its key characteristics, describe the process by which it unfolds, outline the main traps to avoid, and

T. Schlager (✉) · M. Christen
Faculty of Business and Economics (HEC) University of Lausanne, Lausanne, Switzerland
e-mail: Tobias.Schlager@unil.ch; Markus.Christen@unil.ch

© Springer Nature Switzerland AG 2022
C. Homburg et al. (eds), *Handbook of Market Research*,
https://doi.org/10.1007/978-3-319-57413-4_29

provide an outlook into the future. A key concern of this chapter is also to reflect the key challenges in business environments, such as the abundance of data, globalization, as well as the acceleration of different trends.

Keywords

Heterogeneity · Market segmentation · Segmentation basis · Segmentation process · Segment-of-one · Social media

Introduction to the Concept

A key goal of firms is to allocate resources to their best opportunities and efficiently reach their organizational objectives. This requires firms to identify *groups of customers* who would most likely respond favorably to their offers and marketing actions. Market segmentation serves this purpose and is one of the most fundamental concepts in marketing management.

Market segmentation goes back to Smith (1956) and is defined as the identification of groups of customers with similar characteristics or needs who therefore are likely to exhibit similar behavior and reactions (i.e., are homogeneous) and that are distinct from other groups of consumers (i.e., are heterogeneous) in ways that are relevant for the firm. These groups should be mutually exclusive and collectively exhaustive. In other words, every customer should be allocated to exactly one segment. This definition has remained largely unchanged. For example, to Dolnicar et al. (2018), segmentation is *"the process of grouping consumers into naturally existing or artificially created segments of consumers who share similar product preferences or characteristics"* (Dolnicar et al. 2018, p. 11).

Conceptually, market segmentation is a compromise between, on the one hand, considering all customers as unique entities, with their idiosyncratic needs and preferences, enabling a firm to fully *customize* its marketing actions, and, on the other hand, considering the entire population of customers as similar enabling the firm to address them with a set of *standardized* marketing actions. By identifying subgroups or segments that are sufficiently homogeneous and different from other subgroups within a heterogeneous population, a firm can standardize its marketing actions for the subgroup only and still customize marketing actions across subgroups.

For instance, a car manufacturer could group its customers into five segments. In the best case, the car manufacturer should then be able to customize its marketing activities and products to these segments or a subset of them and still benefit from economies of scale. Thanks to market segmentation, General Motors was known to offer a "car for every purse and purpose," which contrasted with Ford's one-size-fits-all Model T, which was famously available only in black.

The key goals of market segmentation are therefore the following (Kotler 1989; Mahajan and Jain 1978):

1. Understanding the range of customer differences
2. Simplifying a market through grouping customers

3. Selecting target segments
4. Developing segment-tailored marketing actions
5. Efficiently allocating the firm's resources towards their target segments and marketing actions

Market segmentation is not only a theoretical concept but also one with high managerial relevance as it serves to develop *marketing strategy and actions* (Kotler 1997; Wedel and Kamakura 2012). The concept has become one of the key pillars of any given marketing strategy (Dolnicar et al. 2018) and significantly contributes to the success of marketing within a firm. Unsurprisingly, market segmentation is one of the tools that entails the largest influence on marketing decisions (Roberts et al. 2019). Among a large set of marketing tools, the respondents rated market segmentation as the most impactful tool or concept. From a strategic perspective, market segmentation allows a firm to capitalize on a superior market position as well as to identify niche segments (Beane and Ennis 1987; Weinstein 1987, 2004).

The logical extension of market segmentation is the segmentation, targeting, positioning (STP) framework (DeSarbo et al. 2008; Lilien and Rangaswamy 2004). The real business value of market segmentation follows from the targeting and positioning decisions. Positioning comprises the development and implementation of marketing actions to communicate a firm's image relative to the competition (Ries and Trout 1980). The STP framework and this chapter's focus are illustrated in Fig. 1.

Market segmentation has come a long way. In a seminal article, Daniel Yankelovich (1964) urged marketing managers to abandon simplistic segmentations based on demographic information and introduced psychographic and values-based segmentation. Despite the importance professed by managers, he argued, 40 years on, that the practice of market segmentation had significant room for improvement (Yankelovich and Meer 2006). Our discussions with leaders in strategy consulting confirm this conclusion. Moreover, novel sources of data nowadays allow creating more elaborated market segmentations than ever.

The rest of this chapter is organized into three parts. We first discuss the key considerations of any market segmentation and the question of whether market segmentation is still relevant in the light of developments such as product customization and personalized communication. We then provide a detailed description of the segmentation process. Finally, we conclude by discussing the effects of newer

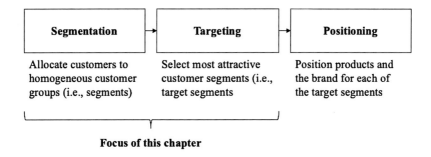

Fig. 1 The segmentation-targeting-positioning (STP) framework and the focus of this chapter

developments on this fundamental marketing concept, managerial implications, and highlight the main traps of market segmentation.

Market Segmentation: Key Considerations

Heterogeneity and Homogeneity

Market segmentation aims at allocating customers into groups based on how similar they are to each other. In technical terms, "similar" refers to homogeneous and "dissimilar" to heterogeneous. Thus, any segmentation, while motivated by the presence of customer differences, has the objective of reducing heterogeneity in the target market by identifying similarities, eventually enabling establishing a marketing strategy.

It would be tempting to start with the premise that customers are different. However, how different consumers are and whether differences are relevant for a firm is a matter of perspective. For example, humans share 99.9% of DNA, i.e., are homogeneous. For many medical problems, therefore, a standardized treatment suffices. For some diseases, however, the remaining 0.1% matter greatly. Likewise, many consumers have similar basic needs, seek similar benefits, but they can differ in terms of their specific preferences for quality, their decision-making process. We all must eat to satisfy our need for calories, but we can still have different preferences concerning the type of food, the way of preparation, and the time, place and form of consumption, creating many opportunities for segmentation.

Moreover, customers' preferences are not fixed and so is the heterogeneity. Firms can influence customer preferences with their marketing strategies. Whether a market consists of substantial heterogeneity and whether recognizing this heterogeneity by a firm is useful depends therefore on its business strategy and competitive situation and its ability to turn it into an advantage.

Segment-of-One

Instead of segmenting customers, a firm could also consider each customer to form her or his own segment. This perspective is often referred to as "segment-of-one," or that each customer forms her or his own segment (Bailey et al. 2010; Peppers and Rogers 1997; Winger and Edelman 1989) challenges the concept of market segmentation, which aims at simplifying the market.

The digital revolution is a key driver of the discussion around the relevance of segmentation because it has a huge impact on the way firms can identify, target, and engage with customers. The data generated by the digital revolution allow for insights into individuals at an increasingly granular level.

To better understand the impact of the digital revolution on the value of market segmentation, it is useful to distinguish between strategic segmentation and *operational* segmentation, i.e., a difference between defining target customers, customizing some marketing actions to individual customers. In particular, product customization (Gilmore and Pine 1997; Kotler 1989; von Hippel 1998, 2001), as well as personalized communication (Ansari and Mela 2003; Arora et al. 2008; Postma and Brokke 2002) allow shifting key components of a firm's marketing program from an aggregated segment level to an individual level. Firms nowadays offer products that can be individualized or customized in response to consumers' idiosyncratic needs, which has been reflected under the term "mass customization" (Dellaert and Dabholkar 2009). Mass customization is a viable strategy, but successfully implementing mass customization requires organizational flexibility, e.g., in the production process (Piller 2004). Related to market segmentation, mass customization can provide the basis for reflecting the heterogeneity between customers by addressing their product preferences on an individual basis. The previously mentioned activities come together under what can be described as one-to-one marketing, which is defined as tailoring one or more dimensions of a firm's marketing mix to individual customers (Arora et al. 2008).

These ideas, however, do not challenge the value of "traditional" segmentation as much as they highlight the importance of distinguishing between strategic segmentation (for hard-to-change and hard-to-customize marketing actions) and operational segmentation (for easy-to-change and easy-to-customize marketing actions). The former makes marketing actions more efficient, while the latter enables customization and makes marketing actions more effective. The digital revolution has certainly shifted a number of marketing actions in many industries from the former to the latter and the combination of the two – a strategic segmentation and an operational segmentation – is key to success (e.g., Bailey et al. 2010). Table 1 outlines the differences between different levels of segmentation:

Concluding Thoughts

The value of any market segmentation ultimately depends on the heterogeneity in the market *and* the firm's marketing strategy. While some firms might even be able to customize their products and personalize their communication efforts, for many firms, "segment-of-one" strategies may be beyond their capacities. Those primarily refer to operational segmentations; however, any firm can benefit from a strategic segmentation.

Market Segmentation: Process

Different suggestions regarding the process of market segmentation exist (e.g., Dolnicar et al. 2018; Wedel and Kamakura 2012). We propose six key phases in market segmentation, ranging from *characterizing the ideal segment* to *implementing the market segmentation* (see Fig. 2).

We will illustrate the process in the domain of the automotive industry and therefore point out the critical factors in each of the phases. For this illustration purpose, we use survey data on 250 consumers that include variables related to:

Table 1 Unsegmented marketing, differentiated marketing, and the segment-of-one

	Unsegmented marketing	Differentiated marketing	Segment-of-one marketing
Unit of analysis	All customers	Groups of customers (segments)	Individual customers, consumption occasions
Target customers	Everyone	Single or multiple segments	Individual customers
Market characteristics	Little heterogeneity	Large heterogeneity	Each customer is unique
Information needs	Low, occasional	High, periodical	Very high, real-time
Granularity of data	Aggregated	Differentiated	Individual
Product	Mass production, physical products	Variety with mass production, physical products, and services	Services and digital products, mass customization
Marketing mix	Same marketing mix for all customers	Several alternative marketing mixes	Each customer receives a different marketing mix
Firm objective	Competitive advantage from low costs	Competitive advantage from differentiation	Competitive advantage from personalization and mass customization
Major disadvantage	Competitor may identify and create segments	Higher complexity and cannibalization	High cost of variety and complexity, no economies
Examples	Industrial commodities (salt)	Most consumer products (detergents)	Most capital goods, luxury goods (yachts)

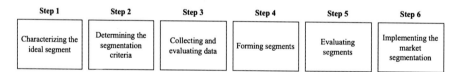

Fig. 2 The process of market segmentation

- Demographics (e.g., gender, age, income)
- Attitudes (e.g., attitudes towards cars as well as the key factors by which they choose a car; e.g., "Image is not important to me in a car")
- Preferences (e.g., concerning the focal product)

Step 1: Characterizing the Ideal Market Segment

The first step in the process of market segmentation is to anticipate and describe the ideal segment as well as the ideal segment solution (Dolnicar et al. 2018).

As market segmentation is characterized by its exploratory nature (i.e., firms normally do not know the final market segments before conducting the segmentation), this step might seem counterintuitive. Omitting this step might lead to firms ending up with a solution that does not fit firm strategy. For instance, while one firm may focus on smaller segments with fewer customers (i.e., niche segments), other firms – the market leaders – tend to only focus on segments that include a greater number of consumers (i.e., mass segments). The decision about which segment to focus on likely depends on multiple dimensions, such as the segments' profitability, the number of consumers firms can cater to, their marketing activities, as well as their value proposition (e.g., for some firms, consumers' response to price elasticity may be more important than for others).

Accordingly, the description of the ideal segment should be done before the actual segmentation and the ideal segment should be characterized by the same criteria that will be used to evaluate it later in the process (see *Step 5: Evaluating Segments*).

In the example of the choice of the car model "Ford Ka," the ideal segment should allow Ford to identify the potential buyers of that new model, which is characterized by a unique design and sporty driving, as opposed to the traditional small car buyer who was a single, first-time or income-constrained buyer. Table 2 illustrates the means and medians of the variables that describe consumers depending on whether they prefer the Ford Ka (listing the model among the top three car choices), no preference for the Ford Ka (listing the model among the bottom three car choices), or middle (none of the previous categories).

Step 2: Determining the Segmentation Criteria

After determining the ideal segment, firms need to select the variables allowing them to identify that segment by distinguishing between consumers. These variables are called "segmentation criteria."

While the literature has proposed many variables that can serve as a basis for segmentation (e.g., Bock and Uncles 2002), this chapter characterizes them using two dimensions (see Wedel and Kamakura 2012):

- *Observability*: The extent to which a variable can be observed without interaction with consumers
- *Consumption-specificity*: The extent to which a variable is related to the specific consumption decision

Table 2 Car preferences and means across variables

Preference	Size	Gender (% female)	Married (yes)	Single (yes)	Age (average)	Income category (median)
Ford Ka top 3	45.6%	53%	56.1%	31.6%	36.8	4.0
Middle	29.6%	51%	48.6%	43.2%	38.1	3.5
Ford Ka least 3	24.8%	35%	43.5%	43.5%	33.4	3.5

Observability. One key distinction between segmentation criteria is whether the segmentation criteria can be easily observed or not (Dolnicar et al. 2018; Wedel and Kamakura 2012). Observability describes a firm's ability to assess a dimension for individual customers without communicating with their consumers. Highly observable variables are visible. The best observable variables are typically related to the "who." Examples of observable segmentation variables include many demographic variables like gender, age, location of the customer, household size, and often culture (Wedel and Kamakura 2012). The combination of these measures can also result in socioeconomic status classifications (i.e., upper-middle class, lower-middle class, etc.). Another advantage is that these variables are stable (Wedel and Kamakura 2012); they do not change much or at all over time. In business markets, an easily observable variable is the industry or the size of the customer. Such observable variables also allow firms to identify any new customers as members of a specific segment. For instance, using age as a segmentation variable allows allocating new customers to specific segments even when they had not been subject to the initiation market segmentation. Accordingly, observable segmentation criteria have various advantages.

Nevertheless, observable variables have disadvantages. One is that segments that are formed based on observable segmentation criteria typically differ less in their responsiveness to firm activities (Frank et al. 1972; McCann 1974). Marketing actions are more effective when they aim at such underlying motivational drivers, the goals customers pursue (Kruglanski and Szumowska 2020). Although this renders observable variables less valuable, firms nowadays still widely apply observable variables as segmentation criteria and their popularity as segmentation criteria is unbroken (Wedel and Kamakura 2012). In sum, unobservable variables related to needs, goals, and benefits are typically more meaningful for the segmentation as they are more closely related to preferences (e.g., attitude towards specific products) or future behavior (e.g., purchase behavior), but it is oftentimes easier for firms to use observable segmentation criteria.

The question "*who* does *what, when, where, how,* and *why?*" provides another classification of segmentation variables into *needs* or *benefits sought* ("why") and the *decision-making process* ("how") of the consumer, *demographic* variables ("who"), and *behavior-specific* information ("what," "when," and "where"). The "why" and the "how" are more related to motivational drivers of behavior but typically unobservable. On the other hand, the "who" and "what" are much easier to observe but are often not closely related to motivational drivers.

Assume using age as segmentation criterion when considering our example of the Ford Ka: Using age, which is observable, as segmentation criterion would unlikely lead to a meaningful segmentation given that reportedly the consumers interested in that model ranged across all age categories. By contrast, consumers' preference for driving pleasure and their ambition to "be different" from others, which both are unobservable to Ford, would be better suited in identifying the segments that are eventually meaningful to Ford.

Accordingly, firms need to assess whether observable variables are sufficient for their market segmentation, or whether they need deeper insights into their customers and therefore need unobservable variables.

Consumption-specificity. The second dimension by which segmentation criteria can be classified is the extent to which a criterion is specific to the consumers' buying and consumption behavior. Examples of criteria with a high consumption specificity are product usage frequency, store loyalty, adoption stage, usage situation, and brand loyalty (Wedel and Kamakura 2012). While some of the variables, and in particular the behavioral variables related to the "what" (e.g., store patronage or online presence visits), are more readily available as they can be observed (e.g., using a CRM system or weblog systems that track consumers' online behavior), others might be more difficult to collect (Payne and Frow 2005; Verhoef et al. 2010). For instance, attitudinal variables, such as ambition to "be different" from other consumers, need to be revealed by consumers in surveys (Wedel and Kamakura 2012). Even more so, consumption-specific variables are often unobservable, especially those related to the "how." Among those unobservable characteristics are variables such as the decision-making process (Blattberg and Sen 1974; Dhalla and Mahatoo 1976), different types of elasticities (and in particular price elasticity; Wedel and Kamakura 2012), and customer perceptions of brand attitudes (Yankelovich 1964).

Using behavioral variables related to the "what" can seem problematic because the exact purpose of segmentation is to identify segments whose behavior can potentially be shaped through marketing actions. While segmentation based on consumption or usage volume, brand loyalty, or customer profitability, a typical segmentation in services or B2B markets to allocate sales effort is relatively easy to implement, and it requires an existing market, available transaction data, stable, hard to change customer behavior, and good coverage of all potential customers. If these conditions do not hold, it can easily result in self-fulfilling "prophecies" (e.g., low users remain low users or brand switchers remain brand switchers), because there is no effort to change behavior, in overlooking a significant part of the market because customers do not appear in existing databases, or in getting blind-sided by competitors, when their actions can change customer behavior. In the end, there is still a need to understand the drivers of the observed behavior to understand customers and guard against these threats.

The variety of the to-date examined measures is so broad that "almost every consumer behavior variable has been proposed for segmenting markets" (Bock and Uncles 2002). The advantage of variables with a high consumption specificity is that they are more predictive of consumer's attitudes and behavior towards a firm's products. However, one downside of high consumption-specificity is that its reliability is questionable (Lastovicka et al. 1990) and may even be negatively related to the stability (Wilkie and Cohen 1977). In particular, consumption-specific variables are often subject to more significant changes given that they depend on characteristics as the rate of innovation or the change of a competitors' marketing communications. By contrast, general, or consumption unspecific, characteristics are typically more stable than consumption-specific characteristics. Among general variables count, for instance, customers' general values, cultural values (Steenkamp and Ter Hofstede 2002), as well as lifestyle (Wedel and Kamakura 2012). Thus, firms need to trade-off whether they use variables that are high in terms of consumption specificity (and thus be more informative for a firm) or that might be more stable (and thus longer lasting).

Table 3 Classification of segmentation variables (see Wedel and Kamakura 2012)

	Consumption specific	Consumption unspecific
Observable	Purchase frequency Store loyalty Online behavior Time spent on the website Purchase amount	Demographics (age, gender) Culture Public social media profile information Industry application
Unobservable	Attitudes toward product/brand Benefits Needs Price sensitivity Decision-making unit and process	Values Lifestyle Opinions Strategic objectives

Building on these dimensions, one can establish a matrix that classifies the different segmentation criteria and thus allows firms to select any of those (see Table 3).

A pitfall of market segmentation is to either *only* use observable (e.g., demographic) or unobservable variables as segmentation variables. A good market segmentation often requires a *combination* of these variables, which allow a firm to form *and* identify actionable, responsive segments.

In the Ford Ka example, the following list is available as segmentation criteria:

- *Demographic variables*: Age, marital status, children, first car, age category, children category, income category, residence, single, marital status, household size
- *Attitudinal variables related to cars and driving* (examples):
  - When it comes to cars, my heart rules my head.
  - I want a car that is nippy and zippy.
  - I prefer cars with high performance.
  - For me, a car is a symbol of freedom and independence.

While the demographic criteria can be (typically) easily observed, the attitude variables require a survey to be evaluated. For the segmentation analysis, we selected three factors that (Factor 1: Value of *small* cars as means of transportation, Factor 2: Seeing a car as a statement, Factor 3: Seeing driving as more than transportation) that summarized the attitudinal variables (an inventory of 100 different questions about transportation, cars, and driving). This approach should allow us to identify segments that have distinct attitudes toward cars and driving.

Step 3: Collecting and Evaluating Data

In this step, firms need to assess the data that are available, as well as identify the need for data that may complement these yet available data (Dolnicar et al. 2018). Firms then collect these data. This step of the segmentation process has significantly changed in the past decades due to new data sources and new data collection methods.

Classical sources of market research remain the most important source of data. To the pillars of classical market research count among others:

- Survey-based methods (e.g., paper-back surveys, web-based surveys)
- Conjoint analysis (e.g., choice-based conjoint analysis, adapt conjoint analysis)
- Other methods (e.g., data from CRM databases, consumers' expressions on social media)

Surveys. Surveys are a method to collect self-reported data and are the most common source of market segmentation also, because they are easy and cheap to collect (Dolnicar et al. 2018). Current and prospective consumers respond to questions on their needs, attitudes (e.g., brand evaluation, customer satisfaction), attitudes and preferences (for product attributes, products, brands), and behaviors (e.g., information search behavior, purchases of the company and its competitors). Notably, those questions should allow for a precise assessment of the dimensions later used for the segmentation. The key advantage of surveys is that they allow to reveal unobservable variables and thus information about the consumers that cannot be easily collected differently. When conceptualizing consumer surveys for segmentation, it is key to allow the collection of unbiased information. This requires considerations about how to recruit respondents (e.g., to avoid biases related to self-selection and representativity), the number of respondents that are recruited (i.e., sample size), as well as how the survey is designed (e.g., to avoid response biases and the effort required of respondents to fill out the survey; Dolnicar et al. 2018).

Conjoint analysis. Conjoint analysis extends these surveys by making a systematic assessment of how individual attributes can affect consumers' choices; eventually, these methods allow to estimate consumers' willingness to pay and thus price sensitivity. Conjoint analysis follows the idea that consumers can assess and compare products as a whole better than individual attributes. Oftentimes, such conjoint analysis starts by requiring respondents to indicate options that they would not consider at all. This allows for more precisely assessing the remaining potentially attractive options. Respondents then evaluate those offers as a package against each other, iteratively comparing different offers. While many methods related to conjoint analysis have been developed, the traditional ones are choice-based conjoint analysis and adaptive conjoint analysis. While the latter only requires respondents to select between two offers at a time while accounting for their previous choices, the former provides multiple profiles of offers (e.g., consisting of a product, a price, a package). Choice-based conjoint analysis is thus typically more demanding. Given that price sensitivity is one of the key segmentation criteria and the importance of individual product attributes allow for actionable insights, conjoint analysis is particularly attractive for collecting data for segmentations.

Other methods. The increase in digitalization and the proliferation of customer relationship management (CRM) databases allow to enrich classical sources with additional segmentation-relevant data from manual or automated recording of *customer observations*. In CRM databases information on a company's current customers is archived and readily accessible, and they typically consist of demographic data, interaction data (previous interactions, such as sales interactions), as well as transaction data (e.g., historic purchases, shopping baskets). Relatedly, weblog systems (e.g., Google Analytics) track consumers in real-time generate detailed behavioral data on individual consumers. Moreover, online social networks nowadays have been established as a source that allows to provide significant amounts of data on both individual consumers as well as their social context (e.g., Casteleyn et al. 2009; Russell 2011). What is more, data exchanges oftentimes allow firms to access information about consumers prior to their arrival on the website.

With an increasing amount of available data, the question for firms shifts from "How can firms access the data?" to "How attractive are the data?" (Cai and Zhu 2015), and ultimately "How important are the data for effectively differentiating between groups of consumers?" (e.g., Haustein 2016; Liu et al. 2016; Tufekci 2014). This section discusses novel data and how firms can use them for market segmentation (Öztaysi and Onar 2013; Netzer et al. 2012) and proposes that these novel data can allow firms to assess previously unobservable consumer characteristics.

A key source of data today are online social networks. Two data types can be usefulness for segmentation:

- Standardized expression of attitudes (e.g., Facebook/Twitter likes)
- Textual data (e.g., Facebook/Twitter comments)

The first, expression of attitudes describe the various ways of expressing oneself on online social networks that are standardized. Examples of those are, for instance, the act of one's liking of a fellow user's comment, of a topic, or even of a brand. While each online social network offers its own labeling of this expression (e.g., Facebook uses so-called "likes"), they often reveal preferences and are easy for firms to collect. The revealed preferences can allow inferring people's personalities, which can be valuable as segmentation criteria.

A large amount of information is posted daily on social in the form of texts (Netzer et al. 2012), for instance, when consumers write status updates (i.e., information about their current activities), comment on others' activities, or engage in conversations. Such data are unstructured, which leaves advantages and disadvantages. While the data potentially contain rich information, the complexity of extracting information may not be trivial and often requires skills and resources (Netzer et al. 2012). Among the common methods of extracting insights from textual data are sentiment analysis (which analyzes the emotional profile of a message; Dhaoui et al. 2017) or advanced natural language processing (Tsai and Chiu 2004), and for more detailed information, please see chapter "Automated Text Analysis" of this handbook. Moreover, to translate this textual data into segmentation criteria, firms also need to deal with multiple key challenges, such as (1) matching people's profiles on online social networks to actual persons and (2) identifying whether consumers state their honest opinion. Despite the previous issues, marketers can take advantage of these new data and also use them as a basis for market segmentation – oftentimes to render observable previously unobservable variables.

In the Ford Ka example, data were collected via surveys. Consumers had to indicate their preferences concerning the car, against different attitudes, as well as whether they listed the Ford Ka among the three most preferred cars, three least preferred cars, or in the middle. Moreover, this survey allowed obtaining information about non-observable variables, such as the consumers' attitudes. However, one challenge related to this survey is the relatively small sample of consumers and the assessment of the representativity. This points to a general problem in data collection for segmentation purposes: creating a sample that is representative to estimate the size of segments, when the segmentation is not yet known. This problem can be addressed with additional market research *after* the segmentation is complete. Alternatively, a commonsense segmentation, which we elaborate on in the next section, can guide the determination of the sample and the sample size *before* the survey is conducted.

Step 4: Forming Segments

The formation of segments, i.e., the actual act of market segmentation, is fundamentally a quantitative task requiring specialized statistical methods. However, any firm can benefit from a market segmentation, even when that segmentation is informal (i.e., lacks sophisticated methods). Dolnicar et al. (2018) propose to distinguish between *commonsense* and *data-driven* market segmentation. While the commonsense segmentation allocates consumers to different groups iteratively using different segmentation variables, data-driven segmentation uses those criteria at the same time along with model-based estimations (Dolnicar et al. 2018). A commonsense segmentation might be as simple as using just paper and pencil by brainstorming about *why* a customer would buy a product or service, derive value from it, and *how* a customer is likely to acquire it.

For using more quantitative market segmentations, multiple methods have evolved over the past decades (Wedel and Kamakura 2000). Initially, researchers used classical multivariate statistical methods such as cluster analysis, discriminant analysis, and regression analysis. More recently, the emphasis has shifted to model-based segmentation methodologies involving more complex optimization and numerical methods, finite mixtures, and Bayesian approaches given the various criteria established for effective market segmentation.

The purpose of this section is to give the reader sufficient insights into different methods to understand their value and offer a guideline to identify the appropriate method for their market segmentation challenge. In particular, it discusses the assumptions of different methods about segments. For detailed technical descriptions of segmentation methods, we refer the reader to other chapters in this handbook (see chapter ▶ "Cluster Analysis in Marketing Research") and to other sources that focus on the description of statistical methods and processes. Forming market segments that are useful for business decisions can be broken into three different but related steps:

- *Creation of market segments:* How many segments do properly represent the customer heterogeneity of a market? What is the unifying need or behavior within a segment and what are the key differences between the segments?

- *Profiling of market segments:* How can firms classify customers into existing segments? What are the characteristics of customers within a segment?
- *Sizing of market segments:* How many customers belong to a segment?

Creation of market segments. Market segmentation is required as a result of the heterogeneity of customers in a market (Kotler 1997). We, therefore, need first a description and quantification of this heterogeneity. The "classic" case of segmentation occurs when the company has no or only limited knowledge of customer heterogeneity, making segmentation an exploratory task. The main goal is to *determine the number of segments* based on the collected data and which segments each customer is assigned to. The most appropriate methods for this task are various existing clustering methods. Cluster analysis is often seen as synonymous with segmentation. It is, however, important to note that clustering methods are most useful for the creation of segments but do not suffice for market segmentation overall.

Different clustering methods make different assumptions about the nature of customer heterogeneity. A first assumption is whether or not a customer belongs to one and only one segment. This leads to the distinction between *nonoverlapping*, *overlapping,* and *fuzzy* clusters (Hruschka 1986). The first type follows the idea that segments ought to be mutually exclusive and collectively exhaustive (MECE) while the other two allow for customers to belong to multiple segments. Fuzzy clustering provides a probability vector for segment membership and can thus be seen as an intermediate solution between overlapping and nonoverlapping clusters.

If a customer can belong to multiple segments, then the customer can be exposed to different, potentially conflicting, marketing actions. On the other hand, it is well known that customers can belong to different segments, especially when we extend market segmentation beyond the grouping of customers to a classification of consumption situations or occasions (Arabie 1977). For example, the same customer can consume beer for different reasons and at different locations. So, the distinction between nonoverlapping and overlapping clustering is closely related to the question of what exactly is the "object" that should be grouped in a market segmentation. This is an important decision that relates to the distinction between strategic and operational segmentation. From a strategic perspective, it is more appropriate to assume a customer belongs to only one segment and therefore assume clusters are nonoverlapping. From an operational perspective, when customer activation requires a combination of marketing actions, forming overlapping clusters can be very useful.

Nonoverlapping clustering methods are the most commonly used methods in marketing for market segmentation. Because the key question when creating segments concerns the number of segments, the distinction between *hierarchical* clustering and *nonhierarchical* clustering methods is very important. Hierarchical methods do not require the specification of several segments. They start with each customer forming a single-subject cluster. These clusters are then linked in successive steps until all customers are in the same cluster. This forms a tree-like structure, hence the term hierarchical clustering. Nonhierarchical methods start from a random initial division of customers, which is then changed until an optimization criterion is achieved given the a priori specified number of segments. Typical optimization criteria involve some kind of distance measure to account for the within and the between variances. Hierarchical methods can therefore be seen as even more exploratory than nonhierarchical methods. Their disadvantage is the lack of a conceptual basis to justify a hierarchical structure among customers to characterize heterogeneity. This structure also implies that a customer stays in the same cluster irrespective of how many clusters are formed as the number of clusters is changed through successive steps of combining clusters.

Determining the appropriate number of clusters is one of the most difficult problems in the creation of segments. The goal, especially for strategic market segmentation, is to obtain the smallest number of segments that makes sense for the firm. A useful approach for this problem is to use multiple methods. Hierarchical clustering gives an initial estimate of the number of clusters which then can be applied to nonhierarchical clustering to refine and verify the segmentation. In the third step, the number of clusters can be systematically increased and decreased. The cost of increasing the number of segments is increased complexity. For example, if an increase in the number of segments yields another segment that would not be targeted, there is little value in increasing the number of segments. Similarly, the size of the additional segment can be too small to be attractive or meaningful. On the other hand, a reduction of the number of segments can eliminate a potentially attractive target segment or an otherwise valuable market insight.

There are statistical methods to determine the optimal number of clusters (e.g., Calinski and Harabasz 1974), but it is important to understand that there is no theoretically correct market segmentation, and the final number of segments is a subjective decision that is based on statistical metrics and business considerations. The final criterion is the utility of a final segmentation for the business and its marketing actions – the business value. For more details about clustering methods, we refer the reader to chapter "Cluster Analysis in Market Research" in this handbook.

Profiling of market segments. This business value also depends on the ability to properly sort customers into the created segments, including customers who were not part of the data used to create the segments in the first place. In other words, market segmentation requires a description or profiling of segment members. For that, we need *observable* variables as outlined the section "Step 2: Determining the Segmentation Criteria."

Clustering and classification methods can be confused because both methods allocate subjects into several groups or segments. In classification tasks, we know the number of groups and the membership of existing subjects to those groups. The objective of clustering methods is to reduce a larger number of items into a smaller number of homogeneous clusters based on collected data. The objective of classification is to assign an item to the appropriate group with the help of a classification model. Using the terminology of machine learning, classification is a typical task of directed knowledge discovery while clustering is an example of undirected knowledge discovery. In a classification task, we have a dependent variable – the existing segments – and independent or predictor variables and we have predictive methods.

The two most common methods are discriminant analysis and logistic regression. Both are used when the dependent variable is categorical. Discriminant analysis creates discriminant function(s) to maximize the difference between the groups on the function and is only used for categorization. Logistic regression works like ordinary least squares regression but on the logit of the dependent variable. It can be used for categorization but more also provides the odds ratio for each variable. Cluster analysis without a subsequent discriminant or regression analysis does not yield properly formed *and* profiled customer segments. An alternative method to clustering plus discriminant analysis is latent class analysis (LCA; see also chapter ▶ "Finite Mixture Models"), which allows for a segmented analysis of customer reactions to various marketing actions, especially price, and an integration of segment creation and profiling (Grover and Srinivasan 1987; Kamakura and Russell 1989).

Predictive methods are also useful in the context of CRM systems when segments can be formed based on past purchase behavior or customer value estimates, which then can be linked to available predictor variables. With today's computing power, very sophisticated predictive models using Markov Chain Monte Carlo (MCMC) methods can be deployed to directly approximate the posterior distribution of a parameter of interest, thereby making the customer heterogeneity visible. Moreover, the possibility to link it to observable predictors greatly facilitates the description or profiling of segments.

Decision trees also provide a powerful and easy-to-implement classification method. The goal is to build a tree that will allow us to predict the dependent variable based on the values of attributes or independent variables. Decision trees differ from logistic regression in the way they generate the boundaries between to separate different classes. Regression "fits" a line to divide the space, whereas decision trees bisect the space into smaller and smaller regions in a nonlinear fashion. While decision trees, especially today's high-power machine learning methods, have superior classification performance, logistic regression accounts for the simultaneous effects of all predictors and is usually less costly in terms of sample size. For a further discussion of the advantages and disadvantages of decision trees, see Berry and Linoff (1997) or Murthy (1998).

Sizing of market segments. Segmentation schemes offered by consulting companies, like the VALS™ segmentation, or simple observable variables like zip codes. The value of these segmentation methods is somewhat limited today. Conceptually, however, these methods play an important role in the segment formation process. First, the selection of *target* segments depends on the evaluation of the attractiveness of the segments. One important determinant of segment attractiveness is the size of the segments (see "Step 5: Evaluating the Final Segment Solution"). An accurate estimation of the size critically depends on the proper sampling of the underlying population, but without some a priori knowledge of the segment structure, it is all but impossible to ensure a representative sample for creating the segments. When Renault launched the Twingo and Ford the Ka, the market segmentation revealed the presence of design-sensitive buyers of small cars. But the size of these segments could not be reliably estimated because the respondents were not recruited with this type of segmentation in mind.

Second, any overall average market research result calculated across a heterogeneous customer group is useless, if not dangerous. The calculation of the average customer satisfaction across all Starbucks customers depends among other things on customer acquisition. The rapid store expansion attracted a lot of convenience buyers who did not value Starbucks as much as the experience buyers, the brand lovers. It is possible that within both segments, customer satisfaction increases, but a faster increase in the number of generally less satisfied convenience buyers would result in a decrease in the average customer satisfaction. Similarly, if Coca-Cola had segmented people before doing taste tests to develop New Coke, for example, on simple variables like their brand preference and attitudes, marketing history might be one disaster shorter.

The third key point is that for *strategic* market segmentation, the key segment formation decision is setting the number of clusters. This is a managerial judgment task guided by statistics. For an *operational* market segmentation, especially in a setting where marketing decisions are automated, statistical methods, like machine learning methods, are essential. They are very powerful, but the daily online experience with retargeting illustrates the danger of very powerful methods: they can be precisely wrong.

It should also be clear that the formation of segments is not a simple sequential process. Segmentation is an iterative process. In particular, the number of segments and the choice of profiling variables also depends on the organizational applicability of the segments. The next step reviews how to evaluate the final segment solution. In sum, it is important to see different methods as complementary and not as substitutes. A good segmentation process requires *descriptive* and *predictive* methods, and without at least some a priori idea of segmentation (see "Step 1: Characterizing the Ideal Market Segment"), any single statistical method can yield incomplete results.

Returning to the Ford Ka example, we conducted a k-means cluster analysis (see chapter ▶ "Cluster Analysis in Marketing Research") to reveal different segments. In a k-means cluster analysis, the so-called k-means algorithm iteratively partitions the data set into a predefined number of groups that are distinct and nonoverlapping. Each data point is then allocated to a specific group.

In a first step, we created the segments using the k-means algorithm and the R package. This step was done to determine the number of segments. We simulated different numbers of clusters and examined to what extent the heterogeneity within the segments was reduced by adding additional clusters with the elbow method (the number of segments was chosen at the kink in the line plot, i.e., at four clusters).

Next, we visualized the segments to provide a profile of those segments (Fig. 3a–c). Specifically, we plotted the segments using the three-, four-, and five-segment solution. As can be seen, the five-segment solution was overlapping for the first two factors, while the three- and four-segment solutions were discriminating well between the consumers on those segments.

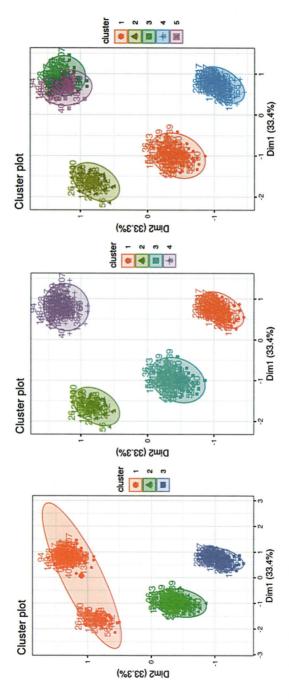

Fig. 3 (a–c) The segments illustrated

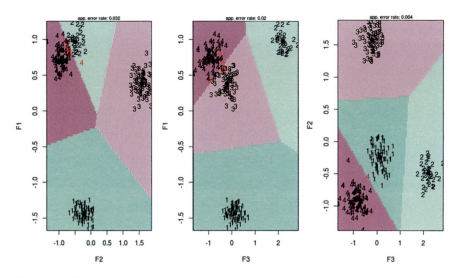

Fig. 4 a–c The discriminatory power of the factors for the four-segment solution

We next used a discriminant analysis to test whether each of the factors contributes to the separation between the factors. The factors discriminated well between segments as the following figure illustrates (Figs. 4a–c):

Step 5: Evaluating the Final Segment Solution

After forming segments, firms need to evaluate the viability of the segmentation. For doing so, several commonly accepted criteria have been established (see Table 4; Pires et al. 2011).

Identifiability. A key criterion for evaluating a market segmentation is the identifiability of the segments (Blattberg and Sen 1974; Dolnicar et al. 2018; Wedel and Kamakura 2012). Identifiability of the segments describes a marketer's ability to identify the segments. Typically, firms can use observable criteria to identify those segments. For instance, when segments differ in terms of age or gender, it would likely be easy to identify the market segments. By contrast, the identifiability is low when nearly no, or no observable criteria are considered in the segmentation. If only unobservable variables such as attitudes are used to distinguish segments, firms are challenged in distinguishing between segments. In practice, firms often either use a combination of observable and non-observable variables (to be able to identify segments without trading off forming meaningful segments) or even entirely use observable variables to ensure the resulting segments are identifiable.

Accessibility. A second criterion is whether a consumer segment can be effectively reached by a firm or its "accessibility" (Kotler 1997; Pires et al. 2011). While the proliferation of new media increases the accessibility of segments and thus this

Table 4 Criteria to evaluate final segmentation

Criterion	Explanation	Ford Ka
Identifiability	Firm's ability to identify the segments using a specific set of observable criteria	Difficult
Accessibility	Extent to which a segment can be effectively reached by a firm	Good
Responsiveness	Extent to which a segment responds to a particular marketing program or product position	Good
Stability	Extent to which a segment remains similar as well as meaningful over time over a specific period of time	Probably good
Substantiality	Extent to which segments will yield enough profits such that they justify being targeted	Unclear

criterion seems to be of less practical relevance, it is by no means given that all segments are equally easy to be reached. Nowadays, consumers can effectively limit the extent to which they are reached by specific communication efforts and thus might be less easily accessible by companies. One way of how access to consumer segments becomes more difficult is the use of ad blockers. Ad blockers restrict the possibility of firms to effectively reach consumers via online advertising (Goldfarb and Tucker 2011). More importantly, some segments are more prone to deter display advertising that they are approached with by a company, i.e., the technology-savvy consumers who are aware of the latest ad blockers. As a result, firms may not be able to reach those consumer segments and thus a market segmentation that results in those segments may create some hardly accessible consumer segments. While this is only one example of how accessibility to segments can vary across segments, multiple others exist.

Responsiveness. "Responsiveness" implies that market segments respond to a firm's marketing activities, such as response to a particular marketing communication campaign, to variations in price, or even the product's features (Myers 1996). Moreover, the segments' responses should also differ from each other, which is sometimes considered to be an extra criterion called "differentiability." Based on the segments' responses, firms can more efficiently specify their marketing activities. For instance, assume two segments differ in terms of their media habits. While the first segment predominantly uses traditional media such as TV and radio, the second segment uses new media and focuses on receiving all information via social media. The difference between the two segments' media usage allows firms to align their media mix in a way that they can reach each of the segments most efficiently. The firm can target the first segment with classical TV campaigns, while it can target the second segment by specifying characteristics for their advertisements on social media. By contrast, if the segments do not differ concerning how they respond to various marketing activities, the market segmentation has failed to attain its goal of more efficiently allocating its resources.

Stability. A criterion of market segmentation is the extent to which the segments are stable (Dolnicar et al. 2018; Hassan et al. 2003; Pires et al. 2011). Put differently, this criterion examines whether the market segmentation as well as the segments it formed remain meaningful over time. Segmentation stability is insofar important for firms as it allows to craft longer-term strategies based on those segments. Dolnicar and Leisch (2010) propose repeating the segmentation when a firm is concerned about changes to assess its stability. Assessing the stability includes evaluating whether the *same* segments will form in a similar structure and size over time. While overall segments might reproduce in different segments over time, individual segments might form less well over time. This segment level stability refers to "how often a market segment with the same characteristics is identified across different repeated calculations of segmentation solutions with the same number of segments" (Dolnicar et al. 2018; p. 167). Notably, the stability of segmentation solutions depends on the criteria chosen for segmentation. A market segmentation that relies on consumers' values, which are characterized to be stable over time, eventually results in a more stable segmentation than one that builds on criteria that vary significantly, e.g., consumers' sentiment expressions on social media.

Substantiality of segmentation. The final and key criteria for evaluating market segments is the "substantiality" of the formed segments. Substantiality describes the extent to which a segment is attractive enough such that it justifies being targeted – which is typically derived by a segment's profitability potential. Substantiality thus depends on a combination of measures, such as the number of consumers assigned to a segment, economic variables as their customer lifetime value, their purchasing power, or their price sensitivity (Hassan et al. 2003). While the number of consumers in a segment is not the only measure, it still remains important as it relates to the firm's strategy: Large segments are typically targeted by market leaders (and thus characterized by more competition), whereas smaller segments form so-called niche segments, which may be more attractive for smaller firms. It is worth noting, however, that recent developments have challenged this idea. Production techniques, as mass customization and personalized communication and dynamic pricing nowadays allow firms to cater to needs of individual consumers. Accordingly, on an operational level, firms are nowadays able to target much smaller segments than previously and to individualize their activities.

We next illustrate the segments using the demographic variables reported at the outset and added the preference for the Ford Ka. In terms of the established criteria for segmentation, it will be difficult to easily identify the segments given that they barely differ in terms of observable attributes such as gender or age. The accessibility to each of the segments is given as follow-up analyses concluded: They can be reached using classical communication instruments. As can be seen by the classification (see Table 5), the segments differ in their preferences for the Ford Ka, thus,

Table 5 Segment descriptions

Segment	Size	Pref Ka	Gender (% female)	Married	Single	Age	Income category
Seg. 1	31%	43.6%	41%	53.8%	35.9%	37.0	3.77
Seg. 2	**13%**	**56.3%**	**50%**	**53.1%**	**37.5%**	**35.1**	**3.59**
Seg. 3	26%	41.5%	62%	50.8%	40%	37.1	3.28
Seg. 4	30%	46.7%	43%	46.7%	38.7%	35.6	3.97

they seem to be differently responsive, with Segment 2 being the one that has the strongest preference for the Ford Ka. While we did not illustrate the stability over time (as this was a cross-sectional survey), one can assess the substantiality of the segments: The smallest segment of the four-segment solution seems to be most likely to consider the Ford Ka among their top three choices. The segment is bolded. This last problem could potentially be alleviated by extending the targeting to include, for example, all or part of Segment 4.

Step 6: Implementing the Market Segmentation

The final step is the implementation of a market segmentation. In this phase, firms need to consider their resources as well as their organization. The key objective of this section is to emphasize that a market segmentation is a means to an end, which is to more effectively serve segments of consumers). Three points require attention:

- Allocating sufficient resources to the implementation (in the short- *and* long-run)
- Closely aligning marketing and sales departments
- Regularly evaluating and updating the market segmentation

To materialize the value of any market segmentation demands to fully embrace it. This may as well imply substantial organizational changes (Croft 1994) and if firms are not willing to bear these consequences and thoroughly implement the market segmentation, even a potentially successful market segmentation may fail (Dibb and Simkin 1997, 2001). While firms may reorganize and align their marketing activities in the short run, they should also consider the long run. For example, in our Ford example, Segment 4 not only seems to be the biggest segment but also the one with the greatest income. However, this potentially profitable consumer segment does not prefer the Ford Ka as much and thus does match the product well. Investing resources to develop a product that meets that segment's needs might not be worth the effort.

One of the challenges when implementing a market segmentation is the alignment of the marketing department and the sales department. Typically, creating a market segmentation is the task of the former, while the implementation primarily concerns the latter. This requires a close alignment between both departments, in terms of its organizational routines or IT systems. The knowledge of the market structure that the marketing department reveals by means of the market segmentation need to be internalized into a firm's a CRM system to grant the sales department easy access. What is more, the operationalization of the market segmentation can be updated in real-time in case a firm's IT systems allow for doing so. For instance, depending on the information that firms have about visitors of their websites (e.g., obtained by Google Analytics), firms could display personalized information. The information though also flows in the opposite direction. A successful segmentation depends on the availability of data within the CRM system, which are primarily generate or provided by sales or customer service.

Besides these formal implementation challenges, the results of a market segmentation should also be actively communicated to a firm's employees (e.g., product developers or customer contact personnel) in a way that it is useful. For illustration purpose, firms can use of so-called "personas" that are actual or fictional profiles (Pires et al. 2011) that portrait the members of each market segment in a representative manner. These personas are typically focused on the attitudes and motivations of that segment and given that they illustrate segments they translate the mere numbers and descriptive patterns of a market segment into useful visualizations. While using actual consumers as personas can be more believable (Judge et al. 2012), fictional ones may fit more precisely and may be dynamically changed to reflect changes in of a given market segment (An et al. 2017). Such illustrations may support the firm in various considerations. For instance, product developers might consider such personas, and their projected motivations and goals, as basis for developing products that appeal to multiple segments (Pires and Stanton 2005). Moreover, personas and their visual characterization may support customer contact personnel in identifying members of individual market segments (Pires et al. 2011) and thus be decisive about whether the market segmentation will be used in practice. While no personas are indicated, we labeled the segments according to their psychographic profiles (see Table 6).

Many firms see market segmentation as something you do "once in a lifetime." Market segments are based on consumer characteristics and these characteristics change over time. As outlined in *Step 5: Evaluating the Final Segment Solution*, a market segmentation should be stable over an extended period of time as it creates the basis for long-term strategic decisions that are hard to adapt or even reverse. At the same time, firms should not ignore the implications of consumer trends for market segmentation. A market segmentation needs to be regularly evaluated against these trends. When new consumers enter a market, the variables used to identify segments may need to be adapted. When new consumer needs emerge, the variables used to create the segments need to be adapted. When both change at the same time, it is time to change the entire market segmentation.

For example, for a long-time, small cars created customer value through a lower price. As a result, all manufacturers segmented consumers based on socioeconomic

Table 6 Segment names and descriptions

	Segment 1	*Segment 2*	*Segment 3*	*Segment 4*
Description	Attention seekers	Freedom lovers	No-nonsense neutrals	Sensible classics
Size	31%	13%	26%	30%
Car preference	Unique car	Funky car	Basic car	Sensible car
Factor 1	Medium	High	Low	High
Factor 2	High	Medium	Medium	High
Factor 3	Medium	High	Medium	Low
Other descriptors	Fashion conscious	Skeptical of government regulation	Can only afford small car	Value conscious

variables and focused on reducing development and production costs. Consider the rising popularity of small cars. Various technological, environmental, and social trends made small cars attractive for other reasons than price (e.g., urban mobility, environmental footprint). These benefits also attracted new consumer segments to small cars. It was not until the introduction of the Renault Twingo and the Ford Ka, that car manufacturers realized the need for new market segmentations.

Conclusions and Managerial Implications

This chapter described the concept and process of market segmentation. The value of market segmentation has been discussed in light of recent developments, like the greater ability of firms to deliver individualized offerings, personalized communication, as well as a much greater degree of price discrimination.

This chapter ascertains that segmentation is as relevant today as it was when the concept was first introduced into management practice. In fact, technology trends have further increased the importance of distinguishing between strategic market segmentation, which guides a firm's long-term decisions (e.g., positioning or innovation and new product strategies), and operational market segmentation, which relates to real-time decisions like personalized communication (Jenkins and McDonald 1997; Sausen et al. 2005). While strategic segmentation is important no matter the firm's strategy or products, operational segmentation intuitively depends on the extent to which firms can adapt to their consumers in real time on an individual basis, which is facilitated by a greater level of digitalization (e.g., of communication). Accordingly, the digitalization provides firms with different abilities to customize their offerings and to personalize their communications and in future, customers will be able to benefit from additional offerings. Nevertheless, developments in the opposite direction exist, too, such as the increased sensitivity for privacy issues (Aguirre et al. 2016; Awad and Krishnan 2006) and data protection (as newer developments like the General Data Protection Regulation). These developments challenge the proliferation of real-time segmentation.

Despite its undeniable value to any business, market segmentation is not without controversy. Because the fundamental goal is to customize marketing actions, at least to some degree, in other words to treat different people differently, segmentation can be viewed as discrimination with another name. By choosing a target segment, firms implicitly choose to serve and focus on some customers and not the entirety of their customers. At a time when society is increasingly sensitive to all forms of discrimination, marketers can face a dilemma. By creating the basis for customization, segmentation creates value for consumers. At the same time, it creates the basis for differentiation and monopoly power, which can be detrimental to customer value. Moreover, marketing actions based on segmentation can reinforce stereotypes that at the root of gender inequality or ethical discrimination.

Even though segmentation is a well-established and fundamental concept in marketing, many firms still struggle with it. Like marketing, successful market segmentation is science and art; it requires judgment on part of market researchers and managers. We conclude this chapter with a list of seven segmentation traps to avoid.

1. *No strategic market segmentation at all.* There is still the belief that market segmentation is something only for big consumer goods firms. Even if the number of customers is small or real-time customization is possible, segmentation improves the quality of marketing and business decisions. All firms can benefit from a strategic market segmentation because the value of segmentation derives not only from the firm's own marketing strategy but importantly from a more detailed understanding of consumers. At least, this can improve the firm's understanding of their consumers, reduce complexity, and simplify internal communications.
2. *Seeing market segmentation as a statistical exercise.* Developing a marketing strategy and selecting target customers are fundamental to the strategy processes of any business. Data alone cannot decide how to segment a market, especially not for strategic market segmentation. Management judgment is part of the process. As a result, market segmentation is always a strategic decision and should not be reduced to a statistical exercise.
3. *Confusing segments and product categories.* Market segmentation groups consumers and leads to strategies and activities that are specific to the needs and behaviors of target segments. This includes adapting products and developing a portfolio of products for the target segments. While a close relationship between target segments and product categories is important, one should not confuse them. There is no "small car" segment; there are consumers – a segment – whose needs are best addressed with a small car – a product category.
4. *Market segmentation solely with demographic variables.* A specific market segment should have a uniform reaction to a marketing action or a set of marketing actions. Consumer behavior is primarily driven by deep motivational and attitudinal factors and not demographic variables. Thus, only using demographic segmentation variables is not promising and likely fails to uncover segments that respond unambiguously to marketing activities.
5. *Segments are not identifiable.* The flipside of the fourth trap is a market segmentation that fails to assign consumers to the created segments. Deep motivational and attitudinal factors are not observable; oftentimes, they are at best revealed over time through consumers' behavior. To implement marketing actions, the target segment must be identifiable, which requires the description of segments with observable variables.
6. *Segment attractiveness is segment size.* The first goal of segmentation is to structure the market into internally homogeneous market segments. The second goal is to prioritize these segments. Segment attractiveness is not just determined by size and growth. The profitability of a market segment also depends on the competition – bigger markets attract more competition – factors as the segment's price sensitivity and whether a firm is able to efficiently serve a segment. Thus, bigger segments might not always be the more attractive ones.

7. *Considering segmentation as a static process.* A key success factor of market segmentation is to keep it relevant over the years while considering how environments and consumers change. It is thus imperative to constantly reevaluate and potentially update the market segmentation.

To conclude, market segmentation is at the core of any market strategy and is rightly considered to be one of the most important marketing tools. Newer developments shape and affect the value of market segmentation and allow firms to customize and individualize their offerings, prices, and communications. The rise of digital marketing certainly had and will continue to have a significant impact on market segmentation, but "big data" and "marketing automation" carry the danger of turning market segmentation into a technical and operational issue instead of cementing its place as the foundation of all marketing strategy and actions. Customers will continue to exhibit similarities and differences and it is up to firms to understand them and harness them for their business strategies and thus the value of market segmentation remains undisputed.

Cross-References

- Analysis of Variance
- Applied Time-Series Analysis in Marketing
- Assessing the Financial Impact of Brand Equity with Short Time-Series Data
- Automated Text Analysis
- Bayesian Models
- Challenges in Conducting International Market Research
- Choice-Based Conjoint Analysis
- Cluster Analysis in Marketing Research
- Dealing with Endogeneity: A Nontechnical Guide for Marketing Researchers
- Crafting Survey Research: A Systematic Process for Conducting Survey Research
- Experiments in Market Research
- Exploiting Data from Field Experiments
- Field Experiments
- Finite Mixture Models
- Fusion Modeling
- Logistic Regression and Discriminant Analysis
- Measuring Customer Satisfaction and Customer Loyalty
- Measuring Sales Promotion Effectiveness
- Mediation Analysis in Experimental Research
- Modeling Customer Lifetime Value, Retention, and Churn
- Modeling Marketing Dynamics Using Vector Autoregressive (VAR) Models
- Multilevel Modeling
- Panel Data Analysis: A Non-technical Introduction for Marketing Researchers
- Partial Least Squares Structural Equation Modeling
- Regression Analysis

- ▶ Return on Media Models
- ▶ Social Network Analysis
- ▶ Structural Equation Modeling
- ▶ Willingness to Pay

References

Aguirre, E., Roggeveen, A., Grewal, D., & Wetzels, M. (2016). The personalization-privacy paradox: Implications for new media. *Journal of Consumer Marketing, 33*(2), 98–110.

Ansari, A., & Mela, C. (2003). E-customization. *Journal of Marketing Research, 40*(2), 131–140.

Arabie, P. (1977). Clustering representations of group overlap. *Journal of Mathematical Sociology, 5*(1), 113–128.

Arora, N., Drèze, X., Ghose, A., Hess, J. D., Iyengar, R., Jing, B., Joshi, Y. V., Kumar, V., Lurie, N. H., Neslin, S., Sajeesh, S., Su, M., Syam, N. B., Thomas, J., & Zhang, Z. (2008). Putting one-to-one marketing to work: Personalization, customization, and choice. *Marketing Letters, 19*(3), 305–321.

Awad, N. F., & Krishnan, M. S. (2006). The personalization privacy paradox: An empirical evaluation of information transparency and the willingness to be profiled online for personalization. *Management Information Systems Quarterly, 30*(1), 13–28.

Bailey, C., Baines, P., Wilson, H., & Moira, C. (2010). Segmentation and customer insight in contemporary services marketing practice: Why grouping customers is no longer enough. *Journal of Marketing Management, 25*(3–4), 227–252.

Beane, T. P., & Ennis, D. M. (1987). Market segmentation: A review. *European Journal of Marketing, 21*(October), 20–42.

Berry, M. J., & Linoff, G. (1997). *Data mining techniques: For marketing, sales, and customer support*. Willey.

Blattberg, R. C., & Sen, S. K. (1974). Market segmentation using models of multidimensional purchasing behavior. *Journal of Marketing, 38*(4), 17–28.

Bock, T., & Uncles, M. (2002). A taxonomy of differences between consumers for market segmentation. *International Journal of Research in Marketing, 19*(3), 215–224.

Cai, L., & Zhu, Y. (2015). The challenges of data quality and data quality assessment in the big data era. *Data Science Journal, 14*, 2.

Caliński, T., & Harabasz, J. (1974). A dendrite method for cluster analysis. *Communications in Statistics-theory and Methods, 3*(1), 1–27.

Casteleyn, J., Mottart, A., & Rutten, K. (2009). How to use data from Facebook in your market research. International Journal of Market Research 51(4):439–447.

Croft, M.J. (1994), Market segmentation: A step-by-step guide to profitable new business. Cengage Learning Emea.

Dellaert, B. G., & Dabholkar, P. A. (2009). Increasing the attractiveness of mass customization: The role of complementary on-line services and range of options. *International Journal of Electronic Commerce, 13*(3), 43–70.

DeSarbo, W. S., Grewal, R., & Scott, C. J. (2008). A clusterwise bilinear multidimensional scaling methodology for simultaneous segmentation and positioning analyses. *Journal of Marketing Research, 45*(3), 280–292.

Dhalla, N. K., & Mahatoo, W. H. (1976). Expanding the scope of segmentation research: Segmentation Research Must Cover More of the Total Marketing Problem if it is to be Operational and Profitable. Journal of Marketing 40(2):34–41.

Dhaoui, C., Webster, C. M., & Tan, L. P. (2017). Social media sentiment analysis: Lexicon versus machine learning. *Journal of Consumer Marketing, 34*(6), 480–488.

Dibb, S., & Simkin, L. (1997). A program for implementing market segmentation. *Journal of Business & Industrial Marketing, 12*(1), 51–65.

Dibb, S., & Simkin, L. (2001). Market segmentation: Diagnosing and treating the barriers. *Industrial Marketing Management, 30*(8), 609–625.

Dolnicar, S., & Leisch, F. (2010). Evaluation of structure and reproducibility of cluster solutions using the bootstrap. *Marketing Letters, 21*(1), 83–101.

Dolnicar, S., Grün, B., & Leisch, F. (2018). Market segmentation analysis. In *Market segmentation analysis* (pp. 11–22). Singapore: Springer.

Frank, R. E., Massey, W. F., & Wind, Y. (1972). *Market segmentation.* Englewood Cliffs: Prentice Hall.

Gilmore, J. H., & Pine, B. J. (1997). The four faces of mass customization. *Harvard Business Review, 75*(1), 91–102.

Goldfarb, A., & Tucker, C. (2011). Online display advertising: Targeting and obtrusiveness. *Marketing Science, 30*(3), 389–404.

Grover, R., & Srinivasan, V. (1987). A simultaneous approach to market segmentation and market structuring. *Journal of Marketing Research, 24*(2), 139–153.

Hassan, S. S., Craft, S., & Kortam, W. (2003). Understanding the new bases for global market segmentation. *Journal of Consumer Marketing, 20*(5), 446–462.

Haustein, S. (2016). Grand challenges in altmetrics: Heterogeneity, data quality and dependencies. *Scientometrics, 108,* 413–423.

Hruschka, H. (1986). Market definition and segmentation using fuzzy clustering methods. *International Journal of Research in Marketing, 3*(2), 117–134.

Jenkins, M., & McDonald, M. (1997). Market segmentation—Organizational archetypes and research agendas. *European Journal of Marketing, 31*(1), 17–32.

Judge, T., Matthews, T., & Whittaker, S. (2012). *Comparing collaboration and individual personas for the design and evaluation of collaboration software.* Austin: Proceedings of the SIGCHI Conference on Human Factors in Computing Systems.

Kamakura, W. A., & Russell, G. J. (1989). A probabilistic choice model for market segmentation and elasticity structure. *Journal of Marketing Research, 26*(4), 379–390.

Kamakura, W. A., & Wedel, M. (2000). Factor analysis and missing data. *Journal of Marketing Research, 37*(4), 490–498.

Kotler, P. (1989). From mass marketing to mass customization. *Planning Review.*

Kotler, P. (1997). *Marketing management, analysis planning and control.* Englewood Cliffs: Prentice Hall International.

Kruglanski, A. W., & Szumowska, E. (2020). Habitual behavior is goal-driven. *Perspectives on Psychological Science, 15*(5), 1256–1271.

Lastovicka, J. L., Murry, J. P., Jr., & Joachimsthaler, E. A. (1990). Evaluating the measurement validity of lifestyle typologies with qualitative measures and multiplicative factoring. *Journal of Marketing Research, 27*(1), 11–23.

Lilien, G.L., Rangaswamy, A. (2004), *Marketing Engineering. Computer-Assisted Marketing Analysis and Planning*, Revised 2nd ed. Trafford Publishing, Victoria.

Liu, J., Li, J., Li, W., & Wu, J. (2016). Rethinking big data: A review on the data quality and usage issues. *ISPRS Journal of Photogrammetry and Remote Sensing, 115*(May), 134–142.

Mahajan, V., & Jain, A. K. (1978). An approach to normative segmentation. *Journal of Marketing Research, 15*(3), 338–345.

McCann, J. M. (1974). Market segment response to the marketing decision variables. *Journal of Marketing Research, 11*(4), 399–412.

Murthy, S. K. (1998). Automatic construction of decision trees from data: A multi-disciplinary survey. *Data Mining and Knowledge Discovery, 2*(4), 345–389.

Myers, J.H. (1996). Segmentation and positioning for strategic marketing decisions. *American Marketing Association.*

Netzer, O., Feldman, R., Goldenberg, J., & Fresko, M. (2012). Mine your own business: Market-structure surveillance through text mining. *Marketing Science, 31*(3), 521–543.

Öztaysi, B., and Onar, S.C. (2013). User segmentation based on twitter data using fuzzy clustering. *Data Mining in Dynamic Social Networks and Fuzzy Systems.* IGI Global, 316–333.

Payne, A., & Frow, P. (2005). A strategic framework for customer relationship management. *Journal of Marketing, 69*(4), 167–176.

Peppers, D., & Rogers, M. (1997). *Enterprise one to one: Tools for competing in the interactive age.* New York: Currency/Doubleday.

Piller, F. T. (2004). Mass customization: Reflections on the state of the concept. *International Journal of Flexible Manufacturing Systems, 16*(4), 313–334.

Pires, G., & Stanton, J. (2005). *Ethnic marketing—Accepting the challenge of cultural diversity.* London: Thomson Learning.

Pires, G. D., Stanton, J., & Stanton, P. (2011). Revisiting the substantiality criterion: From ethnic marketing to market segmentation. *Journal of Business Research, 64*(9), 988–996.

Postma, O. J., & Brokke, M. (2002). Personalization in practice: The proven effects of personalization. *Journal of Database Management, 9*(2), 137–142.

Ries A., and Trout J. (1980). Positioning: The Battle for your mind. McGrawHill.

Roberts, J.H., Kayande, U., and Stremersch, S. (2019). *From academic research to marketing practice: Exploring the marketing science value chain.* In: How to Get Published in the Best Marketing Journals. Edward Elgar Publishing.

Sausen, K., Tomczak, T., & Herrmann, A. (2005). Development of a taxonomy of strategic market segmentation: A framework for bridging the implementation gap between normative segmentation and business practice. *Journal of Strategic Marketing, 13*(3), 151–173.

Smith, W. R. (1956). Product differentiation and market segmentation as alternative marketing strategies. *Journal of Marketing, 21*(1), 3–8.

Steenkamp, J.-B. E. M., & Ter Hofstede, F. (2002). International market segmentation: Issues and perspectives. *International Journal of Research in Marketing, 19*(3), 185–213.

Tsai, C.-Y., & Chiu, C.-C. (2004). A purchase-based market segmentation methodology. *Expert Systems with Applications, 27*(2), 265–276.

Tufekci, Z. (2014). Big questions for social media big data: Representativeness, validity and other methodological pitfalls. In Proceedings of the International AAAI Conference on Web and Social Media (Vol. 8, No. 1).

Verhoef, P. C., Venkatesan, R., McAllister, L., Malthouse, E. C., Kraft, M., & Ganesan, S. (2010). CRM in data rich multichannel retailing environments: A review and future research directions. *Journal of Interactive Marketing, 24*(2), 124–137.

von Hippel, E. (1998). Economics of product development by users: The impact of 'sticky' local information. *Management Science, 44*(5), 629–644.

von Hippel, E. (2001). Perspective: User toolkits for innovation. *Journal of Product Innovation Management, 18*(4), 247–257.

Wedel, M., & Kamakura, W. A. (2012). *Market segmentation: Conceptual and methodological foundations* (2nd ed.). Springer Science & Business Media, LLC.

Weinstein, A. (1987). *Market Segmentation*. Chicago: Probus Publishing Company.

Weinstein, A. (2004). *Handbook of market segmentation: Strategic targeting for business and technology firms*. Psychology Press.

Wilkie, W. L., & Cohen, J. B. (1977). *An overview of market segmentation: Behavioral concepts and research approaches*. Cambridge, MA: Marketing Science Institute Working paper.

Winger, R., & Edelman, D. (1989), Segment-of-one marketing. The Boston Consulting Group, (329).

Yankelovic, D. (1964). New criteria for market segmentation. *Harvard Business Review, 42*(2), 83–90.

Yankelovic, D., & Meer, R. (2006). Rediscovering market segmentation. *Harvard Business Review, 84*(2), 122–131.

Willingness to Pay

Wiebke Klingemann, Ju-Young Kim, and Kai Dominik Füller

Contents

Introduction	970
Conceptual Definitions of WTP	971
Methods for Measuring Willingness to Pay	972
Stated Preference Methods	973
Revealed Preference Methods	979
Summary of Methods for Measuring WTP	982
Drivers of WTP	982
Situational Factors	987
Individual Factors	988
Information-Related Factors	988
Market Research Application	989
Elicitation of Consumers' WTP	989
Application 1: Price Bundling	992
Application 2: Personalized Pricing	993
Application 3: Nonlinear Pricing	993
Conclusion	994
References	995

Abstract

Measuring accurate willingness to pay (WTP) is essential for designing pricing policies, particularly for pricing new products. Neglecting consumers' WTP may lead to unexploited surplus when prices are set too low or to low demand when prices are set too high. Additionally, information on consumers' WTP serves as

---

W. Klingemann (✉) · K. D. Füller
Karlsruhe Institute of Technology, Institute for Information Systems and Marketing – Services Marketing, Karlsruhe, Germany
e-mail: wiebke.klingemann@kit.edu

J.-Y. Kim
Goethe University Frankfurt, Department of Marketing, Frankfurt, Germany
e-mail: ju-young.kim@kit.edu

valuable input to estimate sales and for use in optimization models, thus, to maximize profit. To date, various approaches to measure WTP exist that differ regarding their elicitation approach (direct vs. experimental) and whether they rely on stated or revealed preferences (hypothetical vs. actual WTP). This chapter provides an overview of the most common methods for measuring WTP and further discusses determinants of WTP.

We further provide a practical illustration of WTP measurement. Therefore, we collected data on consumers' WTP for a hypothetical new product offer using two stated preference approaches (open-ended questions and dichotomous choice method following a sequential monadic approach) as well as one revealed preference approach (BDM mechanism). We compare the results of these different methods and discuss how to apply WTP measures in practice.

Keywords

Willingness to pay · Stated preference methods · Revealed preference methods · Hypothetical bias · Drivers of WTP

Introduction

Determining prices is a task that challenges all companies worldwide. As price is the most effective driver of profitability, superior to cost reductions and increases in sales quantity (Simon and Fassnacht 1982, pp. 1–24), optimal pricing can be considered one of the most crucial management decisions. Ideally, pricing decisions should account for production costs and competitors' prices, while also considering how much consumers are willing to spend for the product at maximum (Moorthy 1988). However, the latter, referred to as consumers' *reservation price* or consumers' *willingness to pay* (WTP) (Kalish and Nelson 1991, p. 328), is often neglected, resulting in prices that do not fully exploit consumer surplus: according to McKinsey, 80–90% of all poorly chosen prices are set too low (Marn et al. 2003). This may lead to substantial losses in revenue: for example, the car manufacturer Audi lost more than 200 million Euros because it sold its Q7 luxury SUV too cheap, thus running out of stock. Similarly, Asus, the Taiwanese electronics company, launched its mini-notebook "eee PC" in Germany at a price which was set so low that demand exceeded supply by 900% (Ramanujam and Tacke 2016, p. 22). But even if companies become aware of their undervaluation before running out of stock, they won't be able to easily adjust their prices. Consumers often react negatively to subsequent price increases, consequently leading to lower perceived value, satisfaction, and future purchase intentions (Calabuig et al. 2014). They may even boycott the seller (Sen et al. 2001).

In contrast, an overvaluation, i.e., when prices are set too high, may be adjusted more easily from a consumer's point of view, but it may often lead to market entry difficulties or even product failure. For instance, the introduction of Apple's earlier devices, the handheld Newton (introduced in 1993) and the gaming machine Pippin (introduced in 1995), failed completely as they were perceived as too expensive (Greenberg 2008). Particularly companies that tend to "over-engineer," i.e., equipping their products with features that consumers do not value, encounter the problem of overvaluation. For example, Amazon took a 170-million-dollar write-down in 2014 because its high-end positioned "Fire Phone" was equipped with too expensive features that consumers were not willing to pay for (Ramanujam and Tacke 2016, pp. 16–17).

Without knowing consumers' WTP, it is not only difficult to design a profitable product, it is also impossible to make educated decisions about how a new product should be introduced and offered, such as whether to create product bundles (Chung and Rao 2003), to partition prices (Hamilton and Srivastava 2008), or to estimate the effects of price promotions (Shaffer and Zhang 1995).

Due to the interdependence of price and demand, even small changes in price may significantly influence both the overall market share and profits (Winer 2005). Thus, knowing consumers' true WTP can be considered the most important information for estimating sales (Jedidi and Jagpal 2009, pp. 37–38) and, ultimately, maximizing revenue.

As consumers' true WTP is an unobservable construct, the challenge comprises a valid elicitation manner to find out its true value (Voelckner 2006, p. 137). Therefore, various methods for measuring consumers' WTP have already been developed, with constant efforts to improve weaknesses associated with these measurement approaches, such as high complexity and costs of measurement, biases, lack of realism, or insufficient information specificity.

Therefore, this chapter provides an overview of the most common methods to measure WTP and gives some insights about how to counter these possible weaknesses associated with these methods. We further discuss the importance of context effects. Independent of the method, researchers as well as practitioners have to take into account that consumers' WTP is usually not fixed but dependent on the respective context. Consumer preferences are not stable but are often newly formed during a choice situation, affected by various personal and contextual factors (e.g., Slovic 1995; Bettman et al. 1998; Hoeffler and Ariely 1999). Considering the importance of price to be a profit driver, it is therefore essential to know what circumstances influence consumers' WTP and to understand when and why it changes. In addition to an overview of common methods to measure WTP, we discuss situational, individual, and information-related factors driving consumers' WTP.

To illustrate the theory, we present a simple example and compare the results of three elicitation methods. We measure consumers' WTP for a hypothetical new product offer using two stated preference approaches (open-ended questions and dichotomous choice method following a sequential monadic approach) as well as one revealed preference approach (BDM mechanism). At last, we further discuss how to apply elicited WTP in practice.

Conceptual Definitions of WTP

When estimating WTP, the aim is to determine the maximum price a consumer would be prepared to pay, that is "the maximum sacrifice, in terms of [...] money, that one is willing to make to obtain a commodity" (Donaldson 1999, p. 551). This means that WTP is not necessarily equivalent to consumers' estimation of the value of a product. Consumers may have a WTP below what they believe a product to be worth if they cannot afford to pay more, that is, if their ability to pay is limited (Russell 1996). Therefore, measurements of WTP try to determine "the price at or below which a consumer will demand one unit of the good" (Varian 1992, p. 152). While this implies that a consumer will definitely make a purchase, other definitions state that WTP is the price "at which a consumer would no longer purchase" (Hauser and Urban 1986, p. 449) or "at which a consumer is indifferent between buying and not buying the product" (Jedidi and Zhang 2002, p. 1352).

These marginal technical differences in the definition of WTP illustrate the difficulty of generating a specific point estimate, raising the question whether such a price point exists. From an economic viewpoint, "WTP for a product is the amount of income that will compensate for the loss of utility obtained from the product" (Allenby et al. 2014, p. 430). As it is highly difficult for consumers to determine exactly how much utility they will derive from a product, more recent research suggests that "rather than specific WTP values for products, consumers probably have some range of acceptable values" (Ariely et al. 2003, p. 77). If the price falls below the lower bound of this range ("floor reservation price"), they will definitely buy; if it exceeds the upper bound of the range ("ceiling reservation price"), they will definitely not buy. Within this range, consumers' response is not clearly predictable (Ariely et al. 2003; Wang et al. 2007). Under the premise that the WTP distribution is symmetric within the uncertainty interval, expected WTP is the midpoint of this range (Dost and Wilken 2012, p. 149).

Methods for Measuring Willingness to Pay

Methods for measuring WTP can be differentiated with regard to their elicitation approach (direct vs. experimental) and whether they rely on stated or revealed preferences (hypothetical vs. actual WTP) (c. Miller et al. 2011). With stated preference methods, participants' answers are taken "as stated," and their choices are only of hypothetical nature. Revealed preference methods, in contrast, lead to real consequences and actual purchases.

The following table provides an overview of common methods used to measure WTP (Table 1):

Table 1 Overview of common methods for measuring consumers' WTP

	Stated	Revealed
Direct	Consumer surveys, e.g., – *Open-ended questions* – *Dichotomous choice method* – *Payment card method* Expert opinions	Auctions, e.g., – *Vickrey auctions* – *BDM mechanism* Market data
Experimental	Conjoint analysis Choice-based conjoint analysis	Lab experiments Field experiments

Direct methods estimate WTP by directly asking

- Consumers how much money they are willing to spend (i.e., open-ended questions or closed questions using dichotomous choice or payment card methods; or consumer auctions where consumers have to make bids pursuant to the Vickrey rule or the BDM mechanism)
- Experts about prices they believe achievable (i.e., expert judgments, management discussions)
- The market, by analyzing past (i.e., "natural") market data that give insight about which prices are accepted

Experimental methods, in contrast, actively create or manipulate choice situations that are affected by price, deducting WTP from participants' behavior, without explicitly asking about the price itself.

These can be

- Hypothetical choice scenarios where participants have to evaluate options or choose among options (i.e., conjoint analysis, choice-based conjoint analysis)
- Real, but artificial choice situations where participants have to make actual purchase decisions (i.e., lab experiments)
- Real, natural choice situations, where participants are not aware that their purchase decisions are part of a pricing experiment and that prices are manipulated for experimental purposes (i.e., field experiments)

In the following, we will explain each method in detail, having a closer look on the most popular ones. We then discuss advantages and disadvantages associated with each method and conclude with an overview of method validity and feasibility.

This section concludes with a guide suggesting when to apply which method.

Stated Preference Methods

Direct Stated Preference Methods

Direct stated preference methods can be divided into *consumer surveys* and *expert opinions*. They are usually the fastest and simplest ways to measure consumers' WTP.

The *open-ended questions method* asks consumers directly how much they would be willing to pay for a certain good or service. This is most probably the easiest method to use. A special variant of the open-ended questions is the *van Westendorp method*, a consumer survey that also measures price perception and price sensitivity (Müller 2009). The van Westendorp method generates a pricing corridor based on four questions about what price consumers would consider too cheap vs. attractively cheap as well as expensive but acceptable versus too expensive (van Westendorp 1976). The van Westendorp method thereby generates a price sensitivity meter (PSM). Figure 1 depicts an example on how to interpret the results of such a survey.

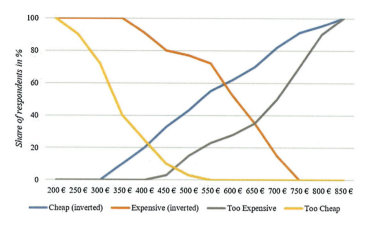

Fig. 1 Example for a price sensitivity meter

The intersection of "too cheap" and "cheap" (inverted) and the intersection of "too expensive" and "expensive" (inverted) mark the lower ends (LE) and upper ends (UE) of the price corridor for optimal pricing. In the example, the product should be priced between 410€ and 650€.

The van Westendorp method allows respondents to indicate a price range instead of one price point, an approach supported by recent research. Wang et al. (2007) argue that consumers are often not completely sure about their own preferences and the exact performance of a product, which means that forcing them to state their WTP as one absolute point does not adequately reflect reality. They therefore propose to ask respondents at which price they would definitely buy/be indifferent between buying and not buying/buy with a very low probability, thereby generating a price range. Dost and Wilken (2012) support this approach by arguing that range-based methods allow consumers to indicate a price range that reflects their decision-making uncertainty, whereas point-based methods ignore this uncertainty and force consumers to make a guess about their WTP that might or might not be true.

However, open-ended questions methods, both point-based methods and price range methods, require high cognitive effort from consumers, who are used to evaluating given prices instead of generating prices on their own (Chernev 2003). Therefore, *dichotomous choice methods* use closed, polar questions, asking respondents whether they would buy a product at a specific price. Dichotomous choice methods are easy to implement; however, the consumer's response only gives information about whether the price is acceptable or not but lacks information on precise WTP. Thus, researchers may work with either a large sample size (*monadic approach*) or with a sequential approach (*sequential monadic approach*). Applying the *monadic approach*, participants are divided into different groups, with each group being confronted with a different price. The amount of price points should be limited, as each requires a new group of participants (Lyon 2002, p. 10). An alternative approach that does not require such a high sample size is the *sequential monadic approach*, sometimes also referred to as *Gabor Granger method*.

Participants who answer that they would not buy the product at the given price will be asked the same question again with a lower price (with the exception that the rejection is based on the fact that the price was too cheap). In contrast, participants accepting the initial price presented, will be asked whether they would buy the product at a higher price, until the maximum WTP is determined (Gabor and Granger 1966).

An undesired effect of this approach is that the price attribute becomes very dominant in contrast to the other attributes of the good or service. This method also suffers from a starting point bias, meaning that the first price serves as an anchor and impacts participants' evaluation of the subsequent prices (Herriges and Shogren 1996).

The *payment card method* avoids this bias by presenting participants with an array of prices, asking them to indicate which of the presented prices reflects their WTP (Fig. 2). However, here researchers must pay attention to select intervals that actually cover participants' differences in WTP, and to choose a decent number of price points manageable for participants (Rowe et al. 1996).

Direct stated methods are the most common method used for contingent valuation, i.e., for measuring the value of goods that cannot be sold, such as public or environmental goods (e.g., air quality) (Mitchell 2013). In contingent valuation, survey participants are asked to imagine how much they would be willing to pay to improve the status quo or to prevent it from deteriorating (e.g., to prevent a reduction of air quality), for instance, through taxes or donations that help to improve or preserve the current status (see Boyle 2017 for a detailed description of how to conduct a contingent valuation study).

While contingent valuation surveys need a sample of participants that represent the respective interest group, companies conducting WTP surveys can also rely on *expert opinions,* thus questioning internal market experts instead of consumers. These experts can be marketing managers or sales people who work closely with consumers and can therefore provide relevant insights for pricing decisions. A disadvantage of working with market experts is that their judgments might be biased. Particularly, when their compensation depends on the number of sales, they may

---

Please indicate how much you would be willing to annually pay to reduce current night-time noise in your neighborhood by 30%:

☐ 0 €   ☐ 150 €
☐ 20 €   ☐ 200 €
☐ 40 €   ☐ 250 €
☐ 75 €   ☐ 300 €
☐ 100 € ☐ more than 300 €
          Please, indicate your maximum amount: _____ €

Fig. 2 Example for a contingent valuation survey using the payment card method

have an incentive to state a lower price than they believe achievable (Hanna and Dodge 1995, p. 70).

Consumer surveys involve a similar incentive problem: as a direct question predominantly shifts attention toward the price, consumers are tempted to act prospectively and state a price lower than their true WTP in order to save money (Lyon 2002, p. 9).

Qualitative research has therefore made efforts to limit strategic answering by improving the formulation of direct questions. For instance, instead of asking what price a respondent would be willing to pay, the researcher could alternatively ask the respondent to state a price that he/she considers fair for both seller and buyer or to ask the respondent to guess at which price the product would sell (see Henderson (2002) for a more detailed description of possible qualitative questions).

Another, although more complex way to eliminate the problems of consumers' strategic understatements of their WTP is to use *experimental stated preference methods*.

Experimental Stated Preference Methods

Experimental stated preference methods, also known as *conjoint analyses*, employ choice scenarios where respondents have to compare and evaluate different options. These methods are decompositional, which means that the respondents' ratings of the presented products, or their choice decisions, are used to deduct WTP for the overall product and its different features ("top-down approach"). Despite being more complex and time-consuming than direct surveys, the holistic approach of these analyses is closer to consumers' actual product evaluation behavior and puts less emphasis on the price attribute. It thereby overcomes most of the previously mentioned problems of direct WTP measurements, such as strategic or biased answering behavior or respondents' difficulties in accurately stating their WTP (Green and Srinivasan 1990).

The underlying idea of conjoint analyses is that consumers' WTP for a product depends on the utility they derive from it, with the overall utility being the sum of the utilities they derive from the different product attributes.

Traditional *conjoint analysis* (CA) (Luce and Tukey 1964) determines these utilities by asking respondents to rank (or rate) different products that are presented through multiple relevant product attributes and product attribute values (e.g., Green and Rao 1971; Green and Srinivasan 1978; see Gustafsson (2007) for a detailed description of different forms and applications of conjoint analysis).

Choice-based conjoint analysis (CBC) (Louviere and Woodworth 1983) does not demand respondents to rank different products but rather to choose among them, including the option to choose nothing (Fig. 3). Therefore, the main advantage of CBC is its similarity to real choice situations (compare Louviere et al. (2000) for a detailed analysis of both approaches).

CA relies on the assumption that respondents derive more utility from the product the higher they rank it. CBC infers that the utility of an option that has been chosen is positive – otherwise the no-choice option would have been selected – and higher

Willingness to Pay

3 Please choose the Bundle you would most likely consider buying.				
Shipping Time	2 Business Days	2 Business Days	1 Business Day	
Shipping Cost	Free of Charge at a Minimum Order Value of 50€	Free of Charge	Shipping Coast charged	
Monthly Bill	✗	✗	✓	
Webinars	✓	✗	✓	I would not consider to buy any of these bundles.
Special online account with access to exclusive content	✗	✓	✗	
Price per Month	9€	39€	29€	
	○	○	○	○

Fig. 3 Example for a choice-based conjoint task for an industrial service bundle

than the utilities of each of the rejected options (Halme and Kallio 2011). Using statistical estimation methods, such as monotonic analysis of variance or multiple regression (c. Green and Srinivasan 1990, p. 5), an additive utility function can then be generated (see Eq. 1).

Equation 1 Exemplary additive utility function of a consumer h for a product i.

$$\hat{U}_{h,i} = \hat{\beta}_{h,0} + \hat{\beta}_{h,j=\text{Price}} * x_{i,j=\text{Price}} + \hat{\beta}_{h,j=\text{Attribute\_1}, m=\text{Value\_1}} * x_{i,j=\text{Attribute\_1}, m=\text{Value\_1}} \\ + \ldots + \hat{\beta}_{h,j=\text{Attribute\_n}, m=\text{Value\_n}} * x_{i,j=\text{Attribute\_n}, m=\text{Value\_n}}$$

Equation 1 shows an exemplary basic formula of a utility function for a consumer h and a product i. It starts with a constant ($\beta_{h,0}$) that represents the basic utility that consumer h derives from product i. The function includes the attribute "price," which is coded with a vector model, meaning that the utility increases/decreases linearly with the attribute value, i.e., the price level. The price parameter ($\beta_{h,j\,=\,\text{Price}}$) is usually negative, meaning the overall utility of a product decreases with increasing price and vice versa (there are rare exceptions, for instance in the area of luxury goods). For example, if $\beta_{h,j\,=\,\text{Price}}$ is estimated as -1.5 and the price equals 10 monetary units, the utility of the product decreases by 15 utility points. Apart from the price attribute, all further relevant attributes must be considered in the function. Nominal attributes are coded with a part-worth utility model, which means that a parameter is estimated for each specific attribute value, with the specific values being incorporated into the function via dummy variables. By offsetting the utility of an attribute with the price that results in a utility of zero, WTP can be calculated for each product attribute and consequently, the overall product if all relevant attributes are considered (Kohli and Mahajan 1991). More precisely, WTP for a specific attribute value is calculated by dividing its part-worth utility through the nominal value of the price parameter of the utility function (compare Eq. 2).

Equation 2 Calculation of WTP using utility parameters

$$WTP_{h,j=\text{Attribute\_}x, m=\text{Value\_}x} = \frac{\hat{\beta}_{h,j=\text{Attribute\_}x, m=\text{Value\_}x}}{\left|\hat{\beta}_{h,j=\text{Price}}\right|}$$

For example, if attribute 1 was color, with value 1 = "red" and value 2 = "blue," a parameter of 3 (6) for value 1 (value 2) would indicate that the utility increases by 3 utility points if the product is red, and by 6 utility points if the product is blue. This means consumer h would be willing to pay 2 monetary units if product i was red ($\rightarrow$ 3: $|-1,5| = 2$) and 4 monetary units if it was blue ($\rightarrow$ 6: $|-1,5| = 4$). Consequently, consumer h would be willing to pay 2 monetary units more if product i was blue instead of red ($\rightarrow$ (6–3): $|-1,5| = 2$).

For a more comprehensive description of how to conduct conjoint experiments, please refer to the chapter "Choice-Based Conjoint Analysis" of this handbook.

Although (choice-based) conjoint analysis relies on several assumptions that are often flawed in reality (e.g., assuming a compensatory relationship between different attributes; compare Srinivasan 1988), it has proven to be a reliable tool for estimating sales and is widely used in both research and practice (Green et al. 2001). However, like all stated preference methods, it suffers from *hypothetical bias*.

Hypothetical Bias in Stated Preference Methods

Stated preference methods suffer from hypothetical bias, which occurs when values are collected in a hypothetical context (Harrison and Rutström 2013). In hypothetical contexts, consumers tend to neglect thinking about what they could alternatively do with the money that is required to buy a product, leading to an exaggerated stated willingness to purchase (Dhar and Gorlin 2013, p. 533). Comparing hypothetical and real purchases, participants more often indicate that they would buy a product in hypothetical contexts (Miller et al. 2011). They further tend to report a significantly higher WTP when they do not have to pay the stated amount in reality (Neill et al. 1994; Voelckner 2006). Consequently, stated purchase intention and related WTP can differ substantially from real behavior (Kalwani and Silk 1982; Morrison 1979).

As stated preference methods are sometimes indispensable, for example to elicit WTP for new products that are not available yet, research has tried to address hypothetical bias in stated preference methods altering qualitative and quantitative aspects.

One simple suggestion is to make respondents more aware of their hypothetical answering behavior. Researchers may inform participants about hypothetical bias and request them to think about what they would really do, i.e., use *cheap talk*. However, results of this approach are mixed, with some studies demonstrating a reduction of hypothetical bias (e.g., Cummings and Taylor 1999) that others could not confirm (e.g., Blumenschein et al. 2008). Another approach is to remind participants of their budget constraints, making them aware that they could also use their money for something else. Effects of this approach are not consistent either, with some research reporting improved results (e.g., Frederick et al. 2009) whereas other research found no difference (e.g., Loomis et al. 1994).

Another alternative to reduce hypothetical bias is the *certainty approach*. The certainty approach only considers data from respondents who are highly sure about their answer. These responses were shown to be closer to real behavior (Blumenschein et al. 2008). Similarly, Hofstetter et al. (2013) note that not all consumers are equally suitable for WTP estimations. Their research on WTP for innovative products shows that individual personal characteristics of respondents regarding abilities and motivation have a positive influence on the validity of their WTP estimates. However, to exclude respondents whose answers are possibly less viable requires a high number of participants.

Quantitative efforts in research may also reduce hypothetical biases. Lieven and Lennerts (2013) present a survey method where participants have to make trade-offs between cash and vouchers that are earmarked for a specific (hypothetical) product/ service. Regardless of its face value, the subjective value of the voucher can naturally never be higher than participants' WTP for the respective product. This method enables researchers to use participants' choice of cash/voucher combinations to draw inferences about their WTP. Ding et al. (2005) have developed an approach that makes conjoint analyses incentive-compatible, leading participants to reveal their actual WTP. Their research suggests to combine conjoint analysis with the Becker–DeGroot–Marschak (BDM) mechanism (Becker et al. 1964; see below for a more detailed description), a revealed preference method (Ding 2007) or to tell participants that they will have the chance of winning their favorite product that will be determined through their answers in the analysis (Dong et al. 2010).

Another option to circumvent the problem of hypothetical bias occurring with stated preference methods is to use *revealed preference methods* instead.

Revealed Preference Methods

Direct Revealed Preference Methods
Direct revealed preference methods are *auctions* or the analysis of *market data*.

Auctions are used in the field (e.g., traditional auctions or online auctions such as eBay) and in the lab as a direct method to elicit WTP, which is revealed through participants' bids and bidding behavior. In the following, we will discuss the most common auction mechanisms.

In *English auctions*, the highest bid wins the auction and determines the purchase price. Competing bidders can overbid each other openly as often as they want what may lead to a systematic overestimation of WTP: they may bid prices that are higher than that of the average consumer, thereby distorting the overall data (Barrot et al. 2010). The phenomenon of auction fever exacerbates this problem. A bidder facing auction fever may be affected by various factors, such as rivalry, social facilitation, time pressure, or the joy of winning, thus leading to overbidding (Ku et al. 2005). However, depending on competition intensity, bidders may also bid below their true WTP.

First-price auctions do not suffer from the problem of auction fever, as they allow only one sealed bid, with the highest bidder obtaining the auctioned good at the price of his or her bid. However, bidders again have an incentive to bid below their true WTP, hoping to still win the auction and to obtain the good at a price lower than their WTP (Hoffman et al. 1993).

In *Dutch auctions*, the auctioneer sets a high starting price and decreases the price by a predetermined increment until one bidder is willing to buy the product at this price. Again, bidders do not have an incentive to bid their true WTP: knowing that they can acquire the good at a lower price if no one else purchases it, bidders may refrain from buying, even if the price matches their WTP. Due to higher transaction costs – with bidders having to wait for the price to decrease – the resulting prices may be higher than with first-price auctions (Carare and Rothkopf 2005) but still not necessarily equal to bidders' actual WTP.

Name-Your-Own-Price (NYOP), also known as *reverse pricing*, can be considered a special kind of auction: consumers do not compete with each other but simply name the price that they are willing to pay, which can be accepted or refused by the seller depending on a threshold value. When multiple bidding is possible, WTP can be derived from the consumers' bidding behavior, assuming that the threshold price is uniformly distributed on a minimum /maximum price interval and frictional costs are constant. As consumers will maximize their expected surplus (i.e., (WTP – price paid) × probability of bid acceptance – frictional costs of submitting bids), it is thus possible to calculate WTP from the number and values of submitted bids (Spann et al. 2004). However, NYOP is also described as "online haggling" (Terwiesch et al. 2005), with buyers trying to make a bargain instead of revealing their actual WTP.

The above described auctions are not incentive-compatible, as bidders may withhold their true WTP. Thus, research has suggested the use of *second-price sealed-bid auctions*, also known as *Vickrey auctions* (Vickrey 1961) and the *Becker–DeGroot–Marschak (BDM) mechanism* (Becker et al. 1964) as incentive-compatible methods.

The mechanism of Vickrey auctions is considered the least prone to biases (Noussair et al. 2004). In the Vickrey auction, each bidder submits a sealed bid. Also here, the highest bidder wins the auction, but the purchase price is determined by the bid of the second-highest bidder (Vickrey 1961). This way, participants do not have any incentive to withhold their true WTP, as they will never pay more than what is necessary to win the auction. If they submit a lower bid than their actual WTP, they may risk losing the auction and the possibility to purchase the product. Bidding above their true WTP is not an optimal strategy either, because participants may win the auction but at a price higher than their WTP. Thus, Vickrey auctions are robust against many kinds of strategic behavior (Barrot et al. 2010). However, there are also limitations associated with this method. Some researchers criticize that bidders assuming that their WTP is too low to win the auction do not have an incentive to bid sincerely (Shogren et al. 2001). They may either submit a lower bid due to lack of motivation or a higher bid in order to increase the price the winning competitor has to pay, leading to distorted WTP results. Further limitations refer to operational problems with the implementation of auctions in general (Wertenbroch and Skiera 2002) and to the fact that auctions typically do not meet realistic decision processes in retailing (Hoffman et al. 1993).

The BDM mechanism (developed by Becker et al. 1964) determines the price of a product through a random draw. First participants submit a sealed bid then someone (e.g., the auctioneer) draws a "market" price. Bidders with bids equal to or higher than the drawn price are obliged to buy the product, whereas those who submitted bids below the "market" price are not allowed to buy it. The mechanism is incentive-compatible, as bidding anything else than one's actual WTP is not an optimal strategy. Bidding more than one's WTP does not affect competing bidders but may result in a purchase obligation at a price above one's WTP. Bidding below the WTP bears the risk of not being allowed to purchase the good. As the price that needs to be paid is determined by a random draw, there is no incentive to deviate from bidding one's true WTP in the hope of impacting the final price. While this mechanism is robust against biases, it suffers from the limitations associated with auctions: the BDM mechanism is difficult to implement in practice and also does not reflect most regular purchase situations, as consumers typically do not have to bid for a limited resource (Wertenbroch and Skiera 2002). Instead, they are influenced by reference prices, deciding whether or not to purchase the product at a given price.

This problem occurs with most direct methods: the generated answers do not fully represent reality. The only direct approach that circumvents this problem is the use of real instead of generated data, that is, the analysis of *market data*. These can be a company's own sales figures, panel data provided by market research agencies, or store scanner data from participating stores (Breidert 2006, p. 39). Based on actual purchase data, market data are incentive-compatible and have high external validity. However, this approach bears obvious weaknesses: first, market data are historical data and are therefore unavailable for new products that have not been put on the market yet. Second, market data only provide information on how many units were sold at a given price, but not on how many people would have paid a higher price, or refrained from purchasing a product due to its price. As this represents a serious constraint to measuring WTP, some researchers have suggested that the analysis of market data should be combined with stated preference methods to generate a more complete picture (Ben-Akiva et al. 1994). An additional severe problem is that market data are confounded by noise, such as promotions or competitor activities, thus, they do not allow for a systematic, clear variation of prices.

One way to investigate actual purchase behavior contingent on price variations is to conduct price *experiments*.

Experimental Revealed Preference Methods

Experimental revealed preference methods estimate WTP using *laboratory experiments* or *field experiments*.

When conducting price experiments, researchers create purchase scenarios that include purchase obligations. Experiments can be conducted in a laboratory, offering the relevant products for sale to the participants, or in the field, selling the products in a real store. When full purchase obligation is not feasible in lab experiments, a helpful solution may be to include a purchase obligation for only a fraction of the participants (e.g., 10%) who are determined by lot (Voelckner 2006).

Assuming that consumers buy as long as the price does not exceed their WTP, the experimenter systematically varies the price and measures the resulting purchase rates and quantities. In laboratory experiments, participants are randomly divided into groups that are confronted with the same purchase situation, but with a variation in price between the groups. In field experiments, prices are usually varied in predefined time intervals. Analyzing the units sold across the different time intervals and prices, the average WTP can be estimated.

Laboratory experiments do not suffer from hypothetical bias; however, participants' WTP may be censored by field opportunities. Participants who know the actual price of a product offered in the laboratory may use this value as a reference and refuse to pay more than it (Harrison et al. 2004). Furthermore, laboratory experiments also suffer from experimental bias: participants may behave not the same way as they would in real purchase settings, knowing that they are participating in an experiment.

In contrast, field experiments have the highest external validity when it comes to measuring true WTP, as they measure WTP under reality conditions. A limitation is, however, that they usually do not allow for the collection of additional controls (e.g., age, income, varying context factors). Field experiments also require high organizational and logistic efforts.

Summary of Methods for Measuring WTP

In the following, we compare the presented methods along main criteria that impact their external validity and feasibility (Table 2).

We then shortly summarize all previously discussed preference measurement methods, presenting examples on how and when to use the methods and provide advantages and disadvantages associated with each kind of approach (Table 3). The tables shall serve as a guidance for academics and practitioners who need to decide which approach is most suitable in which case.

Drivers of WTP

WTP is difficult to measure not only for methodological reasons, but also due to the instability of the value itself. Individual WTP is not constant, but is highly context-dependent and subject to various influencing factors. The following figure provides an overview of important situational, individual, and information-related factors affecting WTP (Fig. 4).

Table 2 Overview of important factors regarding external validity and feasibility of different WTP measurement approaches

Measurement approach	Validity of results					Feasibility of approach		
	Hypothetical bias	Strategic answering bias	Experimental bias	Similarity to real (choice) situations	Consideration of multiple (competitor) products	Applicable for products under development	Complexity/ Costliness
Consumer surveys	yes	yes	yes	low-moderate	no	yes	low
Expert opinions	/	yes	/	/	yes	yes	low
Vickrey auctions	no	no	yes	low	no	no	moderate
BDM mechanism	no	no	yes	very low	no	no	moderate
Market data	no	no	no	equal	yes	no	moderate-high
Conjoint analysis	yes	no	yes	low	yes	yes	moderate-high
CBC	yes	no	yes	high	yes	yes	moderate-high
Lab experiments	no	no	yes	high	yes	no	high
Field experiments	no	no	no	equal	yes	no	high

Table 3 Common methods for measuring WTP in detail: recommended application, examples, and approach-specific advantages and disadvantages

Direct stated preference methods			
Recommended application	– Easy/fast/comparably cheap measurement of WTP – As a starting point, to get a first impression about achievable prices for new products – For contingent valuation		
	Example (WTP for a salad)	**Advantage of specific kind of DSP method**	**Disadvantage of specific kind of DSP method**
Open-ended questions	How much would you pay for this salad?	No starting point bias	Consumers are not used to formulate WTP without reference values
Van Westendorp method	1. At which price would you think that the salad is expensive, but still worth buying? 2. At which price would you think the salad is cheap, without doubting its quality? 3. At which price would you consider the salad to be too expensive? 4. At which price would you consider the salad to be too cheap, in the sense that you would doubt its quality?	Generates a pricing corridor that reflects consumer uncertainty	May result in a very wide price range
Dichotomous choice method	*Monadic approach*		
	Would you pay 4 € for this salad? (group 1)/ …4.50 € for this salad? (group 2)/… n € for this salad? (group n)	Answering is comparably easy for respondents	Requires a large amount of participants
	Sequential monadic approach		
	Would you pay 4 € for this salad? (each participant) → If answer is yes, increase price: … 4.50 € for this salad? → If answer is no, decrease price: … 3.50 € for this salad? → Continue until the accepted price cannot be increased anymore.	Closer to real-choice situations than open-ended questions Requires far less participants than the monadic approach	Starting point bias Puts strong focus on the price attribute

Payment card approach	Which of these prices is the highest you would pay for this salad? 2 €/2.50 €/3 €/3.50 €/4 €/4.50 €/5 €	Answering is comparably easy for respondents No starting-point bias	Respondents' answers are impacted/restricted by the provided range
Expert opinions	In your opinion, which price will our customers pay for this product?	Easy and fast to conduct Expert perspective	Quality of results depends on expertise

Experimental stated preference methods

Recommended application	– If revealed preference methods are not feasible (e.g., unavailable new products; very expensive products) – If multiple (competitor) products shall be considered – To determine not only overall WTP, but also WTP for specific product attributes		
	Example (WTP for a salad)	**Advantage of specific kind of ESP method**	**Disadvantage of specific kind of ESP method**
Conjoint analysis	Please rank the following options according to your preference: – Salad 1: Green salad, tomatoes, onions, 500 grams, organic, 2.99€ – Salad 2: Corn salad, tomatoes, no onions, 400 grams, organic, 3.49€ – [...] – Salad n: ...	Less repetitive for participants than choice-based conjoint analysis	Ranking task does not necessarily reflect actual choice behavior, might be difficult for participants
Choice-based conjoint analysis	Which of these options would you choose: – Salad 1: Green salad, tomatoes, onions, 500 grams, organic, 2.99€ – Salad 2: Corn salad, tomatoes, no onions, 400 grams, organic, 3.49€ – None of the two	Mimics actual choice behavior	Number of choice scenarios must be limited to avoid overburdening participants

Direct revealed preference methods

Recommended application	Auctions – Survey method without hypothetical bias/strategic answering bias – Especially suitable for unique products/products of limited availability Market data – When data about past purchases is available		

(continued)

Table 3 (continued)

Direct stated preference methods

	Example for questions (WTP for a salad)	Advantage of specific kind of DRP method	Disadvantage of specific kind of DRP method
Vickrey auction	Please state the maximum amount of money you would be willing to pay for this salad. In case you are the highest bidder, you must purchase the salad at the price of the second highest bidder. Otherwise, you are not allowed to purchase the salad	Can be put directly into practice for selling unique products	Consumers with low WTP might place a bid that does not correspond to their WTP (lack of motivation/bid with the purpose of raising prices for competitors)
BDM mechanism	Please state the maximum amount of money you would be willing to pay for this salad. We will then determine the price of the salad through a random draw. In case your bid is equal or above this price, you must purchase the salad at the price determined by the random draw. Otherwise, you are not allowed to purchase the salad	Bids are not impacted by beliefs about the behavior of other bidders	Consumers must believe in the randomness of the draw
Market data	Data from purchase panels (e.g., Nielsen), own shop, etc.	Real dataSecondary data (= data exists already)	Historical data To deduct WTP from accepted prices, variation is necessary

Experimental revealed preference methods

Recommended application	– If reduction of biases is more important than costs – If competitor products shall be considered and the product is market-ready		
	Example for questions	Advantage of specific kind of ERP method	Disadvantage of specific kind of ERP method
Lab experiments	Do you want to purchase one of these salads at the prices stated? If yes, we will sell you the salad at the price stated	Control variables (age, gender, income, etc.) can be collected	Experimental bias
Field experiments	Salad is offered in a regular store environment (e.g., supermarket, cafeteria)	High external validity	Collection of control variables often not possible Adequate test store necessary

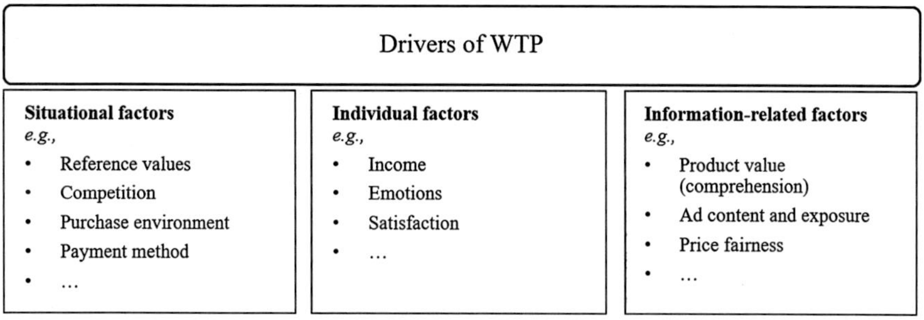

Drivers of WTP		
Situational factors *e.g.,* • Reference values • Competition • Purchase environment • Payment method • …	**Individual factors** *e.g.,* • Income • Emotions • Satisfaction • …	**Information-related factors** *e.g.,* • Product value (comprehension) • Ad content and exposure • Price fairness • …

Fig. 4 Drivers of WTP

Situational Factors

Consumers usually form their WTP at the point of purchase. Therefore, WTP is highly susceptible to situational anchors, that is, prices or other numerical cues that are provided or remembered at the moment of purchase. These can be completely unrelated stimuli, e.g., prices of completely other products (Nunes and Boatwright 2004) or random figures such as someone's social security number (Ariely et al. 2003). However, the effect is strongest when the respective anchor has a direct relation to the source of uncertainty (Simonson and Drolet 2004), thereby providing a reference for a possible price. These reference prices are very important, because without them, consumers may have difficulties translating product value into monetary units and articulate their WTP (Chernev 2003). Reference prices serve as standards when assessing product prices (Monroe 1973) and can be either remembered from past purchases or provided, e.g., by displaying recommended retail prices or the prices of competitor products (for a detailed review of literature on reference prices see Mazumdar et al. 2005). Without the possibility of comparing a product with other alternatives, consumers have difficulties evaluating it and often misjudge its value and their related WTP (Hsee 1998; Sevdalis and Harvey 2006).

Besides from serving as comparative values, the presence of competitor products lowers price tolerance, as switching to another attractive alternative is easy (Anderson 1996, p. 271). This means that market thickness generally lowers WTP (Chan et al. 2007); for example, the maturation of private labels has lowered consumers' WTP for branded products (Steenkamp et al. 2010).

Further, purchase environment and place of purchase play a role, as the same consumer may have different WTP values for the same product, depending on the consumption location and occasion. For example, WTP for beverages increases strongly when they are purchased in a restaurant or discotheque instead of a supermarket. WTP might also depend on the circumstances, e.g., a social or nonsocial setting (Wakefield and Inman 2003), or the surroundings, e.g., store atmospherics (Borges et al. 2013; Fiore et al. 2000). Even subtle cues such as colors may impact WTP: for instance, experiments by Bagchi and Cheema (2013) show that red heightens aggressiveness, leading to higher WTP in auctions, but lower WTP in negotiations.

Furthermore, WTP depends on both where and how consumers purchase products: for instance, consumers' WTP may simply increase by paying with a credit card instead of paying with cash, sometimes to a very large extent (up to 100%) (Prelec and Simester 2001).

Individual Factors

WTP may also vary due to individual factors, such as consumer-specific attributes and emotions.

Consumers' price sensitivity is generally positively related to income (Degeratu et al. 2000, p. 64). Therefore, consumers' tolerance for higher prices and the implied higher WTP increases with rising income, whereas the price search decreases (Urbany et al. 1996). As there are high between-subject differences with regard to income, researchers should control for this variable when WTP is measured. As income is usually relatively stable over a certain amount of time, it is possible to account for different WTP across consumers by using price discrimination (e.g., to offer lower prices for students).

In contrast, emotions vary within consumers, with consumers' WTP changing from one moment to the next. Positive affect (i.e., positive feelings about owning a good) was found to increase WTP (Peters et al. 2003), while positive mood did not seem to have any effect (Capra et al. 2010). Negative mood, however, may impact consumers' WTP: if consumers experience a situation that makes them feel disgusted, they afterward display a reduced WTP, as the experienced disgust has triggered an "avoid taking anything in" goal. Sadness, however, increases WTP because sadness provokes the urge to change one's situation (Lerner et al. 2004).

However, there are also more stable types of emotions, such as general satisfaction with a product or seller. Anderson (1996) shows that consumer satisfaction is likely to decrease price elasticity, which means that satisfied consumers have a higher price tolerance before switching to competitor products. Similarly, Homburg et al. (2005) demonstrate a positive impact of satisfaction on WTP. The underlying relationship can be depicted as an inverse s-form, as disappointment (elation) leads to a strong decrease (increase) in WTP, whereas a mediocre level of satisfaction does not impact WTP.

Information-Related Factors

WTP may also vary depending on the information status. Ajzen and Driver (1992) explain that the WTP that is based on heuristics (i.e., rules of thumb based on few information) deviates from the WTP that is formed after thoroughly considering the value of a product.

Therefore, Smith and Nagle (2002) stress the importance of value comprehension and argue that consumers do not know their WTP until they are fully informed about the value of a product. Thus, due to high costs for information search and evaluation, consumers often underestimate their WTP because they are not fully aware of all the benefits of a product.

Rao and Sieben (1992) support the importance of knowledge. By measuring product knowledge, they show that low-knowledge subjects have a significantly lower WTP than medium- or high-knowledge subjects. Similarly, consumers with higher involvement, i.e., knowledgeable subjects willing to search for information, show a lower price consciousness, and thus, a higher tolerance toward higher prices (Lichtenstein et al. 1988). However, these findings are context-dependent: Chan et al. (2007) show that experience and extensive search lower WTP in the context of online auctions. Here, expertise leads bidders to a more realistic estimation of achievable prices, thus making them more immune to overbidding.

Advertising also plays a decisive role in influencing consumers' WTP. Advertisements communicate information, such as a product's unique selling proposition, advantages, and value, thereby shaping consumers' product perception. Depending on the message delivered, WTP may differ; for example, Kaul and Wittink (1995) show that price advertising increases price sensitivity and therefore lowers WTP, whereas a rise in non-price advertising increases price tolerance. Kalra and Goodstein (1998) refine these results by demonstrating that advertising a minor brand using value positioning reduces WTP, whereas comparisons with premium brands or advertising a unique brand attribute increases it.

In addition to the content of an ad, the ad execution, such as its quality (Hampel et al. 2012) or the chosen medium (Li and Meshkova 2013), may further impact consumers' WTP, as well as the timing of the ad delivery. For example, ads that interrupt current consumer activities may significantly reduce consumers' WTP for the advertised product (Acquisti and Spiekermann 2011).

Finally, understanding the benefits of a product is not necessarily the only information consumers seek when determining their WTP. Consumers may be also concerned with price fairness: their WTP might decrease if they believe prices to be unfair toward consumers. In contrast, their WTP may increase if they feel that the seller does not make an adequate profit (Kahneman et al. 1986).

Market Research Application

In this section, we illustrate how to deal with the information on WTP in practice using some simple examples. Therefore, we collected data on consumers' WTP applying direct stated and direct revealed preference methods, in particular the open-ended question method, the dichotomous choice method, and the BDM mechanism. We then discuss three different application areas.

Elicitation of Consumers' WTP

We collected the data on WTP at a large German university campus. The focal product was described as a fresh, locally sourced salad that was to be offered in three variants (Grilled Veggie, Avocado Superfood, and Caesar Chicken) in the students' cafeteria. The salad was supposed to be sold pre-packaged in standard off-the-shelf sizes, enabling students to not only eat directly at the cafeteria, but also to take the salad with them. We provided further information on the size of the product and the brand (*dean&david,* a restaurant chain specialized in healthy and locally sourced food).

We approached students asking them whether they would be willing to take part in a short study regarding a hypothetical new product offer at the cafeteria. We then explained the new offer as described above and showed pictures of the salads.

Depending on the method we either asked the students to state how much they would be willing to pay for such a salad in the cafeteria (open-ended questions method), to state if they accept or decline a given price (dichotomous choice method), or to make a bid pursuant to the rules of the BDM mechanism, which we explained to them in detail.

Measurement 1: Open-Ended Questions

Using this method, participants directly stated their WTP for the focal product. In sum, 35 students participated and stated prices ranging from 2€ to 5€ for the salad.

Measurement 2: Dichotomous Choice Method

In contrast to measurement 1, participants did not have to state a price, but to agree or to disagree on a given price. To obtain more precise information on their WTP, we further applied a sequential approach. Thus, depending on whether the participants agreed (disagreed) on the given price, they were then asked whether they would be willing to buy the product at a higher (lower) price. The average market price of comparable products in the market (comparable products in university cafeterias: between 3.00€ and 6.00€) was chosen as a starting price, here 4.50€. If participants rejected (accepted) the price, we lowered (increased) the price by 0.50€ until participants changed their mind. We then increased (decreased) the price by another 0.25€. Our chosen ending points equal the margins of the market prices (see Fig. 5 for the price pathways used).

In sum, we interviewed 33 students and collected prices between 3.00€ and 5.00€.

Measurement 3: BDM Mechanism

We conducted the BDM mechanism with 30 students of two marketing classes in the respective lecture rooms. At the end of the classes, we asked the students whether they would be willing to stay to participate in a small experiment that required the use of money.

We needed to provide further information on the procedure, as the mechanism is more complex than the previous methods. Besides giving the students information on the focal product, we explained them that they could actually buy the salads, or more specifically a voucher for the respective salads that could be redeemed at a nearby *dean&david* store. As the offer did not yet exist in reality, we operationalized the purchase by using vouchers instead.

The participants were told that no purchase price had been determined yet, but that one student may draw a price from an envelope containing different price tags. We

Willingness to Pay

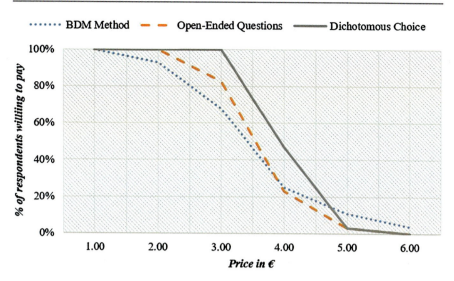

Fig. 5 Tree diagram of price pathways used

pointed out the consequences of bids above or below the price drawn. We then asked students to write down their WTP on an empty paper sheet that had been handed out in the beginning. After a student had drawn the threshold price, all participants disclosed their bids by handing out their sheets. We collected all bids and then sold vouchers to all students whose stated WTP exceeded the threshold price.

Results of the Measurements

A total of 98 students participated in our WTP measurements. Figure 6 shows the demand functions dependent on the elicitation method.

As we can see from Fig. 6, highest WTP are stated in the Dichotomous Choice group with mean WTP that equals 3.80€. In contrast, lowest WTP were elicited in the BDM group (mean WTP = 3.26€). Differences between lowest and highest group are significant ($p < 0.05$, using Satterthwaite approximation). These findings support previous research that respondents in hypothetical settings tend to overstate their WTP compared to the actual cash and incentive-compatible setting of the BDM mechanism, where we observe the lowest WTP. The average WTP is also higher in the Open-Ended Questions group (mean WTP = 3.39€) compared to the BDM group, however, the difference is not significant.

It is also salient that the demand functions are particularly steep between 3.00€ and 4.00€. While 83% of respondents in the Open-Ended Questions group were willing to pay 3.00€ for the salad, only 23% of respondents were willing to pay 4.00 €. More than half of the respondents who were willing to pay 3.00€ were not willing to pay 33% more. Thus, there seems to be a price threshold at 4.00€, which has to be considered when determining prices. Table 4 illustrates the decrease between these price points and the corresponding price elasticities of demand.

In the following we will show how managers can apply this information in practice based on some simple examples.

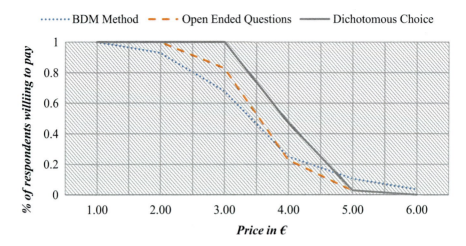

Fig. 6 Comparison of responses depending on method

Table 4 Decrease in WTP

	% of respondents willing to pay		Elasticity
	3.00 €	4.00 €	
BDM	68%	25%	−1.89
Open-ended questions	83%	23%	−2.17
Dichotomous choice	97%	47%	−1.54

Application 1: Price Bundling

Now let us consider that the university cafeteria is indeed interested in expanding the menu by offering the three variants of fresh salads bundled (with a new organic soft drink) and/or unbundled. Suppose that the university cafeteria has additionally identified different segments, which are all of the same size (15,000 per segment) and has collected WTP data on the salad, the new organic soft drink, and the bundle of the two products. Table 5 shows average WTP for the two products in the three different segments.

Let us also assume for simplicity that marginal costs equal zero. Then the cafeteria has three pricing alternatives to choose from. They can apply a uniform pricing strategy, i.e., charge only one fixed price for the salad and for the soft drink, or they can use a pure bundling strategy, i.e., sell the two products in a bundle only. The third alternative is to apply a mixed bundling strategy and to offer the products both separately and as a bundle.

Now let us first suppose that the cafeteria applies the uniform pricing strategy. Then the optimal price for the salad is 3.90€ and for the soft drink is 2.00€, thus

Table 5 Average WTP for unbundled and bundled products

	Average WTP in €		
	Salad	Soft drink	Bundle
Segment 1	4.50	0.50	5.00
Segment 2	3.90	2.00	5.90
Segment 3	1.70	2.50	4.20

resulting in a total revenue of 177,000€. In the second case, the pure bundling strategy, the optimal price for the bundle is 4.20€, resulting in a total revenue of 189,000€. In the last case, the mixed bundling strategy, optimal price for the salad is 4.50€, 2.50€ for the soft drink and 5.90€ for the bundle. This strategy results in a revenue of 193,500€. Consequently, the optimal strategy for the cafeteria is to apply the mixed bundling strategy.

Please note that this a simplified representation of a price bundling case. In practice, managers usually have to deal with more segments and products, and have to consider additional costs, thus making the analysis far more complex.

Application 2: Personalized Pricing

Suppose the cafeteria has additionally collected WTP data for the salad from their university staff as well as external cafeteria visitors who are neither students nor are affiliated with the university. Table 6 shows the elicited WTP and the segment size.

Assume that marginal costs are zero. The cafeteria can now either apply a uniform pricing strategy or charge personalized prices. Using the uniform pricing strategy, the optimal price is 3.50€, resulting in a revenue of 199.500€. However, applying personalized pricing, thus discriminating between the three segments, results in a revenue of 210,700€.

Since personalized pricing is commonly used in this type of service sector, it is easily feasible in this context.

Application 3: Nonlinear Pricing

Now suppose that the student cafeteria on another campus has observed that some students consume more than one salad and thus is interested to give price discounts for a higher amount of purchases, i.e., the second salad is cheaper than the first salad when purchasing two. Assume the following WTP measurements of three different consumer segments which are all of the same size (n = 3000) for different amounts of purchases (see Table 7).

We again assume that marginal costs are zero. Using a uniform pricing strategy without discounting additional purchases, the optimal price would be 2.40€ leading to a total revenue of 50,400€. Considering the changes in WTP with a higher amount

Table 6 WTP for different segments

	Students	Staff	External
Average WTP in €	3.50	4.40	4.60
Segment size	45,000	10,000	2,000

Table 7 Average WTP for different purchase amounts

	Average WTP in €		
	First salad	Second salad	Third salad
Segment 1	4.00	3.50	3.00
Segment 2	3.50	3.10	2.40
Segment 3	2.50	2.00	1.70

of purchases, the cafeteria can also determine the prices sequentially, an approach referred to as "price-point" method (see Dolan and Simon 1996). Following the sequential approach, the optimal price for one salad is 2.50€, the optimal price for the second salad is 2.00€, and for the third salad is 1.70€, resulting in a revenue of 55,800€ (22,500€ + 18,000€ + 15,300€). In this case, the cafeteria yields a higher revenue when using the price-point method compared to the uniform pricing strategy. Using the price-point method, the cafeteria can sell a higher amount of products: all three segments will purchase three salads resulting in 27,000 units sold, whereas in the uniform pricing strategy the cafeteria will only sell 21,000 units.

Also note here that this example is a simplified representation with limited hypothetical data and without considering costs. Managers seeking to measure WTP for product bundles or for different amounts of purchases can, for example, use self-stated data or choice-based data where the design of the offer (bundled/unbundled) or the amount of products offered is varied.

Conclusion

Accurately measuring consumers' WTP is of great importance for pricing decisions and predicting sales. Our chapter gives an overview of common methods for measuring WTP that are widely used in both theory and practice. We discuss the advantages and limitations associated with each method. Stated preference approaches (direct and indirect survey approaches) are advantageous in terms of feasibility but suffer from hypothetical bias and strategic behavior, whereas revealed preference methods may overcome the hypothetical bias, but usually involve more effort (financial and organizational).

We further point to the possible factors influencing WTP and differentiate situational factors, individual factors, and information-related factors. Depending on the situation, on individual consumer-specific attributes and emotions, and on the information status, consumers' WTP may vary. Firms being aware of the drivers of WTP can take advantage of this information and react accordingly.

In the remainder of our chapter, we present a practical application of consumers' WTP measurement for a potential new product offer. We measure WTP via two direct stated preference approaches (open-ended question and dichotomous choice method employing the sequential monadic approach) and one direct revealed preference approach (BDM mechanism). We compare the three different approaches and discuss application areas of WTP using three examples.

References

Acquisti, A., & Spiekermann, S. (2011). Do interruptions pay off? Effects of interruptive ads on consumers' willingness to pay. *Journal of Interactive Marketing, 25*, 226–240. https://doi.org/10.1016/j.intmar.2011.04.003.

Ajzen, I., & Driver, B. L. (1992). Contingent value measurement: On the nature and meaning of willingness to pay. *Journal of Consumer Psychology, 1*, 297–316. https://doi.org/10.1016/S1057-7408(08)80057-5.

Allenby, G. M., Brazell, J. D., Howell, J. R., & Rossi, P. E. (2014). Economic valuation of product features. *Quantitative Marketing and Economics, 12*, 421–456.

Anderson, E. W. (1996). Customer satisfaction and price tolerance. *Marketing Letters, 7*, 265–274. https://doi.org/10.1007/BF00435742.

Ariely, D., Loewenstein, G., & Prelec, D. (2003). "Coherent arbitrariness": Stable demand curves without stable preferences. *The Quarterly Journal of Economics, 118*, 73–106. https://doi.org/10.1162/00335530360535153.

Bagchi, R., & Cheema, A. (2013). The effect of red background color on willingness-to-pay: The moderating role of selling mechanism. *Journal of Consumer Research, 39*, 947–960. https://doi.org/10.1086/666466.

Barrot, C., Albers, S., Skiera, B., & Schäfers, B. (2010). Vickrey vs. eBay: Why second-price sealed-bid auctions Lead to more realistic price-demand functions. *International Journal of Electronic Commerce, 14*, 7–38.

Becker, G. M., DeGroot, M. H., & Marschak, J. (1964). Measuring utility by a single-response sequential method. *Behavioral Science, 9*, 226–232.

Ben-Akiva, M., Bradley, M., Morikawa, T., Benjamin, J., Novak, T., Oppewal, H., et al. (1994). Combining revealed and stated preferences data. *Marketing Letters, 5*, 335–349.

Bettman, J. R., Luce, M. F., & Payne, J. W. (1998). Constructive consumer choice processes. *Journal of Consumer Research, 25*, 187–217. https://doi.org/10.1086/209535.

Blumenschein, K., Blomquist, G. C., Johannesson, M., Horn, N., & Freeman, P. (2008). Eliciting willingness to pay without bias: Evidence from a field experiment. *The Economic Journal, 118*, 114–137. https://doi.org/10.1111/j.1468-0297.2007.02106.x.

Borges, A., Babin, B. J., & Spielmann, N. (2013). Gender orientation and retail atmosphere: Effects on value perception. *International Journal of Retail & Distribution Management, 41*, 498–511.

Boyle, K. J. (2017). Contingent valuation in practice. In *A primer on nonmarket valuation* (pp. 83–131). Dordrecht: Springer.

Breidert, C. (2006). *Estimation of willingness-to-pay: Theory, measurement, application*. Wiesbaden: DUV Deutscher Universitäts-Verlag.

Calabuig, F., Núñez-Pomar, J., Prado-Gascó, V., & Añó, V. (2014). Effect of price increases on future intentions of sport consumers. *Journal of Business Research, 67*, 729–733.

Capra, C. M., Lanier, K. F., & Meer, S. (2010). The effects of induced mood on bidding in random nth-Price auctions. *Journal of Economic Behavior & Organization, 75*, 223–234. https://doi.org/10.1016/j.jebo.2010.04.002.

Carare, O., & Rothkopf, M. (2005). Slow dutch auctions. *Management Science, 51*, 365–373. https://doi.org/10.1287/mnsc.1040.0328.

Chan, T. Y., Kadiyali, V., & Park, Y.-H. (2007). Willingness to pay and competition in online auctions. *Journal of Marketing Research, 44*, 324–333. https://doi.org/10.1509/jmkr.44.2.324.

Chernev, A. (2003). Reverse pricing and online price elicitation strategies in consumer choice. *Journal of Consumer Psychology, 13*, 51–62.

Chung, J., & Rao, V. R. (2003). A general choice model for bundles with multiple-category products: Application to market segmentation and optimal pricing for bundles. *Journal of Marketing Research, 40*, 115–130.

Cummings, R. G., & Taylor, L. O. (1999). Unbiased value estimates for environmental goods: A cheap talk design for the contingent valuation method. *The American Economic Review, 89*, 649–665.

Degeratu, A. M., Rangaswamy, A., & Wu, J. (2000). Consumer choice behavior in online and traditional supermarkets: The effects of brand name, price, and other search attributes. *International Journal of Research in Marketing, 17*, 55–78. https://doi.org/10.1016/S0167-8116(00)00005-7.

Dhar, R., & Gorlin, M. (2013). A dual-system framework to understand preference construction processes in choice. *Journal of Consumer Psychology, 23*, 528–542.

Ding, M. (2007). An incentive-aligned mechanism for conjoint analysis. *Journal of Marketing Research, 44*, 214–223.

Ding, M., Grewal, R., & Liechty, J. (2005). Incentive-aligned conjoint analysis. *Journal of Marketing Research, 42*, 67–82. https://doi.org/10.1509/jmkr.42.1.67.56890.

Dolan, R. J., & Simon, H. (1996). *Power pricing*. New York: The Free Press.

Donaldson, C. (1999). Valuing the benefits of publicly-provided health care: Does 'ability to pay' preclude the use of 'willingness to pay'? *Social Science & Medicine, 49*, 551–563. https://doi.org/10.1016/S0277-9536(99)00173-2.

Dong, S., Ding, M., & Huber, J. (2010). A simple mechanism to incentive-align conjoint experiments. *International Journal of Research in Marketing, 27*, 25–32.

Dost, F., & Wilken, R. (2012). Measuring willingness to pay as a range, revisited: When should we care? *International Journal of Research in Marketing, 29*, 148–166. https://doi.org/10.1016/j.ijresmar.2011.09.003.

Fiore, A. M., Yah, X., & Yoh, E. (2000). Effects of a product display and environmental fragrancing on approach responses and pleasurable experiences. *Psychology and Marketing, 17*, 27–54.

Frederick, S., Novemsky, N., Wang, J., Dhar, R., & Nowlis, S. (2009). Opportunity cost neglect. *Journal of Consumer Research, 36*, 553–561.

Gabor, A., & Granger, C. W. J. (1966). Price as an Indicator of quality: Report on an enquiry. *Economica, 33*, 43. https://doi.org/10.2307/2552272.

Green, P. E., & Rao, V. R. (1971). Conjoint measurement for quantifying judgmental data. *Journal of Marketing Research, 8*, 355–363.

Green, P. E., & Srinivasan, V. (1978). Conjoint analysis in consumer research: Issues and outlook. *Journal of Consumer Research, 5*, 103–123.

Green, P. E., & Srinivasan, V. (1990). Conjoint analysis in marketing: New developments with implications for research and practice. *Journal of Marketing, 54*, 3–19. https://doi.org/10.2307/1251756.

Green, P. E., Krieger, A. M., & Wind, Y. (2001). Thirty years of conjoint analysis: Reflections and prospects. *Interfaces, 31*, 56–73. https://doi.org/10.1287/inte.31.3s.56.9676.

Greenberg, A. (2008). When apple failed. https://www.forbes.com/2008/10/29/apple-product-flops-tech-personal-cx_ag_1030apple, Accessed 18 June 2018

Gustafsson, A. (Ed.). (2007). *Conjoint measurement: Methods and applications* (4th ed.). Berlin u. a.: Springer.

Halme, M., & Kallio, M. (2011). Estimation methods for choice-based conjoint analysis of consumer preferences. *European Journal of Operational Research, 214*, 160–167. https://doi.org/10.1016/j.ejor.2011.03.049.

Hamilton, R. W., & Srivastava, J. (2008). When 2+2 is not the same as 1+3: Variations in price sensitivity across components of partitioned prices. *Journal of Marketing Research, 45*, 450–461.

Hampel, S., Heinrich, D., & Campbell, C. (2012). Is an advertisement worth the paper it's printed on? *Journal of Advertising Research, 52*, 118–127. https://doi.org/10.2501/JAR-52-1-118-127.

Hanna, N., & Dodge, R. (1995). *Pricing – Policies and procedures*. London: Macmillan.

Harrison, G. W., & Rutström, E. E. (2013). Experimental evidence on the existence of hypothetical bias in value elicitation methods. In C. R. Plott & V. L. Smith (Eds.), *Handbook of experimental economics results* (Vol. 1, pp. 752–767). Burlington: Elsevier.

Harrison, G. W., Harstad, R. M., & Rutström, E. E. (2004). Experimental methods and elicitation of values. *Experimental Economics, 7*, 123–140.

Hauser, J. R., & Urban, G. L. (1986). The value priority hypotheses for consumer budget plans. *Journal of Consumer Research, 12*, 446–462.

Henderson, N. R. (2002). Avoiding the pricing trap in qualitative interviews. *Marketing Research, 14*, 38–39.

Herriges, J. A., & Shogren, J. F. (1996). Starting point Bias in dichotomous choice valuation with follow-up questioning. *Journal of Environmental Economics and Management, 30*, 112–131. https://doi.org/10.1006/jeem.1996.0008.

Hoeffler, S., & Ariely, D. (1999). Constructing stable preferences: A look into dimensions of experience and their impact on preference stability. *Journal of Consumer Psychology, 8*, 113–139. https://doi.org/10.1207/s15327663jcp0802_01.

Hoffman, E., Menkhaus, D. J., Chakravarti, D., Field, R. A., & Whipple, G. D. (1993). Using laboratory experimental auctions in marketing research: A case study of new packaging for fresh beef. *Marketing Science, 12*, 318–338.

Hofstetter, R., Miller, K. M., Krohmer, H., & Zhang, Z. J. (2013). How do consumer characteristics affect the bias in measuring willingness to pay for innovative products? *Journal of Product Innovation Management, 30*, 1042–1053. https://doi.org/10.1111/jpim.12040.

Homburg, C., Koschate, N., & Hoyer, W. D. (2005). Do satisfied customers really pay more?: A study of the relationship between customer satisfaction and willingness to pay. *Journal of Marketing, 69*, 84–96. https://doi.org/10.1509/jmkg.69.2.84.60760.

Hsee, C. K. (1998). Less is better: When low-value options are valued more highly than high-value options. *Journal of Behavioral Decision Making, 11*, 107–121.

Jedidi, K., & Jagpal, S. (2009). Willingness to pay: Measurement and managerial implications. In *Handbook of pricing research in marketing* (pp. 37–60).

Jedidi, K., & Zhang, Z. J. (2002). Augmenting conjoint analysis to estimate consumer reservation price. *Management Science, 48*, 1350–1368.

Kahneman, D., Knetsch, J. L., & Thaler, R. (1986). Fairness as a constraint on profit seeking: Entitlements in the market. *The American Economic Review, 76*, 728–741.

Kalish, S., & Nelson, P. (1991). A comparison of ranking, rating and reservation price measurement in conjoint analysis. *Marketing Letters, 2*, 327–335. https://doi.org/10.1007/BF00664219.

Kalra, A., & Goodstein, R. C. (1998). The impact of advertising positioning strategies on consumer Price sensitivity. *Journal of Marketing Research, 35*, 210. https://doi.org/10.2307/3151849.

Kalwani, M. U., & Silk, A. J. (1982). On the reliability and predictive validity of purchase intention measures. *Marketing Science, 1*, 243–286.

Kaul, A., & Wittink, D. R. (1995). Empirical generalizations about the impact of advertising on Price sensitivity and price. *Marketing Science, 14*, G151–G160. https://doi.org/10.1287/mksc.14.3.G151.

Kohli, R., & Mahajan, V. (1991). A reservation-price model for optimal pricing of multiattribute products in conjoint analysis. *Journal of Marketing Research, 28*, 347–354.

Ku, G., Malhotra, D., & Murnighan, J. K. (2005). Towards a competitive arousal model of decision-making: A study of auction fever in live and internet auctions. *Organizational Behavior and Human Decision Processes, 96*, 89–103. https://doi.org/10.1016/j.obhdp.2004.10.001.

Lerner, J. S., Small, D. A., & Loewenstein, G. (2004). Heart strings and purse strings carryover effects of emotions on economic decisions. *Psychological Science, 15*, 337–341.

Li, T., & Meshkova, Z. (2013). Examining the impact of rich media on consumer willingness to pay in online stores. *Electronic Commerce Research and Applications, 12*, 449–461. https://doi.org/10.1016/j.elerap.2013.07.001.

Lichtenstein, D. R., Bloch, P. H., & Black, W. C. (1988). Correlates of price acceptability. *Journal of Consumer Research, 15*, 243–252. https://doi.org/10.1086/209161.

Lieven, T., & Lennerts, S. (2013). Measuring willingness to pay by means of the trade-off between free available cash and specific-purpose vouchers. *Business Research, 6*, 154–171. https://doi.org/10.1007/BF03342747.

Loomis, J., Gonzalez-Caban, A., & Gregory, R. (1994). Do reminders of substitutes and budget constraints influence contingent valuation estimates? *Land Economics, 70*, 499. https://doi.org/10.2307/3146643.

Louviere, J. J., & Woodworth, G. (1983). Design and analysis of simulated consumer choice or allocation experiments: An approach based on aggregate data. *Journal of Marketing Research, 20*, 350–367.

Louviere, J. J., Hensher, D. A., & Swait, J. D. (2000). *Stated choice methods: Analysis and applications*. Cambridge: Cambridge University Press.

Luce, R. D., & Tukey, J. W. (1964). Simultaneous conjoint measurement: A new type of fundamental measurement. *Journal of Mathematical Psychology, 1*, 1–27.

Lyon, D. W. (2002). The price is right (or is it)? Accurate pricing starts with asking the right questions. *Marketing Research, 14*, 8–13.

Marn, M. V., Roegner, E. V., & Zawada, C. C. (2003). Pricing new products. *McKinsey Quarterly, 3*, 40–49.

Mazumdar, T., Raj, S. P., & Sinha, I. (2005). Reference price research: Review and propositions. *Journal of Marketing, 69*, 84–102. https://doi.org/10.1509/jmkg.2005.69.4.84.

Miller, K. M., Hofstetter, R., Krohmer, H., & Zhang, Z. J. (2011). How should consumers' willingness to pay be measured? An empirical comparison of state-of-the-art approaches. *Journal of Marketing Research, 48*, 172–184. https://doi.org/10.1509/jmkr.48.1.172.

Mitchell, R. C. (2013). *Using surveys to value public goods: The contingent valuation method*. Hoboken: Taylor and Francis.

Monroe, K. B. (1973). Buyers' subjective perceptions of price. *Journal of Marketing Research, 10*, 70. https://doi.org/10.2307/3149411.

Moorthy, K. S. (1988). Product and price competition in a duopoly. *Marketing Science, 7*, 141–168. https://doi.org/10.1287/mksc.7.2.141.

Morrison, D. G. (1979). Purchase intentions and purchase behavior. *The Journal of Marketing, 43*, 65–74.

Müller, H. (2009). Empirische untersuchung zur messung der preiswahrnehmung mittels pricesensitivity-meter. *Marketing ZfP, 31*, 171–182.

Neill, H. R., Cummings, R. G., Ganderton, P. T., Harrison, G. W., & McGuckin, T. (1994). Hypothetical surveys and real economic commitments. *Land Economics, 70*, 145–154.

Noussair, C., Robin, S., & Ruffieux, B. (2004). Revealing consumers' willingness-to-pay: A comparison of the BDM mechanism and the vickrey auction. *Journal of Economic Psychology, 25*, 725–741. https://doi.org/10.1016/j.joep.2003.06.004.

Nunes, J. C., & Boatwright, P. (2004). Incidental prices and their effect on willingness to pay. *Journal of Marketing Research, 41*, 457–466.

Peters, E., Slovic, P., & Gregory, R. (2003). The role of affect in the WTA/WTP disparity. *Journal of Behavioral Decision Making, 16*, 309–330. https://doi.org/10.1002/bdm.448.

Prelec, D., & Simester, D. (2001). Always leave home without it: A further investigation of the credit-card effect on willingness to pay. *Marketing Letters, 12*, 5–12.

Ramanujam, M., & Tacke, G. (2016). *Monetizing innovation: How smart companies design the product around the Price* (1st ed.). Hoboken: Wiley.

Rao, A. R., & Sieben, W. A. (1992). The effect of prior knowledge on Price acceptability and the type of information examined. *Journal of Consumer Research, 19*, 256. https://doi.org/10.1086/209300.

Rowe, R. D., Schulze, W. D., & Breffle, W. S. (1996). A test for payment card biases. *Journal of Environmental Economics and Management, 31*, 178–185.

Russell, S. (1996). Ability to pay for health care: Concepts and evidence. *Health Policy and Planning, 11*, 219–237.

Sen, S., Gürhan-Canli, Z., & Morwitz, V. (2001). Withholding consumption: A social dilemma perspective on consumer boycotts. *Journal of Consumer Research, 28*, 399–417. https://doi.org/10.1086/323729.

Sevdalis, N., & Harvey, N. (2006). Determinants of willingness to pay in separate and joint evaluations of options: Context matters. *Journal of Economic Psychology, 27*, 377–385. https://doi.org/10.1016/j.joep.2005.07.001.

Shaffer, G., & Zhang, Z. J. (1995). Competitive coupon targeting. *Marketing Science, 14*, 395–416.

Shogren, J. F., Margolis, M., Koo, C., & List, J. A. (2001). A random nth-price auction. *Journal of Economic Behavior & Organization, 46*, 409–421.

Simon, H., & Fassnacht, M. (1982). *Preismanagement*. Wiesbaden: Springer.

Simonson, I., & Drolet, A. (2004). Anchoring effects on consumers' willingness-to-pay and willingness-to-accept. *Journal of Consumer Research, 31*, 681–690. https://doi.org/10.1086/425103.

Slovic, P. (1995). The construction of preference. *American Psychologist, 50*, 364–371.

Smith, G. E., & Nagle, T. T. (2002). How much are customers willing to pay? *Marketing Research, 14*, 20.

Spann, M., Skiera, B., & Schäfers, B. (2004). Measuring individual frictional costs and willingness-to-pay via name-your-own-price mechanisms. *Journal of Interactive Marketing, 18*(4), 22–36.

Srinivasan, V. (1988). A conjunctive-compensatory approach to the self-explication of multi-attributed preferences. *Decision Sciences, 19*, 295–305.

Steenkamp, J.-B. E. M., van Heerde, H. J., & Geyskens, I. (2010). What makes consumers willing to pay a price premium for national brands over private labels? *Journal of Marketing Research, 47*, 1011–1024. https://doi.org/10.1509/jmkr.47.6.1011.

Terwiesch, C., Savin, S., & Hann, I.-H. (2005). Online haggling at a name-your-own-Price retailer: Theory and application. *Management Science, 51*, 339–351. https://doi.org/10.1287/mnsc.1040.0337.

Urbany, J. E., Dickson, P. R., & Kalapurakal, R. (1996). Price search in the retail grocery market. *Journal of Marketing, 60*, 91. https://doi.org/10.2307/1251933.

van Westendorp, P. H. (1976). NSS price sensitivity meter (PSM) – a new approach to study consumer-perception of prices. In *Proceedings of the ESOMAR congress*.

Varian, H. R. (1992). *Microeconomic analysis*. New York: Norton.

Vickrey, W. (1961). Counterspeculation, auctions, and competitive sealed tenders. *The Journal of Finance, 16*, 8–37.

Voelckner, F. (2006). An empirical comparison of methods for measuring consumers' willingness to pay. *Marketing Letters, 17*, 137–149.

Wakefield, K. L., & Inman, J. J. (2003). Situational price sensitivity: The role of consumption occasion, social context and income. *Journal of Retailing, 79*, 199–212. https://doi.org/10.1016/j.jretai.2003.09.004.

Wang, T., Venkatesh, R., & Chatterjee, R. (2007). Reservation price as a range: An incentive-compatible measurement approach. *Journal of Marketing Research, 44*, 200–213. https://doi.org/10.1509/jmkr.44.2.200.

Wertenbroch, K., & Skiera, B. (2002). Measuring consumers' willingness to pay at the point of purchase. *Journal of Marketing Research, 39*, 228–241.

Winer, R. S. (2005). *Pricing*. Cambridge, MA: Marketing Science Institute.

Modeling Customer Lifetime Value, Retention, and Churn

Herbert Castéran, Lars Meyer-Waarden, and Werner Reinartz

Contents

Introduction 1002
A Taxonomy of Customer Lifetime Value Measurement Models 1003
    Retention Models for CLV Measurement 1006
    Migration Models for CLV Measurement 1010
    Continuous Mixed Models: The Family of NBD Models to Measure CLV 1012
An Application of Stochastic Pareto/NBD and BG/NBD Models for Customer Base
Management 1016
    Data and Methodology 1016
    Estimation 1018
    Results 1023
    Parameter Estimations 1023
    Purchase Prediction Validity 1025
Conclusion 1029
References 1030

Abstract

Customers represent the most important assets of a firm. Customer lifetime value (CLV) allows assessing their current and future value in a customer base. The customer relationship management strategy and marketing resource allocation are

---

H. Castéran (✉)
Humanis Institute, EM Strasbourg Business School, Strasbourg, France
e-mail: herbert.casteran@em-strasbourg.eu

L. Meyer-Waarden
School of Management, CRM CNRS University Toulouse 1 Capitole, IAE Toulouse, Toulouse, France
e-mail: lars.meyer-waarden@iae-toulouse.fr

W. Reinartz
University of Cologne, Köln, Germany
e-mail: werner.reinartz@uni-koeln.de

© Springer Nature Switzerland AG 2022
C. Homburg et al. (eds), *Handbook of Market Research*,
https://doi.org/10.1007/978-3-319-57413-4_21

based on this metric. Managers therefore need to predict the retention but also the purchase behavior of their customers.

This chapter is a systematic review of the most common CLV, retention, and churn modeling approaches for customer-base analysis and gives practical recommendations for their applications. These comprise both the classes of deterministic and stochastic approaches and deal with both, contractual and noncontractual settings. Across those situations, the most common and most important approaches are then systematically structured, described, and evaluated. To this end, a review of the CLV, retention, as well as churn models and a taxonomy are done with their assumptions and weaknesses. Next, an empirical application of the stochastic "standard" Pareto/NBD, and the BG/NBD models, as well as an explanatory Pareto/NBD model with covariates to grocery retailing store loyalty program scanner data, is done. The models show their ability to reproduce the interindividual variations as well as forecasting validity.

Keywords

Customer lifetime value · Customer churn · Customer retention · NBD/Pareto model · BG/NBD model

Introduction

Customers represent assets and the cost of acquiring them relates to the cash flow they are expected to generate over time (Bolton et al. 2004; Tarasi et al. 2011). Customer retention and churn as well as customer lifetime value (CLV), retention, and churn measurement have become a powerful customer valuation metric (Glady et al. 2015; Gupta et al. 2004, 2006; Kumar and Reinartz 2006).

Customer retention refers to the ability of a company or product to retain its customers over some specified period. Defection or churn is the number of customers moving out of a cohort in a firm's database over a specific period of time. CLV is the value of individual customers, based on their past, present, and projected future cash flows (Gupta et al. 2004). To model CLV, it is important to measure customer retention and churn rates. CLV is an important concept on which the customer relationship management strategy; marketing resource allocation (to profitable customers), such as promotions; and the assessment of the marketing efficiency are based on Schulze et al. (2012). The CLV paradigm recognizes customers as the primary source of both current and future cash flows. According to this framework, the firm tries to maximize the net present value of both current and future customers (customer equity, Hogan et al. 2002), which represents a good proxy for the firm's value (Borle et al. 2008; Gupta et al. 2004), as well as an effective segmentation tool. Thus, CLV models offer a powerful means to maximize the return on marketing investments and guide allocations of the marketing budget (Blattberg and Deighton 1996; Reinartz et al. 2005).

A CLV model has prototypically three parameters: (1) margin (purchase baskets minus the costs including retention expenditure), (2) retention probability or lifetime duration, and (3) purchase frequency (Kumar 2007). One way of increasing CLV is to undertake marketing initiatives to reduce churn or the defection rate (and therefore increase the retention rate) of customers – which will have the impact of increase in the customer lifetime periods. Putting it another way, CLV analyses involve distinguishing active customers from defectors and then predicting their lifetime and future levels of transactions according to their observed past purchase behavior. Developing a valid measurement framework that adequately describes the process of birth, purchase activity, and defection is thus a crucial albeit not a trivial task, particularly due to the randomness of individual purchasing behavior and customer heterogeneity (Jain and Singh 2002; Reinartz and Kumar 2000). Whereas the analysis may be easier for contractual, "lost for good" relationships (e.g., subscription markets in which the inactivity date is known), it becomes particularly difficult for noncontractual relationships in which customers do not notify the firm when they disappear (Dwyer 1989; Jackson 1985); in this scenario, identifying active and inactive customers in the database at any given time requires systematic investigation (Schmittlein and Peterson 1994).

The objective of this chapter is to provide a systematic review of the most common retention and churn modeling approaches to model CLV. These comprise both the classes of deterministic and stochastic approaches and deal with both, always-a-share and lost-for-good situations. Across those situations, the most common and most important approaches are then systematically structured, described, and evaluated. To this end, first the retention models, their assumptions, and weaknesses are reviewed and thus a taxonomy is provided. After having presented the taxonomy of CLV, churn, and retention measurement models, this article shows in "A Taxonomy of Customer Lifetime Value Measurement Models" a practical application by using some of the presented stochastic models (Pareto/NBD, explanatory Pareto/NBD, BG/NBD) to model a customer base and the impact of a retail grocery loyalty program on customer churn, retention, and activity. The goal is to show how to implement, use, and interpret these sophisticated models by applying them on firms' frequently used grocery store loyalty program databases and panel data.

This article then concludes with a discussion, some limitations, and recommendations for future research directions.

A Taxonomy of Customer Lifetime Value Measurement Models

In practice, to choose an adequate CLV measurement model, one has to understand whether or not customer defection is observable. One thus has to differentiate between two types of market (Jackson 1985; Dwyer 1989), namely, contractual (*Lost-for-Good*) and non-contractual (*always-a-share*) markets.

In the first type of market, the customer enters into a contractual relationship with a firm (e.g., phone or insurance services, magazine subscriptions, etc.) and is consequently faced with a tangible cost of change. Defection is observable and occurs when consumers end their relationship with the firm. In this scenario, the seller can identify defection as soon as it occurs. This means it is easy to predict defection for modeling purposes and one has to adopt a simple retention model

(Ayache et al. 2006). The notion of *lost-for-good* merges in practice with the contractual situation since it considers that absence of transaction means the customer has become inactive. In the contractual approach, retention is in fact the most important aspect. Generally, it goes hand in hand with a more or less constant flow of income. The models are usually simple with a clear predominance of survival models.

In markets where the customer has no contractual relationship (typically consumer goods), the cost of switching is low and a buyer can simultaneously purchase from different suppliers (*always-a-share*). The supplier has no way of knowing if the customer has defected. The model therefore focuses on churn probability, customer migration, and customer "life span" (Berger and Nasr 1998). The longer the period of inactivity, the more likely it is that the customer has churned. Migration models more specifically cover this scenario.

Fader and Hardie (2009) add an additional distinction depending on whether the purchase occurs at a specific moment (discrete time) or whether it can occur at any time (continuous). This distinction mainly has technical consequences, which can also be computed more or less approximately in a relatively direct way by taking more or less extended periods of time into consideration. Fader and Hardie (2009) themselves admit that this distinction is less meaningful. However, the contractual/noncontractual distinction is conceptually and methodologically fundamental.

The vast majority of markets concern noncontractual markets (Allenby et al. 1999). Many researchers and business practitioners have attempted to develop forecasting systems in this context. Contributions fall into two main categories: purely descriptive approaches (deterministic) and stochastic approaches. Deterministic approaches are primarily based on calculations of actuarial values, reflecting financial flows without the inclusion of random factors or explanatory variables (e.g., expected individual cash flow models as applied by Berger and Nasr 1998). However, they fail to take interindividual heterogeneity into account. Calciu and Salerno (2002) highlighted the relations between these different attempts.

The following table provides an overall view of the models according to the nature of their affiliation with the company and the methodology (deterministic/stochastic) used. Some contributions may be found in two different scenarios, in that they include a comparison of several cases.

Other aspects of model characterization are also included: level of aggregation, inclusion of the competition, return on investment, and the capacity to optimize resource allocation. The nature of the model and the level of aggregation help to determine the model's sophistication and precision. Taking the competition into account is likely to affect the results of the models in that the long-term perspective is more complex when the competitive context is explicitly included. Finally, the capacity to determine return on investment or to optimize the distribution of marketing investment affects the model's operational nature.

Table 1 suggests several trends. The first is the increasing focus on stochastic models as compared to the deterministic models. Since 2005, eight new stochastic models have been presented against only two in the deterministic context. As already stated, probabilistic models are significantly more efficient than deterministic models. This tendency thus seems logical and desirable.

Table 1 Models of customer retention-churn modeling (Adapted from Villanueva and Hanssens 2007)

Authors	Level of analysis	Competition present	Return on investment	Allocation of resources
Deterministic models				
No application				
Rust et al. (2004)	Company	Yes	Yes	Yes
Blattberg et al. (2001)	Segment	No	Yes	No
Application to contractual cases				
Keane and Wang (1995)	Regions	No	No	No
Blattberg and Deighton (1996)	Company	No	Yes	No
Dwyer (1997)	Segment	No	No	No
Ryals (2005)	Individual	No	No	No
Wiesel et al. (2008)	Company	No	No	No
Application to noncontractual cases				
Dwyer (1997)	Segment	No	No	No
Berger and Nasr (1998)	Individual	No	No	No
Stauss and Friege (1999)	Individual	No	No	No
Berger and Nasr (1998)	Company	No	No	No
Gupta et al. (2002)	Company	No	No	No
Gupta and Lehman (2003)	Company	No	No	No
Stochastic models				
Application to contractual cases				
Bitran and Mondschein (1996)	Segment	No	No	No
Thomas et al. (2004)	Individual	No	Yes	No
Lewis (2005)	Individual	No	Yes	No
Villanueva et al. (2008)	Company	No	No	No
Application to noncontractual cases				
Schmittlein et al. (1987)	Individual	No	No	No
Reinartz and Kumar (2000)	Consumer	No	Yes	No
Pfeifer and Carraway (2000)	Segment	No	Yes	No
Libai et al. (2002)	Segment	No	Yes	Yes
Rust et al. (2004)	Company	Yes	Yes	Yes
Venkatesan and Kumar (2004)	Individual	No	Yes	Yes
Fader et al. (2005a)	Individual	No	No	No

(continued)

Table 1 (continued)

Authors	Level of analysis	Competition present	Return on investment	Allocation of resources
Reinartz et al. (2005)	Company	Yes	Yes	No
Villanueva et al. (2008)	Segment	No	Non	No
Simester et al. (2006)	Individual	No	Yes	No
Lewis (2006)	Individual	No	Yes	No
Castéran et al. (2007a, b)	Individual	No	No	No

The second underlying trend involves the increasing disaggregation of the models. From wholly aggregated models, one shifts to an analysis by company, then to one by segment, and, finally and increasingly often, to one by individual. While informational limitations may explain the inclusion of a company level, nothing, on the other hand, justifies grounding a marketing analysis on wholly aggregated models.

Two aspects have been relatively neglected to date, namely, inclusion of the competition and the way managers interpret models for resource allocation. Lack of information is frequently used to explain this shortcoming, but it nonetheless remains detrimental. This is especially true of the failure to include the competition insofar as its absence may substantially impact on conclusions and managerial implications (cf. Fudenberg and Tirole 2000). While the examination of optimized resource allocation remains fundamental, its absence does not, on the other hand, imply an analysis bias.

We present these approaches in more detail in a dual customer relations and methodology framework.

Retention Models for CLV Measurement

These models are divided between deterministic and probabilistic models. To determine CLV, customer retention and churn have to be modeled. Customer retention refers to the ability of a company or product to retain its customers over some specified period. It is measured in the following way (Gupta et al. 2004):

$$\text{Retention rate} = \frac{n \text{ customers in cohort buying in } (t)}{n \text{ customers in cohort buying in } (t-1)} \times 100 \quad (1)$$

The period t can refer to specific durations: months or years are the most frequently used. Customer defection or churn is the number of customers moving out of a cohort in a firm's database over a specific period of time. It is measured in the following way (Gupta et al. 2004):

$$\text{Churn rate} = 1 - \text{Retention rate} \tag{2}$$

Deterministic Models

Berger and Nasr (1998) provide the following general formula for the customer lifetime value (CLV):

$$\text{CLV} = \sum_{t=1}^{n} \pi(t) \frac{\rho^t}{(1+d)^t} \tag{3}$$

with $\pi(t)$ profit generated in period t, ρ the rate of retention, and d the discount rate. If one considers profit stability over time for an annual net gain h, then CLV is formulated as

$$\text{CLV} = h \frac{\rho^t}{(1+d)^t} \tag{4}$$

We have a monetary component h and an expected number of transactions (or products, *discounted expected transactions*). This expression has the advantage of being extremely simple: one just has to estimate the retention rate to obtain the CLV. On the other hand, this approach assumes that the retention rate is stable over time.

However, this assumption fails to take into account the customer base composed of different segments, over and above all considerations of variation in the retention srate at individual level. Imagine that a same cohort of customers is composed of p homogeneous segments, each with an annual retention rate assumed to be constant from 1 year to the next for purpose of simplicity, with ρ_i for each segment i. One also can reason in discrete time for greater simplicity, but the situation can easily be extrapolated to continuous time. Let us assume that by nature segment 1 has the highest retention rate. The average retention rate, for example, in the first year is equal to

$$\bar{r} = \frac{\sum_{i=1}^{p} n_i \rho_i}{\sum_{k=1}^{p} n_k} \tag{5}$$

with n_i the size of segment i. Traditionally, portfolio value is calculated on the basis of this average rate.

However, because of the retention dynamic, the probability of belonging to segment 1 will converge toward 1, and, at the same time, the average retention rate will also converge toward the retention rate of segment 1. In effect, according to Bayes' theorem, one gets the probability of customer c belonging to segment 1 active after t years, formulated as

$$P(c \in S_1 | \text{ active after } t \text{ years}) = \frac{P(c \in S_1) P(\text{active after } t \text{ years} | c \in S_1)}{P(\text{active after } t \text{ years})}$$

$$= \frac{p_1 \rho_1^t}{\sum_{i=1}^n p_i \rho_i^t} = \frac{1}{1 + \frac{p_2 \rho_2^t}{p_1 \rho_1^t} + \cdots + \frac{p_n \rho_n^t}{p_1 \rho_1^t}} \quad (6)$$

$$= \frac{1}{1 + \frac{p_2}{p_1} \left(\frac{\rho_2}{\rho_1}\right)^t + \cdots + \frac{p_n}{p_1} \left(\frac{\rho_n}{\rho_1}\right)^t}$$

However, since, by definition, $r_1 \geq r_i$, $\forall\, i \neq 1$ then $\forall i \neq 1, \lim_{t \to +\infty} \left(\frac{\rho_i}{\rho_1}\right)^t = 0$.

So the more time that passes (t becomes large), the higher the probability of belonging to segment 1, leaning toward a limit of 1. The average retention rate for a cohort thus converges toward the retention rate of segment 1. Variation in the retention rate is linked to the heterogeneous nature of the population. The use of an aggregate rate is not adapted for assessing the CLV. It can however be used by companies as a proxy for business health. Nowadays, adopting a stable retention rate represents a very particular case and is often inadequate.

Probabilistic Models

There are two types of probabilistic models: parametric and semi-parametric.

Parametric Models

In terms of parametric models, more elaborate models than the deterministic ones have been developed in the contractual framework. Thus, Fader and Hardie (2007b) used a survival function to obtain an expression such as (7)

$$E(\text{CLV}) = h \frac{S(t)}{(1+d)^t} \quad (7)$$

considering time as discrete. The link with the preceding form is obvious apart from the fact that $S(t)$ is the survival or retention function on date t and one can no longer speak about CLV but of expectancy of CLV. The authors assume that life span is given by a geometric distribution. The customer remains as such from one period to another with a probability 1-p. In this context, $S(t) = (1 - p)^t$. Interindividual heterogeneity in terms of probability p is given by a beta distribution (with values between 0 and 1). One thus obtains the shifted beta-geometric model (sBG).

Naturally, other expressions of survival are possible, notably with the inclusion of explanatory variables and the shift to continuous time. Schweidel et al. (2008) thus included explanatory variables while retaining a formulation with latent traits in continuous time. They developed the formula

$$S(t) = \int S[t|\theta_i, X(t)] g(\theta_i).d\theta_i \quad (8)$$

with $X(t)$ as all of the explanatory variables for t and θ_i a set of individual latent traits. $g(\theta_i)$ represents the distribution of θ_i. This formulation ensures the harmonious integration of latent traits and explanatory variables, giving us a mixed effects model with fixed and random components.

$g(\theta_i)$ is the distribution that can be used to measure interindividual heterogeneity. It generally involves a gamma distribution for reasons of flexibility and compatibility with most survival distributions. It is expressed as follows:

$$g(\theta_i \mid r, \alpha) = \frac{\alpha^r \theta_i^{r-1} e^{-\alpha \theta_i}}{\Gamma(r)} \qquad (9)$$

One can express the survival function in the form of the hazard function. The hazard function measures the instantaneous risk of mortality.

$$S[t \mid \theta_i, X(t)] = e^{-\sum_{v=1}^{t} \int_{v-1}^{v} h[u \mid \theta_i, X(t)] du} \qquad (10)$$

If one concentrates on the stochastic dimension, the basic hazard function h_0 can adopt the Weibull distribution:

$$h_0(t \mid \theta_i, c) = c\theta_i t^{c-1} \qquad (11)$$

This formulation takes into account risk that evolves over time. Variation in the retention rate depends as much on heterogeneity (interindividual variations) as on intrinsic individual variations. If $c = 1$, one then shifts to the exponential-gamma (EG) model. Note that in continuous time, this model is the equivalent of the sBG model (Fader et al. 2003).

Semi-Parametric Models

The most famous representative of semi-parametric models is the Cox model, often called the proportional hazard model. It models a life span considered as a random variable with a probability density $f(t)$ and a distribution function $F(t)$. The survival function is expressed as

$$S(t) = P(T \geq t) = 1 - F(t) \qquad (12)$$

This function is of course monotonically decreasing.

The hazard function is written as

$$h(t) = \lim_{dt \to 0} \frac{P[(t \leq T < t + dt)(T \geq t)]}{dt} = \frac{f(t)}{S(t)} \qquad (13)$$

Instead of taking the hazard function into consideration in a parametric way as in the preceding point, one estimates it following the Kaplan-Meier procedure. The cumulated hazard function is expressed as

$$H(t) = \int_0^t h(u).du = -\ln[S(t)] \qquad (14)$$

The addition of explanatory variables in the form of an X matrix allows us to adopt a semi-parametric formulation:

$$h(t|\ X) = h_0(t)e^{X\beta} \qquad (15)$$

$h_0(t)$ only depends on time. With Eq. 15, based on expression (11), the survival function becomes

$$S(t|X) = [S_0(t)]^{e^{X\beta}} \qquad (16)$$

with the same formulation logic as the hazard function.

Migration Models for CLV Measurement

These models represent a generalization of retention models. The absence of transactions at any given moment does not mean that the customer has become inactive. This is typically the case in a noncontractual situation, in which customer inactivity cannot be observed.

The main idea is that customers go through different stages in their relationship with the brand with specific characteristics governing each stage. One therefore needs to describe the characteristics of these stages as well as the conditions for the transition from one stage to another.

Deterministic Models

Heuristics are frequently used to identify the situation of a customer in a deterministic context. The best known of these is the RFM segmentation (recency, frequency, and monetary value). Recency is the determinant factor to assess whether or not a customer is active. Customers are segmented on the basis of more or less valid thresholds. Traditionally, one distinguishes three levels per criterion R, F, and M, representing 27 segments. The more recently a customer has made a purchase, the greater his or her purchasing frequency, and the higher the average basket, the greater his or her supposed potential. This apparently logical hypothesis is, as noted earlier, qualified by observation of the behaviors of these different segments (e.g., Fader et al. 2005b).

At managerial level, a customer is traditionally considered as inactive beyond a certain length of time without arbitrarily fixed purchases. This method has been presented to us many times by firms that adopt a customer relation management approach. Schweidel et al. (2008) also noted its predominance in professional practice to determine whether or not a customer is active. Likewise, forecasts of future sales are made through a simple extrapolation of past sales.

Probabilistic Models

Two forms of approaches coexist. The first is in the form of Markov processes and the second in the form of combinations of models.

Markov Processes

In terms of migration models, the most widely used method is certainly that of Markov chains, also called Hidden Markov Models. Popularized by Pfeifer and Carraway in 2000, it has been the object of numerous extensions through the integration of sociodemographic or RFM variables. A customer is assumed to be in a certain relational situation with respect to the company, defined in advance. Naturally, these stages are never observed but remain latent which explains the term "Hidden Markov Models." One can subsequently calculate the probability of transition from one state to another. Thus, Pfeifer and Carraway (2000) identified five levels of customer relations, from the most recent customers to buyers that bought such a long time ago they are considered as "non" or former customers. The transition pattern can be expressed graphically as follows (Fig. 1):

In this framework, there is perfect sequentiality. At stage 5, customers are considered as definitively lost with no chance of reactivation. This hypothesis can easily be changed. These models may be likened to latent class models except that adherence to a segment in the framework of hidden Markov models is dynamic and follows a Markov process.

Adapting Kumar (2007), a customer's CLV may be expressed in the following way:

$$\text{CLV} = \sum_{t=0}^{T} \frac{MM_t P_t}{(1+d)^t} \tag{17}$$

with MM_t the matrix of probability of transition from one state to another at t, d the rate of loss, and P_t the value generated by the customer on date t. Over time, the probability matrices merge with one another. Thus, if one starts from the probability of initial MM_0 transitions, one gets $t = 1$ $MM_1 = MM_0 \times MM_0 = (MM_0)^2$ and so $MM_t = (MM_0)^{t+1}$.

A specific application is that of Rust et al. (2004) with a brand change matrix. Combined with a logit model, this application demonstrates the flexibility and the potential of the Markov approach.

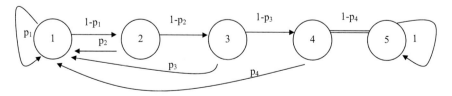

Fig. 1 Transition from one stage to another according to a Markov process

Combinations of Models

This approach was largely developed by Schweidel and Fader (2009). It considers that a stronger customer relationship with a brand (measured by the number of repeat purchases) is expressed through greater purchasing stability and so more stable interpurchase times. In short, it is the transcription of the transition from new customer to existing customer. There are thus two interpurchase periods that follow one another, the first characterized by an exponential distribution and the second by an Erlang 2 distribution. This distribution is a specific case of gamma distributions with a shape parameter equal to 2. The density is thus written as $\lambda^2 x e^{-\lambda x}$.

The transition from one state to the other occurs after each purchase with probability p. One thus arrives at a transition which respects a geometric process.

All the parameters of the different models are assumed heterogeneous. The two parameters transcribing the rate of transactions (exponential distribution and Erlang 2) are themselves gamma distributed, and probability is distributed according to a beta law. This line of research is interesting for several reasons: it takes into account explanatory variables, can be generalized to a larger number of situations and other distributions, etc.

Continuous Mixed Models: The Family of NBD Models to Measure CLV

This term is rarely used but allows us to describe the underlying nature of these models. It involves estimating the different processes simultaneously: consumption, attrition, etc. To this end, each process is assumed to correspond to a specific law. Customer heterogeneity is also expressed by a distribution. All the consumption characteristics are considered to be governed by latent traits. Explanatory variables may be integrated, depending on the degree of sophistication of the different models. Fundamentally though, the introduction of explanatory variables is not in accordance with the philosophy of these models based on stochastic determinants.

The whole palette of statistical tools is used here.

The Pareto/NBD and BG/NBD Model

In this context, continuous mixed models are considered as one of the most promising lines of research, especially the negative binomial formalization (NBD) model. The Poisson distribution of data y is combined with a gamma distribution of purchasing frequency. This approach, developed by Ehrenberg (1959), has been extended by taking into account the inactivity factor: the Pareto/NBD model (Schmittlein et al. 1987; Morrison and Schmittlein 1988; Schmittlein and Peterson 1994; Abe 2009; Jerath et al. 2011) or betaPareto/NBD model-geometric/NBD model (BG/NBD by Fader et al. 2005a). Thus, consumer behavior is represented by a continuous representation that, in theory, takes all of the individual specificities into account.

However, continuous mixed models imply a total parametric specification (generally Poisson with a specific frequency parameter distribution) that is by nature restrictive and very often not very well adapted given the fundamental hypotheses of these distributions. Semi or nonparametric generalizations are naturally possible. However, their introduction requires a highly complex mathematical conceptualization process. In the same way, the introduction of explanatory variables is also possible but always at the price of a demanding mathematical formulation (Castéran et al. 2007a). Consequently, the operational and managerial scope of these models appears to be greatly reduced.

Finite mixed-effect models have been used for many years. The first principles were laid down by Newcomb (1886) and Pearson (1894). Finite mixed-effect models provide a specific case of latent class models (Baltagi 2003). They postulate the existence of latent classes within the population under study and a specific link between explained and explanatory variables within each of these classes. In this way, they underpin the existence of segments with specific behavioral patterns; the marketing implications are clearly apparent.

However, applications in a specifically marketing framework were initiated relatively late, mainly by Wedel et al. (1993). They provide a segmentation of the population beyond traditional behavioral segmentation. While apparently offering less detailed analysis than a continuous approach, segmentation does provide a clear interpretation of the results obtained as well as directly accessible managerial and operational implications. These implications are reinforced by the presence of explanatory variables. Each segment may be studied according to its own behavioral characteristics, which are explained by a set of variables. These explanatory variables help to determine the most effective marketing actions at the level of each segment. Finite mixed-effect models thus appear to be a promising alternative to continuous mixed models.

Nonetheless, to our best knowledge, the comparative efficiency of these models has only been demonstrated one time by Castéran et al. (2008). This comparison in terms of predictive validity between the finite mixed models and models of the NBD family (NBD simple, Pareto/NBD, BG/NBD) is worth exploring further.

The Explanatory Pareto/NBD and BG/NBD Model

The fact that all of these models are purely stochastic implies that they only have limited managerial potential. It is therefore important to reconcile the predictive validity of these purely stochastic models with an interpretative dimension resulting from the presence of explanatory variables. The introduction of explanatory variables within the Pareto/NBD model is a promising approach (Castéran et al. 2007b). This is done by the introduction of the explanatory variables in the gamma-gamma model by breaking down the variability of the scale parameter into two elements by distinguishing two components of parameter λ (purchasing frequency) and by using a regression with explanatory variables as well as a parameter λ_0:

$$\lambda = \lambda_0 e^{X_1 \beta} \tag{18}$$

with β the vector of coefficients and X_1 the individual characteristics and marketing actions. Parameter λ_0 is distributed according to a gamma law of parameters r (form) and α (scale). This parameter captures the residual heterogeneity not taken into account by the explanatory variables. Its density is expressed as

$$f(\lambda_0|r,\alpha) = \frac{\alpha^r}{\Gamma(r)}\lambda_0^{r-1}e^{-\alpha\lambda_0} \qquad (19)$$

with $\lambda_0 > 0$, $r > 0$ et $\alpha > 0$.

Then one has to adopt the same process for inactivity with regard to parameter μ. One notes the matrix of personal characteristics and marketing actions as X_2 (this can partially or entirely correspond to X_1). Inactivity thus becomes

$$\mu = \mu_0 e^{X_2\gamma} \qquad (20)$$

with parameter μ_0 following a gamma distribution of parameters s (form) and δ (scale),

$$f(\mu_0|s,\delta) = \frac{\delta^s}{\Gamma(s)}\mu_0^{s-1}e^{-\delta\mu_0} \qquad (21)$$

with $\mu_0 > 0$, $s > 0$ et $\delta > 0$.

In addition to the explanatory variables X (composed of X_1 and X_2), one needs three additional elements: number of purchases y made during the period [0, T], recency of the last purchase t_y (date of last purchase), and length of the period of estimation T. H is the combination of all three variables, $H = (y, t_y, T)$, and Θ the vector of all the coefficients, $\Theta = (r, \alpha, s, \beta, \gamma)$.

The limitation is due to the fact that one only deals with variables without a dynamic perspective, as they are constant over time.

Finally, Fader and Hardie (2007a) developed a general expression to introduce invariant explanatory variables over time within Pareto/NBD and BG/NBD models. The inclusion of these variables is conducted in a less complex way than the approach of Castéran et al. (2007b).

The Fig. 2 presents an overview of the CLV models.

The fundamental distinction is due to the nature of the relations between the customer and the company: is the customer's inactivity observed (contractual relations) or not? The second criterion comes from the type of model adopted: whole population, segment, or individual.

Finally, the last parameter is the distinction between continuous and discrete purchasing opportunities. However, this distinction is less crucial than the others insofar as certain discrete cases may be considered as continuous cases, while continuous cases can always be "discrete."

Casteran et al. (2007b) did not distinguish between variants with or without explanatory variables in this process. The presence of explanatory variables within purely stochastic formulations presents a methodological as well as a conceptual improvement.

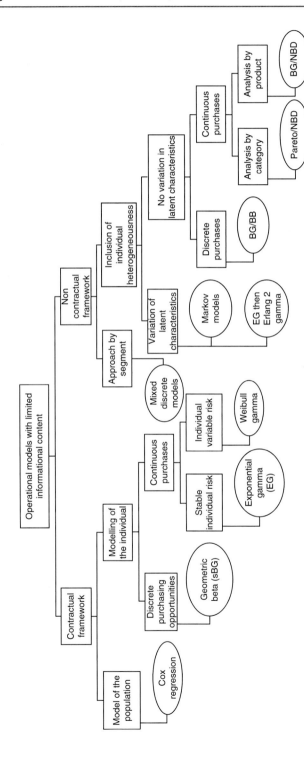

Fig. 2 Overview of the CLV measurement models

An Application of Stochastic Pareto/NBD and BG/NBD Models for Customer Base Management

After having presented the taxonomy of CLV, churn, and retention measurement models, this chapter shows a practical application by using some of the presented stochastic models (Pareto/NBD, BG/NBD) to model a customer base and the impact of a retail grocery loyalty program on customer churn, retention, and activity. The goal is to show how to implement, use, and interpret these sophisticated models by Customer base managementapplying them on firms' frequently used grocery store loyalty program databases and panel data.

Data and Methodology

The data for the practical application of customer base analysis come from a store loyalty program (LP) database of a large French grocery retailer (surface area 9,000 m^2).

An LP consists of integrated and ruled systems of marketing actions (based on collection and redemption rules) that aim to encourage repeat purchases and increase the cost of switching as well as retention and subsequently CLV by providing short- and long-term incentives (Meyer-Waarden 2007; Blattberg et al. 2008; Bijmolt et al. 2010) and enhance "true loyalty," that is, increase behavioral (e.g., cross purchases, repeat purchases, mean basket size) and attitudinal (relationship building through positives attitudes, trust, attachment; Morgan and Hunt 1994) loyalty.

Loyalty programs (LP) are vastly popular – 90% of Europeans and 90% of US shoppers own at least one loyalty card. In 2010, the number of LP memberships in the United States exceeded 2.1 billion memberships, growing by 16% from the previous year despite the worldwide recession (Hlavinka and Sullivan 2011). For example, research estimates that the UK pharmacy chain Boots invested 30 million British pounds in the launch of its Advantage Card LP (Temporal and Trott 2001), and the U.K. retailer Tesco has spent an estimated 60 million pounds to operate its Clubcard LP (Bijmolt et al. 2010).

The store's loyalty program, launched in 1994, is free and provides price discounts, points exchangeable for gifts, and purchase vouchers on a varying set of items. The value of points won increases linearly according to the amount customers spend. Cardholder purchases account for 70% of store revenues. In the analysis, cardholder information is used, identifiable on an individual basis, which includes the majority of customers. The data set contains also information about competing loyalty card memberships and household characteristics (e.g., age, revenue). Scanner data include the transaction details, such as date of purchase and amount paid. Because people often shop on a weekly basis, the daily purchases are aggregated by individuals into a weekly frequency. The transaction data pertain to 5,000 households over a period of 156 weeks (week 2/1998 to week 2/2001).

The LP data is matched with BehaviorScan panel test market data from Angers, France. Scanning technology provides exhaustive recording of the purchasing behavior (95% of fast-moving consumer goods sales in the area) of the panelist households, which are representative of the national population.

The implementation conditions of the models with LP data relate to two aspects: the consideration of new customers that have realized their first purchase, with certainty, and the duration of the estimation period. The date of first purchase in a noncontractual framework may be considered known, whether because of the nature of the data (e.g., Fader et al. 2005b) or the data processing method (Batislam et al. 2007). The Pareto/NBD, BG/NBD, and PDO models forecast all purchases by combining the number of customers at a given date with the unconditional expectancy of the number of purchases, according to the customer maturity level (Fader et al. 2005a). As stated higher, the first purchase is easy to identify in certain settings, when the entire customer history is available. Nevertheless, it is difficult, in most noncontractual relationships, to determine an exact date of the actual first purchase. (An exception are mail order business or e-commerce retail settings, where the shipping address of the customer is known and the purchase can be identified.) In grocery retailing, data from a loyalty program (LP) are left censored, and the first purchase cannot be characterized with certainty, because customers probably purchase before they enroll in a loyalty scheme. Therefore, it is unclear what types of customers are observed: "real" new customers, previously existing customers who have lately adopted the LP or customers who had lapsed or have low usage patterns. Batislam et al. (2007) and Jerath et al. (2011) both resort to drastic truncations to achieve a sample that consists entirely of new customers, who made no purchases in the first 13 months of their observations, whom they logically argue are genuine new customers. This approach means the loss of substantial information and raises questions regarding sample representativeness. For example, consumers who make their first purchases at different times, later or earlier, behave differently in their purchase frequency and loyalty in business settings (Schmittlein and Peterson 1994). The best customers often self-select as early adopters (Meyer-Waarden and Benavent 2009; Rogers 2003), so truncating samples could exclude insights into some of the firm's best customers and earliest adopters. Another option to solve the left-censored data issue is to treat the first customer purchase observed in the LP database as the customer's first actual buying act. This method creates the risk of combining different cohorts though, with different actual dates of first purchase; its consequences for models' predictive validity have never been examined.

Both the Pareto/NBD and the BG/NBD models require tracking customer transactions, starting with their initial purchases, which raises the possibility of left-censored data, because one does not know when people became aware of the outlet's loyalty program and if the first purchases recorded after enrollment are really their first transactions. In other words, households may have bought before adopting the loyalty scheme. Because the store does not have information about the initial purchases of cardholders, this methodological problem treated by left-filtering the panel customer records with transactions before October 14, 1998, which guarantees that the customers in the analysis are newcomers with known initial purchase times data (see Batislam et al. 2007). Thus, 5,000 households of a cohort of 997 new households is extracted that made their first purchases within the same 3-month period (October–January) and realized a total of 6,005 transactions. The panel data is left-filtered and aggregated on a weekly basis, and the final observation window covers 78 weeks, from October 14, 1998, to April 13, 2000. The estimation period is restrained to 26 weeks and the calibration period to 52 weeks (hold-out sample) to establish the predictive validity of the models.

Finally, we get a matrix with one row for each customer, and at least three columns:

1. Customer's frequency, y: number of repeated transactions made in the estimation period
2. Customer's recency, t_y: the time of their last transaction
3. Customer's total time observed in the estimation period, T

Other columns can be added, one for each explanatory variable. The explanatory variables have to be quantitative or dummy variables.

Estimation

Parameter estimation of the Pareto/NBD model is more complex (Fader et al. 2005a; Reinartz and Kumar 2003; Fader and Hardie 2013); in particular, the maximum likelihood estimation (MLE) approach to estimating key parameters used requires a numerical search algorithm that must evaluate the Gauss hypergeometric function (Schmittlein and Peterson 1994).

For the estimation, free statistical software R 3.3.1 (R Development Core Team 2010) is used. Our advice is to adopt a two-step approach. Firstly, we estimate the purely stochastic model parameters (Pareto/NBD or BG/NBD) without explanatory variables. Secondly, we incorporate the explanatory variables and launch a new estimation process based on the results of the first estimation.

Estimation of the Purely Stochastic Parameters

The easiest way for estimating simple Pareto/NBD and BG/NBD models is now to use a dedicated package BYTD (https://CRAN.R-project.org/package=BTYD) "Buy 'Til You Die Models" (Dziurzynski et al. 2014). The estimation of the parameters is made through, respectively, the functions *pnbd.EstimateParameters* (Pareto/NBD) and *bgnbd.EstimateParameters* (NG/NBD).

There are two major estimation issues. First, the procedures are time-consuming, especially with regard to the initial values. Second, depending on these values, non-convergence might be faced, which makes it even more difficult to find an operational set of initial values. Many tries can be required in order to assure a clear convergence. The best choice, even if convergence occurs, is to relaunch with several starting points in order to compare the results and the value of the log-likelihood.

A good starting point is to consider that the average purchase rate is the ratio r/α. It is not sufficient to determine the exact starting values of the parameters, but it can be useful that the initial values of r and α are chosen with respect to the average purchase rate of the dataset.

Since an optimal (in sense of log-likelihood maximization) set of parameters is found, the incorporation of explanatory variables can begin.

Estimation of the Parameters Including Explanatory Variables

The first step is to declare the explanatory variables. If *mydata* is the name of the dataset, the vector of the explanatory variables for the purchasing frequency X_1 could be the following:

```
X1=cbind(mydata$LoyCard, mydata$HhSize, mydata$NumbCard,
mydata$DisStore, mydata$SeniorManager, mydata$Unemployment,
mydata$Income_6, mydata$Income6_12, mydata$Income12_18,
mydata$Income18_24, mydata$Income24_30, mydata$A30_39,
mydata$A40_49, mydata$A50+)
```

Our variables describe:

1. The characteristics of the individuals: the household size (*HhSize*), their age (the *A*... dummy variables), their net wages (the *Income*... dummy variables), and the professional occupation (*SeniorManager, Unemployment*)
2. The relationship to the store: the distance in kilometers from the store (*DisStore*), the owning of loyalty cards (*LoyCard*), and the total number of loyalty cards owned by the household (*NumbCard*)

```
X2=X1 #Explanatory variable vector for inactivity part
```

At the beginning, the explanatory variables for purchasing frequency and inactivity can be the same. Further, during the selection process, the two sets will become different.

In order to incorporate qualitative variables, we divide them into dummy variables (e.g., income or customer age). To avoid overidentification, one modality of each variable shall be excluded from the estimation process. Whatever the modality is, the exclusion of one modality per qualitative variable is mandatory.

The set of initial values (*b0* in the example) is determined on the basis of the first estimation with *pnbd.EstimateParameters* (Pareto/NBD). Those parameters are called *params* here.

```
b0<-c(params, rep(0, ncol(X1)+ncol(X2)))
```

The initial values for the explanatory variables are set to 0 in order to relaunch the estimation process at the same initial state as purely stochastic approaches. The reestimation process can now begin.

For the maximization of the log-likelihood function and estimation of the parameters, two functions are employed: *nlminb* and *optim*. The *nlminb* procedure is more flexible and presents fewer convergence problems. After estimating *nlminb*, the *optim* is used to compute the Hessian matrix for estimating the covariance matrix (standard error of the coefficients). In the following example however, we directly use the *optim* function.

The estimation of the Pareto/NBD model – an effort whose difficulty is frequently cited as a usage limitation – is considerably facilitated by the *gsl* package, with the expression *hyperg_2F1*, that enables the estimation of a Gaussian hypergeometric function to increase external validity.

The final log-likelihood of the explanatory Pareto/NBD model can be written as

$$LL(\Theta_i|H_i, X_i) = \ln \Gamma(r+y) - \ln \Gamma(r) + r \ln \alpha + s \ln \delta + y \ln B + \ln[A_1 A_2 + A_3 A_0] \quad (22)$$

with

(i) $B = e^{X_1 \beta}$ and $G = e^{X_2 \gamma}$
(ii) Due to the presence of the Gaussian hypergeometric function and the form of the integrals, we must distinguish two cases: when $\alpha e^{X_2 \gamma} \geq \delta e^{X_1 \beta}$ and the opposite case. For each case, we note a different expression for A_0:
If $\alpha G \geq \delta B$,

$$A_0 = \frac{\left(\frac{B}{G}\right)^{s+1}}{B} \times \left[\frac{{}_2F^1\left(\frac{s+1}{r+s+y}; r+s+y+1; \frac{\alpha - \delta \frac{B}{G}}{\alpha + t_y B}\right)}{(\alpha + t_y B)^{(r+s+y)}} - \frac{{}_2F^1\left(\frac{s+1}{r+s+y}; r+s+y+1; \frac{\alpha - \delta \frac{B}{G}}{\alpha + TB}\right)}{(\alpha + TB)^{(r+s+y)}} \right] \quad (23)$$

If $\alpha G \leq \delta B$,

$$A_0 = \frac{\left(\frac{G}{B}\right)^{r+y}}{G} \times \left[\frac{{}_2F^1\left(\frac{r+y}{r+s+y}; r+s+y+1; \frac{\delta - \alpha \frac{G}{B}}{\delta + t_y G}\right)}{(\delta + t_y G)^{(r+s+y)}} - \frac{{}_2F^1\left(\frac{r+y}{r+s+y}; r+s+y+1; \frac{\delta - \alpha \frac{G}{B}}{\delta + TG}\right)}{(\delta + TG)^{(r+s+y)}} \right] \quad (24)$$

(iii) $A_1 = (TB + \alpha)^{-(r+y)}$ and $A_2 = (TG + \delta)^{-s}$
(iv) $A_3 = \frac{Gs}{r+s+y}$

Since optimization algorithms classically perform minimization, we use the negative form of the log-likelihood function.

```
library(gsl)
LL_Paretoexp <-function(p) {
# Parameters vector
    r<-p[1]
    alpha<-p[2]
    s<-p[3]
    delta<-p[4]
# Number of covariates
    nX1=ncol(X1)              # for purchasing frequency
    nX2=length(p)-4-nX1       # for inactivity process
# Coefficients of explanatory variables
    b1=p[5:(4+nX1)]           # for purchasing frequency
    g1=p[(5+nX1):length(p)]   # for inactivity process
# Regressions
    B<-exp(as.matrix(X1)%*%b1)
    G<-exp(as.matrix(X2)%*%g1)
#Meta-functions
    A1<-(B*T+alpha)^(-r-y)
    A2<-(G*T+delta)^(-s)
    A3<-G*s/(r+s+y)
# A₀ expression
    coef1<-(B^s)/(G^(s+1))
    arg11<-hyperg_2F1(s+1, r+s+y, r+s+y+1, (alpha-delta*B/G)/
(alpha+t_y*B))/((alpha+t_y*B)^(r+s+y)) # t_y = t_y
    arg12<-hyperg_2F1(s+1, r+s+y, r+s+y+1, (alpha-delta*B/G)/
(alpha+T*B))/((alpha+T*B)^(r+s+y))
    coef2<-((G/B)^(r+y))/G
    arg21<-hyperg_2F1(r+y, r+s+y, r+s+y+1, (delta-alpha*G/B)/
(delta+t_y*G))/((delta+t_y*G)^(r+s+y))
    arg22<-hyperg_2F1(r+y, r+s+y, r+s+y+1, (delta-alpha*G/B)/
(delta+T*G))/((delta+T*G)^(r+s+y))
    A0<-ifelse(alpha*G>delta*B, coef1*(arg11-arg12), coef2*
(arg21-arg22))
# Log-likelihood function
    -sum(lgamma(r+y)-lgamma(r)+ r*log(alpha)+ s*log(delta)+ y*log
(B)+ log(A1*A2+A3*A0))
}
```

The lower bounds are 10^{-3} for the stochastic parameters:

```
min<-c(rep(1e-3,4), rep(-Inf,length(b0)-4))
max<-rep(Inf, length(b0))
```

The selection of the explanatory variables represents a significant challenge. On the basis of the Hessian matrix, small set of variables is kept, though traditionally, modeling purchase behavior is quite complex and the identification of relevant variables very difficult (Ehrenberg 1988).

```
optimal<-optim(b0, fn=LL_Paretoexp, method="L-BFGS-B",
control=list(trace=6, REPORT=1), hessian=TRUE, lower=min,
upper=max)
optimal # Result of the estimation process
```

Let us remind that we get the standard errors by taking the square root of the diagonal elements of the covariance matrix. The covariance matrix is the inverse of the Hessian matrix obtained through the minimization of the negative log-likelihood: *optimal*. All results are presented in a table with the coefficients (*Coeffs*), the standard errors (*StdError*), and the t-values (*t*). The null hypothesis that the coefficients are not significantly different from 0 (β_i or $\gamma_i = 0$) is rejected at a 5% significance level if $t \in\,]-\infty;\, -1.96] \cup [1.96;\, +\infty[$.

We compute also the Bayesian information criterion *BIC*, a common indicator, expressed as $-2LL + k ln(N)$, where k is the number of parameters to be estimated (*length(b0)*), N indicates the number of individuals (*length(y)*), and *LL* is the maximum log-likelihood value for the model (-*optimal$value*).

We recommend a step-by-step descending selection process by removing one variable at each step:

1. We launch the estimation with the whole set of potential covariates.
2. We remove the covariate with the closest to 0 t-value while the t-value belongs to]-1.96; 1.96[.
3. We relaunch the estimation process with the new set of variables.
4. We check for the improvement of the BIC value.
5. While we have t-values comprised between -1.96 (excluded) and 1.96 (excluded) and while the BIC value is improving, we return to step 2.

This selection process can be quite slow but allows an appropriate selection of the covariates.

```
# Computation of the standard errors
inverse<-solve(optimal$hessian)
result<-cbind(optimal$par, sqrt(diag(inverse)), optimal$par/sqrt
(diag(inverse)))
colnames(result)<-c("Coeffs", "StdError", "t")
rownames(result)<-c("r", "alpha", "s", "delta", colnames(X1),
colnames(X2))
print(result)
# Computation of the Bayesian Information Criterion
BIC<-optimal$value*2+length(b0)*log(length(y))
BIC
```

Results

The descriptive results offer a comprehensive overview of the data sets from the grocery sector which is compared with different data used in previous investigations. In addition, the parameter estimation and comparison of the different models is demonstrated.

Of the 997 total customers in the 26-week cohort, 46.3% are zero repurchasers (Means $=1.69$, SD $= 3.59$). The grocery data indicate that the median interpurchase times, even after excluding zero repurchase, is approximately 10.6 weeks, which is low compared with the other applications of the Pareto/NBD model, for which the median interpurchase time is 7 months (office supplies; Schmittlein and Peterson 1994), 17 weeks (catalogue sales; Reinartz and Kumar 2000), or 25 weeks (computer-related products; Reinartz and Kumar 2000). The grocery category features very short purchase cycles, because grocery items are not durable and require frequent replenishment. In addition, the number and heterogeneity of customers is higher in the grocery retail context. For example, the online CD customer base used by Fader et al. (2005a) includes a majority of customers (approximately 85%) who make zero (60%), one, or two repurchases. 46% of grocery retail customers are zero repurchasers, and customers with zero, one, or two repurchases constitute 80% of total grocery retail customers. In contrast, Batislam et al. (2007) find that approximately 40% of grocery retail customers are zero repurchasers, and customers with zero, one, or two repurchases make up around 65% of total grocery retail customers. Such high heterogeneity in grocery purchases decreases the precision of the models.

Parameter Estimations

In order to show a practical application, we interpret the estimated coefficients. They seem coherent for the Pareto/NBD model, with signs in the correct direction (see Table 2).

Purchase frequency is positively influenced by a LP, which is coherent with existing literature (Meyer-Waarden 2007; Leenheer et al. 2007; Liu 2007). The professional occupation of the household members has a direct impact on the purchase activity (frequency) and retention, though a professional situation has the same positive impact on purchase frequency as does lower income. Furthermore,

Table 2 Regression coefficients of the Pareto/NBD model

Frequency regression (β)		Inactivity regression (γ)	
Loyalty card of the shop	+1.01	# of loyalty cards	−0.17
Senior manager	+0.30	Low wage (dummy)	+0.10
Low wage (dummy)	+0.29	Unemployment (dummy)	+1.10
Over 50 (dummy)	−0.73		

Notes: The insignificant coefficients ($p > 0.1$) are household size, profession (employee, worker), wages (1,000–2,000 €, > 2,000 €), and age (30–50 years, < 30 years)

people older than 50 years of age are less mobile than younger people and display lower purchase frequencies. Younger shoppers are more likely to engage in smaller, more frequent fill-in trips than are older ones, probably because the former buyers have more disposable time but less income, which drives them to buy in smaller quantities at higher frequencies (Kahn and Schmittlein 1989; Bell et al. 1998). Financial instability of households (i.e., low wages, unemployment) has a negative impact on inactivity. Grocery patronage behavior depends on the level of education and income, which increase the chances that the consumers uses a more rational purchase process and thus attaches less importance to marketing variables (e.g., store advertisement, promotions, loyalty program rewards). Generally, the more education people possess, the less sensitive they are to a store's promotions or other marketing actions, and the less loyal they are, which means their defection probability is higher and retention is lower (Narasimhan 1984). Less educated households with lower incomes tend to remain loyal, because they experience more influence from store marketing variables. According to an alternative but not incompatible explanation, they also probably have higher switching costs related to mobility constraints (money, transports), which increases the utility of the closest and most familiar store.

Multiple LP memberships relate positively to inactivity, which is coherent with the results of Meyer-Waarden (2007) and may indicate a learning effect with regard to the use of loyalty schemes. Disloyal, opportunistic buyers who regularly shop in several stores and are members of different loyalty schemes (on average, European households possess three grocery retailing loyalty cards; ACNielsen 2005) are more experienced and have smaller switching costs. These purchasers join LP more readily and quickly (Meyer-Waarden 2007; Leenheer et al. 2007).

Table 3 provides the results of the gamma and beta distributions. The parameters for frequency do not vary significantly, despite the introduction of explanatory variables. However, the parameters for the inactivity or dropout rates vary strongly; the drastic growth of δ probably relates to the explanatory variables.

Table 3 Coefficients of the gamma/beta distributions

	Basic NBD	BG/NBD	Standard Pareto/NBD	Explanatory Pareto/NBD
Index of homogeneity in purchase rate: r	0.50	0.43	0.57	0.66
α	5.72	3.94	5.60	6.91
Average purchase rate: r/α	0.09	0.10	0.10	0.10
a		0.22		
b		1.14		
Average inactivity probability: $a/(a + b)$		0.16		
Index of homogeneity in inactivity rate: s			0.63	1.56
δ			30.16	107.55
Average inactivity rate: s/δ			0.02	0.01

The parameters r (which can be seen as purchase rates) and s (which can be seen as churn rates) increase in the explanatory model. Both provide an index of homogeneity (Schmittlein et al. 1987), and their increase denotes more significant homogeneity across customers in the explanatory model. For the explanatory formulation, gamma functions capture residual heterogeneity, not all the heterogeneity, as in the case of purely stochastic formulations.

Purchase Prediction Validity

Empirical analysis carried out for both the 26- and 52-week observation periods for the cohort relies on a popular criterion for adjustment, the Bayesian information criterion (BIC), whose values are based on a log scale. The expression is written as follows: $BIC = -2LL + k \ln(n)$, where k the number of parameters and n the sample size.

The adjustment differences between the BG/NBD approach and the explanatory Pareto/NBD model are not very important, and the BIC is very close for both (see Table 4). If one considers the mean absolute percent error (MAPE) as an empirical criterion, the explanatory Pareto/NBD model has slightly worse results than either the standard or the BG/NBD model (15.5% vs. 12% and 10.5%; the basic NBD achieves the worst results at 38.1%). This result makes sense. According to Fader et al. (2005a), the BG/NBD forecasts are better when purchase frequency is high, as in the grocery retailing context, because of the differences among the model structures. Under the Pareto/NBD model, dropout occurs at any time – even before a customer has made a first purchase. However, under the BG/NBD, a customer cannot become inactive before making his or her first purchase. If buying rates are fairly high, BG/NBD and Pareto/NBD perform similarly well. However, in contexts in which purchase frequencies are low, the BG/NBD model suffers in comparison with the Pareto/NBD approach.

After having tested the robustness of the models, a more thorough investigation of their performance is completed. The accuracies of the different models are not similar (Fig. 3).

During the validation period, the BG/NBD model performs quite well, whereas the Pareto/NBD and explanatory Pareto/NBD formulations underestimate the weekly purchase frequency. The basic NBD model does not perform well at all. With the exception of the basic NBD model, the approaches converge to actual repeat purchases during the forecast period. Weekly sales rise during the first 14 weeks, due to new customers in the cohort and their repeat purchases. All models underestimate the peak in weekly actual purchases in the initial weeks, probably

Table 4 Log-likelihood and Bayesian information criterion

	Basic NBD	BG/NBD	Standard Pareto/NBD	Explanatory Pareto/NBD
Log-Likelihood	−4,954	−4,922	−4,935	−4,900
Bayesian information criterion	9,922	9,872	9,898	9,876

because they miss the increasing trend in repeat purchases due to promotions during the same period. Later in the observation period, all models (with the exception of the basic NBD) match the actual purchases.

The deviation of weekly estimates from actual purchases during the initial weeks leads to an underestimation of the cumulative repeat purchases in the initial weeks as well (see Fig. 4).

During the forecast period (52 weeks), the models underestimate actual purchases (Pareto/NBD model: −9%, explanatory Pareto/NBD model: −14%, BG/NBD

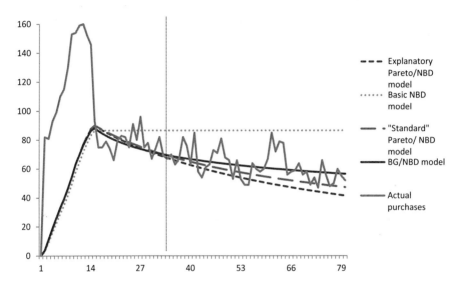

Fig. 3 Estimation of the weekly repeat purchases

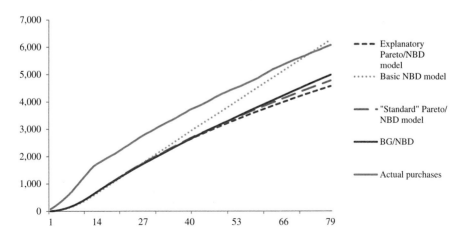

Fig. 4 Estimation of the cumulative repeat purchases

model: −2%). The fairly high purchase frequency rates in grocery shopping may explain the strong results derived from the BG/NBD model. In this case, the assumption that a customer is active until he or she makes a repeat purchase is not a problem. However, purchase frequency is not too high to affect the dropout time ("exhaustion" effect) of the BG/NBD model.

We measure individual-level performance according to the conditional expectations for the forecast period, depending on the number of repeat purchases in the observation period (Fig. 5). That is, for each value of x in the observation period, an average of the actual number of purchases in the forecast period is compared.

The forecasts of the BG/NBD and the standard Pareto/NBD models are very close and provide acceptable predictions of the expected number of transactions in the holdout period, consistent with the results of Fader et al. (2005b). The Pareto/NBD model offers slightly better predictions than the BG/NBD, but it is important to keep in mind that the number of heavy buyers is small. The explanatory model and the basic NBD model systematically overestimate the number of repeat purchases, especially for heavy customers.

Another way to assess the predictive validity of the models is to group customers on the basis of their recency and frequency characteristics. One can then compare the results with traditional recency/frequency (RF) segmentation analysis.

Each of the customers is assigned to a RF segment in the following manner. The terciles for recency and frequency (the customers who made no repeat purchases are coded as R = F = 0) have to be determined. High recency means a low number of days since the last purchase, i.e., a recent repurchaser. At the opposite, a low recency characterizes an exceptional repurchase. In Table 5, the size of each RF group is shown.

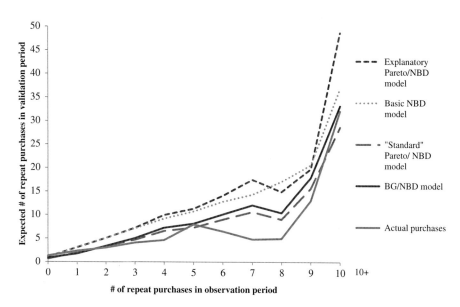

Fig. 5 Conditional expectations

Only 15% of the customers are frequent and recent repurchasers. On the other hand, the zero repurchasers during the estimation period represent almost half of the customers. In a traditional approach, managers in the retailing sector would assume that, after a half year of inactivity, a customer is inactive.

In fact, the average number of purchases made by those customers, during the following 52 weeks, is four times lower in average than the same number made by other segments. However, due to the size of this group, their contribution is really impressive: they represent 18.3% of the total of the purchases of the following 52 weeks, the second contribution of all the segments. This aspect is very interesting. It is taken into account by the models (even the contribution of the zero repurchaser is underestimated between 9.6% and 11.7% instead of 18.3%) (Fig. 6).

Table 5 Repartition of the customers between RF segmentation

Recency	Frequency of repeat purchases (estimation period: 26 weeks)	# of customers
No repeat purchase	0	**46.3%**
Low recency	1	3.0%
	2	0.5%
Total low recency		**3.5%**
Medium recency	1	14.1%
	2	5.6%
	3+	5.1%
Total medium recency		**24.9%**
High recency	1	5.2%
	2	4.9%
	3+	15.1%
Total high recency		**25.3%**

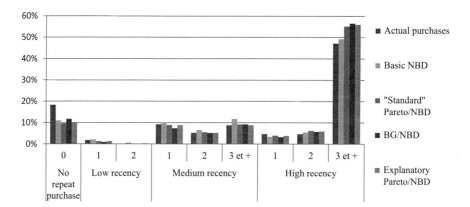

Fig. 6 Purchases by recency and frequency

Conclusion

We have seen an operational form of CLV, retention, and churn models, (namely, the Pareto/NBD, BG/NBD, and explanatory Pareto/NBD models) and their high degree of validity for customer base analysis and for forecasting a customer's future purchasing, conditional on his or her past buying behavior. The Pareto/NBD, BG/NBD, and explanatory Pareto/NBD models systematically outperform the basic NBD model, because it does not consider inactivity.

The Pareto/NBD and explanatory Pareto/NBD formulations underestimate weekly purchase frequency, whereas the BG/NBD model performs quite well. These results show that explanatory variables introduce more information and therefore generate a better forecast.

However, even if the predictive validity of the explanatory NBD/Pareto model is not necessarily better, its performance does not suffer in comparison with the Pareto/NBD and the BG/NBD models. Nevertheless, the advantages of the explanatory approach relate more to the opportunity to explain the impact of personal characteristics and the impact of marketing actions rather than the accuracy of the forecasts at an aggregate level. The ability of the explanatory Pareto/NBD model to predict future purchases is quite good. Even with a reduced set of explanatory variables, the explanatory Pareto/NBD model is as accurate as the standard formulation. Nevertheless, the results are not better than those of the BG/NBD approach. However, improvements are possible with other sets of variables (i.e., more marketing mix variables).

These CLV, retention, and churn models for customer base analysis can help managers understand why their marketing operations work, or do not work, and how and to which customer segments they should improve their efforts. The explanatory model approach represents a promising way to understand buyer behavior. The applications are broad, including segmentation, understanding customer life cycles, determining elasticities and elements that influence loyalty and purchase behavior, the possibility of analyzing marketing actions and personal characteristics, and a means to establish more valid customer CLV models to predict customer value.

Managers should be encouraged to use these models to determine their customer base analysis, CLV calculations, and resource allocations, using their often large longitudinal databases.

Further research should address underlying model assumptions that are unrealistic and not compatible with extant literature about purchasing behavior. For example, researchers could relax the Poisson distribution assumptions and perhaps use a Weibull distribution instead. The BG/NBD formulation suffers a major weakness because its underlying conditions (i.e., dropout rates independent of purchase frequencies) demand inactivity appear immediately after each repurchase act. This behavioral assumption is not compatible with purchasing behavior literature. In the same sense, the Pareto/NBD model supposes independence between purchase frequency and inactivity, which may be reasonable only in "always-a-share" markets (Reinartz and Kumar 2000). Some other authors also suppose a link between both variables (East et al. 2000).

Few current models explicitly incorporate competition, yet heightened competition can affect customer CLV in several ways – shortened expected lifetime, decreased prices, and increased acquisition costs. Panel data provide a promising source for some firms, and surveys can be very useful in capturing the effect of competition. Other empirical investigations should examine in which conditions (high/low purchase frequencies) and with which type of data (internal, panel) the different models perform best.

Compared with predicting purchase frequency and weekly repeat purchases, forecasts of individual purchases include more customer information and should provide higher accuracy in individual-level forecasts. However, it remains difficult to model individual purchase behavior, especially with regard to the highly heterogeneous purchase behavior encountered in grocery sales (Fader and Hardie 2013).

Finally, to allocate optimally, managers cannot simply measure CLV but instead must know how CLV reacts to changes in the marketing mix. Additional research should address this concern.

References

Abe, M. (2009). 'counting your customers' one by one: A hierarchical Bayes extension to the Pareto/NBD model. *Marketing Science, 28*(3), 541–553.

Allenby, G. M., Leone, R. P., & Jen, L. (1999). A dynamic model of purchase timing with application to direct marketing. *Journal of the American Statistical Association, 94*(446), 365–374.

Ayache, A., Calciu, M., & Salerno, F. (2006). Stochastic approach to customer equity and lifetime value calculations with applications to customer retention models and some extensions. *35th Conference of EMAC,* Athènes.

Baltagi, B. H. (2003). *A companion to theoretical econometrics.* Willinston: Blackwell.

Batislam, E., Denizel, M., & Filiztekin, A. (2007). Empirical validation and comparison of models for customer base analysis. *International Journal of Research in Marketing, 24*(3), 201–209.

Bell, D. R., Ho, T. H., & Tang, C. S. (1998). Determining where to shop: Fixed and variable costs of shopping. *Journal of Marketing Research, 35*(3), 352–369.

Berger P., & Nasr, N. (1998). Customer lifetime value: Marketing models and applications. *Journal of Interactive Marketing,* Winter 98, *12*(1), 17–30.

Bijmolt, T., Dorotic, M., & Verhoef, P. (2010). Loyalty programs: Generalizations on their adoption, effectiveness and design. *Foundations & Trends in Marketing, 5*(4), 197–258.

Bitran, G., & Mondschein, S. (1996). Mailing decisions in the catalog sales industry. *Management Science, 42*(9), 1364–1381.

Blattberg, R. C., & Deighton, J. (1996). Manage marketing by the customer equity test. *Harvard Business Review, 74,* 136–144.

Blattberg, R. C., Getz, G., & Thomas, J. S. (2001). *Customer equity: Building and managing relationships as valued assets.* Boston: Harvard Business School Press.

Blattberg, R. C., Kim, B., & Neslin, S. A. (2008). *Database marketing. Analyzing and managing customers.* New York: Springer.

Bolton, R. N., Lemon, K. N., & Verhoef, P. C. (2004). The theoretical underpinnings of customer asset management: A framework and propositions for future research. *Journal of the Academy of Marketing Science, 32*(3), 271–292.

Borle, S., Singh, S., & Jain, D. C. (2008). Customer lifetime value measurement. *Management Science, 54*(1), 100–112.

Calciu, M., & Salerno, F. (2002). Customer value modelling: Synthesis and extension proposals. *Journal of Targeting, Measurement & Analysis for Marketing, 11*(2), 124–134.

Castéran, H., Meyer-Waarden, L., & Benavent, C. (2007a). *Empirical evaluation of NBD models for the estimation of life time value in the retailing sector.* XXIIIrd International Annual Conference of the French Marketing Association, Aix-les-Bains.

Castéran, H., Meyer-Waarden, L., & Benavent, C. (2007b). *Incorporation of covariates in the Pareto/NBD model: First formulations and comparison with others models in the retailing sector.* Third German French Austrian Conference, ESSEC, Paris.

Castéran, H., Meyer-Waarden, L., & Benavent, C. (2008). *Application of latent class models to purchases in the retailing sector and comparison with the Pareto/NBD formulation.* 7ème Congrès Tendances du Marketing Paris Venise (Venise).

Dwyer, F. R. (1997). Customer lifetime valuation to support marketing decision making. *Journal of Direct Marketing, 11*(4), 6–13.

Dwyer, R. (1989). Customer lifetime valuation to support marketing decision making. *Journal of Direct Marketing, 3*(4), 8–15.

Dziurzynski, L., Wadsworth, E., & McCarthy, D. (2014). BTYD: Implementing buy 'Til You Die Models. R package version 2.4. https://CRAN.R-project.org/package=BTYD

East, R., Hammond, K., Harris, P., & Lomax, W. (2000). First-store loyalty and retention. *Journal of Marketing Management, 16*(4), 307–325.

Ehrenberg, A. S. C. (1959). The pattern of consumer purchases. *Applied Statistics, 8*(1), 26–41.

Ehrenberg, A. S. C. (1988). *Repeat buying: Facts, theory and applications.* London: C. Griffin & Co..

Fader, P., & Hardie, B. (2007a). *Incorporating time-invariant covariates into the Pareto/NBD and BG/NBD models.* Working Paper, University of Pennsylvania and London Business School.

Fader, P. S., & Hardie, B. G. S. (2007b). How to project customer retention. *Journal of Interactive Marketing, 21*, 76–90.

Fader, P., & Hardie, B. (2009). Probability models for customer-base analysis. *Journal of Interactive Marketing, 23*(1), 61–69.

Fader, P., & Hardie, B. (2013). Overcoming the BG/NBD model's #NUM! error problem. http://brucehardie.com/notes/027/. Accessed 23 Feb 2015.

Fader, P. S., Hardie, B. G. S., & Zeithammer, R. (2003). Forecasting new product trial in a controlled test market environment. *Journal of Forecasting, 22*, 391–410.

Fader, P., Hardie, B., & Lok, L. K. (2005a). Counting your customers the easy way: An alternative to the Pareto/NBD model. *Marketing Science, 24*(2), 275–284.

Fader, P., Hardie, B., & Lok, L. K. (2005b). RFM and CLV: Using iso-value curves for customer base analysis. *Journal of Marketing Research, 42*(4), 415–430.

Fudenberg, D., & Tirole, J. (2000). Customer poaching and brand switching. *RAND Journal of Economics, 31*(4), 634–657.

Glady, N., Lemmens, A., & Croux, C. (2015). Unveiling the relationship between the transaction timing, spending and dropout behavior of customers. *International Journal of Research in Marketing, 32*(1), 78–93.

Gupta, S., & Lehmann, D. R. (2003). Customers as assets. *Journal of Interactive Marketing, 17*(1), 9–24.

Gupta, S., Lehmann, D. R., & Stuart, J. A. (2002). Valuing customers. *Journal of Marketing Research, XLI*, 7–18.

Gupta, S., Lehmann, D. R., & Stuart, J. A. (2004). Valuing customers. *Journal of Marketing Research, 41*(1), 7–18.

Gupta, S., Hanssens, D., Hardie, B., Kahn, W., Kumar, V., Lin, N., & Sriram, N. (2006). Modeling customer lifetime value. *Journal of Service Research, 9*(2), 139–155.

Hlavinka, K., & Sullivan, J. (2011). The art and science of building customer value. Colloquy.

Hogan, J. E., Lemon, K. N., & Rust, R. R. (2002). Customer equity management: Charting new directions for the future of marketing. *Journal of Service Research, 5*(1), 4–12.

Jackson, B. B. (1985). Build customer relationship that last. *Harvard Business Review, 63*, 120–128.

Jain, D., & Singh, S. (2002). Customer lifetime value research in marketing: A review and future directions. *Journal of Interactive Marketing, 16*(2), 34–46.

Jerath, K., Fader, P., & Hardie, B. (2011). New perspectives on customer death using a generalization of the Pareto/NBD model. *Marketing Science, 30*(5), 866–880.

Kahn, B. E., & Schmittlein, D. C. (1989). Shopping trip behavior: An empirical investigation. *Marketing Letters, 1*(4), 55–70.

Keane, T. J., & Wang, P. (1995). Applications for the lifetime value model in modern newspaper publishing. *Journal of Direct Marketing, 9*(2), 59–66.

Kumar, V. (2007). Customer lifetime value: The path to profitability. *Foundations & Trends in Marketing, 2*(1), 1–96.

Kumar, V., & Reinartz, W. (2006). *Customer relationship management: A databased approach.* Hoboken: Wiley.

Leenheer, J., Bijmolt, T. H. A., van Heerde, H. J., & Smidts, A. (2007). Do loyalty programs enhance behavioral loyalty? A market-wide analysis accounting for endogeneity. *International Journal of Research in Marketing, 24*(1), 31–47.

Lewis, M. (2005). Incorporating strategic consumer behavior into customer valuation. *Journal of Marketing, 69*, 230–238.

Lewis, M. (2006). Customer acquisition promotions and customer asset value. *Journal of Marketing Research, 43*(2), 195–203.

Libai, B., Narayandas, D., & Humby, C. (2002). Toward an individual customer profitability model: A segment-based approach. *Journal of Service Research, 5*(1), 69–76.

Liu, Y. (2007). The long-term impact of loyalty programs on consumer purchase behavior and loyalty. *Journal of Marketing, 71*(4), 19–35.

Meyer-Waarden, L. (2007). The effects of loyalty programs on customer lifetime duration and share of wallet. *Journal of Retailing, 83*(2), 223–236.

Meyer-Waarden, L., & Benavent, C. (2009). Retail loyalty program effects: Self-selection or purchase behavior change? *Journal of the Academy of Marketing Science, 3*(3), 345–358.

Morgan, R., & Hunt, S. (1994). The commitment-trust theory of relationship marketing. *Journal of Marketing, 58*(3), 20–38. doi:10.2307/1252308.

Morrison, D., & Schmittlein, D. (1988). Generalizing the NBD model for customer purchases: What are the implications and is it worth the effort? *Journal of Business and Economic Statistic, 6*, 145–159.

Narasimhan, C. (1984). A price discrimination theory of coupons. *Marketing Science*, Spring 84, *3*(2), 128–147.

Newcomb, S. (1886). A generalized theory of the combination of observations so as to obtain the best result. *American Journal of Mathematics, 8*, 343–366.

Pearson, K. (1894). Contributions to the mathematical theory of evolution. *Philosophical Transactions, A185*, 71–110.

Pfeifer, P. E., & Carraway, R. L. (2000). Modeling customer relationships as Markov chains. *Journal of Interactive Marketing, 14*(2), 43–55.

R Development Core Team. (2010). *R: A language and environment for statistical computing.* Vienna: R Foundation for Statistical Computing.

Reinartz, W. J., & Kumar, V. (2000). On the profitability of long-life customers in a noncontractual setting: An empirical investigation and implications for marketing. *Journal of Marketing, 64*(4), 17–35.

Reinartz, W., & Kumar, V. (2003). The impact of customer relationship characteristics on profitable lifetime duration. *Journal of Marketing, 67*(1), 77–99.

Reinartz, W. J., Thomas, J. S., & Kumar, V. (2005). Balancing acquisition and retention resources to maximize customer profitability. *Journal of Marketing, 69*, 63–79.

Rogers, E. M. (2003). *Diffusion of innovations*. New York: Free Press.

Rust, R. T., Lemon, K. A., & Zeithaml, V. A. (2004). Return on marketing: Using customer equity to focus marketing strategy. *Journal of Marketing, 68*(1), 109–127.

Ryals, L. (2005). Making customer relationship management work: The measurement and profitable management of customer relationships. *Journal of Marketing, 69*(4), 252–261.

Schmittlein, D., & Peterson, R. (1994). Customer case analysis: An industrial purchase process application. *Marketing Science, 13*(1), 41–67.

Schmittlein, D., Morrison, D., & Colombo, R. (1987). Counting your customers: Who are they and what will they do next? *Management Science, 33*(1), 1–24.

Schulze, C., Skiera, B., & Wiesel, T. (2012). Linking customer and financial metrics to shareholder value: The leverage effect in customer-based valuation. *Journal of Marketing, 76*(2), 17–32.

Schweidel, D. A., & Fader, P. S. (2009). Dynamic change points revisited. An evolving process model of new product sales. *International Journal of Research in Marketing, 26*(2), 119–124.

Schweidel, D. A., Fader, P. S., & Bradlow, E. T. (2008). Understanding service retention within and across cohorts using limited information. *Journal of Marketing, 72*, 82–94.

Simester, D. I., Sun, P., & Tsitsiklis, J. N. (2006). Dynamic catalog mailing policies. *Management Science, 52*(5), 683–696.

Stauss, B., & Friege, C. (1999). Regaining service customers: Costs and benefits of regain management. *Journal of Service Research, 1*(4), 347–361.

Tarasi, C., Bolton, R., Hutt, M., & Walker, B. (2011). Balancing risk and return in a customer portfolio. *Journal of Marketing, 75*(3), 1–17.

Temporal, P., & Trott, M. (2001). *Romancing the customer: Maximising brand value through powerful relationship management*. New York: Wiley.

Thomas, J., Blattberg, R., & Fox, E. (2004). Recapturing lost customers. *Journal of Marketing Research, 38*(2), 31–45.

Venkatesan, R., & Kumar, V. (2004). A customer lifetime value framework for customer selection and resource allocation strategy. *Journal of Marketing, 68*(4), 106–125.

Villanueva, J., & Hanssens, D. (2007). Customer equity: Measurement, management and research opportunities. *Foundations and Trends® in Marketing, 1*(1), 1–95.

Villanueva, J., Yoo, S., & Hanssens, D. M. (2008). The impact of marketing-induced versus word-of-mouth customer acquisition on customer equity growth. *Journal of Marketing Research, 45*(1), 48–59.

Wedel, M., Desarbo, W. S., Bult, J. R., & Ramaswamy, V. (1993). A latent class Poisson regression model for heterogeneous count data. *Journal of Applied Econometrics, 8*(4), 397–411.

Wiesel, T., Skiera, B., & Villanueva, J. (2008). Customer equity: An integral part of financial reporting. *Journal of Marketing, 72*, 1–14.

Assessing the Financial Impact of Brand Equity with Short Time-Series Data

Natalie Mizik and Eugene Pavlov

Contents

Introduction	1036
Marketing Academics' Views on the Measurement of Brand Equity	1037
Customer Mindset Brand Equity	1039
Product Market-Based Brand Equity	1040
Financial Market-Based Brand Equity	1041
Assessing Long-Term Impact of Brand Equity	1043
Empirical Illustration	1046
Total Financial Impact of Brand Asset	1048
Heterogeneity in Brand Equity Impact	1049
Conclusion	1051
References	1053

Abstract

In this chapter, we describe an approach to estimating the total long-term impact of brand perceptions on financial performance. The approach relies on modeling the stock market reactions to changes in brand perceptions and allows estimating their total impact even with limited time-series data. We present an application of the method to the Y&R Brand Asset Valuator (BAV) data. The analyses show that, on average, the bulk of brand impact on financial performance is realized in the future and the contemporaneous effects reflect only a small portion of the total impact. The analyses, however, also show considerable heterogeneity across industries: while in some industries the whole impact of brand asset occurs in current period only (restaurants), in other industries it occurs in future periods only (high-tech). Further, some components of consumer perceptions have differential effects in different industries. Returns to brand building, and to

---

N. Mizik (✉) · E. Pavlov
Foster School of Business, University of Washington, Seattle, WA, USA
e-mail: nmizik@uw.edu; epavlov@uw.edu

© Springer Nature Switzerland AG 2022
C. Homburg et al. (eds), *Handbook of Market Research*,
https://doi.org/10.1007/978-3-319-57413-4_31

marketing efforts in general, should not be evaluated based on contemporaneous outcomes, but should rather be evaluated over a long-time horizon.

> **Keywords**
>
> Brand equity · Customer mindset · Financial impact · Heterogeneity · Dynamic panel · Instrumental variables

Introduction

Aaker (2012, p. 7) defines brand equity as a "set of assets (and liabilities) linked to a brand's name and symbol that adds to (or subtracts from) the value provided by a product or service to a firm and/or that firm's customers." Brand equity stems from the ability of a brand to create awareness and favorable image in consumer minds. It allows the branded product to accrue extra profit over an extended period of time compared to a nonbranded product with comparable physical attributes. The benefits of strong brand equity can be observed in greater sales, higher profitability, or greater market valuation of a firm. There is, however, no easy method for assessing financial impact of a brand, and there is no comprehensive and unambiguous approach to the measurement of brand equity.

One reason a standardized approach to brand equity measurement and assessment of its impact on financial performance is lacking is that brand is an abstract construct, a mental structure of values, perceptions, and attitudes that resides in consumer minds (Pavlov and Mizik 2017). The process of brand equity formation is inherently psychological and is very complex (Keller 1993). Much work is still needed to understand the mental structure that represents a brand and to achieve consensus within academic and practitioner community on the concept and general model of brand equity.

Another complication impeding the development of a standardized tool for measuring brand equity stems from the fact that brand equity is often a product of long-term marketing effort. It takes a long time to build brand equity because the effect of marketing effort on consumer perceptions, associations, and attitudes is not immediate, but rather can take a long time to materialize. That is, there is a high level of persistence and inertia to brand equity.

Please consider the case of Martha Stewart Living Omnimedia, Inc. Following the 2002 scandal involving Martha Stewart's sale of ImClone stock – which prompted insider trading and perjury investigations by the SEC and FBI –both the Martha Stewart brand perceptions and the stock price of Martha Stewart Living Omnimedia plummeted (Fig. 1). The negative impact of brand damage on sales and profits, however, took several years to manifest itself (Fig. 2) and in the long run neither the brand perceptions nor firm performance ever fully recovered to the prescandal levels. The Martha Stewart case shows that contemporaneous accounting performance metrics (such as sales or operating income) can severely underestimate the full impact of a brand.

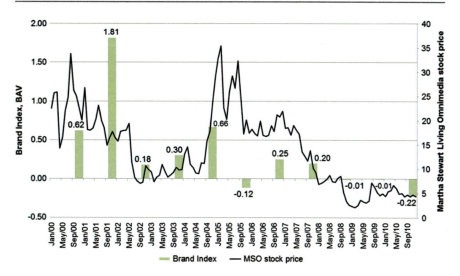

Fig. 1 Martha Stewart Living Omnimedia, Inc. stock price and Brand Perceptions of Martha Stewart brand (Brand Index)Brand Index is computed as a z-standardized equally weighted average of perceived brand Differentiation, Relevance, Esteem, Knowledge, and Energy over the sample of publicly traded monobrand firms in the BAV database in the 2000–2010 period

In this chapter, we describe an approach to estimating the total long-term impact of brand perceptions on financial performance. The approach relies on modeling the stock market reactions to changes in brand perceptions and closely follows Mizik (2014). Just as the case of Martha Stewart's scandal suggests, the analyses show that the bulk of brand impact on financial performance is realized in the future and the contemporaneous effects significantly underestimate the total impact. The analyses also show considerable heterogeneity across industries: while in some industries the whole impact of brand assets occurs in the current period only (restaurants), in other industries it occurs in future periods only (high-tech). Further, different components of consumer perceptions have differential effects across industries.

Marketing Academics' Views on the Measurement of Brand Equity

Academic researchers of brand equity have approached the construct from different viewpoints and proposed various metrics and methods for assessing brand equity. Keller and Lehmann (2003) suggest that brand equity can be measured at three different levels: customer mindset, product market, and financial market. Customer-mindset approach to measuring brand equity stems from the psychological value consumers attach to a branded product, and focuses on assessing two major constructs of brand awareness and brand image. This method primarily relies on consumer surveys. Product-market approach to measuring brand equity (e.g., Kamakura and Russel 1993; Ailawadi et al. 2003; Srinivasan et al. 2005) evaluates

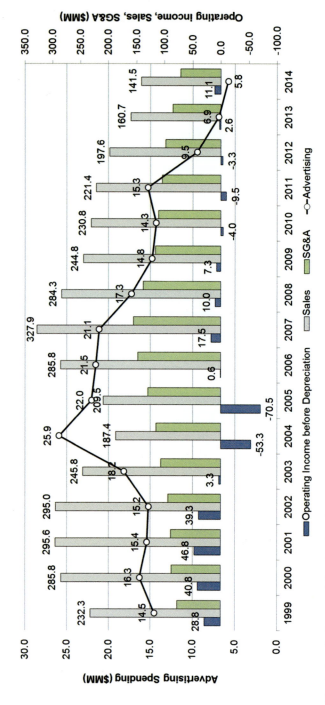

Fig. 2 Martha Stewart Living Omnimedia, Inc. operating performance indicators 1999–2014

incremental preference for a branded compared to a nonbranded product which manifests in incremental market share or price, revenue, or profit premium for the branded product. This approach combines survey-based methods with secondary data and makes use of conjoint analysis or purchase histories and scanner panel data. Financial-market-based approach (e.g., Simon and Sullivan 1993; Aaker and Jacobson 1994, 2001; Mizik and Jacobson 2009) aims to estimate incremental value (cash flows) arising from brand assets. Under this method, survey data is combined with secondary data from the stock market and accounting/financial statements to estimate the total value brand asset is expected to generate for its owner in the long run.

Customer Mindset Brand Equity

From a customer mindset perspective, positive brand equity exists when "consumer is familiar with the brand and holds some favorable, strong, and unique brand associations in memory" (Keller 1993, p. 2). Measuring brand equity from a consumer mindset perspective means dealing with familiarity and associations – constructs which are highly subjective and not directly observable. The abstract nature of consumer mindset-based brand equity gave rise to various proposals on what brand equity components are and what metrics are appropriate (e.g., Pappu et al. 2005; Lassar et al. 1995; Yoo and Donthu 2001). Most discussions of customer mindset-based brand equity center on constructs of brand familiarity and brand associations customers hold. Most of the proposed measurement approaches are, naturally, based on surveys and questionnaires.

Keller and Lehman (2003, p. 27), for example, recognize five components of customer mindset-based brand equity: awareness, associations, attitudes, attachment, and activity. Aaker (1996) advocates the idea of "Brand Equity Ten" – ten indicators contributing to brand asset value. Of the five subcategories (awareness, associations/differentiation, perceived quality/leadership, loyalty, market behavior), the first four are survey-based measures. Aaker (2012) notes that survey-based measures "can be expensive, inconvenient, time consuming, hard to implement/ interpret." Indeed, they are. With advent of the Web 2.0, however, it is becoming cheaper and easier to collect some customer mind-set branding data (Lee and Bradlow 2011; Netzer et al. 2012; Liu et al. 2017). These new approaches are often based on natural language processing techniques. They allow compiling relevant customer mindset-based metrics bypassing costly traditional surveying.

The various approaches to assess customer mindset-based brand equity can be classified into two broad categories: direct and indirect. Surveys fall into the category of "direct" measurement of customer mindset brand equity. Direct approaches also include studying customer response to marketing activities through experiments: the treatment group is exposed to marketing actions attributed to a particular brand, while control group is exposed to marketing actions attributed to a generic or unknown brand (Keller 1993, p. 13). "Blind" tests are examples of such experiments (Allison and Uhl 1964). Conjoint analysis is another direct method, which allows to rank relative importance of product/service attributes/features based on customers' stated preferences and perceptions and to estimate price premium due to the brand (Rangaswamy et al. 1993). Cobb-Walgren et al. (1995, p.35), for example, conduct a conjoint analysis for the hotel industry and find that brand name is the fourth most important attribute after price, bed size, and availability of a pool. "Indirect" approach includes association tasks, interpretation of imagery, brand personality descriptors, etc. (Keller 1993, p. 12), and is far less suitable for translating into financial value.

Some brand perceptions and attitudes are collected through large-scale consumer surveys. Brand Asset Valuator by Young and Rubicam, EquiTrend by Harris Poll, Millward Brown's Brand Z are the main industry providers in this area. While brand attitude and perceptions data can be very valuable for brand management per se, they do not offer direct insight into the financial value of the brand. These perceptions and attitude data, however, can be used as a building block in the development of financial market-based measures of brand equity. We discuss these methods later in this chapter in more detail.

Product Market-Based Brand Equity

Under the product-market approach, brand equity is understood as the incremental value (e.g., in terms of market share, price, revenue, or profit) a branded product generates compared to its nonbranded analogue. For instance, in Park and Srinivasan (1994, p. 273), brand equity is conceptualized as an "incremental preference endowed by the brand to the product as perceived by an individual consumer." The authors suggest that brand equity stems from the difference between the overall product preference and objective preference, which is based on attribute-by-attribute evaluation. They use individual-level secondary data on actual in-store purchases to estimate this difference. Based on an empirical application of the model to the market of toothpaste and mouthwash, the authors found substantial effects of brand's equity on market share. For example, 12.2% of Colgate's 21.8% market share was attributed to brand equity and, compared to the store brand, Colgate-Palmolive was able to charge an estimated 37 cents more. The measures of brand equity obtained using this approach are relative: they do not reflect the absolute value of brand equity for a given brand. Rather, they provide an estimate of brand equity in comparison to another brand.

Srinivasan et al. (2005, p. 1433) define brand equity as an "incremental contribution per year obtained by the brand in comparison to the same product (or service) at the same price but without brand-building efforts (i.e., base product)." Using individual-level data the authors estimate incremental choice probability of a branded versus a base product for an individual customer. Three distinct sources of brand equity value were considered: brand awareness, nonattribute preference, and enhanced attribute perceptions (i.e., attribute perceptions compared to the base product's attribute perceptions). Using consumer data from the mobile phone market in South Korea, the authors obtain estimates of brand equity and its components for four leading companies. Brand equity of Samsung is estimated to provide 34.8% of Samsung's 52.5% market share. Total value of brand equity obtained from incremental choice probabilities is estimated at $127 MM for Samsung, $69 MM for LG, $32 MM for Motorola, and $9 MM for Qualcomm (p. 1445). As for components of brand equity, awareness was found to have the strongest effect, followed by non-attribute preference and enhanced attribute perceptions.

Ailawadi et al. (2003) propose revenue premium – the difference in revenue between a branded good and a corresponding private label – as a measure of brand equity. The advantage of this measure is in simultaneously capturing the effects of brand equity on both price and volume. Studying a major grocery retailer in 1991–1996, the authors calculated yearly revenue premia for 111 brands and documented a median decrease in revenue premia of 11%. One of the challenges for the revenue premium calculation lies in identifying an appropriate benchmark brand or generic to compare prices and volumes with. That is, the revenue premium is a relative and not an absolute measure of brand equity as store brands are brands in their own right. Another challenge is the proper market definition for a particular brand. The revenue premium measure reflects the effect of competition. That is, the same brand might have a much greater revenue premium in the market where few competitors are present versus the market where there are many options for consumers to choose from. Other concerns with the revenue premium model have been noted in the literature and include its failure to account for the costs of brand management and maintenance and the lack of temporal dimension (only contemporaneous effects on sales are captured). For example, Srinivasan et al. (2005) suggest that profit premium would be a better measure of brand equity and advocate for assessing long-term brand-induced incremental profits.

Product-market models for estimating brand equity value provide important insights by leveraging secondary data (often, scanner panel data of actual purchase histories). They allow attributing observed differences in market shares and prices charged by producers in the same product category to psychological value consumers derive from choosing a particular brand. The limitations of product market-based models stem from (1) the relative nature of brand equity estimates (i.e., estimate of brand equity is defined in comparison to another brand) (2) subjectivity involved in the choice of an appropriate benchmark and/or a market definition, and (3) lack of temporal consideration for the brand effects. As the case of Martha Stewart illustrates, a large portion of the brand value might be missing in contemporaneous (same-year) product market performance metrics.

Financial Market-Based Brand Equity

The financial market-based approach to valuing brands views brands as assets capable of generating stream of profits over a long period of time. Financial market-based valuation of brand equity is "forward-looking" (Simon and Sullivan 1993, p. 32) in the sense that it reflects the sum of the discounted incremental future cash flows attributable to the brand. Under this view, the value of brand assets is a portion of the company's stock market capitalization. As such, any changes in the brand assets will be reflected in the market valuation of the company.

Accounting Valuation of Brands

It is important to highlight the distinction between the market-based and accounting-based valuation of brands. Internally generated intangibles, including brands, are not included on the balance sheet. Exclusion of brands and other intangibles from the balance sheet gives rise to sizeable discrepancies between the book value and the market value of a company. For example, Sinclair and Keller (2014, p. 294) discuss the $200 billion market capitalization of Procter & Gamble at the time when its net tangible assets are a negative $18.7 billion.

Although internally generated brand assets are not on the balance sheets, brand assets acquired in business combinations (e.g., acquisitions) are recognized as assets and placed on the balance sheet of the acquirer (Cañibano et al. 2000; Austin 2007). Various valuation methods are used to arrive at the value of acquired brands. The most commonly used approaches employ earnings split (estimating the portion of the earnings attributable to the brand and projecting future earnings and discount factors) and relief from royalty (estimating the "royalty savings" from owning a brand based on a set of comparable brands, where royalty structure is known, and projecting future earnings) analyses. Both types of analyses involve significant subjective judgment in attributing earnings or selecting comparables and projecting future earnings and discount factors. Bahadir et al. (2008) report that the recognized value of brands in M&A transactions varies widely (it ranged from 1.16% to 49.7% of the transaction value) and comment that the value of a brand lies "in the eye of the beholder."

Financial Market Value-Relevance of Brands

Simon and Sullivan (1993, p. 29) define brand equity as "the incremental cash flows which accrue to branded products over and above the cash flows which would result from the sale of unbranded products." They criticize product market-based metrics of assessing brand equity such as price premium. Price premium method (1) does not account for brand's ability to reduce marketing costs in future periods and (2) it might be confounded with high-quality product attributes, resulting in biased estimates of brand equity value. Simon and Sullivan (1993) estimate that brand equity accounts for 19% of tangible asset value for the 638 firms in their sample.

Barth et al. (1998) analyzed stock market valuation of Interbrand's brand value measures. Controlling for fiscal year fixed effect, book value of equity per share, earnings per share from continuing operations, the authors found a significant association between stock price at the end of fiscal year and the Interbrand's brand value estimate. Madden et al. (2006) used World's Most Valuable brands (WMVB) ranking by Interbrand to compare performance of companies owning highly valuable brands to companies that do not. They construct a portfolio of 111 companies on the WMVB list and compare its performance against a benchmark portfolio comprised of all other companies in the CRSP database. The WMVB portfolio outperformed the benchmark and delivered higher returns with significantly smaller risk, as measured by market Beta (the coefficient on market return in Fama-French model). A concern that has been raised with these analyses relates to the fact that Interbrand and other providers are not fully transparent on how brand values are calculated and that they use market capitalization of the firm as one of the inputs in their calculations of brand value (Hrustic 2012).

A few studies have lined customer mindset-based measures of brand equity directly to company stock performance. Aaker and Jacobson (1994) study the association between perceived product quality (EquiTrend) and stock returns. The authors find that perceived quality is significantly associated with stock market returns and has incremental explanatory power over ROI (profitability). Aaker and Jacobson (2001) apply a similar approach to a survey-based brand attitude measure (positive/neutral/negative) for a high-tech company (Techtel) and find a significant positive effect of brand attitude on abnormal stock return.

Mizik and Jacobson (2008) used Young & Rubicam Brand Asset Valuator (BAV) data to assess the financial value relevance of perceptual brand attributes. Based on eight waves of a large-scale annual customer survey, they examined five pillars of brand perceptions (differentiation, relevance, esteem, knowledge, and energy) to assess their incremental information content. Of the five pillars, relevance and energy were found to be significantly positively associated with abnormal stock returns and no contemporaneous effect of differentiation, esteem, or knowledge on stock returns has been found. However, the authors detected a significant effect of prior year change in differentiation on unanticipated changes in earnings, which suggested the existence of a market anomaly: past changes in brand differentiation predicting current abnormal returns. Additional analyses revealed a significant difference in mean abnormal stock returns for companies with brands which gained in perceived brand differentiation in the prior year versus companies with decreased brand differentiation in prior year and attributed this anomaly to the lack of transparency (private information) in brand strategy.

Most empirical studies employing financial market-based approach have focused on assessing the value relevance and incremental information content of various brand metrics (see Mizik and Jacobson (2009) for an exception and an illustration of comparables-based valuation approach to valuing brand assets). Mizik (2014) proposed extending the method to explicitly address their total *long-term* financial impact. We discuss the theoretical and empirical foundations of this approach and present an empirical illustration below.

Assessing Long-Term Impact of Brand Equity

Brands have both contemporaneous and delayed effects on firm profitability. Figure 3 depicts the dynamic framework of brand financial impact. γ_0 is the contemporaneous effect of brand asset on earnings. It reflects both the costs associated with developing the brand asset at time t and the realized incremental revenue which accrued due to the brand asset at time t. γ_0 can be positive or negative, depending on whether the costs or the incremental revenue effect dominates. λ_0 is the contemporaneous impact

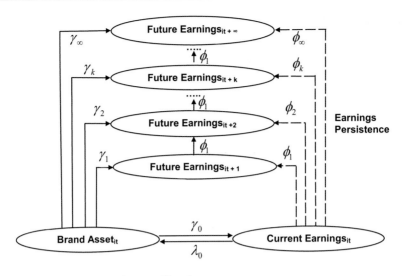

Fig. 3 Dynamic performance impact of brand assets

of earnings on brand asset. It too can be positive (if the firms increase brand asset building effort when profits increase) or negative (if the firms increase brand asset building when profitability falters).

γ_1 represents the impact of brand asset developed at time t on earnings in period t+1. Because the brand asset was developed in time period t (i.e., the development cost occurred in period t), γ_1 is nonnegative for value-generating brand assets (it is negative if the brand asset is value destroying, like poor reputation). γ_k represents the delayed impact of brand asset and is the *direct* impact of Brand Asset (t) on earnings in period (t+k).

The total long-term impact of brand asset on profitability, however, exceeds the sum of its direct impacts described above. Because earnings persist (in Fig. 3, the dynamic coefficients ϕ_k indicate that current level of earnings depends on previous period earnings), a portion of contemporaneous impact of brand asset is carried over to future periods through earnings dynamics. A shock to earnings in period t is partially carried over to period (t+1). The indirect effect of brand asset on earnings in period t+1 equals to $\gamma_0 * \phi_1$ and the total effect in period t+1 is equal to $\gamma_1 + \gamma_0 * \phi_1$. The total long-term impact of Brand Asset (t) on firm financial performance is the aggregate sum over all direct and indirect effects.

The estimation of the total impact of brand asset on profitability as depicted in Fig. 3 with standard distributed lag panel data models is typically not feasible because time series of branding data are often limited. However, under the assumption of efficient markets, the stock market-based approach can be implemented even with limited time-series data.

Under the hypothesis of financial markets efficiency (Fama 1970), the stock market value of a firm incorporates all information and rational expectations of a company's future financial performance. Unexpected changes in firm's brand assets lead to changes in expected future cash flows and induce investors to recalculate company valuation. This change in firm valuation serves as an unbiased estimate of the total impact the change in brand asset is expected to generate in the long run.

Figure 4 summarizes the estimation framework. The interpretation of γ_0 and λ_0 coefficients remains the same as in Fig. 3. The future impact of brand asset (represented by coefficients γ_k, with k>0, in Fig. 3) is now captured in the β_2 coefficient. The framework depicted in Fig. 4 generates the following two estimation equations:

$$StkRet_{it} = Eret_{it} + \beta_1 \Delta ROA_{it} + \beta_2 \Delta BrandAsset_{it} + \epsilon_{1it}, \qquad (1)$$

$$\Delta ROA_{it} = \gamma_0 \Delta BrandAsset_{it} + \epsilon_{2it}, \text{where} \qquad (2)$$

$StkRet_{it}$ is the stock return for firm i at time t, $Eret_{it}$ is the expected return, ΔROA_{it} is the unanticipated change in size-adjusted earnings, $\Delta BrandAsset_{it}$ is the unanticipated change in the brand asset, ϵ_{1it} and ϵ_{2it} are i.i.d. normal error terms.

Several issues arise with the estimation of Eqs. 1 and 2. First, one needs to obtain the unanticipated components of ROA_{it} and $BrandAsset_{it}$ series. Second, γ_0 in Eq. 2 could be estimated consistently only under no simultaneity condition (i.e., no feedback from ΔROA_{it} to $\Delta BrandAsset_{it}$). That is, only if λ_0 is equal to zero.

Estimating Eqs. 1 and 2 generates both contemporaneous (γ_0) and long-term direct (β_2) impact of brand asset on financial performance. The indirect effect of $\Delta BrandAsset_{it}$ on future earnings occurs because the contemporaneous impact of $\Delta BrandAsset_{it}$ on ΔROA_{it} is transferred through the earnings-response coefficient β_1.

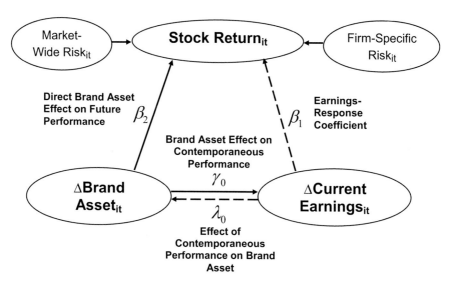

Fig. 4 Estimating framework for assessing the total financial impact of band aAsset using the stock market-based approach

This indirect effect of brand asset on earnings equals to $\gamma_0 * \beta_1$. Hence, the total financial impact of brand asset on profitability is equal to the sum of direct future effect and the indirect effects: $\beta_2 + \gamma_0 * \beta_1$.

Empirical Illustration

The empirical application below draws on several data sources. Stock return data and the Fama-French-Carhart risk factors come from the Chicago's Center for Research in Security Prices (CRSP). The accounting data come from the quarterly Compustat database. Profitability (ROA) is measured as operating income before depreciation over assets. Brand perceptions data come from the 2000–2010 Y&R's BAV database. It includes 444 monobrand publicly traded firms. The measure of Brand Asset Index is a z-standardized index comprised of five brand perceptions of (1) differentiation, (2) relevance, (3) esteem, (4) knowledge, and (5) energy. The perceptual constructs used in constructing the Brand Asset Index and their measurement are discussed in detail in Mizik and Jacobson (2008).

Calculating Abnormal Stock Returns

Abnormal stock returns are calculated using Fama-French (1993) model augmented with the momentum factor (Carhart's 1997) and with risk characteristics of size and book-to-market (Daniel and Titman 1997), but findings are robust to alternative definitions of abnormal returns:

$$Ret_{it} - Ret_{riskfree,t} = a_t + \beta_{mkt}(Ret_{mkt,t} - Ret_{riskfree,t}) + s(SMB_t) + h(HML_t) + m(MOM_t) + \eta_t Size_{it-1} + \nu_t BookMarket_{it-1} + u_{it}, where \quad (3)$$

Ret_{it} is stock return of firm i at period t, $Ret_{riskfree,t}$ is risk-free return at time t, $Ret_{mkt,t}$ is market return at time t, SMB_t is difference between large and small book-to-market ratio firms at period t, HML_t is difference between high and low capitalization firms at period t, MOM_t is Carhart's (1997) momentum at period t, $Size_{it-1}$ is firm-specific risk characteristic of size, calculated as log of lagged market value, $BookMarket_{it-1}$ is firm-specific risk characteristic of book-to-market, calculated as log of lagged book value over market value. Abnormal stock returns are the residuals from this regression, u_{it}.

Calculating Unanticipated Components of ROA and Brand Asset Index

Estimating Eqs. 1 and 2 requires computing a measure of unanticipated change in size-adjusted earnings or "earnings surprise" (ΔROA_{it}). Because ROA series exhibit significant persistence and seasonality, a four-quarter autoregressive fixed effects model is used to approximate the data-generating process:

$$ROA_{iq} = a_i + \sum_{k=1}^{4} \phi_k ROA_{iq-k} + \sum_{q=1}^{Q} \delta_q \times Time_q + e_{iq} \quad (4)$$

a_i is the firm-specific indicator, $Time_q$ is the time period (year-quarter) indicator, and ϕ_k is the quarter k autoregressive coefficient. a_i and ϕ_k can be consistently estimated using Anderson-Hsiao (1982) or Arellano-Bond (1991) instrumental variables approach. First, the data is recomputed in terms of deviations from year-quarter-specific means (to cancel out time-period fixed effects δ_q). Then, first differences of series are taken to remove fixed effects a_i. Lagged values of ROA serve as instrumental variables for the first lag of ΔROA (ROA_{iq-2} and ROA_{iq-3} instrument for $[ROA_{iq-1} - ROA_{iq-2}]$).

Table 1 reports the results of this estimation. The 1st-order and the 4th-order lags of ROA have the highest autoregressive coefficients indicating the presence of strong seasonality. The measure of annual earnings surprise (ΔROA_{it}) is computed as a sum of prediction errors ($ROA_{iq} - \hat{ROA}_{iq}$) over the four quarters in a given year.

With short time series of branding data it is often impossible to use the same procedure to estimate unanticipated components of BAIndex. However, instead of modeling dynamics of the marketing metric directly, one can evaluate the stock market's beliefs about its dynamics. The market beliefs about the dynamic properties of brand equity metric can be assessed with the following model:

$$AbnormalStkRet_{it} = \beta_1 \Delta ROA_{it} + \beta_2^* (BAIndex_{it} - \beta_0 BAIndex_{(it-1)}) + \epsilon_{it}, \text{where} \quad (5)$$

ϕ_0 is the persistence in brand index series.
Equation 5 could be rewritten as

$$AbnormalStkRet_{it} = \beta_1 \Delta ROA_{it} + \beta_2^* BAIndex_{it} + \beta_2^0 BAIndex_{it-1} + \epsilon_{it} \quad (6)$$

A finding of $\beta_2^* + \beta_2^0 = 0$ would suggest that ϕ_0 is equal to one and that $BAIndex_{it}$ contains a unit root. Because that is the case in our data sample, the surprise in brand asset index can be defined as the first difference of Brand Asset Index series: $\Delta BAIndex_{it} = BAIndex_{it} - BAIndex_{it-1}$. If no unit root in $BAIndex_{it}$ is detected, then the surprise in brand asset index can be computed as $\Delta BAIndex_{it} = BAIndex_{it} - \phi_0 BAIndex_{it-1}$, where ϕ_0 is the estimate from Eq. (5). In situations when sufficient time series of a marketing metric are available, the surprise can be

Table 1 Fourth-order autoregressive fixed-effects instrumental variable regression for ROA

	Estimate	SE	t-statistic
ϕ_1[a]	.28131**	.02397	11.74
ϕ_2	.05048**	.01298	3.89
ϕ_3	.01645*	.00989	1.66
ϕ_4	.66795**	.00508	131.39
Number of obs	22,526		
F-statistic	6509.75		

*$p < .10$; **$p < .01$
[a]Denotes the use of IV estimation

computed following the approach described above for calculating ΔROA_{it}: [1] estimate an autoregressive panel model for the marketing metric, [2] calculate the residuals from the autoregressive model. These residuals then serve as $\Delta BAIndex_{it}$.

Assessing the Presence of Simultaneity

Because we are working with short time series of BAIndex, we cannot address potential simultaneity bias in γ_0 directly (an appropriate instrument cannot be constructed due to short time series of BAIndex). But we can assess potential simultaneity between earnings (ROA) and BAIndex by estimating the following dynamic panel models because the ROA time series are sufficiently long such that an instrument for ROA can be constructed:

$$BAIndex_{it} = a_{BA,i} + \lambda_0 ROA_{it} + \lambda_1 ROA_{it-1} + \lambda_2 ROA_{it-2} + \delta_t Year_t + \kappa_{1,it} \quad (7)$$

$$BAIndex_{it} = a_{BA,i} + \lambda_0 ROA_{it} + \lambda_1 ROA_{it-1} + \lambda_2 ROA_{it-2} + \phi_1 BAIndex_{it-1} \\ + \phi_2 BAIndex_{it-2} + \delta_t Year_t + \kappa_{2,it} \quad (8)$$

Here, λ_0 measures the contemporaneous impact of earnings on brand perceptions. A finding of $\lambda_0 = 0$ would suggest that no simultaneity is present (that is, earnings do not have a contemporaneous effect on brand perceptions). Estimating Eqs. 7 and 8, again, requires taking the first differences of the data to remove the fixed effects and using the instrumental variables approach. The estimated coefficient $\hat{\lambda}_0$ is small and insignificant in both models. Estimating model Eq. 7 generates $\hat{\lambda}_0 = 0.98$ (SE=9.90) and $\hat{\lambda}_0 = -15.55$ (SE=12.69) in model Eq. 8. As such, we find no evidence of feedback from contemporaneous earnings to Brand Asset Index.

If $\lambda_0 \neq 0$, OLS estimate of γ_0 in Eq. 2 will be biased and inconsistent due to presence of feedback loop effect. We refer the reader to Chap. 15 in Greene (2002) for the discussion on consistent estimation in simultaneous-equations models.

Total Financial Impact of Brand Asset

The total financial impact of Brand Asset Index can be assessed by estimating Eq. 2 and Eq. 9 below. Because no simultaneity is present in our sample, the total financial impact can also be estimated directly after substituting Eq. 2 into Eq. 9 to obtain estimating Eq. 10:

$$AbnRet_{it} = \beta_1 \Delta ROA_{it} + \beta_2 \Delta BAIndex_{it} + e_{1it} \quad (9)$$

$$AbnRet_{it} = \psi \Delta BAIndex_{it} + e_{2it}, \text{where} \psi = \beta_2 + \gamma_0^* \beta_1 \quad (10)$$

The results of estimating Eqs. 9 and 10 are presented in Table 2. The information content in BAIndex is significantly and positively associated with abnormal stock return of a firm. It is positive and significant in both formulations – with and without including ROA information in the estimating equation. The estimates reported in Table 2 indicate that Brand Asset Index has a direct impact on stock returns of 0.068,

Table 2 Direct future and total performance impact of the BAIndex[a]

	Model Eq. 8	Model Eq. 9
Unanticipated change in BAIndex	.068** .080 (.018)	.07568** .089 (.019)
Unanticipated change in ROA	3.18** .291 (.235)	
F-statistic	99.96	15.67
N	1956	1956

*$p < .10$; **$p < .01$
[a]Standardized regression coefficients are in *italics*, standard errors are in *parentheses*

which is incremental to ROA. The total impact of Brand Asset Index on stock return is 0.07568.

Based on the estimates reported in Table 2, one can ascertain the dynamics of Brand Asset Index impact on stock return and break down the total impact into its direct and indirect components. Difference in the estimates of BAIndex coefficient in Eqs. 9 and 10 is 0.07568−0.068=0.008. This difference is the indirect effect of Brand Asset Index on abnormal returns (which occurs through earnings persistence). That is, the immediate impact of Brand Asset Index on ROA is equal to 0.0025 (0.008/3.184). This suggests that only approximately 3.3% (0.0025/0.07568) of Brand Asset Index impact is realized in contemporaneous operating income, and the bulk of the impact occurs in future periods.

Heterogeneity in Brand Equity Impact

Sector-Specific Differences in the Impact of Brand Asset Index

One interesting research question remains: are the effects of Brand Asset uniform across different industrial sectors? Results of sector-specific analyses suggest that there exists a significant heterogeneity in the dynamics of the Brand Asset Index impact across different industrial sectors. Table 3 presents the results of estimating models Eq. 9 and 10 in six sectors: financial, distribution/retail, restaurants, computer/Internet, pharmaceuticals, and travel/entertainment.

We observe no significant findings for BAIndex for either finance or for travel/entertainment sectors. For distribution/retail sector, the estimates of BAIndex are largely in line with the aggregate findings reported in Table 2: the immediate impact of BAIndex on ROA is small. It can be calculated as (0.101−0.078)/4.125=0.006, which is about 5.5% of the total impact. That is, approximately 95% of the effect of Brand Asset is realized in the future. The pattern for the high-tech sectors (computer/Internet and pharmaceuticals) suggests that all of the BAIndex effect is realized in the future periods. This finding implies that a success or failure of brand-building efforts in these industries cannot be determined using contemporaneous product-market performance measures. Finally, in the restaurant sector, all of the effect of

Table 3 Differential impact of brand asset index by sector

	Finance	Distribution/ Retail	Computer/ Internet	Pharmaceutical	Restaurants	Travel/ Entertainment
Panel A. Direct future impact of the BAIndex (equation model 9)						
Unanticipated change in the BAIndex	0.036 (0.092)	0.078* (0.041)	0.121*** (0.045)	0.141*** (0.050)	0.083 (0.093)	0.116 (0.135)
Unanticipated change in ROA	5.607*** (1.792)	4.125*** (0.565)	2.236*** (0.471)	2.110*** (0.86)	5.968*** (1.103)	3.669 (2.335)
F-stat	5.15	29.79	14.43	6.60	17.06	1.37
N obs	172	379	420	61	106	91
Panel B. Total performance impact of the BAIndex (equation model 10)						
Unanticipated change in the BAIndex	0.066 (0.094)	0.101** (0.043)	0.113** (0.046)	0.144*** (0.060)	0.199* (0.102)	0.069 (0.132)
F-stat	0.49	5.5	6.06	6.58	3.82	0.27
N obs	172	379	420	61	106	91

*$p < .10$; **$p < .05$; ***$p < .01$
Standard errors in *parentheses*

BAIndex (0.199) comes from its effect on contemporaneous earnings and no direct future effect exists. That is, if branding initiatives did not generate immediate (same-year) benefits, there is unlikely to be any benefit in the future periods either.

Component-Specific Differences in the Impact of Brand Perceptions

The insignificant effects of BAIndex for Finance and Travel/Entertainment sector might be suggesting that brand perceptions are not value-relevant in these sectors. Alternatively, the insignificant effects might be masking the heterogeneous impact of the individual perceptual components of Differentiation, Relevance, Esteem, Knowledge, and Energy in these sectors.

Table 4 reports disaggregate analyses for the individual components of Brand Asset Index in six different industrial sectors. Interestingly, three of the five perceptual components in Brand Asset Index – Differentiation, Relevance, and Energy – are significant in the Finance sector. Because they have opposite signs (increases in Differentiation have a negative effect while increases in Relevance and Energy have a positive effect on stock return), their combination in the aggregate Brand Asset Index is not significant. A similar picture emerges in the Travel/Entertainment sector: Differentiation has a marginally negative effect while Esteem and Energy have marginally positive effects. The effect of Relevance is also highly significant in the Computer/Internet and Restaurants sectors and is marginally significant in the Distribution/Retail sector.

There is less consistency in the effects of other Brand Asset Index components across industrial sectors. While Differentiation has a negative effect in the Finance and Travel/ Entertainment sectors, it has a positive effect in the Pharmaceutical sector. Esteem has a marginally positive effect in the Distribution/Retail and Travel/

Table 4 Disaggregate analyses: differential impact of brand perceptions by sector Dependent variable: abnormal stock return

	Finance	Distribution/ Retail	Computer/ Internet	Pharmaceutical	Restaurants	Travel/ Entertainment
Panel A. Direct future impact of the BAIndex (equation model 9)						
ΔDifferentiation	−0.100* (0.061)	0.010 (0.025)	−0.007 (0.030)	0.084* (0.044)	0.011 (0.060)	−0.197* (0.117)
ΔRelevance	0.197* (0.109)	0.109* (0.060)	0.199*** (0.064)	0.033 (0.070)	0.310** (0.130)	0.053 (0.198)
ΔEsteem	−0.000 (0.087)	0.075* (0.046)	0.039 (0.059)	0.004 (0.074)	−0.092 (0.110)	0.255* (0.147)
ΔKnowledge	−0.129 (0.190)	−0.101 (0.096)	−0.095 (0.113)	0.100 (0.135)	−0.145 (0.180)	0.107 (0.356)
ΔEnergy	0.110* (0.067)	−0.019 (0.030)	0.024 (0.027)	0.011 (0.042)	0.004 (0.067)	0.143* (0.087)
Unanticipated change in ROA	5.103*** (1.889)	4.132*** (0.564)	2.379*** (0.473)	1.971** (0.890)	6.152*** (1.126)	3.22 (2.389)
F-stat	2.74	11.01	6.23	2.43	6.55	1.48
N obs	172	379	420	61	106	91
Panel B. Total Performance Impact of the BAIndex (equation model 10)						
ΔDifferentiation	−0.123** (0.062)	0.017 (0.027)	−0.007 (0.031)	0.088* (0.045)	0.020 (0.068)	−0.216* (0.116)
ΔRelevance	0.230** (0.110)	0.105* (0.064)	0.159*** (0.065)	0.051 (0.072)	0.307** (0.155)	0.012 (0.196)
ΔEsteem	0.067 (0.085)	0.086* (0.049)	0.049 (0.061)	0.003 (0.076)	0.062 (0.122)	0.224 (0.146)
ΔKnowledge	−0.229 (0.190)	−0.110 (0.102)	−0.083 (0.116)	0.100 (0.140)	−0.156 (0.208)	0.208 (0.350)
ΔEnergy	0.116* (0.068)	−0.010 (0.032)	0.025 (0.028)	−0.001 (0.043)	0.017 (0.077)	0.141 (0.088)
F-stat	1.76	2.16	2.28	1.8	1.47	1.39
N obs	172	379	420	61	106	91

*$p < .10$; **$p < .05$; ***$p < .01$
Standard errors in *parentheses*

Entertainment sectors only. Energy has a marginally positive effect in the Finance and Travel/Entertainment sectors only. Interestingly, while most models of brand equity focus on the construct of brand familiarity, there is no significant positive association detected between the stock returns and the measure of familiarity (Knowledge).

Conclusion

Brand assets are crucial to firm performance and are a significant component of firm value. They are, however, difficult to value and to quantify in financial terms. The key reasons valuation of brand assets is difficult are the following:

(1) *They are intangible.* They reside in consumer minds and are represented by a mental structure of perceptions and attitudes. Individual components of brand associations and attitudes comprising customer mindset brand equity have been proposed and studied, but the research in this domain in not complete. At present, there is no general agreement on what exactly this mental structure is. Research continues into which components are relevant and which components are not relevant in customer mindset-based brand equity.
(2) *They are an outcome of a complex psychological process.* The mechanism behind the brand equity formation is complex and probably highly individualistic.
(3) *Nonseparable nature of brand and product equity.* The question of whether the value of brand asset is additive and can be viewed and assessed independently of its owner or the product it is associated with is unresolved. Brand characteristics and physical characteristics of the product carrying a brand name are not independent. Consumers exhibit significant biases in evaluating physical characteristics of branded products and also project their personal experiences and product perceptions onto the brand.

Brand equity is now measured at three main stages of the brand value chain (Keller and Lehman 2006). Consumer mindset approach uses survey methods to capture the psychological value consumers attach to a brand. Product market-based approach relies on scanner panel data or accounting data to estimate incremental market share, price, revenue, or profit premium attributable to the brand. Financial market-based approach uses secondary data from the stock market to estimate incremental firm value attributable to its brand assets. All these approaches involve a significant subjective component and judgement in deciding which perceptions to survey, how to define the market or generic benchmark, how much cash flow or market value to attribute to the brand versus other intangible assets the firm owns.

This chapter describes a tool that can be used to assess financial impact of brand perceptions and examine partial dynamics (immediate vs. future and direct vs. indirect) of this impact. This is conceptually and empirically different from measuring the value of brand equity. The presented approach has a limitation in that it allows estimating only partial (not full) dynamics of the effect. It does not allow estimating exactly how many years it will take for full benefits of brand development to be realized or what the pattern of the benefits in each future time period is. Also, the estimates are based on a set of monobrand firms. It is, however, likely (but remains to be confirmed) that the key insights are transferrable to individual product brands in multibrand firms.

With increasing availability of longer time series of brand metrics and brand performance outcome measures, addressing the full dynamics of brand impact will become feasible with standard time series and panel data approaches even at product brand level. Meanwhile, the approach described in this chapter allows assessing the long-term financial impact of marketing metrics with even limited time-series data to derive valuable insights. For example, in the empirical application of the method to disaggregate components of brand asset, important lessons are learned: most of the financial impact of brand typically occurs in the future periods and brand perceptions have very different impact in different industrial sectors.

References

Aaker, D. A. (1996). Measuring brand equity across products and markets. *California Management Review, 38*(3), 102–120.
Aaker, D. A. (2012). *Building strong brands*. Free Press (November 8, 2011). Simon and Schuster Digital Sales Inc. https://www.amazon.com/Building-Strong-Brands-David-Aaker-ebook/dp/B005O315Z2/ref=la_B000APVZQI_1_9?s=books&ie=UTF8&qid=1504831274&sr=1-9&refinements=p_82%3AB000APVZQI
Aaker, D. A., & Jacobson, R. (1994). The financial information content of perceived quality. *Journal of Marketing Research, 31*(2), 191–201.
Aaker, D. A., & Jacobson, R. (2001). The value relevance of brand attitude in high-technology markets. *Journal of Marketing Research, 38*(4), 485–493.
Ailawadi, K. L., Lehmann, D. R., & Neslin, S. A. (2003). Revenue premium as an outcome measure of brand equity. *Journal of Marketing, 67*(4), 1–17.
Allison, R. I., & Uhl, K. P. (1964). Influence of beer brand identification on taste perception. *Journal of Marketing Research, 1*(3), 36–39.
Anderson, T. W., & Hsiao, C. (1982). Formulation and estimation of dynamic models using panel data. *Journal of Econometrics, 18*(1), 47–82.
Arellano, M., & Bond, S. (1991). Some tests of specification for panel data: Monte Carlo evidence and an application to employment equations. *The Review of Economic Studies, 58*(2), 277–297.
Austin, L. (2007). Accounting for intangible assets. *University of Auckland Business Review, 9*(1), 63–72.
Bahadir, S. C., Bharadwaj, S. G., & Srivastava, R. K. (2008). Financial value of brands in mergers and acquisitions: Is value in the eye of the beholder? *Journal of Marketing, 72*(6), 49–64.
Barth, M. E., Clement, M. B., Foster, G., & Kasznik, R. (1998). Brand values and capital market valuation. *Review of Accounting Studies, 3*(1–2), 41–68.
Cañibano, L., Garcia-Ayuso, M., & Sanchez, P. (2000). Accounting for intangibles: A literature review. *Journal of Accounting Literature, 19*, 102–130.
Carhart, M. M. (1997). On persistence in mutual fund performance. *The Journal of Finance, 52*(1), 57–82.
Cobb-Walgren, C. J., Ruble, C. A., & Donthu, N. (1995). Brand equity, brand preference, and purchase intent. *Journal of Advertising, 24*(3), 25–40.
Daniel, K., & Titman, S. (1997). Evidence on the characteristics of cross sectional variation in stock returns. *The Journal of Finance, 52*(1), 1–33.
Fama, E. F. (1970). Efficient capital markets: A review of theory and empirical work. *The Journal of Finance, 25*(2), 383–417.
Fama, E. F., & French, K. R. (1993). Common risk factors in the returns on stocks and bonds. *Journal of Financial Economics, 33*(1), 3–56.
Greene, W. H. (2002). *Econometric analysis* (5th ed.). Upper Saddle River: Pearson Education.
Hrustic, E. (2012). Presentation at the "Brands and branding in law, accounting and marketing" conference. UNC.
Kamakura, W. A., & Russell, G. J. (1993). Measuring brand value with scanner data. *International Journal of Research in Marketing, 10*(1), 9–22.
Keller, K. L. (1993). Conceptualizing, measuring, and managing customer-based brand equity. *Journal of Marketing, 57*(1), 1–22.
Keller, K. L., & Lehmann, D. R. (2003). How do brands create value? *Marketing Management, 12*(3), 26–31.

Keller, K. L., & Lehmann, D. R. (2006). Brands and branding: Research findings and future priorities. *Marketing Science, 25*(6), 740–759.

Lassar, W., Mittal, B., & Sharma, A. (1995). Measuring customer-based brand equity. *Journal of Consumer Marketing, 12*(4), 11–19.

Lee, T. Y., & Bradlow, E. T. (2011). Automated marketing research using online customer reviews. *Journal of Marketing Research, 48*(5), 881–894.

Liu, L., Dzyabura, D. & Mizik, N. (2017). Visual listening in: Extracting brand image portrayed on social media. (May 8, 2017). Available at SSRN: https://ssrn.com/abstract=2978805 or http://dx.doi.org/10.2139/ssrn.2978805.

Madden, T. J., Fehle, F., & Fournier, S. (2006). Brands matter: An empirical demonstration of the creation of shareholder value through branding. *Journal of the Academy of Marketing Science, 34*(2), 224–235.

Mizik, N. (2014). Assessing the total financial performance impact of brand equity with limited time-series data. *Journal of Marketing Research, 51*(6), 691–706.

Mizik, N., & Jacobson, R. (2008). The financial value impact of perceptual brand attributes. *Journal of Marketing Research, 45*(1), 15–32.

Mizik, N., & Jacobson, R. (2009). Valuing branded businesses. *Journal of Marketing, 73*(6), 137–153.

Netzer, O., Feldman, R., Goldenberg, J., & Fresko, M. (2012). Mine your own business: Market-structure surveillance through text mining. *Marketing Science, 31*(3), 521–543.

Pappu, R., Quester, P. G., & Cooksey, R. W. (2005). Consumer-based brand equity: Improving the measurement-empirical evidence. *Journal of Product and Brand Management, 14*(3), 143–154.

Park, C. S., & Srinivasan, V. (1994). A survey-based method for measuring and understanding brand equity and its extendibility. *Journal of Marketing Research, 31*(2), 271–288.

Pavlov, E. & Mizik, N. (2017). Values' voters and their brands, Working paper.

Rangaswamy, A., Burke, R. R., & Oliva, T. A. (1993). Brand equity and the extendibility of brand names. *International Journal of Research in Marketing, 10*(1), 61–75.

Simon, C. J., & Sullivan, M. W. (1993). The measurement and determinants of brand equity: A financial approach. *Marketing Science, 12*(1), 28–52.

Sinclair, R. N., & Keller, K. L. (2014). A case for brands as assets: Acquired and internally developed. *Journal of Brand Management, 21*(4), 286–302.

Srinivasan, V., Park, C. S., & Chang, D. R. (2005). An approach to the measurement, analysis, and prediction of brand equity and its sources. *Management Science, 51*(9), 1433–1448.

Yoo, B., & Donthu, N. (2001). Developing and validating a multidimensional consumer-based brand equity scale. *Journal of Business Research, 52*(1), 1–14.

Measuring Sales Promotion Effectiveness

Karen Gedenk

Contents

Introduction	1056
Sales Promotion Tools and Their Effects	1056
Data for Measuring Sales Promotion Effectiveness	1059
Non-experimental Data on Observed Behavior	1059
Further Sources of Data	1061
Measuring Promotion Effectiveness with Panel Data	1062
SCAN*PRO	1063
PROMOTIONSCAN	1065
Decomposition Based on Single-Source Data	1067
Summary	1070
References	1070

Abstract

Sales promotions are an important marketing tool for both manufacturers and retailers. They include, for example, temporary price reductions, coupons, features, displays, sampling, and premiums. The bad news about promotions is that many of them are not profitable. The good news is that promotion effectiveness can be measured so that managers can identify the promotions which generate a profit and eliminate the ones that do not. This chapter presents data and models that can be used for this purpose. It focuses on panel data which is available at the aggregate (i.e., store) level and at the disaggregate (i.e., consumer) level. While aggregate data is more readily available and easier to analyze, disaggregate data allows for more detailed analyses. Several examples illustrate how models build on these data to measure promotion effectiveness. Since panel data has its limitations, it is often useful to complement it with surveys and/or experiments.

K. Gedenk (✉)
University of Hamburg, Hamburg, Germany
e-mail: karen.gedenk@uni-hamburg.de

Keywords

Sales promotions · Panel data · Surveys · Experiments · Decomposition of promotion effects

Introduction

Sales Promotions are a key marketing instrument for many companies. For example, firms sell their products with temporary price reductions (TPR), offer premiums, sweepstakes, or samples, and use feature advertising and displays to draw shoppers' attention to the promoted products. Manufacturer spendings on sales promotions are high, e.g., manufacturers of consumer packaged goods (CPG) in the USA spend 55% of their marketing budget on sales promotions (Cadent Consulting Group 2017). And retailers generate a large percentage of their sales with promoted products, e.g., in Europe 28% of volume sales in grocery retailing (IRI 2016).

Despite their widespread use, sales promotions are often not successful. McKinsey analyzed 5000 promotions in six European countries in 2002, finding that only 40% are profitable for the manufacturers of the promoted brands (N.N. 2002). Ailawadi et al. (2006) in their analysis of all promotions run by the drugstore chain CVS in 2003, find that less than half of them are profitable for the retailer.

Thus, managers may think that – similar to the famous quote for advertising – half the money they spend on promotions is wasted. Compared to advertising, however, it is much easier to find out which half this is. Effects of promotions are more immediate, so that, it is easier to establish causal relationships. There is plenty of data available for measuring promotion effectiveness, especially for CPG, and researchers have developed and tested models with which to analyze these data. Note that such analyses are not trivial – but given the huge investments in sales promotions, they are typically well worth the effort.

This chapter provides an overview of relevant data sources and approaches for analyzing these data. It focuses on promotions directed at consumers by manufacturers and retailers, as opposed to trade promotions, which manufacturers offer to retailers. The following section presents key sales promotion tools and their potential effects that need to be measured. Next, an overview of measurement approaches with a focus on relevant data sources and the opportunities they offer for analyzing sales promotion effectiveness. Since sales promotions are most heavily used for CPG, and the analysis of promotion effectiveness in this industry relies heavily on panel data, I describe some examples for this type of analysis in the remainder of the chapter.

Sales Promotion Tools and Their Effects

Promotions offered to consumers can be distinguished in price versus non-price promotions (Gedenk 2002; Gedenk et al. 2010). The most common type of price promotion is a temporary price reduction (TPR), where the product is offered at a reduced price for a limited time (e.g., "normally 2.99 € – this week only 1.99 €"). Other types of price promotions include rebates (consumers pay full price and send in their receipt to receive a discount) and multi-item promotions (consumers only get a discount when they buy multiple units, e.g., "buy two – get one free"). Retailers and manufacturers can also distribute coupons through different media (e.g., newspapers, websites, or direct mail) and consumers receive a discount (for one or multiple items), when they present the coupon at the point-of purchase.

Non-price promotions can be "supportive" or "true" (Gedenk 2002; Gedenk et al. 2010). "Supportive" non-price promotions include, for example, displays, features (i.e., retailers' weekly flyers), and other POS materials. They are typically used to draw attention to price promotions, and in most consumers' minds, they are therefore closely linked to price cuts. Note, however, that "supportive" non-price promotions can also stand alone to highlight products at regular price. "True" non-price promotions, in contrast, clearly focus on the brand or store, not on price. Tools like samples, contests, and sweepstakes, as well as premiums, fall into this category. While managers typically use price and "supportive" non-price promotions to achieve short-term increases in sales and profit, "true" non-price promotions often focus more on long-term goals like building awareness for a brand and enhancing its image and thus increasing profit in the time after the promotion. Note that promotion campaigns by manufacturers and retailers often combine several of the above-mentioned tools.

Managers, who want to measure promotion effectiveness, need to make sure that they take into account all relevant effects. Even if the primary goal of a promotion is to increase sales in the short term, potential long-term effects must not be ignored. Also, the short-term sales bump needs to be decomposed to determine which part of it is truly incremental for manufacturers and retailers. Figure 1 details the different effects of promotions on sales of the promoted product in the focal store.

Suppose that chocolate by the brand Milka is on promotion at the German retailer Rewe. In this case, the sales of Milka at Rewe will evince a short-term increase in sales. This sales bump is made up of different components and can be decomposed by asking "what would consumers have done without the promotion?". There are several answers to this question: The bump can occur because consumers otherwise would have bought their chocolate at Edeka (store switching), would have bought chocolate by Ritter Sport (brand switching), would have bought cookies instead of chocolate (category switching), or would have bought later or a smaller amount of chocolate (purchase acceleration). It is important to make this decomposition because effects that are advantageous for the retailer are not necessarily good for the manufacturer and vice versa. For example, brand switching increases sales for the manufacturer but not for the retailer, who only shifts sales from one brand to another. The opposite holds for store switching which increases sales for the retailer, while the manufacturer only shifts sales of its brand from one retailer to another. To determine whether purchase acceleration is advantageous, it needs to be decomposed further. If consumers buy more or buy earlier than they would have done without the promotion, in many product categories this leads to increased consumption, i.e., consumers eat more chocolate. This effect is positive for both manufacturers and retailers. However,

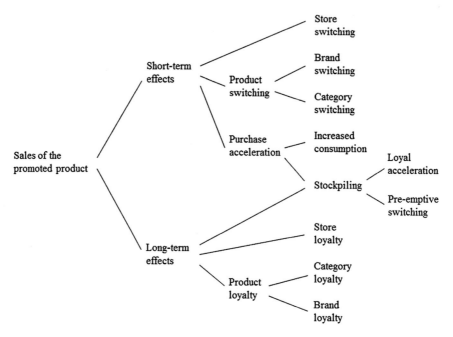

Fig. 1 Sales effects of promotions (Gedenk 2002, p. 104)

purchase acceleration may also result in consumers stockpiling the promoted product. In other words: The promotion steals sales from the future – without the promotion, the consumers would have purchased (more) at a later time. In this case, an interesting question arises: Does the promotion steal sales from the promoted brand in the focal store (loyal acceleration), or does it steal from the competition, i.e., other brands and/or other retailers (preemptive switching) (Ailawadi et al. 2007)? Preemptive switching results in an incremental sales effect for the focal brand/retailer, while loyal acceleration only shifts sales from one period to another.

In the long-term, promotions can affect consumers' loyalty to stores, brands, and product categories. The effect of price promotions on brand loyalty is often negative, in part because price cuts lead to lower reference prices and because consumers learn to buy on promotion (Gedenk 2002, pp. 245 ff.). This can result in conflicts within manufacturing firms, where the sales department often focuses primarily on short-term sales, whereas the marketing department is also interested in brand building. Store loyalty may improve because of a better price image but may also decrease because consumers learn to search for deals.

Note that Fig. 1 only captures effects of promotions on sales of the promoted brand in the store that runs the promotion. In addition, it can be interesting – especially for retailers – to look at effects on other product categories. Promotions can attract customers to the store who then buy other products that are not on promotion. Finally, in addition to effects on sales, managers need to consider prices and costs to determine the profitability of promotions.

Data for Measuring Sales Promotion Effectiveness

Figure 2 depicts a classification of relevant data sources, distinguishing between surveys versus observed behavior and between experimental versus non-experimental data.

Non-experimental Data on Observed Behavior

The large majority of academic research on sales promotions uses non-experimental data on observed behavior (cell I in Fig. 2), i.e., market data, especially panel data. For managers also, this is a key data source, especially for CPG sold through grocery retailers. Such data can have different levels of aggregation.

Sales data aggregated to the level of stores or retailers are available for many industries. Often retailers share their sales data with manufacturers, since both benefit from in-depth analyses of the data. Scanner panels provided by market research companies allow even more meaningful analyses, because they combine data from several retailers and include systematic information on sales promotions. The leading suppliers of such panels are IRI and Nielsen. They collect sales and price data from grocery retailers (including drugstores), who share the information from their databases. The retailers gather sales data by scanning consumers' purchases at the check-out. In addition, employees of the market research companies visit the participating stores each week to collect information on non-price promotions like displays and features.

Disaggregate data that captures purchases at the level of consumers is available to many companies in the form of consumer panels, provided, for example, by

	Non-experimental data	**Experiments** • Field experiments • Lab experiments

Observed behavior
• Store-level data
  - Retailer sales data
  - Scanner panels
• Consumer-level data
  - Consumer panels
  - Single-source panels
  - Loyalty card data
	I
	(majority of promotion research)
		II

Survey	III	IV

Fig. 2 Data for measuring promotion success (Gedenk 2006, S. 586)

GfK. In a consumer panel, a large number of households record their purchases in the focal product categories (typically via in-home scanning), and send that information to the market research institute running the panel. For the analysis of sales promotions, consumer panel data need to be augmented with data on the promotions that were available in the stores where the panelists went shopping. Consumers' self-reports on the promotions they encountered are not very reliable and available only for the products purchased, but not for competing products. Thus, it is more promising to collect promotion information from other sources like retailer features. In Europe, this approach is used, for example, by the data provider FOCUS Marketing Research. It works well if many promotions are featured, which in turn requires coordination across the stores belonging to a retail chain.

A better matching of purchase with promotion data is achieved by single-source panels, like BehaviorScan by GfK. They combine a consumer panel with store panel data. In the German BehaviorScan market in Haßloch (Pfalz), 3000 households participate as well as most of the grocery retail stores in town. Households show ID cards when they go shopping, so that all their purchases are recorded. Retailers provide information on prices, and employees of GfK visit the stores to record non-price promotions. In addition, the participating households can receive targeted advertising – but that is typically only of minor relevance for the analysis of promotion effectiveness.

Loyalty card data also combine purchase with promotion information: Retailers know their prices and promotions, and can observe the purchase behavior of households participating in the loyalty program. The key problem here is that only purchases in the stores participating in the loyalty program are captured, while purchases at competing retailers cannot be observed.

Aggregate and disaggregate sales data allow for different types of analyses. Store-level data are good for measuring the short-term increase in sales caused by promotions. Researchers have also used aggregate data to decompose the short-term sales bump into its components and to measure long-term effects (e.g., Nijs et al. 2001; van Heerde et al. 2000, 2004). However, there is always the danger of an aggregation bias in these approaches. Neslin and Schneider Stone (1996) explain this in depth for the measurement of stockpiling effects. Their starting point is the observation that studies based on aggregate data typically do not find a post-promotion dip, while studies based on disaggregate data do find evidence for stockpiling. Neslin and Schneider Stone discuss several explanations for this phenomenon, mostly related to aggregation bias. For example, households have different interpurchase times, so that each household that stockpiles has its personal post-promotion dip at a different time, and an overall dip is not visible when data are aggregated across households. Also, deal-to-deal buying – an extreme form of stockpiling where households only buy a product when it is on promotion – cannot be detected in aggregate data.

A more precise decomposition of the short-term sales bump can be done with disaggregate data at the consumer level. It allows for a detailed analysis of consumer response to promotions: Researchers can not only model aggregate sales but rather different consumer decisions like store choice, product category purchase incidence, brand choice, and decisions on purchase quantity. Often, researchers use models of purchase incidence, brand choice, and purchase quantity to identify brand switching and purchase acceleration (e.g., Gupta 1988; Bell et al. 1999; Ailawadi et al. 2007). Van Heerde et al. (2003) point out that this decomposition should be done based on unit sales rather than on elasticities. Otherwise, the importance of brand switching relative to purchase acceleration will be overstated.

Thus, researchers face a trade-off when choosing between aggregate and disaggregate data for analyzing promotion effectiveness. On the one hand, disaggregate data allow for more detailed analyses. On the other hand, aggregate data are cheaper, and the analysis requires less effort. Therefore, managers mostly analyze store-level data, while academics also use consumer-level data to provide deeper insights into promotion effectiveness (for a review, see Gedenk 2002; Gedenk et al. 2010). Academic research on sales promotions often relies on market data provided by market research institutes, manufactures, and retailers. An example of a publically available database is described by Bronnenberg et al. (2008), and organizations like AiMark and the Kilts Center for Marketing at Chicago Booth make other databases available to academics.

In sum, non-experimental data on observed behavior can provide many insights into promotion effectiveness. However, it also has limitations:

- Market data is not readily available for all product categories. It abounds for CPG and grocery retailing, but may be difficult to come by in other industries.
- Market data is only available for products that are already on the market and for promotions that have already been used.
- Consumers' purchase behavior is driven by many factors beyond sales promotions, and it is often hard to control for these factors such that promotion effects can be properly identified. Also, endogeneity of the promotion variables may bias results.
- Market data can be used to measure consumers' behavior, but it does not contain information about attitudes, emotions, and motives that may explain this behavior.

Therefore, the measurement of promotion effectiveness is often supplemented by using other types of data.

Further Sources of Data

Surveys can be used to measure attitudes, emotions, motives, and behavioral intentions. They can solve all of the four problems mentioned above: Surveys can inquire into new products and new promotions in any product category and provide explanations for behavior, while controlling for extraneous factors. They can also easily capture characteristics of promotions, products, and consumers, as well as other factors which potentially moderate promotion response. A downside of surveys, of course, is their limited external validity. Do respondents indicate their true attitude, and will they really behave as stated in a survey?

Non-experimental surveys (cell III in Fig. 2) have been used, for example, to measure deal proneness, i.e., to find out which consumers respond most strongly to promotions (e.g., Ailawadi et al. 2001). More frequently, however, surveys contain experiments, in which promotions are manipulated systematically to test the effects of different promotion designs (cell IV in Fig. 2). Experiments attempt to keep all variables besides the treatment variables constant, and therefore allow the diagnosis of causal effects, in this case, the identification of promotion effects and their moderators. For example, Arora and Henderson (2007) study the effect of cause-related marketing campaigns, which is difficult to isolate in field data. Also, many survey-based experiments have looked into the framing of price promotions. They have studied, for example, under which conditions a price cut should be indicated in percent versus as an absolute value (e.g., Chen et al. 1998).

Finally, field experiments with observed behavior (cell II in Fig. 2) are a valuable data source for measuring promotion effectiveness. They combine the high external validity of market data with the high internal validity of an experiment. Compared to non-experimental market data, promotion effects can be identified more clearly. Unfortunately, managers are often reluctant to run field experiments, maybe because they worry about high costs or about offending customers who receive unfavorable treatments. Yet, even simple store tests can yield very interesting results. For example, Wansink et al. (1998) show that quantity restrictions on price promotions ("maximum of X units") can increase the average quantity bought. One explanation for this surprising effect is anchoring and adjustment, such that consumers use the quantity indicated in the restriction as an anchor and adjust their purchase quantity to it.

Note that the discussion so far has focused on promotions in offline retail channels. For digital promotions in the online and mobile channels, managers have some additional options for observing consumer behavior. In particular, they have information not only on purchases but also on consumers' search behavior. In mobile marketing, they can make use of information on consumers' location and target their promotions accordingly. Also, field experiments are much easier to implement and thus less costly than in the offline channel, so that we see more experiments for digital promotions. For example, Luo et al. (2014) and Fong et al. (2015) run field experiments to study how the design of mobile coupon campaigns affects redemption rates.

Measuring Promotion Effectiveness with Panel Data

In this section, I describe the basic ideas behind three frequently used approaches for analyzing non-experimental panel data (cell I in Fig. 2) and provide examples of applications. For a more detailed discussion and further promotion models, see van Heerde and Neslin (2017). Since managers mainly use store-level data to measure promotion effectiveness, I first present two common approaches for this type of analysis: the SCAN*PRO model developed in cooperation with Nielsen and the

PROMOTIONSCAN model developed in cooperation with IRI. At the core of the SCAN*PRO model (Wittink et al. 1987) is a multiplicative sales response function. In contrast, PROMOTIONSCAN (Abraham and Lodish 1993) uses a baseline approach. It determines the effect of a promotion as the difference between actual sales and baseline sales, where the baseline, i.e., the sales level that would have been achieved without the promotion, is estimated based on sales in promotion-free weeks. A third example (Ailawadi et al. 2007) illustrates a more in-depth analysis of promotion effects based on single-source panel data.

SCAN*PRO

In the SCAN*PRO model (Wittink et al. 1987; van Heerde et al. 2002), unit sales are a multiplicative function of price and non-price promotions:

$$Q_{ist} = \prod_{j=1}^{J} \left[\left(\frac{P_{jst}}{BP_{js}}\right)^{\beta_j} \cdot \gamma_{1j}^{F_{jst}} \cdot \gamma_{2j}^{D_{jst}} \cdot \gamma_{3j}^{FAD_{jst}} \right] \cdot \prod_{t=1}^{T} \left[\delta_t^{W_t}\right] \cdot \prod_{s=1}^{S} \left[\lambda_s^{Z_s}\right] \cdot e^{u_{ist}} \quad (1)$$

with:

Q_{ist} = Unit sales of brand i in store s and time period t
P_{jst} = Price per unit of brand j in store s and time period t
BP_{js} = Base price per unit of brand j in store s (median of prices in weeks without sales promotion)
F_{jst} = Indicator variable for feature (1 if brand j is featured but not on display in store s and time period t, 0 else)
D_{jst} = Indicator variable for display (1 if brand j is on display but not featured in store s and time period t, 0 else)
FAD_{jst} = Indicator variable for feature and display (1 if brand j is featured and on display in store s and time period t, 0 else)
W_t = Indicator variable for time period (1 if observation is from week t, 0 else)
Z_s = Indicator variable for store (1 if observation is from store s, 0 else)
u_{ist} = Error term for brand i, store s, and time period t

Wittink et al. (1987) suggest aggregating the data to the level of weeks, stores, and brands, but different levels of aggregation are possible (e.g., days instead of weeks, retail chains instead of stores, and SKUs instead of brands). Typically, researchers pool across stores and time periods, and estimate one model per brand. Sales of the focal brand are a function of prices and promotions of this brand, but also of the prices and promotions of competing brands in the same product category. Prices are made comparable across stores by dividing actual price by base price. The base price captures the regular price in a store and is defined as the median of prices of a brand in a store in promotion-free time periods. Differences in unit sales levels between stores can be accommodated in a similar way: by dividing by base sales. Or the researcher can include store dummies Z_s in the model, as in Eq. (1). SCAN*PRO models can also contain dummy variables for non-price promotions. Often these are "supportive" non-price promotions like features and displays (see Eq. 1), but of course, the effects of "true" non-price promotions can be modeled in the same way, if the respective data is available. Finally, indicator variables for weeks W_t control for seasonal effects and exceptional events.

The effect of price promotions is captured by the price elasticity β_j. For $i = j$, this is the direct elasticity (price of the focal brand i affects the sales of i), while for $i \neq j$ it is a cross-elasticity, (price of a competing brand j affects sales of the focal brand i). The coefficients γ_{1j} to γ_{3j} are multipliers indicating how much larger unit sales are with a non-price promotion than without.

An example for a SCAN*PRO model can be found in the study by Foekens et al. (1999). The authors estimate the model in Eq. (1) with scanner data from 28 stores of a US retail chain for three brands from one product category. Table 1 presents the parameter estimates for price and non-price promotion effects. Direct effects are highlighted by grey shading.

The three direct price elasticities (effect of P_i on sales of brand i) have typical values of around -3, close to the mean short-term promotional price elasticity of -3.63 that Bijmolt et al. (2005) find in their meta-analysis. The cross-price elasticities (effect of P_j on sales of brand i) are also significant. Positive values indicate brand switching – if one brand decreases price, the other brands lose sales. Features only have a significant direct effect on sales for brand C (effect of F_C on sales of brand C). Here, unit sales are 2.12 times as high with a feature than without. Displays cause sales to roughly double for all three brands (effect of D_i on sales of brand i). Some of the multipliers for cross-effects of non-price promotions (effect of F_i, D_i, and FAD_i on sales of brand i) are smaller than 1, indicating brand switching.

Table 1 Parameters of the SCAN*PRO model by Foekens et al. (1999, p. 262)

Independent variable	Dependent variable: Unit sales of brand…		
	A	B	C
P_A	-2.96	0.26	0.54
P_B	0.69	-2.42	1.34
P_C	1.08	0.38	-3.21
F_A	n. s.	1.48	0.63
D_A	1.80	n. s.	0.82
FAD_A	1.75	1.34	0.54
F_B	0.38	n. s.	n. s.
D_B	n. s.	1.54	n. s.
FAD_B	0.33	2.08	0.61
F_C	n. s.	1.42	2.12
D_C	n. s.	n. s.	2.41
FAD_C	n. s.	1.26	3.22

Direct effects are shaded in grey, the remaining effects are cross-effects
P Price, *F* Feature only, *D* Display only, *FAD* Feature and Display, *n. s.* not significant

However, for brand B, Foekens et al. find significant multipliers larger than 1. Thus, brand B benefits from non-price promotions of competing brands. This can be explained by an attention effect. Features for brands A and C (alone or in combination with displays) draw consumers' attention to the product category, and customers with a preference for brand B buy more in the category but stay loyal to brand B. Only price promotions provide a sufficient incentive for them to switch brands. This suggests that brand B is a strong brand. Also, brand A should not pay an advertising allowance to retailers, since features for brand A only benefit brand B.

Many extensions of this simple SCAN*PRO model have been suggested over the years (van Heerde et al. 2002). For example researchers have estimated varying-parameters/hierarchical models where the price elasticity is a function of second-level variables like past promotions (Foekens et al. 1999) or store-size (Haans and Gijsbrechts 2011). Van Heerde et al. (2000) and Neslin and Macé (2004) add lead and lag effects (i.e., effects of past and future promotions) to model purchase acceleration. Van Heerde et al. (2001) show that price cuts with different depths have different effects on purchase behavior. And van Heerde et al. (2004) demonstrate that a decomposition of the short-term sales bump caused by a promotion is possible with aggregate sales data. Note that SCAN*PRO is not only frequently used by academics but also by managers, reflecting the wide availability of store-level panel data and the low effort required for the analysis. Van Heerde et al. (2002, p. 201) report more than 3000 commercial applications by Nielsen, and that number has certainly grown further by now.

PROMOTIONSCAN

With SCAN*PRO, researchers model the effect of promotions on sales directly and estimate it with panel data from all weeks. In contrast, Abraham and Lodish (1993) in their PROMOTIONSCAN model choose an indirect approach. They estimate a baseline which reflects sales that would have been achieved without promotions, using only data from weeks whose sales are not affected by promotions. Specifically, they proceed in five steps:

1. Adjustment of data for trend and seasonality,
2. Elimination of periods where sales is affected by promotions,
3. Elimination of outliers,
4. Calculation of preliminary baseline by smoothing over promotion-free periods and adding trend and seasonality back in,
5. Adjustment for out-of-stock situations and market-specific factors (e.g., marketing activities of the competition).

Some of these steps are performed several times in an iterative process. Together with final consistency checks, this leads to robust estimations that can be automated to a large degree. Once the researcher has estimated a baseline, he can compare it to actual sales to determine the effect of promotions. Typically, actual sales are higher than the baseline during a promotion, and lower afterwards because of stockpiling.

A key difficulty with PROMOTIONSCAN is the identification of periods where sales are not affected by promotions. The researcher needs to exclude not only the weeks during a promotion but also the weeks with a post-promotion dip caused by stockpiling afterwards. In product categories with frequent promotions, there are sometimes only few weeks left with which to estimate a baseline.

Baseline models are also frequently used in practice. A prominent example that combines academic research with a practical application is the study by Ailawadi et al. (2006). The authors use the relatively simple and robust method to analyze all promotions in 2003 of the US drug store chain CVS, i.e., 36 million promotions in 189 product categories and 3808 stores. They determine a baseline for a promotion by computing moving averages across promotion-free weeks before and after the promotion. The number of weeks taken into account varies, depending on the turnover and seasonality of the product. The difference between actual sales and the baseline yields the gross lift in unit sales of a product in a given store. Next, Ailawadi et al. decompose this short-term sales bump and consider a promotion's effect on other product categories. The retailer (CVS) needs to identify the components of the gross lift that are taken from other products in the category (brand switching) and from its future sales (loyal acceleration). These two components do not constitute incremental sales for the retailer, while the remaining components do. Furthermore, if a promotion has a halo effect, i.e., if it increases sales of other product categories (e.g., due to store switching), that is advantageous for the retailer. Therefore, Ailawadi et al. determine the extent of brand switching and halo effects on other product categories based on scanner data from CVS. They isolate loyal acceleration with the help of data from the retailer's loyalty program, since – as explained above – disaggregate data are more appropriate than store-level data for measuring stockpiling (Neslin and Schneider Stone 1996). Finally, the authors have access to data on retailer costs and on trade promotions, so that they can measure not only the net sales effect but also the net profit impact of promotions. Table 2 shows the medians for the various effects for four broad groups of product categories as well as for the full sample.

The gross sales lift, i.e., the short-term increase in sales, is about 300%. Given price cuts of 30% on average, this corresponds to price elasticities of roughly -10. Note that these elasticities capture not only the effect of price promotions, but also the support by non-price promotions like features and displays. A little less than half of the gross sales lift (46% on average) derives from brand switching, and about 10% from loyal acceleration. The remainder – about 45% – constitutes incremental sales for CVS. In addition to these within-category effects, there is a halo effect: In three out of four groups of product categories, promotions in one category also advance sales in other product categories. Across the full sample, for each unit of the gross sales lift, there is a sales increase of 0.16 units of products from other categories. All these effects together (gross sales lift – brand switching – local acceleration + halo) result in a net sales impact of 1.05 units on average. That is, on promotion, CVS sells 1.05 units more per article, week, and store than the baseline of 0.86 units. However, the net profit impact is negative in two out of four groups of product categories. Here, the incremental sales and the trade promotions CVS receives from the manufacturers are not sufficient to compensate for the loss in margin. Overall, more than half of the promotions analyzed are not profitable for CVS.

Table 2 Results of Ailawadi et al. (2006, p. 527) (medians)

Effect	Full sample	Health	Beauty	Edibles	General merchandise
Gross sales lift	310%	264%	314%	308%	421%
Brand switching (fraction of gross lift)	0.46	0.50	0.47	0.40	0.43
Loyal acceleration (fraction of gross lift)	0.10	0.11	0.09	0.15	0.08
Halo (fraction of gross lift)	0.16	−0.04	0.30	0.05	0.28
Net unit sales impact	1.05	0.58	1.35	2.07	1.71
Baseline unit sales	0.86	0.80	0.67	2.00	0.75
Net profit impact	−0.62	−0.93	0.23	−1.14	0.08
Baseline profit	1.29	1.69	1.24	0.91	0.94

Ailawadi et al. also identify drivers of both the net sales impact and the net profit impact of promotions at CVS. Differences in promotion effectiveness are small between stores, but substantial between brands, product categories, and types of promotions. One of the most interesting results of the paper is that the drivers which explain this variance, typically have opposing effects on incremental sales versus incremental profit. For example, the depth of the price cut has a positive effect on the net sales impact of promotions (because it provides more incentive to purchase), but negatively affects their net profit impact (because it cuts more deeply into margins). Also, a brand's market share has a positive effect on the net sales impact, but a negative effect on the net profit impact. This should remind managers of how dangerous it is to only look at sales effects when measuring promotion effectiveness. Also, corporate governance should not focus primarily on sales and market shares, but rather on profit goals. With the wrong incentive system, it is difficult for managers to eliminate unprofitable promotions, because typically this will only be possible by sacrificing sales.

The analysis of promotion effectiveness with models like SCAN*PRO or PROMOTIONSCAN has the big advantage that store-level data are easily available in many industries, especially CPG, and that the analysis can be automated to a large degree. On the other hand, disaggregate data allow for more detailed analysis of promotion effects. The example of Ailawadi et al. (2006) illustrates how both types of data and analyses can be combined. The authors use consumer-level data to measure purchase acceleration. The next subsection describes the study by Ailawadi et al. (2007) as an example of how an even more detailed decomposition of the sales promotion bump can be done with single-source data.

Decomposition Based on Single-Source Data

Ailawadi et al. (2007) analyze the effectiveness of price promotions and "supportive" non-price-promotions from the perspective of a manufacturer. Their model is based on data from a single-source panel and captures consumers' decisions on category purchase incidence, brand choice, and purchase quantity:

$$P_{ht}(i\&q) = P_{ht}(inc) \cdot P_{ht}(i|inc) \cdot P_{ht}(q|\,inc\&i) \qquad (2)$$

with:

P_{ht} (i & q) = Probability that household h purchases quantity q of brand i on shopping trip t

P_{ht} (inc) = Probability that household h makes a purchase in the focal product category on shopping trip t

P_{ht} (i| inc) = Probability that household h chooses brand i on shopping trip t, conditional on a purchase in the product category

P_{ht} (q| inc & i) = Probability that household h buys quantity q of brand i, conditional on a purchase in the category and on choosing brand i

Each shopping trip of a household constitutes an observation. On a given shopping trip, a household first decides on whether to make a purchase in the focal product category or not. If he decides to purchase, he next chooses a brand, and finally, he decides how much of it to buy. The authors use a nested logit model to capture category purchase incidence and brand choice, and a poisson model for purchase quantity.

Ailawadi et al. (2007) are primarily interested in a detailed analysis of purchase acceleration. Purchase acceleration as a whole becomes visible in category incidence and purchase quantity decisions: consumers buy earlier and/or more than they would have done without a promotion. Part of this extra quantity that consumers now have available goes into increased consumption, because consumers have fewer stockouts and increase their consumption rates. Since inventory levels and consumption cannot be observed in panel data, the authors need to make assumptions about the quantities consumed and update inventory levels accordingly. They estimate a model with flexible consumption, and find that households consume more of a product if they have more of it in stock. That is, promotions that increase the inventory of households, lead to increased consumption.

In addition to increasing consumption, households also stockpile, i.e., sales are stolen from the future. Ailawadi et al. (2007) introduce the distinction between sales stolen from the brand's own future sales (loyal acceleration) versus from competing brands (preemptive switching). Finally, they also study how purchase acceleration affects brand loyalty, by including detailed feedback effects in their brand choice model. The respective parameters indicate that promotions decrease brand loyalty, but this effect is smaller when consumers stockpile. An explanation could be that consumers get more used to a brand if they use more of it, and thus are more likely to repurchase out of habit.

Finally, an analysis based on disaggregate data needs to take into account that consumers are heterogeneous in their brand preferences as well as in their response to marketing mix variables. If this heterogeneity is ignored, model parameters will be biased. Therefore, Ailawadi et al. (2007) use a continuous mixture model, where parameters follow a normal distribution (Train 2009). Once the authors have estimated the parameters of their model of purchase behavior, they determine the size of the sales bump caused by promotions and decompose it. Their decomposition approach is based on unit sales and uses a Monte Carlo simulation. The authors simulate purchase behavior with and without a promotion – differences are caused by the promotion, and the authors assign them to the various components of the promotion effect.

Table 3 presents the results of this decomposition for one yogurt and one ketchup brand. The underlying model was estimated with data from a US single-source panel for these two product categories and used a dummy variable for promotions, i.e., temporary price reductions and/or features and displays.

As in the previous examples, the short-term sales bump is large. For the yogurt brand "Dannon," sales increase by 12.45 units in the short run, compared to baseline sales in non-promotion periods of 3.88 units. About one third of this sales bump comes from brand switching and about two thirds from purchase acceleration. Most of the extra inventory that households acquire from purchase acceleration goes into increased consumption. That is, promotions make consumers eat much more yogurt, which is a favorable effect for manufacturers. There is only little stockpiling (loyal acceleration and preemptive switching), and when promotions steal sales from the future, they mostly steal from the competition (preemptive switching), and not from the focal brand's future sales (loyal acceleration). This holds for three out of four yogurt brands investigated. For the ketchup brand "Del Monte," there is less of a consumption effect than for yogurt, and the promotional sales bump is mostly driven by brand switching instead, which is plausible. Again, for three out of four ketchup brands, preemptive switching is larger than loyal acceleration.

Table 3 further shows that promotions affect consumption not only in the short, but also in the long run. Finally, there is a weak positive effect of purchase acceleration on brand loyalty. Note that this is not the total effect of promotions on

Table 3 Decomposition results by Ailawadi et al. (2007, p. 459)

		Yogurt ("Dannon")		Ketchup ("Del Monte")	
		Units	% of sales bump	Units	% of sales bump
Baseline sales		3.88		0.80	
Short-term sales bump		12.45	100%	3.85	100%
Decomposition of short-term sales bump					
Brand switching		4.78	38.4%	2.26	58.6%
Purchase acceleration	Short-term increase in consumption	6.50	52.2%	1.14	29.5%
	Loyal acceleration	0.41	3.3%	0.21	5.4%
	Preemptive brand switching	0.76	6.1%	0.25	6.5%
Long-term effects from purchase acceleration					
Long-term increase in consumption		−1.61	−12.9%	0.04	1.1%
Brand loyalty effect of purchase acceleration		0.20	1.6%	0.03	0.8%

loyalty but only the part that can be attributed to consumers purchasing and consuming more of the brand.

Summary

In order to determine sales promotion effectiveness, marketing researchers need to measure the short-term sales bump caused by the promotion, decompose it into its components, and capture the long-term effects of the promotion. Mostly, this is done based on panel data. Aggregate data at the store level are available either from retailers or from scanner panels, and the best disaggregate data at the household level is available from single-source panels. With respect to these data sources, there is a trade-off between costs and benefits. While disaggregate data allow a very detailed measurement of promotion effects, single-source data is not widely available, costly, and its analysis is difficult as well as time-consuming. Aggregate data yield fewer insights but are more readily available and easier to analyze. Examples illustrate how aggregate and disaggregate data can be used to measure promotion effectiveness. Since all panel data analysis has some limitations, it often is helpful to also use surveys and experiments. Finally, it is important to keep in mind that for monitoring promotions, it is not sufficient to focus on sales effects, since many promotions increase sales but decrease profits.

References

Abraham, M. M., & Lodish, L. M. (1993). An implemented system for improving promotion productivity using store scanner data. *Marketing Science, 12*(3), 248–269.

Ailawadi, K. L., Neslin, S. A., & Gedenk, K. (2001). Pursuing the value-conscious consumer: Store brands versus National Brand Promotions. *Journal of Marketing, 65*(1), 71–89.

Ailawadi, K. L., Harlam, B. A., César, J., & Trounce, D. (2006). Promotion profitability for a retailer: The role of promotion, brand, category, and store characteristics. *Journal of Marketing Research, 43*(4), 518–535.

Ailawadi, K. L., Gedenk, K., Lutzky, C., & Neslin, S. A. (2007). Decomposition of the sales impact of promotion-induced stockpiling. *Journal of Marketing Research, 44*(3), 450–467.

Arora, N., & Henderson, T. (2007). Embedded premium promotion: Why it works and how to make it more effective. *Marketing Science, 26*(4), 514–531.

Bell, D. R., Chiang, J., & Padmanabhan, V. (1999). The decomposition of promotional response: An empirical generalization. *Marketing Science, 18*(4), 504–526.

Bijmolt, T. H. A., van Heerde, H. J., & Pieters, R. G. M. (2005). New empirical generalizations on the determinants of price elasticity. *Journal of Marketing Research, 42*(2), 141–156.

Bronnenberg, B. J., Kruger, M. W., & Mela, C. F. (2008). The IRI marketing data set. *Marketing Science, 27*(4), 745–748.

Cadent Consulting Group. (2017). 2017 Marketing spending industry study. http://cadentcg.com/wp-content/uploads/2017-Marketing-Spending-Study.pdf. Accessed 10 Aug 2017.

Chen, S.-F. S., Monroe, K. B., & Lou, Y.-C. (1998). The effects of framing price promotion messages on consumers' perceptions and purchase intentions. *Journal of Retailing, 74*(3), 353–372.

Foekens, E. W., Leeflang, P. S. H., & Wittink, D. R. (1999). Varying parameter models to accomodate dynamic promotion effects. *Journal of Econometrics, 89*(1/2), 249–268.

Fong, N. M., Fang, Z., & Luo, X. (2015). Geo-conquesting: Competitive locational targeting of mobile promotions. *Journal of Marketing Research, 52*(5), 726–735.

Gedenk, K. (2002). *Verkaufsförderung*. München: Vahlen.

Gedenk, K. (2006). Controlling von Verkaufsförderungsmaßnahmen. In S. Reinecke & T. Tomczak (Eds.), *Handbuch Marketingcontrolling* (2nd ed., pp. 573–592). Gabler: Wiesbaden.

Gedenk, K., Neslin, S. A., & Ailawadi, K. A. (2010). Sales promotion. In M. Krafft & M. K. Mantrala (Eds.), *Retailing in the 21st century* (2nd ed., pp. 393–407). Berlin: Springer.

Gupta, S. (1988). Impact of sales promotions on when, what, and how much to buy. *Journal of Marketing Research, 25*(4), 342–355.

Haans, H., & Gijsbrechts, E. (2011). "One-deal-fits-all?" on category sales promotion effectiveness in smaller versus larger supermarkets. *Journal of Retailing, 87*(4), 427–443.

IRI. (2016). Price and promotion in Western Europe. https://www.iriworldwide.com/IRI/media/IRI-Clients/International/Price-Promotion-in-Western-Economies-a-Pause-in-Promotion-Escalation.pdf. Accessed 10 Aug 2017.

Luo, X., Andrews, M., Fang, Z., & Phang, C. W. (2014). Mobile targeting. *Management Science, 60*(7), 1738–1756.

N.N. (2002, May 24). Promotions – Fass ohne Boden? *Lebensmittelzeitung*, p. 36.

Neslin, S. A., & Macé, S. (2004). The determinants of pre- and postpromotion dips in sales of frequently purchased goods. *Journal of Marketing Research, 41*(3), 339–350.

Neslin, S. A., & Schneider Stone, L. G. (1996). Consumer inventory sensitivity and the postpromotion dip. *Marketing Letters, 7*(1), 77–94.

Nijs, V., Dekimpe, M. G., Steenkamp, J.-B. E. M., & Hanssens, D. M. (2001). The category-demand effects of price promotions. *Marketing Science, 20*(1), 1–22.

Train, K. (2009). *Discrete choice methods with simulation* (2nd ed.). Cambridge: Cambridge University Press.

Van Heerde, H. J., & Neslin, S. A. (2017). Sales promotion models. In B. Wierenga & R. van der Lans (Eds.), *Handbook of marketing decision models* (2nd ed., pp. 13–78). Berlin: Springer.

van Heerde, H. J., Leeflang, P. S. H., & Wittink, D. R. (2000). The estimation of pre- and postpromotion dips with store-level scanner data. *Journal of Marketing Research, 37*(3), 383–395.

van Heerde, H. J., Leeflang, P. S. H., & Wittink, D. R. (2001). Semiparametric analysis to estimate the deal effect curve. *Journal of Marketing Research, 38*(2), 197–215.

van Heerde, H. J., Leeflang, P. S. H., & Wittink, D. R. (2002). How promotions work: Scan*pro-based evolutionary model building. *Schmalenbach Business Review, 54*(3), 198–220.

van Heerde, H. J., Gupta, S., & Wittink, D. R. (2003). Is 75% of the sales promotion bump due to brand switching? No, only 33% is. *Journal of Marketing Research, 40*(4), 481–491.

van Heerde, H. J., Leeflang, P. S. H., & Wittink, D. R. (2004). Decomposing the sales promotion bump with store data. *Marketing Science, 23*(3), 317–334.

Wansink, B., Kent, R. J., & Hoch, S. J. (1998). An anchoring and adjustment model of purchase quantity decisions. *Journal of Marketing Research, 35*(1), 71–81.

Wittink, D. R., Addona, M. J., Hawkes, W. J., & Porter, J. C. (1987). Scan*pro: A model to measure short-term effects for promotional activities on brand sales, based on store-level scanner data, Working paper, Cornell University.

Return on Media Models

Dominique M. Hanssens

Contents

Introduction 1074
The Importance of Reference Points in Media Return Calculations 1075
Fundamental Advertising Response Phenomena 1076
Estimating Media Response Parameters 1078
    The Shape of the Advertising-Response Function 1078
    Advertising-Response Dynamics 1080
    Data-Interval Bias 1082
    Asymmetric Response 1083
    Dealing with Reverse Causality 1083
    Differences Across Media 1085
    Advertising Copy and Creative Effects 1086
    Intermediate Performance Metrics 1086
Deriving Media Returns from the Estimated Response Parameters 1087
Path-to-Purchase and Attribution Models for Digital Media 1088
Media Advertising and Asset Creation 1090
    Brand Equity 1091
    Customer Equity 1092
    Other Response Metrics 1093
Conclusion 1094
References 1094

Abstract

The proliferation of marketing media, especially since the advent of digital media, has created an urgent need for marketers to understand their relative importance in generating revenue for their brands. Ultimately, this understanding should result in managers' ability to project returns from their media investments. This chapter will focus on quantitative methods that enable such media return calculations. We

---

D. M. Hanssens (✉)
UCLA Anderson School of Management, Los Angeles, CA, USA
e-mail: dominique.hanssens@anderson.ucla.edu

© Springer Nature Switzerland AG 2022
C. Homburg et al. (eds), *Handbook of Market Research*,
https://doi.org/10.1007/978-3-319-57413-4_1

begin with a definition of "return on media" and show how it connects to the need of estimating top-line lift, i.e., consumer response to media, from various data sources. We introduce the standard media-mix response model and discuss the estimation of media response elasticities. We extend these models to include brand-building and customer-equity effects and intermediate-performance variables. Finally, we address return to media in the digital era, with specific reference to path-to-purchase models, and we describe how media returns are derived from sales response models.

Keywords

Return on media · Marketing mix · Sales response models · Attribution models · Marketing resource allocation

Introduction

Advertising is one of the most visible activities of companies and brands. Firms and brands advertise for a variety of reasons, among them to help launch new products, to announce price changes, to increase brand awareness, and to protect the brand franchise against competitive encroachment. These efforts are expensive. Worldwide advertising expenditures amounted to about $600 billion in 2015. In relative terms, the advertising outlays in many firms are of an order of magnitude comparable to that of their profitability. For example, in 2015, the worldwide ad spending of Procter & Gamble was about $8.3 billion, while their net income was about $7 billion. Thus, knowledge of the economic impact of, and more specifically, the *return* on advertising spending is of paramount importance to managers and investors alike.

In recent years, there has been increasing pressure on marketing executives to demonstrate the shareholder value created by these investments, which are, after all, discretionary. Not surprisingly, a financial definition has emerged as the key metric for value, viz., return on investment (ROI). This motivates the focus of the current chapter on the models that are needed to obtain reasonable estimates of these media returns.

We start with a concise definition of return on media (ROM hereafter). Consistent with finance practice, return on media is the estimate of the incremental financial value (in monetary terms) to the firm generated by identifiable media expenditures, less the cost of those expenditures as a percentage of the same expenditures (Some firms do not subtract cost of media in the numerator. The resulting metric is still usable, as it merely shifts the break-even value from 0 to 1. However, that definition is, strictly speaking, not a "return" metric and runs the risk of being misinterpreted by financial executives.):

$$\text{ROM} = \frac{\text{Incremental Financial Value Generated by Media} - \text{Cost of Media}}{\text{Cost of Media}} \quad (1)$$

Unlike other types of investments, media funds are rarely tied up in inventories, fixed assets, or receivables, and most media expenditures come from what otherwise would be liquid funds. Therefore, great care will need to be taken to validate comparisons between the return on media and other ROI estimates. In particular, the effects of some media spending may be short-lived, while other media actions may generate revenue and profit returns over multiple years, building cumulative impact and creating assets with future value. What is needed is a strong focus on the first part of the numerator in (1), i.e., the *incremental* financial value attributed to the media spending. This attribution needs to, first, understand the *top-line* effects of media spending, which are typically expressed as unit sales or sales revenues. Unit sales are then multiplied by gross profit margins to obtain gross financial contribution. Sales revenues are multiplied by percent gross margin, or, in the case of relationship businesses, by the margin multiplier (Gupta et al. 2004) (The margin multiplier transforms short-term revenue to long-term revenue by incorporating the expected loyalty levels of newly acquired customers. The section on *"Customer Equity"* offers more specifics.). Once the incremental financial contributions are determined, it is straightforward to do the cost accounting part of the equation, i.e. subtract and divide by media spending.

With respect to top-line media effects, there exists a detailed marketing science literature on the sales response effects of advertising and other marketing drivers, see for example Hanssens et al. (2001), to which we turn next. We will make ample use of this literature in discussing the nature of consumer response to advertising response and its implications for model building. This focus on top-line media effects will also allow us to avoid some misinterpretations in industry's use of media return estimates, which we discuss first.

The Importance of Reference Points in Media Return Calculations

Although the math is simple, the meaning and significance of the ROM metric is anything but straightforward. Above all, the first term in the numerator, "incremental financial value generated by media" needs careful attention. "Incremental" can only be measured if there is a baseline or reference point for comparison, i.e., "incremental compared to what." Second, the metric makes it necessary to make an attribution with respect to media expenditures, i.e., there needs to be a causal link between the two. Finally, there is a time dimension with respect to "incremental value" that could influence the calculations.

Industry studies often result in stated conclusions such as "the return of our TV spending is 45%, whereas it is 32% for spending on print media. Therefore, TV works better for us." Regardless of which medium is more effective, such statements are misleading, because they critically depend on the amount spent on each media. For example, if print is highly impactful, but the firm overspends on print media, its total return will be affected negatively, and could easily drop below that of other, less impactful media. Total ROM comparisons across media can only be made when the spending levels are the same, which is typically not the case.

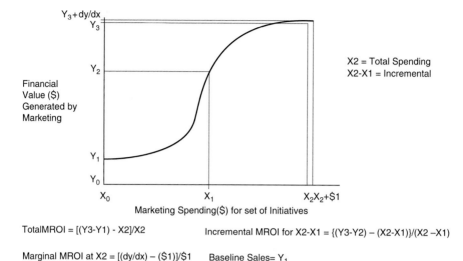

Fig. 1 Total, incremental, and marginal media returns (Source: Farris et al. (2015))

Figure 1 illustrates graphically the distinction between reporting total, incremental, and marginal ROM. Total ROM evaluates return on all spending, incremental for a specified additional spending "increment," and marginal is the estimated return on the "last dollar" of media spending. Total and Incremental ROM are typically easier to estimate and often result from experimental designs (so-called A/B testing), or from models that use linear response functions. Evaluating the marginal returns to spending is more challenging and, with the exception of complex and expensive experiments, will usually involve models that include nonlinear response functions. Conceptually and practically, these three types of returns are different and they should not be compared to each other. Although diminishing returns will eventually be encountered, there is no general rule on which of the three measures of ROM will be higher or lower. Their relative values will depend on the shape of the response function and where on that function the return is evaluated. In other words, the critical difference among the three is the comparison or reference spending level. Because media impact on revenue is nonlinear, it matters a great deal which reference point is chosen. We therefore need to start the discussion with a summary of what is known about the advertising-to-sales response function.

Fundamental Advertising Response Phenomena

As media returns are derived, first and foremost, from the media's impact on top-line revenue, we must recognize the specific nature of consumer response to media advertising. This response is *not* linear. Instead, it is characterized by the following five specific phenomena, which were first summarized in a seminal paper by John Little (1979):

- The steady-state response of sales to advertising is concave or S-shaped.
- Upward response is fast; downward response is slow.
- Competitive spending matters.
- Advertising effectiveness changes over time.
- Response can tail off even under constant spending.

Since this publication, a number of studies on advertising response have provided quantifications of advertising response that put these findings in a sharper perspective.

First, the predominant response function is concave, and the advertising elasticity (Advertising elasticity is the percent change in sales divided by the percent change in advertising. It implies that the sales change can be attributed to the advertising change.) empirical generalization is 0.1 (Sethuraman et al. 2011). Threshold effects that lead to S-shaped response functions may exist, but they are the exception (e.g., Rao and Miller 1975). In terms of overall sales sensitivity, advertising is the weakest of the marketing-mix instruments (see Hanssens et al. (2001) for details). That does not imply, however, that advertising is the least profitable instrument. It does imply that a profit-optimizing level of media spending exists, which we will elaborate on in a subsequent section.

Second, advertising elasticities are demonstrably higher for new products (elasticity about 0.3) than for established products (about 0.01) (Sethuraman et al. 2011). This is explained by the fact that, for both durables and consumables, advertising is stronger in creating awareness than in fostering preference. In particular, advertising has a stronger effect on trial rates than on repeat rates (Deighton et al. 1994). Initial awareness creation is a key for new products whereas, for more established products, prior consumer experience dominates. Indeed, the performance feedback loop (i.e., product usage experience or purchase reinforcement) is much stronger than advertising in determining future consumer choices. Hence, while advertising can be used to initiate trial, it alone is not sufficient to sustain repeat purchase without a favorable product evaluation. This helps explain the declining role of advertising over the product life cycle.

Third, visible short-term lifts are a *condition* for the existence of long-term effects. For example, an extensive experimental study by Lodish et al. (1995) showed that about *one-third* of television commercials showed a significant effect on sales in the first year. The long-term impact of these *effective* commercials is about twice the short-run effect. Thus ineffective media spending in the short run is unlikely to make a difference in the long run.

Fourth, while competitive spending matters, the ultimate effects of advertising are more influenced by the nature of consumer response itself than by the vigilance of competitors' reactions (Steenkamp et al. 2005). A straightforward approach to include competitive media spending is to use a "share of voice" metric in advertising response, i.e., brand spending divided by total (brand plus competition) spending in a certain time period.

Fifth, smaller competitors tend to have higher advertising-to-sales (A/S) ratios than market leaders (e.g., Tellis 2004). One explanation is that these smaller players desire to grow their market share and need to invest in advertising more so than their competitors (in relative terms). Another explanation is that the market leaders have already developed strong assets in the form of extensive distribution and brand equity that make advertising less important for them, again in relative terms.

Finally, advertising wear-in and wear-out patterns help explain why ad response can tail off even under constant spending. For *consumables*, we know that people "learn faster than they forget," which helps explain the different rise/decay rates in ad response. Over half a century after his published experiments, Zielske's (1959) result that three to four exposures is best, still holds. If the brand continues to expose consumers beyond the fourth impression, the impact is expected to be drastically reduced. Furthermore, for *durables*, market rejuvenation is a key concept. Effective advertising for a durable product reduces the untapped market (buyers remaining), resulting in a loss of aggregate effectiveness. After some time has elapsed, the market is rejuvenated with new prospects, and a new campaign can once again be effective.

Many studies have focused on various qualitative aspects of advertising (see Vakratsas 2005 for a review of contributions). Among the most promising is work on eye movements that has revealed which aspects of a print ad (e.g., text, pictures, brand name, relative position on the page, etc.) are the most impactful (Pieters et al. 1999). Their results could well lead to a new, improved practice of copy writing. On the other hand, we know little about the *relative importance* of advertising quality and advertising quantity, e.g., can higher spending make up for poorer advertising quality?

Estimating Media Response Parameters

We now use these qualitative insights into the nature of advertising response to address the specification and estimation of media response parameters. In a subsequent section, we will address how these estimates of top-line impact are used in media return calculations that impact advertising decision-making.

The Shape of the Advertising-Response Function

All else equal, higher advertising spending is expected to increase sales for a variety of reasons. Acquiring previously unaware prospects, increasing purchase quantities, increasing brand switching in the direction of the advertised brand, and retaining a larger fraction of the existing customer base are among the major sources. At the same time, we expect there to be *diminishing returns* to these effects, again for several reasons. Consumers cease to be responsive once they have learned the basic message contained in the advertising (saturation effect), markets deplete as successful advertising causes purchasing which then removes the buyers from the market, at least temporarily (market-depletion effect) and, finally, there are natural ceilings to the number or percent of target customers that can be reached (ceiling effect). While sales then still increase with increases in advertising support, each additional unit of advertising brings less in incremental sales than the previous unit did.

As a consequence, the basic advertising-response function is *nonlinear*. More specifically, it is expected to be concave, as in the following multiplicative model

$$S_t = e^c \, A_t^\beta \, X_t^\gamma \, Z_t^\delta \, e^{u_t}, \qquad (2)$$

where S_t refers to sales or another performance metric in period t (for example, week t), A_t is the advertising support in that week, X_t refers to other elements of the marketing mix, Z_t corresponds to environmental factors, and u_t is an error term. For simplicity of exposition, we list only one X and one Z variable. The base response model may be estimated across time periods t but could also be specified over cross-sectional units $i = 1,\ldots, I$ (for example geographical regions, market segments or individual consumers), or both. We expect $0 < \beta < 1$ in estimation, a condition which results in concavity of response.

The base model (2) implies that with infinite advertising comes infinite sales. In practice, however, there will be a limit or *ceiling* to sales, usually determined by prevailing market conditions. While there are other ways to represent concavity (see e.g., Hanssens et al. 2001, pp. 100–102), the multiplicative function is particularly appealing as it recognizes that media-mix effects interact with each other (i.e., the marginal sales effect of an incremental advertising dollar depends on the other elements in the equation). In addition, taking logarithms linearizes the model:

$$\ln(S_t) = c + \beta \ln(A_t) + \gamma \ln(X_t) + \delta \ln(Z_t) + u_t, \qquad (3)$$

making it more easily estimable. Finally, the response parameters are easily interpreted as response elasticities. An example of an advertising response curve with elasticity $\beta = 0.13$ may be found in Fig. 2a.

In some cases, the response is S-shaped, i.e., there is a minimum or threshold-level of ad spend below which there is little or no impact, followed by a range of advertising spending with rapidly increasing sales response. At even higher spending levels (i.e., past a certain "inflection point"), the usual diminishing returns appear (see Fig. 2b). The base model (2) can readily be extended to an "odds" model that allows for S-shaped response, as demonstrated by Johansson (1979):

$$(S_t - I)/(K - S_t) = e^c \, A_t^\beta \, X_t^\gamma \, Z_t^\delta \, e^{u_t}, \qquad (4)$$

where I is the minimum sales level (e.g., the level at zero media spend), and K is the ceiling level. For example, if sales is expressed in relative terms (i.e., market shares), I could be set at 0% and K at 100%. For advertising response parameters $0 < \beta < 1$, model (4) is still concave, but for $\beta > 1$, the function is S-shaped. Johansson (1979) discusses the formal estimation of (4) with maximum-likelihood methods, as well as an easy approximation based on ordinary least squares.

For all practical purposes, concavity and S-shape are sufficient functional forms to capture the essence of advertising response (We refer to Hanssens et al. (2001) for

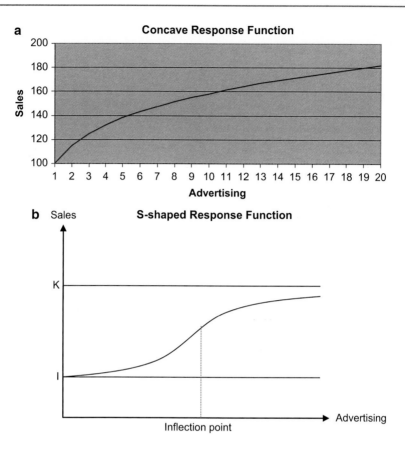

Fig. 2 (**a**) Concave response function (**b**) S-shaped response function

a review of other functional specifications that have been used in the literature.). In some cases, the response may be even simpler; if all the advertising spending observations lie in a restricted range of the data, the response function may well be approximated by a linear function. Of course, one should be careful not to make media effect inferences outside this restricted range.

Advertising-Response Dynamics

Advertising is communication, which can trigger memory, and thus its impact may easily extend beyond the campaign period. Similarly, customers could be exposed to a given advertising message (e.g., a magazine ad insert or pop-up digital ad) on multiple occasions. Therefore, response models that simply relate current sales to current advertising expenditures are likely to underestimate advertising's total impact. Provided good longitudinal data are available, advertising-response dynamics can be represented by extending the core model in (2) to a distributed-lag model over time t:

$$S_t = e^c \, A_t^{\beta(L)} \, X_t^{\gamma} \, Z_t^{\delta} \, e^{u_t}, \tag{5}$$

where $\beta(L) = \beta_0 + \beta_1 L + \beta_2 L^2 + \beta_3 L^3 + \ldots$, and with L the lag operator (i.e., $L^2 A_t = A_{t-2}$).

In this model, the cumulative advertising effects are obtained as $\Sigma_i \, \beta^i$. The time-delayed effects of advertising captured in the lag-polynomial $\beta(L)$ are often referred to as carry-over effects and tend to vary across products, categories, and media. As it is hard to estimate a large number of β-parameters and/or to define a priori a precise cut-off point for the number of lags to consider, one often imposes a certain structure on the various β-parameters. A popular structure is the geometric decay implied in the Koyck model, in that $\beta_{i+1} = \lambda \beta_i$ (see e.g., Clarke 1976). Rather than a priori imposing a certain structure, one could also use empirical specification methods to determine the functional form of $\beta(L)$, such as the Box-Jenkins transfer-function method (see e.g., Helmer and Johansson 1977) or the Liu and Hanssens (1982) direct-lag specification method. A technical description of these methods is beyond the scope of this article but can be found in Hanssens et al. (2001, Chap. 7). We do want to point out, however, that the distributed lag-model in (5) is flexible enough to accommodate the well-known wear-in and wear-out effects of advertising. For example, if it takes two periods for any economic impact to take place, one can specify $\beta(L)$ as $\beta_2 L^2$. If, in addition, advertising effects wear out (decay) at a rate of 10% per period, the lag polynomial $\beta(L)$ can be written as $\beta_2 \, L^2/(1-0.9L)$.

An alternative approach to assessing the dynamic effects of advertising is Adstock (Broadbent 1984), which has gained some popularity among practitioners. The Adstock model rests on the assumption that each advertising effort adds to a preexisting stock of advertising goodwill. Conversely, absent any current advertising, the stock decays at a constant rate. Thus, the empirical specification is

$$\text{ADSTOCK}_t = \alpha \, \text{ADSTOCK}_{t-1} + (1-\alpha) A_t, \tag{6}$$

where α is the decay factor ($0 < \alpha < 1$). Adstock models are elegant in conceptualization and easy to use, as they circumvent the problem of empirical lag specification. However, the decay parameter is set subjectively and that may lead to a bias (usually an overestimation) in the advertising impact. Whenever possible, we recommend that decay parameters be estimated from the data. In addition, Adstock does not make the critical distinction between *purchase reinforcement* and *advertising carryover*. Suppose advertising generates trial for a new product, which leads to a positive consumption experience and, therefore, subsequent (repeat) sales. While advertising should be credited with generating the initial sales, it should share that credit with purchase reinforcement for subsequent sales. Givon and Horsky (1990) developed a distributed lag model to disentangle both effects. Their application in several product categories revealed that the purchase feedback effect dominates the advertising carryover effect.

Research on the dynamics of advertising impact has intensified in recent years, in part because of the availability of high-quality advertising response data, especially from digital media. This has created a need for more advanced estimation methods such as persistence modeling, dynamic linear models, and Bayesian estimation. A detailed comparative review of these methods may be found in Leeflang et al. (2009).

Data-Interval Bias

The determination of advertising response dynamics is closely related to the chosen temporal data interval. In the past, data intervals posed a serious econometric problem because they were too coarse to allow for detailed inference. For example, sales and advertising movements sampled annually, or even quarterly, will almost inevitably represent a mixture of consumer response effects, firm decision, and competitive reaction effects. Thus, the nature of a *contemporaneous* correlation between advertising and sales is difficult to ascertain. Moreover, marketing researchers have long been puzzled by the empirical observation that estimated carry-offer, and hence, advertising-duration effects, differed depending on whether dynamic advertising models were estimated on monthly, quarterly, or annual data. Conventional wisdom was then to use as "preferred" data interval the one that most closely resembled the brand's interpurchase time (see e.g., Leone (1995) for a review). This view was challenged by Tellis and Franses (2006), who showed that one can retrieve the correct carryover effects with aggregate data provided one has information about the exact interexposure times. However, in many instances, applied marketing researchers do not know the exact media insertion patterns, let alone the interexposure time of consumers. In that case, using data at the lowest level of aggregation was found to be a good heuristic.

Fortunately, advertising databases have become available at much more disaggregate sampling levels. For example, weekly media advertising spending data are routinely collected by Kantar Media and Nielsen. When matched with weekly sales numbers, distributed lag models of advertising effects may readily be estimated. Contemporaneous correlations between advertising and sales can then safely be interpreted as consumer response effects, since it would be difficult for most organizations to react to competitive moves and/or to incorporate sales feedback in advertising spending within 1 week. In some cases, the data interval is reduced even further, for example to hourly measurements in the case of direct-response television campaigns (e.g., Tellis et al. 2000). Overall, it is fair to conclude that advances in data collection technology are gradually obsoleting the problem of temporal data interval bias.

Another form of data aggregation bias is cross-sectional. For example, national data may be used in an advertising response model, even though some regional markets receive different advertising exposures than others. In nonlinear models (as the multiplicative core model (2)), linear aggregation (e.g., when data of the individual regions are summed to a national aggregate) will create biased estimates of advertising's effectiveness if advertising spending differed between the regions across which the summation took place. We refer to Christen et al. (1997) for an in-depth discussion of these issues.

Asymmetric Response

The core response model assumes that advertising effects are symmetric, so if adding 10% to the spending increases sales by 2%, then cutting the spending by 10% implies that sales will decrease by 2%. In reality, however, asymmetries may exist.

Consider the case where a successful new advertising campaign first acquires several new customers quickly, then brings in a lower, but still positive number of new customers. Similarly, at some point, a mature brand's sales may have become resistant to further advertising increases but quite sensitive to advertising reductions (Vakratsas 2005), a situation many managers may feel applies to their brand. Representing such a process requires that we model, separately, the effects of "starting," "continuing," and "ending" of a campaign. That problem was tackled by Simon (1982), who extends the core response model (with only contemporaneous response effects for simplicity of exposure) as follows:

$$S_t = e^c \, A_t \, \beta + \theta \, I_t \, X_t^{\gamma} \, Z_t^{\delta} \, e^u{}_t, \qquad (7)$$

where $I_t = 1$ if the period corresponds to the beginning of a campaign, and $I_t = 0$ elsewhere. Similarly, one could add another time-varying dummy variable to denote the ending of the campaign. Thus, the start of a campaign has a total positive impact of $(\beta + \theta)$, and the remainder of the campaign has a "level" impact of β. Simon refers to the asymmetric effect θ as a "differential-stimulus" effect. This model was tested by Hanssens and Levien (1983) in the context of Navy advertising for recruits. Their lead generation model showed, for example, that radio advertising had a θ effect of 0.08 added to its level elasticity β of 0.26.

New data sources could provide even better insights into the asymmetric response nature of advertising. For example, in the case of a durable product or service, a company may be able to separate its weekly sales into two components: sales coming from new customers and sales from existing customers. Since we know that advertising has a stronger impact on trial sales than on repeat sales (e.g., Deighton et al. 1994), we may discover the asymmetries by applying the core model (2) separately to both components.

Dealing with Reverse Causality

Scientists like to make inferences from experimental data, i.e., where the treatment and control conditions are assigned randomly, so that the impact of the treatment is readily isolated from other influences on the dependent variable of interest. Marketing managers, however, would not last long if their allocation decisions were made randomly. In the case of advertising spending, for example, some months of the year may be favored over others, and some products or regional markets will likewise receive preferential allocation over others. In most cases, these allocations are made based on *ex ante expected sales performance*. For example, motion picture studios routinely allocate substantial prelaunch advertising budgets to high-cost productions that are expected to become blockbusters, sometimes as part of their contractual obligations to high-profile actors.

These well-known managerial conditions create an inference problem called endogeneity or reverse causality. Econometrically, it means that the error term in model (2) may be correlated with some of the explanatory variables, in Casu advertising. Ordinary least-squares estimation will then lead to biased estimates of advertising's effects on sales. For example, if management picks successful products to advertise more heavily, an OLS estimator may confuse a true advertising effect with a "popular-product" effect, and thus overestimate the advertising impact.

Endogeneity is most problematic with cross-sectional data, where the modeler lacks the natural passing of time to establish the direction of effects. Standard econometric tests such as the Hausman test are available to diagnose endogeneity, and when detected, alternative estimators such as instrumental-variable methods may be used. We refer to Van Heerde et al. (2005) for an in-depth discussion of these methods. Even so, the most reliable inference of advertising impact on cross-sectional data comes from experimental designs in which some markets or customers are deliberately given different advertising treatments than others. A good example in this context are the V-8 advertising experiments reported in Eastlack and Rao (1986). Advertising experiments are now enjoying a resurgence because of the relative ease with which they can be executed with digital media, see for example Lambrecht and Tucker (2017).

On time-series data, endogeneity is less problematic provided one has sufficiently short data intervals (e.g., weekly data). It is generally the case that consumers can respond to advertising stimuli a lot faster than companies can adjust their advertising spending to changes in consumer demand. Thus, if an application of core model (2) reveals a 0.2 contemporaneous elasticity of advertising, we can be reasonably confident that this is a true advertising response effect. In addition, any lagged advertising response effects are by definition free of reverse causality effects.

It is important to understand that the presence of decision feedback loops and competitive reactions can create a long-run outcome of an advertising campaign that may be quite different from its short-run impact. In order to assess such long-run effects, the single-equation advertising response model in (2) is replaced by a dynamic system with multiple equations, a method called "persistence modeling." A discussion of persistence models is beyond the scope of this chapter and may be found in Dekimpe and Hanssens (1995) (Persistence modeling uses Vector Autoregressive Modeling (VAR) techniques.). Taken together, the combined chain-like effects of consumer response, decision feedback and competitive response to various marketing initiatives, including media advertising, can generate long-run sales impacts that are up to five times that of their short-term response, as demonstrated by Pauwels (2004) in the frozen-dinner market.

Differences Across Media

Not all advertising media are created equal, and in many cases, a marketer will want to understand the differential impact of spending in different media. The core response model allows for this by including as many explanatory variables in the response model as there are relevant media. For example, a media-mix model may be

$$S_t = e^c \, TV_t^{\beta_1(L)} \, PRINT_t^{\beta_2(L)} \, EMAIL_t^{\beta_3(L)} \, X_t^\gamma \, Z_t^\delta \, e^{u_t}, \qquad (8)$$

where the combined advertising expenditures A_t are now replaced by the respective expenditures in three media (as an illustration): TV, Print, and Email. Each medium has its own response elasticity and lag structure. Provided the database has sufficient degrees of freedom, and provided there is natural variation in the media spending patterns, media-mix models can be used to disentangle the relative contribution of each medium in explaining observed sales variations.

Media mix models have a long history starting with Montgomery and Silk (1972) who analyzed a pharmaceutical market and showed the differential impact of print advertising, direct mail, and sampling and literature. Dekimpe and Hanssens (1995) considered both print and TV advertising for a major home-improvement chain and found the medium with the lowest short-run effect (TV) to have the highest long-run impact.

At the qualitative level, one can make predictions of differential media impact by considering the information style delivered by each medium. Advertising is persuasive inasfar as it fosters consumers' cognition, affect, and experience (Vakratsas and Ambler 1999). Specifically, print or internet advertising is strong on *cognition* because readers can absorb factual information about a product as long as they like (for example, reading about the performance characteristics of an automobile). TV, by contrast, is better at delivering *affect* through the use of sound and motion (for example, portraying the thrill of a car's swift acceleration). Communicating *experience* is often achieved with specific advertising content such as consumer testimonials and celebrity endorsements, for which several media may be used. By matching the delivery of cognition, affect, and experience to the needs of the advertised brand, managers can formulate initial hypotheses about media differences that are testable using model (8) and its variants.

Should a company invest all of its advertising spending in the medium with the highest lift? While such a decision rule is simple, it would be incorrect. Not only do sales benefit from synergistic effects of spending across the media but the laws of diminishing returns would make such a rule suboptimal. Instead, managers should allocate their advertising budget to media *in proportion to the media response elasticities*, the so-called Dorfman-Steiner conditions. While a formal proof of this proposition is beyond the scope of this chapter, it is readily obtained by maximizing the profit function accompanying response model (8). See, for example Hanssens et al. (2001) for a more detailed discussion. Explicitly allowing for synergistic effects between two media which are each characterized by diminishing returns, Naik and Raman (2003) demonstrated that, as synergy increases, advertisers should not only increase the total budget but also allocate more funds to the less effective medium.

Advertising Copy and Creative Effects

Creativity of communication is an integral part of advertising design and execution and can have a substantial impact on the persuasive appeal of advertising. From a response modeling perspective, creative impact can be measured in a number of ways. First, one could use categorical variables to distinguish between different creative executions (e.g., campaigns). A simple example with two campaign executions may be

$$S_t = e^c \, A_t^{\beta_1(L) + \beta_2(L) \, E_t} \, X_t^\gamma \, Z_t^\delta \, e^{u_t}, \tag{9}$$

where $E_t = 0$ for the base execution, and $E_t = 1$ for the new execution. Inasfar as the new copy had a different impact on sales than the previous execution, the terms in $\beta_2(L)$ will be different from zero. Alternatively, one could try to directly import creative-quality metrics into the market-response model. For example, suppose a panel of experts rate the creative execution of each advertising campaign on a 5-point scale. Then the basic advertising response model may be extended to distinguish between spending elasticities and creative-execution elasticities as follows:

$$S_t = e^c \, A_t^{\beta_1(L) + \beta_2(L) \, Q_t} \, X_t^\gamma \, Z_t^\delta \, e^{u_t}, \tag{10}$$

where the $\beta_1(L)$ terms now measure the pure spending effects of advertising, and the $\beta_2(L)$ terms measure how these effects increase with higher-quality creative, measured by Q_t. This approach was used in a Bayesian framework for measuring advertising copy effects by Gatignon (1984).

The internet age promises to bring new insights from the measurement of digital communication content in general and the creative quality of advertising in particular. For example, text-mining algorithms are used by Culotta and Cutler (2016) to monitor brand messages on Twitter and by Trusov et al. (2016) to target consumers for advertising based on their web-surfing behavior.

Intermediate Performance Metrics

So far, the core response model (2) and its extensions have focused on cases where the advertising→sales relationship can be inferred in a direct way, which is the most relevant for assessing accountability and financial planning. While these represent the majority of applications, there are instances of relatively long sales cycles, notably in some business-to-business markets, where advertising's impact is better represented in stages. For example, media spending may create awareness of a certain business-to-business offering; however, that awareness is insufficient to create a sale. Instead, there need to be follow-up sales calls to an initial inquiry, sometimes multiple calls, to guide the customer to an eventual product adoption.

Intermediate media performance metrics may include consumer awareness, consumer consideration, and consumer preference metrics. They are generally survey based and are not financial in nature and therefore do not readily lend themselves to return calculations. However, they can be used as intermediate dependent variables in a chain (system of equations), where each equation is similar in design to the core response model (5). For example, media spending impacts consumer awareness in an awareness equation. This, in turn, converts to sales in a separate sales equation. The ultimate return of media spending then depends on their initial impact on awareness multiplied by the awareness-to-sales conversion rate. Hanssens et al. (2014) developed such a system for several brands in four consumer product categories over a 7-year period. They reported that the model with intermediate performance metrics provided superior performance in terms of sales prediction accuracy as well as quality of managerial recommendations.

A major challenge with intermediate performance metrics is that they should be collected at similar data intervals as the sales data, which is often unrealistic. For example, sales data are available on a weekly or even daily basis, but consumer preference surveys are conducted only quarterly. The advent of digital data sources, however, provides new metrics that can prove to be useful. These include Google queries (a proxy for consumer interest) and Facebook likes (a proxy for consumer sentiment). Figure 4 illustrates how different digital response metrics impact the estimation of media effectiveness, as discussed below.

Deriving Media Returns from the Estimated Response Parameters

Having obtained some reliable estimates of sales response to media spending (i.e., the *top-line* effects), how are media *return* estimates derived? Assuming a constant profit margin, the net cash flows (CF) in period t – excluding nonmedia costs – may be expressed as

$$CF_t = S_t^* \text{ margin} - A_t, \qquad (11)$$

where A_t is total advertising media spending.

The *total* return on media spending A is then obtained as

$$ROM = [CF(A) - CF(A=0)]/A \qquad (12)$$

Note that ROM is a ratio, which is useful for an ex-post assessment of the return of a specific media campaign or investment. However, as pointed out earlier, total ROM should *not* be used to determine optimal levels of media spending. Doing so will often result in underinvesting on media, because ROM typically declines monotonically with higher spending (see Ambler and Roberts 2008 for an elaboration). Instead, the optimal media spend A* may be derived from maximizing the cash-flow function (11) based on the response model (5):

$$A^* = \left[e^{c'} * \beta(L) * \text{margin} \right]^{1/[1-\beta(L)]}, \qquad (13)$$

where we have incorporated the effects of other firm-controlled variables X and environmental conditions Z into the adjusted baseline $e^{c'}$ for ease of exposition. It is easy to demonstrate that, at this optimal spend level, the *marginal* ROM is zero.

Importantly, the relationship between media spending and cash flow generation depends on (i) the natural size (the baseline) of the business, (ii) the productivity of media spending β(L), and (iii) the prevailing profit margin. Taken together, they fully determine optimal short-run media-resource allocation. At the same time, these determinants are exogenous; for example, it is assumed that more aggressive media spending has no impact on either the baseline or media effectiveness itself. Thus, the decision rule in (13) may be thought of as a harvesting or reactive view of media resource allocation. We will discuss in a subsequent section how to incorporate *asset-building* effects of media spending, in particular brand equity and customer equity.

The important take-away from the analysis so far is that only *one* ROM definition is useful for media allocation decisions: the *marginal* media return should be zero across all the media in the mix. Positive marginal returns indicate *underspending* and negative values suggest *overspending* in that medium.

A corollary of this basic result is that, while total ROM estimates can always be made, they are useful only for comparing the impact of *equal* spend levels. For example, if total media ROI is 75% for TV spending and 60% for internet spending, you cannot infer that TV is a more effective medium *unless* the two have the same spending levels. Indeed, the internet spending may *appear* to be a less impactful medium, whereas, in reality, the medium is highly effective but offers a lower ROM due to high spending relative to TV.

Finally, note that it is difficult to obtain marginal ROM estimates – and, therefore, optimal advertising spending levels – from advertising experiments, because these generally result in only two or three points of the response curve. Media experiments are more useful for assessing the causal impact of media on sales and for testing different creative executions.

Path-to-Purchase and Attribution Models for Digital Media

The media return measurement approach described above applies to all media and as such is widely used. In recent years, the availability of so-called *path to purchase* data in the online world has resulted in a different approach for ROM assessment. The central idea is that, at any point in time, individual consumers have different purchase probabilities for a given category and brand, and they reveal these probabilities by their online activities, including searching, blogging, and clicking on various online ads. These methods are generally known as *digital attribution* methods.

Initially, digital attribution models used a simple *last click* heuristic, i.e., whichever medium the consumer used just prior to online purchase was given full credit for the purchase conversion. Subsequently, more sophisticated models recognized that prior media interventions may deserve some conversion credit as well, by recognizing that consumers move through various stages in the purchase funnel over time. A well-known digital attribution technique (Li and Kannan 2014) makes the distinction between customer-initiated web actions (e.g., conducting a search, visiting a website) and firm-initiated channels (e.g., delivering a pop-up display ad, sending an e-mail). These actions change the consumer's purchase probability over time, to different degrees. Figure 3 presents the conceptual framework underlying the authors' digital attribution method.

The key challenge in digital attribution is to estimate the *incremental* purchase probability achieved by a certain media intervention. To do so, the authors set up a model that incorporates consumers' movement from brand consideration stage to visit stage to purchase stage and estimate it with Bayesian methods. Their empirical analysis in the hospitality industry revealed strong differences across the media in their ability to convert consumers' apparent interest in a product to actual purchase.

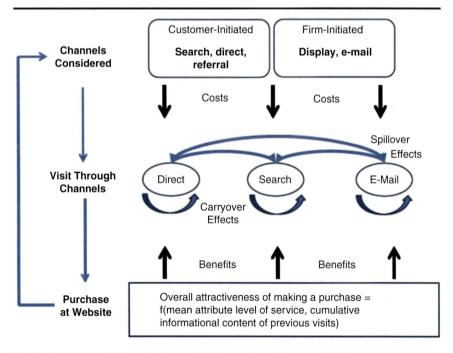

Fig. 3 Conceptual digital attribution model (Source: Li and Kannan (2014))

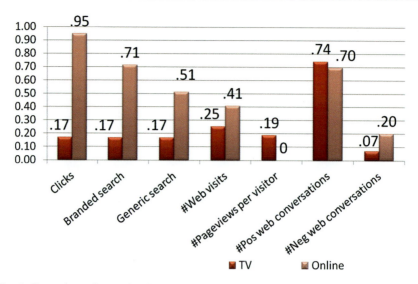

Fig. 4 Comparison of TV and online media elasticities on online performance metrics (Source: Pauwels and van Ewijk (2013))

The differences in estimated response effects of digital media inside the consumer purchase funnel are illustrated in Fig. 4 (Pauwels and van Ewijk 2013). One important conclusion from the figure is that, the deeper one goes into the consumer purchase funnel, the lower the estimated media elasticities. The figure also shows that digital elasticities are generally higher than TV elasticities, *except* on the criterion of generating positive web conversations. This illustrates the principle that traditional media (such as TV) can "drive consumers to the web" and, as such, still provide an important role in the overall media mix.

An in-depth review of digital marketing, including attribution models, may be found in Kannan and Li (2017). Overall, digital attribution models offer substantial promise in the analysis of digital media ROI. At the same time, they depend on accurate clickstream data and, as such, are limited to online purchasing. The use of digital attribution models in industry will increase with their ability to act on consumer actions in a "just-in-time" fashion. For example, *mobile* advertising messages are particularly adept at reaching consumers who are close to a purchase occasion.

Media Advertising and Asset Creation

A prevailing belief among practitioners and academics is that well-placed media spending not only stimulates sales but also builds *future assets* for the firm. In order to represent that capability of media, we must extend the core response model to account for endogenously created assets that, in turn, will generate future cash flows.

Not doing so may result in underestimating media returns, because only the cash flows coming from incremental sales effects are incorporated. By contrast, by considering *stock metrics* of business performance, in addition to cash flows, we may represent important long-term media effects. Among those stock metrics, the most important are brand equity and customer equity.

Brand Equity

Perhaps the most frequently studied stock metric in the marketing literature is the concept of brand equity. An excellent review is given in Ailawadi et al. (2003), who propose the *revenue premium* as a financially relevant measure for the value of a brand in a given industry. The revenue premium is defined as the difference in revenue realized by branded vs. unbranded competitors, i.e.,

$$\text{Revenue premium} = \text{volume}_{\text{brand}} * \text{price}_{\text{brand}} - \text{volume}_{\text{nonbrand}} * \text{price}_{\text{nonbrand}} \quad (14)$$

This reflects the idea that brand equity may boost sales volume, allow for a price premium, or both. Put differently, brand-building activities may enhance future cash flows as a result of realizing a higher sales volume and/or a higher price. The measure is shown to be actionable, stable over time, and to have considerable diagnostic value in terms of the brand's long-run health, thereby conforming to our earlier criteria. Interestingly, Ailawadi et al. (2003) also demonstrate how branded products exhibit asymmetric upward and downward (market-share) price elasticities. Using data from a variety of consumer-packaged products, they derive that low-revenue premium brands have an average down price elasticity of -1.195, and an average up elasticity of -0.921. High-equity brands, in contrast, have an average down share elasticity of -0.747, and an up elasticity of only -0.183. Hence, while brands with a higher revenue premium gain some share when they reduce their prices, they lose comparatively less share when they increase their price. As such, brand equity is a stock metric that enhances future cash flows through three different routes described earlier: higher baseline sales (volume premium), higher profit margins (price premium), and increased marketing effectiveness (differential $\beta(L)$).

Note that some marketing activity may deteriorate brand equity. For example, Mela et al. (1997) used time-varying response models to demonstrate that increasing the frequency of sales promotions may increase customers' price sensitivity to the brand. As a result, either a smaller percent of sales is generated at full price, or the brand's price premium is lowered. Both scenarios result in damage to the brand's equity.

From a media return perspective, the revenue premium that captures brand equity in (14) is typically estimated using the sales-response model (5) for different brands in a category and examining differences in the intercept and slope parameters. A time-varying-parameter version of this model may also be used in this context.

Customer Equity

While brand equity focuses on the supply side, i.e., the offerings of the firm, customer equity (CE) is an asset valued on the demand side, with specific reference to the firm's customer base. Customer lifetime value (CLV) is generally defined as the present value of all future profits obtained from a customer over his/her life of relationship with a firm (Gupta et al. 2004):

$$CLV = \sum_{t=0}^{T} \frac{(p_t - c_t)r_t}{(1+i)^t} - AC \qquad (15)$$

where p_t = revenue generated by a consumer at time t, c_t = direct cost of servicing the customer at time t, i = discount rate or cost of capital for the firm, r_t = probability of customer repeat buying or being "alive" at time t, AC = customer acquisition cost, and T = time horizon for estimating CLV.

Customer equity (CE) is the sum of the firm's customers' lifetime values. CLV and CE measure "net present value" from a customer asset perspective, and thus speak to both shareholder value and customer value.

Marketing spending may impact customer equity in several ways: through acquiring new customers (at a cost AC per customer), through retaining existing customers (at a servicing cost c_t in each period), and through increasing per-customer revenue, which is sometimes referred to as *share of wallet*. In relationship businesses such as insurance and financial services, these effects can be quantified through direct counting of customers and aggregation of their CLVs. In most cases, however, the direct-count approach is not feasible or practical, and we should infer marketing's impact on customer equity at a more aggregate level (see e.g., Rust et al. 2004). This may be achieved by examining marketing's role in *purchase reinforcement*, i.e., using an existing sale to create more future sales from that customer. Purchase reinforcement modeling applies mainly in frequently purchased product and service categories, where consumers have reason to expect a similar-quality experience between one purchase occasion and the next. Givon and Horsky (1990) developed a market-share model that contrasts the impact of purchase experience (β) relative to advertising-induced retention (λ) as follows:

$$\text{Share}_t = \alpha(1 - \lambda) + (\beta + \lambda)\text{Share}_{t-1} - \beta \lambda \, \text{Share}_{t-2} + \gamma \, \text{Adshare}_t + e_t \qquad (16)$$

This model is a special case of the dynamic core response function (5) with two-period dynamics. Thus it lends itself to calculations of the cash-flow impact (and therefore return) of investments in advertising vs. customer service provision. In their empirical investigation of four frequently purchased product categories, the authors reported that $\beta > \lambda$, i.e., the impact of purchase experience exceeds that of advertising spending. As such, even without renewed instantaneous media support, a stock effect is at work that results in future sales.

Since then, more complex models have been developed that infer movements in customer equity from sales transactions data and brand-related marketing actions in a variety of sectors. For example, Hanssens et al. (2008) explored the impact of various marketing activities and external factors on the growth in customer equity for a major financial institution. Customer equity has, in various studies, been found to be an actionable and stable metric, which offers reliable guidance and an explicit linkage to financial performance (see e.g., Gupta and Lehmann 2005 for a review).

Other Response Metrics

Our discussion of return on media would not be complete without considering other, indirect ways in which media spending can enhance firm performance and, therefore, be subject to return calculations. We list below a number of important alternative performance metrics, discussed in Dekimpe and Hanssens (2011), and we make some observations about how advertising is known to affect them. Note that the response models for these alternative metrics are generally similar in nature to the models we have discussed in this chapter.

Protecting or enhancing price premiums. There is evidence that, ceteris paribus, nonprice advertising leads to lower price sensitivity and hence the ability to charge higher prices (e.g., Farris and Albion 1980). Note that, by the same token, price advertising may *increase* price sensitivity (see also Kaul and Wittink 1995).

Enhancing sales-call effectiveness. Advertising support may pre-educate a prospect so that subsequent sales calls have a higher chance of success. For example, Gatignon and Hanssens (1987) found this to be the case in military recruitment, i.e., the effectiveness of recruiting efforts increases with higher levels of media support.

Building distribution. When the trade makes stocking decisions based on anticipated consumer demand and when they perceive that demand to be influenced by advertising, higher distribution levels may be obtained (e.g., Parsons 1974). Since the distribution-to-sales elasticity is known to be high, this indirect route of media impact can be quite substantial.

Motivating employees. Advertising may have an "internal" audience in addition to its usual external audience (e.g., Gilly and Wolfinbarger 1998). This is particularly important in service-intensive industries, for example the hospitality sector, where "happy employees" can contribute to customer satisfaction.

Lifting stock price. Investors are exposed to advertising as much as consumers are. Evidence from the PC industry suggests that advertising may increase stock prices above and beyond the effect expected from an increase in sales and profits (Joshi and Hanssens 2010). In addition, advertising can reduce earnings volatility, which also impacts stock prices positively. This is because media spending is relatively easily manipulated and is fully amortized in the period in which it occurs. That makes it a convenient expenditure category to expand in times of strong earnings and reduce in times of weak earnings, thereby reducing the firm's earnings volatility and its cost of capital. This strategic use of advertising is enhanced by the finding that, over long time periods, higher media expenditures are associated with lower systemic risk of the firm (McAlister et al. 2007).

Conclusion

This chapter has reviewed the analytical aspects of determining the return on media (ROM), which is a managerial task of increasing importance given the proliferation of new, technology-enabled advertising media. We first provided a tight definition of return on media that allows marketers to speak the language of finance, which is important in budget allocations. We then reviewed some common mistakes in ROM interpretation found in industry and concluded that media return measurement should start with assessing the top-line effects (i.e., on brand sales revenue) of media spending. This led us to formulate the key phenomena of advertising response that should be present in models of media return. Next, we reviewed several challenges that arise in the measurement of advertising effects, including the shape of the advertising response function, dynamic effects of advertising, optimal data intervals for measurement, asymmetric response, reverse causality, differences in media effects, copy and creative impact, and intermediate performance metrics. Next, we derived media return values from sales response models and discussed their use in media mix allocation. Finally, we extended the measurement of media returns to purchase path analyses of digital media, to the incorporation of asset building effects such as brand equity and customer equity, and to the use of various alternative business performance metrics.

Acknowledgment I am grateful to coauthors in other publications that have helped shape the content of this chapter, in particular material from Hanssens et al. (2001), Dekimpe and Hanssens (2007, 2011), Hanssens and Dekimpe (2008), and Farris et al. (2015).

References

Ailawadi, K. L., Lehmann, D. R., & Neslin, S. A. (2003). Revenue premium as an outcome measure of brand equity. *Journal of Marketing, 67*, 1–17.

Ambler, T., & Roberts, J. H. (2008). Assessing marketing performance: Don't settle for a silver metric. *Journal of Marketing Management, 24*(7–8), 733–750.

Broadbent, S. (1984). Modeling with Adstock. *Journal of the Market Research Society, 26*, 295–312.

Christen, M., Gupta, S., Porter, J. C., Staelin, R., & Wittink, D. R. (1997). Using market level data to understand promotional effects in a nonlinear model. *Journal of Marketing Research, 34*(3), 322–334.

Clarke, D. G. (1976). Econometric measurement of the duration of advertising effect on sales. *Journal of Marketing Research, 16*, 286–289.

Culotta, A., & Cutler, J. (2016). Mining brand perceptions from twitter social networks. *Marketing Science, 25*(3), 343–362.

Deighton, J., Henderson, C., & Neslin, S. (1994). The effects of advertising on brand switching and repeat purchasing. *Journal of Marketing Research, 31*, 28–42.

Dekimpe, M. G., & Hanssens, D. (1995). The persistence of marketing effects on sales. *Marketing Science, 14*, 1–21.

Dekimpe, M. G., & Hanssens, D. M. (2007). Advertising response modeling. In G. Tellis & T. Ambler (Eds.), *Handbook of advertising*. London: Sage Publications.

Dekimpe, M. G., & Hanssens, D. M. (2011). The hidden powers of advertising investments. In J. Wierenga, P. Verhoef, & J. Hoekstra (Eds.), *Liber Amicorum in honor of Peter S.H. Leeflang*. Groningen: Rijksuniversiteit.

Eastlack, J. O., Jr., & Rao, A. G. (1986). Modeling response to advertising and pricing changes for 'V-8' cocktail vegetable juice. *Marketing Science, 5*, 245–259.

Farris, P. W., & Albion, M. S. (1980). The impact of advertising on the price of consumer products. *Journal of Advertising Research, 44*, 17–35.

Farris, P., Hanssens, D. M., Lenskold, J., & Reibstein, D. R. (2015). Marketing return on investment: Seeking clarity for concept and measurement. *Applied Marketing Analytics, 1*(3), 267–282.

Gatignon, H. (1984). Toward a methodology for measuring advertising copy effects. *Marketing Science, 3*(4), 308–326.

Gatignon, H., & Hanssens, D. M. (1987). Modeling marketing interactions with application to salesforce effectiveness. *Journal of Marketing Research, 24*, 247–257.

Gilly, M., & Wolfinbarger, M. (1998). Advertising's internal audience. *Journal of Marketing, 62*, 69–88.

Givon, M., & Horsky, D. (1990). Untangling the effects of purchase reinforcement and advertising carryover. *Marketing Science, 9*(2), 171–187.

Gupta, S., & Lehmann, D. R. (2005). *Managing customers as investments*. Upper Saddle River: Wharton School Publishing/Pearson-Financial Times.

Gupta, S., Lehmann, D. R., & Stuart, J. A. (2004). Valuing customers. *Journal of Marketing Research, 41*, 7–18.

Hanssens, D. M., & Dekimpe, M. G. (2008). Models for the financial performance effects of marketing. In B. Wierenga (Ed.), *Handbook of marketing decision models*. New York: Springer Science. Second edition forthcoming, 2017.

Hanssens, D. M., & Levien, H. A. (1983). An econometric study of recruitment marketing in the U.S. navy. *Management Science, 29*, 1167–1184.

Hanssens, D. M., Parsons, L. J., & Schultz, R. L. (2001). *Market response models* (2nd ed.). Boston: Kluwer Academic Publishers.

Hanssens, D. M., Pauwels, K. H., Srinivasan, S., Vanhuele, M., & Yildirim, G. (2014). Consumer attitude metrics for guiding marketing mix decisions. *Marketing Science, 33*, 534–550.

Hanssens, D. M., Thorpe, D., & Finkbeiner, C. (2008). Marketing when customer equity matters. *Harvard Business Review, 86*, 117–123.

Helmer, R. M., & Johansson, J. K. (1977). An exposition of the box-Jenkins transfer function analysis with application to the advertising-sales relationship. *Journal of Marketing Research, 14*, 227–239.

Johansson, J. K. (1979). Advertising and the S-curve: A new approach. *Journal of Marketing Research, 16*, 346–354.

Joshi, A., & Hanssens, D. M. (2010). The direct and indirect effects of advertising spending on firm value. *Journal of Marketing, 74*(1), 20–33.

Kannan, P. K., & Li, H. (2017). Digital marketing: A framework, review and research agenda. *International Journal of Research in Marketing, 34*, 22–45.

Kaul, A., & Wittink, D. R. (1995). Empirical generalizations about the impact of advertising on price sensitivity and price. *Marketing Science, 14*(3), G151–G160.

Lambrecht, A., & Tucker, C. E. (2017). Field experiments. In N. Mizik, & D. M. Hanssens (Eds.), *Handbook of marketing analytics: Methods and applications in marketing management, public policy and litigation support*. London: Edward Elgar, forthcoming.

Leeflang, P., Bijmolt, T., van Doorn, J., Hanssens, D., van Heerde, H., Verhoef, P., & Wierenga, J. (2009). Lift versus base: Current trends in marketing dynamics. *International Journal of Research in Marketing, 26*(1), 13–20.

Li, H., & Kannan, P. K. (2014). Attributing conversions in a multichannel online marketing environment: An empirical model and a field experiment. *Journal of Marketing Research, 51*, 40–56.

Leone, R. P. (1995). Generalizing what is known of temporal aggregation and advertising carryover. *Marketing Science, 14*(3), G141–G150.

Little, J. D. C. (1979). Aggregate advertising models: The state of the art. *Operations Research, 27*, 629–667.

Liu, L.-M., & Hanssens, D. M. (1982). Identification of multiple-input transfer function models. *Communication in Statistics Theory and Methods, 11*(3), 297–314.

Lodish, L. M., Magid, A., Kalmenson, S., Livelsberger, J., Beth, L., Richardson, B., & Stevens, M. E. (1995). How TV advertising works: A meta-analysis of 389 real world split cable TV advertising experiments. *Journal of Marketing Research, 32*, 125–139.

McAlister, L., Srinivasan, R., & Kim, M. C. (2007). Advertising, research and development, and systematic risk of the firm. *Journal of Marketing, 7*(1), 35–48.

Mela, C. F., Gupta, S., & Lehmann, D. R. (1997). The long-term impact of promotion and advertising on consumer brand choice. *Journal of Marketing Research, 34*(2), 248–261.

Montgomery, D. B., & Silk, A. J. (1972). Estimating dynamic effects of marketing communication expenditures. *Management Science, 18*, B485–B501.

Naik, P. A., & Raman, K. (2003). Understanding the impact of synergy in multimarketing communications. *Journal of Marketing Research, 40*, 375–388.

Parsons, L. J. (1974). An econometric analysis of advertising, retail availability, and sales of a new brand. *Management Science, 20*, 938–947.

Pauwels, K. (2004). How dynamic consumer response, competitor response, company support and company inertia shape long-term marketing effectiveness. *Marketing Science, 23*(4), 596–610.

Pauwels, K., & Bernadette, van E. (2013). Do online behavior tracking or attitude survey metrics drive brand sales? An integrative model of attitudes and actions on the consumer boulevard, Report 13–118. Cambridge, MA: Marketing Science Institute.

Pieters, R., Rosbergen, E., & Wedel, M. (1999). Visual attention to repeated print advertising: A test of scanpath theory. *Journal of Marketing Research, 36*, 424–438.

Rao, A., & Miller, P. B. (1975). Advertising/sales response functions. *Journal of Advertising Research, 15*, 7–15.

Rust, R. T., Lemon, K. N., & Zeithaml, V. A. (2004). Return on marketing: Using customer equity to focus marketing strategy. *Journal of Marketing, 68*, 109–127.

Sethuraman, R., Tellis, G., & Briesch, R. (2011). How well does advertising work? Generalizations from meta-analysis of brand advertising elasticities. *Journal of Marketing Research, 48*(3), 457–471.

Simon, H. (1982). ADPULS: An advertising model with wearout and pulsation. *Journal of Marketing Research, 19*, 352–363.

Steenkamp, J.-B. E. M., Nijs, V. R., Hanssens, D. M., & Dekimpe, M. G. (2005). Competitive reactions and the cross-sales effects of advertising and promotion. *Marketing Science, 24*(1), 35–54.

Tellis, G. (2004). *Effective advertising*. Thousand Oaks: Sage Publications.

Tellis, G., Chandy, R. K., & Thaivanich, P. (2000). Which ads work, when, where, and how often? Modeling the effects of direct television advertising. *Journal of Marketing Research, 37*, 32–46.

Tellis, G., & Franses, P. H. (2006). Optimal data interval for estimating advertising response. *Marketing Science, 25*(3), 217–229.

Trusov, M., Ma, L., & Jamal, Z. (2016). Crumbs of the cookie: User profiling in customer-base analysis and behavioral targeting. *Marketing Science, 25*(3), 405–426.

Vakratsas, D. (2005). Advertising response models with managerial impact: An agenda for the future. *Applied Stochastic Models in Business and Industry, 21*(4–5), 351–361.

Vakratsas, D., & Ambler, T. (1999). How advertising works: What do we really know? *Journal of Marketing, 63*(1), 26–43.

Van Heerde, H. J., Dekimpe, M. G., & Putsis, W. P., Jr. (2005). Marketing models and the Lucas critque. *Journal of Marketing Research, 42*, 15–21.

Zielske, H. (1959). The remembering and forgetting of advertising. *Journal of Marketing, 23*, 239–243.

Index

A
Abnormal stock return, 1043
A/B test, 4, 32, 39, 43, 44, 46, 47, 51–55, 57, 60, 823, 825
Accessibility-diagnosticity theory, 72
Acquiescence, 83, 84
Adapted etic model, 125
Adaptive Conjoint Analysis (ACA), 785
Adjacency matrix, 698
Adjusted R-squared (Adjusted R^2), 304, 305, 308
Advertising, 671–672
    elasticity, 187
    endogeneity, 189
    visuals, 680
Aggregate regressors, 169
Aggregation bias, 1060
Akaike information criteria (AIC), 259, 485, 499
Akaike weights, 611
Alpha inflation, 276
Ambiguous temporal precedence, 49
Amoroso-Robinson theorem, 188
Analysis of covariance (ANCOVA), 267, 292
Analysis of variance (ANOVA), 266
Anderson-Hsiao, 1047
A priori contrasts, 276
Arellano-Bond approach, 460, 1047
Artefactual field experiments, 19, 42
Attenuation bias, 443
Attribute importance, 804
Attribute levels, 783
Attribution models, 1089
Augmented Dickey Fuller (ADF) method, 473, 474, 495, 497, 520
Autocorrelation, 310, 311, 313–316, 321, 325
Autocorrelation function (ACF), 475–477, 495, 497, 498
Automated content analysis, 645, 657, 658
Automated text analysis, *see* Text analysis
Autoregressive (AR), 471, 472, 497, 498
    coefficient, 1047
Autoregressive integrated moving average (ARIMA), 474
    ACF, 475–477, 495, 497–499
    log transformation, 495
    PACF, 475–477, 495, 497–499
    stationary tests, 495–497
Autoregressive moving average (ARMA), 471–474
Average treatment effect (ATE), 44–47
Average variance extracted (AVE), 565, 578, 604

B
Back-translation, 135
Barplot, 268
Baseline model, 382–383, 1066
Bayesian estimation, 387
Bayesian inference
    beta-binomial model, 732–734
    binomial probit likelihood, 736–737
    conditional posterior distributions, 742–744
    conditional posterior distributions in hierarchical models, 745–746
    data augmentation, 740–741
    Gibbs sampler, 738–740
    Metropolis-Hastings algorithm, 746–748
    normal-normal model, 734–736
    software implementation, 765
Bayesian information criterion (BIC), 259, 485, 499, 540, 611, 1025
Bayesian missing data, 169
    problems, 149–152
Bayesian model
    Bayesian estimation, 721, 731–732
    computational resources, 721

Bayesian model (*cont.*)
  developments in, 759–761
  goals, 723
  hierarchical multinomial logit model, 766–769
  inference about parameters, 721
  likelihood function, 722
  mediation analysis, 769–771
  popularity, 720
  predictions, 744–745
  prior distributions, 722–724
Bayesian shrinkage, 161
Bayesian structural equation modeling (BSEM), 570
Becker–DeGroot–Marschak (BDM) mechanism, 798, 979, 980
BehaviorScan, 1060
Bernoulli experiment, 732
Best-worst scaling, 797
Beta-binomial model, 732–734
Beta-geometric/NBD model, 1012
  See also Pareto/NBD model
Beta-prior, 733
Between-subjects design, 25, 266
Between variance, 376, 377, 379, 382, 384, 395
Bias, 187, 192, 201, 214
Bias-corrected and accelerated (BCa) method, 605
Biases, in survey research
  measurement errors, 74–85
  representation errors, 85–89
Big data, 720, 854
  analytics, 38
Binary data, 164
Binomial logit model, 209
Binomial probit likelihood, 736–737
Blind tests, 1039
Blocked Gibbs samplers, 741–742
Blundell-Bond approach, 460
Bootstrapping, 606
  approach, 865–867, 875
  confidence interval, 605
  techniques, 208
Business field experiments, 38
Business optimization, 60

C

Canonical correlation coefficient, 338
Carryover effects, 27, 527
Categorical data, 163, 167, 168
Category equivalence, 127
Cauchy prior, 157

Causal inference, 44, 186
  blockage design, 893
  causal design, 39
  causal indicators, 592
  causal statements, 828
  causal steps approach, 863
  challenge to, 844
  concurrent double randomization design, 893
  consistency design, 893
  double randomized experiments, 892
  effect, 40, 43, 44
    of marketing, 191
    of prices, 194, 195
  enhancement design, 893
  experimental methods, 891, 893
  measurement-of-mediation design, 893
  in mediation analysis, 891
  from non-equal groups, 829
  parallel design, 893
  pattern matching, 893
  prerequisite of, 853
  in quasi field experiments, 841
  requirements for, 839
  specificity design, 893
  within-subject design, 894
Cause-effect relationships, 5, 14, 19, 32
Cause indicators, 552
Centering, 395, 389-390, 896-897
  group mean centering 389, 390, 395, 403
  grand mean centering 389, 403
  standardization 306-307
Centroid scheme, 596
K-centroids cluster analysis, 245
Certainty approach, 979
Chi-square goodness-of-fit test, 558, 561, 567
Choice-based conjoint analysis (CBC), 783, 976
Choice design, 795
Choice experiment, 795
Choice model, 787
Choice set, 784
Classification matrix, 686
Closed questions, 98
Closeness centrality, 701
Cluster analysis
  applications, 226
  k-centroids, 240
  characteristics, 222
  history, 222
  of market basket data, 229–244
  partitioning, 229
  steps to conduct, 224

Index

Cluster-robust standard errors, 428, 430, 433, 443, 445, 449, 453, 455
Cluster sample, 51
Coefficient of determination ($R2$), 304, 609
Cointegration test, 481, 483, 521
Collaborative translation, 135, 136
Collinearity assessment, 606
Color histograms, 681
Common method bias (CMB), 571, 580
    categories, 75
    conceptualization, 75–76
    definition, 75
    different data sources, 77
    proximal separation, 78
    psychological separation of scale formats, 78
    reasons for occurrence, 76–77
    statistical remedies, 78
    temporal separation of measurement, 77–78
Communality, 604
Competitive market structure (CMS) analysis, 222
Competitive mediation, 869
Competitive reaction effects, 528
Complete mediation, 869
Composite indicators, 552, 593
Composite reliability, 564, 565, 578, 603
Computer-assisted text analysis, *see* Text analysis
Computer vision, 686
Conditional direct effect, in mediation models, 881
Conditional Granger causality test, 482
Conditional independence assumption, 166
Conditional indirect effect, in mediation models, 881
Conditional moderated mediation, 888
Conditional posterior distributions, 742–744
Conditional process analysis, 885–887
    conceptual description, 879
    statistical description, 881
Condition (experimental), 63
Confidence interval, 268
Configural equivalence, 139
Configural properties, 379
Confirmatory composite analysis, 601
Confirmatory factor analysis (CFA), 575
Confirmatory factor model, 555–556
Confound checks, 13
Confounding variables, 13, 41, 49, 859
Confusion matrix, 164
Congeneric factor model, 564

Conjoint analysis (CA), 57, 574, 782, 949, 976, 1039
    adaptive, 785
    choice-based, 783, 976
    traditional, 976
Consistent Akaike information criterion (CAIC), 259
Consistent estimate, 194
Consistent PLS (PLSc) approach, 598
Constant conditional variance, 489
Constrained prior, 723
Construct(s), 590
    equivalence, 126
Consumer images, 676
    direct elicited images, 677–679
    images from internet and social media, 676–677
Consumer preferences, 971
Consumption-specificity, 945, 947–948
Contemporaneous effects, 527
Content analysis, 635
    automated, 645, 657, 658
    computer-assisted, 635
    modern, 635
    traditional, 635, 637
Context effect, 50
Control function (CF) approach, 200, 207–209
Control group, 41, 45–47, 51, 58, 61
    nonequal, 829
    suitable, 833
Control variables, 13, 41, 49, 94, 859
Convenience sampling, 23, 51
Conventional lab experiment, 42
Convergent validity, 564, 565, 567, 604, 606
Convolutional neural networks, 682
Cook's distance, 317
Correction-based marker variable technique, 78
Counterfactual, 832
Covariance-based SEM, 588
Covariates, 13, 41, 49, 94, 203, 859, 859
Cox model, 1009
Cronbach's alpha, 603
Cross-cultural research, 130, 132
Cross-level interaction, 380, 385, 390–392, 398, 400, 403
Cross-level models, 380
Crossover designs, 27
Culti-units, 129
Cultural dimensions, 130
Customer base management
    data and methodology, 1016–1018
    estimation, 1018–1022

Customer base management (*cont.*)
  parameter estimation, 1023–1025
  purchase prediction validity, 1025–1028
  results, 1023
Customer lifetime value (CLV)
  continuous mixed models, 1012
  measurement models, 1015
  migration models, 1010–1012
  retention models, 1008–1009
  taxonomy, 1003–1006
Customer loyalty
  antecedent of, 912
  conceptualization of, 914
  customer satisfaction and, 910
  definition, 911
  measurement, 921–925
  satisfaction and, 911
Customer mindset, 1037
  associations, 1039
  blind tests, 1039
  conjoint analysis, 1039
  surveys, 1039
Customer relationship management (CRM),
      947, 949, 954, 960
  data, 148, 170
Customer retention-churn modeling, 1005
Customer satisfaction
  conceptualization of, 910, 914
  CRM-Outcome Chain, 912
  cumulative perspective, 917
  and customer loyalty, 910
  definition, 911
  indices, 918
  level of, 918, 919
  loyalty, relationship of, 911
  and loyalty, 910
  measurement, 102, 910, 915
  multi-item scales, 96, 915
  novel and existing, 910
  ratings, 170
  requirements, 910
  scales, 915
  surveys, 102
  transaction-specific, 915
Customer scoring, 160
Customer targeting, 160
Cut point model, 154, 166, 169

D

Data augmentation, 151, 166, 740–741
Data collection, 23, 32, 104
Data equivalence, 124

Data fusion, 152, 164, 167–169
  classic problem, 148–151, 167
  mixed levels of data aggregation, 151–152
  multivariate normal model, 153–163
  multivariate probit model, 163–165
Data generating process (DGP), 194, 721
Data visualizations, 493–494
Debriefing, 31
Deception, 31, 32
Decomposition, 1057, 1061
Deep neural networks, 682, 683, 686
Degenerate prior, 723
Degree centrality, 699
Degree distribution, 703
Degrees of freedom, 271
Delta method, 864
Demand curve, OLS, 185
Demand effect, 27, 49, 75
  categories, 75
  conceptualization, 75–76
  definition, 75
  different data sources, 77
  proximal separation, 78
  psychological separation of scale
      formats, 78
  reasons for occurrence, 76–77
  statistical remedies, 78
  temporal separation of measurement, 77–78
Dependent variable, 266, 300, 302, 304–306,
      310, 311, 314, 316, 319, 321,
      324, 326
Design effect, 378
Design matrix, 54
Design of experiment (DOE), 55
Detailing endogeneity, 190
Deterministic models, 1007–1008, 1010
Deviance, 388
Dichotomous choice method, 971
Dictionary-based methods, 636
Difference in coefficients approach, 863
Difference-in-differences estimator, 456,
      834–835
  application area for, 831
  approach, 829, 832
  critical assumptions, 832–834
  designs, 829, 832
  methodology, 830
  regression, 830
  requirements, 829
  staggered designs, 831
Difference-in-means, 45
Differential attrition, 48–49
Diffuse prior, 723

Index 1101

Digital experiment, 39
Direct data fusion method, 165, 168
Directed network, 699
Direct effect, in mediation analysis, 860, 862, 863
Direct surveys, 973
Disacquiescence, 83–85, 91
Disaggregated approach, 377
Discontinuity
    plausibility, 839
    regression designs, 835
Discrete mixture model, 167
Discriminant analysis, 331, 951, 954
    applied examples, 357–359
    concept of, 332
    discriminant function coefficients, 339–340
    discriminant function estimation, 334–337
    discriminant function performance, 337–339
    model formulation, 334
    objectives, 331–332
    prediction, 341–343
    problem and group definition, 333
Discriminant validity, 565–567, 604
Distance-based clustering methods, 227
Distance concept, 341
Distribution of the product approach, 865
Domain-sampling model, 98
Double-asymmetric structural VAR (DASVAR) model, 529
Double randomized experiments, 892
Dummy-coding, 293
Dummy variables, 324
Durbin-Watson statistic, 314
Dutch auctions, 980
Dyad, 697
Dyadic data, 77
Dynamic multiplier analysis, 535
Dynamic panel, 1048
    models, 457–461
Dynamic systems, 471, 477, 481, 482, 485, 486, 491

E

Effect-coding, 278, 293, 800
Effect indicators, 552, 592
Effect size, 294
Eigenvector centrality, 701
Elasticities, 307, 309, 312, 319, 355
Emergent variables, 593
Emic concepts, 125, 126, 135

Empirical identification, 167
Endogeneity, 301, 309, 321–324, 413, 567–569
    advertising, 189
    advertising elasticity, 187
    correction, 204
    description, 183–187
    detailing, 190
    Hausman test, 202
    interaction term, 210–211
    measurement error, 444, 463, 464
    multiple endogenous regressors, 210
    omitted variable bias, 441, 442, 449, 450, 456, 458, 459
    price, 188
    price elasticity, 187
    problem on survey data, 191
    regression model, 192–198
    in survey research, 106–110
    of treatment, 844
Endogenous latent variable, 591
Endogenous variables, 527–529
Engle and Granger approach, 522
English auctions, 979
Error term, 184, 302
Ethnocentrism, 140
Etic concepts, 125, 126, 135
Event study, 832
Evolving series, 519
Exact fit test, 600
Excludability, 45, 46
Exclusion restriction, 192, 196, 846, 847
Exogeneity, 847
Exogenous latent variable, 591
Exogenous variables, 523, 526, 527
Experimental bias, 982
Experimental-causal-chain designs, 16
Experimental design, 6, 47, 53, 793
    dependent variable, operationalization of, 14–15
    environmental setting (*see* Experimental environment)
    experimental units and assignment to treatments (*see* Experimental units)
    extraneous variables, 13–14
    independent variable, 7–13, 29
    mediators, 15–17, 30
    preliminary testing, 27–28, 30
    research question, definition of, 6–7, 29
Experimental environment
    field experiments, 19–20
    laboratory experiments, 17–19
    online experiments, 20–21
Experimental factors, 266

Experimental units, 21–22, 30
  experimental treatments, participants to, 25–27
  incentivization of participants, 24–25
  participants and sampling procedure, number of, 22–24
Experimenter bias, 49
Experiments, in market research
  and causality, 5
  ethical issues, 31–32
  experimental design (*see* Experimental design)
Explanatory power, 595, 609
Exploratory structural equation modeling (ESEM), 570
External validity, 18, 44, 51, 85
Extraneous variables, 13
Extreme response style, 84, 91
Eye-tracking, 15, 22

F
Factor, 53, 54
Factor-based SEM, 588
Factorial Design, 793
Factor weighting scheme, 596
F-distribution, 271
Feasible generalized least squares estimator, 436
Feature extraction, 681–683
Feedback effects, 523, 527
$f2$ effect size, 609
Field experiments, 19, 40, 192, 215, 825–828
  average treatment effect, 44
  in business, 57–60
  causality and internal validity, 48
  classification, 825
  definition, 40–41
  experimental design and multivariate experiments, 53
  features of, 42–43
  generalizability of findings and external validity, 50
  vs. lab, 41–42
  natural, 826
  offline, 60
  online experiments, 43
  quasi, 826
  quasi-natural, 835
  sample size, 51
  types of, 825

Financial impact, 1043, 1046, 1048–1049
Finite mixture models
  applications in multivariate methods, 260–262
  description, 252
  example, 253–254
  and likelihood function, 254–256
  segmentation variable and mixed density function, 256–257
  segment determination, 258–260
Firm images
  advertising databases, 680
  firm brand communications, 680
  images on social media pages of firms, 680
  product images on retail websites, 679–680
First difference estimator, 455
First-price auctions, 980
First-stage regression, 193, 195, 207
Fisher's classification functions, 341
Fixed-effects estimator, 211, 432–435, 451, 454
k-fold cross-validation, 610
Forecast error variance decomposition (FEVD), 504–505, 519, 537
Forecasting, 685
Formative measurement model, 552, 592
  assessment, PLS-SEM, 606–608, 617–619
Four-way interaction, 56
Fractional factorial design, 8, 56
Fraction of missing information, 163
Framed field experiments, 19, 42
F-test, 195, 273, 305–308
Full factorial design, 8, 29
Full information maximum likelihood (FIML) test, 483, 522
Full model, 351
Functional equivalence, 127
Fusing media and purchase data, 148

G
Gabor filter, 681
Gabor Granger method, 974
Gaussian copulas, 215
Generalized autoregressive conditional heteroskedasticity (GARCH), 490, 491
Generalized forecast error variation decomposition (GFEVD), 487–488, 537, 538
Generalized impulse response functions (GIRFs), 485–487, 534

Generalized method of moments (GMM) estimator, 460
General linear model (GLM), 270
Geo-experiments, 61
Geographic proximity, 703
Geweke and Meese's criterion (GM), 611
Gibbs sampler, 155, 166, 168, 738–740
   blocked, 741–742
      Metropolis-Hastings (MH) algorithm, 746–748
      Monte-Carlo-Markov-Chain (MCMC), 748–749
Gibbs sampler proposal density, 749–759
GLOBE study, 131
Goodness of fit, 304–305, 319, 600
Grand mean, 270
   centering, 389, 403
Granger causality tests, 481–482, 519, 535
Group mean centering, 389, 390, 395, 403

H
p-Hacking, 607
Halo effect, 1066
Hamiltonian-Monte-Carlo (HMC), 759
Hannan-Quinn (HQ) criterion, 485
Hausman-Taylor approach, 450
Hausman test, 200, 202, 203, 206, 208, 442, 444, 449
Hawthorne effect, 49
Hazard function, 1009
Heterogeneity, 942, 943, 951–955, 1049–1051, 1068
Heterogeneous customer group, 955
Heteroskedasticity, 310, 315–317, 325, 326, 444, 454
Heterotrait-monotrait ratio (HTMT), 604
Hidden Markov models, 1011
Hierarchical Bayes models, 730
Hierarchical Bayes (HB) procedure, 811
Hierarchical clustering, 253, 952, 953
   agglomerative algorithms, 228
   agglomerative clustering, 232
   application of, 240
   K-medoid clustering, 236–240
   linkage criteria in, 233
   outcome of, 233
   techniques for, 228
Hierarchical data structure, 371, 376, 381, 403
Hierarchical models, 745–746
Hierarchical (or multilevel) random effect models, 573, 574
Hierarchy of effects (HoE) model, 541

Hit rate, 352, 799
HLM, 396, 397
Hofstede cultural dimensions, 131
Holdout-sample validation, 204, 799
   sample, 610
Homogeneity, 942
Homologous models, 380
Homophily, 695, 702
Homoskedasticity, 309
Hosmer-Lemeshow test, 353, 359
Hotdeck, 150
Hubs, 696, 699
Hue, saturation, value (HSV), 681
Human-coded features, 682
Human development indicator (HDI), 130
Hypothetical bias, 978, 979, 982, 994

I
Ideal market segment, 944–945
Ideal point model, 789
Identifiability, 944–945, 958
Identification strategy, 192
Ignorablility, 150, 167, 169
Image processing, 668, 678, 679
Image tagging, 668, 669, 687
   advertising, 671–672
   branding, 672–674
   consumer perspectives, 675
   consumer *vs.* firm images, 675–681
   feature extraction, 681–683
   future research in marketing, 669
   model application, 685
   model evaluation and validation, 684–685
   model training, 683–684
   online shopping experience, 674–675
   product design, 670–671
Immediate effect, 486, 507
Imposed-etic approach, 125
Impulse response function (IRF), 478, 485, 486, 505–509, 519, 530
Incentive(s), 89
   alignment, 798
Incentivization, 24
Independent variable, 266, 300–302, 304–307, 309–314, 316, 317, 319, 321, 324, 326
   coding scheme, 897–898
   fractional factorial designs, 8–9
   multi-factor designs, 8
   number of levels, 9
   operationalization of treatments, 10–13
   single-factor designs, 8

Index of moderated mediation, 882, 886
Indicators, 591
Indirect effect, in mediation analysis, 860, 862
Indirect surveys, 976
Individual-item reliability, 564
Individual-level constructs, 378
Inference-by-eye, 269, 276
Informative prior, 723
Informed consent, 31
In-sample model fit criteria, 204
In-sample predictive power, 609
Instructional manipulation checks, 11
Instrumental variables (IVs), 183, 192, 195, 568, 1047
  applications in business research, 850
  area of application, 845
  in field experiment, 849
  graphical illustration of, 845
  method, 853
Interaction(s), 8, 9, 20, 28, 29
  effect, 49, 50, 53, 319, 324, 356, 790
  term, 210
Internal consistency reliability, 603
Internal validity, 17, 44, 47, 86
International market research
  challenges, 123
  conceptual framework, 124
  data analysis, 138
  data collection, 133
  interpretation, 140
  units and drivers, 127
Interpretable features, 668, 679, 682, 687
Intervention, 825, 826, 830, 831
  analysis, 478
Intraclass correlation coefficient (ICC), 377, 395, 436
  ICC1, 379
  ICC2, 379
Invariance of parameters across groups, 572
Inverse square root method, 599
Item parcels, 570
Item reversals, 100
Iterative translation, 135, 136

J

Jaccard similarity coefficient, 226
Jackknife method, 356
JAGS, 166
John Henry effect, 49
Joint data fusion method, 167
Joint endogeneity, 480

K

K-centroids cluster analysis, 240–244
Key informant bias, 79
  conceptualization, 79
  procedural remedies, 80
  reasons for occurrence, 79
  statistical remedies, 81
K-means clustering, 639, 642
K-medoid clustering, 236–240
KPSS tests, 520

L

Laboratory experiment, 17, 41, 48, 63
Lagrange multiplier test, 439, 562
Latent class analysis (LCA), 809, 954
Latent constructs, 292
Latent curve models, 573
Latent Dirichlet allocation (LDA), 639, 642
LatentGold®, 261
Latent growth models, 380
Latent instrumental variables (LIV), 215
Latent semantic analysis (LSA), 639, 642
Latent variable model, 344, 551, 556, 564, 567
  empirical example, 579–581
  extensions of, 571
Latent variables, 154, 163, 590
Least squares dummy variables (LSDV) regression, 433
Least squares method, 302, 307, 311, 315
Levene's test, 295
Likelihood-ratio test, 351, 353, 354, 388
Linear mixed models (LMMs), 294
Linear regression model, 300, 301, 304, 307, 312, 317, 319, 321, 322, 324, 326, 722
  aim of, 302
  benchmark, 610
  goal of, 317
  goodness of fit for, 304
  results of, 308, 318
LKJ prior, 157
Logistic probability unit, 345
Logistic regression
  applications, 343
  applied examples, 359–364
  coefficients, 353–356
  function estimation, 349
  latent variable model, 344–345
  model formulation, 348
  model performance, 349–353
  prediction, 356
  probability model, 345–347
  problem and group definition, 348

Index

Log-likelihood, 1025
Long format, 286, 287
Longitudinal data, 374, 375, 380
Longitudinal mediation analysis, 890
Long-run cointegrating equilibrium, 523
Long-term effect, 486, 504, 507

M

Machine learning, 729
Mahalanobis distance, 317
Main effect, 56
Manipulation, 10, 13, 14, 16–18, 23, 27–29
    checks, 11–13, 29
    effectiveness of, 30
Marginal effects, 354
Marketing and mindset metrics models, 541
Market response modeling, 148
Market scenarios, 783
Market segmentation, 222, 783, 941
    accessibility, 957–958
    a priori idea, 955
    conjoint analysis, 949
    consumption-specificity, 947–948
    creation of market segments, 952–953
    CRM databases, 949
    customers as unique entities, 940
    data-driven, 951
    digitalization, 949
    formation of segments, 951–957
    goals of, 940
    heterogeneity and homogeneity, 942
    ideal market segment, 944–945
    identifiability, 944–945
    implementation, 960–962
    observability, 946
    profiling of market segments, 953–954
    responsiveness, 958
    segment-of-one, 942–943
    sizing of market segments, 954–957
    stability, 958–959
    standardized, 940, 942, 950
    substantiality, 959
    surveys, 949
Market simulations, 806
Markov chain Monte Carlo (MCMC), 151, 153, 155, 159, 160, 166
Markov processes, 1011
MATLAB, 157, 166
Maximum likelihood estimation (MLE) approach, 254, 386, 462, 802, 1018
Mean absolute error (MAE), 610

Mean centering, in conditional process analysis, 896–897
Measured latent factor, 82
Measured response style technique, 85
Measurement equivalence, 139
Measurement errors, survey research, 186
    CMB, 75–78
    key informant bias, 78–81
    response styles, 83–85
    social desirability, 81–83
Measurement models, 564–567
    confirmatory factor analysis, 575
    extensions, 569–571
    observed variables, 563
    types of, 552
Measurement-of-mediation design, 16
Measurement theory, 72–74, 592–594
Mechanical Turk (MTurk), 23, 91, 93
Mediated moderation, 880
Mediation analysis, 769–771, 859
    causal inference, 891–894
    classification, 869–870
    complete mediation, 869
    conditional direct effect, 881
    conditional indirect effect, 881
    conditional process analysis, 885
    direct effect 860, 862, 863
    effect size measures, 870
    indirect effect, 860, 862
    longitudinal and multilevel, 890
    regression analysis vs. structural equation modeling, 898–899
    sample size and power, 895–896
    software tools, 900
    time and nested data in, 890–891
    variable metrics, 870–871
Mediation models, with multiple predictor/outcome variables, 889–890
Mediator, 15, 859
Meta-analysis, 375
Method effects, 570, 571
Metric equivalence models, 139
Metropolis-Hastings (MH) algorithm, 746–748
Midpoint responding, 84
Missing by design, 151, 165, 167
Missing completely at random (MCAR), 150
Missing data, 149–150, 152–155, 158–159, 161, 163, 165, 169–170
    mechanism, 167, 169
Missing regressors, 169
Mixed aggregate-disaggregate data, 152, 167, 168
Mixed-ANOVA, 289

MLwiN, 397
Model chi-square, 351
Model comparisons, 611
Model estimation, 385, 390, 556–558
Model fit, 387, 388, 394, 399–401
Model identification, 554
Model modification, 562
Model overfit, 609
Model training, 683–684
Moderated mediation, 879, 880
Moderated moderated mediation, 888
Moderation-of-process designs, 16
Moderator, 325, 859
Modification index (MI), 562, 572, 577
Modified Akaike information criterion, 259
Monadic approach, 974, 995
Monte-Carlo-Markov-Chain (MCMC) techniques, 748–749
  binomial probit without data augmentation, 772–778
  convergence, 754
  graphical inspection, 759
  iterations, 766
  traces, 753
Monte Carlo simulation approach, 534
Moving average (MA), 472, 497, 498
Mplus, 397, 399
MTurk, see Mechanical Turk (MTurk)
Multicollinearity, 310–313, 326
Multi-factor designs, 8
Multilevel mediation analysis, 890
Multilevel modeling, 398–400
  aggregation, 379
  assumptions, 386
  baseline model, 382–383
  conceptual relevance, 372–375
  configural properties, 379
  cross-level interaction effects, 385
  cross-level models, 380
  global properties, 379
  homologous models, 380
  independent variables, at level 1, 383
  independent variables, at level 2, 383–384
  individual-level constructs, 378
  intraclass correlation, 379
  latent growth models, 380
  longitudinal data, 380
  model estimation and assessing model fit, 386–389
  multilevel structural equation modeling, 392–396
  random slopes, testing for, 384–385
  sample size considerations, 390–392
  shared properties, 379
  single-level models, 379
  software, 396–397
  statistical relevance, 375–378
  unobserved heterogeneity, 379
  variable centering, 389–390
Multilevel structure, 372
  equation modeling, 392–396
  in marketing organizations, 374
Multinomial logit (MNL) model, 791
Multinomial regression model, 209
Multiple endogenous regressors, 209–210
Multiple imputation, 167
Multiple linear regression (MLR), 495, 500, 502
Multiple regression model, 500
Multiple time series models, 479–481
  cointegration test, 483
  GFEVD, 487–488
  GIRFs, 485–487
  Granger causality tests, 481–482
  VAR model, 483–485
  VEC model, 484
  volatility models, 489–491
Multiplicative sales response function, 318, 326
Multi-sample models, 573
Multi-stage random sampling, 23
Multivariate analysis of variance (MANOVA), 267, 293
Multivariate experiment, 53–57

N
Natural experiment, 41
Natural field experiments, 19, 42
Nested data structures, 371–373, 375–377, 379, 383, 389
Net acquiescence, 83
Network analysis, 694
Network density, 703
Nonconvergence, 558
Nonexperimental approaches, 192
Non-hierarchical clustering, 228, 952
Non-ignorability, 151, 169
Non-interference, 45, 47
Non-overlapping clustering approaches, 228
Non-parametric model, 166
Non-probability sampling, 104
Non-response bias, 85, 87
  conceptualization, 87–88
  organizational factors, 88
  personal factors, 88
  procedural remedies, 88–89

Index   1107

statistical remedies, 89
survey-related factors, 88
Non-sampling bias, 85
   conceptualization, 85–86
   procedural remedies, 87
   reasons for occurrence, 86
   statistical remedies, 87
Normal distribution of the residuals, 309, 311
Normal-Inverse Wishart prior, 746
Normal prior, 157
Normal regression likelihood, 734
No U-turn Sampler (NUTS), 759, 761

O
Object detection, 677, 686, 688
Observational data, 94, 183
Observational investigations, 40, 41
Omitted variables, 107, 196, 203
Omnibus test, 276, 293
Online collages, 668, 672
Online experiment, 20, 43–44, 47, 51
Online social networks, 950
Open-ended questions, 98
Operational segmentation, 942, 943, 952, 962
Opinion leaders, 696
Optimal design, 56
Optimal number of clusters, 953
Ordered-categorical (discrete-ordinal) observed
      variables, 569
Ordinary least squares (OLS) approach,
      184, 484
Orthogonality, 56
Out-degree, 699
Outlier detection, 317
Outliers, 310, 317–318, 321, 325, 326
Out-of-sample predictive power, 610
Over-identification test, 200

P
Pairwise Granger causality test, 482
Panel data, 211–213, 380, 1056, 1059, 1060,
      1062, 1065, 1070
Panel-internal instrumental variables, 450, 459
Panel vector autoregression (PVAR), 484, 541
Parallel multiple mediator model, 871–875
Parallel trends assumption, 832, 833
Parametric probabilistic models, 1008
Pareto/NBD model, 1012–1014
   customer base management (*see* Customer
         base management)
   regression coefficients, 1023
Partial autocorrelation function (PACF),
      475–477, 495, 497, 498

Partial least squares (PLS) estimation, 557
Partial least squares structural equation
      modeling (PLS-SEM)
   algorithm, 595–598
   bias, 594
   considerations using, 598–601
   corporate reputation model, 612–614
   distributional assumptions, 598
   formative measurement model assessment,
         606–608
   goodness-of-fit, 600–601
   measurement theory, 592–594
   methodological reason for, 589
   model complexity and sample size, 599–600
   model estimation, 615
   procedure for evaluation, 601–602
   reflective measurement model assessment,
         603–605
   research application, 612–621
   results evaluation, 616–621
   statistical power, 599
   structural model assessment, 608–612
   structural theory, 591–592
Partial mediation, 869
Partial moderated mediation, 888
Partworth model, 789
Partworth utilities, 784
Path, 700
   coefficients, 592
   weighting scheme, 596
Path model
   estimation with PLS-SEM, 594–601
   with latent variables, 590–591
Payment card method, 973, 975
Percentile method, 605
Persistence modeling, 481, 527
Pilot tests, 28
Placebo effect, 49
PLSpredict procedure, 610
Poisson regression model, 209
Polar extreme approach, 348
Policy simulation analysis, 481
Pooled OLS (POLS) estimator, 427, 430, 452
Population heterogeneity, 572–574
Posterior, 151, 153, 161, 163, 164
Post hoc tests, 276
Power, 52, 286, 558, 567
Prediction, 205
   accuracy, 684, 687
   error, 610
   power, 610
Preference measurement, 782
Preliminary testing, 27

Pretesting, 28
Pre-trained models, 683, 685
Price elasticity, 182, 187
Price endogeneity, 188
Price experiment, 981
Price promotions, 1057, 1058, 1062, 1066
Price sensitivity, 959, 963, 973, 988, 989
Prior, 157, 166
Probabilistic latent semantic analysis (PLSA), 639
Probabilistic models
  parametric, 1008
  semi-parametric, 1009
Probability concept, 342
Probability density function, 273
Probability model, 345
Probability samples, 104
Probit model, 209
Product attribute, 976, 977
Product of coefficients approach, 863
Profiling of market segments, 952–954
Prolific Academic (ProA), 23, 92, 93
Promotion effectiveness, 1056, 1057, 1059–1062, 1067, 1070
PROMOTIONSCAN model, 1065–1067
Proportional chance criterion (PCC), 352, 353, 358, 359
Proportional hazard model, 1009
Proportional random sampling, 23
Proximity measures, 225
Pseudo-etic, 125
PSPP, 325
Psychology of survey response, 71–72
Pulse effect, 478
P-value, 273
Python, 157, 166

Q

Quantification, 952
Questionnaire design, survey research process
  pre-test of questionnaire, 103–104
  question content, 95–98
  question format, 98–100
  question sequence, 101–103
  question wording, 100–101
  survey content, 94–95
  survey layout, 103
Question wording
  neutrality, 101
  simplicity, 100
  unambiguousness, 101
Quota sampling, 24

R

R^2, 304, 305, 307, 308, 311, 318, 319, 388
Random assignment, 40, 41, 43, 45, 46, 58
  of prices, 191
Random cluster-specific slope coefficients, 461
Random coefficient modeling, 371
Random effects, 213
  estimator, 432, 436, 438, 452
Random intercept, 382–385, 387, 388, 403
Randomization, 5, 13, 19, 30, 40, 42, 44, 47, 60
Randomized experiment, 61
Randomized response techniques, 82
Random slope models, 461, 462
Random slopes, 384–385, 389, 394, 400, 403
Random utility theory, 787
Receiver operator characteristic (ROC), 352
Recursive model, 553
Reduced-form VAR, 483, 486, 519, 527
Redundancy analysis, 606, 618
Reflective indicators, 592
Reflective measurement model, 552, 592
  assessment, PLS-SEM, 603–605, 616–621
Regression analysis, 56, 192, 270, 726
  autocorrelation, test for, 313
  dependent and independent variables, 310
  efficiency of estimators, 311
  endogeneity, 309, 321
  goodness of fit, 304
  heteroskedasticity, test for, 315
  implications, 320–321
  interpretation of results, 307
  multicollinearity, test for, 311
  objective function and estimation of regression coefficients, 301–303
  outliers, identification of, 317
  problem statement, 300–301
  residuals, 309
  results, 307–309
  significance testing, 305
  software, 325
  standardization of coefficients, 306
  transformation of variables, 318
Regression discontinuity
  approach, 838, 839
  bandwidth selection, 839
  designs, 835, 838
  method, 841
  setting, 835
Regression weights, 597
Regressor-error dependencies, 187
Relevance condition, 846

Index

Reliability, 72, 73, 75, 79–81, 96–99, 104–106, 557, 564, 565, 567, 570
   coefficient, 603
Relief from royalty, 1042
Repeated measures, 375
Repeated-measures analysis of variance (RM-ANOVA), 267, 286
Representation errors, survey research
   non-response bias, 87–89
   non-sampling bias, 85–87
Representativeness, 85
Residual, 302, 303, 305, 309, 311, 313–317, 321, 322
   analysis, 562
Response range, 84
Response rates, 87
Response styles, 83
   acquiescence, disacquiesence and net acquiescence, 83–84
   extreme responding, midpoint responding and response range, 84
   procedural remedies, 84–85
   statistical remedies, 85
Responsiveness, 958
Return on media (ROM), 1074–1076
   advertising copy and creative effects, 1086
   advertising response dynamics, 1080–1082
   advertising-response function, shape of, 1078–1080
   asymmetric response, 1082–1083
   brand equity, 1091
   building distribution, 1093
   customer equity, 1091–1093
   data-interval bias, 1082
   enhancing sales-call effectiveness, 1093
   estimated response parameters, 1087–1088
   fundamental advertising response phenomena, 1076–1078
   intermediate performance metrics, 1086–1087
   lifting stock price, 1093
   path-to-purchase and attribution models for digital media, 1088–1090
   protecting/enhancing price premiums, 1093
   reverse causality, 1083–1084
Revealed preference methods, 972, 979, 994
   direct, 979
   experimental, 981
Reverse pricing, 980
Root mean squared error (RMSE), 610
   of approximation, 560
Root-mean-square deviation (RMSE), 501

Root mean square residual covariance (RMStheta), 600
R-package bayesm, 721, 728, 745, 750
RStan, 155
R statistical language, 157, 166

S

Sales contests (SCs), 357
Sales promotions
   academic research on, 1059, 1061
   analysis of, 1060
   characteristics, 1056
   effectiveness, 1059–1062
   investments in, 1056
   manufacturer spendings on, 1056
   marketing budget on, 1056
   systematic information on, 1059
   tools, 1056–1058
Sales response function, 318, 320, 326
Sales response models, 1094
Sample size, 22, 42, 51–53
   considerations, 390–392
Sampling frame equivalence, 136
Sampling frames, 86
Sampling methods, 151
Sargan-test, 201
SAS, 325, 397
Satisficing, 11
Sawtooth®, 261
SCAN*PRO model, 1063, 1065
Scanner panel, 1059, 1070
   data, 1041
Schwartz' Bayes Information Criterion (SBIC), 259, 485, 499, 540, 611, 1025
Schwartz cultural dimensions, 131
Second-price auctions, 980
Segmentation criteria, 945–948
Segmentation, targeting, positioning (STP) framework, 941
Segment-of-one, 942–943
Segment size, 963
Selection bias, 46, 48
Self-reports, 14, 29, 71
Semi-parametric probabilistic models, 1009–1010
Sensitivity analysis, 355
Sentiment analysis, 640
Sequential approach, 990, 994
Serial correlation, 426, 428, 430, 436, 437, 444, 454
Serial multiple mediator model, 875–878

Significance testing, 52, 53, 305–306
Simple random sampling, 23, 51
Simplicity, 100
Simultaneity, 187, 714, 1045
Single-factor designs, 8
Single items, 96
Single-level models, 379
Single mediator model
  assumptions, 867–869
  conceptual description, 879
  description of, 881
  statistical description, 881–885
Single-source panels, 1060, 1063, 1067, 1069, 1070
Singular value decomposition (SVD), 639
Sizing of market segments, 952, 954–957
SMARTPLS, 261
Snowball sampling, 705
Sobel test, 864
Social desirability, 81
  conceptualization, 81
  procedural remedies, 81–82
  reasons for occurrence, 81
  statistical remedies, 82–83
Social influence, 696
Social learning, 696
Social network, 695
Social normative pressure, 696
Software, 396–397
Specific indirect effect, multiple mediator model, 878
Sphericity, 288
Split-plot ANOVA, 289
Split questionnaire, 149, 153, 163, 166–168
SPSS, 307, 325, 326, 397, 825
Stability, 947, 958–959
Stable Unit Treatment Value Assumption (SUTVA), 47
Stan, 155–157, 163–166, 721, 759, 775–776
Standard error of mean, 268
Standard errors, 202, 208
Standardized regression coefficients, 306–307
Standardized root mean square residual (SRMR), 600
STATA, 307, 325, 326, 397, 825, 849
Stated preference method, 972
  direct, 973
  experimental, 976
  hypothetical bias, 978
Stated preference methods, 973, 978
Stationary, 473, 475, 478, 481, 483, 495–497, 519

Statistical power, 391
Step effect, 478
Stimuli, 795
Strategic answering, 976
Strategic segmentation, 942, 952, 962
Stratified sample, 51
Structural breaks, 521
Structural equation modeling (SEM), 392–396, 550
  empirical example, 574–581
  extensions of core structure equation model, 569–574
  latent variable model, 567
  measurement model, 564–567
  problem of endogeneity, 567–569
  submodels, 551–556
Structural model, 169
Structural model assessment, PLS-SEM, 608–612, 619–621
Structural theory, 591–592
Structural vector-autoregressive model (SVAR), 519, 529
Student samples, 104
Subcultures, 129
Subgraph sampling, 706, 707
Substantiality, 959
Sum of squares, 271
Supervised classification task, 683
Supervised learning, 684
Support vector machine (SVM), 638
Suppressor variables, 13
Survey(s), 949
  design, 69, 88, 110
  non-response, 151, 170
  research, 149–151, 163, 170
  subsampling, 150, 167
Survey bias
  fundamentals of survey research, 70–71
  measurement theory, 72–74
  psychology of survey response, 71–72
Survey research process
  data analysis, 106
  data collection, 104–105
  measurement evaluation, 105–106
  questionnaire design, 93–104
  selection of research variables, 89–90
  selection of survey method, 91–93
Synthetic controls, 833
Systematic biases, 74
Systematic errors, in survey research
  measurement errors, 74–85
  representation errors, 85–89
Systematic random sampling, 23

Index

T

Target variable, 686, 687
T-distribution, 270
Technology acceptance model (TAM), 554, 574, 580
Temporal causality, 536
Testing the global fit of model, 558–561
Text analysis
    approaches to, 635–636
    classification methods, 638
    construct, 647–648
    data collection, 646–647
    dictionary-based methods, 636–638
    history, 635
    interpretation and analysis, 650–657
    operationalization, 648–650
    organization and firm environment, measurement of, 642–643
    research question, 645–646
    sentiment analysis, 640–641
    textual data, 643–644
    topic discovery and positioning maps, online text, 642
    topic modeling, 638–639
    validation, 657–659
    word of mouth communication, 641–642
Three-way interaction, 56
Ties, 697
Tie strength, 701
Time effects, 49
Time fixed effects, 213
Time sampling, 150, 167
Time-series analysis, in marketing
    multiple time series models, 479–491
    univariate time series treatments and diagnostics, 471–479
Time series processor (TSP), 539
Time trend, 831
Tolerance, 311
Topic modeling, 638
Total effect, in mediation analysis, 860, 862
Total indirect effect
    multiple mediator model, 878
    parallel multiple mediator model, 872, 873
    serial multiple mediator model, 876, 877
Transfer function, 478, 479
Transformation of variables, 310, 318–320
Treatment effect, 830
    local average treatment effect (ATE), 44–47, 829, 848
Treatment group, 40, 41, 45, 46, 825, 826, 828–831
T-test, 270

Two-level regression model, 381–392
Two-stage least squares (2SLS) approach, 194, 199, 202
Two-way fixed effects model, 212
Two-way interaction, 56

U

U-method, 356
Unambiguousness, 101
Undirected network, 699
Unit root test, 473, 481, 483, 494, 502, 519
Univariate time series models
    autoregressive and moving average process, 471–473
    autoregressive integrated moving average model, 474–476
    evolution *vs.* stationarity, 472–474
    single equation time-series models, exogenous variables, 476–479
Unobserved demand shocks, 189
Unobserved effects models, 211
Unobserved heterogeneity, 379
Unobserved population heterogeneity, 574
Unsupervised learning, 684, 687
Utility, 782
    function, 783, 977
    model, 787

V

Validity, 69, 72–75, 81, 85, 86, 95, 96, 104–106, 785
Value comprehension, 988
van Westendorp method, 973
Variable centering, 389–390
Variance inflation factor (VIF) value, 311, 312, 347, 606
Vector autoregressive (VAR) models, 483, 484, 502–504, 518
    dynamic system of equations, 523
    investor response models in marketing-finance, 539
    in levels, 484
    marketing studies, 524
    order of lags, 484–485
    software programs for estimation, 539
    VAR-in-difference model, 483, 484
Vector-error correction model (VECM), 481, 484, 523, 530
Vector model, 788
Vector moving average (VMA), 486
Vickrey auctions, 980

Videos, 668
Visual data, 668
Visual features, 672
Volatility, 471, 489–491
Volunteer sampling, 23

W
Website test, 57
Weighted PLS-SEM approach, 598
Weight matrix, 698

Wide-format, 286, 287
Wilks's lambda, 338
Willingness-to-pay (WTP), 798, 970, 971, 973, 976–982
   definition, 971
   drivers of, 982–989
   measurement methods, 972–986
WinBUGS, 155, 166, 765
Within-estimator, 212
Within-subjects, 25–27, 266
Within variance, 376, 377, 382, 384